Of Law and Life

UPENDRA BAXI in Conversation with

ARVIND NARRAIN
LAWRENCE LIANG
SITHARAMAM KAKARALA
SRUTI CHAGANTI

Orient BlackSwan

OF LAW AND LIFE: UPENDRA BAXI IN CONVERSATION WITH ARVIND NARRAIN, LAWRENCE LIANG, SITHARAMAM KAKARALA AND SRUTI CHAGANTI

ORIENT BLACKSWAN PRIVATE LIMITED

Registered Office
3-6-752 Himayatnagar, Hyderabad 500 029, Telangana, India
e-mail: centraloffice@orientblackswan.com

Other Offices
Bengaluru, Chennai, Guwahati, Hyderabad, Kolkata, Mumbai, New Delhi, Noida, Patna

First published in Hardback by Orient BlackSwan in 2024
This Paperback edition published by Orient BlackSwan in 2024

ISBN 978-93-5442-813-5

042845

Typeset in
Adobe Jensen Pro 11/13.5
by Le Studio Graphique, Gurgaon 122 007

Printed in India at
Replika Press Pvt. Ltd.

Published by
Orient Blackswan Private Limited
3-6-752 Himayatnagar, Hyderabad 500 029, Telangana, India
e-mail: info@orientblackswan.com

Of Law and Life

Contents

Plates

between pages 266–267

1. Early life. Prem Mandir: The house at Rajkot (1922)
2. Upendra Baxi's grandmother, Kashibahen Venilal Baxi, the 'storyteller', in centre, at Prem Mandir
3. Upendra Baxi's father, Vishnuprasad Baxi
4. Upendra Baxi's mother, Muktaben, on the left
5. Upendra Baxi on the right with his brother, Madhusudhan Baxi
6. From left: Madhusudhan Baxi, Upendra Baxi, Kirit Swadia, Asghar Ali Jasdanwala, Jayant Swadia
7. Learning the law. Senior L.L.M., Branch 1, 1962–1963, Government Law College, University of Bombay. Upendra Baxi is in the second row, second from the right
8. At the National House, University of California—Berkeley, 1964
9. Hans Kelsen Inscription, reads 'to Mr. Upendra Baxi, with kindest regards, Hans Kelsen, Berkeley, 19 October 1964'
10. Berkeley student protests (from Upendra Baxi's Berkeley album)
11. The Australian interlude. Teaching at the Sydney Law School, from left: Garth Nettheim, Upendra Baxi, Julius Stone
12. In front of the New South Wales Supreme Court
13. Letter to the Editor, *Sydney Morning Herald*, 14 September 1971. 'Head tax on Jews: an appeal', signed by Upendra Baxi, Noel Sydney Hush, and Julius Stone
14. Return to Delhi. Upendra Baxi with Professor Sarup Singh, former Vice-Chancellor, University of Delhi
15. First Curriculum Development Committee, UGC: includes (facing camera) Lotika Sarkar, B. S. Sivarammayya, Upendra Baxi

16. Indian Legal Theory. Participants at a seminar on Judicial Process and the Law (Vizag), includes (seated) B. S. Sivarammaya, T. S. Rama Rao, Alice Jacob, Lotika Sarkar, S. N. Jain, D. K. Singh, M. L. Upadhyaya, V. S. Murthy. Upendra Baxi is centre, second row
17. Upendra Baxi, on the right, with Justice Krishna Iyer, centre
18. Conference of the International Political Science Association (IPSA) study group on political philosophy meeting at Vadodara, 1984. Upendra Baxi is in the second row, second from the left
19. What indigenous law can teach us. The Lok Adalat at Rangpur, with Harivallabh Bhai Parekh
20. The Bellagio Declaration, 1993. Includes Peter Jasszi and Rosemary Coombs (third and fourth from left, seated). Upendra Baxi is third from left (standing)
21. Gwyer Hall, 1996: From left: Upendra Baxi, André Béteille, and Justice Ranganath Misra
22. Asian Coalition of Human Rights Organization workshop on Effective Human Rights in Asia, October 1988. From left: Upendra Baxi, Clarence Dias
23. Workshop on Gender Justice: Role of the Law Commission, from left: Lotika Sarkar, Justice D. A. Desai, Upendra Baxi
24. University of Warwick: From left: Upendra Baxi, Abdul Paliwala, Issa G. Shivji, and William Twining, at a conference held in the memory of Dwijen Rangnekar
25. Giorgio Agamben, Università IUAV di Venezia & Collège International de Philosophie Paris on *What is a Dispositif?*, 16 January 2007, Centre for the Study of Law and Governance, Jawaharlal Nehru University. From left: Upendra Baxi, Niraja Gopal Jayal, Giorgio Agamben

Abbreviations

AALCO	Asian–African Legal Consultative Organization
AIR	*All India Reporter*
ALF	Alternative Law Forum
APCLC	Andhra Pradesh Civil Liberties Committee
BDO	Block Development Officer
BHU	Banaras Hindu University
BISA	Brazil, India, South Africa
BJP	Bharatiya Janata Party
CAH	crimes against health
CBI	Central Bureau of Investigation
CEDAW	Convention on the Elimination of All Forms of Discrimination against Women
CJI	Chief Justice of India
CL	customary law
CLS	Critical Legal Studies
CPI	Communist Party of India
CPV	Collective Political Violence
CRPF	Central Reserve Police Force
CSCS	Centre for the Study of Culture & Society, Bangalore
DU	Delhi University
DUSU	Delhi University Students' Union
EPW	*The Economic and Political Weekly*
FAO	Food and Agriculture Organization (of the United Nations)
FCRA	Foreign Contribution Regulation Act
GOI	Government of India
HAP	human animal persons

HRE	Human Rights Education
HRI	Human Rights Institutions
HUF	Hindu Undivided Family
IAS	Indian Administrative Service
ICES	International Centre for Ethnic Studies
ICJ	International Court of Justice
ICSSR	Indian Council of Social Science Research
IL	indigenous law
ILI	Indian Law Institute
JILI	*The Journal of the Indian Law Institute*
IMF	International Monetary Fund
JNU	Jawaharlal Nehru University
KCOCA	Karnataka Control of Organised Crime Act, 2000
LAWS	Lethal Autonomous Weapons Systems
LGBTQI	Lesbian, Gay, Bisexual, Transgender, Queer, Intersex
LSCP	Law, Society and Culture Programme
LTTE	Liberation Tigers of Tamil Eelam
MDG	Millennium Development Goals
MIC	Methyl isocyanate (gas)
MISA	Maintenance of Internal Security Act
MLA	Member of Legislative Assembly
NHAP	non-human animal persons
NHRC	National Human Rights Commission
NHRI	National Human Rights Institutions
NLSIU	National Law School of India University, Bangalore
NUJS	National University of Juridical Sciences, West Bengal
NREGA	National Rural Employment Guarantee Act, 2005 (later renamed as the Mahatma Gandhi National Rural Employment Guarantee Act, MGNREGA)
OPPI	Organisation of Pharmaceutical Producers of India
OUP	Oxford University Press
PIL	Public Interest Litigation
PPT	Permanent People's Tribunal

PUCL	People's Union for Civil Liberties
PUDR	People's Union for Democratic Rights
RSS	Rashtriya Swayamsevak Sangh
SAHMAT	Safdar Hashmi Memorial Trust
SAL	Social Action Litigation
SALT	Strategic Arms Limitation Treaty
SHO	Station House Officer
SP	Superintendent of Police
TULF	Tamil United Liberation Front
TWAIL	Third World Approaches to International Law
UAPA	Unlawful Activities Prevention Act
UCC	Uniform Civil Code; *also* Union Carbide Company
UCIL	Union Carbide India Limited
UDHR	Universal Declaration of Human Rights
UNDR	National Union for Democracy and Renewal
UNFPA	United Nations Population Fund (formerly, United Nations Fund for Population Activities)
WIPO	World Intellectual Property Organization
WSF	World Social Forum
WTO	World Trade Organization

From the Series Editors

Turns of millennia are usually occasions to review forms of knowledge production for what they have achieved. The end of the twentieth century was, however, an unusual one in India. Its last decade has often been seen as politically bracketed by globalisation at one end, and the onset of religious majoritarianism at the other. However, as the following century wears on and we look back at our own *fin de siècle*, perhaps the crisis of this time seems to be rather different, and also rather more foundational.

We may well be witnessing something far more significant than merely a political crisis as we come to terms with the insufficiency of several founding concepts of modernity, such as nation, freedom, identity, governance, and indeed of power, as they try to account for our condition. We may therefore have to engage in a struggle that is as much of method as of means, as crippling political developments are exacerbated by the inability of 'big' academic disciplines to adequately perform their primary tasks. Paradoxically, this struggle is rendered especially stark when placed alongside a contrasting, and widespread, optimism that *also* defined the era. The sudden availability of new open-access research tools that were once only to be found in wealthy Western universities now promised a delirious new freedom, as the archives opened up, and transdisciplinary and transnational access led to the crumbling of time-worn disciplinary silos.

This moment in history can be variously characterised. Its simplest description, perhaps, was that it was the time of the 'internet'. Being the era of the internet, it was also a time of new trans-border conversations that were inconceivable a scant decade earlier. It was a time of the globalisation of capital and in its wake, of translational flows of information. As methodological negotiations with the contemporary became linked to strategic coalitions within and outside the university system, the growing inability of established State-supported universities to manoeuvre through new challenges, such as that of privatisation, set the stage as much for the entry of private universities as it did for the short-lived rise of independent research spaces heralding a different energy. Fruitful interactions now began between human and natural science academics, artists, and political activists, initiating conversations between new theoretical frameworks, and drawing in new political movements willing to engage with such frameworks. Directly facilitating their existence in the 1990s were new agencies on the academic scene: large and small donors, international and national, together with diverse 'venture' initiatives—all invested in the idea of change, looking actively to partner, to fund, and to house new kinds of interdisciplinary research, to wager on its transformative potential to both understand social phenomena and fashion new strategies for social intervention. Autonomy from the State, or at least 'arm's length' distance from it, defined an era as much by arguments for the privatisation of education as by the entry of non-governmental and community-based organisations into the areas of research and pedagogy.

Another possible way of characterising this moment, then, was through its pluralisation: of both the *spaces* for doing theory and of the *means* by which theory could be done. While the many books in this series define these spaces and means diversely, a possible common thread that runs through them will be a focus on new practices of trans-institutional knowledge production, typically brought together by the triad of *pedagogy*, *research*, and *public engagement*, often contextualised by the onset of mass public digitisation.

It is clear that this period did not last. One sign of its demise may well be the loss of faith in the internet's neutrality, signalled by the meltdowns, the funding crises, the corruption, the fears of neoliberal excess, the terrorist threats, the surveillance mechanisms, and the new global ecologies that would soon engulf us in the new century. Several millennial goals have since been abandoned or declared unfeasible; the research they generated unsustainable. State-driven nationalism has staged a major comeback, and the draconian implementation of laws, ranging from the Unlawful Activities Prevention Act (UAPA) to the Foreign Contribution Regulation Act (FCRA), have made the very existence of small private institutions a perilous one.

Of relevance to this present series is one such institution, the Centre for the Study of Culture & Society (CSCS), founded in Bangalore in 1998 and effectively closed in 2014, where the editors of this series worked in this time. A significant part of CSCS' self-identity was derived historically, from the tradition of an earlier generation of social science research centres (albeit State-supported ones), themselves products of no less tumultuous a history—that of the Emergency and the years after. If that era had seen the reinvigoration of the disciplines of history, political science, economics, and law, this one would now see transdisciplinary work coming together under the broad heading of 'Cultural Studies'. This domain now included—to take the example of CSCS alone—integrated science education, interventions into the overall emerging field of higher education, the creative economy, critical legal studies (and new directions in economic, social, and cultural rights), new media practices, mental health/psychoanalysis, digital democracy, and Asian cultural theory, apart from the fields of enquiry—such as cinema studies and gender studies—for which CSCS faculty were already known.

It was in the spirit of the times that CSCS, together with a range of new institutions, initiatives, and projects across India, saw its role as moving beyond the limits of the orthodox institution: inventing the term 'inter-institutionality', contending that the array of research resources and networks, which proper interdisciplinary work needed, could never be supported within any single institution, however large or well-funded. Through the late 1990s and the early 2000s, such inter-institutional and interdisciplinary engagements took place in ways both academically conventional and unconventional. Major conferences and workshops were organised in all of the above areas, as were workshops on curricula and research methodology, outreach programmes in undergraduate colleges, student and young researcher conferences. Project implementation strategies were experimented with in areas such as higher education, cultural policy, mental health, and critical legal studies, using means ranging from judicial activism to tactical media.

As we turn back to the millennial moment, then, such diversity of both location and method may need to be placed alongside, and indeed viewed as an elaboration of, the dilemmas faced by academic practice in this fraught era of modern political history. The diversity of means in the expanded space of the human sciences, together with the claim that new practices of pedagogy and public engagement receive full recognition as research domains, were—this series proposes—part and parcel of the larger academic response mounted to the political challenges of the time. Although each of the different books in the series will define its own contours, across all of them we will find outlined an era that was politically fraught, facing crises that were at once of the moment and requiring a larger historical frame; capable of some radical inter-disciplinary/institutional barrier-breaking; sustained, if only momentarily, by the temporary convergence of academic-activist drive and independent support. They will also track, on occasion, the fashioning of several interventionist strategies of both pedagogy and dissent that were adapted to new use within State-funded universities as the 2000s wore on.

The present series revisits the initiatives, practices, and several of the conversations that characterised what it outlines as 'Culture and Democracy at the Millennial Turn'. Although no claims are made towards exhaustiveness, it expects to cover key disciplinary, institutional, and public locations where knowledge practices were assembled in India in this time.

This Volume

In August 2008, CSCS, together with the Alternative Law Forum (ALF), invited Upendra Baxi to Bangalore. He was, in those days, a frequent visitor here, and his visits were always viewed with considerable excitement. This time, however, something new was being attempted.

From 2000, when CSCS and ALF collaborated on a year-long seminar, titled 'Law and Society', several initiatives in the broad area of critical legal studies had taken place under the 'Law, Society and Culture Programme' (or LSCP). In August 2005, LSCP, ALF, and the National Law School of India University had jointly put together the major conference titled 'Enculturing Law: New Agendas for Legal Pedagogy'. Over the following decade, LSCP housed several major projects; for example, the 'Promoting Pluralism Knowledge Programme', an academic-practitioner collaboration to map and generate knowledge addressing identity, social prejudice, and intolerance of faiths other than one's own.

All of this work had happened with Professor Baxi's guidance and support. He had become something of a father figure as he brought his vast institution-building experience to help our fledgling experiment. That August, however, a further step was taken as a series of conversations was planned between Baxi and four young lawyers and legal researchers, to get him to talk about his life and work. The idea began simply enough, to better understand the history he literally embodied. It was preceded by a mammoth effort to assemble and spiral-bind as many of Baxi's writings—the several books that were now out of print, the academic texts, the newspaper articles, the petitions, the letters—as could be managed.

These conversations happened over several days, recorded on a small portable device. There were the usual accidents, and a few conversations were drowned out by ambient noise. Most of the discussion was retained, captured, copied, and eventually transcribed. The result is here, a debate for the ages, ranging from intense to reflective, emotional, confrontational even, as Baxi relived some seventy years of his life and with it, key moments in the legal and political history of independent India. The transcriptions themselves took a while, and the ensuing editing process involved multiple researchers and spanned across India, the UK, the USA, and Australia, as every reference of events, places, people, movements, texts was painstakingly worked out.

Of Law and Life: Upendra Baxi in Conversation with Arvind Narrain, Lawrence Liang, Sitharamam Kakarala, and Sruti Chaganti is an epic retelling: of a life of a person as much as it is of a nation, a saga of India's post-Independence legal history told from within.

The Editors: Tejaswini Niranjana
Ashish Rajadhyaksha
S. V. Srinivas
Sitharamam Kakarala

February 2024

Acknowledgements

This book began as an idea in 2008 and over the past sixteen years, when it has had to traverse the distance from idea to reality, it has accumulated many debts.

This project would not have seen the light of day if it had not been for the commitment of the Series Editor, Ashish Rajadhyaksha, whose incomparable enthusiasm and boundless generosity ensured that the book became reality.

Our Editor, Proteeti Banerjee, has gracefully accommodated our many requests and yet ensured that the book was on track.

Pratiksha Baxi dug through her family archives and made available to us the photos which are reprinted here. Upen captured in what Pratiksha described as 'a conversational mode' on the cover page comes from the family archives as well.

The diligent work of Sean Fuller, who tracked down references and did interviews with key respondents in Australia to shed light on dimensions of Australian law and politics, has been of inestimable value.

Many interns at both the Alternative Law Forum and the Center for Study of Culture and Society have been part of the sixteen-year journey of this volume, from interview to transcript and finally to manuscript, complete with footnotes and references. Their work and labour are gratefully acknowledged.

Introduction

ARVIND NARRAIN AND SITHARAMAM KAKARALA

Professor Upendra Baxi (henceforth Upen) is perhaps the best-known figure in Indian law. 'His decades of towering scholarship,' writes Pratap Bhanu Mehta, 'has said all that can be potentially said about the Indian judiciary' (Mehta 2016). His writings now cover several volumes, and there is no area of law on which one cannot find something of his germinal (a term he prefers to 'seminal', which he considers sexist) contributions. At a time of super-specialisation, Upen has written on vast and diverse areas of what he has titled as nothing less than the 'crisis of Indian law'. His perspectives are multidisciplinary, drawing from sociology, anthropology, philosophy, political economy, and literature, among other disciplines. He has been a well-known commentator on significant legal controversies, writing and speaking extensively in the media over the past fifty years. He has, over the course of his career, been somewhat of a legendary teacher, inspiring thousands of students.

This part is well-known. Less known is what made him the person he has come to be. How do you understand the forces that made Upen, which are only hinted at in his writings? Is there a link between the inner world of passions, the world of thought, and the actions that define an engagement with the external world?

Any link between the internal and the external, passion and reason, thought and action, is complicated, and occurs less in published academic work and more often through biography and autobiography. Ray Monk (1991, xviii) writes in his exemplary biography of Wittgenstein that

> there are... many excellent introductory books on Wittgenstein's work that would explain what his main philosophical themes

> are, and how he deals with them. What they do not explain is what his work has to do with *him*—what the connections are between the spiritual and ethical preoccupations that dominate his life, and the seemingly rather remote philosophical questions that dominate his work.

If a scholar's work does not on its own yield up secrets of the author's passions, the difficulty—especially with respect to legal writing—is multiplied. Conventions of legal writing, the use of the third person, and the displacement of the personality of the author, often provides no clue to authorial motivation. While the Hart-Devlin debate is well-known in jurisprudence, the question as to what impelled H. L. A. Hart to theorise on the separation of law and morals was only answered after Nicola Lacey's biography, when we came to know of the connection between a theoretical position separating law and morals and a deeply personal and intimate aspect of Hart's personality, namely his homosexuality.[1]

This book is not a biography in the conventional sense, nor is it a reconstruction based upon letters, memoirs, personal interviews, interviews with friends, interlocutors, and family, the usual sources of a biography. What you have before you is primarily a product of in-depth conversations that took place over two weeks in 2008. The idea of the conversation developed over a cup of tea at the Alternative Law Forum when some of us felt that there was a unique quality to his speech, familiar to generations of students but perhaps lost to those who had known him only through his writing and not encountered him in person. These conversations reflect some of our preoccupations, and the responses are stimulated by the tenor and nature of the questions. We have tried to preserve the informal quality of the conversations even as we undertook to edit the manuscript. However, although the conversation took place in 2008, some of the literature referenced has been updated till 2023. The transcript, while retaining its quality of speech, was reworked and updated by Upen

[1]'I am or have been a suppressed homosexual (I see you wince) and would become more so (I mean more homosexual and less suppressed) in Oxford' (Lacey 2006, 221).

over a period of time, right up to 2023, accounting for some more contemporary references. As such, the book we present is the product of an affectionate conversation over shared concerns and themes, and thus falls somewhere between biography—really a third person's view of the subject's life—and autobiography, based on the subject's own view of his or her life. Perhaps the closest description of the nature of this conversation is outlined by what Edward Said wrote about a collection of interviews with him.

> All of these pieces occurred, so to speak, in a face-to-face situation. Necessarily then, they reflect the immediacy of such encounters, the back-and-forth, the informal question-and-answer language, the circling around, making, and remaking of a point or argument, the challenge and counter-challenge of interviewer(s) and interviewee.... As such... they are a composite of direct discourse and later clarification. No effort at all has been made by anyone involved to make these interviews seem more 'writerly'. (Said and Viswanathan 2001, Preface)

We try here to capture an oral voice, distinct from the voice of a writer who is well-known in the legal world. The passion, the humour, the spontaneous erudition—qualities that communicate powerfully in the voice, but may not easily translate into the written work—are, we hope, to be found here. He speaks of his work as an activist, academic, and teacher over the past fifty years. He also speaks about the questions—ethical, spiritual, and political—which preoccupied him and the passions that dominated his life. The conversation moves easily between the personal to the political, and then to the larger philosophical. The lens through which we see things is not merely a factual narration of events, but rather 'event' as seen through the Baxi lens, inevitably bringing together politics, activism, and philosophy. There is the expected ease with the discipline of law and yet, at the same time, the ability to cross over into the realm of philosophical reflection, and then again back into a detailed discussion of activist strategies.[2]

---

[2] Upen distinguishes between activist tactics and strategies. In his opinion, 'tactics are things like press notes, lobbying, etc.', which are about 'skill set competence', whereas he asserts that 'strategies are different from tactics'. The

Upen's is a singular subjectivity, and a conversation that has opened doors for each of us on ways of being in the world.[3]

The Air Around Us is Not an Empty Void: Characterising Upen

> *For the air around us is not a dead and empty void, it has in it the rhythm and vibration of the time. We absorb them unconsciously into our bloodstream as the air carries them deep into our hearts and minds.*
>
> Stefan Zweig (2009, 219)

Although specific areas of Upen's work have been engaged with by scholars over the years, few have engaged with the whole of his oeuvre. Three who did so are William Twining, who has described him as a 'protest theorist', Oishik Sircar, who names him a 'professor of pathos', and Adil Hasan Khan, who considers him something like a Don Quixote figure, 'who rebels sans any certainty of success'. To Sircar, 'Baxi's single-most important contribution to jurisprudence in India has been to infuse legal scholarship with pathos—the pathos of suffering, resistance, responsibility and care.' This 'pathos' has been 'disarticulated' by a 'theoretical silence towards the aesthetics in and of Baxi's jurisprudence'. Referring to it as a minor jurisprudence, not 'necessarily (to) mean the opposite of major, or lesser and insignificant', Sircar draws on Deleuze and Guattari to speak of a 'sub-text that comes to the fore only when you look for pathos on the margins of Baxi's writings, or in his marginal writings or read his major works against the grain' (Sircar 2018, 209).

initiation of Strategic Action Litigation or the writing of an open letter on the Mathura rape judgment are strategies and are really means one utilises that can best achieve the desired outcome. See Chapters 13 and 10.

[3] As Said put it, 'many ways, interviews are sustained acts of discovery, not only for the person being interviewed but for even the well-prepared interviewer' (Said and Viswanathan 2001, Preface).

Sircar is of course right to assert that the Baxi corpus cannot be read without attention to its embedding in the 'pathos of suffering, resistance, responsibility and care'. All of Upen's texts, be they doctrinal analysis or interdisciplinary, have these thematics embedded in them. In some texts, suffering is expressly articulated, while elsewhere it remains an unarticulated premise. These conversations only prove Sircar's thesis that a redressal of suffering, a concern with resistance, a need to take responsibility, and an ethic of care are central: his activist work is nothing if not an engagement with suffering and resistance. Early texts like *Crisis of the Indian Legal System*, though grounded strongly in criminology, law, and sociology, is based on an ethic of taking suffering seriously. The 'ethic of care' forms the substratum of the one text that defines his work best: the famous Open Letter on the Mathura judgment, discussed later in this Introduction and in the book itself.

In Khan's complementary text, Baxi's argument for 'a heterogenous multitude of struggling peoples and their communities' is at war with an international law 'common sense' of postcolonial States as sole representatives of their peoples. It is a 'knight errantry' that consists of rebelling against the global *status quo* in an attempt to 'bring about other worlds and futures to come' (Khan 2018, 155, 164). There is indeed something of the quixotic in Upen,[4] but characterising a man at war with the common sense of his time, a man who refuses to be bound by 'what is' and constantly puts forward an imagination of a 'future', may miss out the basic fact that, far from a lonely struggle, Upen's battle is forged in solidarity with 'people in struggle and communities in resistance' (Baxi 2013c, xxxiii). There is a love of reading, as we shall

[4] In *Mambrino's Helmet?* (Baxi 1994c), Baxi refers to an incident from *Don Quixote*, when the Don charges at a poor peasant wearing a barber's basin as a headgear, thinking that the peasant is wearing the famous Mambrino's helmet. Khan argues that 'this taking up of the persona of Quixote by Baxi as an example of Baxi both forming a constellation with a past historical moment of crisis and also instructing others in forming such constellations with his times and their own' (Khan 2018, 161).

see, which parallels the Don's fascination with chivalric romances, but there is also a concrete and passionate engagement in struggle.[5]

The voice we hear is remarkably sensitive to the rhythm and vibration of the time, to quote Zweig, picking up on their pulsations and responding to their felt necessities, responding to concrete historical events as an activist, academic, and as a public intellectual. The uniqueness of Upen's response to various crises in the Indian context is to turn to both the institutional *avatar* of the law and to its utopian and creative energies, bringing together social sensitivity with legal imagination (see Santos 1995). This conversation will insistently return to certain moments in the larger history of the nation, whether it be the Mathura rape case, the Bhopal Gas catastrophe, or the Emergency, each of which have been experienced at a visceral level and end up being life-defining and life-altering.

Three Passions, and Reading as 'Manthan'

In his autobiography, Bertrand Russell summed up his life as a story of 'three passions', namely 'the longing for love, the search for knowledge, and unbearable pity for the suffering of mankind'. He says he 'sought love' because it brought 'ecstasy' and with 'equal passion' 'knowledge', because he 'wished to understand the hearts of men' and wanted to know 'why the stars shine'. While the passion for 'love and knowledge' 'led upward toward the heavens', what brought him down to earth was the third passion of 'pity'. As he puts it, 'echoes of cries of pain' of 'children in famine' and 'victims tortured by oppressors' 'make a mockery of what human life should be', and he longs to 'alleviate this evil', but he cannot and suffers. He concludes that 'this has been my life. I have found it worth living and would gladly live it again if the chance were offered me' (Russell 1994, 1).

[5] As Upen himself notes in response to Hassan Khan, 'quixotism may indeed be tragi-comic but this does not detract from solidarity of sentiment'.

Here, too, we encounter three passions, a testament to a 'mind on fire': a love of knowledge as much as a love of the law, both leavened by the need to redress human suffering.[6] The first two, the passion for knowledge and for law, might have produced a gifted academic residing in an ivory tower. It is ultimately the third, the empathy for the suffering other, that turns Upen towards innovating with the law and insistently bending it towards justice.

What began in early life at the age of five or six is the habit that we shall now term impassioned reading, uncompromised either by the high pressures of activism or the duties of Vice-Chancellorship and rigorous teaching schedules. He claims that this was made possible because he sleeps three-and-a-half hours a day and, as he only half-jokingly told us, 'sleeping long hours is a crime against humanity. Present company included!' (Chapter 13, 459).

Reading becomes an activity through which the self is constituted and reconstituted. 'There is a Sanskrit word called *manthan*,which means churning,' he tells us. 'There is a legend in which elixir is only produced when the ocean is churned with a mountain. Reading must be a churning' (Chapter 9). Books are not transitory experiences to be swallowed and regurgitated: they form his worldview. The thinkers traverse disciplines, from legal scholars like Judith Shklar, Julius Stone, Hans Kelsen, Roscoe Pound, and Niklas Luhmann, to philosophers like Jacques Derrida, Hannah Arendt, Michel Foucault, Jean Paul Sartre, and Peter Winch, to Marxists like E. P. Thompson and Nicos Poulantzas, and writers of fiction like Mahasweta Devi and J. M. Coetzee. Within the Indian canon, Gandhi looms large, as does Ambedkar. While it would be impossible in the Introduction to even inventory the range of references, what we aim to do is to point out that the thinkers invoked are those who contributed to the making of Upen. They are invoked with a passion that makes them not just bit-actors in his universe; rather, they constitute a part of his self.

This is a universe peopled by a range of influences, but one figure traverses the conversation: that of Karl Marx. 'I am yet to find a

---

[6] See Rajni Kothari's autobiography, in which he also talks about three passions: for ideas, for politics, and for institution-building (Kothari 2002).

comparable thinker to Marx,' he says, for 'you then have to read all the others in light of our understanding of Marx. You have to resituate Foucault or, as Agamben said, have to "complete Foucault". You should resituate Agamben through an original reading of Marx' (Chapter 9, 314).

The act of reading Marx was a transformative experience. Upen read *Capital*, Vol. II, over six or seven weeks, and they

> were the worst period of my life, I could have committed suicide I was so unhappy. I neglected my teaching because I could not say I was a teacher when, in the privacy of my own room, I could not understand a book. It was that bad. Reading is difficult... I don't believe one can ever fully understand Marx.

Reading Marx exemplifies 'reading as *manthan*'. The opposite of 'reading as *manthan*' is the method of Jon Elster, who wrote *Making Sense of Marx* (1985). 'Elster,' Upen observes, 'treats Marx as if he was submitting several separate dissertations. Rather than being a student of Marx, you make Marx a student of yours. This to me is the wrong way of going about it.' Reading is being a student of a great mind. 'I am a student of Ambedkar,' he says, 'and every time I read him, I discover something new.' To him, Ambedkar's writing is 'oceanic',[7] for it leads to an understanding of how structural violence works in India. Referencing 'the great book' by Ambedkar, *What Mr Gandhi and the Congress have done to India's Untouchables*, he says that 'there is no book in my esteem more worthy of repeated reading than that. He was no Marxist or Marxian, but he provided embodied, erudite and organic narratives of structural injustice.'

What does reading do for the self? Just as the 'initial endowments of suffering' may sometimes pass on into later life, empathetic reading can broaden and deepen the notion of what it is to be human. Upen's wide reading opens out the domain of passionate engagement. One

[7]'The ocean as a collection of suffering people's tears, constantly replenished, is a powerful imagery and I am of the opinion that Babasaheb's oceanic writings express the power of hope as well as of despair—civic lamentation at the continuing acts of injustice. Civic lamentation has been a powerful voice of subaltern protest' (Baxi 2020b, 15).

remembers his invocations in class of Shivarama Karanth's memorable portrayal of a bonded labourer in *Chomana Dudi* (*Choma's Drum*) as a way to understand the nature of feudal oppression, or of Rohinton Mistry's *A Fine Balance* as the text to read if you are to understand the Emergency. Reading opens out the world beyond one's direct experiences, and replenishes the reservoir of emotions and thoughts which feeds into his teaching, his activism, and his writing. If, as Susan Sontag (Sontag, et al. 2007, 164) puts it, 'a writer is first of all a reader', here we perhaps are justified in saying that all three, activist, teacher, as well as writer, are formed by Upen the reader.

A Lover's Quarrel

Pratiksha and Viplav[8] tell us that Upen's favourite poem is Robert Frost's, *Lesson of Today*.

> And were an epitaph to be my story
> I'd have a short one ready for my own.
> I would have written of me on my stone:
> I had a lover's quarrel with the world. (Baxi and Baxi 2018)

Given that his life's work involves a serious engagement with the continuing project of thinking about what law is, what it should be, what it does, and what it should not do, one may well summarise Upen's lifelong engagement as a lover's quarrel with the law. He is, simultaneously, the harshest critic of the law as well as the one most invested in what it can do for those who suffer. Quoting Benjamin to make the point that one cannot think of the law without at the same time thinking of the police, he exposes what Benjamin calls 'the foundational violence of the law' and what Marx would have called the 'terror of the law', even as he pursues a 'people's law' and 'alternative law'.

[8] Refers to Baxi's two children. Pratiksha Baxi is a noted legal anthropologist, author of *Public Secrets of Law: Rape Trials in India* (2014) and faculty at the Centre for the Study of Law and Governance, JNU. Viplav Baxi is a well-known EdTech Professional and Researcher.

This is not merely an instrumental relationship, but an affective one. He critiques the law and exposes its violence, even as he is committed to working with it. The struggle is not merely how to *use* the law as it exists, but rather to *renovate* it and make it something *other than* what it is. His quarrel with the law has been to push it to be better: in this case, to get it to conform to the ideals of justice. But of course, as any lover knows, you not only transform the loved one, but are yourself also transformed by the encounter with the loved one.

Inevitably, these conversations include a long meditation on the nature of love.

> If you are not vulnerable to love, you are truly post-human in a very pejorative sense. This vulnerability, openness is terribly important. It is not consistent with good moral character, not consistent with the ethic of public standards. But it is this openness to the love of a stranger, a distant third, refusing to regard him/her as an object, a thing—this openness to others is always terribly important. (Chapter 1, 70)

Love can show us a way of being in the world: it is, he said in one public event, 'infinite justice'. Such an idea permeates his often near-lyrical writing on the Constitution.

> ...we also have to rebuild the Constitution and reinterpret what constitutional law is for. That's a kind of constitutional love because it is irredeemably related to justice.... That's what makes it beautiful, and that's what enthrals me, engages me, makes me a kind of perpetual labourer.... That is the only way I can relate to the Constitution. That is a wonderful feeling. (Chapter 10, 347)

The Constitution, or what Baxi would famously call its 'C3' aspect—as we discuss at some length below and in Chapter 10 of this book—represents hope, aspiration, and struggle. One has to 'own' the Constitution, in terms of 'caring for it' and 'living within it'. This habitation within the Constitution, this care of it, produces a politics of 'invention'. Both the Mathura Open Letter and Social Action Litigation (Chapter 10), the two legal interventions most directly associated with Upen, are, as examples of C3, the result of this 'lover's quarrel', which bends the law towards justice.

Experiencing Suffering

In these conversations, Upen shares memories of his childhood in Rajkot in a joint family. To him, it is in part a realm of politics where 'there was bickering and backbiting' and it was his 'mother who was the object of a particularly malignant misunderstanding'. Upen attributes his ease with Roman law to his experience of the joint family as embodying the power of the head of the household over life and death. 'Homo Sacer is not very different from other ancient traditions of law,' he says (Chapter 1, 61). To see one's life through the lens of theory and to respond with a conceptual imagination to the experience of the past: this ability marks a specifically Upenian characteristic, of an incessant recasting of personal experience into a wider worldview.

The deeply personal experience raises a more abstract question: whether the 'initial endowments of suffering... carry on in later life'. 'What moral residue does this early experience leave us with is the question' (Chapter 1, 69). The formulation is really about the role of suffering in human existence. Does suffering really broaden our ethical horizons, deepen our capacity for empathy, and enhance the possibility of solidarity? Is it true that, because I know what it is to suffer, I have an enhanced ability to put myself in your skin when you are suffering? Do we go along with Stefan Zweig (2009, 48), who said that 'crises and problems that oppress the human heart at the same time greatly enlarge it'?

Responding to the Suffering Other

Or one could weep because another wept.

W. H. Auden, *The Shield of Achilles* (1952)

Central to the development of a worldview is the need to alleviate the suffering of the other. 'The constant making and remaking of the self in response to a genuinely shared sense of suffering, isn't that what we call being human?' (Chapter 6, 192). Suffering, be it of the indigenous people in Australia or the young tribal woman called Mathura, triggers the insistent Leninist question, 'What is to be done?'

To answer this question, one needs to first feel the problem intensely. What does it mean, to feel a problem with intensity? For Nietzsche, 'the problem itself is experienced deeply, and only problems that are experienced so deeply are given consideration. Only problems that present themselves so forcefully that they threaten the thinker's present mode of life lead to philosophic inquires' (Kaufmann 2013, 89). The sense one gets in the course of the conversation is a similar conflict, into which the self is flung in response to suffering humanity.

> When I read the Mathura judgment, I could not for days together eat, drink, or even sleep.... I was not in a place where I could embody my pain in the larger universe, but I was very hurt and upset because the High Court convicts the policemen, but the Supreme Court says there are no marks of resistance on this tribal girl, and therefore it must be deemed that she consented. I had never heard of this kind of injustice. So I said what should I do, write a monograph, write an essay, a newspaper, or a learned journal article? Will any of this work?... And, after a week of anguishing about this after my classes every day, I hit on the idea of an open letter to the Chief Justice of India.... (Chapter 10, 335)

Bhopal produces a similar impact:

> I went to Bhopal on the third or fourth day after the gas leak. I was in South Gujarat University at the time; I just took a plane and went to Bhopal. I saw contingency-fee lawyers right on the roadside. I saw bodies piled over each other in hospital or being taken in public trucks for mass cremation.... I stayed there two or three nights talking to people, they did not know me, I did not know them. I just had to do it, I had to go. It is kind of a strange happening, you would say.... (Chapter 12, 446–447)

So does the condition of the women in the Agra Women's Home:

> We were concerned about what was happening in the Agra Women's Home. We got to know that there were hundreds of women living in a space the size of a small room, some of them suffering from STD and other physical ailments. (Chapter 10, 340)

It is this deep engagement with human suffering, with the question of what one can do at the back of one's mind, which leads one to innovate. As Upen puts it:

> In retrospect, this ability not just to produce results through an engagement in an instant exchange, but in a dialogical terrain that nobody had thought of travelling was a direct result of the thorough immersion in the immiseration of the Agra Home women's lives. It is not a question of my brilliance or anything. So, citizen interpretation is a passionate engagement with the suffering of the other. This is the key to the whole thing. And when you are really immersed, it is unlikely that you will be impoverished in your imagination or your articulation. (Chapter 10, 341–42)

'One must still have chaos in oneself to be able to give birth to a dancing star' (Nietzsche). The chaos into which the self was flung was what produced the Mathura Open Letter and the initiation of what Upen would call 'social action litigation'. These creative responses to crises resulted in innovative activist forms and practice. The Bhopal struggle produced the notion of absolute liability and the Public Liability Insurance Act.

Humour as 'Lightness'

Perhaps the most fundamental of the many qualities that communicate the unique spoken voice that we present here is the sense of irreverent humour: one quality not amenable to easy translation into Upen's written work. As we see repeatedly, what humour does is to subvert, and transform, the idea of authority. As an Associate Research Professor and Joint Editor of the *Journal of Indian Law Institute*, he worked under the 'brilliant scholar', 'charismatic teacher', but 'authoritarian leader', G. S. Sharma. Sharma would go away for long periods from the Institute, often taking the key of the mailbox with him. As editor, it was impossible for Upen to carry out his job when incoming articles were locked away in the mailbox. So he just 'overturned the mailbox' and 'took all the letters related to the journal'. When 'Sharmaji' returned, he was furious. Upen, when confronted, defended himself by saying that it was his job to keep to the schedule, and he had no other way to do his job. When Gianiji thundered that 'you are undermining my authority', Upen's quick response was that 'authority may reside in many strange places, but it surely does not reside in a mailbox'! (Chapter 3, 102)

On another memorable occasion (described in the same chapter), Upen talks of how he went along with Sharmaji to meet Chief Justice Hidayatullah in his chambers regarding the journal of the Indian Law Institute. After the customary pleasantries, the Chief Justice offered them something to eat, when suddenly he saw a big rat and said that for 'the first and only time... shrieked in the Chief Justice's chamber'. When normalcy had returned, the Chief Justice asked whether he had never seen rats in his life. He had, he replied, but not this big. To which Hidayatullah said, 'Do you think the Chief Justice of India can work with rats of a lesser size?' Upen says, 'He had the liveliest sense of humour, and that's why we got to be good friends'! (Chapter 3, 104)

In one (presumably serious) conversation with feminist colleagues, when Upen suggests that they read bestselling author Lawrence Sanders' book, *The Passion of Molly T*,[9] and his suggestion is received with bemusement, he reflects that 'the trouble with me... is that people cannot make me out—when I am actually joking, they take me seriously, and when I say something serious, they think I am joking'!

[9] As Upen puts it,

> Lawrence Sanders has a marvellous account in this book of militant anti-liberal feminism, the whole idea and programme of which is the violent destruction of sex industries, especially of Playboy. They are not asking for anti-pornography legislation like Catherine Mackinnon, they just blow up the headquarters of Playboy, and there are all kinds of violent insurrections by women for equality. It is a marvellous story. Then the question arises: Why doesn't one of us contest the US Presidency and bring about change from the top rather than from below? I won't tell you the second part of the story. Anticlimactic. Obviously, the system captures you more often than you capture the system. It is the name of the game. So, there comes the stress of disenchantment with reformism. (Chapter 8, 267)

(Chapter 8, 267). Upen's approach embodies what Susan Sontag called having a sense of 'play', which can 'dethrone the serious'. He is, to the chagrin of the humourless, 'frivolous about the serious' and 'serious about the frivolous'. Underlying this sense of play is a recognition that one needs to develop a 'new, more complex relation to "the serious", because "Sincerity can be simple philistinism, intellectual narrowness"' (Sontag 2009, 514).

Humour can transform both activism and teaching, as in Sontag's phrase it introduces a 'new, more complex, relationship to the serious'. Too much seriousness may disguise a dangerous narrowness of vision, a monomania that refuses to see other perspectives. To be playful about serious subjects can be an act of profound and meaningful subversion. To humorously subvert authority, to poke fun at self-important persons, can be a way of asserting a radical equality. Humour's importance is really about an outlook on life: it is, for Wittgenstein, 'not a mood but a way of looking at the world'. To say that 'humour was stamped out in Nazi Germany' did not mean that 'people were not in good spirits'. It rather meant 'something much deeper and more important' (Monk 1991, 529).

What is the 'deeper and more important'? What can humour truly contribute? A disposition of lightness as a 'reaction to the weight of living'? Calvino outlines 'lightness' as one of his memos for the new millennium, a disposition that does not deny 'the reality of the world of monsters' in which we live, but rather, a method that entails a 'subtraction of weight'. For Calvino, 'there is a lightness that is thoughtful and that is different from the frivolous lightness we all know. Indeed thoughtful lightness can make frivolity seem heavy and opaque' (2016, 6).

There is a real danger, especially for activists, of taking oneself too seriously. Such activists are likely to be weighed down by the feeling of 'doom and gloom', producing 'cynicism instead of hope'. Approaching the world with a sense of humour dispels heaviness in the air and opens the possibility of hope. Nobody who meets Upen goes away with a sense of doom, inspite of talking about difficult, if not impossible, situations: a tribute to what 'lightness' as a way of approaching the world can contribute.

The Hedonist Teacher: Teaching as Provocation

The most significant parts of a legacy may also be among the most ephemeral. Upen has taught thousands of students from many regions of the world in the course of his long teaching career. The importance he gave to teaching is evident from the fact that even when he had to discharge the onerous responsibilities of a Vice-Chancellor, he would still teach.

An important part of being a teacher involves the act of engaging the class repeatedly, over a period of time. The classroom interaction is rarely recorded and often only survives in the memories of students. Teaching, for Upen, 'in the profoundest sense of the word, has always appeared ... to be sacrificial, a process in which the best articulation of personality is achieved in the least lasting form, a process in which the teacher herself is, as it were, fire at the altar of knowledge' (Baxi 1990a, 152).

This classroom performance is slowly finding its chroniclers, for instance through recent essays by Amita Dhanda[10] and Mathew John[11] in the *Jindal Global Law Review*. While generations of law

[10] Amita Dhanda recollects Upen as a charismatic teacher, doctoral guide, and a presence in her own teaching of law. She provides a recollection of Upen in class.

> I, yet again, realised the social situatedness of scholarship when in a 'Distributive Justice' class, I made a class intervention, which stridently endorsed some version of formal equality. Baxi heard me out and then wryly remarked that my opinion evidently emanated from my privileged middle-class background. It was a punch in the stomach, which brought home to me that I did not just have to be cognisant of the social backgrounds of the authors I was reading but needed to be equally cognizant of my own background. Both the theorist and the reader exist in a context and that context should not be rendered invisible in the process of learning. (Dhanda 2018, 260)

[11] A stirring recollection of Upen as a teacher is provided by Mathew John.

> One such tale of hope that continues to remain with me was the Canadian Supreme Court's recognition of native title in the now well-known case of *Delgamuukw v British Columbia*. We did, of course,

students have benefitted from Upen as a teacher, his own theorisation of the practice of teaching has found admirers from beyond the law. Brinda Bose, in her meditation on Upen's piece, 'Teaching as Provocation', picks up the contemporary relevance of what Upen names the 'hedonist teacher', as compared to a 'rationalist teacher'.[12] The hedonist teacher challenges the status quo of teaching and is an 'adventurer who, above all, derives irrational pleasure from her teaching activities, which always challenge proscriptions on behaviour and method' (Bose 2018, 284).

This conversation lingers over the hedonist teacher who worked in Australia with students to challenge the status quo of indigenous exploitation, inspired students to initiate what he would later go on to call 'social action litigation', challenged hierarchies in the classroom, and deployed humour as a learning tool.

The hedonist teacher embodies the idea of teaching as ethics. For Upen, it is a search for 'moral perfection', and 'if you cannot bear to look at your face because it makes visible the agonies of millions, then you have arrived as a teacher'. The shift is really from the idea of doing justice to 'some congregation that you call the class', to doing justice to oneself. The question for Upen is whether 'you have been true to your vocation'.

> discuss the technical detail of the case like any good lawyer must, but we were intrigued by the way in which Baxi started us off in reading that case by taking us to its schedule. Hidden in that schedule were the names of almost fifty tribal chiefs who had brought that case to court. By making us read those unfamiliar names Baxi taught us the perennial importance of reading the law as form of mediation through which lives and worlds of 'little people' were often shaded into the margins. (John 2018, 328)

[12]'If the "rationalist" teacher is governed strictly by the rules of a discipline, she is also governed by strictness and correctness of demeanour and method. The "hedonist" is like the humanities, employing modes that combine intensity and precision, abandonment and depth; and so also, as Baxi says, "Bonds of sharing so conspicuous among the 'hedonist' teacher-taught relationships are seen as threatening with anarchy the manicured garden of ideas in the rationalist processes of 'teaching'"' (Bose 2018, 283).

Upen is driven by the need to establish a connection with his students, not speak over them or at them, but to them and with them. It is this worldview that leads him to make a link between the world of contemporary politics and that of the syllabus. The daily newspaper becomes a pedagogic tool to initiate students into new fields of law. Contemporary developments, from the Gulf of Tonkin Resolution, the SALT talks between the US and the USSR, to the arrest of Pinochet in London, become 'gateways to jurisprudence'.

When he began teaching in Sydney, Upen initially filled in for the legendary Australian legal scholar Julius Stone, and had to lecture on Maine and Savigny. 'I looked at this sea of faces, they were not interested in Maine, they were not interested in Savigny, and there was no way I could interest them in these texts.' He ploughed on, but 'was deeply dissatisfied'. When he taught the course to another batch of students, he recollected that that was the time that the struggle for self-determination in Papua-New Guinea was on.

> There was a lot of discussion in the papers, in the *Sydney Morning Herald*, and so on. I asked the students to bring the daily newspapers to class. From the debate on Papua-New Guinea, I led them back to Maine and Savigny. My route to the texts was through these contemporary debates. The students, they just loved it. (Chapter 4, 119)

Upen enjoys teaching and is able to communicate that enjoyment to students. Humour becomes a resource for teaching.

> For example, in many Indian languages, instead of saying 'state', one says 'estate'. Many people, and not just from Haryana, say 'estate' instead of 'state'. Hegel has a theory where he says that the State emerges from estates. So, I used to say that many folks thought of that distinction, thus bringing Hegel down from his high pedestal! So, misspellings, mispronunciations can be resources for teaching law and human rights.
>
> Different styles of spoken English are gateways to jurisprudence. These are just minor things, but it gets the class interested. (Chapter 13, 490)

For Upen, teaching is not only about what the law 'is', but equally about what it 'ought to be'. Education is a 'high art of speaking to the future':

one that Upen pursues through many techniques. One technique is getting the students to 'think in pairs'. Students are asked, 'What is the other of colonisation? What is the other of globalisation, that is, colonisation without colonisers? What is the other of exploitation? If you think exploitation has no other, then virtually the struggle for justice ends.' Opening out these questions in class has incalculable effects, and teaching itself can become 'a resource for the movement'.

Conceptualising teaching as a form of ethics, striving to establish a connection with your students, and a willingness to go beyond conventional pedagogies mark the 'hedonist' teacher. In Bose's prognosis, this ideal of a hedonist teacher is under threat in campuses around the country.

> Teaching and learning spaces in the university are closing in on us inexorably. We are gasping to survive a death-grip on the idea of a democratic classroom, a classroom in which ideas soar and dip with freedom between student and teacher, student and student. Instead, we find ourselves mired continually in seeping suspicion, dread and venom on our campuses, most perhaps among erstwhile comrades turned combatants. (Bose 2018, 280)

Today, knowledge is becoming increasingly professionalised and dominated by experts in narrower and narrower domains. There is a growing disconnect between the world we live in and the world we study, appositely described by Amitav Ghosh (2016) as the 'Great Derangement'. It is in this context that the romantic call of the 'hedonist teacher' is more important than ever before.

The Legal Activist: Social Action Litigation and the Open Letter

Of particular importance to the *oeuvre* is the use of the law to challenge forms of societal and State oppression. A motivating force has been the question which an activist with the Bhoomi Sena, named

Kalu Ram, once asked Upen: How, he wanted to know, could one 'use the law of the oppressor on behalf of the oppressed?' (Chapter 5). A particular niche, that of a legal activist, opens up: the legal activist is specifically committed to thinking about and innovating strategies in the law to deploy on behalf of the oppressed, and as such, can be traced back to the pioneering work of both Gandhi[13] and Ambedkar.[14] Contemporary histories of legal activism still need to be told.[15]

Central to the imagination of a legal activist is a commitment to struggling with the law to wrest space within it for those who are on the margins. As K. Balagopal put it:

> Courts say they do their job within the four corners of the law, but the four corners are only corners. The space enclosed may be quite wide, and can permit divergent tendencies, all of

[13] Arvind Narrain (2013) argues that

> In his lifetime, Gandhi engaged, creatively, passionately and subversively with law. This engagement was varied and creative and included his civil rights work in South Africa, his crucial role in preparing a fact-finding report after the Jallianwala Bagh massacre, his use of legal journalism to generate popular support for the independence movement, leveraging the theatrical potential of the court and making an argument that the law to be law must be connected to justice. These demonstrate an alternative Gandhian conception of the law.

[14] Baxi writes: 'At least till recently, Ambedkar was "ritually celebrated" even as he was "intellectually marginalized"'. He notes that 'the Indian social science landscape has disarticulated Babasaheb Ambedkar by studious theoretical silence'. In this climate of silence, he asserts that Ambedkar was the originator of the idea of the 'lawless laws of Hinduism', which not only denied 'equality before the law as a principle to the untouchables, thus erecting a permanent edifice of subalternity over them down the ages', but also 'inscribed the extra territorialisation of whole communities of human beings and their castigation as being outside the pale of humanity' (Baxi 1995).

[15] For some initial work based on interviews with fifty human rights lawyers in India, see Narrain and Uma (2016). Like Upen, some of the figures who have been influential in multiple roles as lawyers, activists, and public intellectuals include K. Balagopal, K. G. Kannabiran, and Nandita Haksar. For a collection of writings by them, see www.balagopal.org and Balagopal (2011), Kannabiran (2004, 2022), and Haksar (2007).

> them passing for interpretations of the law or the Constitution. (Balagopal 2009, 16)

For all their strong critiques of the law, for both Upen and Balagopal, much can indeed be done within its four corners. Neither belong to the Critical Legal Studies tradition, or indeed to any postmodernist tradition that might, in Upen's words, 'curl up on this chair, have a nice smoke of whatever kind, and pooh-pooh the idea of civilisation or modernity'. Rather, legal activism becomes a passionate and relentless engagement with the idea of the future. Upen illustrates this approach in his discussion around the idea of a just war. The notion of a just war restricts the ability to wage war. If the war is just, then the legal activist cannot give up, but has to come back with a formulation about the injustice of the means used to prosecute what may be, in its aims, a just war.

> Thinking is saying, if you accept the first half, we come back to you on the second half. You appropriate our notion of just war for your own expedient purposes, then we come back and say, a just war becomes unjust because you have used unjust means. This is what I call thinking. For most of us, thinking is a one-shot activity. But thinking is a paired concept, always raising the question of alternatives. If you say that unnecessary suffering should be minimised in acts of war, unjust means should not be deployed in the act of war, you very nearly render almost all acts of war unjust by another move, a narrative, textual, tactical move. (Chapter 8, 253)

To be a legal activist is a commitment to bending the law towards justice: to produce 'alternative law'. 'It must be alternative to the existing indifference to certain central problems of law and state,' he says (Chapter 13, 496). To be alternative is to 'draw the curtain not down but up on things that are taboo, like sexuality, terror, CPV [Collective Political Violence], etc.' This can happen from many strategic vantage points. Upen's preeminent contributions to innovating the forms of legal activism in the Indian context were what he was to call 'social action litigation' (SAL), as well as the form of the 'Open Letter' post the Mathura rape case.

The first social action litigation he initiated was on the condition of the protective homes in Agra, reported as *Dr Upendra Baxi vs. State of Uttar Pradesh*.[16] He was 'very upset' when his name was cited as Dr Upendra Baxi, as this implicitly put one person in front. What needed to be done was 'to collectivise' (Chapter 12). All the SALs he would now be involved in had the name of an organisation which represented the issue. This is the salient distinction between *public interest* and *social action* litigation that became—and this is why he called it that—not merely on *behalf of* a public, but a mode through which a *collective* could come into being, to take forward the struggle.

The other dilemma of SAL has been that of representation. Who was he to speak on behalf of a suffering community, especially as he did not live amongst them or share their pain? He 'has been haunted by this question'. The tentative answer to the problematic of representation is never to speak on *behalf of* a community, but rather, speak *with* that community. Speaking *with* is 'a phrase, but it is also a real and engaged set of practices of material labour, and not just a metaphysical set of thoughts and ambitions' (Chapter 6, 196). The impact of SAL should be judged not purely from the question of a victory or a loss. Taking the example of the Narmada Bachao Andolan, which challenged the construction of a number of massive dams on the Narmada river through a SAL and finally lost the case, he speaks of how, during the pendency of the litigation, the Court granted a stay order which was in effect for four-and-a-half years: 'it was at this time that the Narmada Bachao Andolan became a nationwide movement' (see Chapter 12, 431).

> Delay is very critical to creating the social space and political time in which to create linkages among suffering people. Delay is a very important resource for people's movements.... When you have this political time and social space, you cannot be repressed. It is a non-repressive space. When you are before the court, you are protected.

Perhaps the most innovative of all forms was the Open Letter: devised first in a joint letter written to the Chief Justice following the decision

[16] (1981) 3 Scale 1137.

in the 1974 Mathura case when constables were acquitted of the rape of Mathura, which occurred inside a police station. Once the Supreme Court gave its decision upholding the acquittal of the accused, he was in a dilemma as to what to do. This discontent, and the form it took, has had incalculable consequences, picked up by the feminist movement in India that went on to campaign against the injustice done to Mathura as well as for a reform of the rape law. The campaign led to amendments to the law and to the recognition of custodial rape as a form of rape. This result leads him here to distinguish between what he calls 'episodic' and 'structural' activism: while justice for Mathura may have been episodic, the demand for law reform is structural. It is not a question of prioritising one over the other; rather, it is how the episodic must 'become a gateway for the structural moment... must flow into the structural'.[17]

The law can be used to 'create a new social consciousness' even in a conservative social and political system. The first attempt at a Public Interest Litigation (PIL) when he was a teacher in Australia 'broke the conspiracy of silence on the issue of aboriginal rights in the academia'. If the law has to be seen as a catalyst in transforming social consciousness, its impact needs to go beyond narrow quantitative parameters. Its impact is often wider than merely a victory or defeat, and impacts the way society looks at an issue. It is this lens that must be used to assess issues where the fundamental battle may well be to

---

[17] Balagopal also reflects upon the relationship between the episodic and the structural in his work, which began with preventing the torture of political prisoners in police lock-up.

> In the beginning police used to make fun of us. That look when you come to a police station asking for the release or somebody to be produced in court who happens to be a radical, he is in the lockup, there are ten more people in the lockup along with him, why don't you talk about them? Police, of course were not interested that we should talk about them. They were interested in exposing our one-sidedness. But we learnt a lesson from that. So we started saying that torture is wrong. And if torture is wrong, then you have to answer many more questions. Because you are saying torture not only of a political revolutionary, but also of a criminal is wrong. (Transcript of interview with Deepa Dhanraj, www.balagopal.org [accessed January 2022])

change societal mindsets. This is particularly evident when we assess the impact of the long battle against criminalisation of LGBTQI lives, which finally resulted in the decision of *Navtej Singh Johar vs. Union of India* that decriminalised LGBTQI lives in India.[18]

The battle to change social consciousness cannot stop at a judicial decision. How, Upen asks, 'do you convey a Shah Bano, a Bandua Mukti Morcha, an Unnikrishnan or any major decision, to those beyond the ones who may be immediately involved in the litigation?'[19] In *Navtej Singh Johar vs. Union of India*, Justice Nariman pays heed, in his concurring opinion, to the same problematic by ordering that

> The Union of India shall take all measures to ensure that this judgment is given wide publicity through the public media, which includes television, radio, print and online media at regular intervals, and initiate programs to reduce and finally eliminate the stigma associated with such persons.[20]

This issue of communicating the constitutional implications of a judgment is really about 'transmitting the social meaning of the constitution', and in effect fostering a constitutional consciousness founded on a respect for the inherent dignity of the human person. This is a task that legal activists have to attend to if they are to ensure that a judgment in the books transforms attitudes on the ground. This calls for creative communication strategies that use a multiplicity of forms, including theatre, art, and social media.

While legal activism is of course premised upon a victory, more often than not the result may be defeat. When such is the result, what is the way forward? For 'each institution of governance, there might be corresponding modes of public influence and articulation' (Chapter 12, 440). The first response to a decision one does not

---

[18] (2018) 10 SCC 1. For Upen's contribution to this process, see S. Narrain (2018, 299).

[19] *Mohd Ahmed Khan vs. Shah Bano Begum and Ors*, AIR 1985 SC 945, *Bandhua Mukti Morcha vs. Union of India*, AIR 1984 SC 802, *Unnikrishnan P.J. and Ors. vs. State of A.P. and Ors*, AIR 1993 SC 2178.

[20] *Navtej Singh Johar vs. Union of India*, Concurring Opinion of Nariman J., (2018) 10 SCC 1.

agree with cannot be a *dharna*, as that may not be 'a responsible way of relating to the court or of changing its behaviour'. In Upen's thinking, 'these practices go against the very idea of public reason or deliberation that the court is supposed to embody. Courts may not be reduced to political parties.' The form and scale of the protest have to be commensurate with the nature of the case (Chapter 12).

Legal activism is also about innovating the forms of the law in a bid to generate a public consciousness around pressing human rights challenges. The work of the Permanent People's Tribunals (PPTs) is one such experiment with which Upen has been deeply involved.[21] In a recent session of the PPT held on 14–18 May 2018, Upen was one of the judges who wrote the Advisory Opinion on the activities included under the label of 'fracking' and other unconventional oil and gas extraction techniques, and on climate change, with the objective of generating a public consciousness around fracking as an issue with serious human rights implications.[22]

---

[21] The precursor to the PPT is the Russell Tribunal, which was initiated by Betrand Russell and had eminent members like Jean Paul Sartre. The Russell Tribunal began its work with adjudicating the legality of the American war in Vietnam and several other issues of mass human rights violations in the Latin American context. The Permanent People's Tribunal was established in 1979 in Bologna, and its statute elucidates the objectives as follows:

> a tribune of visibility, of the right to speak, of the affirmation of the rights of peoples exposed to severe and systematic violations by public and private actors, at national and international levels, who have no possibility of referring and having access to competent organs of the organised international community;
>
> an instrument of explicitation and verification of the existence, the severity, the responsibilities, and impunity of the concrete violations, as well as of the due measures of justice and reparation;
>
> a witness and promoter of research aimed at filling the institutional and doctrinal gaps in existing international law.
>
> (http://permanentpeoplestribunal.org/wp-content/uploads/2019/05/Statute-of-the-PPT_ENG_FINAL.pdf [accessed January 2022])

[22] See http://permanentpeoplestribunal.org/47-session-on-human-rights-fracking-and-climate-change-14-18-may-2018/?lang=en (accessed January 2022).

The legal activist stands in a slightly different relationship to the constituency s/he claims to represent, as compared to a social activist. The best of social activists often have close and intimate ties with the communities they claim to represent. However, for legal activists who are not community-based lawyers, but rather work with High Courts and the Supreme Court or with law reform, the link to the communities they claim to represent may be more distanced. This democratic deficit in the power to represent is something that Upen is acutely conscious of, and as he puts it, 'It torments me even now.... If I am not tormented by deep ethical anxieties, then I am not an activist' (Chapter 12, 413–414).

Legal activism as a domain is by and large an under-theorised practice. In this context, Upen's body of work provides an important vantage point from which to begin theorising the field, including questions such as what might count as legal activism, the strategies of a legal activist, and the ethical dilemmas a legal activist encounters.

The Administrator

Upen was the Dean of the School of Law, Delhi University from 1975–78. After that, he was the Vice-Chancellor of the University of South Gujarat, from 1982–85. Finally, he was the Vice-Chancellor of Delhi University from 1990–94.

To all these administrative duties, he brought his own worldview. These conversations document his instinctive aversion to what he calls the 'semi-feudal nature of the university system', and the propensity of those in power to hold a *durbar*.

> People have their own followers. The Dean would have some teachers always in his office, whether they worked or not, carrying tales about other colleagues, a kind of durbar. You cannot imagine a feudal system without a royal court. Holding court with people sitting around. Whether they were doing any work, academic, administrative, scientific, was not the question. (Chapter 14, 461)

He sets about trying to 'defeudalise the university and its administration'. He decides to be 'ruggedly democratic' and ensures that 'everything is transparent'. Criticism is welcome and he begins a monthly newsletter named *Outlaw*, in which criticism, including of the Dean, could be printed. Colleagues are referred to by their first names, for 'the marker of our relationships cannot be titles such as Dr, Prof., etc.' These are 'small steps of communicative courtesy', and they work (Chapter 13, 462).

A feudal mindset sees the university as a system in which one can exercise power: a space in which power can be exercised to 'raise somebody's marks, to give jobs, to make somebody from temporary to permanent employee'. 'I would say, you are kidding yourself if you think this is power. This is the lowest form of power.... With the captive audience of a maximum of 100 in a classroom, one does not capture or exercise sovereign power of a state or peoples.' He quotes anthropologist Margaret Mead, a visitor to his office, to make the point that 'if you want money, you do not go to the university, if you want power, you do not go to the university. The only reason you go to the university is if you like thinking and reading and writing. Money and power are not consistent with a university career' (Chapter 14, 463).

His most challenging administrative post was the Vice-Chancellorship of Delhi University, with its enrollment in the lakhs. Delhi University then had 2,50,000 students and ninety affiliated colleges. To the challenge of administering what was in effect a sub-political system was added the fact that shortly after he assumed office, the implementation of the Mandal Report was announced, and student protests broke out on the issue. He reminisces about the 'burden' of dealing with a system of such 'scale and complexity' (Chapter 13), but in a typical Upen touch, leavens the burden through humour.

> One day, after the first one-and-a-half years of Vice-Chancellorship, I felt truly liberated when I met a person who was associated with the University of Iran. It turned out that he was the VC of all the Iranian universities. He said he must have 600,000 students. I made the mistake of asking him: Do you have any leisure time, and what do you do in your leisure time? He said, the Iranian revolutionary council has entrusted me with

> the job of Islamising science and technology. I had no problems compared to that! DU's problems did not exist compared to the kinds of problems he had to face. So, after that, like Bertie Wooster, I had a song on my lips, tra-la-la, without a care in the world. It's all relative. (Chapter 13, 461)

Although teaching is an 'ephemeral practice' and legal activism is under-theorised, there is at least some writing on both aspects. When academics choose to take on administrative burdens and sully their hands with the nitty-gritty of administration, the underlying motivation is a commitment to nurturing academic spaces, nourishing public educational spaces, and creating a 'fellowship of learning'. This aspect clearly needs to be better understood and discussed.

The Scholar: Situating Upendra Baxi's Work in India and the Global South

Although firmly grounded in the Indian context, Upen has also taught in Australia, the United Kingdom, and the United States of America. It is hard to either summarise or locate the prolific scholarly contributions in these spaces, but it may be possible to outline a schema and capture some key intellectual contributions of his work.

William Twining (2009) says that 'dominant scholarly and activist discourses about human rights' have developed without reference to scholarly voices from within the global South. Upen's work, according to Twining, needs to form part of a global intellectual conversation. In the ignoring of 'southern voices', Twining recognises what Upen later calls 'epistemic racism' within global scholarship, and warns that 'claims about universality sit uneasily with ignorance of other traditions and parochial or ethnocentric tendencies'.

> Baxi moves smoothly from his Indian intellectual heritage (Gandhi, Ambedkar, the Supreme Court of India) to Western (especially Anglo-American) jurisprudence (he has written about Bentham, Kelsen, Rawls, Dworkin, and Stone), through Marxian theory (Marx, Gramsci, Benjamin) and Natural law

> (Aquinas, Gewirth), drawing on contemporary sociology (e.g. Beck, Bourdieu, and Castells) and Continental European philosophy (Foucault, Derrida, Laclau, Levinas), engaging with but distancing himself from post-modernism (especially Rorty) and critical legal studies, and dealing more sympathetically with Nussbaum and Sen. (Twining 2009, 219)

The uniqueness of the Southern voice is not just in the intellectual traditions brought to the table, but equally in the concerns around injustice and dehumanisation that emerge from the global South. Twining describes Baxi as a 'protest theorist', and his voice as 'an impassioned plea that human rights discourse should first and foremost be interpreted and used to further the interests of the worst off' (ibid., 220).

Unique to Upen's work is not only a deep-rooted sense of place, but also the imagination to move beyond one's own location and make connections with other Southern contexts. Coming from a subcontinent with a rich and complex history, he repudiates specialist credentials, preferring instead to 'understand the struggle of the Zapatistas in some uncommon yet common place'. Social movements 'have to narrate the experience of localised struggle, but they should also be able to relate to similar localised struggles elsewhere'. The legal imagination, although forged in the fires of the local, should not be limited to the local; and so the venerated Subaltern Studies movement is critiqued for its 'inability to enable and forge links between similar narratives from, say, Latin America. This might be its strength, but it is also its limit.... If you take the local as a unique property, then it is also the limit of your universe' (Chapter 6, 191).

Doctrine, Necessary but not Sufficient

At the heart of his contribution to the study of law is a methodological approach that distinguishes Upen from his predecessors (and many of his contemporaries): the emphasis on both the study of doctrine and its contextualisation within the study of other disciplines.

Following the dominant tradition, the doctrinal approach has a significant place in the study of law, for Upen as well. Thus, the germinal studies of Indian law, *Supreme Court and Politics, Courage, Craft and Contention*, or *The Little Done, The Vast Undone*, take forward their larger research agenda of demonstrating the politics of the judicial role and of constitution-making, based on a penetrating exposition of legal doctrine. His accurate prediction of the disqualification of Indira Gandhi for corrupt practices by the Allahabad High Court, described in this book, which surprised everybody, and led to him being feted as a legal 'genius' by the then Vice-Chancellor, Sarup Singh, was (to him) no more than a reading of precedent and an understanding that an order of the Supreme Court on corrupt electoral practices was akin to a 'sheet of instruction' to the Allahabad High Court, which was bound to decide the way it did.

It was a similar grasp of doctrine and knowledge of *May's Parliamentary Practice* that led him to 'play a small role' in the Haryana MLA Hardwari Lal's successful challenge to his expulsion from the state legislative assembly in 1975 (see Chapter 7). This grasp of doctrine is also evident in the complex Bhopal litigation, which demanded a mastery over many areas of law, including private international law, civil procedure, tort law, criminal law, and constitutional law. As a lawyer's lawyer—writing for lawyers, parsing the law, distinguishing precedents, keeping up to date on the latest case law, both nationally and globally—he is second to none. It is also central to his career as a legal activist.

The earliest insight that we have into his dissatisfaction with doctrinal law was his angry response to his mentor Julius Stone's essay supporting a minority dissenting judge in the German South West Africa mandate case (Chapter 2). That dissent had in effect justified South African sovereignty over Namibia, and Upen says that he was 'stunned... could not believe Stone could be so colonial'. This prompted him to write a response that went beyond doctrinal law to understand the roots of legal reasoning in colonial ways of thinking.

His encounter in Australia with the dispossession of indigenous people by the rule of law led to a critique of the 'Blackstonian doctrine of *terra nullius*, which made possible the acquisition of territories, jurisdictions, resources, and peoples of non-Euro nations, and the concepts of free markets, free contract, and private property as essential attributes of the rule of law' (Baxi 2018a).

Thus, Upen emerged as a critic of the dominant legal theory that answers the foundational question, 'what is law?' as comprising of 'rules', 'principles', 'commands', etc. Upen sees law as going beyond its positivist and functional dimension. The respect that law commands depends equally on how people receive, internalise, and reinterpret the meaning of law in the everyday. Thus, there is attention to the performative circulation (the ways and means of its circulation and meaning-making) of (what anthropologists and sociologists call) legal cultures.

For Upen, a proper and adequate understanding of law requires an understanding of law both as doctrine and as 'lived experience'. Such an approach places him in a unique position *vis-à-vis* the dominant traditions of Western scholarship, such as the analytical traditions of jurisprudence/legal theory and black letter doctrinal restatements of laws, which continue to theorise law in its doctrinal essence, as well as those who advocate a pure sociological/anthropological view of law. This unique methodological approach—the conviction that an adequate understanding of law in the global South (and in other postcolonial societies) needs the strength of doctrine as well as the theoretical tools of human sciences—exists as an unbroken intellectual thread in the entire corpus of his writings.

'Law in Context'

The tradition of writing known as 'law in context', which brings the human sciences into the study of law, is not new. From the beginning of the twentieth century, there has been a growing body of literature that falls broadly within this rubric. Upen's approach to 'law in context' is distinct in at least three important ways. First, the interdisciplinarity that his work presents is diverse. Concepts like the Marxian notion of 'force of phrases' or 'force without phrases', the Ambedkarite notion of 'lawless laws', the feminist engagement with 'partition violence', or the insights that Manto's fiction offers while thinking about the Constitution inform his writings (and these conversations). Whether it be *Towards a Sociology of Indian Law* (1986b), *Crisis of the Indian Legal System* (1982a), or *Future of Human Rights* (2013c), we are presented with a fascinating ability to traverse human science subjects, from philosophy to linguistics, from literature to sociology, and from political theory to history.

A second aspect that defines his approach to law in context is his fascination with the unique colonial experience of making law and the subjects of law. The 'colonial question' has emerged from the 1980s as a critical area in the understanding of law and legal cultures, and Upen's own journey may well have begun with his engagement with the Subaltern Studies collective and more substantially through the *Sociology of Indian Law*. Upen argues that the colonial journey of law is hugely formative in shaping both the idea of modern law in India and its post-independence journey. As a 'lived experience', both the doctrine and its colonial journey (the framing of the norms in the English Parliament as well as its interpretations in the evolving modern court system in British India, and equally the codification of personal laws) is as important as the ways in which people at large received, represented, and redeployed the modern law.

Both of these inform a third dimension of his law-in-context approach: the need for a 'grounded approach' to analysing the law's lived experience in the global South. Research and reflection on the law begins not from abstract theories, but rather from what it means to people on the ground. This is used as a means to critique the conventional model of legal scholarship, as happened in a keynote titled 'What Can the Convicts of Rajahmundry Teach Us?', at a forum named the Association of Indian Law Teachers.[23] In his words,

> [T]his was regarding the prison revolt in Andhra. In this keynote, I talked about two kinds of consciousness. One, I called an AIR [All India Reporter] consciousness, in which the entire world of 'law' consisted of the pages of the AIR. In the second,

[23] Unfortunately, all efforts to trace the paper have failed.

> we learn the law not from the imagination of lawpersons, but from the experience of law by 'common' people, the subjects of law. (Chapter 11, 373)

Critical Engagement with the Courts

As with other legal academics, Upen begins his career with a sustained focus on the legal system and the decisions of the courts. In *Supreme Court and Politics* (1980), he notes that the responsibility of the legal scholar is to 'study the Court as an institution, not just a factory manufacturing legal and constitutional norms', and to 'develop a theory of evaluation of the judicial role' and 'to develop a body of standards' by which to evaluate the role of judges and courts (Baxi 1980, 6). He seeks, in works as diverse as *Supreme Court and Politics* (1980), *Courage, Craft and Contention* (1985b), 'Taking Suffering Seriously' (1985c), and others, to make sense of the output of the judiciary. He gives the go-by to conventional truths such as the problems of an activist court or the theory of separation of powers. The key concept used here is the notion of *politics* and the assumption that judges do politics, even as they work within the discipline of the law with its own rules. The parallel commitment to the idea of law as a system with rules, codes, players, and ways of decision-making, and hence to the idea of law as a system with a relative autonomy and integrity of its own, means that politics needs to be viewed as *inflecting* judicial decision-making, but not *determining* it.[24]

As such, the output of the Court is discussed with a sensitivity to political history, with political analysis and doctrinal analysis informing

[24] The law is a system with its own rules, codes, and ways of decision-making, which are relatively autonomous. Upen often invokes Marxist scholar Poulantzas's interpretation: that 'the state should be relatively autonomous of capital, market and labour. Only then can it function as a useful arbiter. They all need some agency to help them sort out problems without necessarily appropriating them' (see Baxi 1993b, Ch. Nine).

each other. A central insight is his contention that SAL began as a response to the excesses of the Emergency, the efflorescence of human rights jurisprudence after its lifting being a way of relegitimising a Court that had suffered severe damage to its reputation, given its failure to defend the rights guaranteed by the Constitution. SAL becomes an 'expiatory syndrome' for the wrong of having abdicated the judicial responsibility of protecting fundamental rights during the Emergency.

In 'Taking Suffering Seriously' (1985c), SAL is seen as 'symbolizing the politics of liberation', where 'the ruled and misruled have added to the might of the adult franchise the quiet dignity of constitutionalism in their struggle against the myriad excesses of power'. The Supreme Court 'at long last' has become the 'Supreme Court for all Indians' (ibid.). The SAL moment, which he would later characterise as C3, has been challenged by younger scholars such as Anuj Bhuwania, who critiques how the loosening of procedural requirements has had deleterious impacts on the urban poor. In Bhuwania's analysis, the reign of SAL has enabled judges to disguise class-driven prejudices against slum dwellers and allow the demolition of slums in the name of public interest. Bhuwania sees the High Court of Delhi becoming a slum demolition machine (Bhuwania 2017).[25]

---

[25] However, this perspective is being questioned by emerging research. Lekha Adavi argues, based on a study of litigation concerning slums in Bangalore:

> While Anuj Bhuwania, Asher Ghertner and Usha Ramanathan, in their studies have predominantly stated that the Courts are not in favour of slum residents and do not recognize their right to housing or shelter, in case of Karnataka, the Courts have mainly recognized that the slum residents have a 'right to shelter' and as a result, a right to be rehabilitated .... What has been an important learning from the cases observed in Karnataka High Court is that strong sociopolitical movements of slum residents coupled with legal representatives who use strong legal frameworks to interpret the sociopolitical and economic rights of slum residents for the consumption of the Courts, have resulted in achieving a fair bit through interim reliefs and rehabilitation. (Adavi, on file with the Alternative Law Forum)

Even prior to Bhuwania's critique, Upen himself had acknowledged the changing nature of SAL under globalisation, noting that there has been a 'structural adjustment of the distinctively Indian judicial power, process, and activism' (Baxi 2007d). And now in his response to Bhuwania, he continues to stress the distinction, making the case that Bhuwania's critique is actually referencing PIL and not SAL (Baxi 2017c). Upen remains a defender of SAL, and in particular its potential for redressing human suffering. His contention that it was SAL that transformed the Supreme Court into a 'court for all Indians' has also been critiqued by new historical scholarship. For example, Rohit De, in his book *A People's Constitution* (2018), makes the point that the Constitution has, ever since its inception and even before the rise of SAL, functioned as a tool that ordinary people have utilised to strike down arbitrary State laws that limited their rights. De illustrates this point by referencing how marginalised groups, including butchers, sex workers, and petty traders, have used the Constitution to assert their rights under the constitutional clause on the freedom of trade and profession.

Redefining Constitutionalism in the Global South

Studying the Constitution lies at the heart of legal studies. Yet, a majority of the Constitutional law texts confine themselves (inevitably with honourable exceptions) to studying the text and its interpretations by the courts. The concept of constitutionalism is rarely paid attention to in Indian law schools and colleges. Upen's work, from his review-response to Granville Austin's *The Indian Constitution: Cornerstone of a Nation* in the mid-1960s, to his profoundly insightful contribution to the *Cardozo Law Review* in 1999, to recent reflections on the idea of transformative constitutionalism, have provided a new lens through which to understand constitutionalism as an abstract idea, as material practice, and as a lived experience in the global South.

Upen introduces a threefold way of thinking about the Constitution: as text (C1), as interpretation (C2), and as constitutionalism

(C3). In most cases, its teaching is confined to C1 and C2. C3 represents constitutionalism, which is almost never consciously articulated or examined. C3 brings to the fore the idea that the Constitution may look very different from the vantage point of the disadvantaged. To study the Constitution is now to study a 'series of state formative practices' in which C1, C2, and C3 have to be brought together (Baxi 1999).

And so the journeys of Indian constitutionalism are charted through reference to the 'constitutional hardware that is designed to combat challenges to the life of the sovereign state', including the police and the military, which often function outside the authorisation of C1 and C2. The hardware of the military and the police, what E.P. Thompson would have called 'the secret state', while integral to the functioning of constitutionalism, never figures in the grand narrative of the Indian Constitution, he says. This links to rule by decree and the rule authorised by the Emergency provisions of the Constitution, which, Upen argues, have hardly been written about, other than in the 'great book' by Nasser Hussain on 'States of Emergency' (2003). Going further yet, he notes that the 'founding of modern Constitutionalism' is often accompanied by invisible 'genocidal violence'. We owe a debt of gratitude to feminist scholars of the Partition, says Upen, who have signposted the gendered genocides that attended the birth of the nation. The horrors of Partition were preceded by the wilful dispossession of the original inhabitants of India from their land, legitimised by the Constitution. We are reminded of the speech by Jaipal Singh in the Constituent Assembly, that 'the making of the Indian Constitution was itself an act of theft, taking away the forms of nationhood from the indigenous people of India' (Baxi 2005c).

Liberal constitutional scholarship turns a blind eye to this history of violation and dispossession which accompanies the birth of Constitutions; and this is not unique to India. In fact, in a searing critique of the work of Kenneth Karst on the US Constitution, Upen poignantly asks,

> If there was a reference to *Bury My Heart at Wounded Knee*, I somehow missed it. If there was a reference to the unscrupulous annexation of Hawaii and the symbolic shredding of its flag into

> so many souvenirs (a memory of hurt still alive among many native Hawaiians), I again missed it. (Baxi 1999, 1183)

Upen's constitutional studies alert us to the contradiction between justice texts and governance texts in C1, demonstrate the politics of the judicial role in C2, and alert us to the ideologies of domination and the possibilities of resistance in both C3 and C2. Although Upen, in sharp critiques of contemporary constitutional scholarship, may appear to conclude that C1 and C2 are hopelessly compromised, he does not quite provide that easy conclusion. He goes on to say that even though it may be a mask hiding the 'face of raw and bloody power', the law begins, 'despite its intentions', to acquire the 'visage of benign justice' (Baxi 1993d). He implies that despite the well-worn critique of the rule of law as a mere charade, in the playacting, certain forms of justice for the oppressed may open out.[26] The main challenge is to bring C1, C2, and C3 in conversation with each other: we have scholars who are 'expert' in one of these domains, but who rarely traverse all three domains and produce insights that are the result of yoking together different domains of knowledge.

Upen's approach to the study of constitutionalism uniquely locates it within the context of the global South. What defines the global South is a shared history of colonialism and a history of a long struggle against colonial oppression. This struggle against colonialism is what marks the Constitutions of the global South as 'inaugural' documents, which re-invent constitutional concepts like equality, dignity, and fraternity.

---

[26] This seems to parallel E. P. Thompson's conclusion in his study of the Black Act. Thompson argues that the Black Act was an unconscionably bloody legislation which created fifty new capital offences. Clearly, it was meant to consolidate a form of class power, but because this assertion of class power took the form of a law, it meant that it had to function within the forms and procedures of law. As he puts it,

> The essential precondition for the effectiveness of law, in its function as ideology is that it shall display an independence from gross manipulation and shall seem to be just. It cannot seem to be so without upholding its own logic and criteria of equity; indeed on occasion by actually *being* just. (Thompson 1975, 205)

Human Rights and Human Futures

Upen's work on human rights is complex and vast. One important source of understanding it is, as mentioned earlier, his public engagement with rights violations. Another is his work on the systemic nature of the crisis of law in the colonial Indian legal system and its institutions, be it the police, prisons, or the court system itself, and how these colonial institutions operate to prevent any meaningful delivery of justice. Human rights are now placed within a larger frame of reference, but as always, combined with an insistence on taking their logic, language, and institutions seriously. 'The model of universal human rights for all human beings contradicts the idea that all human beings without exception, have the right to be human,' he would write (Baxi 1987b, 191). In this important early reading, he argues that India, with its entrenched inequalities based on status and class, prevents a vast majority from availing of even a minimum dignity, making the promise of human rights illusory for most people. This critique of how the *rhetoric of universality* bases itself on the *reality of deprivation* recalls earlier formulations by Marx on the limitations of the bourgeois nature of rights,[27] Arendt's formulation on the right to have rights,[28]

[27] Upen in fact references Marx's essay on 'The Jewish Question' and says that the current human rights model 'diminish the very notion of humanity from species life to class life' (Baxi 1987b).

[28] Arendt argues that minorities and the Stateless are dependent upon the State for rights. The State in turn is taken over by the nation, which determines who in the territory of the State can have rights. The Stateless as well as minorities, dependent as they are on the State for any rights, are deprived of the very 'right to have rights'. Ayten Gundogdu, in her reading of the Arendtian conception of the 'right to have rights', argues that,

> What this term captures within the contemporary context is not the absolute loss or lack of rights such as legal personhood but instead their increasing fragility. 'Rightlessness' alerts us to the precarious legal, political and ontological standing of many migrants (and some citizens) in an age that is simultaneously defined by the proliferation of human rights and the globalization of immigration control. These challenging

and the capabilities approach of Amartya Sen and Martha Nussbaum. Although critique is at the heart of the approach, the central concern as an activist is to ensure that 'the state incrementally become ethical, governance just, and power accountable' (Baxi 2013c, 18).

This double insight is key. In *The Future of Human Rights* (2013c), Upen subjects human rights to critique from many standpoints, from the perspective of the global South. He engages with globalisation and how it manifests itself in the dominance of international economic institutions and economic laws, and the ways in which they impact human rights standards. He also addresses several fundamental questions that have troubled the global human rights movement: for example, the origin of human rights, universal rights and relativism, and human rights movements versus human rights markets.

At the heart of the book is a recognition of two faces of human rights—one that is clearly a justification of oppression and power, and the other that is about the struggle against it. He constructed this duality by distinguishing between what he terms *modern* and *contemporary* human rights, a politics *of* human rights and a politics *for* human rights, reason of human rights and the 'unreason' of State sovereignty, as well as the 'globalization of human rights' and the 'universalization of human rights' (Uma and Narrain 2018, 288). While *Future* engages with postmodern critiques, it is not postmodern enough to abandon the project itself. Just when you think that for Upen, human rights is a method to make power accountable, he introduces the idea that the advent of a 'trade-related market-friendly human rights' may mark the end of the Universal Declaration of Human Rights (UDHR) paradigm. Upen's corpus on human rights is endlessly fascinating, for one cannot quite box the writer as belonging to any one ideological current. Its strength comes from bringing a salutary sense of critique to what might otherwise be a mere celebration of the 'age of human rights'.

Even *Future* does not remain a final statement; for what one gets from Upen's corpus is a willingness to think afresh about new and

---

problems highlight that the universal human rights framework falls short of guaranteeing 'a right to have rights', or a right to citizenship and humanity. (Gundogdu 2014, 122) emerging questions. He is sensitive to emerging issues and constantly willing to engage with challenges thrown up by emerging movements, be it the nascent LGBTQI movement (S. Narrain 2018, 299) or animal rights discourse,[29] or contemporary questions related to ecology, technology, and climate change, and as always, to what he was to name the post-human question.

In all of Upen's work, there is something of what can be called the integrity of thought. Upen's ways of thinking about an issue are not predetermined by a series of ideological commitments, even though they are rooted in a commitment to redress suffering. This allows him to engage with a certain freedom of the mind, with which to address emerging issues and new challenges and constantly reinvent human rights as a way of responding to human suffering.

Law and Development: The Other Side of the Law

While the phrase is now well-worn, there are at least three ways in which Upen explicates the concept of development as it relates to the law: what it may say to human rights, to people's participation, and to underdevelopment. Development, as an idea, occupies hegemonic

[29]See Upendra Baxi, 'Animal Rights as Companion Human Rights', Nineteenth I. P. Desai Memorial Lecture, Center for Social Studies, South Gujarat University, 12 August 2008 (unpublished lecture on file with the editors). One gets a sense of a mind constantly willing to challenge itself as Upen acknowledges the limitations of the analysis in *Future of Human Rights* and attempts to go beyond. Upen notes that,

> I must here acknowledge that in critiquing the three generations of the CSR and in analysing the United Nations Draft Norms concerning human rights responsibilities of multinational corporations and related business entities, in chapter nine of *The Future of Human Rights*, I missed this crucial dimension [of animal rights]. Since global agribusiness, food, pharmaceutical and technoscientific industries stand to benefit the most for the exploitative practices of animals as systems of production surely more is needed in terms of an Animal Rights Theory and Movement (ARTM) based discourse.

force in the world today, including every aspect of the law, not least of which is human rights. While the concept often functions free of constitutional controls and sanctions, Upen has instead been concerned to see how the idea might be made to conform to constitutional limitations. Described as the development of the 'right to development' at the international level, he sees the normative enunciation of the Declaration of the Right to Development, especially with its centring of the right of people to participate in development, as an important signal to the idea that people should be the *subjects* of development and not its objects. Even as he welcomes this normative enunciation, he points to its limitations in the time of globalisation (see Chs 4 and 5, this volume. Also see Baxi 2007a).

The Declaration of the Right to Development, with its enunciation of people's participation, while an important step forward, cannot step outside the discursive framework within which the idea of development is embedded. Upen, in a second reading of development, is one with Arturo Escobar and his critique of the discourse of development and its many presuppositions. In the building of big dams, in the forcible eviction of people, as well as during the Bhopal catastrophe, Upen sees the side of development that the mainstream would want to cover up. Impoverishment is often the other side of the Development coin, and so the third thread that runs through his critique of the development discourse is the critique of capitalism itself: the recognition that the idea of development cannot be understood outside the idea of the 'development of underdevelopment'.

In Conclusion

'The old world is dying and the new world struggles to be born. Now is the time of monsters' (Gramsci, as translated by Žižek 2012, 42). The 'time of monsters' is a particularly apt metaphor for the rise of right-wing forces around the world, powered by a form of nationalism based on a hatred of the other. The old verities, be they the ideas of universal human rights, of justice, or the necessity of truth, are under normative challenge. What, in this period of flux, is the value of a book that charts the story of an engagement with the law with a view to redressing human suffering, and is in part personal reminiscence, in part activist narrative, and part academic reflection?

Upen's reflections provide many pegs on which to hang a critique of the contemporary order, even as they goad us on to imagine possible futures. The incitement to imagine futures is best illustrated through Upen's gloss on the Gramscian dictum of 'pessimism of the intellect, optimism of the will', as a summons to those 'who would dare to practice the optimism of the intellect' (Baxi 2016f).

The 'optimism of the intellect' lies at the core of this book. It is a commitment to the belief that human suffering should not be a matter of indifference, and that the law with all its problems has the potential to redress human suffering.

In moments of darkness, sometimes we have to return to history. Hannah Arendt penned a book called *Men in Dark Times* (1968), about the lives of figures such as Rosa Luxemburg, Walter Benjamin, and Bertolt Brecht, and her hope was that the telling of the stories of these lives would provide some illumination in dark times. As she puts it:

> That even in the darkest of times we have the right to expect some illumination, and that such illumination may well come less from theories and concepts than from the uncertain, flickering, and often weak light that some men and women, in their lives and their works, will kindle under almost all circumstances and shed over the time span that was given them on earth—this conviction is the inarticulate background against which these profiles were drawn. Eyes so used to darkness as ours will hardly be able to tell whether their light was the light of a candle or that of a blazing sun.... (Arendt 1968, ix)

One hopes that for the reader, the light emitted by Upen's passionate engagement with law and suffering will trigger reflections and kindle some ways through which the darkness can be illuminated.

One
Early Life

Bringing Philosophy to Its Source

Lawrence Liang: In our own personal division of work, we first divided the areas of your work into different segments of possible conversation, which we realised quickly would not stand because of the crisscrossing of themes—the idea of Indian constitutionalism, Baxi the activist, Baxi the teacher, law and the unfinished project of democracy, global concerns, the future of human rights, etc. We will begin with the autobiographical, not in any straightforward biographical sense of the word, but rather in exploring an intellectual history, the history of activism, etc.

I want to read a small extract from Stanley Cavell's autobiography, where he speaks on the idea of philosophical authority. He says, citing Emerson: '... the deeper the scholar dives into his privatest, secretest presentiment, to his wonder he finds this is the most acceptable, most public, and universally true' (Cavell 2010, 432).

And he says: '... The autobiographical dimension of philosophy is internal to the claim that philosophy speaks for the human, for all; that is its necessary arrogance' (Cavell 1994, 8, 10).

We are interested in posing a similar question. When one claims to speak about the kinds of issues, and the range of issues, that we speak for, we are interested in aspects of the autobiographical that form us. Pratiksha (Baxi) has also helped us to identify a set of questions:

1. What do you remember about growing up and studying in Rajkot? Were there any significant influences that you can recall?
2. What was it like growing up in early postcolonial India? What was the political and intellectual climate in school and college?
3. When was Baxi the avid reader made? What were the intellectual resources that were available to you when you were growing up in the 1940s and 1950s?
4. Why did you decide to study law at a time when Nehru was calling for everyone to become an engineer?
5. What was the situation of legal education when you studied law? Do you recall any significant influences on you when you were studying law?

Upendra Baxi: First, let me say how much I appreciate your great effort in seducing me to this conversation. No modesty on my part is needed—at any rate, modesty is not a postmodern virtue—in saying that many other common friends of ours would have been more worthy of your endeavours, nor am I sure that what I say in response will turn out to be as exciting as you all think.

Second, I—indeed, none of us—know where, how, and why these conversations may go! But a loose framework—making our sandwiches as we go—is a good idea because none of us is a professionally trained historian, biographer, or autobiographer (although I wonder how one can quite be trained in the autobiographical role!).

Third, autobiographies can be read in many ways—as acts of self-conceit, confession, narrative of past life, as didacticism, history, therapy, aesthetics, prophecy. In contrast, 'conversations' mean just talking about things, events, oneself and or as others (as Jean Paul Gustave Ricœur would prefer)—a narrative which may be shaped and reshaped across past, present, and future.

I am afraid I have not yet read Cavell as closely as you all, especially Lawrence, have done. Because I did not do justice to your recall of Cavell in our early discussions, allow me to speak to it now a trifle more elaborately.

His distinctive concern is, I think, to trace the relationship between philosophy and autobiography—a critical concern, of course. A cogent case is being made here concerning why 'the autobiographical dimension of philosophy' is internal to the claim that philosophy 'speaks for the human'. He has in view not so much the uses we can make of autobiography as grasping philosophy, but rather making one's practice of thinking as decisive to how one makes one's own 'philosophy' and more widely put, the concern with the status of 'sceptical' thought within the Western philosophical canon.

But what moves me in Cavell is this somewhat paradoxical position between the 'universal' and the 'particular'. There is a tension here in the conception of philosophy as a quest for that which is universal and autobiography's struggle to make a particular into a universal. Thus arises the notion of the 'normal' and the pathological in doing 'philosophy'—the suspicion of the 'malady of thought' (Hume) or its 'madness' (Descartes). What may be thought—the limits of 'rational' doubt—and must remain philosophically unsaid, even *unsayable*, is here entirely at stake in the doing of metaphysics or ontology.

In his famous *A Pitch of Philosophy: Autobiographical Exercises* (1994), Cavell says (as you know) the following:

> An obvious first is that a blessing has to be seen to be offered, a promise of an authorization for me to become what I am, which will be expressed as establishing my right to exist, to have a birth; a second, that the authorization is marked by the sense that I have arrogated the right to it, itself attested, third, by my having intercepted the conversation of my parents and translated their words by finding, fourth, a version of perfect pitch; and that this movement is, fifth, a process of passing again into my neutrality, which, sixth, bears testimony of the world I think. (ibid., 38–39)

One may incidentally note in the above quotes how in being alive, being a philosopher, and writing one's autobiography, the language of human rights gets entangled. There cannot be an autobiography unless the political and judicial/juristic system produces an affimation of the 'right to exist', which biologically means a right to birth. Second, the human right to memory and its public attestation necessarily entails freedom of speech and expression. (Let us leave aside, for another time, the examination of the 'right to be born' in the context of abortion or women's reproductive freedom). Third, the human right to the attestation of personal and intersubjective memory; this brings to mind all sorts of questions about the structures of social and State censorship and freedom of speech. And, finally, the human right to communication, expressed by Cavell in this passage as a 'process of passing into neutrality', which 'bears testimony of the world I think'. Cavell may not have thought of all this, but he speaks of a right specifically and the use of the terms 'arrogation', 'promise', 'and 'authorization' allows at least to read him as implicitly speaking of a human rights framework. So, autobiographies presuppose (as well as affirm) a given set of the idea and ideal of human rights.

Philosophical biography stands rather differently, signified by Richard Rorty in speaking to us of his early socialist years and his affairs with Euro-Marxism in *Philosophy and Social Hope* (2000). Here, the art of self-presentation remains 'internal' to doing philosophy, but differently than in Cavell. The contrast is rich as well as extraordinary, isn't it? Insofar as I grasp Cavell's remark that you present, the contestation is no longer between that which is internal and that which may lie outside the doing of philosophical autobiography, but is, with Rorty, the question of bringing philosophy back to its source, to the sufferings and agonies of actually existing peoples, and the travails of fashioning solidarity amidst contingent yet often catastrophic hegemonies.

One also ought to accord a co-equal dignity to the pluriverses of organic thought-practices.

Talking about this reminds me of Mahatma Gandhi's unique text, *My Experiments with Truth* (2013 [1927]). As an *infinitely* lesser mortal in every way, I follow ways of telling the stories about my life in this narrative vein. Even as I thus proceed, one large remark deserves a dignitary mention. Autobiography generally remains a sphere of narrative endeavours in which the fragments aspire to lay claims to forms of unitary, yet chaotic, totality. I have lots to say about all this (for example, that totality is elusive, and indeed that which is considered totality is best grasped as a series of fragments; we have still to develop styles and habits of reading fragments rather than finished products; and all life, I believe, consists of fragments rather than totality), but this must remain a task for another day.

Allow me, then, for better or for worse, to now address largely some specifics of your interlocution!

Let me then at the outset compliment you all for innovating a relatively new genre called 'Conversations', which straddles many forms—biography, autobiography, oral history, for example. This format allows a relatively unstructured dialogue amidst us. I know how massive labours were undertaken initially by Sruti and Arvind to transcribe an unwieldy dialogue into a written text and the travails involved in a little more than a decade in many a revision of the text. But for Arvind's editorial exertions, and provision of documentary footnotes and a long bibliography, a near final shape to the text now in your hands would not have seen the light of day. The more than generous introduction tries to bring some order in the chaos of conversations. And Ashish has not merely added the pictorial content (in collaboration with Pratiksha), but also gently insisted on the publication; Orient BlackSwan has shown unparalleled editorial indulgence and I would be remiss if I were not to acknowledge Ms Nilanjana Majumdar and Ms Proteeti Banerjee for their arduous and valiant effort to bring the manuscript to a final shape. This work is, then, a truly composite effort and I hope will prove as enjoyable and creative for the readers as it has been for the participants in this unusual publication venture.

Rajkot

UB (*contd*): Rajkot names a place where I was born, or (to deploy a telling Heideggerian phrase) thrown into being, as far back as

November 1938. In his *Being and Time* (1962), Heidegger talks about contingency as radical: the idea that we are thrown into this world in which we would have our being and vanish without a trace (when finitude beckons) shows fully the radical contingency all mortals live under and with; these are happenings over which we have no control. Every person's life, I add, is a struggle for peace and justice within this interregnum—the time and space between life and death—each of which is uniquely our own and no one else's. That which we call our uniquely own life, are not commodities in the market, but reflexively akin to a 'well of loneliness', of an existential and ethical kind. (The phrase I derive, as you all will know, from the lesbian novel by Radclyffe Hall first published in 1928, describing the life of an Englishwoman from an upper-class family, whose 'sexual inversion' manifests in an early age.)

How does one talk about one's place of birth when one is nearing the end of one's life? Especially, when it covers the most formative years, and joys and sorrows of one's life? Can it just be summed up in a single brief sentence: 'I went to a municipal and then a secondary school, and had my college education in Rajkot'?

What now follows is much longer version, though not in all details of life, which may not engage you or the future reader.

It was only gradually I learnt that Rajkot was then a Princely State of Kathiawar, much later named as Saurashtra, and was one of more than 500-odd such states (mostly spread across the region now comprising Gujarat, Rajasthan, and Madhya Pradesh). Princely States were parts of British India, yet they retained some degree of autonomous governance within a regime of British paramountcy over matters of defence, security, and currency, and included regions (like Junagadh, Hyderabad under the Nizam, and Jammu and Kashmir) whose accession to India was contested, but which now stand declared as integral parts of India under the Indian Constitution. These were ruled by erstwhile monarchs and princelings at the sufferance of the British Empire, and governed indirectly by relations of paramountcy, that is, they were not directly administered by the British but indirectly by a royal agent called the Resident, an officer who vigilantly negotiated imperial suzerainty. It would be far-fetched for me to say that the experience of my infancy had anything to do with my later development. But then, who knows all the causal mysteries of life and living?

Even so, I can't help wondering why, at Berkeley, I named my doctoral studies then a non-existent field—'Indian Private International Law'. I discovered that much of the law of enforcement of foreign judgments and choice of law originated under the princely rule. All through my life, Rajkot has taught me to pursue micro-histories of these forms and formats of juridical administration and imperial governance. In turn, this may also explain my political unconscious in encouraging my students at Sydney Law School to study the so-called 'micro-mini' states of the South Pacific. Now this recall, truth to say, also stands with a sense of guilt at my own scholarly itineraries—that the cosmopolitan mode of production of scholarship carries inveterate costs of so unwholesomely neglecting the profoundly local.

Rajkot means far too many things to me than I can describe here. In adulthood, I visited Rajkot briefly three times, twice from Bombay before leaving for Berkeley, and once much later when I was the Vice-Chancellor, South Gujarat University. The first visit was personal—to lead a somewhat reluctant father, and family, to sign away all claims over Prem Mandir, our ancestral property, in Rajkot in favour of my uncle, in order to discharge all the debts owed to the young widowed aunt. The second time was to collect proxies for Sumati Morarji, Chairperson of the Scindia Steam Navigation Company. The third, and the last time I visited Rajkot was in late 1983–84, when I was member of the Second Gujarat Labour Law Review Committee. It was a three-member committee comprising, in addition to myself, Justice M. U. Mehta (retired from the Gujarat High Court) and the Labour Secretary to the Government of Gujarat. The First Labour Law Review Committee was headed by Justice D. A. Desai; incidentally, this is one of the few governmental law reforms that I have been a part of. We visited several sites across Gujarat. I went to the Bhuj and Kutch areas where salt-mine workers were kept in cages so that they would not run away. India never ceases to update the narratives of primitive accumulation so horrendously depicted by Marx in *Capital*, Vol. One!

This was a formative experience. Here, state managers and 'civil society' combined to continually produce some contemporary instances and regimes of sustained slavery. On my way back from Bhuj, I stopped at Rajkot.

The last chapter in the Report was on the State as the saboteur of labour laws. It was written by me, as was much of the Report, and and I appreciate that the colleagues in the Committee, while making valuable suggestions, reposed such a lot of trust in me. The Gujarat government yielded to our insistence that the Report be published unexpurgated, although its compliance was at best reluctant. The print order was minuscule. And now of course no one looks at it, even as history. I always stand reminded of the saying in *Hamlet*: 'There is a destiny that shapes our ends/rough, hew them as we will.' Of course, Shakespeare originally said 'divinity', not 'destiny'. Is there a difference between the two? I do not know, but since early days, as a child of contingency, I believe with the Bard in a soliloquy (in *As You Like It*) that begins:

> All the world's a stage,
> And all the men and women merely players;
> They have their exits and their entrances;
> And one man in his time plays many parts,
> His acts being seven ages.

I do not know about the 'seven ages', but the soliloquy was among my favourites. Forgive me this digression, which all acts of living are!

My first visit to Prem Mandir was to repatriate a family debt of honour. Bit chivalrous, no? Chivalry was a medieval feudal virtue, which like honour has disappeared from our vocabulary in the neoliberal, or even post-industrial era. But in those heady days at Rajkot, these words made a special sense.

My second visit to Rajkot was a short one, directed to collect some proxies for Sumati Morarjee. Incidentally, this was my first introduction to the dynamics of company law. It is in major respects unrecognisable today, but company law was an elaborate articulation of governmental control and direction of private capital—those were early but heady socialist days of license-quota *raj* and the planned socialist economy (which needed to be revisited as modern legal history). I do not recall why proxies were needed, but usually shareholders authorised the proxy holder to vote for him/her at these meetings.

I met many people in Rajkot whom I had heard of as community elders, with other people whom I had never heard of. But this knowledge came in handy when some of us decided to take proxies at the Union Carbide Corporation Annual General Meeting at Danbury, Connecticut, where we raised concerns about the Bhopal catastrophe [narrated later]. At Rajkot, I was received kindly, and particularly the elders received me with some affection (the 'Baxi' name was, I suppose, endowed with some local magical properties!). Folks who ran an institution named Pensioners' Paradise at the end of the road of Prem Mandir (and near Choudhry High School) displayed the early forms of struggle for pensioner's rights, and pension justice. They also held weekly elderly gossip sessions—and were particularly delighted to see me and facilitated the work a good deal.

My third visit was a different experience for me. Although by then I was the Vice-Chancellor of the University of South Gujarat, many fond memories overcame me. Profound memories of my Platonic romantic attachment to my teachers, both men and women, overcame me. On that occasion, at a reception in my 'honour' hosted by the Vice-Chancellor of Saurashtra University, a noted literary and aesthetic figure, a faculty member made a somewhat belated appearance. To the overall astonishment of all present, I ambled across and we hugged each other. It was my Sanskrit teacher, a beauteous person. She taught us the *Bhava* and the *Rasa* of the great poet Kalidasa. We all were in love with her, perhaps entirely unbeknownst. She let me visit her often at her beautiful home and we had many conversations concerning the Kalidasa motifs. From her, I surely learnt the importance of grace within and beyond classroom discursive relations. In this recall, I thank her for her contribution to my own making as a teacher, a being who knows how to be loved by her students, yet not be enamoured of them!

The birthing of my adolescent sexuality at Rajkot was complemented by yet another romantic attachment, this time around a Professor J who initiated us into the romantic era of English Literature. As one coming from a Gujarati-medium school, where the height of my distinction in the sixth standard was pronouncing and correctly spelling the word 'cage', I became very devoted to this teacher, who took us on the magic tradition of literature. One day in class, he announced that he was leaving. I remember leading a weeping brigade in class, saying, you can't go, Sir, leaving us thus entirely forlorn. I had tears welling in my eyes years later when I watched the English movie, *To Sir with Love* (and likewise, its Bollywood equivalent).

On none of these Rajkot visits could I revisit the shrine of Gabensah Pir, whose Dargah I visited every so often, particularly on Thursdays. I used to observe a fast without water or food the whole day at the shrine. Although not myself religious, my family was so, especially my grandmother and mother. Perhaps my love for them made me do this. I must say that it gave me a lot of strength and peace, but it was very hard in summer, when the mercury touched 43 degrees Celsius, and when the river Aji used to dry up. I also used to visit the great Panchnath Mandir in the centre of the town, which had a life of its own. A big, bustling place, where ceremonies and rituals took place and constantly. This is a temple where Lord Shiva reigned and ruled, but it also had other deities, including Ram and Sita. What struck me deeply was the ability to learn solitude among crowds, an inner serenity amidst constant activity, and tranquillity in the noise of the present.

But the question nags: Why did I not visit these shrines? Had I totally become a *Sheri Babu*, an urban dweller, who had difficulties finding/making time? Did I not wear the cloak of solitude to cover the bareness of my existence? For those of us who migrate from rural/rurban settings to really urban sites, the question, when did I become a city-dweller (from remaining a 'caveman'!) is important for the sociology of urbanisation. The question may also affect us who are born and brought up in cities or urban conglomerations: Is there something exotic (or sad) in the search for 'roots'? In this context, how may one think of the global Indian diaspora—as civilisational, cultural, religious communities reinventing nostalgia, or merely as political and market-friendly and trade-related global political para-communities? Even brief visits to Rajkot raise so many thematics for thought!

Rajkot for me meant a college education, livened by an intense engagement with different personalities and the blossoming of many enduring human friendships. In my first year of college, when the principal told me that I was not eligible to take the exam because I had failed both in geography and mathematics, my world came crashing down. I was wounded and shocked by this decision, as I had passed in seven subjects out of nine, which resulted in a pass as per the rules then prevalent, and the Gujarat University owed me a threshold decision on eligibility of admission; but the University took its own time in coming to the final decision that geography was essential to offer an arts degree course. This meant that mid-year, I could no longer be a student in that College until I had 'cleared' those subjects, taking again a partial matric examination.

This suddenly made me a tragic figure of exile in the eyes of my teachers, peers, and myself. The experience of being totally institutionally cut off from my peers is also an experience of exile from a community. Aside from the pain of isolation, one also felt stigmatised, wearing the badge of inferiority. Perhaps that's when I started writing verses in Gujarati about the emptiness of the world, the loss of meaning of life, etc.

It made me determined to fight all academic injustices in the name of the retrospective application of so-called educational standards. I learnt early what injustice meant in academic life, and the memory and messages from that exile into ethical loneliness have served me well later during my various avatars as an educational administrator. Of course, rules decide who should be a student, for what, and how long, but this does not determine that educational standards must remain the domain of discretion, and subjective decisions by a few authorities. One ought to also be guided by some norms against causing any unnecessary suffering, or preventable harm, hurt, and trauma to young students, often called 'the future of India'. Avoiding surplus suffering through mindless and even soulless administrative decisions for all should become the norm of all governance, resistance, and reconstruction of governance in its myriad forms; it is the *leitmotif* of Universities, and other educational systems. This is the idea of human rights itself—the progressive elimination of arbitrariness in social action (as I tried later to demonstrate in *The Future of Human Rights* [2013c]).

I have plenty of other memories of my college days. One striking memory is that of an absentminded yet a semi-authoritarian principal. When he got flustered and angry, he led students one floor down to the threshold of the College, and he used to say that if a student, like a good dog, were to sniff the threshold every day, she will eventually get a degree without having to listen to lectures or to study! The other memory I had was the constant supply of Gandhi caps he seemed to have: he often used his caps to mark a page in large file folders which went to administrators in the College, and when he could not find his old cap, he wore a new one. One thing I succeeded in was never to wear a cap, although absentmindedness was a deliciously edible virtue, which simply meant that your mind was someplace else. Incidentally, is it not always elsewhere? Any kind of mindfulness requires great discipline and determination not to let your mind wander; and often one wonders whether that exercise is worthy when a vagabond consciousness is found equally creative. Much later, I was to learn at Sydney from some Australian indigenous peoples, friends, and folks about the notion of the *walkabout*—to roam freely, to journey without a destination, and to arrive nowhere in particular. A teleology of new sprits, then, where 'all that is solid melts into air' (to evoke Prince Hamlet?)—I do not know if I should prefer to read this as 'solid', when other renderings of the soliloquy read as—'O, that this too *sullied flesh* would melt'). Anyway, this is now a subject of modern meditation for Marshall Berman in a book by that title, subtitled as *Experience of Modernity* (*All That Is Solid Melts into Air* [1983]).

Among teachers I fondly remember are Professors S. T. Buch (English, who, among other precious things, taught me how to take care of borrowed books and how to read literary works) and Prabhu (logic and philosophy), from whom I tried to learn the importance of avoiding logical fallacies in thinking and writing. There was a teacher of Persian and Urdu, who wrote excellent Gujarati ghazals; Professor Khalifa spoke about vengeance and its limits. I still recall one of his verses, which said: 'My friend, there are some limits even to revenge/it is futile to light again and again the funeral pyre.' The idea of limits to revenge is still present with me when I say and write that it is ethically and juristically wrong to view law as a programme of revenge. It is not; and better thought of as a changeful instrumentality for doing justice.

Impassioned Reading Habits

UB (***contd***): I must have read almost every book there was; and there were plenty in the then-named Laing Library at Rajkot. A kind librarian allowed even adolescents to read adult books; he thus contributed to the production of my bibliophile self. I started reading at the age of six or seven. I read a lot in English. I read Scott, Hardy, Wilde, the Brontës, a bit of Jane Austen (though I have never been able to relate to her fully). Not everything could I understand, yet I did very well in English literature studies because of this. Thanks to my father, who read constantly, I read almost all P. G. Wodehouse books—I still read these—and authors now forgotten, especially Hall Caine's *The Eternal City* and Marie Corelli's *The Soul of Lilith*. My introduction to Shakespeare was through Charles and Mary Lamb's *Tales from Shakespeare* (a great little book, indeed) and through his *Sonnets*, which for a strange reason I was able to read only furtively.

I began to read serious poetry only in my college days—mostly the romantic poets. I was introduced to Milton via his masque *Comus* (on which I wrote a long essay), and my quartet of wordsmiths was formed by Wordsworth, Tennyson, Arnold, and Pope—a curious juxtaposition, you would say, and so in some ways it is. In part, didactic poetry made a considerable impact on me, though it was Coleridge who remained, to use a quaint phrase from Rajkot college days, my 'favouritest'. His phrase, 'the willing suspension of belief', which has stayed with me all this long life, is important to understand not merely for poetry or literature, but every form of the enchantment with this life. Gayatri Chakraborty Spivak now talks in an interview about the 'structures of engagement' and 'structures of postponement'. I do not know whether she had Coleridge in view, but the schoolboy in me still thinks of the poet, even as a postmodern self reads Gayatri. I often feel that a motley collage of selves shaped by habits of slow and careful reading is better than the development of a strong unified self. Some self-serving recall this, don't you all think!

I read a bit of his essays and those of Shelley as well (and later, T. S. Eliot), and always wondered why so many fine distinctions were made between 'poetry' and 'prose'. Shelly's essay, *In Defence of Poetry*, would assume several meanings in my later life; he concluded that poets are the 'unacknowledged legislators of [hu]mankind'. Later, I was able to grasp the category of 'unacknowledged legislators' more fully—people who have not just a will to power, but also who inspire us all to develop a will to justice.

It was thanks again to my father that I discovered the works of Shri Aurobindo, and especially the great epic *Savitri*, perhaps the only one of the last century CE? Do we live in the era of the end of the epic, as both Mikhail Bakhtin and Georg Lukacs differently forecast? Lukacs clearly stated (I rely on J. M. Bernstein's analysis in *The Philosophy of the Novel: Lukacs, Marxism, and the Dialectics of Form* [1984]), which concludes that the novel of today is the epic of yesterday. And what other forms of social loss are incurred, besides the death of a literary genre? But the loss is partly occasioned by our not knowing even the bare facts of cultural production. I had the great privilege of reading Umashankar Joshi's great *Viswa Shanti*, which is considered a 'long poem', but can still be considered an epic. Unfortunately never translated in any international language, this poem/epic dwelling on the message of peace has not won international notice. There may be other examples from the Global South. Epic as a form may have existed in Europe; but Europe, as we now understand, at last, is not the entire world. A comparative concern is framed by a change of literary forms and fashions of law, which says: Is there any correspondence between the canons or fashions of thought that concern literary change and legal change?

There were no comics, save some in Gujarati, and I avidly read these, though rather stealthily. We had no sense then of people living with disability and I used to enjoy reading *Chakram*, which told us about the exploits of a 'lunatic' or an 'idiot'! Now, we speak about people not of lunacy or unsound mind, but in terms of stigma-free medical illness.

At the time I grew up, there was no word such as 'ableism', but discrimination and stigmatisation against the disabled was very common. But in this respect, the large family at Prem Mandir, about which I have much to say anon, was extraordinary and exceptional.

The experience of growing up included being introduced to twins of my second aunt; they had no visible ankles and legs, stumps of which were enfolded to their torso, and they could not walk but learnt to slither and slide, and had to be carried across thresholds and steps by her younger brother. Their mental faculties were sharp, and conversation fluent, and they enjoyed their lives with gusto. They were much senior to me and when I bowed my head in reverence to them, each time they held my hand and took it to their foreheads, by way of mutuality of affectionate greetings. I used to go and meet them often, and their joyous resilience spread throughout my heart. The great thing about Bachiba and Neeluba (as they were called) was that everyone enjoyed their companionship and no hurtful remarks at their ailments were ever expressed. Indeed, they were treated affectionately as members of the family and with dignity. I still feel bereaved, though they left the world after half-a-century of zestful life.

Of course, there was no television; there was the radio, which was a family thing, only the elders could control it. For them, of course, it was a symbol of authority. Listening to the radio was, unlike in the vastly changed circumstances of today, an opportunity locked by parental controls. This suggested early the problem of leisure and work—in fact, my first essay in life was on 'leisure'. It was published in the college magazine. I do not have a copy of it, but generally recall that it was a writing on the concept of leisure, as play and work and emptiness of time. We all had some experience of 'time literally hanging on our hands' (as the expression goes)—and everyone had different ways of 'filling it'. Some did it by resort to rituals, others did it by idle (and very often hurtful) gossip, some with movies, and others by reading. I could see even then that the problem of what to do with emptiness of time did not arise for certain classes of people: domestic labour, professionals, women—in short, people who had to labour, though not always for gainful employment.

I had not read Veblen or Marx then, and therefore could not have distinguished (and commented on) between productive and unproductive leisure, or the class-bound nature of that distinction. Looking back, I now realise why the importance of conceptualising leisure in law—the times of *legislative* law, the times of *administration/enforcement*, the time of *adjudication*, and *constitutional times* have been among the central themes on thinking about law and jurisprudence.

Growing up then presented no alternative to cultivating (what now parades itself so conveniently as) a resistant subaltern self (although the marks of a subaltern being were readily masked within the large and reputed family).

Women in Enforced Temporary Exile

UB (*contd*): We lived in a joint family, which comprised a very large number of uncles, aunts, and cousins all together. The big house was called Prem Mandir, *lit.* the Temple of Love. And 'love' of all sorts was always around us, enveloping us.

Most of the time, it was conjugal love—it must have been so—given the regularly occurring reproductive events. I have two early memories of childhood. The first has to do with a sweet that was made of honey, *gur*, gum, and *methi*, and it was only prepared when there was a pregnancy at home. In such a large family, I always had a constant supply, someone or the other was always pregnant. This is my first memory of women.

My second memory is of my mother cooking. She was the eldest of the daughters-in-law, and hence oversaw the kitchen. In Gujarat, we eat very early—and lustily—in the morning. The food had to be hot, the *phulkas* (the *Guju* chapattis) soft, and a continuous supply kept up. This poor woman worked like a galley slave, there was no gas stove in those days, and she had to work on a *chullah*. There was a lot of smoke from the cowdung cakes, and later from the coal and the primus stove which worked on kerosene (whose design, in those times, was so faulty as to cause many fatal accidents). I was always concerned about her, and wanted to help, but she never shared my concern, and would ask me to go play or do something else with my time!

Talking about fatal primus stove accidents, a tragedy hit me when I was in college: an out-of-station student, an intimate friend of mine living in a rented room, was killed by a stove explosion. For a long time, the injustice of his death haunted me. He came to Rajkot from a small nearby town and had huge ambitions of what to do with life. His death affected me powerfully, as the law was altogether ineffective in rendering the manufacturer liable or punishing him. Much later, when I studied and researched into law, I realised why tort law has not grown in India. It quite bluntly celebrates what I have called (Baxi 2017a) the corporate, trade, and business right to do human rights wrong. And why, socially, we accept as 'accidents' what are really perpetrations of destruction, disability, death, and injustice for profit.

Going back to her, I felt very happy that for three days in a month, my mother was not allowed into the kitchen. I was very pleased for her. However, even in the room to which she was 'confined' for three days (with other women at times), she was put to work re-laying the mud flooring. After the three days, it was of course business as usual. But no one explained why women were segregated for three whole days, and it was much later that I came to learn that they were considered ritually unclean. How religion and culture can become fate was a lesson I learnt very early, although it was only later, with the first-wave feminists, that 'biology is not destiny' became a compelling slogan.

I only knew what happened inside Prem Mandir and not in the wider world, except for the fact that I was aware that the sweeper woman who came every day to clean our large courtyard and the women who 'cleaned' our latrine (there were no dry latrines even then in our house) did not seem to have these three benign days. I wondered why it fell to her to clean the huge sandy courtyard and backyard (within the vast range that we called the compound) of a rather large house; I wondered why only one domestic help had to go to market, sweep the inside of a large home, wash so many clothes, and clean all the utensils twice a day. I wondered how much they were paid and whether they got any leave. As children, we were not supposed to ask these questions, and there was no one in this large family I could ask questions that thus arose, nor were there friends or teachers at school with whom I could have discussed these. All I figured out then was the fact that women in this condition were somehow regarded as unclean and impure, and less than eligible for daily household chores. They were also to be 'kept away' from their husbands, lest they pollute the entire household by touching things or persons.

Allow me to make a rather heavy digression. When I first read Article 17 of the Indian Constitution (incidentally, I think it is *the* Constitution), I was more or less immediately able to understand the reason why the term 'untouchability' was placed within severe constitutionally ordained quotes. The constitutional parenthesis thus made a distinction between temporary and more abiding states of impurity. I was going to frame the second limb of contrast as millennial or historic forms; but this would be incorrect, surely, because women's confinement is quite similar. In both cases, what is today named as biopower/biopolitics—signatures of subjugation—reigned supreme.

Why the menstruating bodies of 'Hindu' women did not constitute 'untouchability' worthy of militant constitutional action still remains a question for me. Of course, I continued to bring it up, rather unconventionally, in my law-teaching days, years, decades at Delhi University, but there were few takers.

One colleague, now awarded with the dignity of the title 'Living Legend in Law', felt continually exasperated by my asking him how, as a proclaimed 'liberal', he could undertake the rigorous pilgrimage to the temple at Sabarimala, which denied access to menstruating women. He thought I was being both stupid and offensive. That was in the late 1970s at Delhi Law School; perhaps he now thinks differently, given the judicial challenges confronting this and similar verdicts forbidding such practices. Or, perhaps not! Some people like gender justice, but within prescribed limits that maintain the 'purity' and 'superiority' of the masculine and State power, even if often appropriated by the 'male in the State' (as Wendy Brown puts it). Or there are different ways of reading Lord Ayyappa's commandments, which the impious or not-so-pious may never fully understand. In any event, this is a conflict for constitutional political actors and the activist adjudicatory leadership to authoritatively resolve.

Allow me to add that in the 1960s, as a keen student of Roman Law (at the University of Bombay), I had no difficulty, compared with almost all my classmates, in understanding the doctrine of *patria potestas*, the power of the head of the household over life and death. And decades later now, I have become very fond of Giorgio Agamben's *Homo Sacer*, which revives the understanding of this integral aspect of the Roman Law, not very different from other ancient traditions of law. In both, being the head of the family and/or the religious organisation bestows some special powers. Are the custodians of traditions and religions to decide who are the *homo sacrii* or the orders/disorders of State sovereignty? The question may not be new, but the contexts in which it may be answered vary from time to time and are very different.

Family as a 'School of Morals'

UB (*contd*): I evoke here a deeply contested phrase of John Rawls. Deeply contested because the background question is *what*, *whose*, and *which* morals may regulate that 'school'? I speak to my own formative experiences rather than entering the thicket of post-Rawlsian debates. For me, the critical term is not so much 'morals', but rather the term 'school'.

The lifelong headmaster of that school was my own grandfather, Venilal Baxi, a strict disciplinarian. Love for him consisted in imparting a 'moral character' to us all. This signified diverse things, but for me, as a growing youngster, above all, it meant the cultivation of habits of obedience and of deference to one's elders. In this, there was concealed the greatest affection especially for my elder brother, Madhusudan Baxi—and vicariously for me, of course. My grandfather always took his side when we brothers disagreed with each other. Perhaps this was not so much because he was my elder brother, but rather because of Krishna Kumar—the eldest brother, who died early. I never knew him, but heard constantly about this absent other. In some raw ways, I thought this entirely unjust.

If only I had been born before my elder brother, I felt I too would have reaped the harvest of affection heaped by everyone on him! In a marked contrast, my grandmother always privileged me as the younger sibling. This was for me what we today name as the principle of affirmative action, working the wonders of its compensatory justice in full measure. Perhaps, more concretely put, I must have then thought that I was worthier of affection than my elder brother? To take recourse to pop psychology, perhaps much, if not all, our 'fondnesses' begin their itineraries in sibling rivalry?

My vivid last memory of my grandfather is also of his absolute partiality. Let me explain this a bit. Once—and as it turned out, on his last night—Madhusudan and I, as we were wont to do, played a mock archery game under his benevolent superintendence. 'Archery' puts the matter too robustly; it was in fact a game of makeshift bows and arrows in which we had to assail an easily marked object on a wooden stool. The arrows were of course blunted, because grandfather was a few paces away, swinging on his *jhoola*. The game ended with the declaration of my having lost, as always. I carried this 'defeat' into tearful sleep. But what I witnessed one next morning was calamitous indeed.

My grandfather was laid prostrate in a white shroud; one was not allowed to see his face. Later, he was taken away, and I was borne away by wailing bereaved women someplace else. He was never to be seen or heard again. I felt both ashamed and guilty that I had doubted the integrity of my grandfather on the very eve of his dying, and to this day the image remains of his body taken away inexplicably without an opportunity to say 'sorry' to him. I do not know how all of you—my favourite interlocutors—would prefer to frame similar narratives of death in the family. As concerns me, at least, this was my 'first death', which variously haunts me even today.

My *dada* (paternal grandfather) was a dignified person, by profession a lawyer, a pleader—as non-barrister *vakils*, or pleaders, as they were then called. I also recall him being involved in the nationalist movement. I do not know much about his practice, apart from the fact that it was mostly on the civil side, but he would have done well by all standards since he sired four sons and seven daughters, educated them (although the women were educated only up to a certain school level), and contracted marriages for them all. Marriages were costly affairs even then and customary *kanyadan*—golden ornaments—were expensive. So my grandmother (*dadi*) would tell me. She was a great storyteller, most (of her stories) of a 'never-ending' genre.

My early enduring impressions are also of many people staying at Prem Mandir, frequently visiting kin, and the politics of it all. Not in any sense national, or even local, politics, but of the other kind—intensely personal competition for 'superiority' achieved by putting down others; this was politics because it involved power and domination, yet it also lay beyond the political (in the sense of the struggle for truth, rights, and justice).

In fact, representations of family politics (sans the political) is now a multimillion-rupee Hindi soap opera bonanza, offered to us on national and regional 24x7 TV channels. If the record viewership (judged by the advertisement revenues generated) is to be decoded as a contemporary cultural fact, little has changed by way of family mores overall. I said the soap was devoid of the political, but this is not entirely so, given how upholding family integration and family values remains the principal message of the TV *parivar* women.

There was always a lot of politics and bickering and backbiting in a joint family, but what I found hurtful was that it was often my mother who was the object of a particularly malignant misunderstanding, and I decided very early that I would break out of this system given the first opportunity. It was a kind of cultural malignancy, when there was nothing good you could say about the other person. I was very tired of this at a very young age, which is perhaps why I turned to obsessive reading and to some obsessive friendships as well!

I may add that I used to go regularly to the only bookshop (near the beginning of Rajkot market). That was the only academic bookshop, and I used to see many a book, and read some partially in the bookshop. This was because for a long time I was not allowed to buy books, nor had I the money to buy them. But I recall I could buy some later in my college days: compared with today's prices, the books were not expensive, but anything beyond Rs 15 was considered very expensive. I used to buy only those books which I had seen or read in the library, because I wanted to read and mark them. I had developed a well-bred horror of marking books that I did not have in my own collection, because I always thought that other people's markings and notes adversely (most of the time) affected my reading of the text. Even now, when a friend asks for a book, one of my conditions is, 'Please do not mark it'.

I have been thinking a lot about inscription: When the author does it, it is called 'writing', when the critic does it, it is called a 'review', and when the reader does it, it is called 'reading'. Is there any difference between this? How may writing differ from reading? Is all activity some form of action and inscription? Many such questions arise, and which I have fitfully pursued later with thinkers as different as Jacques Derrida, Gayatri Spivak, and Stanley Fish.

Stories of Deprivation

UB (***contd***): I went through a bad spell around the time I was nearly approaching school board examinations at the Shree A. S. Chaudhary High School, and lasted till almost my graduation. And what some of us had to endure for what seemed to us then as eternity but passed away only in a few years' time. On sound second thoughts, it occurs to me that it would not be fair to anyone, and above all to the family, to talk about concrete contexts of what really happened. But it may not be too unfair to anyone to refer to the experiences of deprivations with the near and dear ones that one had to suffer.

I began to live apartheid, although the full horror of that term as racism became clear to me only later in my life. Even today, violent social exclusion of others, and of any kind, hurts me because I know what the privation this entails. More than what I know; I still bear the marks of that early pain inside me. I am surprised I am saying this to you all because I thought I had overcome this personal side of the story as much as one can. But it is still there, and it hurts.

I learnt from my mother that all traumas pass—leaving a massive residue, of course. She was, and remained, a deeply spiritual person, investing whatever time she had in some religious rites. She used to regularly visit temples and she used to fast. She used to fast on an average for 265 days a year, she did not need an excuse to not eat! But she knew what hunger meant to us, and the meagre rations provided to us had to be constantly supplemented by *Bai* (my mother's nickname in the family). There were many days when there wasn't much to eat, and some days where there was literally nothing to eat!

But I also learnt the value of generosity. Occasionally, I was furtively handed over some money. That helped; sometimes *Bai* would go to Prem Mandir, walking the long distance, and bring us leftovers. Many times, her elder and younger brothers (from Jamnagar, a distance away from Rajkot) would come with sweets and presents of cash, which was a great help indeed. I also learnt the hard way how to be an elder at a very young age myself. It was all complicated and created lots of confusion and cross-purposes.

This experience of systematic injustice within the family developed in me a sense of just indignation and anger, and this might have something to do with my multiple senses of injustice, of understanding their sources, and their complexity, in kinship ties, local networks, local cultural mores, and so on. I developed early an attitude of critical empathy, solidarity, and compassion.

With all this going on, I applied myself to study. When it came to my studies, I was a single-minded student, but a vagabond learner. It was almost that I developed a dislike for discipline (long before Michel Foucault, who taught us about both the coexistence and conflict between disciplinary power and sovereign power). It is not the case that only those who have suffered injustice and humiliation can talk about it and do something to ameliorate or annihilate it as a social condition or relation. [One realises the epistemic folly of so thinking: clearly, an oncologist, for example, does not have to suffer cancer in order to provide diagnoses, or therapy, or even prediction of demise!] If that were so, the mission of comparative human rights discourse and development would be unintelligible. But it is true that lived experiences of conditions and contexts of injustice and humiliation enable enhanced understanding of rights, justice, and constitutional resistance.

K. M. Munshi and Other Matters

UB (*contd*): Through all this, I must say that my father was very fond of me. He worked as a civil servant, and he worked for a while with K. M. Munshi in the central government.[1] That was when we all went to Delhi and stayed with him on Pandara Road. This was the only period of respite for me. I recall how my elder brother and I walked from India Gate to Feroz Shah Kotla Stadium (travelling by foot, it seemed a long way away) to see our first Test match. All of us had great passion for cricket, both listening to commentaries and when permitted, watching the game. It was a great moment to go to Feroz Shah Kotla Stadium, but we were about an hour late. There were no proper seats left, aggressive chaps bullied their way through the queue; inside the stadium, they threw things from the top seats at many of us. That was their way of showing contempt for those who they thought of as country bumpkins, as some us were not elegantly dressed for the occasion!

My father was working with Munshi, India's first food minister and author of great Gujarati historical novels. I read him alongside with Walter Scott (and Alexander Dumas), and instantly discovered how well-read he was in their storytelling ways. Walter Scott of Gujarat that he was, I do not think he ever fully expressed his debt to Scott. Still, he inaugurated the art of the historical novel in Gujarati literature. He had a vivid style of writing and the books were mammoth: the chapters were short and titled after some description of event or action. He was great at portraying characters and what we know from literary studies now as the art of 'emplotment'. He served as a member of the Constituent Assembly where he made valued contributions to the making of the Indian Constitution, the Nehru Cabinet, and later, as the 'Kulpati' of Bharatiya Vidya Bhavan. He

[1]K(aniyalal) M(aneklal) Munshi (1887–1971), Gujarati novelist and major political figure, part of the independence movement and a member of the Constituent Assembly.

took pride in the syncretic character of Hindu religion and culture and sought to educate all Indians about the *Wonder that Was India* (to pinch the title of Professor A. L. Basham's great work).

Anyway, we eventually returned to Rajkot, and one of the things I saw with my own eyes was this whole business of integration of states. It was quite a job. My father was working with K. P. S. Menon[2] to get the instruments of accession signed by the princely states (under the vigilant care of the great Sardar Vallabhbhai Patel) in Saurashtra and parts of (now) Rajasthan. He used to go to various places, carrying these papers for royal signatures. One story I recall even today is of a Maharaja, fond of sport as he was, absent-mindedly signing the accession papers on the tennis court, irritated momentarily by the intrusion! I cannot vouch for this story, but the folklore of state accession is as fascinating as its actual history is complex.

I do recall that as a child, I accompanied my father to Sirohi in Mount Abu, where he had the papers signed very quickly. Some of these princes immediately complied as they seemed to be in awe of the post-independence period, and were mainly concerned about their privy purses.

The other memory I have of K. M. Munshi is the Somnath Temple, which was long in ruins. The government's concern—even during the immediate aftermath of the Partition—was to rebuild or restore the temple. And the prime mover of this idea was Sardar Vallabhbhai Patel, with the blessings of the first President of India, Dr Rajendra Prasasd. Patel oversaw every aspect of the *jirnodhar*, the work of restoration, ably supported by Shri K. M. Munshi (see Munshi 2016; Thapar 2005). In retrospect, I think this had the blessings of Sardar Patel rather than of Jawaharlal Nehru. U. N. Dhebar,[3] a veteran Congress leader and later the first Chief Minister of Saurashtra state,

---

[2]Kumar Padmanabha Sivasankara Menon (1898–82), career member of the Indian Civil Service and independent India's first Foreign Secretary (1948–52).

[3]Uchharangrai Navalshankar Dhebar (1905–77), former Chief Minister of Saurashtra (1948–54), President of the Indian National Congress (1955–59), and member of the Lok Sabha representing Rajkot.

and my father went to Rajkot railway station to greet Munshi on his way to the site of the temple. Somehow, I was allowed to tag along with my father. I remember vividly Munshi's anger. He was very angry, though I now forget what triggered it. He shouted, 'I will blow your brains out', or something like that, at my father or at Dhebar, I can't recall now. And I had these enormous tears welling in my eyes; Munshi perhaps saw this and smiled blankly at me. This scene made an impression on me. I always thought that such a display of anger was unjust, all this blowing someone's brains out, etc. I get very angry myself, but instantly calm myself down, with Munshi's threat echoing in my ears.

But I often wonder whether outbursts of anger are ever justified. Perhaps there are mood changes that one may never wholly control. But these interactional events also constitute aggression and violence. Very often, anger takes the form of intimate violence; very often, it is a violence that stems from occupying an office or a status (or authority exploitation). As concerns rather infrequent angry outbursts, I apologise for them almost instantly. But the ideal is not to minimise such events but altogether eradicate anger. Professor Lotika Sarkar,[4] a dear friend and a colleague at Delhi Law faculty, often recalled her father (she used to fondly call him 'Chelku', whereas in outside life he was Sir Dhiren Mitra, a senior crown law official), who counselled her to count till ten before getting angry!

But there is the other side of anger: anger at injustice and unfairness. There are many people who maintain majestic calm at precedents of gross injustice. That has never ceased to amaze me. Does the lack of anger at injustice betoken a complicity with it? Or does it have to do with one's own finitude, which also encourages the avoidance of exposure to excesses even of just protestation, and perhaps even the risk of martyrdom? Or is it fatalism—entrusting some Big Other with the task of combating the evil of injustice? I do not know the answers,

[4] Lotika Sarkar (1923–2013), noted Indian feminist, social worker, educator, and lawyer, founding member of the Centre for Women's Development Studies (CWDS) and Indian Association for Women's Studies. Her father, Sir Dhiren Mitra, was a leading lawyer in late colonial India.

save positing that the feeling of anger and indignation is essential to identifying circumstances and conditions of recurrent injustice in any society and fighting against it.

LL: The sense of compassion that you talked about, it is a very similar experience for me. Very often, in discussions, you are asked this question: When did you become political, or when were you politicised? I find it an unintelligible question, because it assumes a clear moment when we are suddenly made aware of ideas of justice and injustice. For me, it was very similar—my grandmother was a domestic worker, she shot herself in the Chinese embassy, and this was something we didn't know about for the longest time. But growing up with a domestic help, like most kids, I was always very nasty to our help. Till my mother sat me down one day and said, you don't know much about your grandmother since she died when I was very young, but whatever little I remember of her, I want to share with you. She then told me about her working in houses, washing clothes, etc. So she said, the next time you speak to our maid, just remember your grandmother, whom you never saw. This is a pre-political sense of justice.

UB: Yes, it is very important to share personal genealogies of suffering and injustice. But I do not see this early signal as a sense of 'pre-political' indignation at acts of injustice. Yes, they are pre-political in the sense that given one's infancy or early adolescence, there is an experience of powerlessness at changing oppressive circumstances. But sharing of experiences (as your mother did with you) forms a powerful sense of treating others fairly in later life; that moral pedagogy is very important. It is also a way of disciplining.

I recall how my mother slapped me hard when, at the age of six (though this was the only instance of corporeal violence I suffered), I asked her for the meaning of a slang/abuse: I have never uttered an abuse in my whole life as a result! But moral pedagogy of six years old aside, a feeling of just compassion at the events of injustice begins then to develop. The initial endowments of suffering, do they carry on in later life? In some cases, they do not. What moral residue does this early experience leave us with is the question: How, then, does one transform this experience into the latter-day agenda of social struggles?

LL: There is a scene in *Citizen Kane* in which one of the characters, an old man, says that when he was a teenager, he was travelling on a ship, and the ship passed by another ship. He was standing on the deck, and he saw a girl on the other deck. He says, I must have seen her for five seconds, and I don't think she even saw me, but there isn't a single day that has gone by in my life when I have not thought about her.

UB: Terrific, the imagery of ships passing by in the night is a powerful one. Abstract, pure love is a powerful force: you do not ask for reciprocity, even recognition; in fact, one does not ask anything. One just receives the grace.

If you are not vulnerable to love, you are truly post-human in a very pejorative sense. This vulnerability, openness is terribly important. It is not consistent with good moral character, not consistent with the ethic of public standards. But it is this openness to the love of a stranger, a distant third, refusing to regard him/her as an object, a thing—this openness to others is always terribly important. Ram, what about you, do you have any personal experiences to share?

Sitharamam Kakarala: I wanted to ask you if you remember any significant influences from that period with whom you are still in touch.

UB: Yes, I was very fond of my youngest aunt, I still am, though not as an aunt but as a close friend, we are on first-name terms. There is an older aunt, who used to adore me—and still does—and now, at the age of ninety, she has many stories to tell, especially of my growing up. Above all, I recall warmly the Bohra family that lived opposite Prem Mandir, the old grandpa called *Abba*, his son Akbarali Jasdanwala, his daughters—Sara, Dayam, and a younger one whose name I will soon recall—and, of course, the son Asgharali, and the Ammijaan. Their family was heaven compared to mine, closely-knit, caring of each other and of their friends, and above all, loving. From them, I learnt many a thing—the virtue of commensality, eating together from a common *thali*, a certain catholicity of outlook, a sense of laughter, and a certain gentle unobtrusive practice of faith—virtues that do not often find expression in all our fond talk of Constitutional secularism. Akbarali Saab suddenly discovered his genius in Gujarati verse/poetry; he had great creative potential and became Gujarat's leading poet, a Shayar, who composed Ghazals. In his warm companionship, I also learnt to be a minor poet in Gujarati. And Sara was the lodestar of my life—she held my hand through some of my most difficult moments.

Love and Justice

LL: Love and justice! Can anyone understand justice if they do not understand love?

UB: Nothing more true can ever be said, dear Lawrence. Both love and justice remain the provinces of heart and soul. The rest is mere conversation of and about the 'rational' and 'reasonable'.

This we know differently, yet precisely, from my favourite saint, St. Francis of Assisi, and from Kabir to Mother Teresa. From Sabari, to Mira, Chaitanya, Kabir, and the Sufi saints. For each one of them, justice was as much an abstract virtue contrasting with love as it was an embodied one. The power of love confronting State sovereignty has been exemplified through the ages in the meditations on Antigone. Contemporary feminist discourse takes up the theme in addressing us on the relationship between *justice* and *care*, or in my way of feeling, on *justice as care*.

One ought to immediately distinguish, with Rousseau, between 'official' and 'non-official' forms of love relationships. No doubt this troubled terrain admits of no easy articulation. I think that I derive this distinction partly from the treatment of Rousseau by Derrida in his *On Grammatology*, noting here the germinal contributions of Peter Goodrich, which you obviously have in mind. The laws against treason and sedition, for example, obligate us all to bear affection to the lawfully constituted sovereign everywhere; this is a form of abstract citizen love, always pitted against the cacophonies of voices of suffering and communities of resistance.

The love/justice dichotomy now re-enacts itself in a post-metaphysical discourse. I have in mind the recent writings of so diverse a range of thinkers as Antonio Negri and Alain Badiou. I had better leave this remark un-supplemented any further in terms of the present conversation, except to say that I trace this complexity in my 'Aspects of Justice: A Tale of Three Cities', the 2009 Tagore Law Lectures (Baxi 2023, forthcoming, I hope!),[5] where I fully address the pertinence of your interlocution.

LL: I wanted to ask you about your writing. It is marked by a sensuality that informs unexpected areas. Constitutional law is not meant to be written sensually, but you write about it sensually when you talk of ideas of Constitutional grief, and ingraining forms of remembrances within the Constitution. There is an inflection of your affectivity in bits of your writing.

UB: You are right; it is perhaps nothing new, when we recall that the making of the Indian Constitution was dipped in the unbearable violence of the Partition. If I had indeed to use/evoke the dignity of large words, I might even say that our collective experience then and since indicates that there is nothing to the life of law but the messy and cruel litanies of the governance of desires, or serial protestations against the overweening rationalism of the State/law combine.

We surely learn from Jacques Lacan the crucial importance of sovereign desire that rewrites our bodies as theatres of the governed populace; the State does more—it constantly recomposes bodies and their truths by an 'anti-law' that always masquerades as so many instant incarnations of the 'rule of law'. This remark scarcely warrants

[5]Upendra Baxi note: 'This is a long-belated publication. A chief reason for this delay is a conceptual one. The two halves of the book tracing the geographies of justice (both imagined and real) do not match: one is about ancient theories of justice and the second are the more contemporary approaches, aggravated by the installation of anthropogenic harms and accelerating the Anthropocene. I am long in search of a narrative bridge that connects the two. Many friends have made constructive suggestions, especially Professor Allan Norrie at Warwick. I hope at last to work this out!'

further elaboration in a world constantly re-ordered, constantly in the making even while being unmade.

I feel that the relationship between law and desire is very crucial, but yet not fully explored, except by those writing on psychoanalysis and the law, and of course on law and Lacan, and humanising law and justice. There is obviously desire for love and justice that motivates peace and harmony among oneself, the other, the other of the other, and a distant third. There is also governance and the disciplining of desires in civil society, religious, political, and State spheres. There is also a distinct desire for social order. I spoke a long time ago about the *constitutionally desired social order* (Baxi 1967a). One of the questions is how the production of law as love pertains to a desire for order (which a moderniser of social theory, Talcott Parsons [Parsons 1970], described as pattern-maintenance, which leads to the integration of social order) and the desire of/for justice. The two are often antagonistic and much depends on how we define/describe that 'order'. One can maintain a strong order that is unjust (at least as maintaining and fostering violent social exclusion), or one may aspire to a just order with just means. It is not always the case that most people prefer justice over other desires, especially in situations of civil war or outright wars. Also, in ordinary times, people might desire order over justice. How these desires manifest themselves and alternate from time to time, and how they are reproduced over generations are extremely important areas of exploration. The relation between violence and desire needs also to be explored more in legal studies.

I will not pursue this theme any further here, save to say that the production of desire for law and justice in any society needs to be carefully explored, including the modes in which religion, education, and law participate in acts of such production.

I think writing with the body is a very important statement to make; I have never done it consciously. I am glad you noticed the politics of affect; this does not normally get commented on, except by people who say this is not the way to write about Constitutional law. There are welcome exceptions now. Some of my friends teaching American Constitutional law are now openly abandoning their fascination with *Marbury vs. Madison*[6] and are beginning to discover *Dred Scott*[7] as a starting point for teaching American Constitutional law, although I often wonder why it took so long to start the right way. The production of governance desires is one way of grasping law; but so are the modes of production of desires and passions for justice within and beyond law and sovereignty.

My friend, Anna Grear (Grear 2010), has written a very profound series of essays concerning the practices of embodiment/ disembodiment via the very languages of contemporary human rights.

If you are concerned with suffering, you have to start with (what Deleuze calls) the logic of the senses. You simply cannot start with the abstract logic of reason (and recall the 'terror of reason' that post-Auschwitz thinkers constantly and fearfully assail). The meaning of suffering poses some inordinate analytical and historical questions. I understand that. Essentially, it is a state of embodiment, a state

[6] *Marbury v. Madison*, 5 U.S. 137, 1803. This case established the principle of judicial review in the United States. Chief Justice Marshall reasoned that the Judiciary Act of 1789 conflicted with the Constitution and that Congress did not have power to modify the Constitution through regular legislation. Widely considered the most important decision in American Constitutional law, the decision established the power of the Supreme Court to declare laws passed by Congress null and void if they, in the Court's opinion, violated the Constitution. As the Court put it, 'Thus, the particular phraseology of the constitution of the United States confirms and strengthens the principle, supposed to be essential to all written constitutions, that a law repugnant to the constitution is void; and that courts, as well as other departments, are bound by that instrument.'

[7] *Dred Scott v. Sandford*, 60 U.S. 393, 1857: The Dred Scott decision was a widely criticised decision by the United States Supreme Court, which held that African-Americans whose ancestors had been imported to the US and sold as slaves could not be American citizens—whether enslaved or free—and therefore had no standing to sue in court. The opinion of the Court by Chief Justice Taney pronounced that, 'We think they are not included, and were not intended to be included, under the word "citizens" in the Constitution, and can therefore claim none of the rights and privileges which that instrument provides for and secures to citizens of the United States.'

of embodied intersubjectivity in which you feel the pain of others. Wittgenstein offers some very good reasons for why you cannot feel the pain of others inside you—it is a logical impossibility, you can imagine it, but you can never feel it. Stanley Cavell (1999), and in a different mode, Veena Das (2016), have written on this. But I am simply saying that here at work in statements of protest, an intrusion into the life of reason, lies a desire, a passion for justice. And it is important to realise the deep relation between desire, the body, and the senses. It must be a wider pedagogic project, to impart a sense of law as a sensory experience, not as a dogma or as an abstraction, as power or resistance, but of law as it affects your body. Law is only moved with the sense of the body and with the sense of its profound trans-reason.

What is at stake indeed are the roles of political passion, always in contrast with those of political reason. Both move and shape the world, often decisively. As we all surely know, different logics of love as justice animated the French, American, the Socialist, and postcolonial revolutions. More crucially, it is only the rejection of colonising reason by the struggles for love and justice that makes the idea of the post-colony an idea of justice. Love and justice are perhaps what made Tilak's slogan possible: 'Swaraj is my birthright and I shall have it', and the Mahatma's subsequent pragmatic mutations of this battle-cry. The labour of thought of Frantz Fanon, Amílcar Cabral, and of other African leaders is to cultivate a grasp of love and justice in their determined struggles against the preordained Euro-Enlightenment idea of progress.

I may say, summarily, that love/justice talk and action remains (to evoke Gramsci) the province of organic thinkers more than that of the erudite ones. What we today name as acts/performatives of human rights and social movement solidarity are initially born out of empathy and protest at what Maurice Merleau-Ponty described as the 'injustice in/of the flesh' (Baxi 1994b). Put another way, we must keep in mind that injustices inscribed on bodies without language often precede the writing of constitutions in languages of abstract ideals as rational guardians of the people and resist the erasure of the 'vital' difference between writing with the body and writing the body into the text.

Two
Learning the Law

Working with Scindia Steam Navigation Company

SRK: How did you get interested in maritime law?

UB: It was a concatenation of circumstances. Many things happened. My father was transferred to Bombay after Saurashtra became a part of the state of Bombay in November 1956. In 1958, I came to Bombay. He left for Ahmedabad later, for Gujarat state (which was formed on 1 May 1960). Coming from a small town, Bombay was a scary wonder. The population of Rajkot was estimated at 193,500, whereas for the same year it was 4,152,056 for Bombay. But it was not a mere matter of demography. Although a small city, Rajkot then had many things to its credit: it housed the famous Watson Museum (containing items of interest for human history and that of the city), was known for the late schooling of Mohandas Gandhi, and its aesthetics made it, in popular parlance, a 'colourful' city (*Rangeela* Rajkot). The scholar and writer Malcom Pasley,[1] who earned fame also as a translator of Kafka,

[1] Sir John Malcolm Sabine Pasley (1926–2004).

was born there. But the cultural riches of Bombay were immense in comparison.

Bombay was simply overwhelming, spatially and aquatically; the city stretched miles and miles and was surrounded by sea and ocean on all sides. We lived in a very central location: 1st Pasta Lane, Colaba, and Churchgate area was nearby, only a few kilometres away; the station was huge with many platforms, and connected to many parts of the city by local trains—and these lifelines, the local trains, crisscrossed the city like a big python, lissom as well as firm, and the BEST headquarters was nearby, with its fleet of buses. From Rajkot (literally, a city of princes), the move to Bombay was also like dipping into an ocean of urban anonymity. News substituted gossip (although the distinction and 'transaction' between gossip and news is always worth pondering).[2] In Bombay, although large families stayed together (mostly because of the housing situation), each member of the family had an individual identity and parental control was greatly loosened at an early age; the network of friends mattered a great deal; intimacy was replaced by increasing alienation; and time suddenly became important, even crucial. There was nothing laidback about Bombay;

---

[2] Upendra Baxi note: The relation of 'news' to 'rumour' stands brilliantly analysed by Ranajit Guha in his *Elementary Aspects of Peasant Insurgency* (Guha 1999). He says:

> To regard rumour as lying is not merely a measure of the distance between a typical site of collective discourse and an ideal seat of official truth—between the bazaar and the bungalow, so to say. But it is also the result of an ill-conceived assimilation of rumour to news. Kaye in characterizing the former as 'a certain description of news' shares with other elitist writers the fairly common error of lumping these together and identifying one as merely a corrupted version of the other. In fact, however, no two kinds of verbal communication could be more different. They differ in two important respects.... In the first place, the source of news is necessarily identifiable: its message is open to verification by being retraced to the point of its origin and the bearer is considered accountable for its accuracy in most cases. By contrast, rumour is necessarily anonymous and its origin unknown (even though on occasion .... a fictive source may be assigned to it).... (ibid., 258)

everyone was busy doing something... I sensed, and began to live, a great difference.

Many things happened to me there; may I mention only a few here? I met Prema; incidentally, she was the first woman secretary to be assigned to a sessions court. She had passed, of course, the BPSC examinations and resumed her studies in graduation and law. Later, I asked her whether she could get me a copy of the judgment banning *Lady Chatterley's Lover*, later overruled by Justice Hidayatullah (*Ranjit D. Udeshi vs. State Of Maharashtra*, 1965).[3] As you know, District Court judgments were then almost impossible to get, but she made for a copy somehow through great effort. But I am running ahead of the story... let me return later to Prema.

I wanted to study English, but out of the blue I got an offer to join the Scindia Steam Navigation Company headed by the first and only woman shipping director, Ms. Sumati Morarjee. Everyone told me I should accept the job; this was Lady Luck knocking on the doors, and one must gracefully allow her to enter with good tidings.

I went to Elphinstone College and met Principal G. C. Bannerjee who said, you have very good marks in English Literature and I would love to admit you, but you cannot do your job while you study. (Yes, I was not 'graced' into a first class, though I was on the edge.) Part-time students were not enrolled for the M.A. programme. I had very few friends in Bombay, partly because I was a Rajkot fellow and very uncouth by Bombay standards until I learned how to dress well. Still, the few friends I had persuaded me not to give up the Scindia job. Sumati Bahen took a great interest in me and suggested that I do something other than be an assistant to the Publicity Officer Mr I. M. Choksi, since I was a 'man of literature'. She put me in touch with Mr Jhaveri, who was a good personal friend of hers. The two of them encouraged me and asked me to draft a history of the shipping company. I enjoyed the task of drafting.... The book emerged a few years later as the *Saga of Scindia* (Jog 1969). It was published much later, but I like to think that it is mostly based on my narrative. It tells the story of how nationalism and shipping came to be related. One of

[3] *Ranjit D. Udeshi vs. State Of Maharashtra*, AIR 1965 SC 881.

the few first demands in 1931 was for the freedom of coastal shipping for Indians. It was fascinating for me to learn how important shipping was to the freedom struggle, and how crucial the latter was to the development of *Scindia* in particular, and Indian shipping in general. Of course, the book was published later by Sumati Morarjee, and at that point in time it did not bear any direct or explicit acknowledgement of my early literary efforts.[4] What I recall even today is her personally conveying warm appreciation of my labour of love.

Government Law College, Bombay

UB (***contd***): My second year there, I decided to study law at the Government Law College in Bombay. I was utterly horrified by Contracts and Torts and the way people taught it, and so I took to reading and writing some poems about the imponderables in life in class! After the first six months. I quit the law college. Yet, the first two papers I wrote in my life—one was even awarded a medal—had to do with law. The first was written for an essay competition on leisure. The second was a speech I made on the concept of truth in law and literature. This was long before the law and literature movement developed. I am proud of these papers, but they were handwritten and are now lost. I always thought that law would be a good option to fall back upon, but the teaching was so dreary.

[4] The Foreword to the book *Saga of Scindia*, written by Sumati Morarjee, concludes thus,

> We are thankful to Shri N.G. Jog, author and well-known journalist, for having agreed to write this history of our company at short notice. How well he has done it, I leave it to the reader to judge. [I]t would not have been possible to bring out this volume but for the unstinted co-operation of many trusted friends and colleagues in and out of the company and to them I am grateful. [O]n this auspicious occasion our hearts go out in salutation to those—ashore and afloat—who have kept our flag bearing the Swastika flying high with faith and courage. (Jog 1969, vi)

Since I had done this manuscript for the book, Ms. Morarjee made me the youngest officer in the shipping company. She said I had to do the round of the various departments doing the charter party, bill of lading, etc. I was told that I would be sent to Hamburg and London, for two years each, and would come back as assistant manager. She kindly permitted me to join the law college again. This time, I had fun because I did not take it seriously—I just sat in the library of the law college and went to a few classes. I had some funny teachers, such as Professor S. D. Balsara[5] for Tort law, who had a great sense of humour. The next year we did transfer of property, we had five teachers, and every teacher would start with Section 53 on part performance (The Transfer of Property Act 1882)! Ranganath Rao (hailing from Bangalore) taught us private international law; he was an irascible teacher and a brilliant man. Principal (T. K.) Tope was a good teacher, but he was stern as a Principal. I easily broke all records, standing first in the first-year examinations.

I was privileged to read in the College library some classics in jurisprudence and political theory that were borrowed and read by Professor, later Principal, Dr B. R. Ambedkar. He was not just an avid reader and a good bibliophile, but my later reading of his oceanic collected works brought me his implicit and incipient theory of creative reading—reading like an untouchable. Reading was a creative act of suffering which also furnished a resilient way of overcoming the 'frustration' experienced by the Untouchables as '*frustration forever*', '*unrelieved by space or time*'. Drawing upon P. B. Shelley, who said imperishably that poets are the 'unacknowledged legislators of the world', and Mathew Arnold who famously said, 'Failure to affirm one's own essence is simply another name for frustration', for Dr Ambedkar, reading was not only resistance, but also delineated future histories of emancipation (see, Moon (ed.), *Collected Works*, Vol. 12, Chapter 7, 733–736).

The law college library was good on traditional jurisprudence and I read a lot of it. But I really wanted to read more systematically, and the University library had a richer collection on Roman law, and

[5]S. D. Balsara, author of *A Textbook on the Criminal Procedure Code* (1973).

comparative jurisprudence. I joined the L.L.M. programme where we had a very good teacher, Phiroze K. Irani.[6] Irani was also a solicitor and practised law as such. Dr M. J. Sethna taught us jurisprudence, and a young man called S. P. Sathe[7] was also my teacher.

I have two stories. One is about Sethna, who wrote a book called *Synthetic Jurisprudence*. The Foreword for one of his books by that title was written by Roscoe Pound[8] (Sethna 1962). One day, Sethna was going on in the class about Roscoe Pound and jural postulates of civilised societies. I raised my hand and said, Professor Pound does not know enough about the Third World. All his premises are suspect when you apply his theory to India. Pound says that legislatures make law in response to social demands, and that is completely untrue in India. Rather, laws advance a social demand, such as the Untouchability Offences Act, Hindu Code, etc. He was very upset and angry and asked me to leave the class, and he went to the head of the department and said that I needed to be disciplined for criticising Pound! What gumption, he said.

Phiroze then spoke to me and told Sethna Saheb that I would not do something like that again. I was restless and decided to write a long letter to Roscoe Pound, and to my surprise I got a reply two-and-a-half pages long in which, after explaining in some detail why he was only engaged with the theory of interests and jural postulates in the context of Western societies, he said, 'I need to think about some of the points you have raised, why don't you come to Harvard when you have finished your law studies in India?' Sethna was angrier when he found out that I had written the letter, it was like a nuclear explosion!

The second story is in relation to this young teacher, Sathe. He was teaching us principles of legislation and Roman law. Roman law is

[6] Phiroze K. Irani, former Head, Department of Law, University of Bombay.

[7] Satyaranjan Purushottam Sathe: former Principal of the ILS Law College (1976–91) and later Pro-Vice-Chancellor of Pune (now Savitribai Phule) University.

[8] Roscoe Pound (1870–1964), former Dean of Harvard Law School (1916–36) and member of the faculty at UCLA Law School (1949–52).

my passion, and I read it even now. He was teaching this one day, and I knew where it was coming from, so I decided to read something else, it may have been *The Times of India*. He got very upset and said, Baxi, I am telling you something about Roman law and you are reading a newspaper. This is an insult, you cannot read a newspaper, why are you not attending to me? I said, sir, I am attending to you, I can tell you what you have been telling us; what is more, I can tell you the page numbers of the relevant book from which you are teaching. If this is not enough, I can tell you what other pages you are going to present to us in the next half hour. And if I am wrong, you can take action against me. It was very impertinent, and it is not done as a student, but I was bored. He said, never come to any of my classes again! I went out and thought nothing about it, I did not go back to his classes, I went to the library instead. Probably, my attendance record for a couple of weeks was, for this reason, questionable, so Phiroze must have talked to Sathe. Sathe insisted that I apologise to him as I had insulted him. I had not insulted him, but I had been angry. Clearly that was no way of teaching. Phiroze said, he had some discretion but first of all, I should convey my apology. I recall saying that you will never get a first class in your L.L.M. programme in international law and jurisprudence if you do not put me up as a candidate for the exam, you will lose that prospect. Some cheek! But that was the result ultimately. I set a new record. I knew I would.

Following Brahmananda Reddy[9] (a politician from Andhra Pradesh and sometime Union Cabinet Minister), who invented a classic form of the Indian apology, I said to Dr Sathe, I apologise *if* I have hurt your sentiments. But then I said to him, I don't want to apologise in this manner, that is a wrong way of doing it, let us put it this way: you were right in your way, and I was not altogether wrong in my response. He probably agreed to this.

I had forgotten this incident, but was reminded of it by Sathe publicly at a Law Faculty seminar lecture series in the 1990s, when he said that he was a better teacher as a result of this encounter. He said,

---

[9]Kasu Brahmananda Reddy (1909–94), Chief Minister of Andhra Pradesh (1964–71) and Home Minister of India (1974–77).

my teaching was mechanical, I thought teaching consisted of passing on information from old notes. I disliked then what Baxi said, but he made a substantial difference to my teaching. Only a rare teacher has the moral courage to do this—auto-critique, the ability to say one was wrong, and transform her/himself, both in pedagogy and research.

We had this lovely system of examination in Bombay University whence we were directed to: 'answer at least one, but not more than four'. The exams were meant to be written in three hours. In my Jurisprudence exam, there was this one question on relativism, and I wrote an answer on relativism in ancient and modern contexts, comparing Gustav Radbruch with Sage Parasara. I could not finish it, and three hours went down in a twinkle of the eye! The examiner (as I learnt later) was a man called G. S. Sharma,[10] a doyen of Indian jurisprudence teachers. He contacted Irani and invited me, even before I had graduated, to Kasauli for a workshop on advanced legal education, and I wrote an article for it on patterns of postgraduate legal education in India. I vividly recall Professor Bertram Wilcox from Yale who corrected the paper on a train to Kasauli; he scored out all unnecessary words and generally sought to tighten the prose. He did not tell me in words that I did not know how to write, but in effect, that was what he was telling me. Dr Sharma was later to publish a rigorously edited version of that article in the *Jaipur Law Journal*.

It was a great learning experience for me to be part of the national seminar and to rub shoulders with some of the leading lights of the Bench and the Bar. There were many highlights. I met with Justice Gajendraragadkar, who was kind enough to ask me to study the dynamics of constitutional justicing. I also met Dr L. M. Singhvi, then a rising star at the Bar and a zestful young Member of Parliament, and the national seminar marked the beginning of a creative law and society engagement and the privilege of personal friendship. I met also senior law academic stars on the scholarly firmament.

I know that times have changed and now we can readily meet on the computer screen all the folks one wants to see and hear and should

[10]Gyan Swaroop Sharma. Baxi refers to him variously as Gyan Swaroop, Gyani-ji, and G. S. (see Baxi 2002d).

you have access to library platforms, get most of their writings. More awaits information on open access and routine web search engines. But I still believe in the individual contact with senior lawyers, and erudite Justices, as a part of legal learning. I still regret that the Indian Law Institute has ceased this seminar programme and I hope that some well-resourced Universities and National Law schools will adopt this.

Berkeley: Of Vietnam, Kelsen, and Others

UB (*contd*): I have another story about Pound and India—I was admitted to Columbia, Harvard, Yale, and Berkeley with a fellowship on my L.L.M. results. I was going to go to Pound at Harvard, but we killed him! Did you know how? Pound came to give the Tagore Law Lectures. This story is probably an exaggeration. But I have found it pedagogically useful, and makes teacher and learner rethink, and Pound exemplified rigorous thinking and rethinking. Pound walked up and down during the lecture and said how wonderful it was to be in Calcutta. At precisely thirty minutes he stopped and said, now ladies and gentlemen, any questions or comments? He waited for five or ten minutes, and there were no comments. He was pacing up and down. One finger went up and Pound jumped up and said, sir, speak loudly, I will come as close as I can to you, sir, tell me. He was dying to hear the first Indian reaction. The questioner said, Professor Pound, the University of Calcutta has gone to great pains to invite you, it has paid airfare for you and Ms. Pound, you have a contract to deliver five lectures of one hour each, you have spoken for thirty minutes, and you ask us to participate! Why so? My spin on that is that Pound returned to Harvard and died a few months later, perhaps of what we know as a culture shock!

Anyway, coming back to the point, in my choice of university, I settled on Berkeley. I told Ms. Morarjee that I have got this invitation and she said, come back tomorrow, in a very brusque manner. The next day, she said, I would give you leave, but you are not coming back. I said, I tell you, I will come back, and I will go to Hamburg, I owe it to you. She was a devotee of Lord Krishna, she prayed for two hours every day, all her major decisions were based on what Thakhurji said, and Thakhurji had said to her that I would not come back. I said, this is too much, I will prove your Thakhurji wrong, I will come back.

She gave me one year's leave with lien and put me on a cargo boat with twelve officers and crew, on which I was the only passenger for thirty days. My first long voyage, and I saw the horror—the people who really ran the ship were ghettoed in the crew quarters while I had a whole cabin to myself. The officers ate, played cards, drank beer, and were served by these people. There was a storm in the Atlantic for five hours, and they had to put chains on everything, it tossed the ship so much I thought I was going to die. That was where I learnt the actual meaning of the expression, 'sailing into the eye of the storm'. When confronted with a big storm, you have to go right into the centre of it, where there is utter calm.

Incidentally, I recall the voyage and the storm when I read of what Heidegger once said about the hermeneutical circle:

> [W]hen confronted by it, it is best to stay within it and reach near its heart in order to tear it asunder. This circle of understanding is not an orbit in which any random kind of knowledge may move; it is the expression of the existential fore-structure of Dasein itself. It is not to be reduced to the level of a vicious circle, or even of a circle which is merely tolerated. (Heidegger 2001 [1962], 195)

But let us resume the narrative of events: Then we reached Boston, and it was my first day in America. We had a few hours to go ashore and I ventured out as a pedestrian: my first footfall in the US. At the signal, I did not know how to cross and I stood there for what seemed like hours (until a good Samaritan showed me how a signal button is to be pressed when you want to cross roads). Then I met a white man old enough to be my father, who was eating slices of stale bread from a garbage trash can—what they call beauty cans—he put his hand out, but I had only traveller's cheques. I felt so miserable. I had not heard of this sort of absolute, dire poverty in America; I had only heard of race. I apologised in Bombay English. And then I went back on the ship to go on to New York. I had a few hours before taking a flight to Berkeley and I recall taking the time off to visit the UN building. It was colossal, and so was everything else. Even the blocks of road down which I had to walk were very long.

At Berkeley, I was assigned Room 661 in the International Students House. I opened my closet to put my things in, and saw a plaque that said this was the second most earthquake-prone building in the Bay Area. I ran down seven floors and asked the director about the plaque, what about the first most earthquake-prone building, I asked? He said it had been destroyed in the previous earthquake! There was no twinkle in his eyes; so I took him at face value! But later research that I conducted showed that he could not have been referring to the 'great' San Francisco earthquake in 1906 because the international student house was established in Berkeley only on 18 August 1930—some years before I was born! However, one knows now that the Bay area is a seismic zone where low-intensity earthquakes occur regularly. The United States Geological Society's Working Group Report (1999) finds '0.70 probability (± 0.1) of at least one magnitude 6.7 or greater earthquake before 2030' within the region. One hopes that in the future, the International House at Piedmont Avenue will be saved by more earthquake 'proof' technologies, from earthquakes so far predicted.

Incidentally, I also found that the building at Piedmont Avenue has been constructed 'because it was the home of fraternities and sororities, which then excluded foreigners and people of color'. By proposing this site, the founder of the I. House movement, Edmonds, 'sought to strike bigotry and exclusiveness…right hard in the nose' (as per the website of I. House in Berkeley). Most of us who formed a fellowship of learning then had no access to this information, now freely available on the worldwide web. Readers may acclaim (as I sadly, but also lustily, do) this access, even when the truths of Shoshana Zuboff, *The Age of Surveillance Capitalism: The Fight for a Human Future at the New Frontier of Power* (2019) may not wholly forget the dangers posed by digitalisation to democracy.

The other experience was that I was vegetarian, so we had to have mashed potatoes, spinach, and tomato sauce every day. Not even broccoli. The worse aspect was that there were no green chillies, to which I am addicted even now! I started a movement with the following slogan on the billboard: Vegetarians of the world, unite. You have nothing to lose but your mashed potatoes! That attracted a lot of South Asian students and some American nuns who were studying in the Divinity School.

I had foster parents, they tended to adopt a few students at the International House. The husband was Professor Albert Lepawsky from Political Science.[11] They had a nice place. I vividly recall my first dinner there. They passed the food around, but nobody urged you to eat some more. I did not eat, I was snobbish about spinach even then. At 12.30 AM that night, I simply could not stand the hunger anymore, I went across the hall to an Italian chap who, it turned out, was doing a doctorate in maths, and said, I am very hungry. He said, you Indians are always hungry. He took me several blocks down and I had my first vegetarian pizza!

Initially, I thought these fellows are uncivilised, but later on I had a moral conversion and realised that the culture in which I had been brought up was based on hypocrisy. If you want something, you say, no, I don't want it, so the host can have the satisfaction of giving it to you. It is a ritual transaction between the host and the guest. I learnt this *samskara* (good manners, upbringing) at my mother's knee, to my disadvantage, in Berkeley at least. But sometimes, I still like to be asked. Old habits, as they say, die hard. However, I saw to it that our children (later on in Sydney) were never brought up on lies.

LL: I have a quote from your 'State Formative Practices' article:

> Belonging to an adolescent generation of *Midnight's Children* that made Salman Rushdie an overnight celebrity, and having been shaped at Berkeley (though at Boalt Hall) during the height of the anti-Vietnam protests, I encounter these presentations in the context of many a postmodern nightmare. (Baxi 1999, 1183)

UB: Did I actually say this? But I can say that you are all well read! The anti-war protests were the highlight of my time at Berkeley. I was

[11] Albert C. Lepawsky (1908–92), organisational theorist and Professor of Political Science at the University of California, Berkeley.

the only law student and one of the very few South Asians, and hardly any Indian, to take part in the movement. It was a very demanding movement, but there was also a great romanticism to it. It was demanding in the sense that though there were different views on the Vietnam War, on campus, there was no disagreement on the technical issue of the deferment of draft. So many did not have to take a position on the war, but only on the deferment of the draft of young persons. Eventually, this became a fully anti-war struggle. What emerged was the Free Speech Movement. It was a coalition of people—Mario Savio, Angela Davis (from the Black Panther movement), Joan Baez (singing protest songs), so many young peaceniks. It was fantastic!

I was then also misdiagnosed with a cardiac problem that I never had. I was in Bay Area Hospital all by myself, and I was released after ten days with massive medication. The reason I mention that is because I was able to get permission to have a phone in my room and I used to get a call in a husky voice saying, sir, I am forbidden to disclose my name, but you must not do what you are doing. I said, please give me your name; he never did, it was intimidation. The man called me a few times; the next time he called me, I said, sir, this is too much, you have to tell me why you are calling me. If you do not give your name, I will have to go public. He said, sir, you have come here for an education, and that is what you should do. I said, this is my education, through solidarity and protest, fine, I am on the campus radio tonight, and I will repeat this conversation on radio. The conversation ceased after that and he never called me again! But I have never been quite able to distinguish between intimidation and lawlessness. Is there any difference? Is it of degree or of kind? How may we differentiate between the perpetrator and the victim perspectives?

There were a lot of attempts at managing protests, cordoning off protest areas, not allowing the use of a microphone, and so on. All the things which universities use to manage dissent. I was surprised at that, given the First Amendment, but it was a sensitive issue, they were not going to allow students to lead a revolt against the State. I do not think I have shouted slogans or carried protest flags again after that. The other occasion I remember is marching to Shastri Bhawan (in the early 1980s, after I returned from Sydney) with eminent friends and historians such as R. S. Sharma and Irfan Habib. We had 150 CRPF (Central Reserve Police Force) personnel escorting us, and I said to them, most of us are past our prime. They said, we are here for your security. A posse of 150 armed police for about fifteen professors from DU (Delhi University), AMU (Aligarh Muslim University), and JNU (Jawaharlal Nehru University), most of whom had never marched before or after and were (barring me, the youngest among the lot) on the wrong side of their fifties at least. It was quite an experience because one began to relate education to social action in a very interesting way.

In Berkeley, I had done all the difficult undergraduate courses, but I never could understand how discussions in the classroom could go on without reference to the war powers of the President, the Gulf of Tonkin resolution, the legality of the war or the moral/ethical status or legal status of conscientious objection, the Seeger case (*United States vs. Seeger*),[12] and all that. It was discussed episodically outside the classroom, but in a very anodyne way, as if we lived in a different kind of universe. This is what the difference between professionalism and politics is, and I was puzzled by it. Obviously, the Constitution did not seem to have any relevance to the lives of the people affected.

I audited a course by a gifted teacher, David Daube, on 'Greek and Roman reflections on Impossible laws' (Daube 1967). One day I asked him, what is this, Professor Daube, people are marching and getting killed, and you are talking about some period in the Roman Empire, why don't you talk about what is going on and the impossibility of law during the state of war? He said, yes, I could do that, but I would rather you listen to what I am saying, and someday in life, you will begin to think how important this was for you also.

I took that as a kind of challenge, but I did not like his refusal to get engaged. In many ways, I now understand how right he was. Giorgio Agamben discovers in *Homo Sacer* the roots of a 'lethal state' in the private Roman law institution named *patria potestas* and inverts in the process many institutions of public Roman law. David also wrote a small book on form criticism in Roman Law, which is a minor

[12] *United States vs. Seeger* 380 US 163 (1965).

classic and worth reading even today, in these halcyon days of law and literature (Daube 1956). In many ways, Roman law and jurisprudence is the fount of modern law and at this time it may be worthwhile to study the difference in categories of law in Ancient and modern law, beyond the work of modernisers and orientalist discourses.

I still run into some of my colleagues from the Vietnam years. Michael Tigar, who wrote that book on law and the rise of capitalism (Tigar 1977), I met him briefly in Austin, Texas where he was a popular teacher. Angela Davis, the prominent Black Panther, I met her twenty or so years later in Samarkand and she asked me, Baxi, do you remember me? That was Angela Davis all over, a photographic memory and an unfailing love for difference!

The first week in Berkeley, I was terrified. I had broken all records in Bombay, but I had never read a case, a statute, or a law and policy report. I read more important things, I believe, but I had not read those. I met my guide, Professor Albert Ehrenzweig,[13] and told him I wanted to study jurisprudence. He got up, shook my hand and said, have a nice holiday in California, your records show that you topped Bombay University in jurisprudence, you are obviously here for a holiday. I was really upset at this ruthless comment. I went back to him with another list of subjects—admiralty law, conflict of laws, etc.—but this time there was no jurisprudence on my list. He was surprised, but he was his ruthless self when it came to his course in comparative private international law. This cannot be your forte, he said, even some American students fail it, you cannot study conflict of laws, it is too difficult.

Ultimately, I persuaded him. And then my terror began. When I went to the library, the students, they had done speed reading courses, they would zoom through the page using marker pens; by the time I had read ten pages, the guy next to me would have read fifty. I stopped reading in the library and almost had a breakdown, a cognitive crisis. I was a slow reader. I still am! And hopefully no worse because of it!

[13]Albert A. Ehrenzweig (1906–74), legal scholar and author of *Psychoanalytic Jurisprudence: On Ethics, Aesthetics, and 'Law'—on Crime, Tort, and Procedure* (1971).

In class, you took the seat labelled by your name. Professor Steve [Stefan] Riesenfeld,[14] who taught us admiralty law, would ask me, what do you think of this, and I would have no idea since I was still struggling to read. Some professors, like John Fleming in Torts,[15] were kinder, but generally I got some version of the third degree in class. After four weeks of this, I pulled myself together. I said to myself, these people here, they do not have even 200 years of constitutional history. I come from a culture and civilisation that is more than 5,000-plus years old! I come from a different learning tradition. I said to myself, don't be terrified, just read at your pace and use your mind, don't worry about keeping pace with the class. I followed my own advice. What cheek!

With a fellow student called Ron Hacker, I formed a reading group in private international law. Ron is now a practising attorney in Los Angeles and still writes to me occasionally. His wife and he looked after me affectionately and became good friends. The term passed, I thought I would flunk, but I got law review grades, including in conflict of laws, the highest grade you can get. My trick worked: I said, I am not going to be intimidated by American students, I had to uphold the honour of Bombay University, the honour of India, and so on, a pep talk worthy of Dale Carnegie! It worked. I relaxed. I was told I did not have to do my second term, I would be promoted. This was an extraordinary proposition; in the last twenty-eight years, they had not admitted any person to the Ph.D. programme in this manner. I refused, I told him that I would like to complete my L.L.B. I said, I am Indian, we like our degrees!

Then came the traumatic experience of writing. I wrote—my typing skills were poor—on Kautilyan principles and the law of nations (Baxi 1967b) and on the doctrine of *professio juris* (the autonomy of contracting parties to stipulate law governing the agreement) in private international law (Baxi 1967c). When I entered Albert's room, he said,

---

[14] Stefan (Albrecht) Riesenfeld (1909–99), international law expert, known for having helped frame the Constitution for West Germany after World War II. He joined the faculty at Berkeley in 1952 as a professor of law after teaching at Harvard and the University of Minnesota.

[15] John G. Fleming (1919–97), author of a classic, *The Law of Torts* (1971).

stop there, don't enter the room. He had thirty-five pages of my class paper with him, he threw them at me and said, take this away, I don't want to ever look at this again. I was aghast, this was so undignified. I had two choices: to leave without picking up the pages, or to pick them up. My curiosity won over my dignity and I collected the papers. What was his problem? A silly problem, at that time. I did not know the difference between *op. cit.* and *loc. cit.*, *supra* and *infra*, and there were a few typing errors. I tried to give him a withering look, but it was wasted on him, he did not look at me. I banged the door and went out, what does he think of himself, I even fumed! Nothing wrong with the substance, the form can certainly be improved, I thought, but such an extreme reaction? I wasn't going to leave it there, I resolved to get it right. I learnt the citation formats from the Harvard Bluebook and left him a second draft with this note: should you prefer to throw it at me, kindly staple it! We became friends, and he said, don't call me Professor, call me Albert. I realised how this misbehaviour was pedagogic—one must not be sloppy in one's writing. I was deeply offended at the time by that pedagogic offensiveness or discourtesy, though. And of course, there is still some sloppiness in my writing, I guess by way of eternal protest at perfectionism.

I told Ms. Morarjee, I am coming back next year. She was so kind to me, she would ask the company's agent in San Francisco to enquire if I needed anything from India! Although she knew I wasn't coming back, she had not forgotten me, she and her Thakhurji. The second term was a lot more relaxed, I spoke and wrote with more freedom. I also officiated at a wedding in International House, and when I caught sight of the bride, already a married woman, in her bridal sari, I said to her, my god, you look absolutely dazzling. I must have said dazzling with an extra touch of enthusiasm; in Marathi, she said, Baxi, *jaasti bolu nako* (don't talk too much!), and with that, my honeymoon with the Marathi language ended.

The highlight of my Berkeley years was Vietnam, but it was also Kelsen. I had decided to go to Berkeley because Hans Kelsen[16] was

[16]Hans Kelsen (1881–1973), Austrian jurist, legal and political philosopher, one of the authors of the 1920 Austrian Constitution and

associated with Berkeley, and I read a lot of Kelsen while in Bombay. But when I got there, I found there was no Hans Kelsen around, he never was with the law school in the first place. There was only a Kelsen Hall, where he had taught political science. I said, what is to be done, I have come all the way to learn at the feet of Kelsen. Ultimately, I discovered that he was in fact in Berkeley, only not on campus. He was a frail man and he did not see students. I got his number and rang him. I said, Professor Kelsen, I have come all the way from India to study jurisprudence with you. He said, what can I do if you have come all the way, it is not my fault. I said, can I at least talk to you for ten minutes? He said, I don't see students anymore. I was really hurt. I was very upset; he was not rude, but he just didn't want to see me. I asked Albert, who was also Austrian, and he said, forget about Kelsen, he is at the end of his life, he doesn't meet scholars and students, he thinks nobody understands him.

I wouldn't give up, and I found a way. The crafty Oriental that I was, I established contact with Ms. Kelsen! She said, there is not the slightest chance that he will see you or talk to you. Given the fact that you have come all the way from India to work with him, all I can do is invite you over for a cup of tea. He works in the garden when he is in a good mood; he may or may not have anything to do with you, but that is all I can do. I powdered my nose, put on my best shirt, and took a taxi. He came over to look at this foreign object in his house with a gleam in his eye and said, who are you? Are you the one who has been calling me, why have you come? I said, Ms. Kelsen invited me. He said, I will give you five minutes. That was the start of a beautiful friendship. I don't recall now what I said in those five minutes, I must have showed off my knowledge on the pure theory of law or something. He weakened and said, come again in two weeks, on the Saturday. From then on and until I left Berkeley, for nearly three years, we met regularly every fortnight, initially for half-an-hour, then an hour, sometimes for two hours. He was happy and surprised that someone from so far away knew so much about his work. When I was

---

among other valued works, the book, *Pure Theory of Law*, originally published in 1934 (Kelsen 1967).

leaving, I asked him for his autograph. He refused at first, he didn't believe in such sentimentalism, he said. And then, he gave me one any way. It is on the first page of *Jaipur Law Journal*, which carries his elegant photograph; I have framed it and maintained it in my study all these years. It is my proud possession.

There is the extraordinary story of Julius Stone[17] having met with Kelsen. Stone warmly complimented Kelsen to his face, using some very flowery language. I am sure Stone meant every word of what he said, but Kelsen wasn't overly impressed, he didn't have a very high opinion of sociological jurisprudence. The next thing Kelsen knew, he had received a copy of an article published in the *Modern Law Review* by Stone, titled 'Mystery and Mystique in the Basic Norm' (Stone 1963). He writes in it of the great honour he had of meeting Kelsen. The article was not nasty, but it was a sustained critique of Kelsen. The article arrived when I was there. I have never seen a man so distressed. There was a certain naiveté to him, a definite charm. Kelsen wrote a rather nice response to the article and sent it to the *University of California Law Review*. The student editorial board returned his response, saying that the law review was not a personal forum for airing personal grievances among eminent professors. He was very hurt. His response was published eventually in the *Stanford Law Review* (Kelsen 1964).

---

[17]Julius Stone (1907–85), Challis Professor of Jurisprudence and International Law at the University of Sydney from 1942 to 1972. According to his biography at the University of Sydney's Julius Stone Institute, his appointment in 1942 was controversial due to his 'perceived radicalism' and his Jewish identity. David Armitage and Jennifer Pitts note that in his Sydney role, he 'made imaginative—often international' faculty appointments, and 'attempted to bring law into closer dialogue with philosophy and history in the Australian legal academy' (Alexandrowicz, et al. 2017, 12). A 'staunch supporter of Israel', he influenced Australian political policy on that topic, particularly in the 1980s (Blackshield 2012). In 1960, he proposed, in lectures given for the Australian Broadcasting Commission, the establishment of a hotline between Moscow and Washington as a safeguard against nuclear war, which was adopted by President Kennedy in 1963 (ibid.).

There are many other anecdotes. He asked me whether I had read his one-sentence review. I had not, and Kelsen had indeed a two-line review of a book titled *The Secrets of Hegel's Philosophy*, and his one-line review was a note of congratulations to the author for keeping it a secret for over 600 pages!

When we became more friendly, he frequently asked me whether I thought there would be a third World War. I was unnerved by the question because no one before (and, as it happened, since) had asked me such a question. But I later understood that war, and being an émigré, were terrible realities for Hans Kelsen, who had to leave Austria during the Nazi times and begin life all over again in the USA. War was a terrifying reality for an earlier generation, and some lived in terror of its return and the might of nuclear weapons. It is astonishing how far the Cold War has become a World War II substitute (through the so-called low-intensity conflict) and nuclear war has been averted by a balance of terror (or MAD, mutually assured destruction).

Only once was Kelsen monumentally cross with me. He had kindly read through my handwritten manuscript on validity and efficacy, where I said (among other things) that it was a distinction without a difference. He asked me as a logician: How can there be a distinction without a difference? More vehement was his insistence that I read the original text in German. He was deeply disappointed to learn that I did not know the language. I said he was right on both counts, and promised to rectify some of my positions. This I have fully done in my jurisprudence teachings, but I have yet to finalise my paper (the original text has not survived as many as seventeen house changes across continents!). However, the general point is the tendency towards the 'normative force of the factual' (Eugen Erlich stated this in terms of the sociological theory about the law) and the materiality of law.

LL: What was your Ph.D. on?

UB: On the spur of the moment, I said that I wanted to work on Indian conflict of laws. There was no such area, I had to invent it! The normative idea of a Ph.D. is that it should be a contribution of knowledge that has so far not been made. I collated some decisions, all rather dispersed, on the recognition of foreign decrees, recognition of marriages, etc. These were on the conflict of laws as it relates to the Constitution of India, especially to Articles 2, 3, 4, and 5.[18] My first article was called *Alleppey Turmeric Fingers and Arbitral Awards: Spices in the Conflict of Laws* (see Baxi 1968b). I contributed major studies to the *Annual Survey of Indian Law*, the Journal of Indian Law Institute, as well as to the Houston Law Review (see Baxi 1967a, 1967b, 1967c, 1967d). The administration of the School decided to have the viva before the submission of my thesis, and to examine me not only on writings on conflict of laws in India, but also my writings generally and some of the courses I had taken at Berkeley. That was a very wide range indeed. And the viva was long, lasting for about three hours. There were nine examiners at my viva. From the law school, there were, of course, Professors Albert Ehrenzweig, John Fleming, Richard Buxbaum, Herma Hill Kay, Stefan Riesenfeld, and some others. Professors Ralph Retzlaff and Gerald Berreman were there from Anthropology. They asked me wide-ranging questions from all sides: from the recently delivered decision in the United States on immunity (*Banco Nacional de Cuba vs. Sabbatino*[19]) to *Nyaya Panchayats*. It was a gruelling discussion, and I was, to my mind, not up to the mark in some areas. But, as it turned out, they unanimously thought well of me.

---

[18] In a recent conversation, Upen relates how his degree came to be awarded to him:

> I was very heavily involved with the Vietnam War protests in Berkeley. I was supposed to leave for Australia. I didn't have a written thesis, but they held a viva voce on the basis of my writings, on the understanding that the result would be declared on submission of written thesis. John Fleming came to Australia a year later, and he asked Julius Stone to persuade me to complete my thesis. I said, such 'clerical labour' is not of interest to me now. The committee met again, and they decided my basic work qualified for award of degree. My 'thesis' was eventually published as a series of articles. (21 October 2017 at Upen's house [LL and SC])

[19] 376 U.S. 398 (1964).

First Visit to Sydney: Stone and the German South West Africa Decision

UB (*contd*): Julius Stone then invited me to spend six months (which became a year) in Sydney. It was a great honour. That year in Australia, I wrote a lot of papers. I did not teach, I was a researcher. Charles Alexandrowicz,[20] the founder of Madras University's Department of Legal Studies and its programme in international law, was there. He is one of my heroes because he was interested in sources of international law other than European (Baxi 2019d). Both of us were interested in the Kautilyan notions. Pieter Drost—he wrote, among other things, a germinal book in two volumes on ethnocide (Drost 1959)—was also there.

In Sydney, I got into a big maelstrom with Julius Stone. This was with respect to the decision of the International Court of Justice in the German South West Africa mandate case. An Australian judge gave a dissenting judgment in which he favoured South Africa, and Julius Stone wrote three articles in *The Australian* favouring that kind

[20] Alexandrowicz, Charles Henry (1902–75). Polish-British scholar and lawyer, born Karol Aleksandrowicz in Lemberg, in Austrian Galicia. Austrian citizen of Polish descent, a 'member of a suppressed nationality, part of a nation without a state' until 1919, when Poland was restored statehood after World War I. 'He spent the bulk of his career on what might be called the intellectual semi-periphery, first in India (1951–1961) and then in Australia (1961–1967).' He moved to Madras in 1951 at a time when, soon after the new Indian Constitution had come into effect in 1950, 'the expertise of European and American lawyers who were not indelibly associated with the former colonial power was in particular demand'. Creating and teaching at the Madras School of Law, he wrote widely and advised the Indian government and Prime Minister Nehru. He moved to Australia in August 1961 and took up a post as Associate Professor of International Legal Organization at the University of Sydney, in part following the efforts of Julius Stone, who had 'developed strong contacts in India' (Alexandrowicz, et al. 2017, 4–12).

of view.[21] I was stunned. I could not believe Stone could be so colonial. I got into a frenzy.

At the time, I was reading a lot of books on Western classical music, so I used what Debussy said about Wagner, that his music was a beautiful sunset mistaken for a dawn. I wrote a piece titled 'Sunset or Dawn? Reflections on Julius Stone's Remarks on the German South West African Case',[22] and it was a full forty-five pages long. I typed for six days and got it out of my system. I gave it to Stone, he asked me what this was about, I said this is about you. It was a rather polemical article and the refrain was, idols have feet of clay. For six days, Stone would not even talk to me.

I gave notice to my landlord and said, I am leaving next Sunday. Stone finally met me and said, I understand your criticism, but I don't understand the acrimony, the bitterness. I said, this is how I feel. He said, I hear you are leaving me. I said yes, I must have caused you great offence, we may differ, but if we cannot relate to each other then there is no point in staying back. Stone said, you shall not go, stay till the

---

[21] Dissenting opinion of Sir Percy Spender (Australia) in the South West Africa Cases, Preliminary Objections, I.C.J. Reports, 1962, 319. Sir Percy Spender was President of the Court by the time the South West Africa Cases, Second Phase, [1966] ICJ Rep 6 came to be heard and reversed his opinion here.

[22] The International Court of Justice made a series of decisions in the 1950s and 1960s regarding the Union of South Africa's management of its territory of South West Africa (now Namibia). In particular, the governments of Ethiopia and Liberia brought a proceeding before the court in November 1960, alleging maladministration of the territory. Elizabeth S. Landis notes that the 'South African preliminary defense was based on procedural objections' and was dismissed in December 1962 in an 8-7 decision (Landis 1964, 10–12). The case then proceeded, and when it was finally resolved in 1966, the court found in favour of South Africa, also by an 8-7 decision, ruling that these governments were not the proper parties to bring the case of mismanagement of a territory. Julius Stone writes about this in 'Reflections on apartheid after the South West Africa cases' (Stone 1966a). Baxi's essay was titled 'Sunset or Dawn? Some Reflections on Julius Stone's Remarks on the German South West African Case'. All efforts to track down that essay have failed.

end of your term here, unless you get a good assignment elsewhere. I see potential in you.

His point was that the issue was not our disagreement, it was the diplomacy (or in this case, the lack thereof) of scholarly communication. He said, you should not be polemical, for then your point is lost. Of course, I did not agree with him. There were masters of polemics like Marx. He did not closely read Marx or Lenin either. He said, you should never write just as you feel, you should always write just as you think. The worst remark that he thought you can get about your writing in the English language is that you have written poetry. If somebody says that to you, he said, it is the end of the conversation because it means there is no rationality. (That is what was said before the feminists elevated emotional intelligence and sentimental reason to their rightful place.) I said, look, South West Africa was gobbled up in the most extraordinary scramble for empire, they were called savages, and they were treated savagely by so-called civilised people. I said, I have read your work, you write about justice, my blood boils, you have forgotten about colonisation. He said, here you go again. I said, of course here I go again, I think with my blood. He said, that's not thinking.

That's when he started calling me 'son'. He said, son, that's not the way to write, I have never been attacked so viciously in my life, I don't understand why you do so. I understand you carry the burden of the colonised people and so on, but this is not the way to go about it. If you are making an argument, it is not visible in the way you write. You should make your argument visible in your writing. That's another component of diplomacy and scholarly communication. He was Julius Stone and he found it difficult to acknowledge that he could be mistaken. But my love for him and his scholarship never ebbed.

I must here also mention Ms. Zena Sachs, who was a friend of, and secretary to, Julius Stone. She was a mainstay of Julius. She did all the drudgery for Julius, with constant smiles. Her dedication to Julius was legendary. It is impossible to think that Julius would have achieved so much without her.

THREE
The Indian Law Institute

Authority Does Not Reside in a Mailbox

LL: This is all pre-marriage?

UB: No, I was married by then. Prema was studying law in the morning college, while working at the same time, and I was a scholarship student. So, for around three years, we were severely alone. It was difficult; there was no email, we had no phone in our home in Bombay, but Prema and I corresponded with each other fairly regularly. It was a wonderful epistolary reunion. It is a rollicking story, our relationship survived. You should ask her more about that. She was very young. She enjoyed her studies and spiritual pursuits, but obviously we missed each other.

After a year in Sydney, I came to the Indian Law Institute (ILI) in Delhi, but I was not entirely finished with Sydney. G. S. Sharma, who was my jurisprudence examiner in Bombay University, invited me to join ILI as Associate Research Professor and as Joint Editor of JILI (the *Journal of the Indian Law Institute*). I asked Julius Stone and he said, I don't want you to go, but you can go for a year; I want you back after that. I thought, oh no, here we go again. This reminded me of the time I was leaving for the US and recalled what Sumati Bahen said about her Thakhurji. Stone told me to come back to Australia and raise a family there.

I decided to go back to India. I wrote to Ms. Morarjee, saying that I wanted to go see her in Bombay and apologise. She wrote me only one sentence in response: 'You are always welcome to come and see me, but it is not appropriate to apologise for what Thakurji has already decided.'

We had a good time in those ILI days. We lived in Jangpura, behind Vikram hotel. Prema took up a job in Daryaganj, I had to go to the ILI, and we had no vehicle. This was 1966, one year before I published 'The Little Done, the Vast Undone' (Baxi 1967a). My salary was Rs 1,100, Prema's was around Rs 2,100. The taxi fare was steep and cost a lot of our monthly earnings. So, by the twenty-first of each month, we had no money left. It was the old early childhood cycle again, how to make do, but mercifully for shorter periods!

Delhi was a sprawling city but manageable, and it did not overawe me (as Bombay had) because of the sojourn in Sydney; the sea and sheer diversity of peoples were common between Sydney and Bombay. Of course, there were un-commonalities. There was a lot more air and noise pollution in Delhi, although we lacked the social consciousness and organisation to fully measure and combat it. The city transport was rickety, and traffic was chaotic. On the whole, it was green and there were many forest areas, now all yielding to dense housing, roads, flyovers, and consumerism. At that time, Delhi seemed a very bucolic and even rustic, yet overgrown capital. I learnt the virtues of underdevelopment then; 'sustainable development' was not yet the policy and market buzzword. Unlike Sydney, history called from every nook and corner of this imperial centre of power; it was much later (and particularly reading Khushwant Singh's *Delhi*) that I glimpsed the history of violence that the city had witnessed and endured.

Unlike Sydney and Bombay, where we used buses and suburban trains, both Prema and I travelled separately by taxis and occasionally by two-wheeler scooters, which were cheaper but fully exposed to wind and weather. The experience of bumpy rides through Delhi led me to invent a privatising phrase: 'Baxi taxi service'; when my Berkeley friends had difficulty in spelling and pronouncing my last name, I used to say, 'Baxi as in taxi'! The fare was expensive by the cost of living in those days, but the rupee was a strong currency and kept middle classes content. We managed, and if some visitor came, we would take them out for lunch or dinner. That was pretty expensive, but in those days there were no takeaways or home deliveries on cell phones.

The interesting part of the ILI experience was working with G. S. Sharma, a brilliant scholar and charismatic teacher, but an authoritarian leader—actually feudal, not authoritarian. There was a mailbox at the entrance of ILI, to which the proofs, etc., of the articles we edited for the journal would be delivered. Professor Sharma would go away for long periods from the Institute, and he would take the keys away with him. We were on a schedule for the journal and the keys would not be available to open the mailbox. This one time, I just overturned the mailbox and took out all the letters related to the journal. When Sharma-ji came back, he was told what had happened and how this was Baxi's doing. He called me and demanded to know how I dared do this. I said to him, is this the way to run an institution? I am a joint editor, I have come from Australia to work with you, do you want me to run on schedule or not? How am I to keep to schedule if you go away without leaving me the keys? Who will edit the proofs, who will read them? I said, if this is an affront to your dignity, here is my letter of resignation, I will leave. He said, that is not my intention, but you are undermining my authority. I said, authority may reside in many strange places, but it surely does not reside in a mailbox!

I learned much of Indian law by reading Indian law reports. I was not keen on source checking, but it had to be done: it was a way of involuntary learning that I did in the companionship of R. K. Raizada, a gem of a human being and a very good scholar in criminal law and criminology. Then we would check whether the judgment quoted in the text corresponded with the citations and internal quotations from judgments. I would edit the papers and send them back to their authors, most of whom were established senior teachers. There were a lot of complaints about this young man who had taken over, and G. S. said, Baxi, you are ruining my journal, this is very bad. I said, if you want an editor, then this is his job. I said, all the letters of complaint that come to you, either you deal with them or let me deal with them. He said, I cannot antagonise my colleagues. Even so, I would write the letters. I wrote long letters to authors pointing out technical problems, seven or eight pages full of reasons for why this case was cited in this fashion, why a comma was placed here, etc. To tell you a secret, the longer the letter, the more likely it was that they would agree with the edits!

I had to submit all the material before a three-member committee, which included the Attorney-General and the Chief Justice of India. I would send them 200–300 pages for every issue. G. S. had no time, the Attorney-General never replied, but Chief Justice Hidayatullah (whom I was later privileged to call Hadi[1]) always replied. He corrected my English and syntax. I wondered what to do about the other two gentlemen. I finally wrote a polite note to Setalvad,[2] the Attorney-General at the time, saying that *if I do not hear from you in the next two weeks, I will take it that you approve the draft*. Sharma was very angry. He said, how dare you write to the Attorney-General! There were lots of people in earlier generations who did not like the written word. If you said, write this, they would say, let us talk it over. Anything but write. Teach but do not write, research but do not write!

The Chief Justice later asked us to come to his chambers at the lunch hour. G. S. said, you have ruined my career. I said, you are getting so combustible, he has not told us why he has called us. He said, I am sure it is a complaint about your impertinence. I said, it is my funeral, you relax, I will handle it, I did not ask you to protect me. And that was the first time I entered the Chief Justice of India's chambers. He was a very pleasant man, he offered us sandwiches and tea, but even today, I remember shrieking (my first public shriek in India)—the first and only time I have shrieked in the Chief Justice's chamber. I shrieked, you see, because a large rat jumped in front of me,

---

[1]Hidayatullah, Mohammad (1905–92), eleventh Chief Justice of India (1968–70) and sixth Vice-President of India (1979–84). See 'Remembering Justice Hidayatullah' (Baxi 1993a).

[2]Setalvad, M. C. (1884–1974), Attorney-General for India (1950–63), Chairman of the First Law Commission of India (1955–58), and first Chairman of the Bar Council of India (1961).

I had never seen such a rat. Hadi said, sit down, haven't you seen a rat in your life? I said yes, but not one this big. He said, do you think the Chief Justice of India can work with rats of a lesser size? He had the liveliest sense of humour, and that's why we got to be good friends!

Dr Sharma said, I apologise for the letter that Professor Baxi wrote to the Attorney-General, I advised him not to do it. Hadi looked at me and actually winked at me. He said, have you finished, Professor Sharma? I called you here today because Setalvad was to come as well, but he could not make it. He wanted to know who this young man was, and to congratulate him for having proper procedures in place; he wanted to say he was sorry that he could not meet the deadline, but he had an important case. I was in seventh heaven! Incidentally, I have learnt that it was Setalvad, Irani, and Sharma, along with C. R. Das (who was then the Visitor's nominee) who, in 1972, decided to invite me as Professor to Delhi University, by which time my claim to fame was 'The Little Done, The Vast Undone' and many other articles.

This was my first experience in editing a learned law journal. I streamlined the journal. I must have made many mistakes, but I was very ably assisted by R. K. Raizada, who was then an assistant editor and schooled in the meticulous art of editing with Krishna Mohan Sharma. Krishna later moved to the University of New South Wales in Sydney, where he also edited LAWASIA, a scholarly journal of repute, where justices and lawyers from Australia and Asia often wrote. Dr Raizada was a noted scholar in criminal law and wrote a stupendous thesis on the death penalty, a landmark study. I wish he would have heeded my frequent suggestion that he publish it, but he was such a perfectionist that he never did.

The year 1968 was an eventful one, in which people like Pandit H. N. Kunzru[3] and R. P. Anand[4] organised a conference on Eurocentrism

[3]Hridya Nath Kunzru (1887–1978), long-time Parliamentarian, member of the Constituent Assembly of India, the Legislative Council of the United Provinces (1921–26), Central Legislative Assembly, the Council of States, the Provisional Parliament, and the Rajya Sabha.

[4]Ram Prakash Anand (1933–2011), Professor at the Centre of International Legal Studies (CILS), Jawaharlal Nehru University, New Delhi,

in international law. I wrote a short piece, which turned out to be one of the foundational texts of the movement later called Third World Approaches to International Law (TWAIL), and the piece is still read (Baxi 1972a). It was great fun. As usual, I was attracted to a lot of people who were very bright and articulate, but as always, they were not 'fatal attractions' (to adopt the title of a 1987 film starring Michael Douglas). That was Delhi circa 1967.

LL: Who was ILI set up by?

UB: K. M. Munshi (see Chapter One). ILI became instantly famous because of the foundational speech given by Dr Rajendra Prasad, the Chair of the Constituent Assembly and the first President of India, where he expressed the view that under the Indian Constitution, the President was not just a titular Head of the State, but stood vested with certain independent discretionary constitutional powers.

This speech was later utilised in the decision by Sir John Robert Kerr in Australia when he dismissed Gough Whitlam, who led the Labour party as the Prime Minister. Gough's exit was a great loss to the Australian liberal world and to a majority of academics and students, who were also traumatised by the manner of his sacking by the Governor-General. Many years later, in my Australian sojourns, I witnessed the continuing trauma and grief and the general experience of grief among friends, and held their hands in solidarity.

The Indian Law Institute became a great centre of learning. It attracted India's front-ranking scholars and thinkers as Directors, among whom were Gyan Swaroop Sharma, A. T. Markose, M. P. Jain, S. N. Jain, and Alice Jacob. It also had eminent visiting scholars like S. S. Nigam, R. S. Tewari, Lotika Sarkar, D. K. Singh, R. K. Misra, and others. One of its principal features was holding seminars or conferences of law teachers, lawyers, and Justices, where each learnt from the others. *The Journal of the Indian Law Institute* (JILI) became the prominent Indian Law Review (as did the companion *Annual Survey of Indian Law*).

---

and author a.o. of *Studies in International Adjudication* (1969) and *International Courts and Contemporary Conflicts* (1974).

Much later (in the 1980s), when I delivered a course of lectures (Sulakshana Devi Mahajan Memorial Lectures on Legal Professions in India),[5] the ILI seminars, where I began to get acquainted with many senior lawyers, and the discussions that I had with them and others came to be of great help. To make an important digression here, my main thesis was, there is no Indian legal profession, but there are many and varied Indian legal professions.

One lecture (out of five, some presided over by Justices of the Supreme Court) was on the myth, particularly contributed by the Bombay Bar, that lawyers were the main force behind the Mahatma's independence movement! I did some archival work, drew on secondary sources, and I can say that it was completely untrue. When Gandhi called for a boycott, it was roundly criticised by leaders of the Indian bar. Then Mohandas Gandhi wrote an article in the *Harijan* titled 'Lawyers and Cobblers' (Gandhi 1921). It was an explosive article. He said, both serve society, what is the difference between the two? The cobbler is more honest. There was a contempt petition that was sought to be filed, and he was asked to apologise.

We may ignore at our own peril that legal professions had their own evolutionary histories, which I described in some detail in the Sulakshana Devi Mahajan Memorial Lectures in the 1980s; I regret that I have not yet published them save in fragments, despite his friendly prodding and the urging of Professor Wes Pue, and many significant others.

My principal thesis in the lectures was that (1) although the Indian legal profession is legally a united profession, it is sociologically misleading to speak of a single legal profession because what we have are varying professions according to political and social cultures, which needs a fuller study; (2) law practice, apart from being regarded as a learned profession, has also become a trade and business and with aspects of a labour movement; (3) the Indian legal professions carefully cultivate their own foundational myths such as playing a

[5] A series of five lectures delivered in 1986–87 on the Indian Legal Profession at the ILI. Barring one (Baxi 1986f), the other lectures are in unpublished form with the author.

lead role in the nationalist freedom movement and subsequent Indian development, as compared with others; and (4) the professions remain a congregation of 'striking' professions in both senses—and they go on strike very often and also constitute an epistocracy of their own,[6] which emerges as both repressive and emancipatory. Yet, it cannot be denied one bit that eminent lawyers of the nation were involved in the drafting committee of the Constitution.

I also requested the Bar Council to publish the proceedings of disciplinary hearings in their journal. And they did.[7] What came out was mind-boggling. Based on some of these, I published an article on 'The Pathology of Indian Legal Profession' in their Silver Jubilee Number.[8] That also unfortunately marked the end of association with the journal and the publication of disciplinary proceedings!

A Thesis so Strained

LL: Back to 1967 and the context just before 'The Little Done, The Vast Undone.'

UB: I was there in ILI when the article was published, but I wrote a further supplementary concerning the Jagat Narain rejoinder (Baxi 1969a).

LL: Footnote No. 110?[9]

---

[6] See, on epistocracy (expert-based rule of the people), Estlund (2008).

[7] 3 J. Bar Council of India 272 (1978).

[8] *Supra* note 11, 479; Proceedings of the Disciplinary Committee of the Bar Council of India were published from 1972–78 in the *Journal of the Bar Council of India*, and then again from 1987–89 in the *Indian Bar Review*. See also Baxi (1986f).

[9] The text of footnote 110 reads thus:

> It is in this context, that we should take into account the strange thesis of Mr. Jagat Narain that from a 'juridical viewpoint ... it makes sense to say that the "Directive Principles" do constitute part of Indian constitutional law and that they are in no way subordinate to the "Fundamental Rights."' Narain urges that this is so because article 37

UB: What a good memory you have. Julius again reminded me of the diplomacy of communication. He said, tone it down, tone it down, don't write so polemically. That footnote went through seven drafts at least. It was the weakest version, yet caused him the strongest offence. There is no telling!

LL: Who was Jagat Narain?

UB: I have asked myself this question. He taught public law in Ireland, at Queen's University in Belfast. I have never met him. He probably liked controversy. I subsequently heard stories about him from William Twining and other colleagues. He was actively involved in civil rights issues during the Northern Ireland conflict.

'The Little Done, The Vast Undone' was a longish paper—a monograph, almost—and I was very worried whether, among the many themes I had touched upon, I had got the bit on the *Quareshi* case (on cow slaughter) right (*Mohd. Hanif Quareshi vs. The State of Bihar*, 1958).[10] I got my copy of the issue in which it was published on a Sunday. I rushed to the ILI library, it was very difficult to get a

> lays down in a language that 'could not have been more explicit,' that the directives shall be fundamental in the governance of the country. Moreover, the directives are 'law in the real sense of the term' because 'most of them have been followed and practised by the Government since the inception of the Constitution' and such directives as have not been followed so far are still in some sense 'rules of law' since they remain in the text of the Constitution and cannot be deprived of their legal character save by an amendment. All through his discussion, Narain relies heavily on the analogy between rules of international law and the directives. (Narain 1966, emphasis added).... The whole thesis is so strained that to state it afresh is almost to answer it. Whether or not Narain's thesis makes sense 'juridically,' it is clear that the learned writer has preferred to overlook both the constitutional history and the decisional law on the subject and has let his enthusiasm to infuse life in the directive principles (which we share) import meanings into the text of the Constitution that it cannot bear. Besides, state practice does not make law in the municipal sphere if anywhere; and the analogy between the directives and rules of international law is infirm and proceeds on a basic misunderstanding of both. (Baxi 1967a, 362)

[10] *Mohd. Hanif Quareshi vs. The State of Bihar*, AIR 1958 SC 731.

taxi. With my heart in my mouth, I found the judgment; I was not too far wrong, but I could have done better. It was not a misstatement, at least. I have this panic about misreading a text, it has always been my constant companion, often a nightmarish companion.

Granville Austin[11] was at the University of Texas—and a good friend of Lotika and Chanchal Sarkar—and on their urging, I sent this huge article to him by airmail. It cost me a lot of money. I never received a word of acknowledgment. Not one word did I hear from him, till he came to Delhi in the 1980s on another Ford Foundation project, planning his second book. R. Sudarshan of the Ford Foundation called for a meeting at ILI, and I was asked to say a few words about the project. I said, please don't write another word on the Indian Constitution, please don't, that's my advice, if you want it. He was startled, everybody was startled!

I said, your liberal interpretation of constitutionalism has been ruling the roost for the last twenty-five years, it has painted a picture of constitutionalism as a smooth surface without any contradictions. We are just coming out of it, some of us, at least. We are moving away from the consensus model. I told him to write a novel, write poetry, or do something else. He didn't like it, and I didn't like saying it! But despite this difference, we became good friends. He met me several times and interviewed me for his book in the early 1990s. He wrote the book, and he did a good job of it. I never asked him why he didn't acknowledge my article for twenty years, and he never told me. One of those little unresolved perplexities! Later, I reviewed this second book, *Working a Democratic Constitution*, for *The Economic and Political Weekly* (Baxi 2001a).

Despite many a fundamental difference, how I wish that there were many Granville Austins in India, who would rectify and evaluate at the same time the great craft of constitutional historiography.

[11] Granville Seward Austin (1927–2014), author of *The Indian Constitution: Cornerstone of a Nation* (1966) and *Working a Democratic Constitution: The Indian Experience* (1999).

The Rule of Law Must Run with the Rule of Life

UB (*contd*): At ILI, we founded the Indian Society for Legal Philosophy with G. S. Sharma as President.[12] R. K. Misra from Benares, an exciting jurisprudential thinker who wrote these studies on judicial process in the *Annual Survey of Indian Law* by weaving Max Weber, et al. into his writing (Misra 1965). We also roped in Professor Daya Krishna, a great philosopher.[13] We had an inaugural meeting in ILI, which turned out to be the valedictory meeting as well! It was a good initiative, though. Around this time, Julius Stone visited India, too, he was at the conference on the rule of law organised in Delhi at which Nehru famously said, *the rule of law must run with the rule of life*. It was a landmark conference in Asian discourse.[14]

LL: Who organised the conference?

UB: The conference was convened, I think, by the Asian–African Legal Consultative Organization (AALCO) headquartered in New Delhi, and the Sapru House. The School of International Studies had a great presence as a centre of learning. I organised the ILI conference for launching the Indian Chapter of Legal Philosophy. Some very nice people were a part of it, such as Professor Tiwari from Gorakhpur; his articles in the *JILI* are still worth reading (Tiwari 2001, 2002, 2003, 2010). There was a nucleus of early thinking about Indian legal theory, but these efforts unfortunately did not gain momentum.

[12] The Indian Chapter of the Society for Legal Philosophy, formed by Baxi with G. S. Sharma, R. K. Misra, K. K. Nigam. Julius Stone inaugurated the Society (discussed in Baxi 2002d).

[13] Daya Krishna (1924–2007), philosopher, pro-Vice-Chancellor of Rajasthan University, editor of the *Journal of Indian Council of Philosophical Research*, author of, among other major texts, *The Nature of Philosophy* (1955).

[14] International Congress of Jurists, New Delhi, January 1959. Nehru's speech, 'Law and the Changing Values', is reprinted in *Jawaharlal Nehru: Selected Speeches, Vol. 4* (1964).

I was at ILI for one year. It was getting increasingly irritating, though, working with the institute. This was because my role required me to have a continuing correspondence with authors, and maintaining a dialogue was virtually impossible. The grapevine was abuzz with rumours of my imperious ways of editing and of my lack of respect for seniority and hierarchy. As if editing could maintain these virtues!

Nevertheless, I enjoyed my stint, there were many good sides to it. One clear memory is of my trip to Mussoorie for a seminar on the teaching of contract law. I wrote a paper for the seminar, which was eventually published (Baxi 1968a). Arshad Hidayatullah, the son of the then Chief Justice, and I went climbing on China Peak and we lost our way. The Hidayatullahs were very protective of Arshad and always grieved the early sad demise of their daughter. On our return, I got an injudicious reproach from the Chief Justice![15] But for this, it was a very good conference where I met a number of Ford Foundation professors, including Friedrich Kessler from Yale, an eminent teacher of contracts.[16]

LL: Did you give him 'The Little Done, The Vast Undone'?

UB: No, no, the paper I wrote for the seminar was on whether contract is a principle of order or a principle of freedom, a contrast which I had picked up from Friedrich Kessler's writings. The paper was on contracts, but it was also on the pedagogy of it. I described most teachers of contract law as Indian Rip van Winkles. In hindsight, if I had described them as Kumbhakarnas, the analogy would have been more readily grasped!

---

[15] Upen narrates this episode thus in 'Remembering Justice Hidayatullah':

> I came to know him and adore him for his non-hierarchical, fraternal approach at my first national seminar on Contract Law in India. Arshad, his son, and I hiked our way through China Peak in Mussoorie, it turned out that Pushpa's and Hadi's (as he was fondly called by his friends) anxiety was equally divided for both of us! A new social contract, as it were, was born out of this adventure. (Baxi 1993a)

[16] Kessler, Friedrich 'Fritz' (1901–98), Professor at Yale Law School (1935–38, 1947–70), and author (with Malcolm Sharp) of *Cases On Contract* (Chicago: Distributed by the University of Chicago Bookstore, 1946).

One of the great contributions ILI made at that point in time, despite resource constraints, was organising this law teachers' seminar. Young and old teachers alike met at some nice place, and several volumes were published as a result of these meetings (Indian Law Institute 1966, 1969a, 1969b, 1970, 1973a, 1973b, 1978a, 1978b, 1983). I remember this one time it was a seminar on urbanisation in India. If I ever think of my good writing, my piece on public purpose in land acquisition for this seminar is one such (Baxi 1969b). The seminar was in Allahabad, I went there by train, I reached in the morning, but nobody came to meet me. There were no taxis at that time. I did not know how to reach this place, there were no taxis, no scooters, only human pedalled rickshaws. I never appreciated this idea of being carried on the back of another human being. I did not know what to do.

I waited for forty minutes, a rickshaw puller ultimately appeared, and he did not haggle about the fares or the destination. I told this old man, who was old enough to be my father, you ride in the back, I will pull the rickshaw. He thought I was pulling his leg, and said, 'Son, don't worry, I will take you, this is my business.' I asked him how long it takes, he said about an hour or so. I measured the time by my watch, and after exactly half the distance, I told him, stop the rickshaw and come sit in the back seat. He did not take me seriously at first, but then yielded, complaining that he would lose his license. I said, nothing will happen to your license. He very reluctantly sat back. For the first and last time in my life, I pulled a rickshaw, which I must confess was a heavy-duty task!

I rode it right up to the gates of the High Court where Chief Justice M. H. Beg[17] and Professor Sharma and other luminaries were waiting. They were not waiting for me, but embarrassingly found me! And Gyan Swaroop Sharma had another fit and said, you wretch, what are you doing? We had a lovely relationship. I always scandalised him. I could never do right by him. I said, this is a seminar on urbanisation, and we have a situation where a person the age of my father has to earn

[17] Beg, Mirza Hameedullah (1913–88), judge of Allahabad High Court (1963–70) and Chief Justice of the Supreme Court (1977–78).

a living by pedalling on a cycle rickshaw, while we all drive in cars. I am not a saviour of anybody. I am not making a dramatic statement. I just could not have let him carry me, I said. And it is true, I have always been puzzled, especially by young and able people who ride cycle rickshaws.

I asked Chief Justice Beg for help in remedying this situation. Beg Sahib said, I cannot help you directly, but you can speak to the manager of some nationalised bank, maybe of the State Bank. There was no Social Action Litigation (SAL) then. I talked to the manager and requested him to advance loans to rickshaw pullers. He said, this is a very good idea in principle, but it will prove difficult to implement. Motorisation is not very common, what collateral will there be for the loans; what will happen if the debt is not paid back, and what about returns? I said, you are a nationalised bank, you were nationalised for the service of the impoverished: the old banking rationality has to change.

I was very new. I was in India for the first time in a position other than as a student. I had this label of Associate Professor of the Indian Law Institute. Anyway, I talked with someone in a bank. I said to him, make some plans for doing this, the Chief Justice is with us on this, you will be covered in glory if you succeed in this. I could not understand how this situation had been allowed to continue thus. But nothing much came of all this. G. S. Sharma said to me, this is not something you can change, do you think no one has thought about it before? I said, that's all very well, but what has been done still so far? There is no point in discussing urbanisation without looking at the dark side of it.

There the matter ended for a while. In fact, the situation became worse, as the cycle-rickshaw pullers became hired labourers, from having ownership of their rickshaws. It fell to the Supreme Court of India to constitutionally rescue the rickshaw pullers.

Justice Krishna Iyer (and Justice R. S. Pathak, who concurred in a very brief opinion) wrote:

> [T]hese writ petitions compels to remind ourselves that under our constitutional system courts are havens of refuge for the toiler, not the exploiter, for the weaker claimant of social justice,

> not the stronger pretender who seeks to sustain the *status quo ante* by judicial writ in the name of fundamental right.

He enunciated a 'higher duty' and a 'solemn responsibility' of the apex Court 'to uphold every State measure that translates into living law the preambular promise of social justice reiterated in Article 38 of the Constitution'. Instead of examining the *vires* of the Punjab Cycle Rickshaws (Regulation of Rickshaws) Act, 1976, which was legally appropriate, 'constitutional humanism' required a 'symbiosis of legislative embargo on exploitative working conditions and viable facilities or acceptable alternatives whereby shackles are shaken off and self-ownership substituted'. Court and counsel

> agreed on this constructive approach and strove through several adjournments, to mould a scheme of acquisition of cycle rickshaws by licensed rickshaw pullers without financial hurdles, suretyship problems and, more than all, that heartless enemy, at the implementation level of all progressive projects best left unmentioned.[18]

Notable also are the labours of some high courts, especially the Delhi High Court.[19]

As there are no empirical studies, it is difficult to know the actual results; but the normative revolution in adjudication is here to stay. Some comfort. Isn't it? Even so, we must never stop asking whether that 'heartless enemy at the implementation level' may still be active.

[18] *Azad Rickshaw Pullers Union vs. State of Punjab and Others*, AIR 1981 SC 14.

[19] See also Kishwar (2006).

Four
The Australian Interlude

Teaching in Sydney Law School

UB: And then I went back to Sydney, Julius Stone asked me to join the faculty as a lecturer. G. S. Sharma was not too unhappy to release me from ILI. This time, Prema and I went together. Earlier, when I was by myself in Sydney, I lived in a single-room apartment in Thrupp Street. I chose it only because of the name, 'Thrupp'. It comes from one of Dickens' books. It was uphill—Sydney is very uphill anyway—and everyone would ask me why I was living in this inconvenient one-room place. I said, it is because the name reminds me of Dickens! But a year later, after the ILI interlude, Prema and I found a nice apartment in Cremone. North Sydney, and then a wonderful interwar house in much further Chatswood. Both were on a very steep road and we were in the middle of it. We did not need to exercise or go to the gym; just reaching—walking up and down the hill, often with heavy paper bags from shopping—was good enough, and the days (Sundays and holidays, which were very few) were pretty blissful.

The most enjoyable aspect of staying in Thrupp Street was access to Kiribilli Wharf and a steamboat and Hovercraft that would take us to Circular Quay (the main station via three stops), and the most majestic site was of course the great Sydney Harbour bridge, which we could sight from various perspectives at different parts of the day. It was a short walking distance to the wharf, which also had the mom-and-pop shop where I could buy local groceries and vegetables from day to day. I used to not sit in the cabin (save on rainy days) and would let the tremendous ocean breeze talk to me and run all through the body. From the Circular Quay one changed ferry boats to go to many parts of Sydney; going to a bustling part of Sydney—Manley—by boat was one of my little pleasures. It took about an hour's voyage. The admiralty person in me liked traversing the Pacific Ocean and the sounds and smell of the ships, some distance away from the local maritime traffic. It was this maritime sub-conscious that perhaps led me in the early 1980s at Surat (South Gujarat University) to Dr Mahida,[1] who had written extensively on inland river traffic (of persons and things), and hoped that his studies would revive maritime traffic that would benefit south Gujarat and more. Of course to no avail, but I like to believe that the seeds thus sown by him will someday yield full results.[2]

This was my first proper teaching job. I was asked to teach international law and jurisprudence to Masters' students. I did experimental courses at that time on SALT (Strategic Arms Limitation Treaty) negotiations. People said, this is not international law. I said, international law in the making should not be just left to the diplomats, strategists, and international relations specialists.

---

[1]U. N. Mahida, author of *Water Pollution and Disposal of Waste Water on Land* (1980). Dr Mahida had a concern for inland waterways and was a prominent advocate of inland maritime traffic. He was a member of the Committee (1957) appointed by the Union of India, which made several important recommendations in this regard. He also wrote on environmental pollution and degradation.

[2]Upendra Baxi note: The amended National Waterway Act, 2016 contemplates at least five rivers of Gujarat—including Mahi, Narmada, Sabarmati, and Tapi—that flow into the Gulf of Khambhat. Of course, it remains crucial that the ecological aspects are also considered as decisive as the economic ones, both at the national and local levels.

International law is based on negotiations, and disarmament is one of the most fundamental issues for the world we live in today.

It was a small group. A well-dressed person in a bowler hat always attended this course. His name was Michael Kirby, who later became a very distinguished judge in the Australian High Court and delivered many interesting and significant judicial opinions.[3] As I later developed an understanding of Australian law and jurisprudence, I realised the many splendored contributions he had made to Australian law and life. He was an early pioneer of the LGBTQI rights movement and a fervent advocate of the HIV/AIDS movement. Michael visited Delhi often and I still recall how he shocked the students by taking a condom out of his coat pocket! He has written widely on law and other things and is very fond of the progressive activism of the Supreme Court; his adoration of Justices Krishna Iyer and P. N. Bhagwati is well-known. He is one of the few justices in the Anglo-American orbit to have taken a full note of Indian judicial and juridical discourse.

I taught another Master's course on law and social development. I was particularly fascinated by Professor S. F. C. Milsom's then recent work on feudalism and forms of the common law (Milsom 1969, 1976). Those were good courses.[4]

---

[3] Kirby, Michael Donald (b. 1939), former Justice of the High Court of Australia (1996–2009). Taught by Baxi at Sydney Law School (1967–68), Kirby recalls that since Julius Stone was regularly overseas, much of the teaching load was carried by Tony Blackshield, Don Harding, and Dr Ilmar Tammelo, and Baxi was one of the tutors working in Professor Stone's department. Kirby writes that Baxi was 'the more memorable and outstanding (not only because of his extremely strong intellect) but because he was Indian and these were the years of White Australia', and that it 'was very unusual for Australians at that time to see or hear from people who were not "white"' (Sean Fuller, verbatim quote from conversation with Michael Kirby, email dated 1 November 2017).

[4] The Sydney Law School prominently advertises a Social Justice programme on their information page, and offers two elective units specifically related to this programme (Legal Clinics A and B). These involve students working with disadvantaged members of the community, and there is a list of affiliate organisations that students are encouraged to work with

The undergraduate classes were large, with 100-plus students to a class. Some of the students were articled clerks to practising lawyers: they came in for the afternoon classes at 4 o' clock or so. Tony Blackshield was a very popular teacher[5] and Julius Stone, of course, was teaching undergraduate classes. When Stone was away, I would stand in for him in his jurisprudence classes. The first time I had to stand in for him in an undergraduate course, I had to lecture on Henry Sumner

---

on the page. There is also a chair position in 'law and social justice' among University staff—the Kim Santow Chair in Law and Social Justice. There is some discussion of the Law and Social Justice course in newspaper writings about the future of the Jurisprudence department. A letter to the editor written by John Purnell in October 1972 says that: 'One of the side issues resulting from the debacles over the future of the Jurisprudence Department at Sydney University's Law School is the law-and-social-justice option.' He also notes that this option is 'novel to legal study in Australia', that it is 'known colloquially at the Law School as poverty law', and on Baxi, says that: 'The course proper has been developed largely and almost solely by Dr Baxi, who is leaving Australia at the end of this year to take up a Chair at Delhi University' (Purnell 1972).

[5] Blackshield, Anthony (Tony) (b. 1937), attended The University of Sydney, where he worked as a part-time research assistant to Julius Stone after his graduation (Kirby 2013). Kirby characterises the Department of Jurisprudence and International Law where Blackshield worked at this time as 'exotic', in comparison to the 'monochrome racial and social uniformity' of Australia in the mid-1960s (ibid.). Along with Stone and Blackshield, Tammelo, Alexandrowicz, and Baxi all worked there, in addition to a 'constant stream of international visitors'. Blackshield went on to have a prominent legal academic career (at the universities of Sydney, New South Wales, La Trobe, and Macquarie). His association with the Australia Party led him to become involved with political issues of the day, including the treatment of indigenous people, censorship, and opposition to the Vietnam War. In an effort to condemn a prosecution for publishing an 'obscene' student magazine, Blackshield sold copies of the magazine outside the courthouse where the publisher was being sentenced, and was arrested, although the charges were later dropped. According to Kirby, Blackshield emerged from these events 'with authority and without the blemish of a criminal conviction' (Sean Fuller, verbatim quote from conversation with Michael Kirby, email dated 1 November 2017).

Maine and Friedrich Carl von Savigny. I looked at this sea of faces, they were not interested in Maine, they were not interested in Savigny, and there was no way I could interest them in these texts. I just dug in anyway and talked my way through the class. I was deeply dissatisfied after. I asked Julius to let me teach a full semester. He was sceptical. I wasn't sure myself, but I knew I wanted to do something different.

That time, I taught the law and society part. Tony taught the analytical part. And Stone would come back in time to teach a part of the course on law and justice, too. This was the period when the struggle for self-determination in Papua New Guinea was on. There was a lot of discussion in the papers, in the *Sydney Morning Herald* and so on. I asked the students to bring the daily newspapers to class. From the debate on Papua New Guinea, I led them back to Maine and Savigny. My route to the texts was through these contemporary debates. The students, they just loved it. Then Tony, Stone, and I had a meeting, a moderation meeting of sorts. Julius said, son, what have you done, the students are full of contemporary references, Papua New Guinea and so on, what has all this got to do with Savigny and Maine? I said, look at the content of their answer scripts and then decide. He said, surely you cannot do jurisprudence by reference to contemporary newspapers. I said, why not, there is no given pedagogy. If I can lead them to your books, rather than lead them away from your books, it should not matter. When I taught straight from the books, the students were not interested. As it turned out, my class got the best marks of the three sections!

Experience of 'Mild' Racism

UB (*contd*): But I soon ran into academic hatred and thinly disguised racism. I earned the nickname of BB—Black Bastard—in Sydney Law School for several reasons. Some of the first- and second-year students came up to me. I was, like them, very young, and we had a rapport. They said, Upen, we want to do a survey of the teaching here. I helped them design a questionnaire for the survey on a ten-point score, and lo and behold, all the senior guys scored badly, while the younger faculty did very well. It was an objective exercise, nothing rigged in it; the survey covered issues like clarity of presentation, invoking interest, ability to think out of the box while responding to queries in class, etc. Now there was this marvellous man, Ken [Kenneth Owen] Shatwell, he taught contract law and was also the Dean of the Law School. He, like most senior colleagues, did not do too well in the survey, and he was very upset. It is very hurtful, let me tell you, for anyone to receive a negative ranking by students in public, particularly if you have been teaching for long years.

Now, it was widely known that I had helped with the questionnaire, but it was a student initiative first and last, I just helped them; the UN would call it technical assistance! My support of the initiative was not anti-anyone, and such surveys were routine in the United States, from where I had just come. The Dean, he said in a faculty meeting that he wanted permission to sue those of us who were involved with the survey for libel. I was quite taken aback, and wiser counsel eventually prevailed. This was around the time when the idea of Baxi the Black Bastard began to take shape.

Then we had the first ever Papua New Guinea student, called Bernard Narokobi.[6] He was a lovely man, a poet, and he wrote spiritual essays. Bernard, he did well in most of his subjects. In one or two subjects, however, he consistently failed. And one of them was the law of succession and death duties. He got in the vicinity of 42–46,

[6]Narokobi, Bernard (b. 1937 in Wautogik Village in Papua New Guinea). According to Jean Zorn's memorial for Narokobi (Zorn 2010), his education far outstripped the expectations for people from PNG at the time. 'In the 1960s, when few Papua New Guineans had been outside their home villages ... he was in Australia, doing a law degree at the University of Sydney.' PNG was moving towards independence at this time, and Narokobi became a consultant to the Constitutional Planning Committee and had a personal hand in writing parts of the PNG Constitution when independence was achieved in 1975. He went on to become a prominent political figure in Papua New Guinea, serving as Speaker in Parliament, as well as a lecturer at the University of Papua New Guinea and a writer of several books.

and kept on failing. The pass mark was fifty. The question arose as to whether he would get his degree. At the time, I didn't speak very much at faculty meetings. But the third time this happened, I decided enough was enough! I said, you should be proud of having the first black student, who incidentally was a native informant for Margaret Mead (that's another story, but it will keep for now). This man, he is a really deep human being.

The argument then was: On passing, he is entitled to practice at the New South Wales bar, and knowledge of death duties is very important for a practising lawyer. I said, look at the context he comes from, his tradition: death has no property connotations in it. Death is a very different category among the highland tribes in New Guinea. Death, even if it were to be associated with devolution or succession of property, is a collective notion, and the idea of a State charging death duties, and lawyers fighting over it, is culturally incomprehensible to him. Even so, his performance has been consistent—from 42–46 per cent is the limit of his cognitive comprehension, not because he has a low IQ, but because there is a cultural barrier. This was an argument ahead of its time! I said finally, as a measure of desperate recourse, that if the faculty does not award him his degree, it will clearly be a case of racial discrimination, and I reserve my right to go public on this.

This was too much for them. I was in my second year of teaching. Julius said, son, what are you doing? I was determined; gradually Garth Netteheim, Tony Blackshield, and others joined me. I answered every objection rationally. And I could sense that many members of the Faculty came round to question the strictness and even rigidity on this score!

Eventually, Bernard became Attorney-General in the Government of Papua New Guinea. I also heard that he became a judge, but gave it up. He has now gone back to his poetic-meditative existence. He had a disdain for Western/modern law as an argumentative culture. These labels were not around then, but these days he may have been termed a 'Crit' or a 'postmodern' legal mind in the Western world. He was a real gem of a person and never sought recognition or affirmation outside. His genius lay in serenity of the inner world. It was my good fortune to have his brief companionship.

Indigenous People's Jurisprudence

UB (*contd.*): Around this time, in the second year of my teaching, a group of students approached Tony Blackshield and I with a proposition. We were perhaps the two teachers in the faculty the students related to the best. They said, we are interested in studying poverty law. We brainstormed this over a number of meetings. I said, the course cannot be about poverty alone, it has to be on something called social justice. By that time, I was becoming aware of the plight of the Australian indigenous people, but there was little public discourse about it. Some of us wanted to call it 'Law and Indigenous People'. But the course had to be passed by the faculty, and we decided to name it 'Law and Social Justice'.

Tony and I (although it was mostly me) prepared a syllabus covering issues like—how criminal law treated indigenous people, how modern law perpetrated violence against the First Nations peoples, public health problems, etc. There was very little material of direct relevance. We presented it to the faculty, and needless to say, there was opposition, the capital 'B' was growing in font size by the minute! There was a round of meetings and almost everybody, including those who had backed me on earlier issues, said, what do you know about indigenous people, and how is the legal system relevant to them in any case?[7]

By this time, Tony was busy with other things, particularly with his association with Kerry Packer of World Series Cricket fame. Kerry

[7] Blackshield: 'The two years when Upendra and I taught "Law and Social Justice" together were a very special experience for everyone concerned. Among the students involved were the journalist David Marr, the solicitor Eddy Neumann, the law lecturer Denis Harley (UNSW), and Alan Cameron, currently the head of the NSW Law Reform Commission' (Sean Fuller, verbatim quote from conversation with Michael Kirby, email dated 1 November 2017).

Packer was trying to create a third party in Australia,[8] and Tony was a trusted associate, he ran a paper with him called *Reform*.[9] Tony, unlike me, does nothing halfway: he got fully involved in the running of the paper. But the students, they were very determined. The student effort

---

[8]The Australia Party that Blackshield mentions above was conceived of as an alternative 'third' political party, originally called the Liberal Reform Group. They splintered off from the dominant political party of the period, the Liberal Party, over Australia's involvement in the Vietnam War, among other things. Later, they were known as the Australian Reform Movement (this is the name which Michael Kirby associates with Blackshield in a lecture about Blackshield's life), and later still became known as the Australia Party (this is what Blackshield was mostly formally involved with). According to the state library records, Blackshield was the Joint State Convenor for the Australia Party in 1969. The party merged to form the Australian Democrats in 1977, who remained a relevant political force in Australia into the twenty-first century. The Liberal Reform Group was founded by a number of people, including Gordon Barton, who, in addition to being a founding member of this political party, also managed a range of newspapers, including the *Sunday Review* and the *Nation Review*.

[9]Blackshield: '*Reform* was the fortnightly newsletter of the Australia Party (the predecessor of the Australian Democrats). For a couple of years around 1970 I was the NSW State Convener of the Australia Party: I had joined it when it was called the Australian Reform Movement. I had always said I would never join a political party, but ironically, I helped to preside over the negotiations to transform the 'Movement' into a 'Party'. For a year or so, I was working almost full-time on Australia Party work. It got to the stage where I had to choose: I could either be a full-time academic or a full-time politician, but I couldn't be both. I decided I wanted to be an academic, and immediately cut back my party work and resigned from my position as State Convener. Instead, I took over from Robert Horn as editor of *Reform*. *Reform* had actually been started a few years earlier by one of the Victorian members of the Reform Movement, Laurie Hill. He was a believer in a radical version of grassroots democracy: all policies of the Australia Party were supposed to be decided upon by the grassroots membership voting in an Australia-wide ballot, and as well as being a newsletter, *Reform* was designed as the mechanism through which those ballots were conducted. So it was a very interesting exercise' (Sean Fuller, verbatim quote from conversation with Blackshield, dated 7 November 2017).

was led by Jim [James] Spigelman, who would go on to become the Chief Justice of the Supreme Court of New South Wales. Now, like in India, the faculty could not believe that students could have any urges without somebody inciting them.

To cut a long story short—or to make a long story longer—I ultimately managed to convince two or three senior academics! I said to them, all right, we won't compete with any other course. We won't take more than twelve students. It is your choice whether you give them credit for the course or not. We won't interfere with your curriculum. Watch us for two years, and then take an academic call on whether to keep the course or not. If no student is willing to take the course as a labour of love, without the promise of credit, the course collapses, so why all this hostility? We are not damaging the structure of law or legal education. It was a ploy, one that worked. And wow! The course spread in time. Monash University and other law schools also started a course like this.

An Incipient Attempt at Public Interest Litigation

UB (***contd***): And so it was that I taught the course. The issue of indigenous people's land rights was obviously very prominent. In the context of my newspaper-based teaching, I came across the activities of this multinational called Nabalco Private Limited, a leading multinational in mining bauxite. It was invading the Northern Territory. Of course, I mean invading as a figure of speech, the company had a license to mine bauxite there. Australia is a huge continent with a small population, and very few people cared about what was going on. There was no political representation from the Northern Territory. I saw the news and said, we may do something. We formed a committee, some interested students and myself. Fortunately, we were able to locate the legal challenge filed by three Elders Milirrpum Marika (the Rirratjingu clan); Munffaraway (the Gumatj clan), and Daymbalipu, (of the Djapu clan), represented by Edward Woodward,

Frank Purcell, John Little, and John Fogarty. We, in the class, did much background research and worked assiduously—in a kind of first attempt (at least in substance, since the form was a regular law suit) an association with what is now called Public Interest Litigation (PIL) (*Milirrpum vs. Nabalco Pty Ltd*, 1971; see Baxi 2014; Sharp 1996).[10] The basic question was this: There is no bill of rights in the Australian Constitution, so what do you do? But from the freedom of religion clause came to aid their idea of Dreamland as a sacred trust, a sacred land, which was visited by the spirit of their ancestors. The guarantee of freedom of religion means that this, their relation to the land, cannot be violated. We also found that they were denied all norms of natural justice—they were not consulted, there was no collective consultation before the license was granted. I don't think there was much concern with indigenous peoples' rights in 1968–1969, but what little there was, was confined to a few. There was no way then in which we could, in Australia or in any other place, file a petition like that. Justice Richard Blackburn of the Federal Court heard this case over weeks.

This is *Milirrpum vs. Nabalco*, I wrote about it in my paper on the 'Lost Dreamtime' (Baxi 1972b). Blackburn went a long way in his judgment, but not all the way. In effect, he said, I recognise that, and the evidence shows that the indigenous people have a system of law. It is not right for the Western, legal system to say they do not have a system: sacred property is still property, and therefore, they have a notion of rights. But he said the difference is—and as a Western judge, this difference is material to him—that property has three incidents: the right to possess, the right to use, and the right to alienate. In the indigenous people's legal system, the third component is missing. This is a classic response. I was marginally involved in a similar case in Canada, *Delgamuukw vs. British Columbia*, 1997,[11] where we got a similar response from the Supreme Court: the land is sacred, it

[10] *Milirrpum vs. Nabalco Pty Ltd*, (1971) 17 FLR 141.

[11] *Delgamuukw vs. British Columbia*, (1997) 3 SCR 1010.

cannot be sold as a commodity, but it can be used in the traditional civilisationally and culturally justified mode.[12]

The Canadian judicial discourse of course goes further. It is very progressive because (*i*) it takes folk song and dance as evidence, in an oral culture, of possession and ownership of land; (*ii*) it attributes to the Queen a lofty motive in entering into treaties with indigenous peoples and denigrates the imputation of dishonourable intentions to her; (*iii*) it recognises a full customary right to indigenous title, although structurally subject to traditional usage.

In Australia, we lost, but not entirely. Not entirely because we broke the conspiracy of silence on the issue of indigenous people's rights in the academia. The argument we made over indigenous people's land rights in *Milirrpum* matured twenty years later in *Mabo vs. Queensland* (No. 2, 1992),[13] which overruled the former decision. I am not saying there is any causal connection, which declared that 'The common law cannot be "frozen an age of racial discrimination"'. *Milirpum* started it

[12] This case, from 1997, discussed the nature and source of indigenous people's land rights, and its impact lay in an increased value given to the oral history of indigenous people as evidence in native title cases. The Supreme Court 'acknowledged the conventional evidentiary difficulties' associated with oral histories, but also their 'importance in the adjudication of aboriginal rights'. The judgment noted that 'the laws of evidence must be adapted in order that this type of evidence can be accommodated and placed on an equal footing with the types of historical evidence that courts are familiar with'. As with the *Milirrpum vs. Nabalco* case in Australia, this was an influential step towards native title without being a decisive victory (Blake, et al. 1998).

[13] *Mabo vs. Queensland (No. 2)*, (1992) HCA 23. This is a landmark native title case in Australia, which officially recognised native title for the first time. The most notable part of the judgment was that the doctrine of *terra nullius*, which had been used to justify importing the laws of England to Australia, did not apply if there were already inhabitants living on the land, and therefore the customs and laws of the native people would apply in all cases where the land was not now owned by the Crown. The case famously received historical evidence about the ways of life in the disputed region prior to European settlement, and accepted that these ways of life constituted relevant laws and customs that English law did not, by default, supersede. See also Ivison (1997).

all. It was a great revelation to me that one could use the law to create a new social consciousness even in the most conservative political and social system. Australia at that time was really conservative—white Australia policy, immigration restrictions, you name it, they had it.

And then, in the third or fourth year of my teaching, a student asked me: We have learnt so much from you about our tribal people, can you tell us something about yours in India? I felt [as though] I was struck by a thunderbolt. I realised I knew very little about India in this regard. I made do with some kind of response about indigenous peoples' land rights, the Fifth and Sixth Schedules of the Indian Constitution, but I knew that I was inadequate. That was the moment in the classroom when I felt I should return to India whenever the opportunity arose and do something about my inadequacy. We are talking about location and commitment, and this woman student, she didn't mean badly, she didn't intend to produce the effect it produced in me, but there are these moments of revelation, I can't describe it. I am grateful to her; she is a friend now, but I didn't burden her with that responsibility. She said what she did out of a just curiosity about the Indian people.

Learning to Drive and Becoming a Father

UB (*contd*): And then, the most brilliant thing happened, Prema was pregnant!

The second most brilliant thing to happen at the time was that I learned to drive. I went through six driving tests. Sydney is a very hilly city, like San Francisco. I did everything right, except for two things: I could not go up a hill without slightly sliding back (which I soon learnt to control) and I was terrible at reverse-parking. Prema was getting heavier and heavier with the first child and I was no nearer to my license. My friends could not understand why I couldn't get one. The sixth time I tested for it, I climbed the hill all right, I was even able to reverse-park, but when the instructor asked me to take right, I turned left at the Sydney Harbour Bridge. The traffic was colossal, I could not reverse in it, so I went into the city, went several streets across, took a U-turn, went again to the Harbour Bridge, and then went back to the RTO. He said, fail! I said, excuse me! I took you in the car, I didn't fumble on the hill, I did the reverse-parking right, I even took you through the city in peak-hour traffic with superb confidence and without the slightest inconvenience to you, and brought you back in record time, what do you mean by fail? He said, you didn't know left from right. I said, this is too much. If you want me to be a perfect driver, I am very close to it. Racism is a very deep word for this encounter, but there was, I felt, some discrimination. Anyway, I got my license, and thanked him most profusely!

But the real test was on the bicentennial of Captain Cook's landing in Australia. I wanted Prema to see the fireworks. What I did not realise was that the whole of Sydney had run amok and everyone was going to the same destination. On the main road, there was a veritable sea of cars; you had no choice but to inch along; there was no way other than going ahead. It took us nearly four hours returning, after a lot of stops-and-starts, and a handbrake spree. My six driving tests definitely proved handy! And, collars up, I emerged as a fine driver of cars!

When Prema went into labour, there was a taxi strike, but I was able to drive her to Mater Hospital at Crow's Nest. The air-conditioning in her hospital room was terribly cold, she slept fitfully, and I was reading a very interesting book, *The Idea of a Social Science* by Peter Winch (1958), a first-rate book. And Pratiksha was born in the early hours of the morning, we were happy and excited. Around that time, I received an invitation from the University of Chicago, from Marc Galanter, to a conference on unobtrusive social science method, and I told Prema, Pratiksha is one day old, there is no question of my going. She said, no, you must go. I said, you are very brave, but this is not right. She literally pushed me out, saying, I gave birth to this child, don't you think I can look after her? So I had to go to the University of Chicago leaving Pratiksha and Prema behind, and at the conference, everybody congratulated me on the birth of a son. I inadvertently broke a Western custom by passing around cigars, one apparently does that when one has a male child. This was quite a spectacular meeting because Neelan Tiruchelvam and Sithie, who were newly married, were there, and they were totally in love.[14] When we had a leisurely stroll in the evening on the Lakeside drive, they would be (as the expression goes) billing and cooing and hugging and kissing. I used to tease them about this long afterwards!

LL: Is this the first time you met them?

UB: Yes, indeed, they were a lovely couple and very passionate. Such displays of affection in Sri Lanka were, in all likelihood, rare, and they must have felt liberated, except they had this Indian hanging around them. Although I do not think this fact cramped their style one bit!

At the conference, we were asked to do a research proposal each, and I worked on one on protests and anomie. Rajni Kothari had, in his *Politics in India*, which was then a raging classic, popularised the concept of anomie.[15] In it, he sought to 'marry' Durkheim-da with Almond and Verba's *Civic Culture*. My question was, how can protests be considered anomic in a country which owes its independence to Gandhi? I think the question is a valid one, but the Chicago workshop was all about 'methods' of study and the substantive point got lost.

Our friend Madhava Menon was at the conference.[16] Also attending was Dalveer Bhandari, L. M. Singhvi's cousin, a nice gentle

---

[14]Tiruchelvam, Neelan (1944–99), director of the Colombo-based International Centre for Ethnic Studies (ICES), member and later Chair of the London-based Minority Rights Group International (MRG), and Member of the Sri Lankan Parliament representing the Tamil United Liberation Front (TULF). He was tragically assassinated in July 1999 by the Liberation Tigers of Tamil Eelam (LTTE).

[15]Kothari speaks of how a 'strategy of mobilization' based on 'reservation of jobs, educational openings, and legislative seats for backward castes' tends to 'resolve an important dilemma for traditional societies: the dilemma of one or two ethnic groups getting all important rewards and others being relegated to subject category and virtual non-membership in the nation, leading to a deep schism in society and to violence and anomie' (Kothari 1970, 96).

[16]Neelakanta Ramakrishna Madhava Menon (b. 1935–2019), Founder-Director of the National Law School of India University (NLSIU), Bangalore, the National Judicial Academy, Bhopal, and the founder Vice-Chancellor of the West Bengal National University of Juridical Sciences (NUJS).

person—he wrote a proposal on the food and drug adulteration law in India. Bhandari's rather playful hypothesis (we all had to have one) was that the law for the prevention of adulteration could not work in India because if you want to commit suicide and ask for poison, even the poison would be found adulterated! Later, Bhandari was among the youngest judges in the Indian Supreme Court. He wrote a very good dissenting judgment (in *Ashoka Kumar Thakur vs. Union of India*,[17] on why, instead of reservations, there should be primary education and a deadline of six months should be set to achieve the right to education in elementary and primary schools. His opinion is really about the wider implications of justice. He is now on the International Court of Justice at the Hague, serving a second distinguished term of the high office, developing not just multinational justice among the state parties but multicultural jurisprudence as well.

I hurried back to Sydney to find Prema very upset because she and Pratiksha had been moved to a small house for post-maternity care, which she didn't care much for. When I telephoned her from the airport, she was in tears, saying, where the hell were you. I picked up my car from the airport and drove back to retrieve them from there and take them home.

I was walking on air with Pratiksha, a lovely child! But I had to teach, so I went for my classes. Then Julius called me to his office and said, son, we are very happy you have a girl child, you know my first-born was an equal delight. I didn't know where he was going with this. He offered me a glass of sherry and said, you are going to your jurisprudence class and speaking on international law, you are going to your international law class and speaking on jurisprudence! The students are no doubt enjoying this slightly out-of-sync performance, but alas, there are institutional limits! I said, I am dreadfully sorry, I am just beside myself, I have never been like this. Then Ms. and Mr Cooper, our landlords who lived on the floor above us, both came to our place one Sunday. We offered them a cup of tea, and after a while, I said as a concluding gesture, please do come again. As they finally got up to leave, they said, there is just a small matter, this small

[17] *Ashoka Kumar Thakur vs. Union of India & Ors* [2008 (56) BLJR 1292].

matter of rent, you are overdue by six weeks. I was never late in the payment of rent, but I was just not in this world!

It had a terrific impact on me, and I always felt—and I say this to everyone I meet—remember, you can be the parent of your first child only once. It cannot recur. So, she received the warmest affection anyone can give to her those first few months (and obviously beyond). It really went to her head! By the time she was three or four weeks old, she already knew what worked and what didn't with me. She figured it out quietly. She wouldn't sleep at night until I cuddled her and sang her a song that woke other people up! When she wouldn't stop crying, we had no one to consult; there was no fairy grandmother. I bought a book by Dr Benjamin Spock, entitled *Baby and Child Care*, the Vietnam edition. I flipped through the pages to see what to do when the baby cries, and on page 503 or thereabouts, there was this whole list of suggestions, do this, that, and the other, but if nothing works, maybe the infant wants a breath of fresh air, so take her out. I did that, and it worked. Pratiksha had some kind of understanding of this, so after that, I had to take her out every time, in fact, drive her around the corner. Pratiksha was also the reason for my first involuntary encounter with non-vegetarian food. She had to be fed baby food, strained turkey, strained chicken, etc. And she wouldn't eat unless I ate a bit with her. If ever I was going to enjoy non-vegetarian food, that put an end to it. Those things were inedible. But it was a lovely time in our lives.

And then we decided to move house. Prema (who is a very spiritual person, but she also learnt to take an interest in the material things of life) decided we must have our own place. We raised a loan and bought a house, it was an interwar house, a huge house with a big garden. Viplav was born there. Much later, I took Pratiksha and Viplav to show them the houses they were born and raised in. But then we realised that this place was filled with toxic spiders, certainly not fit for a house with growing infants! One was called the Redback; if it bit you, you died instantly. Another was the equally toxic Funnel-web spider. After that, whenever I am asked to maintain a garden, I plead a right to life! Eventually, I found a way to collect these toxic spiders, and we sent them to an anti-virus lab in Melbourne.

Viplav was not a demanding child, but there was always love and mischief in his eyes, like now, but it was even more pronounced then. Compared with Pratiksha, who was quite a heavy infant, Viplav was slimmer; now, of course, the roles are beautifully reversed! He was most happy to sit on his rocking chair in the sun, and when I heard that a person called Timothy Sun was interested in buying our house in Chatswood, I composed a ditty (which he seemed to like, and which I still recall): 'Oh my Son/Rocking in the sun/In the House/of Timothy Sun.' It felt good to see them through the mirror of the car in their car seats when we went out long distances to meet our friends. There was a good bonding between them, and early on, the brother and sister developed a fond but critical stance towards the world of elders; they were to nurture secrets among them which never were (in terms of Pratiksha's book, much later) 'public secrets'. I have known few siblings without mimetic rivalry, and yet capable of such intense relationships over a long time. I have grown up a second time round in their companionship and have been, I hope, a better human being than they found me.

Viplav is now a respected figure in E-learning, runs a blog of what he calls 'meanderings', and is working on a book on education, captivatingly titled *What If*—a series of counterfactuals about educational innovations. No mention of him is complete without a recall of three independent beings: Shalini, his partner, who teaches chemistry at one of the most renowned colleges on the campus and is an accomplished musician, and Paripoorna and Sambhav, the two beautiful teenaged grandchildren of whom we are extremely fond and proud. And one hopes that they will recall us in the future as persons who tried to change things a little better than they found them.

I was in Sydney for about five years. During this time, Tony Blackshield left for a newly founded law school at the University of New South Wales, Charles Alexandrowicz died, Pieter Drost went to Netherlands law school and he died there, and Ilmar Tammelo was appointed Professor in Salzburg, Austria. I was by then a senior lecturer. I was very happy with my work and my students.

Around then, I received a letter from the Registrar of Delhi University inviting me to be Chair of Law. I rolled it up and pushed it into the wastepaper basket, thinking that this was some sort of a joke: who would invite me to Delhi, I thought. Julius saw this and said, son, what are you doing? He read the letter and said, it may be genuine, why don't you respond to it? I said, I will look at it later. I just slept over the letter, until another letter arrived, reminding me of the first one!

Writing for the Newspapers

UB (***contd***): But before that second letter arrived, Julius Stone also left for New South Wales University, and I was the sole survivor from the old days. All the anti-Julius Stone forces decided to wind up the Department of Jurisprudence and merge it with the Law School. I felt an institutional loyalty to defend the honour of the department. I led a single-person movement against the abolition within the faculty. I insisted on both an intra-faculty and a public debate. Julius Stone had served this institution, and through it, Australia and worlds beyond. I had many disagreements with him, all of us had disagreements with him, but this is a legacy which shall not be sidelined. We had an enormous public meeting at the Law School. It was quite a performance on both sides. I learnt public speaking and then I decided to carry this battle into the newspapers. This intra-university conflict was widely covered by the media.[18]

[18]John O'Hara (see O'Hara 1972a) speaks about the planned abolition of the Department of International Law and Jurisprudence, and also mentions Baxi. The article discusses the appointment of some new Law Chairs, including one which is to replace the retiring Julius Stone. It is largely about a statement made by the Leader of the State Opposition in the Legislative Council, who had called for a review into the decision. O'Hara (1972b) quotes the Leader of the Opposition, N. K. Wran, as saying that the abolition of the department would 'be a step backwards towards legal orthodoxy', and that 'The teaching of jurisprudence, concerned as it is with social injustices and human rights, should be encouraged'. The article also quotes a public statement from Baxi, in which he criticises the Vice-Chancellor of Sydney University, who had said that there was no intention to abolish teaching or

This wasn't the first occasion on which I wrote for the newspapers, I used to write regularly on High Court decisions.[19] I particularly went to town on the strange judgments the High Court delivered on the question of the interpretation of the term Commonwealth 'place'. The other occasion on which I wrote for the papers, I almost ended up being charged for the crime of obstructing the course of justice. It came about this way. The State police had put in place a radar system to track drivers speeding over the Sydney Harbour Bridge. Some young people, including some of my students, took to standing in the pedestrian area with a sign saying, Slow Down! Radar Ahead! So speeding drivers slowed down, and they could not be prosecuted. The police decided to prosecute these young people instead for obstruction

---

research in jurisprudence. Baxi says that 'The statement carries no assurance that jurisprudence will be taught in depth or with the highest scholarly competence'. He also said that the three new chairs in law were 'neither interested nor qualified in jurisprudence', and asked, without a professor who is appropriately interested in jurisprudence, 'who can be the intellectual vanguard of social change through law?' O'Hara characterises the debate around the department merger as follows:

> The main official reason for the move is that the present division of the Faculty of Law into two separate departments—the Department of Law and the Department of International Law and Jurisprudence—is wasteful of resources. Opponents of the move see it as an attempt by conservatives to remove the spirit of philosophical inquiry.

The article also notes that the future of the chair of International Law and Jurisprudence came into question with Julius Stone's impending retirement, and that no member of the department sat on the committee that made the decision to abolish the chair. A student is quoted, referencing the international reputations of Stone, Tammelo, Drost, and Baxi, and comparing the abolition of the department to banning Socrates, 'because he asks too many searching questions'.

[19] Baxi appears with mentions in articles in *Sydney Morning Herald* around this period on various topics. For example, calling for an inquiry into the ill-treatment of prisoners in Bathurst Jail, quoted in the article 'Labor to attack on jail decision' on 22 July 1971. He is also a signatory on some letters to the editor on political topics.

of performance of police duty. I wrote a long article in a national paper on why this would not amount to obstruction.

My argument was, what the students were doing would be obstruction only if you considered the whole purpose of the law to be to prosecute people for speeding. But if the purpose of the law is to keep people from speeding, then what was done was to help the police in enhancing safety and not an obstruction. I wrote this article, even though the matter was technically *sub-judice*. There was some action contemplated against me for interference with the course of the administration of justice. But fortunately nothing came of it.

Coming back to my fight to save the department, I went to see the Vice-Chancellor, who was also an economics professor. The great thing about these places is that Vice-Chancellors are not visible. If you want them, they are there, otherwise they are not seen. I sought him out and he said, yes, I have been reading your statements, it is an implicit policy that you don't take our affairs to the public. I said, that is why I have come to you, I have come to invite your attention to the fact that this is a great endowment. Even if you want to merge it with the Law School, you must take some time to look for a successor to Stone; nobody can replace him, that's for sure, but there may be somebody you will find to take on the role.

Ultimately, they did find someone, and the department was saved. Stone's successor, Alice Tay,[20] kept the department going for many more years. Alice was a Singaporean-Australian, married to a very well-known Marxist thinker, Eugene Kamenka, who pursued a distinctive field called History of Political Ideas. She was teaching in Canberra when she was offered the chair in Sydney.

By the end of 1972, my appointment was in process. I had received the second letter from Delhi University, so I decided to go back with the two young people in tow. But even now, on an average of three years, whenever I go to Sydney, all former students from within Australia congregate and we have a meeting and dinner. They have each distinguished themselves in their chosen careers and we go

[20] Alice Erh-Soon Tay (1934–2004), jurisprudence and comparative law scholar, Challis Professor of Jurisprudence at the Sydney Law School.

down memory lane, which is at once joyous and cathartic. I would not embarrass them here, but a particular mention needs to be made of lifelong friends and colleagues: Anthony R. Blackshield and Oliver Mendelsohn. With them, we launched a comparative study of the Australian and Indian Constitutions, and they were kind enough to endorse the plurality/multiplicity of the Indian Constitution as a paradigm of a 'postcolonial Constitution' in the modern era, beset with the antinomies of four mutually contradictory ideas and ideals: governance, development, rights, and justice. The project never fructified, but the discussions we had left a creative residue. Oliver has been a help in many ways, but spectacularly so in terms of tending to (as an editor) the Oxford University Press (OUP) series on Indian law and society. Tony has been keeping abreast of the Indian constitutional developments, alongside keeping a hawk's eye on the Australian High Court. Both deserve a lot more recognition in India and elsewhere, but they are content at the same time with the international esteem they have already obtained.

I have many fond stories of my days with students and friends; that would require a different monograph. But I must not leave the Sydney story without mentioning how, within the space of five years, Sydney, and Australia, was changing. Perhaps small pathways to the future globalising world: electronic typewriters, credit cards, withdrawals of cash from banks by bank cards through special machines that operated them, new departmental stores supplementing local shops (not supplanting these), rapid demolition and construction activities, new monumental symbols (such as the Sydney Opera House, then still under construction), and constant highways and flyovers. The material culture of society was changing fast, with considerable changes in social organisation and consciousness. I witnessed this change in my own working life. The first time I went to Sydney Law School at 167 Phillip Street, it was a dingy old building, with rickety stairs and large rooms. In less than a decade, the School had moved to the end of that street, to a new and modern matchbox building of thirteen floors with separate staff and general lifts, where no fresh air, dust, and noise were allowed to enter and smoking was allowed in the rooms, but was quite hazardous. Some middle rooms had no windows and lecture theatres were fitted with new gadgets: overheard projection and other devices, which required a new engineering training of teachers on how to operate various consoles and keys. Gone was the old blackboard and white chalk method, together with the old duster. On a different register, I still recall how we all flocked to see, on the department store TV, the broadcast of Commander Neil Armstrong landing on the moon and saying to an American home crowd, among all earthlings, how that celestial void was soft and mushy like American cheese.

Kingsford Smith was the homely airport where Prema and I had arrived in Sydney, and where, during short visits within Australia and outside, it was safe to leave the car in a parking lot and drive to and fro. In 1973, we left by the same airport, but now it was totally refurbished with a large number of airbus hangers and terminals. I still vividly remember how many students and friends who had come to see us off had to walk long distances within the airport, and how Sue Armstrong was to walk even faster and help us to the right boarding area.

Even as the world was changing fast, good human hearts kept the same rhythm of friendship and solidarity/sorority, and their hearts beat with love.

Five

Learning from the Australian Experience

Indigenous People's Jurisprudence

Comparative Indigenous People's Jurisprudence

LL: Your involvement with the rights of indigenous people, and the entire experience with indigenous people's law teaching, is clearly something that stayed with you for a long time to come. Because in a number of your articles, some of the criticisms you have, even of something like CLS (Critical Legal Studies), is that (*a*) they never ever developed a perspective of the Third World, and (*b*) they are never even jurisprudentially multicultural in their ability to take on the cultural imagination of indigenous peoples' rights. So I was interested in how your involvement with the rights of indigenous people shaped your own legal cosmology, as it were.

I am also interested in the differences between what happened in Australia and Canada in terms of the jurisprudence of indigenous peoples' rights. Although it begins from the land question, it goes on to take on the cosmology question. This, we have not quite been able to articulate in the same way in India. So, for example, in the Courts, we have never gone into the question of a very different relationship to land, the idea of property, etc. I am interested in the differences between Australia, Canada, and Indian jurisprudence, and the reason for that.

UB: The second part of your question is a tough one, we will try and come to that later. With regard to the first part, there are two critical moments in my life with respect to law and teaching: the first was Vietnam, and the second was this encounter with the indigenous people's rights issue. In the latter case, what struck me was the long story of exploitation and the accompanying regime of silence in White Australia. It was not just the issue of land rights, that was only one aspect. What emerged with time was also the story of stolen generations, the taking away of indigenous children by missionaries, so-called suicides in custody by indigenous prisoners, and other dimensions of the politics of ethnic cruelty. It was the massive colonial continuity that was shocking in Australia. It was all the more scandalous when compared to the difference in the treatment of Maoris in New Zealand, as I came to learn from my friend Jane Kelsey[1] and others. The Treaty of Waitangi was a legal instrument and the Government of New Zealand was held to account by the Maori movement.

Australia was thus a unique case of continued colonial exploitation. There were of course some efforts aimed at indigenous people's welfare, primarily missionary (in the better sense of the term), which tried to give them literacy, numeracy, and some education, take them away from liquor, etc. Alcohol was a big problem with the indigenous peoples in Australia, as was public health. But there was no agency to really deal with the magnitude of the problem. Both meandering State indifference and missionary efforts proved only marginal to the existence of the remote populations of indigenous people.

---

[1]Jane Kelsey, Professor of Law at the University of Auckland, and major activist campaigning for the New Zealand government's full recognition of the Treaty of Waitangi. Signed in 1840 by the British and Maori chiefs of the North Island, this document is of central importance to the history and political constitution of the State of New Zealand, and has been significant in framing the political relations between New Zealand's government and the Maori population.

The indigenous people, they have a distinct cosmology, what they called the great chain of being. Ancestral spirits inhabit the land, the places these spirits visit are sacred, the land is a figure of the mother in some senses. There are many indigenous communities, and each god-spirit has its own mythology. Dreamtime is their notion of the sacred. These were people, communities, which were colonised and marginalised. They lived as much as they could in their own world until the intrusion began in terms of resource hunting, for mining and extraction. That's the site where legal and juristic struggles began.

Apart from land, the other growing concern was with the commoditisation of the sacred iconography of the indigenous people as tea cosies, table mats, and so on. This was, of course, offensive to the tribal elders, as such commercial endeavours were deeply profaning of cultural icons. The issue emerged later as one of intellectual property rights, and began, like land, to relate to collective identity and historical memory. Much later, I was interested in Australian law reform concerning the collective intellectual property rights of indigenous communities. Group royalty for the use of co-actively preserved cultural property is a very interesting and innovative conception, which is important because it imports pre-liberal aspects into the models of liberal human rights traditions in the West and makes these, in a certain sense, postliberal. I also contributed somewhat to the then discussion in the World Intellectual Property Organization (WIPO) concerning the draft treaty on cultural intellectual property. In the book that Oliver Mendelsohn and I edited, *The Rights of Subordinated People*, we have some excellent chapters on indigenous folklore (see essays by Crawford and Tatz, in Mendelsohn and Baxi 1997).

The question of race and gender was also coming to the fore, and the feminist effort was to reappraise the protection of rights of indigenous people with the demand for the equal treatment of women. The responses of indigenous women varied. Some of the categories of Western feminism were irrelevant to them. There was no problem with pre-marital sex, for instance. In the collection that Mendelsohn and I edited, there is a very poignant article by Diane Bell, which narrativises the situation from the perspective of indigenous women (Bell 1997). Bell poses various ways in which voices of discriminated and brutalised women rarely come to the fore.[2] The question of an alternate—feminist—cosmology still remains for the first-nation women (Allen 1986; Crenshaw 1991; Brown 1992; Butler 1993, 2004).

These are, by several millennia, the oldest people in the world. Australian indigenous people have a very long history. What was done to them is a story of unspeakable, unnameable horror. In the island of Tasmania, I heard that the settlers in the eighteenth century, bored with nothing to do, no public entertainment, actually hunted down indigenous persons as sport; there is no single full-blood indigenous people in Tasmania anymore. They liquidated the whole community. Recent historical accounts suggest different stories: see the moving tribute to Truganini, the last full-blooded speaker of the Tasmanian language, when she died. Born in 1812, 'she was witness to British invasion and colonisation' (Lindall 2008; Morris 2017).

Christian missionaries who worked with some indigenous communities made traditional motifs and beliefs compatible with biblical Christianity. It is an extraordinary story. In the process of working on land rights, I engaged in what the Crits (Critical Legal Studies movement) would call interdisciplinarity or multidisciplinarity. There is no way in which you can study indigenous communities outside the unity and totality that constitutes the people in their environment, life, nature, custom, community. You cannot do it by any one disciplinary framework alone. I understood and lived well with this principle.

The situation in India is slightly different, because we had revolts and insurrections by indigenous peoples against the British. It is a long and complicated history, the history of the interaction between

[2]'Gender and race intersect in ways which permit the abuse of aboriginal women to be rendered almost invisible.... Add race to gender and you have created an extremely marginal voice' (Mendelsohn and Baxi 1997, 225). See also the fine anthology by Dianne Bell and Renate Kline, *Radically Speaking: Feminism Reclaimed*, (1996), and their Foreword, 'Beware: Radical Feminists Speak, Read, Write, Organise, Enjoy Life, and Never Forget', is unforgettable. One hopes one never recovers from this text!

the colonising power and first-nations peoples. I may not be wrong in saying that there were very few similar militant assertions of identity in Australia, for obvious reasons. Settlers were invaders and colonisers, and there was a certain degree of remoteness in large continents. The points of collision were necessarily few and far between. Economically speaking, also, Australia was kind of a dependent semi-periphery State in the world economy. All this began to change after World War II, but there were early signs during the interwar period as well. Australia is a land of migrants and there was a heavy post-war influx. Melbourne, for example, has the second largest population of Greeks outside Greece. There is a strong Eastern European population as well. They have people from many parts of the world. I don't know what implications this really had, but it certainly pushed Australia towards a greater degree of tolerance. Migrants from Hong Kong, Eastern Europe, in fact all parts of the world, brought skills and resources which Australia was in need of. So the White Australia policy remained in place, but it was breached in several places after the war. The incoming migrants were not always indifferent to the plight of the indigenous people.

In India, we had a very strong tradition of insurgent identity formation in relation to dominant power. I am not an expert in this area, but I do know that not all groups had a distinct cosmology at this point in time. Ramachandra Guha's book on Verrier Elwin and Nehru (a very good book, probably the finest he has written) shows how the inheritors of political power from the anti-colonial nationalist independence struggle took a paternal approach to the plight of India's indigenous peoples (Guha 1999). You cannot understand the Fifth and Sixth Schedules of the Constitution without understanding this approach of the Nehru government. The Sixth Schedule gives the hill councils of Northeast and elsewhere the power to override not only state law, but also federal law. Today, we don't study these Schedules. I am not being romantic about it, but I think it is symbolically, as well as instrumentally, very important to recognise what the Fifth and Sixth Schedules mean.

Australia did not have a history at all of the Hinduisation of English law. If we look at the Criminal Tribes Act, it makes the fact of being born into a criminal tribe a criminal act (The Criminal Tribes Act

1871).[3] This is a strictly Hindu notion, which has found its way into English law. The Act has rarely been studied by lawyers, but historians have, on the other hand, looked at it. We all study the adverse effects of colonisation on people like us; however, the most affected people are always the other. The styles of colonial administration were very different with regard to different groups. The missionary activity was larger in this respect in India. If you have read the old classical works of anthropologists like *Morals and Merit* (Furer-Haimendorf 1967), a classic book whose themes I juxtaposed with contemporary studies in *Towards a Sociology of Indian Law* (Baxi 1986b), you find a lot of commonalities among the indigenous groups. However, there is also an encyclopaedic diversity. Not every indigenous group regards—as most indigenous communities do, or as Canadian Indians used to do—land as sacred. Not every community has that worldview. Some do and some don't. If you ask me for one great book about the religious traditions of indigenous peoples, I cannot name it. You might have a book here and there, but no volumes outlining the cosmologies of law.

I did this study of the Lok Adalat at Rangpur (Baxi 1976b). I looked far and wide for an understanding of the Bhils. In Madhya Pradesh and Gujarat, the Bhils are the largest formation, and there was only one book (by T. B. Naik of Gujarat Vidyapith, the Gandhian University; *cf.* Naik 1956) and two articles. I must be clearly wrong when I say that there are no books. But really, if you compare the literature on the cosmology and religion of Australian indigenous people with the Indian scene, we will fully realise the lack, although students and scholars of cultural anthropology may have contrary views.

[3] The Criminal Tribes Act of 1871 applied to the Northwestern Provinces, Punjab, and Oudh. By 1911, it extended to the entirety of British India. It referred to 'a gang, tribe or class of people addicted to the systematic commission of non-bailable offense'. It empowered local governments to notify an entire gang, tribe, or class of people as criminals. The Act put several restrictions on the movements of the members of the notified tribes, including requiring members of such communities to report their movements to local police stations, being forcefully resettled as the government saw fit, and being subject to arbitrary police action (Nigam 1990).

In contrast, we are strong on the history of revolts and insurgency. It is a very fecund area of political theory-based research. I have explored this in my study, as also the constitutional coupling of Scheduled Castes (SCs) and Scheduled Tribes (STs) and the whole idea of the constitutional repudiation of caste, which ironically creates a secular caste—the Scheduled Caste—and lists those who belong to it. But this assimilates, for official purposes of beneficence, a whole variety of different civilisational traditions under the label of Scheduled Castes and Scheduled Tribes, not to speak of the Other Backward Classes.

There are differences between the Australian context and the situation of indigenous people in India. For example, while in the Indian context there is a lot of folklore and legend and traditions that form their belief systems, so far as I can remember, the idea of sacredness of land is not writ as large as it is in so many indigenous communities in Australia. The idea of human-nature linkage, of unity, is there.

Which is why I always say to people, if anybody wants to study the idea of sustainable environment and so on, these are the places to go to. This should be their role model. This harmonious relationship between nature and human beings. I am not really answering your question. There are important, different areas of concern, in different settings. Your second question was related to—tell me again?

LL: How did this affect your legal cosmology? This engagement with indigenous law.

What Can Indigenous Law Teach Us?

UB: I suppose your reference here is primarily to my writings and work with the Lok Adalat at Rangpur. Yet there are other referents as well. Let me put these briefly.

First, the convention in India is to use the term 'customary law' (CL) instead of 'indigenous law' (IL). This usage remains problematic insofar as it suggests that 'they' (the 'tribal') have 'custom' and we (the 'non-tribal') have 'law'. If so, this is erroneous in the extreme because custom dwells at the very heart of so-called modern law as well—think about judicial customs (the doctrine of precedent, of reticence in judicial action, for example) or legislative customs (three readings of the Bill, parliamentary privileges, and so on). Further, I believe the expression 'indigenous law' is important as it gives dignity to alternate forms of legal imagination and tradition.

Second, IL also enables us to better address the politics of constitutional and legal change. This is a vast and complicated theme in itself, but in the main, it is fair to say that the redrawing of the federal map of India, especially for the Northeast, has mediated what is now called the politics of identity. So have the provisions of the Fifth and Sixth Schedules of the Indian Constitution, and of course legislative reservations and related affirmative action programmes for Scheduled Tribes. Militant movements for secession have been converted into demands for autonomy within the Union of India. Even so, neither expression—politics of identity/difference or reinforced federalism—may be understood fully outside the creeping forms of the militarisation of the ways of Indian governance and a coequal militarisation of collective political action. Of course, 'tribal' militancy pervaded aspects of colonial governance, but, as noted before, it now militarises rather heavily the habitus of postcolonial Indian governance. The discourse of the unity and integrity of India prevails over all else, of course, given the geopolitics with the People's Republic of China and other forms, as well, of borders/boundaries governance. Mainstream Indian legal scholarship remains overwhelmingly concerned with affirmative action programmes for STs which is, incidentally, a most peculiar expression substituting the rights of indigenous peoples by the languages of governance beneficence and State largesse, concealing from view integral aspects of Indian economic 'development' that seek to ameliorate, but also at times alienates, even annihilates, the indigenous culture and civilisation.

At long last, State/official languages now at least recognise this fact. I have in view two occurrences: former Prime Minister Manmohan Singh's address suggesting the need to *somehow* ameliorate the exploitation of IP resources, and the proceedings before the Indian

Supreme Court concerning both the illegality and unconstitutionality of the mining leases in IP areas, as also the Ambani brothers' litigation before the Court. A noted Assamese legal scholar, Professor Sanajaoba, whose writings remain consistently ignored by us all, frequently reminds us that Indian federalism at work constantly promotes the systematic underdevelopment of the Northeastern states and peoples. How else, he asks, do all of us routinely accustom ourselves, year after year, to the flooding of the Brahmaputra river and the unequal sharing of royalties from petroleum and oil resources? To say all this is not to deny the enormous accomplishment of the constitutional Fifth and Sixth Schedules, the legislative reservations for the Scheduled Tribes, and the eventual federal devolution of power. Yet the problematic of IP human rights still fully stares us in the eye.

Third, the politics of constitutional and legal change as concerns the fond talk about the Uniform Civil Code (UCC) presents the constitutional idea of India where only 'majority' and 'minority' communities matter. The UCC discourse, as I have reiterated in my writings, almost entirely ignores the jurisprudential formations of IL (Baxi 2006a). This is a matter of grave constitutional misfortune. IL jurisprudential formations hold much potential for otherwise 'progressive' UCC-talk. Its histories of governance of sexuality offer many a precious lesson for re-imagining UCC-talk, exceeding some easy-minded and flattening discourses of the right to equality talk. For example, 'customs' of pre-marital sexual cohabitation in some IL formations, as precursors to a future happier married life, are jarring to sexually constipated high-caste ears! No doubt, if judged by the flattened narrative standards of Indian constitutional law and jurisprudence, gender discrimination in inheritance in some IP formations seem to present issues that may never be fully grasped outside the sphere of the IP nomos. Some easy-minded liberal legal feminist practices may themselves appear as discriminatory, and even violative, of the cultural logics of some IP formations. I name thus a difficult issue between *horizontal* and *vertical* forms of the idea and ideals of gender equality, at least as promoting in this conversation the cause of a more nuanced grasp of what John Rawls and particularly Michael Walzer (2008) name as concerns for 'complex equality'. It is counterproductive to constitutional good governance to say that articulation of specific cultural diversities is itself a crime against national unity and security! The Constitution variously protects what Article 51-A (*f*) calls 'the composite culture' of India, and what is more, obligates all citizens of India to 'value and promote' it.

But, coming back to my work with the Rangpur Lok Adalat, this profoundly shaped my legal cosmology, as you describe it. I have narrated the experience in several articles, especially in the 'Epilogue' to the *Crisis of the Indian Legal System* and in 'Popular Justice, Participatory Development and Power Politics: Lok Adalat in Turmoil' (Baxi 1982a, 1985a). And yes, though in a different vein, in my contributions to *Asian Indigenous Law* edited by Professor Masaji Chiba (Baxi 1986a), which I partly reproduced in *Towards a Sociology of Indian Law*, and in my response to Ranajit Guha's cameo study of colonial adjudicature, 'Chandra's Death', published as 'State's Emissary' in *Subaltern Studies VII* (Baxi 1986b, 1992). If you will allow me a moment of authorial vanity, these are writings that I remain most fond of.

I wrote about IP imageries and practices of the Lok Adalat when these were not known at all, even by progressive justices of the Gujarat High Court, later elevated to the Supreme Court of India—Justices P. N. Bhagwati, D. A. Desai, and M. P. Thakkar. Nor did justices from other regions know much about similar experiments in Mirzapur in Uttar Pradesh, and in Nagaland. Indeed, these began almost simultaneously with the Indian Constitution, and therefore deserved a greater dignity of juristic and juridical attention. This simply did not happen, given the colonial legacies which derive inspiration for legal reform from 'Old' and 'New' Commonwealth regions, now of course fully obscured in these days of the Americanisation of Indian law and jurisprudence. Alternative dispute resolution talk continues to dominate, organising further the complete amnesia of distinctive Indian alternate neo-Gandhian traditions and experience. If anyone wishes to understand these, one has to have recourse to the rich repertoire of thought practices of Mohandas Gandhi, Vinoba Bhave, and Jayaprakash Narayan (see Chapter 9).

To be sure, the imagery of Lok Adalat was fully utilised by State agents and managers of the Indian law reform portfolios. Thus, we have the Lok Adalat Act[4] and its various aftermaths (The Legal Services Authority Act 1987). Further, forum-shopping overseas for designer goods of law reform models and action programmes extravagantly ignores the wholesome wisdom of neo-Gandhian inventions of grassroots justicing. Allow me, please, to mention the poignant fact that all my efforts for the establishment of Family Courts in India by inviting the richest attention to the Lok Adalat at Rangpur excited little advertence, despite the fact that it remains the best exemplar of communitarian 'family courts.' I do not know how to frame this agony over such a conspicuous lack outside of a fully-fledged reference to Fanon's critique, entitled *Black Skin, White Masks* (1967). But I must mention here two exceptions among the Bar and the practitioners of human rights activism: Shymala Papu, Senior Advocate of the Supreme Court, and Vasudha Dhagamwar. Vasudha has done excellent work showing both aspects of liberation and suppression in her classic work, *Law, Power, and Justice* (Dhagamwar 1992) And Shymala (in a refreshing change from the attitude of senior lawyers towards IP) became sensitive to these aspects when they were brought to her attention.

Arvind Narrain: Mathew John worked with the Kashtakari Sanghatana[5]—he was there for a year, researching precisely this

[4]The Legal Services Authorities Act, 1987: Enacted in furtherance of Article 39A of the Constitution of India, this Act establishes statutory bodies (known as Legal Services Authorities) to provide free legal services to citizens. While legal aid schemes and activities pre-dated this statute—legal aid was introduced by Justice P. N. Bhagwati under the Legal Aid Committee formed in 1971—it was enacted to give a statutory basis and a uniform pattern to such programmes. The Act establishes a nationwide network, at the apex of which is the National Legal Services Authority, for the provision of legal aid and assistance. See Baxi (1975b).

[5]Kashtakari Sanghatana: Organisation started in 1978 in Dahanu, Maharashtra, to work with the tribal landless, marginal peasantry, and migrant labour in the predominantly tribal blocks in around 600 tribal villages in Thane district. It is an organisation of the Adivasis of the region,

question of tribal cosmologies, worldviews, and their relation to law and legality. And the answer he came up with is that, because of the spread of capitalist relationships, tribal customs were not what they might have been at an earlier point in time. He was saying that there was a large number of tribals in the Kashtakari Sanghatana who were in the wage labour economy. So their consciousness itself is very different, it is not the romantic notion of a different worldview, as it were. He was describing the complexity of the current lives of indigenous people in Dahanu. For example, someone like Pradip Prabhu is very strongly rooted in the understanding that the indigenous people have a different cosmology. His point was that the actuality of people's lives is not lived within this form of consciousness or worldview.

UB: Things change, yes, you are right. I am glad Mathew is working on this. I lack access to his texts, so I can here only infer that what he is describing are the processes of de-tribalisation. In a sense, it is an ongoing process of de-culturation, more 'properly' speaking. Or a different kind of enculturation, perhaps? Yet, I simply don't know how Mathew is thus engaged with the 'specificity of the political'. I do not know whether Mathew says that being appendages of a wage economy meant also a loss of belonging to ancient civilisations and distinctive cosmologies.

Resisting the everyday, and yet ever changing, forms of exploitation on the ground provides us different historic landscapes of understanding than those present in forms of 'snapshot' understanding. Mathew, as you mention, invested just a year. This is no criticism of Mathew, yet there is this difference between historically grounded and merely episodic research of a social movement.

I honestly cannot respond to your point about Mathew's findings about 'capitalist relations' affecting 'customs' or 'cosmos'. In general, this may be said about almost any situation of transition from one mode of production to another. There has been a lot of talk of 'mixed modes' or 'intermediate regimes' among economic historians. One is here not

---

committed to fighting the exploitation of the Adivasis through collective action. It was started, amongst others, by Pradip Prabhu, who was then a Jesuit priest, with an ideology of liberation theology.

talking about remnants or residues, but rather of the coexistence of different civilisational traditions and social formations. If so, we must think, not of 'custom', but of the political values of indigenous peoples which animate so much their conduct within the group and in relation to others.

Movement and struggle on the ground almost always change with the immediacy of contexts. Yet, 'contexts' also somehow endure beyond this poignant immediacy of tactics and strategy. What thus remains somewhat enduring is the imagination of social movements and of action in the Kashtakari Sanghatana or Bhoomi Sena movements. Far from constituting any de-tribalisation or de-customisation, what we have here is a re-articulation of the innately participatory cultures of many and most Indian indigenous peoples. These remain broadly participatory. Take the example of Bhoomi Sena: it had these *mandals*—committees—of elders, of young people, of women workers. Every action had to be approved by these committees.

This was a kind of federalism, an authentic federalism, that you do find among American Indians also. They, in fact, invented federalism, and that is how it came into American law. I cited this extraordinary book (Johansen 1982) on American Indian contribution to the theory of federalism in my article on Ronald Dworkin (Baxi 2003a).

How Can the Same Law that Oppresses Us be Turned against the Oppressors?

UB (*contd*): I had heard of Bhoomi Sena from many friends—Professor Arindam Das Gupta and Niranajan Mehta (formerly of the National Institute of Banking), Dharam Ghai, and Anisur Rehaman (ILO). Das Gupta conveyed to them that this man, Baxi, was interested in helping out and that he was a good fellow. I did not hear from them for many months. Then one fine morning Kalu Ram Goghade was at my doorstep, and he was among the architects of the movement. I was greatly moved by their adopting non-violence in demands for implementation of the idea of rule of law (see Calman 1985; Silva, et al. 1979).

He said, I have come as a member of Bhoomi Sena, we have received your 'application'! I have never made an application anywhere. It is a circumstance of my life that I have never appeared for any interview. It is just a freak occurrence that it is so, and I accept it. So, I am very careful about interviews. I ensure that they are not hegemonic occasions. If I had wide power, I will dispense with them. Mere change in naming—from interviews to interaction—does not change the structure or institutional cultures.

I said, what, I never applied to Bhoomi Sena! He said, I don't know what you understand by application, but we were told that you were interested in working with us. I said, yes, I am. He said, we consider that an application. And we have discussed your name in our *mandal* circles, and we have a strong objection to your American degree. I said, what has that got to do with anything, I have learnt some law, that should be useful enough. He said, no, we don't like this kind of thing, but we are not saying no, we will try you out on some kind of probation. I had at the time some incipient professional ego, and so I said, look, this is going too far, let's end this conversation. In return, he said, you cannot end this conversation. I began it, I have come all the way representing a movement and you are an applicant, you better behave!

We will try, he said, and overlook your American degree, provided you don't behave like an expert. We don't want you to define our problems for us, don't define our solutions for us, don't tell us what to do; as and when we need you, we will communicate with you, somebody will come and tell you. Whatever you say will be discussed among us. I said, okay, fine.

The question, however, that the Bhoomi Sena put to me changed my life and my understanding of the life of law. They were not trying to throw away the bourgeois like those engaged in 'revolutions'. Kalu Ram said, we are not asking you to help us with our cause, howsoever described but since you know a bit of law (a bit of law!), tell us within the next six months how the same law which oppresses us can be peacefully turned against the oppressors. That is the question and if you can answer it, it is fine. Otherwise, we go on doing what we do. Amazing! He taught me more than I fancied I had learnt from more erudite discourses on metaphysics, meta-ethics, and on the high tables of social theory! My whole idea of law, and of law reform, comes from that question. I won't go into the details, but later I gave them several suggestions, some of which may be debatable, but only if you consider there is more than just the one system of ethics and morals which no one should ever transgress.

Only if you were to accept one notion of ethics and morals, totally excluding other worldviews, only then a singular yardstick will emerge. But what if you were to introduce plurality? Would there then arise different yardsticks with which to judge morals? Would you change the system through a conflicting conceptions of morality? To come home to law, is a motion for adjournment, or bail, always a 'misuse' of a legal provision authorising it? More generally, if 'misuse' is to be inferred by a conduct or a pattern of conduct, this entails a general theory of legislative intent. But, as has been pointed out, it is not always clear what the intent is. Is it the intent of the regime which proposes a Bill? Or the intent of the opposition proposing several amendments to it, or the intent of a Parliamentary committee? How is the legislative intent to be established? The point is that an intent is always polycentric and remains a matter of retrospective construction. Adjudication very often *imputes* a legislative intent, as Hans Kelsen categorically stated often. For example, the Government of India prints the Constitution of India as from time to time legislatively amended by Parliament, but to read the Constitution as if the Court had never laid down the doctrine of the basic structure in, and since, 1973, is misleading! The same may be said about reading Article 21 (judicial substitution of 'due process of law' for procedure established by law), Part IV (the slow but steady incorporation of Part IV into Part III), Article 142 (power to do complete justice), or Article 124 (invention of judicial collegium). Is this judicial action ever to be regarded as any 'misuse' of high adjudicative power?

The category of 'miuse' of law is itself, perhaps, a misuse! And in any event, would there be any difference between 'misuse' and 'abuse' of law?

It remains true that many tribal cultures in India, even today, have a great sense of honour. Honour is something that we today don't quite understand. Dealing with middle-class people as we do, we don't understand the idea of honour. We understand best the language of principles. I used to say whenever I was angry in the DU academic council (sometimes I did get angry, but rarely!) that the university would be a happier and more creative place if there were fewer people with principles and more with a sense of honour. You have to make a difference between commitment to principles and to honour. Bhoomi Sena were willing to take recourse to the decadence of the legal system, but not at the cost of truth and honour. These are related. How did you think the system of bonded labour has survived? Because you swear on the honour of your mother or grandmother to bind yourself to your creditor. Thus, debt bondage survives in India on this notion of honour. Your mother's or grandmother's name is on paper, and their honour must be defended at all costs, including that of one's own slavery. There is a high intensity democracy in this that you will never see in civil society.

There is a difference between exploitation that is obviously contrary to honour and exploitation as violative of law and as inviting penal sanctions. The latter is an affair of evidence and representation by lawyers. Even if some social stigma accompanies fine or punishment, the modern reformative punishment approach would want us to believe that no question of dishonour survives undergoing a legal punishment. It is different in the case of honour; the loss of 'face', the internal mechanism of shame, justifies self-wounding or even dying. The stigma of acting in breach of the code of honour is often more severe than legal punishment. Anthropologists often have distinguished between the cultures of shame and cultures of guilt (Benedict 1946; Vanderheiden and Mayer 2017). What if a given culture lies beyond shame and guilt: is it entitled to be called a legal culture at all?

One may put a more theoretical gloss on it by saying that honour is a feudal virtue, a medieval virtue. The language of honour prevailed in a system of production which was not capitalist. The language of honour disappears in the industrial West, though not in all advanced societies (Japan is prominent example), where the rise of capitalism marks the end of honour. Some chivalry persists, of course, for example in the terms of international humanitarian law against the killing of non-combatants and such-like. But what prevails is the language of competition overlaid with the language of principles. One way of understanding the Bhoomi Sena in this great global age is as a pre-industrial culture versus an industrialising culture. I don't want to go into all these directions just now. There is always the risk of generalising too much.

In contrast, the precursor Lok Adalats (before the State misappropriated this concept) used the idea of the decadence of the State legal system as a resource, used it in the way they issued summons. In Rangpur people's court, they would say, we are poor and marginalised people, it is best we settle our disputes with minimal cost. So please come to the Lok Adalat, let us talk about it for one last time. If you do not come to the Lok Adalat on such-and-such a date, it is with a heavy heart that we will take this matter to the state courts, which you know will be ruinous for you and for us. I have reproduced the same text in my Lok Adalat paper (Baxi 1976b). The Lok Adalat is using recourse to the Indian State legal system as a threat to secure compliance with its own organisation. This is another way of using the decadence of the Indian legal system.

To come back to the question of changing customs, it was the night Pratiksha was born, when I was reading Peter Winch (1958), that I really understood the idea of custom. There is no better book than that in the whole English-speaking world! But to understand changing customs, one doesn't have to be a social theorist, one just needs to know a little bit of international law. A governing problem in international law is: When can you say that a custom is breached? The same problem is there with indigenous law. Here, too, the moment a custom is breached, a new custom arises. Customs do not change; they are replaced by other customs. This process is very complex; the breach of a custom is the progenitor of another type of custom. The important question is, how does the social understanding of change, and the political understanding, converge and conflict? The process of changing customs is supple, it is a dynamic process.

So yes, there is the wider phenomenon of what M. N. Srinivas calls *Sanskritisation*, we can even say of *Islamisation*, some would speak further of Anglicisation, all occurring not only within communities, but also spreading outwards to non-Hindu, non-Muslim communities. How about de-tribalisation? Does it mean one loses one's customs on which one's rights and identity are based? Can you tell me the name of one author who has extended the notion of Sanskritisation to indigenous peoples? In which directions are indigenous customs going? Are they taking the direction of Hinduisation? I think this is a very big problem affecting the solidarity of the subaltern. The politics of communalism is leading to a completely different ethos. The radical right, all over the globe, is now confronting legal liberalism of plurality and diversity with practices of social exclusion and 'ethno-nationalism', which affirm the integrity of the national majoritarian culture of violence. That culture does not believe in colonial racism but in the violent exclusion of the other. What the future may unfold is anyone's guess, but so long as the Indian Constitution exists in its present frame, it is unlikely that ethno-political practices (of exclusion and expulsion) can occur or continue without any limits imposed by the judiciary.

The Indian Law Institute (ILI), while I was there as Honorary Research Director, promoted some studies of 'codification' of 'tribal law' in the Northeast. We published many monographs on tribal law and custom in several Northeastern states. ILI branches in Assam and sister states promoted these studies. Justice B. L. Hansaria,[6] was interested in this, and so were others. There is a lot of work to be done, particularly in the context of codification. The ILI studies adopted a somewhat mechanical jurisprudence approach, in that they presumed that there was a mass of customs waiting to be codified, but each community had a different understanding of that mass. Friedrich von Savigny, the German founder of the historical school of jurisprudence in the nineteenth century, said that we must distinguish technical from political dimension to codification. The technical aspect is more

[6]Banwari Lal Hansaria. He was, prior to being elevated to the Supreme Court, the Chief Justice of the Orissa High Court (1990–1993).

evident in the ILI studies; generally, it is presumed that reforming lawyers' law—custom, in this case—is all there is to this enterprise. This is obviously not true and much more is involved. Did you mean all this, Lawrence?

Re-enchanting the World

LL: I was going to pick up a strand from what Arvind said to tie it up to some aspects of what you have written about, which is this entire issue of romanticism or romanticising something that is not there. The opposition which is often set up is between some idea of the real and some idea of the enchanted. Peter Fitzpatrick (1992) critiques modern law in terms of its own mythology. What you do by setting up the opposition between the modern real and the political enchanted which erases its own mythology. There is a kind of call in your own work about a certain re-enchantment. I want to now understand that the absence of this enchantment, that this romanticism, might actually be what is needed. When you hold on to a romanticised past, you are still holding on to the idea that you have a past. Hannah Arendt's critique of modernity is that it leaves you with a history, but not a past (Arendt 1961). So you will easily be consigned to history, but when you talk about a past, you are actually talking about the ability of a temporal relationship that acts as a normative basis for the future as well. I think, in some aspects of your writing, there is a call for a 're-enchantment', as it were, of the world.

UB: Well, yes, this is a deep question indeed! The question of history is very important, especially for courts and justices when they have to decide on complex issues of fact and law, as in the Ayodhya-Babri Masjid dispute. This involves, in particular, the relation between law and archaeology. The focus of some literature I have read is, however, on law and history. I have not come across similar concerns relating to archaeology. There is more to be said, of course, on how far archaeology shares the view of meta-history: is there an Arendt school of archaeology, for instance, that draws such a vivid distinction between 'past' and 'history'?

I do believe in 're-enchantment'. True, in many ways re-enchantment is opposed to 'dis-enchantment' with the world, in the sense that Max Weber gave to it. I think this is an important dialectic, although many Weberian scholars name it as 'antinomic', not as a 'dialectic'. There are many difficulties with the use of this dialectic. One such is illustrated in (Ramachandra) Guha's book on Verrier Elwin. Elwin has been criticised as having Nehru's romanticism, a constitutional romanticism about—that awful phrase!—'bringing people into the mainstream'. But what do we do when that mainstream itself is no more than a cesspool? Or, to sharpen the provocation a bit, what if the traffic is between one cesspool and another, something that we are apt to call 'progress' nevertheless?

There is now prevalent a certain vision of India which is meta-cultural, civilisational, and so on. When Nandita Haksar[7] was an M.Phil. student in JNU, she rang me and said, I want to read something about Nehru and Gandhi. I said, ask Sarvepalli Gopal.[8] He was her supervisor. Ultimately, I said, I read *The Discovery of India*. She read it and besieged me with the question, why did you ask me to read this? What/which India did Nehru *discover*? There is no mention of criminal tribes, very little mention of indigenous people either. This anecdote is a good enough antidote to large stories, to erudite descriptions of diversity and inclusiveness. What if these stories do not convince different others? What if they have large stories of difference to tell us? The principal question is: How do we deal honestly with *difference*, and if facing it fully leads to disenchantment, so be it.

[7]Nandita Haksar: human rights lawyer, teacher, and activist, and author of *Demystification of Law for Women* (1986), *Framing Geelani, Hanging Afzal: Patriotism in the Time of Terror* (2007), *Rogue Agent: How India's Military Intelligence Betrayed the Burmese Resistance* (2009), and other texts on human rights.

[8]Sarvepalli Gopal (1923–2002), historian, author of *Jawaharlal Nehru: A Biography* (1976), and co-editor of *Selected Works of Jawaharlal Nehru* (1972–82) and *The Essential Writings of Jawaharlal Nehru* (2003).

On the point of romanticisation, yes, I think that it is a problem. David Maybury-Lewis,[9] an anthropologist friend who founded an organisation called Cultural Survival, reminded us of this by taking a decennial census of tribal groups liable to extinction. All the hunting peoples worldwide have become extinct. One curious consequence of this concern with cultural diversity is the gold rush for genetic information by multinationals. They are taking their germplasm so that they can all, severally and jointly, as the case may be, appropriate it by patenting it. So the point about David Maybury-Lewis is that enchantment comes not in talking about diversity, culture, and custom. Very much like one may rent-a-crowd, one may rent-a-culture. Rather, enchantment comes from a discredited word called 'civilisation'. They are civilisationally different. And, on the whole, more civilised. That's where the enchantment comes from. Incidentally, I dealt with three related notions—euphoria, chaos, and enchantment, disenchantment—in my article, 'The Avatars of Indian Judicial Activism' (Baxi 2007d), of which I am very fond!

There is a core of something called Indian civilisation which is different from culture, State, Constitution, law. I had a long discussion with Bhikhu Parekh,[10] and he further developed this idea and wrote about it. Are we primarily a civilisational community or a cultural community or a political community or a market community? What, then, is the idea of civilisation? Civilisation is a dirty word after the

[9] David Maybury-Lewis (1929–2007): British anthropologist, ethnologist of lowland South America, activist for indigenous peoples' human rights, Professor Emeritus of Harvard University, and author of *The Attraction of Opposites: Thought and Society in the Dualistic Mode* (1989), *Millennium: Tribal Wisdom and the Modern World* (1992), *The Savage and the Innocent* (1965) and *Indigenous Peoples, Ethnic Groups, and the State* (1997).

[10] Bhikhu Chotalal Parekh (b. 1935), political theorist and Labour member of the House of Lords, and author of many valuable books, including *Colonialism, Tradition and Reform: An Analysis of Gandhi's Political Discourse* (1989), *Gandhi's Political Philosophy: A Critical Examination* (1988), *Rethinking Multiculturalism: Cultural Diversity and Political Theory* (2006 [2000]), and *A New Politics of Identity: Political Principles for an Interdependent World* (2008).

Third Reich. It has become responsible for many, many holocausts. And then again—his name I rarely mention—Samuel P. Huntington, you cannot use the word 'civilisation' without his name cropping up. He wrote a much-cited book titled *The Clash of Civilizations and the Remaking of World Order* (1996). My point is, you have to rescue the notion of something larger than politics, law, State, whether you call it 'civilisation' or something else. You need to re-discover D. D. Kosambi and Ananda Coomaraswamy because civilisation is the place for many things other than power, money, hegemony; the life of the spirit is the life of civilisation itself. People these days don't read books that were dated from before they were born. But many authors have carefully revived the notion of civilisation, anthropologically. That I think is a part of the project that re-enchants. What follows after you re-enchant? A hell of a lot follows—law, State, reform, etc. But probably the use of the word 'civilisation' is today globally heavily occupied in the service of oligarchy that purses ethnic solidarity and supremacy and is placed at the altar of populist nationalism', often endangering pluralism and diversity everywhere globally. So you have to find a different notion related to it.

LL: Like Simmel's notion of moral memory. He says: 'Gratitude is the moral memory of mankind'.

UB: Wonderful! Moral memory, future histories, whatever. We can go to folks like Aurobindo who have a lot of words for that. Another discredited word now—discredited by policy research (terrible stuff!)—is nostalgia. And nostalgia is a reinvention of the past, a reimagination of the past. This can only be done by going beyond all these little bits and pieces we call the State, law, institutions, ideologies, and so on to something wider and deeper.

I tried and failed. The only limited success I had was in partly organising the Melbourne conference on the Rights of Subordinated Peoples.[11] I have tried several times, with several people, to convene an international meeting in Delhi, or elsewhere in India, on the forgotten peoples—the Banjaras, the 'gypsies', or the Romanis. If we only were

[11] At La Trobe University, 1988; see Mendelsohn and Baxi (1997).

to list the forgotten peoples of the world, it would be a very large list. We talk so easily of universality, of humanity, of humankind. But re-enchantment is a serious business. Disenchantment is perhaps easier—one can curl up on this chair, have a nice smoke of whatever kind, and pooh-pooh the idea of civilisation, or modernity, or whatever!

Disenchantment is a work of history as well, and not just a theory. That's what industrialisation does. The whole relationship between yourself and others and the objects of the natural world and the world of nature is transformed. So we can talk about industrial civilisation and pre-industrial civilisation—economists do talk about it. The markers of an industrial civilisation in economic history are different; in postmodernism, it is a different kind.

It is a question not of rational thought but of pre-rational thought, of sentimental thought. It is very important. It is wrong to say that the only thing there is instrumental (or calculative) reason. In the relationship of means and ends, to say that there is nobody above us or below us who defines these ends and means, that verily we define our ends and means, is very often a performance of rationalisation, fragmentation, alienation.

You referred to Peter Fitzpatrick's idea (Fitzpatrick 1992) of the mythology of modern law, and how all law has a myth at its foundations. One of the difficulties I have is that there are so many notions and ideas of what a mythology means, and what myth means. I have found useful Roland Barthes' idea that ultimately the best way to understand mythology is that it furnishes a political language. Peter elaborates this, but does he foreground this idea of myth as a sociolinguist or an ideologue, as a new kind of language that brings in contradictory elements into a single whole? How do we fully grasp the myth of free trade, the myth of liberalism, the myth of socialism? This is an activist understanding, not an erudite understanding of what perhaps mythology means, and this is a good starting point. I don't know why I was thinking about it this morning, I normally don't think about what we will discuss, and I normally don't think as to how I should speak. This sudden act of thinking surprises me!

LL: (Michael) Taussig also has this bit on how dreaming has lost its dreamlike quality. And how can one have hope, if one does not dream? He calls for a re-enchantment of the world.

UB: Let's take the World Social Forum and its idea that other worlds are possible. If you begin to examine this idea closely, you are lost, there is nothing in it. Once you get into these other worlds, worlds other than capitalism, you are already boxed into non-utopian forms. But if you let those four words stay with you, and you don't let them collapse into neat analytical categories, it is a very powerful slogan, and therein lies its appeal. There are different kinds of founding myths. There is a creativity which is at the heart of enchantment, not a canon, not a laid down truth, but a process of becoming. The making of a myth is not always being, but becoming. There are different kinds of myths; if you deploy a binary, these fall neatly into the categories of founding myths of emancipation and myths that foster repression. Things become more complex when one introduces subaltern myths, which imagine different forms of emancipation and repression. One has to begin to think not only of the promises of enchantment and re-enchantment, but also of their perils. This is the big problem.

Not Land for Land, but a Running Brook for a Running Brook

LL: I will read a bit from a post sent by a friend on the *Sarai Reader* List. This is about ongoing land acquisition conflicts in Himachal Pradesh. A journalist friend recounted an encounter. He went to find out about the land acquisition conflicts in Himachal on account of a big skiing resort that is being planned there. There were many claims and counterclaims. What strongly stayed with him as a puzzle was this old man of about ninety years. He gently said that he does not see the urgency to move from where he is now. On being asked why, as the compensation package was good, he explained that the *dhoop* (warmish sunlight) that he was used to for the last twenty years in the patch where he sits every day will disappear from his life, and that he was not keen to lose it. Now, my friend was a bit bemused by this response. It may not come into his manifest account of the troubled times, but it had definitely arrived in him as a lifelong puzzle. I was trying to understand this strange presence in my friend's mind amidst stories of violence and injustice, which he has been encountering in his travels within India. In a landscape overflowing with the language of scorn, the gentle remark of the man takes our mind to another way of thinking.

UB: Beautiful! This is an act of affectionate intelligence. Not empathy, but intelligence of a different kind. It does not think *appropriation* (taking away) without talking/thinking about its other, *re-appropriation*.

This reminds me of what should really be a footnote! I was in Surat when the Narmada movement was just about beginning (see Chapter 12). Hardly four-and-a-half people were involved at the time—one was a sociology student, there were three others, and the half was me. We were trying to prevent the early process of land acquisition, and we were getting nowhere. The compensation (if it can be called that) offered for the acquired land was around Rs 5,000.

We discussed what should be done. I said, let us go to the High Court in Gujarat. Before that, there was no SAL in an otherwise progressive High Court (see Chapters 10 and 12 for SAL). I filed the petition as a citizen of India, not as a law teacher or as the Vice-Chancellor of South Gujarat University. Justice M. P. Thakkar heard the case. I had put forward the argument for the Right to Life under Article 21 [of the Constitution] in the following terms: I want, not land for land, but a running brook for a running brook, a sunset for a sunset, and a grove of trees with shade for a grove of trees with shade. So my Right to Life is a right to my specific civilisational mode of being in the world. And I cannot be rehabilitated or compensated outside a recreation of what life means to me. Justice Thakkar did not know what had hit him. I knew that because of the sheer enormity of this argument, it would never be accepted. It was not a rational argument, it was an enchantment argument. We got some results—an injunction here and there—and the movement of four-and-a-half people found space to grow.

As this incipient struggle grew, the then Chief Minister of Gujarat, Madhav Singh Solanki, was persuaded to declare a whole lot of areas where land was acquired as a 'prohibited place' under the Official Secrets Act of 1923. Once these areas are thus notified, any movement within which is not authorised by the authorities is a serious offence amounting to treason. The idea was to prevent activists from coming in to try and prevent acquisition. Inhabitants of that place were moved out of there to other areas. I was approached by some activists, and I thought about what I should do. I did not fancy going to the High Court again.

There is a section in it on sedition, Section 124A. If you look at Macaulay's language, the offence is of the creation of disaffection against the State. Disaffection means you have a duty to love your government. I was enchanted. I fell in love with the idea of love in the Indian Penal Code. I said, *voila*! and wrote an article in a national newspaper which was in the form of a notice to the Chief Minister of Gujarat. Take notice, I wrote, that by your actions in this area invoking the Official Secrets Act, you and your Council of Ministers have created disaffection against the lawfully elected government and, therefore, unless the order is withdrawn in a week's time or reasons are given for the continuation of this regime, we will be compelled to file a prosecution for seditious behaviour against you and your government. I don't know if it was because of that, but the order was withdrawn with lightning speed! Under Section 124A, the State wants its citizens to love it. Otherwise 124A does not make sense. While treason is an act of war against the State, sedition is withdrawal of affection.

This is perhaps what the project-affected people are saying. They don't merely want land for land. They want their ecology back. One of the issues with resettlement in the Narmada movement (it boggles the mind) was the question of cremation and burial grounds. They said, we cannot cremate or bury our dead here, we can only bury them where they were born. We cannot allow this area to be submerged because that is where the spirit, the roots, lie. This is a romantic argument, it is an argument deeply held, sacred. You have to bring a lot of emotion into it, a lot of passion, a lot of non-instrumental reason. Many others have said we want a return, not to pre-modern, but to primitive rationality. This is the enchantment. What matters is not being *original*, but being *ab-original*. This is stepping into a different world, or trying to do so. And you can only do it with aesthetics: with art, literature, poetry, painting, sculpture; you cannot do it with words alone. Put another way, when one develops the idea of justice as beauty! And the notion, so central to critical aesthetics, of chaosmos (disordered order). One can also produce a new ordered chaos! Recall what Friedrich Nietzsche said in *Thus Spake Zarathustra*: 'one must still have chaos in oneself to be able to give birth to a dancing star'.

Six

Love, Suffering, and Justice

Meeting Prema

LL: Getting back to 1967, you have returned to ILI after a year in Sydney. What was your motivation in coming back to ILI?

UB: Partly, it was simply the desire to get back to Prema. I left for Berkeley soon after getting married. Call it a homing instinct. The other context in which I wanted to return to India was to follow up some themes sounded in *The Journal of Indian Law Institute,* titled 'The Little Done, The Vast Undone' (Baxi 1967a). This article has been noted often, but most of its themes have been unjustly neglected.

I must say a little bit more about Prema. She stayed back to pursue her studies, a two-year degree course in law which she much later in 1985 completed with first class first and gold medal at the South Gujarat University, and she enrolled at the Delhi Bar. She was a keen debater and won a prize at an inter-collegiate competition at Nagpur. She won many laurels at the college, but her ideal preference was medicine, for which she was unfortunately not fully eligible. She rued it as she always wanted to follow her father in the medical profession and research. But she was also interested in printing, proofing, and she pursued these in proficiency courses offered at JJ Arts College Campus. She also did a certificate correspondence course in Homoeopathy. Her interest in photography led her to join the programme at *The Indian Express* as late as 2013, interrupted by the cerebral stroke that I suffered in early 2013. Even if caring involved a lot of drudgery, she never let anyone know! She looked after me with great devotion for months together and gave me a new life.

She was very proficient in shorthand and typing and she is also a conscientious reader; she is well-read in most of the Indian scriptures—*Gita*, *Upanishads*, *Yoga Vashishtha*, *Ramayana*, *Guru Granth Sahib*, etc. Her book, *My Spiritual Journey with Swami Satyananda* (2013), has been a runway success with all kinds of readers across the world. She has also written a book titled *Uma Tuli: Lighting Many Lives* (2019) about Ms (Dr) Uma Tuli, who is known as a founder of inclusive education in India for all children. Prema has written many poems, both in English and Hindi. What is extraordinary is her style: she writes graciously and effortlessly, straight from her soul. Such writing is hard to come by.

She went painstakingly through some of my papers, and especially through my second article on Kautilya, published in the *Indian Yearbook of International Affairs* by Professor T. S. Rama Rao.[1] She does not read everything that I write, and every time she does read a draft, she reprimands me for residuary typos. She also wonders aloud why I can't write more simply and explicitly.

An excellent chef and host, she has entertained generations of friends and colleagues in India and overseas, fondly inviting the title Annapurna. And combined gracefully the work of hospitality with the function of breadwinner (because most of the time, she supplemented my meagre earnings from professional income as a lawyer). Not merely this: she accomplished the care of children as they grew up and was a caregiver to us all in desperate times. I owe her more than what these words may ever express!

---

[1] T. S. Rama Rao, Professor of International Law and Constitutional Law at the University of Madras.

During this period, I also wrote on the judgment in *State of Gujarat vs. Shantilal*[2] in the *Jaipur Law Journal* (Baxi 1969c). While I was halfway through writing this article, I said to myself, oh dear! Who am I to criticise Supreme Court judgments? Why should they listen to me? What business do I have to judge the judges? They have arguments and facts before them. So I said, I must have a theory of justice with which to question their approach to compensation in Article 31. It took me six months to write; I went through the literature on analytical welfare economics and the like, which was unfamiliar to me. In retrospect, it is one of my best contributions. I felt that if this is the kind of work I am doing—addressing Indian law and the Constitution—then Sydney is probably not the best site in which to do so. When Professor G. S. Sharma said to me, you have held up my volume for six months, this is not done, I have to publish it, I said to him, hang on, hang on, G. S., you will never get an article like this in your lifetime. I was so modest! I made sure that it was one of the best things I could write at that point in time. I thought if G. S. Sharma was in India and was inviting me to ILI, why not join it? I had no career plan, I was a nomad. I always have been. In retrospect, a foolhardy nomad at that time.

LL: So, you came back to be with Prema?

UB: Yes, for us to be together. We were separated for about three years. But it was also an academic event for me. I thought Sydney was fine, but I didn't know Delhi at all, I had never lived in Delhi. That explains my travelling in taxis. I had no idea of Delhi, I spent a decade in Bombay, and Prema always remained a Bombay person. The thing about people who come from coastal towns in India is that they feel choked if there is no sea, no water. Today one chokes for a different reason: mindless globalisation, extreme weather pollution, advancing Anthropocene, and accelerated anthropogenic harm to the planet. But we behave as if everything is 'normal' where nothing really is: a disjunction that Amitav Ghosh has called the 'Great Derangement'. I still miss the sea. In a sense, it is the collective unconscious of coastal people.

---

[2] *State of Gujarat vs. Shri Shantilal. Mangaldas*, AIR 1969 SC 634.

LL: How did you meet Prema?

UB: You must ask her. I must respect her privacy, but she will be here in Bangalore soon and you can talk to her as well about it. When I was in Bombay, doing my law degree while working with Scindia, I invisibly met her during a trial in the district court (she was a secretary in the court, although I did not know it at the time), and I met her visibly in an unusual situation which I will describe now.

I was invited to go to the *satsang* or congregation of Swami Satyananda Saraswati, who was a disciple of Swami Sivananada Saraswati, the founder of Divine Life Society. I went to the congregation where he was conducting Yoga classes, and everybody, including the women, was wearing white. So my first impression of meeting Prema is from amongst a whole lot of people doing an *asana*. They were raising half their bodies, legs up in *Sarvangasan*. I didn't know who she was, but I saw a lot of people in that posture. There was not much to write home about at that point in time. It was a close friend of mine who introduced us. Thereafter, we met a number of times and fell in love with each other; a little flirtation was allowed, but even a cosmopolitan centre (soaked with sentimental Bollywood movies and love songs—and provocative dances) did not then permit of much public display of it. Social mores and folkways effectively did the job which moral policing now seems to do by way of governance of sexuality.

Our marriage was solemnised at Sadhubella Temple, Bombay. I recall that the wedding was very simple and Professor Prabhu (who was my good teacher in logic at Rajkot, and who was a celibate, a *bhakt* too of Lord Hanuman) was the only non-family person whom I had invited. I have seen no simpler ceremony than the one I attended.

Link between Biography and Social Text

LL: It's become much clearer through the conversations that in your writing, how important the idea of suffering is to you. From the writing alone, you don't always get a sense of the personal genealogies of your engagement with suffering. Can you elaborate a bit more on that? We will come back to this, the idea of the renunciation of self as a form of sovereignty, or as a form of moral perfectionism. You can see the lineages in your conversation with Levinas emerging.

UB: This is a multiple comment, and one that is difficult to respond to in conversation. We will return to it, as you say, in many different contexts.

On the point of transit between individual biographies and social text, obviously there is a connection; the question is, how do you decipher this? One way of deciphering this is in a purely autobiographical sense, with which your project has some resonance. In a sense, all of this is the problem of coping with the here and now of suffering, the problem of relating to the prospect of redemption. This is the problem for applied spirituality, be it for the man on the cross, or for Gandhi, or for any other.

This is the problem. It is very important for redemptive politics, for transformative politics. I think this form of politics is a quest to reorient State, law, society, writing, technologies of self, and so on, to the other, to the suffering other. There are various ways of doing or not doing this. I found some ways of doing this in my encounter with Swami Satyananda Saraswati. These are life experiences that shaped or dis-shaped me; I include here, of course, my Rajkot days. There is something that distances discourse and event. I know that some people talk about discourse in terms of an event. What Jean-François Lyotard and Michel Foucault have said is that discursivity is not to be separated from real life or experience, but there is a degree of distance—some may say alienation, contradiction, ambiguity, in-organicity—between the biography and the social text.

It's a very difficult journey when one asks the question: How does one connect accidents of life, its textuality and intertextuality, which is both a form of commoditisation of knowledge and a communication of knowledge, with one's intellectual products? The textuality of knowledge production entails a certain kind of distance, objectification, even alienation from lived and embodied life—that is called 'discipline' in the truest sense of the word. How does one live a disciplinary life and connect the lived life (autobiography) to social texts? To what extent is genealogy distinct from writing about the self? Perhaps it is writing about several enmeshed selves, or is it about selves who use a common word or a world?

Maybe it is not wrong to distance the two. Imagine if everybody embodied and carried forward the biographical into their work, it would never stop, it would become impossible. Look at Derrida, how often does the Algerian encounter figure in his writing? Look at Foucault, how often do his travails against homophobia figure in his work? Foucault led marches in the streets of Paris, how often does it actually inform about this when he writes? Did he really mean to denounce Western—or, indeed, any other kind of—feminism when he praised Ayatollah Khomeini for inaugurating the first non-Western revolution in Iran? If you read biographies of Foucault, you will know this, you will sense this, you will share the connection. It is a big problem, it is a question of how much weight narratives of the self would actually carry in the production of abstract knowledges. The only exception is Mohandas Gandhi and his experiments with truth; there is no difference between text and man. I don't know about feminists and LGBTQI writers. There is the problem of everydayness, how does one enchant it? There is a big issue of the *ensoulment* of writing. Of course, I don't mean soul in the traditional manner. Embodied writing is also a huge question. I am not able to cope with it. But such distancing is the very site for the production of erudite knowledge. It is a fact that much of knowledge production must translate itself beyond the biography/autobiography of suffering. This distancing is considered an epistemic virtue in all the reading of feminists, post-feminists, critical theorists, postmodernists, everybody.

Where it is breached in aid of solidarity, that is also important. I mean, for example, the great tradition of telling stories, of sharing stories, which was started by the critical feminist thinkers. The idea being that knowledges are secreted in intimate conversations, or what happens to people in everyday life. My friend Smadar Lavie, an anthropologist, she wrote an excellent book on Bedouin Palestinian suffering (Lavie 1990), and she has enriched anthropology today because she has chosen the path of archiving raw texts of suffering. There is another example, albeit of a slightly different kind: Pierre Bourdieu and Alain Accardo depicted modern modes of suffering [*The Weight of the World*, 1999]. Despite the fact that there is now a considerable body of work on the anthropology of violence, and some on suffering, there is little work on how belligerent occupation is lived. You have to go to literature, not to philosophy or postmodernism or social movements, to know where you come from.

Look at Gabriel Garcia Marquez, Rohinton Mistry, Mahasweta Devi, Eduardo Galeano. You have to combine both law and literature, and meta-ethics and meta-philosophy. I think it is very important to look at the other, at embodied narratives of other peoples' sufferings, and you have to go to literature for this. I am among those who can study literature of this kind, speak about it, but I don't write it. There are different kinds of intellectual upbringing, others are more fortunate, they have received different kinds of education. Hegel or Marx or Spinoza or Gayatri Spivak, many others indeed, can take the autobiographies of suffering and translate them into high meta-theory. It is a great gift. I pay homage to it, but I don't have it.

LL: Across your writing, there is a constant refrain of literature being the moral understanding of the law, particularly in your writings on Constitutional law. References to Manto, Mahasweta Devi, Rohinton Mistry, etc. A particularly poignant moment in your 3Cs article is when you mention:

> If there was a reference to *Bury My Heart at Wounded Knee*, I somehow missed it. If there was a reference to the unscrupulous annexation of Hawaii and the symbolic shredding of its flag into so many souvenirs (a memory of hurt still alive among many native Hawaiians), I again missed it. The American impoverished figure, portrayed as a fugitive figure of 'have-nots' unburdened by an archive of pain, is even evident in John Grisham's *Street Lawyer*. (Baxi 1999, 1183)

UB: In my mind, I am saying, so what? High theory, gifted theory, great narratives miss the underlying question: the denial of suffering. The question of what is, or can be, considered suffering is one important question. The other, raised a long while ago by St Thomas Aquinas, is: Why should just persons suffer, and the wicked prosper?

Now that 'just' which determines the others 'wicked' is not always easy to configure. For example, some believe in harmony as the principal end of justice, while others believe justice to be a virtue of struggle. Some believe that justice is a cosmic virtue, while others say that it is merely earth-bound or terrestrial. Some believe that existing people owe duties of justice to compatriots (justice within actually existing social orders), others theorise justice as also entailing duties to non-nationals, as having duties of justice to all individuals. Some think of values of justice as entirely a matter of the basic structure of society, others think that justice is a virtue of individual conduct. Those who believe in world justice, the global distributive justice, think that not only are tasks of justice owed to States by other States, but also to non-nationals as well as co-nationals, and to address past discrimination through affirmative action in the present generations, and to future peoples, other species, and objects in 'Nature'. The new accents in which business ethics discourse is now conducted enjoins the human rights responsibilities of multinational enterprises and corporate social responsibility or business voluntarism.

On the first question, some believe that suffering can sometimes be pleasurable, and even joyous, as, for instance, in sports, when sportspersons, referees, and spectators consider violence inflicted within the rules of the game as pleasurable or just. Students of warfare, to take another example, consider killing within the rules of war as pleasurable or just. Depending on your morality, masochistic pleasure is just. One can also take a determinate range of examples to maintain that there is a moral human right to do a moral wrong.

Finally, without being exhaustive, as argued by some 'left legalist' friends, in the five situations I set out in the Preface to *The Future of Human Rights*,[3] the problem of suffering almost vanishes, or, at any rate, it does not loom large. But it is recognised that exploitation, at

[3]"'Left legalists" now tell us that unless the politics for human rights remains vigilantly self-reflexive, "a politics organized around publicizing pain constitutes a further degradation of subaltern selves into a species of

least the imposition of one's will on the other, without any sustainable ethical or moral justification is an evil to be avoided or justly condemned. So, for example, slavery or slave-like labour, trafficking in human beings, forced sex, torture, create suffering that ought to be avoided and condemned. That is also the discursive normativity of human rights.

Derrida and many others talk to us about *writing as violence*. Writing is a kind of violent inscription, and written law is often one such form of violence. I have a friend, Jan Breman, a distinguished student of bonded labour in India, who has done some very good work on what I call disorganised labour. I prefer to call it disorganised labour, not unorganised labour, because it is systematically disorganised. If you use the term unorganised, you are already complicit in the system. You fragment and pulverise associative movements, and then you call it unorganised. This is not my language.

I met Jan Breman in Surat, and I liked his contribution on sugar industry workers (Breman 1978, 1979, 1990, 1994). He has re-crafted labour history in India. You must someday talk to him. Jan wrote a book on the *Dublas*, who are bonded labourers in south Gujarat (Breman 1974). *Dubla* means meek, weakened, and emaciated. I was reading this book, and halfway through it, I was absolutely scandalised. I have never done this before to any book, but I put it away. It is a blasphemy for me to do this, but I was really scandalised. Breman describes the system in south Gujarat whereby the upper castes gain access to the first night of a newly married bride of the *Dublas* as customary law. In south Gujarat, he wrote, it is customary that the first night of the bride is offered to the upper caste.

---

subcivilized nonagency". What, however, if relief of suffering is not the sole basis of worthy political work?' (Baxi 2013c, xxxvii).

'One way to measure the social effect of human rights, Baxi says, is to "index the new forms of justifiable suffering it invents". "Human suffering oriented towards, and caused by, human rights implementation is both creative and destructive of human potential... it is jurisgenerative in a constitutive sense being a form of imposition of secular social suffering"' (ibid., 30–32).

My heart stopped. What does this word 'custom' mean? You give the authority of high social theory to a practice that is bloody and unconscionable. I have not quite understood this, although I understand the research canon that says that you report facts as you find them. In this sense, value-neutrality in description is a virtue. But a discipline, I believe, has also some social responsibility which can be discharged by questioning that practice in so many ways. Particularly the standpoint of the suffering other is quite important. In any event, aren't the facts themselves 'theory-laden'?

There are other examples. I was invited, but I didn't go, to an international conference in Delhi on the sexual trafficking of women, where half the papers said that the problem of sexual trafficking of women is an 'interesting problematic'. These are languages which are bloody-minded and implicated in the very order that they seek to expose.

This could be seen as a certain kind of insistence on semantic purity. There is a problem with the linguistic markets, the semiotic markets of suffering. The commoditising of suffering is seen as a necessary precursor to addressing it. I am not imputing any motive; one needs funding, conferences, etc., to highlight injustice, and commodification is not necessarily a bad term with me. The insensitivity of languages used to produce commoditisation is a problem.

Funded Thought vs Ab-original Thought

UB (***contd***): There would be no history of thought if funding were a requirement for thinking. Take Aristotle, Plato, much of the Western pantheon, take the Upanishadic thinkers, take Gautama Buddha or Prophet Mohammed (among the most inaugural thinkers in the world)—they were all unfunded thinkers. Now does one need a lot of resources for thinking, even about suffering, which is all around us? I think that is the ultimate obscenity. All my life I have avoided it, although it is not considered a great virtue.

I must confess, though, that I have supported anyone who wants funding. As for me, barring the $400 that the US-based Asia Foundation gave me to support my visit to Berkeley, I can honestly say, somewhat proudly, that I have shunned funding for thinking or doing things. The point is that of putting yourself in the difficult situation of penniless thought. I think unfunded thought creates a fiduciary bond between the sources of your thought and suffering humanity, if suffering humanity is the source of your thought—I am not presenting myself as a moral exemplar to anyone, how indeed may I! The question, however, is: Do you need to think about moral questions always with the support of funding, whether it is national or foreign?

There is a difference between philanthropy-endorsed thought and original thinking or (my preferred term) 'ab-original' thinking. 'Original' is already implicated in the networks of knowledge production. 'Originality' is already a set, as Michel Foucault says, of 'certificatory sovereignty'. Originality is that which is certified by knowledge as a commodity produced in the epistemic market. How do you practice ab-original or pre-original thought? One is here reminded of Peter Buffett talking about 'colonial philanthropism'[4] and one may add to his description examples of what might be called the 'cognitive philanthropist'—the so-called gifts of knowledge which are merely variations on orientalisms and accents of paternalism masking varieties of governance and domination.

I think the great merit of LGBTQI thinking, more than that of women's liberation or of animal rights thinking, is that it practices the virtue of ab-original thought in its foundations. It is not a thought that is supported by the governments; it replenishes the very idea of being human at its core. In different ways, though, they all present to us the limits of thought. At stake is the point I am making; the point is that they are engaged in challenging the very idea of thinking in a way that I would say has never really happened before. How do our thought

---

[4] Peter Buffett, son of Warren Buffett and Chairman of NoVo Foundation. See Buffett (2013).

and research practices become examples of unfunded thought, away from our networked thought?

To me, the nearest analogue is the great movement of workers around the world. The movement of the working classes was not funded; the theory produced by it was not funded. Of course, Engels helped Marx, he was a factory owner, and Marx belonged to the bourgeoisie (like most of the academic class or those who belong to the commentariat). But the fact is, the rupture that happened through Marx's work was not dictated by the power of funding. I have here in view the great work of E. P. Thompson, *The Making of the English Working Class* (1991a [1966]), and Jacques Rancière, *Proletarian Nights: The Workers' Dream in Nineteenth-Century France* (2012). Rancière expounds (in the Preface to the new English edition) that: 'For the workers of the 1830s, the question was not to demand the impossible, but to realize it themselves.' And that

> it becomes apparent that workers had never needed the secrets of domination explained to them, as their problem was quite a different one. It was to withdraw themselves, intellectually and materially, from the forms by which this domination imprinted on their bodies, and imposed on their actions, modes of perceptions, attitudes, and a language. (ibid., 10)

I am not talking here of distractions from mass solidarity, such as the formation of labour aristocracy or mercantile or corporate philanthropy elites. I see great parallels between these movements as they begin to define the horizons of thinking. (One may think of many movements, like Dalit movements, 'waves' of feminist movements, the First Nations struggles, the racial equality movement, the movement by people living with disability, and the movements for the integrity of the environment, both late Holocene and early Anthropocene).

A great German thinker who died recently said among the most poignant things I have heard. He said, 'If my friends want to remember me, they should only write this much on my tombstone: "I never asked for a grant to do theory".' I think the craze for funding, as opposed to thinking on your own, is a great misfortune.

To be Human Means to be Open to the Suffering Other

LL: You said that the LGBTQI movement and the animal rights movement poses afresh the question of what it means to be human. The core of your question, of what does it mean to be human, is related to the question of what it means to understand suffering.

UB: To me, it is that simple. Ideas of equality, fraternity, dignity, human rights, what have you—they are related notions. So, the question is: What are they related with? That brings to mind the different histories of emancipation from terror, the French Revolution, the great October Revolution, and so on. So, in answer to your question, if you are not open or vulnerable to the suffering other, you have to ask why you think you say you are human, why are you not a stone, what differentiates you? There are degrees of human-ness. There is a distinction that Martin Heidegger draws between inanimate objects like stones and animals and humans. That is a paradigmatic case. Animals and humans are suffering beings. It is assumed that stones do not suffer. Stones do not have agency or rationality of their own. The question then is: What is the distinction between being a human and being a stone? Assuming these ontologies are correct, what makes us and others 'humans' is that we are different from some orders of inanimate things. I say 'some orders' because it is not just a question of what a 'thing' is; the work of people like Bruno Latour has complicated this question.

The first issue is the question: What constitutes the meaning of the word 'human'? If you say some beings/entities are human and others are not, you must ask a few questions. If you believe that God made man in His own image (*imago dei*), then the discussion ends there. Is it a kind of speciesism (like racism and patriarchy) that says that human beings are the end of creation because the Lord created them? If you think differently, and you ask what makes me say I am a human being, or rather, what it is that makes one human, one way to look at this is to ask: What is the other of human? The other can be many things: an inanimate object in nature, an animal human person, migratory species, predatory species, companion species, and an agent of the anthropogenic harm now threatening life and planet to extinction.

Now what is animate and inanimate is a much greater question. You take the paradigm case of a stone or a rock, why is it inanimate? Is it because it has no agency, it has no language, it does not suffer? Can we say a stone does not suffer when subjected to the meteorological activity of mining? You can say that human beings are different from non-sentient beings and entities. This is a question of naming.

What is a sentient being? Is it having the potential for language? If you do not have language to express your pain, are you sentient? Are rivers, oceans, deserts, mountains sentient? It was once not regarded as obvious that even when they looked like humans, the aborigine peoples, slaves, colonised subjects, and even women and children were not considered fully sentient. This is obvious if you look at all the early accounts of the Spanish Inquisition or of the so-called New World. My favourite writer is Eduardo Galeano. But we do not read Galeano! This is a situation of institutional non-camaraderie where South thinkers do not read other South thinkers, Asian Subaltern Studies does not read Latin American Subaltern Studies. But perhaps that is beside the point here.

Returning to our question, why is language important? What is language? There are sign languages, there are other means and forms of communication, birds and some other species have some form of communication. There are codes which are all sensory communication. I am fascinated by modern biology and life sciences. My favourite thinker is Stephen Jay Gould, who wrote on the life sciences and was a post-Darwinian. There is a human-centred assumption that other sentient beings have no language. We are talking of languages that express pain. It is plainly wrong to say that most animals don't feel pain when they are killed. But one may still want to argue that if they feel pain, they have no language in which to express pain, and that is the distinction between human and non-human.

When Bodily Pain Becomes Social Suffering

UB (***contd***): There is an important distinction here between pain and suffering. Pain is a physical fact. It is a pre-linguistic fact. The whole science of anaesthetics is built on the management of pain. Pain is not linguistically expressed, but it is a phenomenon that can be understood. The question now is: When does pain become suffering? For the moment, the answer is: when sentient beings have a code, which translates bodily pain into social suffering. This is a code which some animals (incidentally, I use a longer description: non-human animal persons contrasted with human animal persons—NHAP/HAP, respectively) don't have, which some birds don't have, which earthworms don't have. That is a serious issue! And here, though I am a severe critic of Jeremy Bentham, he was dead right—more right than he is dead on this score!—when he put forward his theory of utilitarianism and his concern with minimising pain and suffering. He said, what makes human animals and non-human animals comparable is that they can both suffer pain (Bentham 1907 [1789]).[5]

A radical egalitarianism is at work here. He was the first person in the Western discourse to say that what is common between human and non-human animals is the capacity to suffer. Out of that comes the animal rights movement of today. From Peter Singer in the early years, to Martha Nussbaum who has done great work on the frontiers of justice, the question of the translation of pain into suffering continues to persist (Nussbaum 2006; Singer 1990).

[5]Bentham writes::'...What else is it that should trace the insuperable line? Is it the faculty of reason, or, perhaps, the faculty of discourse? But a full-grown horse or dog is beyond comparison a more rational, as well as a more conversable animal, than an infant of a day, or a week, or even a month, old. But suppose the case were otherwise, what would it avail? The question is not, Can they *reason*? nor, Can they *talk*? but, Can they *suffer*?' (see Bentham (1907 [1789], Ch. XVII ('Of the Limits of the Penal Branch of Jurisprudence', n122, para 6). Upen has also edited, and has an introduction which links law with expectation in, Bentham's work (see Baxi 1986e).

This, however, is not an issue only for animals and for non-sentient beings, it remains a question for humans as well. The pain of Bhopal is not translated, even by human rights and constitutional languages, into social suffering (see Chapter 12, this volume). The pain of the 1984 massacre—the genocide—of Sikhs is not regarded as social suffering. The pain of Gujarat, 2002 is scarcely rendered into social suffering. There are other vast examples worldwide of 'mass atrocities,' 'ethnic cleansing,' and gross violations of basic human rights. There are everyday ecological atrocities aggravating the pace of the anthropogenic harm. There are vast issues of how one migrates from individual biographies to social texts.

LL: Then is the core of what it means to be human linked directly to the question of what it means to be able to experience pain?

UB: Yes, at least the capability to translate this into social suffering. I have been attacked by good friends as a suffering-monger, of essentialising the idea of suffering. I am called a negative utilitarian because Bentham built his idea of utilitarianism on the idea of maximising pleasure and avoiding suffering. Avoiding suffering is the negative part. I am characterised as being among suffering-mongers because I speak about suffering at every stage of my writing. Good friends of mine, whom I respect deeply, tell me that it is possible to enjoy life under late capitalism. So my emphasis on suffering is said to diminish the agency of those who are said to suffer. The Planning Commission says the poverty ratio has declined. The average unorganised worker gets more money; everybody has a television, a cell phone. Global capitalism today is in fact replete with stories of access to opportunities and experiences of enjoyment which were denied to the early industrial worker. So they say I am a suffering-monger because I do not look at biophilic possibilities, at life-sustaining possibilities. I have been attacked on the ground of essentialising suffering.

In a Belfast Law School discussion, a question was put to me by some human rights activists. The question was: Suffering is infinitely various, it exists even without capital, so how does anyone speak about it? If suffering is context-bound, agency-bound, history-bound, there cannot be a universal theory of suffering. This is absolutely post-Marxian. The great Uncle Marx spoke about the growth of capitalism as the universal history of immiseration. 'Immiseration' is his word; 'suffering' is perhaps a bourgeois word. And immiseration was for him a cousin to the term that he used with great care, 'exploitation'. In my book on Marx, I narrate my understanding of Marx's notion of exploitation in seven ways (Baxi 1993b).[6] In a post-Marxian world, all this will perhaps become meaningless. But making human misery meaningless, making it invisible, converting it as lying outside history (or its peripheries) is the combined labour of governance, the free market, and neoliberalism. The task of human rights everywhere is, and was, to make it visible. The managers of State, captains of trade and industry, and the gurus of globalisation do not like human rights activists and social movements. That is understandable because it disturbs the present moment of the new normal. But we must also understand that the rightless co-creates the other, and demands the right to decreate the existing world and recreate a new one.

[6]In *Marx, Law and Justice*, Upen elaborates three notions of exploitation in Marx and four Marxian notions of exploitation. Exploitation, according to Marx, has three meanings. First, exploitation may mean the economic use of a resource or an advantage. Second, it may also mean 'turning into account for selfish purposes' or using human beings as means rather than ends. Third, it may mean 'taking unfair advantage of someone'. The four Marxian meanings of exploitation have been elaborated by Arun Bose, G. A. Cohen, John Roemer, and Geoff Hodgson. Bose contends that 'exploitation consists in depriving labour of any significant degree of self-determination relative to the direction of the capitalist production'. Cohen argues that it is the labourer who creates the product; however, the labourer receives less than the value of his labour, and this amounts to exploitation. In Roemer's analysis, exploitation flows out of the fact that the means of production are concentrated in a small group of capitalists and the natural concomitant of this concentration is exploitation. According to Hodgson, exploitation can be pre-contractual or post-contractual. An individual worker is always pre-contractually exploited since he faces the Hobson's choice of starving or selling his labour power. Post-contractual exploitation occurs through the robbery of the time of the labourer, exposure to unsafe conditions of work, and through a possible lack of clarity in the contract, which is often exploited by the employer.

Marx had a whole taxonomy, he did not stop with the swear word—immiseration. Rather, he did two things. He archived ways in which immiseration occurs and how it continuously reproduces itself. He was not concerned with the production of suffering as such, but with the reproduction of suffering. Mohandas Gandhi said much the same thing, and so did B. R. Ambedkar, but in very different accents and modes.

This, to my mind, is a very important notion. Production cannot be separated in Marx from the other key ideas: exchange/distribution, consumption, and reproduction. It is a continuum. Those people who say I don't understand that people may actually enjoy life under capitalism only look at the consumption dimension. I am referring to all four dimensions, particularly reproduction. When I speak of the reproduction of human rightlessness, this is what I mean.

Speaking For and With Others

UB (*contd*): I am not only concerned with the production or consumption of suffering, but also with the reproduction of suffering. When I say that someone else suffers, the question is: Who am I to say that s/he suffers? Who am I to translate that suffering for social action? I would like to have been challenged on this, but it has not happened. I have challenged myself, but I have not been frontally challenged. Maybe it means that what I write is not sufficiently important to provoke this challenge. I accept it. Perhaps I sent you this essay on 'Re-Silencing Human Rights', where I raised the question of the representation of suffering (Baxi 2009c).

Who are you to speak on somebody else's suffering? Instead of going to the root of what suffering is, human rights establish a clear hierarchy of suffering when it says that civil and political rights are to be protected in the here and now, while socioeconomic rights can wait. You are implicitly saying that the suffering involved in the denial of the human right to shelter, food, nutrition, health, etc., is constitutionally legitimate, at least for the present. The Millennium Development Goals are obscene statements. They say, reduce the absolute starvation of 800 million people by 2005. Then they say, by 2010. Then they say, by half. You have a complete immunity to languages of suffering in the codification of the social in international law and policy. That's partly my discontent with Amartya Sen, but that is another story. Nobody said you can reduce suffering overnight, but the question is: How many long nights must pass before you truly attempt to overcome it? How many generations must one endure? That is the important question.

Here we should take some account of organised denial of suffering, and its impacts on those immersed in it already. Organised denial takes State or corporate or combinatory denialism (as most recently in the case of President Donald Trump, who denounced climate change and global warming as a 'hoax' and initiated the process of termination of USA's association from the Paris Agreement, 2005, a process reversed later by President Biden). One does not here subscribe, of course, to any excesses of epistocracy (rule by experts) or legitimate insistence on technoscience accountability and answerability. But the fact that only 3 per cent of concerned scientists disagree on models, methods, and measures needs to be taken seriously; not one scientist denies the facts of accelerating anthropogenic harm.

My favourite, and poignant, work on denialism is Stanley Cohen's *States of Denial* (2001), where he studied at least three forms of human rights denialism: 'Literal, Interpretive and Implicatory denial'. In the first form, 'the fact or knowledge of the fact is denied'; in the second, 'the raw facts (something happened) are not being denied', but 'they are given a different meaning from what seems apparent to others'; and the third form is where 'there is no attempt to deny either the facts or their conventional interpretation', but stand 'denied' or 'minimized are the psychological, political or moral implications that conventionally follow' (pp. 7–8). Cohen's insights remain critically relevant also to new assaults on climate change amelioration (CCA) now. In fact, there is need to relate much discourse on climate change denial (CCD) to violations of core human rights by governmental and corporate denial cultures.

Banishing justice-talk from climate change/global warming is another form of CCD. As Klinsky, et al. (2016) recall, at the Durban Platform Negotiations Todd Stern, US Special Envoy for Climate Change, is said to have declared, 'if equity's in, we're out', and that 'discussions of justice ought to be left out of both academic work and policy discussions because they are conceptually flawed', could 'derail the negotiations,' and 'erode political will'. They rightly contest these views and 'sentiments' as marking 'the emerging post-Paris discourse which suggests that we are in a post-equity era of a voluntary and universal climate agreement'. All these enfeebles ethically viable global social change policy formation, agency-based aggressive institutional and programmatic decarbonisation action, local policy action, and forms of civic engagement urgently required for the prevention of present and near future anthropogenic harm.

Coming back to your point, how do we represent suffering? What is the narrative agency here? In this essay I was just referring to, I look at a distinction of great importance between representation as speaking *for* and speaking *with* other people. I add a further distinction, which I name as representing *after* the event. I ask myself: Have I in all honesty represented anyone in my life? What complicates this is the question: How may anyone represent me? This conversation will show that it is impossible for me to represent myself. The self is postulated as a centrality. But am I the same Upen Baxi since I was born? That's definitely absurd. If I am ever changing, I am not an essence, I can't represent myself. If I can't represent myself in whatever meaning I give to the word 'represent', how can anybody else represent me, or how may I represent any other person?

Now whether this question is metaphysical, epistemological, or ontological, it is, nevertheless, a pressing political question—politics of the normal and the exceptional. And it is certainly a question for activists. What is important for me is not metaphysics or ontology, but this: What burdens does it entail for me to say I represent Bhopal, for example? This is a fiduciary question for me, not an epistemological question. The question is of my moral worth and my moral responsibility when I say that I speak *for* others, *with* others. For me, representation at this level is no more a metaphysical or ethical question, it is a question of social, or intra-subjective, trust. Why should I be trusted when I say I represent you?

LL: Why do you distinguish between the two forms?

UB: I will tell you why. You know the law of contract deals also with agency and the responsibilities of an agent. The question to be determined, often, is: Has the agent fulfilled the mandate? It's a question of mandate. Who gives the mandate? In the world of activism, we give ourselves the mandate to represent others. Mandate is a problem for social contract theory in thinking the State, and so on, but I am thinking here of mandate in the context of social movements. Who has mandated us? We are non-representative persons, we do not belong to any political party.

We set ourselves up as representing somebody else, and contest, on that basis, the actions of representative political institutions. Now, the question is: Who gave us the mandate? The fallback answer is: I am a constitutional being, a sincere moral agent, I need no authorisation. As the Zapatistas said, we don't care for recognition by government, these are our rights, we claim them. The best discussion of this problem of mandate in India is in three opinions, written by Justice M. H. Beg, Justice Jaganmohan Reddy, and Justice K. K. Mathew in *Kesavananda Bharati* (1973). You cannot find a judicial discourse as exciting as this, but who reads it? The question was of mandate and mandatory power—can changing political regimes change the Constitution, and if yes, to what extent? It has largely not been written about, except for some sundry comments by Yours Truly (Baxi 1978b)!

I represent the suffering other, not by virtue of any shared public trust, but because of my individual conscience. What is that individual conscience? Emmanuel Levinas would say, it is an ethical conscience open to the vulnerability of the suffering other. What is the claim of activism in comparison to that of institutions of representational democracy? Activism is a self-defined act. I do not need to contest elections, I do not need any qualifications, I do not need to attend election rallies in hot summers, I do not need to get assassinated, persecuted for corruption, and all those things that go with politics in India today, which we criticise. Just imagine addressing a rally of one lakh people in Uttar Pradesh or Andhra Pradesh or Telangana in May in pursuit of an electoral victory. It's a very difficult and demanding turf.

LL: I asked why you separate the two, the ethical and the activist. The reason is because of what one finds in the world of activism; I will give you a recent example, I was in Delhi for a meeting and Dunu Roy was there.[7] He said, I am not alone here, I speak for 40,000 people. I don't understand that.

UB: I will share with you a letter addressed by Binayak Sen's brother, who is a stockbroker in Canada.[8] It is a very poignant letter, I just read it this morning. He said, my dear brother, *tum akele nahi ho, hum tumhare saath hain* [you are not alone, we are with you]. It is a very nice warm feeling. The question here is of the connection between representation and solidarity. The issue becomes that of mobilising solidarity, rather than representation. The collectivisation of one's energies to fight evil is what I call solidarity. When something we describe as evil needs to be fought, and we get together to do that, that is solidarity. The question of representation can fade into the background.

I have always been careful not to raise the distinction too articulately in the Indian context because it is said to diminish solidarity. Metaphysical or epistemological interrogation will of course expose this duality. Obviously, the concern there is not with solidarity as such, but with representation as generative of solidarity. If you say what you mean by representation, they will say, *hum tumhare saath hain* (we are together, we walk with you).

---

[7] Dunu Anorbotto Roy is Director of the Hazards Centre, Delhi.

[8] Binayak Sen: paediatrician, public health specialist and activist, national Vice-President of People's Union for Civil Liberties (PUCL). He was sentenced to life imprisonment in 2010 by Raipur Sessions Court, Chhattisgarh under the sedition law, which was later upheld by the High Court of Chhattisgarh. This conviction triggered a campaign for his release. He was granted bail in April 2011 by the Supreme Court of India.

Let me tell you a favourite story. When I was Dean of Delhi Law Faculty (1973–1975), the stunning Tarkeshwari Sinha,[9] former Member of Parliament from Patna, came to visit us. She went into *shairi* mode, praising my hair, my beauty, and all that! After a while, I said, Tarkeshwari-*ji*, this is very kind of you, but let us talk about something else. She said, yes Professor, what would you like to talk about? I said, you are an MP and a poet, let us talk about the problems of India. She had this big beautiful smile, and she said, Professor, how can you talk about 700 million people through this one mouth? She was a parliamentarian, not a Hegel, or a Spivak, or a Derrida, or a Foucault.

I was stunned by what she said. That representation as speaking *for* is an inconceivable standard. You can't speak *for* indeterminate, innumerable, unnameable groups of people whose first names you don't even know. This is the most gigantic hoax. But liberal politics is based on the idea that some people can speak *to* and even *for* others during the mandated term of five years. Obviously, they don't speak for them. So, you have a crisis of liberal representation all the time. You have all these articles exposing the perfidies of representation, nepotism, corruption, etc. The question, however, is not about the perfidies of representation, but of how you can ever speak for people you don't know, have not met, and will never meet? Yet 'representation'/'mandate' are what Castoriadis maintained are 'socially necessary illusions' (Castoriadis 1998 [1987]). Or we may put these as necessary legal, and even social, fictions, which nevertheless play an important role in constituting the law and the social.

That is where we move on to the question of speaking *with* people, as Gayatri Spivak says.[10] Speaking *to* the people is politics, speaking *for* them is social activism, speaking *with* people is the new politics. We are

[9]Tarkeshwari Sinha (1926–2007), member of Lok Sabha from Patna and later from Barh, Deputy Finance Minister in Nehru's union cabinet (1958–1964).

[10]'Law, Social Movements and the Subaltern: Articulating Postcolonial Predicaments', Conversation between Gayatri Chakravorty Spivak and Upendra Baxi on 25 June 2006, at the Max Mueller Bhavan, Bangalore.

out here because we think we are the better half. We have never soiled our hands with dirty politics. Theoretical minds are unsullied by the very democratic process they otherwise so eminently seek to serve. The distinction between menial and mental labour is acute in modern democracies. The menial labour, the dirty work, that is all done by those involved with electoral politics, which we are quick to scoff at or condemn. We, the NGOs (non-governmental organisations), the progressive intellectuals, hold a mirror up to them. We speak *with* the people, and they speak *for* the people.

This is what is at the heart of *Supreme Court and Politics* (Baxi 1980) as well as of *Courage, Craft and Contention* (Baxi 1985b). In a different vein, so is it at the heart of my book on *The Future of Human Rights* (2013c).[11] I talk in it about politics *of* and *for* human rights. Let us assume you can speak *with* others, then the question is one of the ethics of speaking *with* others. That is why I distinguish, in Chapter 7 of *The Future of Human Rights*, between human rights movements and human rights markets. Human rights markets cannot speak *with* others almost by definition. Human rights movements may and can. Now what does this mean? What is the ethic of speaking *with*? Of course, answers may differ, this may be answered very differently in Latin America or Africa. We must ask the question, what are the Indian instances of speaking *with* people? I would like to find five examples in India in recent times, outside the romantic parade of participation in the World Social Forum (WSF). Is it Bhopal, is it the 1984 or the 2002 'riots', is it PUCL (People's Union for Civil Liberties)/PUDR (People's Union for Democratic Rights), is it the LGBTQI movement, the feminist movement? This is in part a rhetorical question.

I can definitely situate some answers, but that is not the point here. The point is to illustrate that we enter a stormy voyage when we speak of the ethics of speaking *with* others. There are histories and intellectual traditions of speaking *for* others—Rousseau, Locke, Hobbes, Gandhi, Mandela—hundreds, there are thousands of such people. It is a rich heritage. But there is very little craft, and very little theorising, of speaking *with* others. You can say *X* does not speak *for*

[11] Also discussed in Baxi (2009c).

Narmada, you can say *Y* does not speak *for* Bhopal, and so on. We have opinions, but no articulation of the ethics of speaking with others.

LL: The tension is, as it were, also where the answer seems to lie. The question of 'what does it mean to represent another' is this: 'what does it mean to count yourself' is indistinguishable from 'what does it mean to speak with others'. Because the problem seems to be the ethical grammar by which one can speak with others and account for oneself. What is lost in the politics of mobilisation, the politics of NGO language, mainstream politics, or the language of certain large-scale State interventions is that it does not have the grammar with which you have to account for yourself as being linked to how you speak for others.

AN: Would you refer to Gandhi as in some senses speaking *with*? He has this ability to break this representation question. Your actions change with the response of people around you.

UB: Mohandas Gandhi and Martin Luther King Jr. are probably the most contemporary exemplars of speaking *with* others. Mobilisation for emancipation, a tidal wave of ethical solidarity. But that is totally romantic. Mohandas has been criticised as speaking *for* others. For example, he was criticised by Ambedkar for speaking *for* Dalits. On the other hand, Ambedkar's main claim to eminence was that he spoke *with* them, never *for* them. If you see, Mohandas' *satyagraha* was about challenging ideas of purity, fighting for temple entry, etc. In contrast, Ambedkar's first *satyagraha*—the Mahad *Satyagraha* of 1927—was not about temple entry, it was about access to drinking water in the village well.

Now you tell me who spoke *for* or *with*. Ambedkar's jurisprudence of basic needs is a speaking *with*, while Mohandas' jurisprudence of sacred equality is a speaking *for*. This is a very delicate difference to decipher. The more we attempt to read through discursive events, the less we can decide on a universal strategy of struggle. So, how do we get there? I think the way to get there is to study actual discursive formations; for instance, did Jyotiba Phule speak *for* or *with*? All the early nationalist leaders, did they speak *for* or *with* the people? And then compare this with the later generation of leaders, with Nehru,

Jinnah, Bose. All this present discourse on postcoloniality in India is not really addressing this question, this boundary, because this distinction is not really made apparent.

AN: Speaking *with* is not a question of representation.

UB: No. But one way to make it intelligible to the modern mind is to approach it via representation. Are 'speaking *with*' and 'representation' contradictory or complementary? Some people would say they are complementary because speaking *for* generates the need for speaking *with*. But it is also contradictory, because we contest the dominant politics of representation by finding alternate modes of representation. NGO-ised political speech is not that alternative. That alternative is 'speaking *with*'.

AN: When you say speaking *with*, you also link it back to the question of location. If you are embedded in a certain kind of milieu or context, are you better able to speak *with*? For example, if you look at Ambedkar's submissions to the Simon Commission on the conditions of the depressed classes in the cotton mills, he understands caste dynamics in the industry and how even within the labouring class, the upper caste monopolises the better jobs and perpetrates a caste-based discrimination against the Dalits. Ambedkar had not met all the Dalit communities, yet he has a fine-tuned sense of the experiences of Dalit communities because of his location.

UB: The important thing is to understand the voice of anguish of the immediately affected person, the cry. Voice and cry are very complicated things. Location is absolutely critical to be able to engage with this voice or cry. In solidarity movements, and amongst activists, it becomes possible only when they are localised and they are trans-localised at the same time. So, for example, your struggle needs to understand the struggle of the Zapatistas in some uncommon yet common place. Social movements have to narrate the experience of localised struggle, but they should also be able to relate to similar localised struggles elsewhere. What then constitutes local and international solidarity networks is already defined as trans-local. The local is very important, but if you are in the business of linking up severally placed locals, how will you go about it? That is a very difficult question.

The crisis of subaltern studies, South Asia style, is exactly this—its inability to enable and forge links between similar narratives from, say, Latin America. The focus on the local might be the strength of subaltern studies, but it is also its limit. The globalisation of subaltern studies becomes a problem; I am very sensitive to this. I have discovered a lot of South Africans through Anglophone African studies. There is already a restlessness about the hegemony of South Asian subaltern studies. If you take the local as a unique property, then it is also the limit of your universe. If we take the specifically local which E. P. Thompson (Thompson 1991b) describes as the commons, then it is also important to look at the uncommon commons of many locals. And it is there that we may want to build bridges of solidarity without becoming global or globalised. That is another kind of resistance.

Coming back to Ambedkar, if Bhimrao was anything, he was completely local. But the Dalit movement is also intensely global or trans-local. It looks at the African experience, it contrasts itself with race. Dr Gnana Aloysius and Josna Jacob have produced a series of brilliant monographs called *Critical Quest*.[12] As early as in 1975 or 1976, Josna Jacob came to a convention on unorganised (I call it 'disorganised') labour, where she asked a profound question on the experience of being rights-violated. It struck me then that you cannot speak about the experience of rights without the experience of certain molestations. The experience of starvation, of sexual exploitation. If you have not experienced this in your own lifetime, then speaking *with* others requires a very high degree of moral engagement. Speaking *with* others means sharing their pain and suffering in autobiographical terms, which then lends itself to emancipatory possibilities. This may be one logic for the link between biography and social texts. Another logic may be that of empathy and fellow feeling, but they are different.

Coming back to the ethic of speaking *with* others, it is not pre-given. There are some people like Gayatri Spivak and others who converse with us on whether the subaltern can speak (Spivak 1988). The question is, how may this contribute to solidarity struggles which

---

[12] See http://www.criticalquest.info/aboutus.html (accessed February 2022).

are also instances of speaking *with* others? How do we speak a non-UN language through an exchange of narratives of intensely local and autobiographical experiences? How do we attempt to speak outside of the languages which are hegemonic? I really have no answer to this. But maybe this names the struggle. The point of struggle is, to put it very crudely, that you only know it by doing it.

The constant making and re-making of the self in response to a genuinely shared sense of suffering: isn't this what we call being human? That is not easily translatable, and it cannot be. So we have to get to someplace else, beyond this local and trans-local. The question is not of the primacy of the local, or of other sites such as the global or the trans-national. The question is: How do we invent languages of sharing pain beyond these maps?

We have languages of human rights, we have languages of justice, of solidarity, but are they good enough? That is why I like Julius Stone's idea of the fellowship of learning.[13] A fellowship of learning is at all times a process of mutual unlearning. So, what are these languages, then? There is an increasing sense that all ethical languages, the languages of welfare, of human rights, of justice, are now coming to an end in this, our post-human era. These are all complicated processes. The question persists, nevertheless: What forms of languages may we bring to the world of suffering?

LL: Bhrigupati Singh is doing his thesis[14] in Rajasthan on farmer suicides, and he seems to be asking a similar question. He contrasts, for example, the right to food campaign, which attempts to speak to the very material conditions of suffering, but there is a big gap between the conditions of its own representation form, whether in a court of law or as a public mobilisational strategy, to actually speaking with people. There isn't any ability to speak with people, even though there is an attempt to address their material conditions. In his own experience of spending time with the people, it seems that the condition of speaking with occupies an impossible domain which often takes the realm of

[13] Fellowship of juristic learning. See Stone (1965), discussed in 'Revisiting Social Dimensions of Law and Justice in a Posthuman Era' (Baxi 2007e).

[14] Now published as Singh (2015).

spiritual experience and the careers and lives of gods and goddesses in a local area. There seems to be a disjunct between the human rights language and languages that are required to speak with people, because the cultural forms of languages which communicate beyond the immediacy of pain and suffering is what one does not have access to in the language of human rights.

UB: Yes, speaking *with* others requires an immersion, and immersion cannot happen if it is entirely secular. That is the point he is probably making. People who are in desperate straits often take recourse to other worlds beyond this one, in search of succour in the face of suffering. In any case, peoples of faith are not easy to communicate with if your credentials are entirely and radically 'secular'. Whether one wants to validate this discourse or not is a different question. The work that anthropologists do in speaking of suffering from within the world of magical beliefs and support systems is alien to contemporary human rights languages. The end result of human rights logics and languages is the secularisation of beliefs and practices.

Beyond the fold of the surface (isn't it that Michel Foucault acutely spoke of depth as a fold on the surface), when you immerse yourself within the local in order to come to terms with—even, perhaps, to actually experience the deprivations of others—you don't do it only to establish relationality, but also to engage in an intense questioning of the authenticity of the self. The ability to say, trust me, I am with you and almost like you, is also an act of transformative politics. God-persons offer the possibility of redemption and transformation through an engagement with the other-worldly. Human rights activists do not have that kind of trust. Some would say that the poverty of human rights discourse is this distance between suffering and its redress. To be noted also is the insensitivity of alienated human rights discourse, particularly the complex law of human rights or the Spartan beauty of the moral idea of human rights. Then there are always competing claims in social activism. A long time ago, I read this book by the Swiss psychologist Eric Berne, called *What Do You Say After You Say Hello?* (1969). Your own groups, your own people, they want to know, at the end of the day, how all this translates their experience of pain and suffering. This is where reflexive activism takes its first steps. If we don't grant this, we are almost at the borderline of speaking *to* the people when we imagine we are speaking *for*, or *with*, them.

This has always worried me. I appeared as party-in-person in the Supreme Court in [the Narmada dam case] (see Chapter 12). Our line of argument was a fundamental one. We were saying that the Madhya Pradesh government was in violation of the orders of the [Narmada Water Disputes] Tribunal and of the Supreme Court. We were saying, a rehabilitation programme that does not give land for land, but gives cash for land which is easily spent, falls foul of the Constitution, even of the Tribunal Award. Hence, the special rehabilitation packages must be invalidated. I argued this passionately and vehemently on behalf of eminent persons who filed the writ petition.

In my written submissions, I argued that the concept of republican citizenship is the concept of equal regard for all citizens. Those in peril here are not only project-affected persons, but they are also citizens who are project-affected. And I said to the court, you are not justices, but rather, citizen justices. At the end of a book by William Dicey, who wrote of the idea of law and public opinion in the nineteenth century, is this ghastly quote: 'You should never make the mistake of weighing butcher's meat on diamond scales',[15] 'butcher's meat' being colonial subjects, and 'diamond scales' being the rule of law. I quoted this before the court and argued that in a republic, there is no butcher's meat, there are only diamond scales. This bewildered and scandalised some 'super citizen' law persons assembled in the Court!

Then I asked myself the question: Was I speaking *for* or *with* the people? What were the consequences of my submissions before the court? All these people were being parted from their land, they were being offered peanuts in cash in lieu of land, and the dam was under construction. Did we put them back at the tender mercy of the Government of Madhya Pradesh? We won a symbolic victory; the court, without stating this in so many words, invalidated the fraud.

[15]'The homely saying, that you ought not to weigh butcher's meat in diamond scales, has a practical weight which is overlooked by paradoxical thinkers.' In Dicey (1919 [1905], 141), discussed in Baxi (2016c).

But the question remains: What entitles me to present this argument on their behalf? I don't know a single person from there. Not one tribal from Madhya Pradesh affected by the dam knew us. This was not the case in other situations [like the Agra Protection Home Case], but generally I have been haunted by this question, for Social Action Litigation has been bedevilled and tormented by this question (see Chapters 10 and 12).

In a letter petition, the *Agra Home* case, Lotika Sarkar and I went to Agra to visit the women in the protection homes and met 100 women there at the cost of my teaching commitments.[16] Five of us went, we spoke to these women, and asked them, is this something you want us to do, we don't know what we can do, but we will try. Finally, what is it that we did? There were 100 women in a very small room, with one toilet and one kitchen next to it, and many of them were victims of STD [Sexually Transmitted Diseases]. We later discovered that some had AIDS. It was a devastating experience, we found it very difficult.

I did it again in Bhopal, I did it consistently for many decades. I would still do it. This question is not only about what I did, but it is also now a methodological, epistemological, even philosophical question. It is the question of the material labours of representation.

---

[16]See *Dr Upendra Baxi (I) vs. State of Uttar Pradesh and Anr.*, (1983) 2 SCC 308.

> Similarly, in Dr. Upendra Baxi v. State of U. P. (1981) 3 Scale 1137 when it was found that the inmates of the Protective Home at Agra were living in inhuman and degrading conditions in blatant violation of Article 21 of the Constitution and by reason of their socially and economically disadvantaged position, they were not in a position to move the Court for judicial redress, two law professors of the Delhi University addressed a letter, to this Court seeking enforcement of the constitutional right of the inmates under Article 21 by improvement of the living conditions in the Protective Home, so that the inmates can live with human dignity in the Protective Home. This Court treated the letter as a writ petition and permitted the two law professors to maintain an action for an appropriate writ for the purpose of enforcing the constitutional right of the inmates of the Protective Home and providing judicial redress to them.

Of actually lived labours, of the embodied labours of representing somebody, of speaking *with* others. 'Speaking *with* others' is a phrase, but it is also a real and engaged set of material practices of labour, and not just a metaphysical set of thoughts or ambitions. That's where I differ from most of the other discourse on this question. For me, it is about embodied labour and practice. The next question then is, what is embodied labour? I do theory also, that is embodied labour; you record all of this, that is embodied labour; there is nothing in life that is not embodied labour. If that is so, you can ask: What is the great thing about this notion? To which my answer is, embodiment or disembodiment lies in the way of exemplifying the vulnerability of the suffering other. It is an exemplification, not a virtue to be broadcasted. It is worth trying, worth attempting.

In retrospect, I have had a rich life, a life rich in suffering with others. We still receive letters and postcards from people, saying you have made some difference to our lives. This is more of a return than all these publications and honours, and these are more precious testimonies, if only because they intimate that you actually spoke *with* others, not just *for* others. That is the only symbolism of it. Not anything else, not that the system has changed, or that there has been a revolution. Nothing of that sort.

My great example is of Justice D. A. Desai and Justice Chinnappa Reddy *garu* in their judgment in *D.S. Nakara vs. Union of India*,[17] the case on the denial of fixed pension benefits in the wake of the recommendations of the Third Central Pay Commission. The judgment in this case was an ironical instance of Gandhian socialism in the Supreme Court, but *Nakara* worked, and the decision made the government restore pension benefits to all pensioners. The loveliest story in my life is that Dhirubhai not only received a large number of letters from senior citizens, but they also met annually across India to thank Justice Desai for his act of justice. They never met this man, they never understood the court decision, they only knew the facts. Now the question is, did Dhirubhai speak *with* or *for* the other?

[17] AIR 1983 SC 130.

There is also what I call speaking *after*, as with the Bhopal victims, victims of the Skih massacres in Delhi, 1984, and the victims of the 2002 Gujarat riots. We were not there speaking *with* them, but we were there speaking *after* what happened. I agree that this is not a very neat theoretical category. Speaking *after* the event is also an act of solidarity; in a sense, it is an act of speaking *with*, although one is speaking *after* the event. Although this is very nebulous, I distinguish between features of speaking *for* and speaking *with*, and of speaking *after* the event. You cannot always be in the place where injustice happens. In fact, you are always somewhere else when injustice occurs. Not being in the business of representing people, we do not speak *for* them, we are speaking *after* them. Speaking *after* is in fact a way of speaking *with* them.

LL: We have now arrived at a slightly perverse place in the post-identity world. There is always this anxiety about speaking *for*, such that you don't even speak *with*. You are so self-conscious about representation politics.

UB: Yes. It has become an enormously stylised discourse. In the real world, it matters a great deal. Is Mother Teresa speaking *with* me or *after* me on the streets of Calcutta? It matters a great deal to sex workers that they are helped with access to antiretroviral drugs. Gayatri Spivak has a very good phrase, 'strategic essentialism', which I often use. There is something wrong with essentialising identities. It is, of course, essentialising to say that certain communities are suffering. As Arvind has pointed out in his work and activism, we know LGBTQI communities are not homogeneous. They are diverse, yes, but to say that the rights of minorities to their sexual conduct affects different communities differently can be an act of strategic essentialism.[18]

The Convention on the Elimination of All Forms of Discrimination against Women (CEDAW) is another example.[19] It speaks for women

[18] See Baxi's Forewords to *Human Rights Violations Against the Transgender Community* (PUCL-K 2003) and *Queer: Despised Sexuality, Law and Social Change* (Narrain 2004).

[19] The Convention on the Elimination of All Forms of Discrimination against Women (CEDAW), adopted in 1979 by the UN General Assembly,

across the world when it says, do not discriminate amongst women. We know there are rural and urban women, white and coloured women, and the CEDAW is a comprehensive encyclopaedia essentialising the notion of women, yet it is considered a radical human rights document. We know there is no such thing as Indigenous People, and the Tribal People's Convention 1989 floundered for twenty years before the notion of a trans-local Indigenous Peoples' movement came to be accepted. An indigenous person is one whom the community accepts as such. There cannot be a mechanism of identification from the outside.

Sometimes essentialising is a way to write the future of resistance, and that's what strategic essentialising means. You know what you are doing is not right in terms of stabilising identities, but it is the right thing to do for movements which offer a new register of difference. This is what I call activist pragmatism and human rights pragmatism. Postmodernists say that all our identities are non-essentialised, everything is a floating signifier, but where do we get from here? It is, however, very important as an activist to be aware of the hegemonic ascription of identity.

In *The Future of Human Rights* (2013c), I speak of the human right to identity in many ways. Identity consists of practices of identification. So the human right to identity means the right to choose practices of identification. The ability to say I am, this is important, but the right to exit such chosen identities, which I call the right to vanish from one's own identity, is equally important. There is a third right to manage the conflict of identities. Also important is the right to switch identities and the right to fight against primordial identities. Speaking *with* people gives you these kinds of dilemmas. Speaking *for* people gives you identity politics. This is a very important distinction.

The most important problem is not the floating signifiers in the shopping mall of identities, but that of movement. A born untouchable remains an untouchable. This exclusion needs to be attacked. This

---

consists of a preamble and thirty articles that define discrimination against women and set up an agenda for national action to end such discrimination. It is often described as an international bill of rights for women.

so-called primordial identity is a violation of the right to choose practices of self-identification. Identity as a category is nothing but a set of practices of identification. This provides agency against history. History gives me certain identities, but the right to identity gives me a repertoire to challenge history, to challenge primordiality. This is what you learn from Babasaheb Ambedkar, but also differently from Freud, Jung, or Lacan.

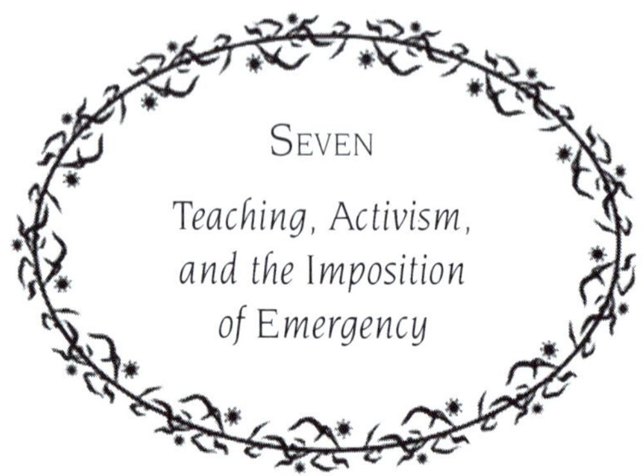

Seven

Teaching, Activism, and the Imposition of Emergency

Return to Delhi

LL: When you decided to return to Delhi, what were they offering you?

UB: A professorship in law in the Delhi Law Faculty. I arrived there on 8 January 1973, just before noon. I will tell you how I remember the date. We were going to stay in the Delhi University guest house for a little while at least, but I did not know where it was. Dean K. B. Rohatgi said to me, come to my office first, somebody will take you to the guest house from there. And when I got there, he said, Baxi, don't go anywhere until you write a joining report. I said, my children are in the car, they are very tired. He said, no, you must write the joining report before 12 PM. If you join in the forenoon, you will be said to have joined the faculty on the eighth, but if you join in the afternoon, you will be deemed to have joined on the ninth. I asked how it mattered. He said, it matters for seniority. He kept me there while he dictated my joining report and had me sign it. This was my first encounter with Delhi University bureaucracy! I have never filed a joining report elsewhere, save again at DU when I re-joined the Faculty after resigning the Vice-Chancellorship; but this report was probably lost *en route*, wreaking havoc with the fixation of pension, which is perhaps amongst the lowest among Professors in DU.

Long before this day, however, around the middle of 1971, I had come to Delhi to meet the Vice-Chancellor, Sarup Singh,[1] because someone wrote to me saying there was some time frame within which I must accept the offer. I was going to New York from Sydney, and I decided to go from New York to Delhi. I suffered from terrible sinusitis in Sydney, I think it must have been those long flights that cured me forever! Sarup Singh was a lovely man. He said, you are the youngest person I have invited to be professor, you must have some regard for Delhi University, you should join us within six months, that is only appropriate. I said, thank you very much Vice-Chancellor, you are quite right, it is a great honour indeed. Now, if I was in the business of selling potatoes in Sydney and you had asked me to come sell potatoes in Delhi, I would have packed my bags immediately and come here. Unfortunately, I am a teacher, and our academic calendar runs from January to December. I feel responsible for the courses I teach, and some of the courses I do, nobody else can do—for example, the course on law and indigenous people. He rose from his chair and said, young man, are you suggesting that we are selling potatoes in Delhi University? I said, far from it, nothing like it, that is just an analogy. He didn't care much for the analogy!

In any case, he went on to say, we would like to have you. I said, I would like to join you in the fall, but I have two other stipulations. One, I don't want to be involved in any administrative work, give me five years before that, and put me at the most on one or two committees. He said, you cannot stipulate conditions so early. I said, no, this is why we are talking. What is your second condition, he asked me. I said, this

[1]Sarup Singh (1917–2003), faculty member at Kirori Mal College, Vice-Chancellor of the University of Delhi (1971–1974), member of the Rajya Sabha from Haryana (1978–1984) representing the Lok Dal party, and Governor of Gujarat.

one, it is not a condition, it is merely a request. The paygrade for this job is from Rs 1,100–1,500. As a senior lecturer in Sydney, my salary is several times more, there is no comparison, and I am not comparing. It would, however, help, what with having two children and all, if you can put me at the top of the grade at Rs 1,500 so that I can at least make do. He said, this is not possible, we have only two professors, and the one makes Rs 1,300 and the other Rs 1,350. I said, forget it, I don't want to create bad blood for a few hundred rupees, no problem. As it happened, I was illegitimate in the eyes of my senior colleagues; the others had been teaching for twenty to twenty-five years, I was a rookie in comparison, and I had also never taught in India before.

LL: You were just thirty-five then?

UB: I don't remember, I must have been thirty-four or thirty-five, yes. Sarup Singh made me the Professor-in-charge of Law Centre 2, where the evening classes were run. So I was Professor in the Law Faculty which was in Old Delhi, and Professor-in-charge of Law Centre 2, which was in Dhaula Kuan in south Delhi.

We found a house in East of Kailash. Delhi is a city of distances. The problem was how to get around the city, taxis were expensive. I had my first superannuation from New South Wales, 5,000 Australian dollars, and I was told that would pay the price of a car, a Fiat maybe, or an Ambassador. I went to Udyog Bhawan, but I was warned that I would have to bribe someone before I got my foreign exchange permit. I met this undersecretary, Ganesh Pandian, I still remember his name, a very bright young man. After I had explained the purpose of my visit to him, he asked me to go have a cup of tea and come back in half-an-hour. I was not sure what to make of this. Imagine my surprise when, in less than half-an-hour, he had my permit ready. I said, Mr Pandian, this is unbelievable! I was told all kinds of things. He said that it is our misfortune that the bureaucratic classes are all tarred with the same brush, but are not all the same!

My experience with Customs, however, was not the same at all. My baggage arrived from Sydney and there was nothing in it to levy duty on, it was all books, clothes, and so on. But I was very fond of classical music, I had a player and nearly 1,000 LP records. The player looked new. I said, fine, charge me duty on that. But then they claimed the records were also new, there are no scratches on it. I said, they are not new, I have been playing them. They levied a heavy duty. I didn't have that kind of money, so I let them put my baggage in the godown while I went on appeal. I met the Assistant Commissioner of Customs, I waited for two hours to meet him, and I said, I am a teacher of law, this is wrong. Everyone tells me I should grease some palms, but I am not going to do that, you can put it to auction if you like, but these are my life's treasures. What will you do, he asked me, if you don't get them back? I said, I may write about the episode later on, that is all I can do! After studying the matter for some time, he said, I am ashamed of my staff's behaviour. He reversed the order and made sure the goods came to East of Kailash. He became a very good friend of mine, and probably studied law later on.

Driving in Delhi was very difficult, people overtook you from all sides, no one followed any rules. I would turn off the car in the middle of the road and let traffic overtake me from all sides to make a scene. I must have made twenty such scenes. Street theatre, Baxi style! To those who challenged me, I would say, you cannot overtake from the wrong side. And they would say, there are no lanes in Delhi. For three years I suffered from massive colon problems, until I found out that among the eighteen reasons for them, the seventeenth was stress related to driving. I then decided to 'join' them, since I could not beat them!

SRK: Were you thirty-two or so when you joined DU?

UB: Ram! This is a bit much; my age at any given time is a matter of public record! Anyway, I think so.

SRK: When you became the Vice-Chancellor in Surat, you were thirty-nine?

UB: From 1982–1985, I was Vice-Chancellor, South Gujarat University. In 1991, I was hit by the Delhi University Vice-Chancellorship.

I also travelled briefly and was at Duke University, and in NSW Law School in Australia.

Teaching in Delhi Law Faculty, Law Centre 2

LL: We were talking about the Delhi years, and Pratiksha helped by sending us a list of milestones and signposts.

UB: More like millstones!

LL: The list we have goes like this:

- Emergency 1975
- Mathura 1980–1983
- Bhagalpur
- 1984 riots in Delhi
- 1985 riots in Gujarat
- Bhopal
- Oleum Gas Leak
- Mandal
- Babri Masjid demolition 1992
- Gujarat pogrom 2002

What were the defining moments from the time you came back?

UB: These are lots of questions! Many of these touch on my life. Let us try and reach out to some of these experiences.

The university gloriously breached its promise to not give me any administrative assignment for a few years and put me in charge of Law Centre 2, which was in Dhaula Kuan, quite far in south Delhi and away from the campus. The college did not want us, so it gave us one office room, one room for all the staff to share, and one mid-sized male urinal, which was closed up and made into a library. That is where I began my first administrative labours. I was very perturbed by it, not because the office wing should be a palatial place, but because it should have been less crammed and the library should have been larger. We had a lovely group of students and I taught jurisprudence and all kinds of other things, but it was difficult to get in and out of a one-room office because students jostled at the entrance for various services!

Both the law school and the Centre had to make allocation choices. There were certain subjects that no one wanted to teach, like income tax, sales tax. Due to my inability to keep my mouth shut, I said there must be some principle by which we choose who should teach such subjects, since somebody must teach it. Since it was unfair to impose it on anybody, I proposed that the responsibility should rotate, and that the youngest to senior-most should take turns in teaching them.

I had no idea that I was sealing my fate when I proposed this rotation! The suggestion was received most happily, since I was the youngest; but also, by virtue of my rank, I was the senior-most! This ended with my being landed with the task of teaching estate duty. I had, however, neither taught nor studied the subject before. But after teaching it, I realised how important the implications of estate duty were for Hindu Undivided Families (HUF), and my colleague Baldev Kohli, who taught Hindu law, was very glad that this allocation had happened. Each lecture of forty-five minutes roughly took nine hours of reading—a working habit I developed early. For estate duty, I made myself familiar with the first fifteen sections, and that consumed a whale of further time. Little was I prepared to discuss the principles of charging and exemptions thereto. In the first class, some students asked me how much duties will be levied, and I said I had not travelled beyond fifteen sections! I was also not prepared to find some assistant controllers of estate duty; they obviously knew all about the incidence of levying. Learning and co-learning law with a mix of students, some young and some more experienced in the working of the law, was a great experience, and I am sad that evening law has been abolished altogether now. Anyway, I must have taught the subject with such passion that in a few years the death duties were abolished, so I must have contributed to law reform indirectly! Not a small contribution to legal reform, won't you say?

I also taught legislative drafting and statutory interpretation. It is a silly Neanderthal manner of law teaching that separates statutory interpretation and drafting from jurisprudence. When you speak of the judicial process, you are speaking of how judges interpret the law, and you cannot study judicial interpretation separately from legislative drafting and from jurisprudence. Subsequently, I was alloted teaching of administrative law, without which I also believe one may not fully understand the relation between the State and the law.

In running the institution, I made the 'mistake' of following the rules with respect to attendance, examinations, etc., with the consequence that for the first time in the history of the institution, 100 or so students were found not eligible to take their exams. One day, when I came home from the Centre, I found Prema struggling to give tea to 100 students who were outside my house. All the students who were not allowed to take their exams were there. We had just returned from Sydney, and Prema was saying apologetically, I will give you all tea in a moment, it is just that we do not have so many cups. I said to them, why are you here, this is not my office, you cannot come here. They said, we cannot ask you for favours in the office as it has now become a rule-bound place. I said, I cannot do anything, I am not the only authority, there is the Vice-Chancellor, and there are Bar Council rules which I have to follow. I found that the faculty dealt with such matters case by case as a matter of discretion and I had a huge normative conflict. I was very cross with my friend K. B. Rohatgi, the Dean, for the relaxed attitude. (I should perhaps have been more informed by my own experiences in Bombay University.) I said to Dean Rohatgi that the difference between us is that I am practising a rule of law jurisprudence and you are practising Kunj Behari jurisprudence (I also practised their first names arduously because they were not easy to access in the pre-internet era. I developed very early the habit of calling my colleagues by their first names!)! Ultimately, I have come to see that the difficulty of legal education in India is not just that of pedagogy and of curriculum, but it is also of the failure to implement rules. If the whole point of legal education is to teach the virtue of performing rules, then we have not succeeded in imparting legal education. Or, the other view is simply that it is the number of humane exceptions that determine rule-following cultures—quite a different meaning from what Carl Schmitt means when he writes about 'states of exception'. In the case of student 'sovereignty', it is the sovereignty of the multitude that determines, from time to time, what the rule means. Michel Foucault had a poignant phrase in *Discipline and Punish*—'mass illegalities'. I wonder at times whether this is a problematic of State formation in India, or if the problems are more accurately summated by reference to the illegality and impunity of the powerful.

Judith Shklar says, in her great book titled *Legalism* (Shklar 1964), that following rules is not merely a technical or mechanical matter, but is an ethical virtue. One ought to follow rules because they are rules. Legalism, in an ethical sense, does much of the world's work. In the armed forces and the police, 'yours is not to reason why, but to do and die'. You follow rules because following rules is a good thing, not because it is instrumentally useful or beneficial. Max Weber also thought of bureaucracy as an affair of rules; a rule-governed bureaucracy is his description of the judiciary. His entire analysis of *stare decisis* in common law and the antinomy between formalism (the formal rationality of law) and substantive law (the purpose of law) is based on this dichotomy. Following rules often results in injustice (assuming that everyone thinks with justification that a conduct is unjust), but then the theory of justice has a good deal of injustice built into it, always! After all, canons of equity in Roman, as well as in English, law arose out of the formalism of rules, but later, equity also became strict and rigid. The battle between rules and discretion is the stuff that law is made of.

An unbridled rule of discretion worried me. But there were other concerns too. I had a number of contests and conflicts with the Dean, and with others. It is a long story. My other major concern at the time was that I felt the University was not interested in solving the problem of suitable accommodation for Law Centre 2. I went to the Vice-Chancellor, Sarup Singh. His cleverness comprised in this: he would first ask after your family, and then about the problems facing the nation. Of course, once we expatiate on the nation's problems, one's own institutional problems seem too small to mention, and one even risked incoherence! I realised he was sharper than me, so on the next visit, I said, Mr Vice-Chancellor, we will not discuss the nation's problems, I am going back to Sydney unless you give me better shelter, not for me, but for my people. That led to some movement. I struggled a lot, I met H. R. Gokhale, the then Union Law Minister.[2] He was my uncle's colleague in Baroda when he, P. C. Hathi, and H. R. Gokhale practised labour law. I met the Minister for Education, [Saiyid] Nurul Hasan.[3] I realised that rule following in legal education was not the only problem, straightforwardness in the administration of education was also a problem.

I also became the Provost of Gwyer Hall, and there arose the question of visiting hours for women students. My predecessor was a professor of psychology, and he had decided to allow visiting hours provided that room doors were kept open at an angle of 45 degrees, so the *chowkidar* and warden could check that relations between the male students and their female visitors were sufficiently chaste. This was called the '45-degree rule'. By then, I was going to become Dean by rotation. I said, no 45-degree rule, there will be an honours system, regulate yourselves, no complaining, no over-staying. The only problems were from the women's hostel and the parents of women students. And then a group of residents came to me and said, nobody comes to visit us. I said, how am I going to help with that? The new system lasted a fair while, but came to nothing after all, because the residents could not agree on the minimum norms for just social cooperation!

UB (*contd*): We also started a faculty club, which unfortunately ended up being used only as a marriage hall, whereas I had wanted it to be an intellectual space. However, we devised the idea of a club, and this was perhaps the first and last time it happened in Delhi University. Sarup Singh was a Haryanvi, and so a club of senior professors was formed called the Thalwa club (the word for elderly people in Haryanvi), and we went once a fortnight to a different member's house. The rule was

---

[2]H. R. Gokhale (1915–1978), leader of the Indian National Congress from Maharashtra, member of the Lok Sabha representing Mumbai northwest, and later Cabinet Minister of Law and Justice in the Indira Gandhi government during the Emergency.

[3]Saiyid Nurul Hasan (1921–1993), historian, member of the Rajya Sabha and Union Minister of State (with Independent Charges) of Education, Social Welfare and Culture before and during the Emergency, and later Governor of Bengal and Odisha (1986–1993).

that there would be no discussion of university business. I mention this because, this one time, while Ms. Gandhi's case was being heard in the Allahabad High Court,[4] Sarup Singh said to me, you are a professor of law, you are well-known, tell us what will happen. Without batting an eyelid, I said, she will be indicted for corrupt practices and will be unseated. They were surprised; they said, how can you say that? I said, it will happen, maybe not all the way, but in some way, it will happen. And, on 12 June 1975, it indeed happened.

They all later came to me in surprise. I said to them, I am not a practitioner, but I am a student of judicial behaviour and, as such, I should be able to forecast how judges will decide. They said, explain! This was my explanation. While the judge in the Allahabad High Court was hearing this matter, a point of civil procedure was appealed before the Supreme Court. Justice K. S. Hegde heard this appeal. In the Supreme Court, Hegde had to decide whether a provision of the Civil Procedure Code applied to the election petition or not, and he decided the point, but he went on to write several more pages, a massive *obiter dicta*, in which he laid down the jurisprudence of corrupt practices.[5]

Now I knew that this was a direct intervention, a sheet of instruction, and the judge of the High Court, Justice Jagmohanlal Sinha, would have been bound to follow it. I would have been very surprised if he had not. Ms. Gandhi was disqualified on two minor grounds: appointment of the election agent and a *shamiana* provided by the State.

---

[4] *State of Uttar Pradesh vs. Raj Narain*, AIR 1975 SC,865.

[5] The order pertained to how a charge of corrupt practice in an election petition is to be dealt with. It was held that regardless of how it is drafted, an opportunity to prove corrupt practice must be given to the petitioner due to the seriousness of the charge. However, allegations of such nature must disclose the constituent parts of the corrupt practice alleged. The High Court had refused the petitioner the chance to amend the charges on the grounds that the limitation period had passed, and the matter thus came in appeal to the Supreme Court, which held that the court may allow particulars of the corrupt practice to be amended or even amplified. The petitioner in this case had challenged Indira Gandhi's election to the Lok Sabha (*State of Uttar Pradesh vs. Raj Narain*, AIR 1975 SC 865).

Challenging a Legislative Expulsion: The First Forensic Victory

UB (*contd*): So my reputation for legal acumen grew. Sarup Singh was a great communicator, and he spread the news that I was a legal 'genius'!

You want me to discuss the internal Emergency of 1975–1976, and it is a wearisome discussion. But it cannot be comprehensive, for many reasons which I hope will became clear as we go along. Here, I prattle about my own experiences as an educational administrator and as a pedagogue, and I hope this will encourage others who lived those days to narrate their own stories. It is as important to leave the bouquet of individual memory and engage with acts of official/institutional memory. I will address the more theoretical questions later in this continuing conversation.

No one expected this political development, which came suddenly on 25 June 1975. But apprehensions about how long the democratic experiment in India would last was a political constant in Indian, and comparative, studies during the Cold War. The question was constantly raised during the Nehru decades, and certainly 'After Nehru, who?' was a question on which books and scholarly articles abounded. For example, Selig Harrison's book, *India: The Most Dangerous Decades* (Harrison 1960), was widely read in India and the emerging Third World. [See also Perry Anderson's 'After Nehru' (Anderson 2012) and Michael Brecher's *Nehru: A Political Biography* (1959)].

I expressed similar apprehensions on the occasion of the Silver Jubilee of the Constitution in 1975.[6] I was the lead speaker and I said, there would be no Golden Jubilee of the Constitution if some of the trends of the time continued. My first instance of this was of Morarji Desai's threat to do a *dharna* on the floor of Parliament. If

[6]The conference was organised by the then Head of Law Centre 1, Professor M. P. Jain, in the South Indian Association Hall, Mandir Marg, New Delhi.

senior leaders do that, I said, how may we contemplate a future of parliamentary democracy?

My second instance was an Amnesty International Report on Naxalites in Bengal. *The Economic and Political Weekly* (EPW) had reprinted the report (Amnesty 1974). I decided to send it around to 100 people, but there was no email or xerox, so I paid someone to stencil it. It cost me a fair bit of my monthly salary, but I sent it out to eminent senior lawyers, judges, and others who I thought would be interested. I did not get a single reply. So I said, in a country in which eminent law persons (and others) are indifferent to the alleged torture and terror, how can you have a Golden Jubilee of the Constitution? I am glad that, barring a savage interruption, we have seen not merely the Golden Jubilee, but are on the verge of a Diamond.

My third example pertained to Hardwari Lal, who was a writer, an erudite man, a principal of a leading campus college in Delhi University, an activist public citizen, as well as a member of the Haryana Legislative Assembly. Hardwari Lal published an exposé of the alleged corruption of the then Chief Minister of Haryana, Bansi Lal. Now, barring a few exceptions which included Hardwari Lal, not too many legislators in the Haryana Assembly had little or no grasp of legal English. Bansi Lal was a strong-headed ruler, and he later became the Home Minister during the Emergency. The allegation against Bansi Lal was that he maintained his power by threatening false criminal charges against dissident MLAs. Hardwari Lal had published a booklet named *Chief Minister Runs Amok—Indian Democracy in Danger—Appeal for Succour*, followed by yet another booklet, *Emergence of Rough and Corrupt Politics—Anatomy of Chief Minister*. On 8 January 1975, a resolution for the expulsion of Hardwari Lal was moved, and it was adopted by the House. As Hardwari Lal demonstrates in his book, *Myth and Law of Parliamentary Privileges* (Lal 1979), not only did the Hon'ble Speaker not allegedly apply his mind to the contents of the breach of privileges motion, but the report of the Committee was also allegedly rushed. However, the issue of whether the legislature possessed the power to expel was contested, and in that I had a small role because I sent him some materials and also a note on the grounds of challenge to the expulsion order to his emissary, as he was then ensconced as a MISA (Maintenance of Internal Security Act) detenu in a Rohtak jail. My basic legal advice, as elaborated in the note, was that the law of privileges and expulsion had now to run the gauntlet of the basic structure doctrine, as democracy which entailed adult suffrage (a right to contest and vote) was an essential feature of the basic structure. A full bench of five judges of Punjab and Haryana High Court held, by a majority, that the State Legislature was not competent to terminate the membership of Hardwari Lal. The court observed: 'When the law regarding disqualification and vacation of seats has specially provided in Articles 190 and 191, there is no warrant for pressing that Article 194 (3) was intended to override them or to operate independently.'[7]

The argument from basic structure was finally, but erroneously in my view, negatived by the Supreme Court in *Raja Ram Pal vs. Hon'ble Speaker, Lok Sabha and Others*,[8] in a 2007 decision by a three-judge Bench in the Supreme Court, comprising Chief Justice of India (CJI) Y. K. Sabharwal, K. G. Balakrishnan, and D. K. Jain.

That goes back to one of your questions on State terror. When does law become terror is an important question. Surely, the answer is straightforward: when the threat or use of force-monopoly of the State is used against any person without any reason or justification at law, it is terror, at least in the eyes of the tormented.

A privileges committee comprising of ten MLAs (Members of Legislative Assembly) met for some time and expelled Hardwari Lal for five years. I looked at the law relating to the expulsion order. It was based upon a book called May's *Parliamentary Practice* (May 2011, 496). There are two books that originated in England and have since ceased publication in England and all other colonies, but are runaway successes in India! One is May's *Parliamentary Practice*, and the other perhaps is *Salmond on Jurisprudence* (Salmond and Williams 1957).

May's treatise continues to be relevant to us because of our decision to continue the law of privileges as it applied to the House of Commons in 1947. It is a big thick book. And there was no question

[7] *Hardwari Lal vs. Election Commission of India*, LAWS(P&H)-1977-4-19.

[8] (2007) 3 SCC 184.

of non-English speaking/knowing people having any legal or historical literacy in the law of privileges. So I narrated this and said, where the power of parliamentary privileges is used to expel members as a way of controlling political dissent, there cannot be any future.

A small sequel to this narrative. On 10 May 1979, I received a typed note from Shri Hardwari Lal which, besides inviting me to the book release function by the prime minister on 22 May 1979, also said the following:

> I have freely used your views regarding the power of Indian Legislature to expel duly elected members. I am sorry for omitting to acknowledge your help in the 'Acknowledgement'. The omission occurred to me only after I had sent the text. I hope you will excuse me.

It was very kind of him to write to me; this is also what we otherwise celebrate as intertextuality in friendship!

I was also struck by this alleged deployment of the State law as a threat, and I began to formulate the lack of distinction in India between *prosecution* and *persecution*. Law without law is what the fiat of a ruler means. Law as a means of *prosecution* with due process can never be a means of *persecution*.

Declaration of Emergency

UB (*contd*): One of the problems was the growing number of anonymous calls telling me to watch out for having interfered in political matters. Sometimes Prema received these calls. I was not yet, at this time, accustomed to receiving threats. By this time, I had been diagnosed with very bad rheumatoid arthritis, so I was taking cortisone pills. Now cortisone is a steroid, it produces certain hormones and shuts down natural hormonal production; you must taper off the dosage when you stop taking it, you could even die if it is withdrawn suddenly. My only preparation then was to get a large supply of cortisone, for I wasn't sure there would be any provided in Tihar Jail.

At the time the Emergency was declared, I had started a programme for conducting seminars on social science, legal research, and methods for young teachers, addressing themes in sociology and law. There were two Indian Council of Social Science Research (ICSSR) workshops that were held in May. One was on law, society, and agrarian reforms and the other was on collective violence and minority rights. Law people and others like Andre Beteille took part. It was a faculty seminar where you worked from 9 AM to 6 PM, and no outside news came in. Nobody was supposed to be distracted. When I heard about Justice Krishna Iyer's stay order in the middle of our seminar, we did not let anyone out, we continued. The discussion was not disrupted, and the news reached the participants only in the evening.

These seminars were among our most interesting achievements. We really struggled to make a connection between law and the social sciences. A man called J. P. Naik,[9] the father of the ICSSR, financed these seminars, and subsequently insisted on a monograph on socio-legal research, which was duly published, first by the ICSSR and then by the Indian Law Institute.[10]

Meeting Ms. Gandhi

UB (*contd*): Coming back to the Emergency, sometime between the twelfth and twenty-fifth of June 1975, my colleague, Vidya Prakash Dutt,[11] the then pro-Vice-Chancellor and the Head of Department of Chinese Studies, asked me to join him and some of his friends

[9]Jayant Pandurang Naik (1907–1981), educator, founder of the Indian Institute of Education (1948), Member-Secretary of the Indian Education Commission (1964–1966), and the first Member-Secretary of the ICSSR.

[10]Monograph on Socio-Legal Research in India. Originally published as Monograph no. 12, ICSSR, republished in a special issue of JILI on legal methods (Baxi 1982b).

[11]Vidya Prakash Dutt (b. 1925), former Pro-Vice-Chancellor of Delhi University and member of the Rajya Sabha.

in meeting Ms. Gandhi to discuss something or the other. Several colleagues from JNU turned up as well. I understood too late that this was a political mission. I was rather naïve.

Professor Dutt introduced me by saying, Professor Baxi is a legal wizard. In a very brief exchange, I first apologised for remaining seated because of my severely arthritic knee, and then said, I want to congratulate you because you had the courage to decry the effigy burning of Jagmohanlal Sinha (the judge of the Allahabad High Court who had rendered the judgment that unseated her). I had never seen a person so angry or outraged. She said, Professor, first you must get your facts right. There is no question of my condemning any effigy burning of a judge before my house, because no effigies were burnt. So I said, in that case, my esteem for you rises even higher, because you have condemned an effigy burning that never happened, and all future events of this nature.

Then somebody prompted me and said that I should merely offer legal analysis. So I said, the legal analysis is quite clear. You have got a very grudging stay order from Justice Krishna Iyer;[12] whether you regard it as unfortunate or not, you are no stranger to parliamentary and democratic traditions. This is a law passed by Parliament, people might say, that the courts have got it wrong, but it is the final outcome. So, coming from the tradition that you come from, I don't have to advise you about the right course of action. To this, there was a storm of sycophantic withdrawals, contrary advice, etc.

The next day, the press reported that a delegation of Delhi University and JNU teachers had met Ms. Gandhi and advised her not to resign. Topping the list of names was Upendra Baxi. Somebody had briefed the press, I was very furious at this inaccurate reportage, but there was very little I could do.

In the post-Emergency period, the report of the meeting has been the one element which has stood as a black mark against me, with my detractors accusing me of having legitimated the decision to impose the Emergency. There could not be wilder speculation!

[12]Stay Order *Indira Nehru Gandhi vs. Raj Narain & Anr*, AIR 1975 SC 1590. See Baxi (1980).

Permission Denied

UB (*contd*): The second or third day after the Emergency was declared on 25 June 1975, standard warrants were issued. I don't know about anywhere else in India than Delhi where *pro-forma* warrants were cyclostyled. The standard warrant stated that X was addressing an anti-government rally at odd hours at the Arts Faculty or in the University library. These were *pro-forma* warrants. Everybody was alleged to be addressing a rally, and there was, I was told, no variation in detail of time or place or in the substance of it. In the first week of Emergency, there was also this system of midnight knocks. At 1.30 or so in the morning, I was disturbed by these loud knocks by a Superintendent of Police [SP] who said we have come to pick up one of your residents. I shall not name him.... We said, why have you come to me? He said, we want your permission. I said, permission is denied, no question. You cannot come to me in the dead of night and ask me to let you pick up one of my colleagues. He presented me with the warrant, and I said, this is not a warrant, I know what a warrant is. I said, go away, and he said, sir, this is a very serious matter, and we will have to make a mention of this. I said, by all means, and they left. I went back to sleep as best as I could. In half-an-hour came another pounding on my door, I thought, what the hell now! It was the concerned teacher, in *kurta* and *pajama*, and he said, what business is it of yours to prevent my arrest?

There were certain people who wanted to be arrested, because it suited their image and that made a political statement. So I said, they came to me and asked me, which was very nice of them, they could have come straight to your room. He replied, no, this is very unfair, you had no business to interfere with my decisions. I said, you should have told me that you want to be arrested, I would have called the SP first thing. He then walked to the police station and got himself arrested!

So much for my principles and all that! Then they picked up one of our law teachers, who was broadly right-wing, ideologically. He had a foot problem. They picked him up and made him stand for long, they treated him very badly. He had an ideology but no politics, he never discussed politics. When he was arrested, I was already Dean of the law school as well, so I stated in my official capacity that he was a good teacher and a man of sterling character. Fortunately he was released on bail and cautioned.

Then one day in the law school, several students came on to the roof of the Law Faculty building, shouting Rashtriya Swayamsevak Sangh (RSS) slogans. I was in my room, and the police were in hot pursuit. I didn't know what was going on, but I came out, and the police were going into the library, and I said, you cannot do this.

They said, who are you? I didn't look like a Dean. I didn't know how to look like a Dean, so I repeated! I am the Dean of the Faculty. I asked whether they had any permission, and they said, no offence, it is not necessary. So we had a big altercation, and I said, go and get an order from the Vice-Chancellor. He wouldn't come on the phone, nor the pro-Vice-Chancellor; they were all very worried. I said, sorry, you can't go in, get a proper warrant. I said, in case you have not heard, I belong to those who believe in the autonomy of the University, and this is what [Sarvepalli] Radhakrishnan did when he was the Vice-Chancellor of Benares Hindu University (BHU) in colonial times: he wouldn't let the police on the campus. It is an Indian tradition. We cannot give you permission without a proper case being made out. But these chaps were very clever. So they went back, and within ten minutes, they had reliable information that the students were hiding in the library. Somebody had gone inside the library and locked it. My library staff was in there, and they were worried. So the police said, we will not go into the library, but if something happens there, that will be your responsibility. I weakened, and I said, I am coming with you. They said, that is up to you. They opened the door and started beating people left and right and picking up people. They even picked up my library staff. I went to the police station. I stopped their vehicle and said, you cannot make arrests randomly, Emergency or no Emergency, these are my co-workers. So they had to release them.

This was directly reported to the home ministry. By this time, we had a new Vice-Chancellor, a man called R. C. Malhotra. He called me to his office later, and said, what are you doing, the University will be in trouble, you will have the force against you, you are getting involved in politics. I was really upset. I said, look here, we are not in a direct employer-employee relationship. We are all employees of the University as a whole. If you ask me to wear a uniform and you wear a uniform, then we can have no discussion, because then there is a hierarchy. But if you wear civilian clothes and you ask me what I am doing as the Dean of the law school, then I am just an official like you are. I said, you should be ashamed that you take note of insinuations against your colleagues and call them to ask them to account for themselves, rather than rebut those insinuations. You should uphold the dignity of the colleague, howsoever difficult the time. I said, never call me again, and stormed out of his office!

Two days later, he came to me and apologised. I said, this is not the right way to go about it. By then I had already collected a substantial number of bad reports from the local police. Because of my reputation, they came to my jurisprudence class, posing as LLM students. Two people looked very odd, very strange, they were sitting and taking notes. So I said, why are you taking the trouble? They said, we are interested in jurisprudence. I said, you are not my students. They said, no. I said, it does not matter, come and have a cup of tea. You are interested in jurisprudence, I can give you some materials.

Their interest stemmed from the fact that I was teaching Hart's notion of recognition in *The Concept of Law*, and Hart's debate with Fuller on unjust laws, and in this context, I was discussing Jayaprakash Narayan [JP] and his Total Revolution. I was not discussing the Emergency. I was discussing JP as a jurisprudential thinker. They came to me after a week and they said, this is very unfortunate, we understand what you are saying, but we have to report it. So I said, go ahead and report it. And, by the way, I am breaching the rules of the University, but I can tell you, if you want positive evidence for your report, there may be a question on JP in the LLB jurisprudence exam paper, which I did put in there. I said, come on the day of the exam and take it from me. I was not being heroic, I was just being what I should be.

One of the major incidents was the arrest of the DUSU [Delhi University Students' Union] President. He was put in jail, obviously, as a youth leader of the Bharatiya Janata Party (BJP). He wrote to me from jail saying, I want the case materials as I want to study for the examination. A number of students from the BJP wrote postcards to me, thanking me for my support to them. Now, support was clearly seen as political support. I was sending them the study materials. All those guys who, pre-Emergency, had an open-door policy, now said, during the Emergency, that rules are rules! I said, come along, you cannot be serious. They thought it was a politically serious situation. I agreed, but I regarded detention as 'an involuntary action', as *force majeure*, the standard 'act of god'. It was my duty to help them within the rules. I prevailed upon the University to let them come and take the examination. We said, the exam cannot be taken in jail, they have to come to the examination centre. They were my students, whatever their political views. So they appeared (for their exams). All of this aggravated the astonishment and suspicion of my being a worker or sympathiser. All this happened.

I still remember the day they were all released from jail, and this particular leader thereafter came with lots of other students and thumped the desk in the Dean's office, saying I must remedy the 'emergency excess' of removing most of the supplementary examinations. This decision was taken responsibly by all members of committee of courses and the faculty, and duly ratified by the Academic Council. I looked at the student leader and asked him to tell me why he had preferred preventive arrest and detention for so long. He said: 'What a question! The whole world knows that I was protesting against the arbitrary regime of Emergency.' Fine, I said, but what you are doing now is to act in that regime style, asking me to reverse a decision that had passed through duly authorised academic statutory bodies. How may I just by a stroke of pen undo these? Won't that be arbitrary? To the eternal credit of that student leader, he realised the error of their ways, and agreed with my suggestion that five of them address the relevant bodies, pleading the best justifications for a modification of that decision. This is what they did, ultimately to everyone's satisfaction.

Then there were sundry pressures to write, endorsing the emergency, including a felicitation volume for Ms. Indira Gandhi on jurisprudence of the 20-point programme; this last came from some eminent scholars as well. I refused. And then I started receiving messages and calls saying, you are pushing things a bit too far, you are pushing your luck a bit too hard. By that time, I knew. On an impulse, I wrote a short letter explaining why I cannot write on the jurisprudence of the twenty-point programme as The Directive Principles of State Policy contained these and more, and so did the two covenants of human rights and the National Union for Democracy and Renewal (UNDR). Within about a week, the matter was resolved and the pressures and calls ceased. I knew that I had taken a one in a million chance, and this is not what things ought to be! But these were absolutely irrational and arbitrary times to improvise social action for a change in the situation.

Swaran Singh Committee Report

UB (***contd***): I also wrote about the Swaran Singh Committee Report (Baxi 1976a). Now, there were two extraordinary things about that report.[13] What I didn't find extraordinary, I criticised. I did praise the audacity of the Committee for two things: for making agrarian reforms and education concurrent subjects. Although there were land reforms at the ground level, the State did not do much to fulfil the objectives.

These didn't go through, but at the time I wrote the article, it was not in any sense a support of the Emergency. It was support for certain types of constitutional change, to which I am still committed. But that created a deep misunderstanding. On the one side, I was being labelled an opposition Professor, and on the other side, I was already being labelled as pro-Emergency in that period!

[13]Swaran Singh Purewal, former member of the Akali Dal, member of the Punjab Partition Committee, Home Minister in the state of Punjab after Independence. Chair of the committee entrusted with the responsibility of recommending changes to the Constitution of India in 1976 during the Emergency. Based on its recommendations, the government introduced the Constitution (Forty-Second) Amendment Act, 1976.

Then came the final story. When the Forty-second [Constitutional] Amendment was being made, P. K. Tripathi,[14] Swaran Singh, and others invited me to speak. And I said, this is not what you proposed, why are you standing by this? There is no mention of agrarian reform, nothing of what you proposed is in there. They said, you come, you have written on our proposals. So I went, and I criticised severely the proposed Forty-second Amendment, and this was reported only in one paper, *The Statesman*. Justice Durga Das Basu rang me up from Calcutta and applauded my courage and conviction.[15] I said, what courage and conviction? I had praised Swaran Singh for good proposals, and now this is an ominous development. Who wants it? But the mere fact that I spoke up mattered to him.

So these were the major incidents. I learnt a lot from this about the nature and forms of campus politics.

Doing It with Your Hand

UB (*contd*): We had to decide Chairs and Professorships at the Law Centre, and as Dean, I was part of this process of decision-making. C. R. Das was the Visitor's nominee, and the great judge, Hidayatullah, the Expert. There was one person whose name evoked huge debate, somewhat even acrimonious. But I maintained that my role was to ensure only the academic merit of performance, not politics, which landed me in the crossfire of other colleagues differently inclined.

Then Hadi (Hidayatullah; those who had the privilege of affection called him Hadi) told us a story, which I have never forgotten. There was a young couple who had just got married. They went to a movie,

[14] Pradyumna Kumar Tripathi (1924–2001), former Professor of Law, Delhi University. See Singh (2011) for a volume of essays on comparative constitutional law, as a Festschrift to Professor P. K. Tripathi on his retirement in 1989. For Baxi's obituary to Tripathi, see Baxi (2001c).

[15] Durga Das Basu, jurist and author of *Commentary on the Constitution of India* (1965).

they had a tough time choosing their seats, but they finally seated themselves. Every once in a while, the wife said to her husband, darling, the man next to me is not all right. He asked, what he is doing? She said, he is masturbating. The husband said, don't worry, let him do what he wants. Five minutes later, the wife made the same complaint, and then again, another five minutes later, the same complaint. The husband got very angry and said, what is this, leave him alone. And the wife said, darling, you don't understand, he is doing it with my hand!

Das was so angry. He said, how dare you tell such awful stories to this young Dean, you are corrupting these young people. But that was Hadi's way of saying, just let things be, and oppose only certain points. The appointment was made, and I was silently reviled by many of my colleagues. It was a very stressful period, during which I learnt several things.

During the Emergency, I proposed several discussions among the faculty on constitutional change, on the Forty-second Amendment, on legislation during the Emergency, but we never had any discussion. People were scared. There was self-censorship. I cannot blame anyone. The day the Emergency was over—when it was withdrawn in January and Ms. Gandhi called general elections on 18 January 1976—then, the whole campus was abuzz with all the taboo subjects. How terrible was the Forty-second Amendment, what business had Baxi to support it (which I did not!), and so on. This was greater than normal because the lid had been taken off.

I then realised that the system gives you the appearance of free speech when it is not needed. It then gives you the unreality of free speech when it is most needed. This is a part of the process of mystification.

Outlaw

UB (***contd***): The Emergency was said to be for the benefit of all, particularly of the poor. And it is true to say that the English language national dailies carried news about bonded labour and and about the 'weaker section of society'. Freedom of speech and criticism of the regime were labelled anti-poor, exploitative acts, and so most people censored themselves and renounced free speech. This is the irony of free speech, and that is why I like very much Foucault's opening line in *The History of Sexuality*, where he says, you can only understand freedom of speech through the codes of censorship, you cannot understand the idea of freedom outside constraint (Foucault 1978).

Then, of course, a lot of things happened. There was the Shah Commission, in which I was cited by various teachers, saying that I had led the law school in participation in the Emergency excesses.[16] Shah, of course, did not take any notice of this, and neither did I. Post the lifting of the Emergency, there was also a big debate between a veteran editor of a national daily, Rajni Kothari, and I, with Rajni Kothari in the Chair. During the debate, I do not know what overcame him, but he made the most vicious, brutal attack that anyone had ever made on me in public! He even dragged in the fact that I had written a book on Justice Mathew (Baxi 1978a). He said, Mathew has been made the Chairman of the Law Commission, and your Dean is a sycophant. He said this publicly, Baxi is a sycophant, a sycophant of the regime, he has done this, he has done that... I was stunned. Rajni Kothari enjoyed himself; I valued him as a friend and he was also among the PUCL (People's Union for Civil Liberties) founders and a staunch civil rights movement person. He didn't protect my honour. I did not know how to respond. I can deal with facts, but not demagoguery. But the stage had been set by the vicious attack, and it would have been completely counterproductive for me to defend myself. The Mathew book was also taken into this kind of quarrel. I was asked by some colleagues

[16]Justice J. C. Shah Commission: appointed by the Government of India in 1977 to inquire into the excesses committed during the Emergency. The first interim report was submitted on 11 March 1978, which dealt with the lead-up to the declaration of the Emergency and initial curbs on press freedom. The second interim report discussed the role of Sanjay Gandhi at the Turkman Gate incident, when the police fired on people protesting the demolition of their houses. The final report, issued in August 1978, covered prison conditions, torture, and family planning atrocities.

when the book had been published, why have you written this book on a judge who is retired? I was told, it must be because the judge is still powerful. You are writing this because you want to go places, when he becomes Chairman of the Law Commission, you will become a member. Many colleagues echoed this and asked, why should we read the book? So I said, fine, don't read it. Six months later, when nothing happened, I visited each one of them and said, start reading at least my critical Introduction now!

There was this reductionist approach that writing had an overt political motive, and therefore, that our reading will contaminate us. This was remarkable, this was not a serious academic atmosphere. I worked very hard, and not for myself. My effort was not about the reading of my book, but it was to clean up this atmosphere. I also brought out a monthly newsletter called *Outlaw*[17] for the faculty, during and after the Emergency, in which people could write and criticise the Dean or anyone else they liked, and this person would have the right to reply. I said, there is no use in gossiping and 'grape-vining', people did not have the courage to speak during the Emergency, but now there is no Emergency, so speak. Be brave and reply if somebody attacks you. It went very well. Unfortunately, it all disappeared eventually. When I compare my time at Delhi Law Faculty and the ILI, its cohesion lay in an elastic band. If you keep it stretched, it remains stretched. You leave it, and it collapses. There is no enduring institutional orientation or culture that develops. Whatever takes place is at the level of individuals. This is how things ought not to be.

[17] Upendra Baxi note: 'This was a stenciled magazine shared with all law colleagues, including external members of the faculty and distinguished academic members of the Committee of Courses, which included some Justices of the Supreme Court and the High Courts, eminent external academics, as well as the University administration.'

Evolutionary Social Change versus Revolutionary Change

AN: The Emergency itself is very distant for us. Most of us were not even born at the time. I was trying to think from the point of view of that moment in time. When you are talking about the post-Nehru period, there is a certain sense of frustration as land reforms have not worked, and there is no substantial change in the lives of the majority of people. So, would it not be feasible to say that the system encouraged the belief that violent, coercive, and draconian measures may actually bring about substantive change, because a revolution is always linked to violence? For example, in a country like South Korea, land reforms happened not through land reform legislation, but through an act of violent State intervention. The history of the French Revolution and the Russian Revolution tells us that change has always been linked to violence. Even when we are thinking progressively in terms of the large majority of the people, is it not possible to think that maybe it is only this process which will bring about substantive change? Hindsight, of course, may give you different answers.

UB: Yes, yes, I see what you mean. You were not there when the 1975–1976 Emergency was imposed. Likewise, although I was born in 1938, I have no memory of World War II or even of anticolonial struggle. So there is a disconnect between 'memory' and 'history'. What is 'history', and how is it different from 'memory'? Is 'history' disembodied memory, and 'memory' embodied history? What is the meaning of the maxim that history occurs the first time as farce, and the second time as tragedy? And what is the import of the statement that those who do not recall history are doomed to repeat it? What are the relations between memory, history, and human rights? My friend, the art historian Geeti Sen, has written an interesting book with an arresting title: *Do Not Let Your History Get in the Way of My Memory*.[18] What are we to make of Milan Kundera's famous remark that the struggle of men (and, I add here, women and the transgender)

[18] Refers to *Your History Gets in the Way of My Memory*; see Sen 2012.

against power is the struggle of memory against forgetting? These are some of the crucial questions, the last especially, that I have re-visited in my teaching, public lectures, and writing.

You are also right about something called the 'system'. Evolutionary social change proceeds infinitely slowly. Edmund Burke called such change 'growth by insensible degree'. In reality, it is slow democratic change, the system remains almost intact while undergoing some miniscule and gradual change. Yet, we consider its *dramatis personae* interesting; even as the script remains the same, there is immunity and impunity for the managers of the system.

The other is revolutionary change, the opposite of evolutionary democratic change. Revolutionary change is almost always violent and undemocratic, but seeks to change the present system through a series of violent breaks. Often, it thrives upon, and leaves behind, more debris than structures. Many of the system changers detest violence as a mode of social change, but they leave intact the structure that produces injustice and human rightlessness. Votaries of non-violent democratic social change rely more upon individual transformation to change institutions of governance and obedience. Again, I have dwelt on these matters in my writings and teaching.

Coming to some of your questions or concerns: Nehru cared a lot about *agrarian* reform, but he accomplished only *land* reform. His greatest success was to abolish zamindari, which was by and large only a tenure measure. It was not an entitlement measure of security of tenure for agricultural labourers, and abolition of zamindari was a process that had, perhaps, begun with the Permanent Settlement itself. The British were never able to do it again after the late nineteenth century. It was relatively easy to break up very large estates into smaller ones. But if you read Nehru carefully, he was always committed to his kind of socialism, which was compromised by his own hand in the making of the Constitution, with the right to property and full compensation.

In one of my speeches on patent law in The Philippines, I quoted this story by Stanley Kochanek. He wrote a history of [the Indian National] Congress and business in India (Kochanek 1974; see also Markovits 2009, 128–149). He tells you the story of how, when the Constitution was being made, the Chambers of Commerce and Industry sent a telegram saying, we must keep Nehru on the rails, he is a flaming socialist. As India became independent, Nehru had a priority list of law reforms, and agrarian reform was one of them. Hindu law reform was another. Patent law reform was at the top of the list. And the fourth was, I think, the abolition of the Criminal Tribes Act. And he faced a very big struggle.

With respect to Hindu law reform, the opposition came from Rajendra Prasad, Shyama Prasad Mukherjee, and others. Five years and more had passed and it was still not completed, and Ambedkar resigned in protest. With respect to patent law reform, I have evidence from the archive that the OPPI (Organisation of Pharmaceutical Producers of India), the consortium of chemical and other industries, made sure through USAID that Nehru would not change patent law to aid development. So what he did was to appoint a committee, the Rajagopala Ayyangar Committee on the reform of the Indian Patent Law in 1956, but nothing happened.[19] It required the Bangladesh war and the emergence of Indira Gandhi as the undisputed leader of the party and the nation to get the Patents Act of 1972. And, I swear to you, this was the most radical patent legislation in the whole of the Third World. This legislation has undergone many free market-oriented/neoliberalisation changes.

Nehru was constrained, *one*, because of developmentalism, and *two*, because we needed foreign aid, apart from all the other things in the first few years. He was committed to land reforms, but he couldn't go beyond zamindari reforms. So what does he do—and that is where his progressivism lies—he says, I will use national power to protect whatever legislations there are from judicial intervention, and that is the story of the First Amendment (Baxi 2002b, 2010a, 2016a). He said, however limited the Bihar and the Punjab laws are, Parliament had to do something about it, and the ouster of courts from this arena was the best option for social justice.

[19] Report on the Revision of the Patents Law, by Shri Justice N. Rajagopala Ayyangar (Ayyangar 1959).

Nehru introduced measures, especially the constitutional amendment that gave Parliament the power to add legislations in the Ninth Schedule. Justice Hidayatullah was later to inimitably say—from the highest Bench in the land—that ours is the only Constitution that needs to protect itself from itself.[20] However, Nehru never had the imagination to bring land into the Concurrent List. He could have got it in there anytime. Maybe, after all, he thought it appropriate that it should be a state subject.

Postcolonial governance has been largely—until now—a story of Congress governance. It does not really matter where the power is. But Nehru did many exemplary things: for example, he started writing these fantastic letters to the chief ministers, and meeting with IAS officers, and addressing panchayats or whatever local self-government agencies there were. He believed in hegemony, not in domination. As a result, what happened? Land reform and agrarian reform ran aground. Then he used the Planning Commission as an elaborate mechanism for setting up the blueprint of what land reforms in a state ought to look like. He set up model elements of law reform.

Gramsci has a marvellous term, the 'Modern Prince'. In our case, Nehru was a Postmodern Prince, who balanced elements of hegemony and elements of coercion. So, to cut a long story short here, yes, Nehru was committed, but he was not always effective. The style of conversation and dialogue, of letters, of providing blueprints, was for him the model of liberal democracy. The style of the Emergency was of violent imposition. However, the idea that land should be made an entry in the Concurrent List is fascinating, and one should look at this.

What were the social forces of the time? Animating the insertion of the 42nd Amendment and particularly Article 51, crystallising the fundamental duties of each and all citizens? Not forgetting the 'socialist' inheritance of the Congress since Jawaharlal Nehru and later the legendary influences of Rajni Patel, Mohan Kumaramagalam, and the 'Young Turks' in the Congress, the addition of fundamental duties of citizens may not be understood only as a device for legitimacy

[20]'The Judiciary as a Resource for Indian Democracy' (Baxi 2010a).

of authoritarian emergency rule. Were distinctive civilisational influences at play? Was the emerging culture of global human rights and responsibilities a factor? Were the duties a blend of the ancient and contemporary values making the Indian constitutionalism more complete? We must, however, not overlook changes in the Preamble, which added the words 'socialist' and 'secular' to the phrase 'sovereign democratic republic', and the addition of Part IV-A, which enshrined the fundamental duties of all citizens. It is noteworthy that these key normative changes have not since been undone.

Eight

Emergency, Collective Political Violence, and Balagopal

Emergency as a Form of Commissariat Dictatorship

UB: On Arvind's and Ram's question yesterday on the Emergency and larger ways of understanding, it just occurred to me to say that there are frames—analytical frames, comparative frames, philosophical frames—through which to look at the events of 1975–1976.

Those born in or after 1975–1977 will have little or no idea about the dark chapter of the Emergency. But we must never be allowed to forget that our Constitution still allows for the imposition of Emergency and martial law. And even today, millions of impoverished Indian citizens live under a state of undeclared Emergency, amidst the myths and rituals of State sovereignty and civil society suzerainty. No doubt partisan politics will continue to attack and appropriate the Emergency. No one today defends it. Even the Congress, through the President of India (Pranab Mukherjee had been a veteran

Congressman), has found ways of saying 'sorry', and Pranab Mukherjee admitted that it was a sad 'mistake'.[1]

But few make the wider point that what is really wrong is the not-so-secret desire of all political leaders to rule by states of Emergency, mostly undeclared, but no less real. Democracy is now said to be in the DNA of the Indian people. But should not all of us then be reading *My Experiments with Truth*, rather than *Mein Kampf*? Have the wielders of power fully internalised, beyond competitive politics, the lessons of the Emergency? And while we must never forget the principal political actors, the central role in repression that the bureaucracy launched has also to be noted.[2] It would take this conversation far afield to include here the pro-Emergency elements in civil society, religious organisations, the media, and the regime-oriented worlds of non-governmental organisations (NGOs).

That is the declared regime of Emergency—officially declared, constitutionally declared. But official declarations do not exhaust the

[1] See https://economictimes.indiatimes.com/news/politics-and-nation/emergency-could-have-been-avoided-pranab-mukherjee/articleshow/69433058.cms?from=mdr.

[2] Upendra Baxi note: I must add that the Justice J. C. Shah Commission report, today all but forgotten, on the Emergency's excesses should be compulsory reading in our schools and colleges, and for our political parties and leaders. It gives us a full judicial picture of how despotic power can be constitutionally acquired, and how dictatorial powers are actually misused. While the political detention of party members, leaders, students, and related others was repressively commonplace, a recent study of the 'scrutiny' files of detention suggests that it was more frequent in the south (321 of 477 in Karnataka, 709 of 1,017 in Tamil Nadu). A non-political approach dominated many states (Uttar Pradesh recorded only 19.5 per cent politically motivated detentions [1,405/7,185], and Bihar, 25.4 per cent [593/2,333]). Most detentions were for 'general types of criminal and antisocial behaviour, or any behaviour that would bring individuals into conflict with the district magistrate'. According to political scientist Alexander Lee, 'the district officials were detaining people simply for making their job more difficult', suggesting that for the bureaucracy, the Emergency was 'more a liberation than an imposition'. (See, for a wider analysis, Lee 2015, 20–21)

genre. As Dalit literature reminds us, as does Rohinton Mistry's *A Fine Balance*, there is also a permanent state of Emergency. Masses of children, women, disabled denizens, and all victims also say so, and so do India's disposable peoples. They endlessly suffer and are vulnerable to the estate of rightlessness, although constitutionally speaking, they do not live in a state of Emergency. But they point to a vital social fact. As Walter Benjamin says, the 'traditions of the oppressed' teach us that the rule of law notions really camouflage a permanent state of Emergency against the have-nots. So, the arbitrary use of power, often cruel and despotic, matters, even when the distinction between *de jure* and *de facto* of the Presidential proclamation of Emergency also matters. *De facto* Emergencies may occur regionally or nationally. The question, in a sense, boils down to the difference between what constitutional, anti-constitutional, or other 'Emergencies' might prevail within a society, and whether these would result in a massive and unproductive confusion and mix up the juridical with the sociological: Is it wise to incur this risk of confusion, which extends and expands the expression for all situations of human rightlessness?

This question is crucial and should be contemplated thoroughly. It should be well-known that the Constitution empowers national emergency (Article 352), state emergency (Article 356), and financial emergency (Article 360). We deal here briefly with only the first category.

Constitutionally, there can never be an 'undeclared emergency' [UE], all emergencies must be declared/promulgated. The only form recognised is that of declaration/promulgation, or the lawful imposition of emergency. The grounds for declaring this are those specially mentioned in the Constitution. In the Constitution as adopted, the President may declare it if 'the security of India or of any part of the territory thereof is threatened, whether, by war or external aggression or armed rebellion', but the 44th Constitutional Amendment Act, 1978 now limits the grounds to 'armed rebellion', along with war and external aggression. National Emergency cannot any more be proclaimed on any other ground.

Further, Clause 3 of the amendment provides that the President can issue multiple states of national emergencies in addition to the existing one if the Union Cabinet (that consists of the Prime Minister and other ministers of Cabinet rank appointed under Article 75) recommends the action in writing. The duration of such declaration is initially one month, unless a special majority by each House of Parliament (by a majority of the total membership of that House and by a majority of not less than 2/3rd of the member of that House present and voting) so decrees. There are no specific time limitations prescribed as to the continuation of a National Emergency, more than the initial six months' time-frame. It can be continued for even an indefinite period until the President is satisfied that the threats to the national security no longer exist. The Courts shall not review the proclamation except to examine whether the limitations conferred by the Constitution have been observed or not. It can, however, check if the satisfaction of the President is valid or not—that is, whether the satisfaction is based on *mala fide* or absurd or irrelevant grounds. If the latter, it is no satisfaction at all (as laid down in *Minerva Mills vs Union of India*.[3]

One of the major impacts of the promulgation is to suspend Article 19, but now every such law that transgresses Article 19 must recite that it is connected to Article 358. Further, Article 359 provides that the President cannot suspend the right to move the Court for the enforcement of fundamental rights guaranteed by Articles 20–21. All other laws can still be challenged if they violate Article 19.

Forgive me this rather brief excursus full of legalese! Whole books have been written on the subject, which cannot be here summarised. But even this barebone glimpse should reveal that the Indian Constitution does not contemplate UE.

This said, it should also be accepted that imposing emergencies and continuing these for generations raises problems with constitutional powers. Certainly, problems concerning the constitutionality/legality of such emergency impositions may arise in India on the grounds of the doctrine of basic structure and essential features.

But these may also occur elsewhere, bereft of such a doctrine. Long before the Trump era in the United States, a group of liberal

[3]AIR 1980 SC 1789.

US senators anxiously noted (in 1974) that US law included 'at least 470 significant emergency statutes without time limits', offering by delegation to the Executive a 'vast range of powers', which 'confer enough authority to rule this country without reference to normal constitutional processes' (United States Senate 1974).

Even in relation to terrorist attacks in the US, it has been well asked: 'If the main reason, for example, for redesigning US institutions is to ward off future terrorist attacks, is not the most immediate task at hand reforming our political and social order, or at least altering US foreign policy so as to minimize the likelihood of terrorist attacks in the first place?' (Scheuermann 2019). And we should retain always the Schmittian (as well as now Agamben's) insight: 'Though inscribed within the law, the emergency is simultaneously external to it; the emergency explodes the confines of the legal order while necessarily resting and thereby belonging to it' (ibid., 294). This is another way of saying with Mark Tuhsnet that: 'Emergency power is inherently "extra-constitutional," congenitally flawed attempts to restrain it by legal and constitutional mechanisms" notwithstanding' (Tushnet, quoted in ibid., 297).

But should emergencies necessarily assume the form of 'legal black holes'? The Constituent Assembly, which initially drafted these provisions, and Parliament, which subsequently amended these, were familiar with the dire and persistent facts of absolute power. Hence, it chose the idea of constitutionally limited promulgation of emergency. The choice has now been named as the choice made by 'democratic institutionalists' who insist that the 'most basic legal freedoms would continue to operate under an emergency, though there would have to be some relaxations' (Scheuermann 2019, 303). They provide other means of pursuit of very vast executive and administrative powers of non-emergency governance by Directive Principles of State Policy and pro-impoverished and developmentalist ways of the amendment of the Constitution.

Democratic liberal competition for power has been oriented towards impoverishment alleviation and disagreement lies on how much has been achieved in terms of meeting the basic material as well as non-material needs of the impoverished everywhere. The oppressed everywhere tell us that the measures adopted are far from adequate. The oppressors tell us that impoverishment ratio is steadily declining. The point here is stark: Does naming this UE help anyone, excepting as inter-party polemics of certain practices competition for power? More generally, the issue is: How may one draw bright lines between 'polemics' and 'critique'?

I do not here talk about the situation of asymmetric terrorist attacks by non-State actors that have grown apace since 9/11, which has been named as 'the crime of New York'. This is now a menacing global reality, and such groups marshal the power to trigger a state of emergency in affected States, some of these lasting for a long period as such threats multiply insecurity. How far terrorist attacks, or threats of such attacks, relate to the justification of states of exception and how the exception assumes the visages of protecting the human right to collective security are questions that deserve very careful study.

It is true in particular that de-subjectification (the production of the 'abject subject', to use Judith Butler's term) occurs, and is sustained in all states of Emergency. In terms of method, if you were to revisit the Emergency, what are the discursive terms in/at hand?

Looked at from the standpoint of the sovereign, Emergencies signify crisis and change in governance. The other approach is to see it in the distinctive terms of Carl Schmitt, as reworked by Giorgio Agamben, of normalcy and the state of exception. The Indian Constitution, as noted, originally permitted the promulgation of Emergency on grounds of internal rebellion and external aggression (war), but ever since the Forty-fourth Amendment, Emergencies can only be declared on the latter ground. A whole range of laws (and security forces, including the army) are responsible for maintaining internal security.[4] The 1975–1976 Emergency was directed towards 'internal rebellion', even when an external Emergency had been in force since 1971 due to the conflict between East Pakistan and Pakistan, and the former's eventual emergence as the State of Bangladesh. The Emergency was presented to us as a moment of exception in terms

[4] Upendra Baxi note: See Shylashri Shankar, *Scaling Justice: India's Supreme Court, Anti-Terror Laws and Social Rights* (2009).

made familiar to us by Carl Schmitt, whom we briefly mention in the next paragraph.

I am tempted to talk about Walter Benjamin (who advocated the real state of Emergency), Carl Schmitt (the state of exception), and the mediation endeavoured by Giorgio Agamben via his notions of biopolitics and *homo sacer*. But I will have to rest content with a barebones summation of Benjamin and Schmitt, whose works remain essential to understanding the dialectics of sovereignty and law-making, as well as law-preserving violence. Benjamin maintained that 'the tradition of the oppressed teaches us that the state of emergency in which we live is not the exception but the rule' (Benjamin 2003, 392). A 'conception of history that accords with this insight' would show that 'it is our task to bring about a real state of emergency' (ibid.), which would 'improve our position in the struggle against fascism' and a revolutionary politics which will 'brush history against the grain', 'blast open the continuum', and 'leap into the open air' (ibid., 392, 395–396). Benjamin thus endeavoured to ensure the 'possibility of a violence that lies absolutely outside and beyond the law and that could transcend or shatter the dialectic between "lawmaking violence" and "law-preserving violence"'. Schmitt, on the other hand, insisted that when the sovereign 'decides on the exception', his decision establishes a rule over what does not belong to the general norm of 'ordinary legal prescription' (Schmitt 1985, 5–6). Schmitt distinguished between commissariat dictatorship and popular sovereignty dictatorship. Commissariat dictatorship, according to Schmitt, was a regime: a normative regime or a political regime, in which one suspended the Constitution in order to nourish its better future. Popular sovereignty dictatorship entailed the overthrow of an *ancien regime* and the effort to substitute it by a newer one. In one reigns the re-working/re-assemblage of institutions and/or processes of governance, while in the other lies the reconstitution of—even episodic deliverance from—anti-people governance, of the politics of massive immunity of the managers of the people. If in one form the establishment reason rules, in the other it is insurgent reason that reigns.

I think you should press to full use this inherited distinction, in descriptive and empirical terms, when it was said of Indira Gandhi that there would be order out of chaos. Dev Kant Barooah[5] from Assam, the then Congress (I) President, coined this slogan that Indira Gandhi stood between 'order and a chaos'. He embodied the notion of commissariat dictatorship. He gave it substance. He genuinely believed in it; many people genuinely believed in it. Vinoba Bhave called it a 'festival of discipline' (*anusashan parava*). The maxims/slogan of a Party President and a saint were on billboards all over the land.

Arvind's invocation yesterday of the discursive terrain on which one might have an understanding of the Emergency, outside the political biographies of X and Y who initiated the regime, is very important. But personalities played a large part, too. I think we must look at Dev Kant Barooah, the fact that he comes from Assam and defended it. And discipline was the watchword of Vinoba.

A soft State is a concept coined by Gunnar Myrdal (1968). A soft State, peculiar to South Asia, is a formation which is too lenient and does not enforce social discipline. Put more rigorously, Myrdal offers two markers: (*i*) policies are poorly enforced, and (*ii*) authorities 'are reluctant to place obligations on people'. The impression had steadily grown that India is a soft State, whether or not this is an impression that is backed by evidence.[6]

What kind of commissariat dictatorship did Indira Gandhi enact in 1975–1976, as for example, when compared with Burma, Pakistan, the rest of South Asia? It is an objective issue, not a hagiographic one, not an antinomic issue of good or bad kind of political judgment. In what ways can one compare states of Emergency conceived as commissariat dictatorship? How does one isolate elements of predatory power as outright lust for power in one person or a clique from commissariat dictatorship? How does one compare the emergencies in Sri Lanka, in Burma, in Bangladesh, with the Internal Emergency in 1975–1976? Whether this was a different imagination

[5] D(ev) K(ant) Barooah (1914–1996): Assamese politician, President of the Indian National Congress during the Emergency (1975–1977), chiefly remembered for his 1974 proclamation that 'India is Indira. Indira is India'.

[6] Upendra Baxi note: But see, for example, the study by Manuel F. Montes, 'Six Development Paths in Southeast Asia: Three plus Three' (2018).

of commissariat dictatorship in Schmittian terms is a theoretical question, and it is a question of practical reason for human rights and social action. I don't speak to the bankruptcy of collective cognitive performances. What matters is that Schmitt only formulated this in terms of saving the Constitution from itself. The objective question is: What did 1975–1976 do? One straw in the wind is—I won't call it evidence—that the post-Emergency scenario is bursting forth with new democraticity, with new human rights futures, new forms of investigative journalism, new types of judicial activism; name it, and you have it. This may not have been intended—one is not talking only of intentions, one is talking of structurally cumulative impacts, both intended and unintended. Did that Emergency have latent (unintended) functions that highlighted the plight of the rightless peoples? To raise this question is not to be a sycophant of Indira Gandhi or compliant with the State or the regime. This is absurd. This is meaningless. This is not the beginning of a conversation. This is the end of any possibility of non-partisan conversation. What one seeks to assess is the overall effects of the state of Emergency on Indian politics/law and society. To begin to study the impact of a large constitutional event, one has to first learn to compare.

I am thinking of the question that Ram and Arvind formulated late afternoon yesterday: What are the varieties of commissariat dictatorship in South Asia, in the Third World? Or, put differently, when does that notion break down? What is an exemplary terrain of understanding constitutionalism, human rights, new politics? We should look at other regions. Nasser Hussain has written a great book on states of Emergency, related primarily to South Asia (Hussain 2003). It provides a dangerous supplement to Agamben, Schmitt, and so on. Very important. Nigerian authors, Tanzanian authors, Latin American authors have also written on this question. The question here is one of methodological individualism, of methodological regional individualism. A South Asia-bound understanding of states of exception versus others. So we need to ask if we are serious about the issues. We should ask, more crucially, how does the commissariat Emergency count its victims, the human rights-violated, and the new rightless peoples? Second, one has to look at the outcomes structurally, and across various sectors, particularly change in the expectations of the least advantaged people in society (as John Rawls names this in proposing his difference principle) or the 'weaker sections of society' (as a Directive Principle of State Policy in Part IV propounds). Third, how far has the Emergency resulted in constitutional reforms? Fourth, to what extent did it foster an activist pro-poor judiciary and a radical constitutional construction? Fifth, how far did it achieve the purposes outlined in the Twenty-Point programme? Undoubtedly, there are other fields of crucial interlocutions regarding the impacts on human health, fertility control (mainly through vasectomy and tubectomy 'camps'), economic growth and development, education, social equity and equality measures, and the agrarian situation.

There have been some scientific studies and many more should be in the pipeline. From this distance of time, I very briefly make some remarks concerning the third and fourth dimensions mentioned above (Granville Austin has focused on these admirably; Austin [1999], also see Baxi [2001a]). Austin seems to normalise the narrative of the Emergency. We are thus told that 'ugly as the Emergency was, New Delhi in 1976 was not Berlin under Hitler' (ibid., 343), and that 'the emergency had its limits', in ways that exemplified considerable 'individual and political freedom [that] existed within it'. Further,

> ...ideological purity was not demanded, opponents were not shot. And the Forty-Second Amendment, with all the ills here described, did not abolish the Supreme Court; left the judiciary with considerable power; did not end the elections and legislatures of representative government; and did not abolish the Fundamental Rights. (ibid., 389)

Undoubtedly, these are valuable comparative approaches. But plenty of people were affected by the heavy hand of the State, arbitrary arrests and detention, and for the next of kin and other rightless humans, the story was not so roseate. It just shows the distance in the perspectives of those who suffer and the comparative observational standpoint.

There is no doubt that the scope for constitutional dictatorship has been reduced for the future by the Forty-fourth Amendment and fundamental rights and freedoms made more robust (immune from drastic Emergency powers). And jurisprudential leadership of adjudication has now yielded to demosprudential judicial co-governance of the Nation (Baxi 2014a, 2016a, 2016b): the direct effect has been the rise of judicial power and activism. The constitutional courts (writ jurisdiction) have been made a medium of judicial activism and an NGO-judicial partnership has grown to a point where the Court has assumed visages of a new social movement. Indeed, new human rights, a regime of appropriate remedy-structure, and wholly new jurisdictions have been invented. Social action litigation (SAL) has expanded its scope and judicial power has expanded in an era of demosprudence. It would be rather difficult to imagine, by way of imaginary history, wherein one takes a counterfactual—it would be hard to tell whether adjudicatory power would have acquired such a salience in governance and development. I always say that every activist Justice since 1976 has been a residuary legatee of Jayaprakash Narayan.

This is just a long footnote saying nothing new, but I felt it necessary for me to say this. Some of my remarks yesterday about my fungible memory were titbits about doing this and that in DU. It is important to carry many messages of deep ambivalence, of even the radicalised middle classes before, during, and after the Emergency. This needs to be noted more fully in the 'Emergency chronicles', to borrow the title of a recent book by Gyan Prakash (2019), in different and richer ways than I did. But this does not quite address the analytical, the analytic of power.

Just to conclude very quickly, I mentioned the degeneration of commissariat dictatorship. Was the Constitution suspended in order to save it from itself? Did we need or have the Emergency to abolish bonded labour, or to set an expiry date on legislations for debt relief and things like that? Did we need it to have Sanjay Gandhi's Five Point Programme, vasectomy, etc.? With all this, we also enter the realm of bio-sovereignty. Is commissariat dictatorship really about instituting a new biopolitical sovereignty, a new regime of sexuality, social reproduction, a very violent and bloodied social structure?

The Emergency as a Regime of Biopolitics

UB (*contd*): The Indian situation is distinct, but not unique. The promulgation or the installation of a new regime of biopolitics is rather common, nationally and internationally. So, Arvind, this is my response, belated but more refined, to your question. It is not only a question, Ram, of DU and JNU or PUCL/PUDR, of the trajectories of intellectuals pre/during/after Emergency, although these are all important. It is also a question of political theory or philosophy, or more importantly, political ethnography, which is very different.

Let us say we all missed the boat on memorialising the Emergency. Too late, we cannot revive it. But not everything is lost. Now we have to revisit the reconstitution of Indian constitutionalism and sovereignty into an installation of biopower. That's what fertility control meant. It is precisely for this reason that I have worked on this. I wrote my first ever review article on a demographer called S. Chandrasekhar, a fantastic mind, and he wrote on population control and the law during the Emergency (Chandrasekhar 1976).

And then I moved in the 1980s to the consideration, in an United Nations Population Fund (UNFPA) lecture, of the reproductive rights of women and State policy (Baxi 2001b). And then, in a *Seminar* article in 2002 or thereabouts (Baxi 2002c), I wrote on the comparison between national and state regimes of reproductive rights, where the language of possible sterilisation is replaced by the language of disenfranchisement. It has the same violent function—biopolitics. I also analysed six or seven state government policies which varied from the national policy. And in fact, in the *Seminar* article, I spoke of the place of human rights in reproductive policies and politics, and what an empty signifier that place was in the Indian discourse. I didn't do it in an Agambenian or Schmittian way, but I am saying I made some movement, uneasy and scattered in my thoughts, in my relation to what might seem a forbidding sphere of social construction. You may not know enough of Schmitt or Agamben, or other such people, but your experiences and narratives of pain and suffering and policymaking are aggravated, and some of it is visited in theoretical discourse with the experience of humiliation.

Emergency as an Assault on Traditions of Humiliation

UB (*contd*): Humiliation is an unknown category in Indian discourse. Long years ago, I wrote a paper on the humiliation and suffering of women and spoke about dignity in the discourse of human rights (Baxi 1996b). We don't talk about humiliation. Humiliation of the other. I looked at the Untouchables; the Indian story of Untouchables is an exemplar of systemic humiliation. There cannot be a greater practice of humiliation. In my *Law and Poverty* (Baxi 1988b), I illustrated how numerous committees, including, most notably, the Malkani and Salappa[7] committees, all tried to regulate human beings carrying human excreta and waste in torn wicker baskets.

I looked at all those reports and how there was very little being done on the ground. I looked at humiliation in the specific unconstitutional Indian context.[8] I raised the issue of a correlation

---

[7]Scavenging Condition Inquiry Committee, chair N. R. Malkani (report submitted in 1966); Report of the Committee on the Improvement of the Living and Working Conditions of Sweepers and Scavengers, Chair I. D. Salappa (Report submitted in 1976).

[8]The concern with the plight of those in manual scavenging continues to draw Upen's attention. In 2019, he authored a blurb to a PUCL-K Report on persons in manual scavenging, titled 'A millennial struggle for dignity', saying:

> This is a heart-wrenching narrative of deaths of persons in manual scavenging in Karnataka, which unfortunately symbolizes the situation in India. It poignantly depicts the conversion of constitutional co-citizens into rightless and disposable peoples by the state and markets, and archives the sad story of how a law becomes non-law (even anti-law) by the cruel reproduction of social callousness and indifference. Why do we treat those in manual scavenging as the wretched of the earth, and the attendant horror and impunity with such apathy, bordering on animosity, is a central moral question in the 70th year of the Indian Republic. One hopes against hope that this monograph will explode the

between humiliation and justice. Can we ever speak of justice outside of humiliation? Then I explored aspects of the global sex market and hardcore pornography markets, and there was this startling instance of a young Hong Kong-Chinese woman whose great claim to glory was the fact that she had been recorded in 155 sexual acts in under three hours on live camera. She is not unique. Why did she do it? How does pornography become a thriving business? Not because of the degeneration or regeneration of otherwise respectable women, it is the market. Now, what supports that market?

On one side, you think of the multinational video business, the internet, and social media, of aggressive proselytisation of soft porn and hard porn. On the other side, there is all this structural knowledge of the subjectivities involved. What also supports this is what the young woman in the video sex market did in order to support her parents and grandparents, from whom she concealed the fact of the source of her income. I think it is important to say that despite the Constitution, humiliation remains a central category of dominant Indian culture. And I ask myself if the Constitution, the activist judiciary, the social movements, the human rights movements, the new social movements, even lisp the alphabet of humiliation, outside of the sexual orientation discourse. We only speak about discrimination. Discrimination is important, but undergirding discrimination is humiliation. And I think this is important, if only because humiliation is not a bloodless category.

The events of 1975–1976 may be read in terms of a contradictory register of biopolitics—on the one hand, a State and law assault on sexuality and reproduction, a violent lumpen assault, and on the other, an assault on the tradition of humiliation, of bonded labour, and of similar things. Arvind, I am riding on the back of the question you raised about a possible radical understanding of the Emergency outside the *dramatis personae*, on how to read the script of the Emergency against the actors, if they betrayed the script or re-improvised the

---

indignation of new social movements and fill each one of us with such shame and sorrow impelling us to a path of concerted social action here sadly but wisely blueprinted. (PUCL-K 2019)

script. How do we read the Emergency in a larger frame? This is a very important question, and we should revisit it as absolutely singular.

Feminising the Narrative of Partition

LL: Are there any subaltern histories of the Emergency period which are not accounts, for example, of rehabilitation and displacement like Emma Tarlo's, or the biopolitics of Sanjay Gandhi's birth control programmes? Are there any other accounts that exist?

UB: Well, there are lots of them, anthropology was reborn in India after the Emergency. Veena Das (2011) had accounts of Shahjahanpura, of the new colonies, and you mentioned Emma Tarlo (2003)—these are both Delhi-based ethnographic works, but I am sure there is national ethnographic detail as well as the archiving of internal displacement. The importance of this new ethnography was its focus on the sufferings of women, and it goes a long way back to the Sikh widows of 1984, and to women in Partition. There is this genealogy, but I think what accentuates post-Emergency ethnography is the use of those odd words: rehabilitation, resettlement, compensation; in my day, women's bodies were the site of competitive liberal politics. Ethnographers are careful not to use these kinds of words, but this is my take on it. Indian women during Partition are a clear example of the language of honour; there were Hindu women in Pakistan and Muslim women here, and Veena Das (2007), Ritu Menon (Menon and Bhasin 1998), and Urvashi Butalia (2000) have analysed this discourse.

It is of great importance for me to continue to say till my dying day that the greatest contribution of Indian feminism has to do with Indian Partition. Constitutional lawyers do not talk about Partition, H. M. Seervai being a solitary exception. He devoted a whole chapter on Partition and its legal and constitutional dimensions (in his magisterial treatise on Constitutional Law).

Partition remains in six novels in English that I know of. Among them, Partition remained a vivid literary memory in Manohar

Malgonkar's *A Bend in the Ganges,* Khushwant Singh's *Train to Pakistan,* Krishna Sobti's writings, and Manto's stories. We talk about law and literature, but still remain disconnected from the imagination of law and justice. The great gift of these three or four feminists [Das, Menon, Bhasin, Butalia] is not merely bringing Partition back as an arena of worthy enquiry, of social science enquiry, but the feminisation of the narrative of Partition.

The importance of feminising the narrative of Partition is not confined to that period of time in history; it invites continual attention to the recurrence of Partition-type violence, which, in the distant languages of Benjamin and Derrida, is reiterative violence. Reiterative violence is a form that re-enacts foundational violence. Foundational violence is the birthplace of law and the State everywhere. To rashly generalise, you cannot have a new State, a new future, without destroying the *ancien regime,* whether you take the case of the French Revolution, the American Revolution, or of postcolonial revolutions. So, outside the foundational violence of law, law is impossible, the nation-State as a site of re-distributive justice is impossible. Not only impossible but unimaginable, I would say.

The Foundational Violence of Partition

UB (*contd*): For us, in India and elsewhere, when we think of Derrida's notion of reiteration or Benjamin's notion of police (in that wonderful essay of his [see Benjamin 2021 [1921]), we say this foundational violence is routinised. Each small routinised act of political violence, dispersed, unnameable as such, yet performing a refurbishment of that paradigm case. Gujarat 2002 is a complete and full enactment of that. The Sikh massacre of 1984 is a complete and full enactment of the violence of Partition. To describe these events as uncritical events, as the failure of politics, as pathologies of power, is precisely the site of wrong and injustice, instances of narrative wrong and narrative injustice. You have to hark back to the fact that it is reiterative, not reiterative of the violence of law, but a re-enactment of foundational violence. Take your question about State terror. When is terror distant from the use of legal force? Look at 1984, 1993, or at 2002. So it is terribly important for me to use this esoteric idea. Because European thinkers, the best of them, and some of them we all love, have no time for the Third World, no energy. When you look at their discourse, you think of the story of Lord Hanuman and the pearl necklace. Hanuman-ji throws away all the pearls in a necklace he is gifted; he is asked why he is doing this, and he says, there is no image of Lord Rama in any of them!

In this echo or shadow of lived suffering dwell the marginalised communities of the Third World. Obviously, we have to provide a bridge, and rework these categories. Partition is not a typically European concept, the Camp is. The Camp is not a terribly distinctive Indian concept, Partition is. So, we are mouthing Agamben, Schmitt, and others—how do we critically revive these categories, resituate them? Just as Agamben says he wants to complete Foucault or resituate him, we need to resituate him in the post-national Third World context. We need to rethink the category of 'failed States' (or mostly, in my lexicon, Southern States made to fail by the Global North) and new disciplinary bio-regimes. That's what I have been feebly trying to do in my work. Seeking to do, not even fully trying to do. And that is important. These prefatory remarks will have to do for today.

SRK: This is excellent because this is a very different take from what we discussed yesterday.

UB: One can always immerse oneself in the contemporary context with all the available repertoire of analytical tools and lament that we have not exploited them fully. I would urge you to return to them, but if this is not possible or considered worthy by our peers, where do we go next? What is the next stop? So, it is a continuation of your valuable interrogations.

[Long pause in the conversation]

UB: It should not take so long to say what you think. At this rate, our conversations will go on till 2050, and you will then have to talk to a disembodied entity!

AN: Post-Upen!

UB: That is a great idea! Post-Upen has arrived some time ago. But when communication is not confined just to the conditions of mortality, how may it be understood as situated? The notion of spirit, spirituality, soul is something that we have lost. Activism is here and now, not intergenerational, let alone extraterrestrial (see Mani 2013a, 2013b).

AN: I was only thinking of some articles on the entire issue of violence, which you have written quite a bit about. And I was thinking about the liberal understanding of violence and what we were just thinking of outside the frame of liberalism. I think here of the article in *Law and Social Change*, where you make the point that a certain idea of democratic violence could be legitimate (Baxi 1988a). In our conversations, you have talked about the French Revolution and the Russian Revolution where, I would imagine, violence and terror are integral to the regime, because there cannot be revolution without violence. There are ways in which one can maybe look at violence outside the frame of liberalism. When I think of it, even in the entire discussion on the Emergency as well, which violence is legitimate is the question which comes in; and how would you evaluate this form of violence? If you bring forth a radical programme, does that in some sense give legitimacy to the violence? The violence of the French and Russian Revolutions is different, they were popular outbursts which became a form of violence, which is different compared to, maybe, the Emergency, which was a more top-down kind of violence. How, then, does one evaluate this violence?

The Descriptive Register of Violence: When is the Body in Pain?

UB: This will take 100 days, if not more, to respond to fully, but I recognise the importance of your comments/question. Leave aside words like liberal, socialist, revolutionary, just for the sake of understanding. There are two issues at least here, two contentious registers.

One is the issue of the languages of descriptive realism about something we call violence. Whose experience is the experience of violence? The question of subjectivity. Is the administration of pain and suffering ever justifiable from the point of view of suffering people? If one loses this subjectivity, would there be any pain or suffering? The Seventh Day Adventists, I am told, refuse any anaesthetic when they go to the dentist. There are issues, and some concern religious and mystical traditions, all along the way. Let me mention two experiences, both involving the Jaina faith. I was in office in South Gujarat University when we went to a place called Jambusar. I was taken to the ashram of a Jain *muni*, a sage, who had taken a vow of silence for two years, during which time he had never spoken to anyone. I did not want to disturb him, just wanted to pay my homage. I don't know how to pay my homage. I would be a better human being if I did. I know humility but not homage.

But I saw in the compound young Jain *sadhvis*, nuns, who were being inducted into the order. They were teenaged women. Their hair was being plucked one by one, it was a fearsome sight. In my mind was the question, which I didn't ask anybody—why can you not apply a razor, wouldn't it be less painful? Then they took me to this *muni*, and, to the astonishment of everyone, including myself, when I folded my hands ritually, he broke his vow of silence and said, son, you had a question. I said, I had no question, I was just offering my *pranams*. He said, you had a question, you were wondering why they pluck their hair out. I was astonished that he could read my mind, obviously that's what they do at a certain stage of discipline in meditation and even attaining trans-human consciousness.

And he said, the answer is simple. When you are initiating yourself into a language and a code of *ahimsa* or non-violence, you must eschew violence against all forms of life, including those you cannot imagine. Now this hair is a live ecosystem in which co-exist many forms of insects, lice, etc. When you use a razor, you kill them, and if at the starting point of initiation into *ahimsa* you are not willing to bear the human pain to avoid the sacrifice of microbial forms of life, you are inauthentic.

So one is the descriptive question, what is violence, in which coded language is this violence? Is labour pain in the act of delivering a child an act of violence? You give birth to a new life, but I said to Prema that I shared her labour pains with her, and she said I was a pretentious patriarch! I don't believe so because I understand what I was saying. Of course, I didn't bear her labour pains, but I felt she was in labour and shared some of her agony.

This is a big conceptual question, whether you bear the pain of the other in your own body, Wittgenstein and all that, I am not going there. The question is: Is the experience of reproduction, the biological reproduction of humans, an act of violence? Now some radical feminists say it is. That's why extreme radical feminists say that the greatest sexual liberation occurs with the possibility of human cloning. The womb becomes absolutely superfluous when human cloning in non-human animal persons becomes possible. The repudiation of the womb is the repudiation of the violence which says that biology is destiny.

When is a body in pain actually a body in pain? You all must have read Elaine Scarry, *The Body in Pain* (Scarry 1985). Without reflecting further, allow me to say that Talal Asad directs our attention to the colonisation of pain, a big problem.

Talal asks if self-flagellation is religiously/divinely sanctioned as an act of mourning, is it an act of violence ('Thinking About Agency and Pain', in Asad 2003)? For the colonialists, for the paternalists, for the human rights activists, it is the same discourse on female genital cutting. The African sisters say to their Northern feminist sisters, their human rights sisters, that they have got it all wrong. So we have a great problem here. From whose standpoint, and when is violence an act of violence? I am not saying that there is no such thing as pain and suffering, or that there is no possibility of talking about the violence of the State, far from it. But I am saying that one needs a little vigilance, a little red mark going out, when we talk about violence as an uncomplicated, always condemnable category. In the practices of sado-masochism, violence is said to give birth to pleasure.

I am sure you have read this very good article, 'Kant with Sade' (Lacan and Swenson 1989). So there is this whole area of—how do you describe violence not from the point of view of the perpetrator, but from the point of view of the experience of the subject of violence? We are not always the objects of violence, we can be the subjects of violence. That's the descriptive part.

The Juridical Register of Violence: When is the Infliction of Pain Unjust?

UB (***contd***): I am not running away from your question, but that is the first issue. The second is this: there are some just forms of violence, they are contrasted with something called unjust forms of violence. Now, who decides which is which? The answer is sometimes very clear, and not clear, in terms of what Foucault calls polymorphous sexuality. That's a different issue. So you say, all right, violence is that which is non-consensually imposed, it is a structural act of domination. I am avoiding 'liberal' and all such qualifiers. Non-consensual structural acts of domination. That's a mouthful, isn't it?

Slavery, sex trafficking, commercial paedophilia (lust markets for human chattel, sexual slavery), and so on. This is the Kantian answer, that you are treating human beings as means and not ends; certain humans become disposable material, waste materials after you enjoy them, use them. It doesn't matter how you describe it. That is what Marx would ask, whether it is possible to have capitalist production treating human beings as ends rather than means. The answer is no, the whole idea of entitlement, progress, of colonisation, of globalisation is the repudiation of the idea that human beings should never be used as means. In everyday life, we don't treat people as ends, but as means. There is a certain romance to the ethical idea that while we cannot help using human beings as means, there is a possible world beyond our imagination where you treat all human beings as ends. Ethical enchantment is this. So now the question is: Is violence a problem of judgment, not of description?

Take the case of war. War is nothing but a series of horrible acts of violence against the other. The other may be the enemy, the terrorist, the insurgent co-citizen, etc. Sustained and unsustainable acts, practices of horrible uncontrolled violence against the other. Does not matter who they are, whether liberal or socialist or post-socialist or post-Marxist—all agree, that is the Cold War history. You have the great slogan of the bourgeoisie, of the world's capitalists, 'Make the world safe for democracy'. Cold War is not just a phrase, it is an enormous reality. Cold War is a very misleading expression. We have many phases of the Cold War, from Korea to Afghanistan. They were crueller, and in terms of casualties and violations, the unending Cold War death toll transcends the history of both World Wars put together by a million or so.

I ask progressive thinkers from Agamben to Žižek (the A to Z thinkers, as I fondly call them), people from whom I have learnt a great deal, where is the history of imperialism, where is the history of colonisation, where is the history of the Cold War? The idea that postmodernism is a critique of totalitarian reason and its multiple histories of cruelty is precious. After all, thinkers lost their faith in reason because under its name, unspeakable mass atrocities were committed in Germany and other parts of Europe, during especially World War II. The question was poignantly raised: *Can we reason at all after Auschwitz?* And so also, we may add, after the invention of the atom bomb and its use, after the attack on Pearl Harbour, and the horrors of Hiroshima and Nagasaki? And of the early Cold War? And also, the ever-present possibility of a catastrophic nuclear annihilation of the world? This possibility was especially real for Europeans who were *emigres* to the United States. Hans Kelsen, whom I was privileged to visit at his home, every so often asked me this question: What did I think about such a war breaking out (see Chapter 2)? This question did not make much sense to me then as my reading of world events was different, and certainly far away from the actual experience of genocide and involuntary migration.

It is in this mood that early postmodernism [hereafter, POMO] emerged. The dread of totalitarianism was very real for the first generation of POMO. It is with them that the question of the subject, of de-centring the subject, of working classes no longer being the privileged actors of history, began. POMO exponents of the European variety are gifted, but theirs is generally an act of collective organised amnesia on the structural violence of colonisation, imperialism, and the Cold War. They were familiar with the practices of the colonial next door (as the French in Algeria) and conscious of racism's relation to imperial domination and governance, but it is only with the modern generations of POMO thinkers that we find some engagement with colonialism and apartheid in distant countries.

I am sorry, but this is my end-of-life statement on this. I still wrestle with these texts. But we are told that the word is the world. Derrida, for example, ends his *Grammatology* by meditation on the aphorism that there is nothing outside the text. But pain and suffering in the body testify to a material world of things, objects, and processes, a non-discursive realm. Does deconstruction erase materiality, then, or merely evade it?

Thinking is a Paired Concept

UB (*contd*): But the question is, can war and the violence of the war, the structural violence of war, be justified? War is not just one event, it is a series of events, and it recomposes what it destroys. War is not a zero-sum game in which one wins and the other loses. It is a chain of historic consequences. The first question, then, is of the justification of cross-border violence, of global structural violence. That is war. Hinduism, Islam, Buddhism, Catholicism, and many other traditions of faith have elaborated doctrines of just war. Of the justification of going to war. That is, war is an unceasing infliction of violence. War is just a word to be decoded. And just wars are justified by the thinkers. 'Thinkers' is a big word for me. I use it sparingly. We all think that we think, but that does not make us all thinkers, including myself.

Thinkers often justify the unjustifiable, whether it is war, or war-like states of affairs, or situations of cross-border terror. This is also true of those who develop the Buddhist, Hindu, or Catholic doctrines on just war. In so doing, they talk of creating restraints on unethical power by saying that this is a just or an unjust cause of war. You must have another script to fall back on. A thinker, in my view, is not for all or nothing; a thinker says, if not this, then what? The next best step is to apply restraint on force—that is called *Temperamenta Belli*, the doctrine of minimisation of unjust suffering. The war might be just, but the means by which you pursue this war might still be unjust. And that is a piece of thinking.

Thinking is saying, if you accept the first half, we come back to you in the second half. You appropriate our notion of just war for your own expedient purposes, then we come back and say, a just war becomes unjust because you have used unjust means. This is what I call thinking. For most of us, thinking is a one-shot activity. But thinking is a paired concept, always raising the question of alternatives. If you say that unnecessary suffering should be minimised in acts of war, unjust means should not be deployed in the act of war, you very nearly render almost all acts of war unjust by another move, a narrative, textual, tactical move. This is what I think lies at the base of Kant's distinction between pure and practical reasoning. Pure reason attends to that which is unjust, particularly unjust. Practical reason shares the task of pure reason, pure judgment, to say, that is not the end of the story. This has enormous messages for activism, human rights, and social movements. We study human rights with this all or nothing mindset—State bashing, negative utopia, end of human rights, no future of human rights, etc., etc.

The point is not endology, the point is not negative utopia, the point is to retain another place of agitated thought. It then seeks to achieve the purposes of pure reason via instrumental reason. I am sorry to be so ponderous, but I think I perhaps make a point.

Lapsarian Violence versus Structural Violence

UB (*contd*): So, the question of judgment: *first* is the situation of law, and *second*, the issue of structural political injustice—slavery, untouchability, patriarchy, slave-like labour, sexual exploitation, disability. Now, one may ask, in what way is this the fault of the structure, it could be—what is it called?—one rotten apple in the barrel. Individual lapses. The third degree, torture, disappearances, etc., they are acts of individuals, the system is said to be fine. This is one move by which to say that there is no structural violence. One would call it lapsarian violence, to use that basic Catholic term. So a given state of affairs becomes the consequence of an individualised sin of commission or omission. This is very important for it might be the critique of activism in India, the distinction between episodic activism and structural activism, which I mentioned yesterday. It is a lapsarian activism that says, get this police commissioner, get this fellow, get this passport officer in *Maneka Gandhi*,[9] get those little guys.

It is an activism which says, there is a state of grace, and there is a state of fall. And our tasks are performed in understanding and fighting violence at the second level—that of the fall from grace. The idea of structural political violence disrupts the idea of paradise, the idea of the state of grace itself.

Incidentally, I owe this to my teaching in Delhi University. Nobody wanted to teach legal history, I said I would do it. It was a very boring subject, what with the *Sadr Diwani Adalat* and what not, all that institutional history of colonial law, so I taught a much-revised version—to follow not the miscellany of jurisdiction of courts, but to attempt to learn the social history of law (Baxi 2018a).[10]

[9] The reference is to *Maneka Gandhi vs. Union of India*, (1978) 1 SCC 248, in which Maneka Gandhi was denied a passport and the Supreme Court held that the denial followed a procedure that was not just, fair, and reasonable, and hence violated Article 21 of the Constitution.

[10] Before I narrate the classroom incident, I need to clarify that while Babasaheb Ambedkar used terms such as 'untouchables' or '*Atisudras*' (the social and economic proletariat classes), or 'disadvantaged' or 'broken people', the more contemporary usage is Dalits, which covers a larger heterogeneous category of peoples, and essentially signifies 'oppressed' or 'broken' and is the name members of this group gave themselves in the 1930s.

See Shah (2001); Jodhka (2002) describes it as an 'extremely useful' work, though in need of supplementation 'of comparative perspectives from other

A first-year law student—this was sometime in the early 1980s—who had studied commerce before coming to law, she said, all this is fine, Professor, but is there anything in Hindu law or in the Manusmriti or whatever which makes intercourse between a Brahmin man and an 'untouchable' woman an offence? The question was held to be settled in Hindu law on as high an authority as Yagnavalka, according to whom 'a son begotten by a Shudra on a Brahmin woman becomes a chandala, the most degraded of human being', and therefore 'outcaste to all religion', and is due to the fact that the 'connection of the parents is contrary to the Shastras and therefore unlawful'; the Bombay High Court held that 'defendant No. 1 being born of a Shudra male and a Brahmin mistress is not a *dasiputra* who alone among the class of illegitimate sons would be entitled to a share in the inheritance, and that defendant No. 1 is not therefore entitled to any share in his father's property.'

I added that all this is overrun now by the Constitution of India, which, as a matter of fundamental rights, not merely abolishes discrimination on the ground of 'untouchability' as an offence, but casts a duty on Parliament to make, as soon as possible, a legislation so decreeing (Articles 17 and 35). What impressed me then was the sensitivity with which the young woman student pursued the situation of caste-based discrimination in ways that did not offend anyone in the class, but invited attention to the problems of feminising governance, development, rights, and justice.

---

regions' beyond 'Western regions and U.P.' (p. 1257). See also Ingole (2021); Guru and Sarukkai (2020).

The Manusmṛiti (Sanskrit: मनुस्मृति), also known as the *Mānava-Dharmaśāstra* or *Laws of Manu*, is believed to be the first ancient legal text and constitutional discourse and is considered a code of conduct and contains prohibitions and penalties, which have been considered a part of the Hindu law as administered by Indian Courts. I do not recall whether I was discussing the specific case (see *Ramchandra Doddappa Naik v Hanamnaik* [1935] 37 *Bombay Law Reports*, 920). but was generally conversing about the situation of hypergamy on which the entire discourse of *anuloma* (permitted) and *pratiloma* (prohibited) marriages was constructed.

So I say, if you want to understand structural violence, the first thing to do is to learn to listen and to stop talking. Absolutely minimum. Go to Marx, post-Marxians, liberals, all the subaltern historians, and our friend E. P. Thompson of the *Whigs and Hunters*, and yes, that's all that it takes, listen to new voices. Understanding needs to be dialogical, not monological or unilateral.

You may think that unilateral understanding is important when you describe a structure like Marx did, but Marx never engaged in a unilateral presentation of structural violence. For example, he tells briefly the story of Mary Anne Walkley in Chapter Ten of *Das Kapital*, but with such huge impact. She is this 20-year-old young girl who had to sew some dancing gowns for a ball for the Duchess of Edinburgh. He describes who Mary Ann Walkley was.[11] You have

[11]'In the last week of June, 1863, all the London daily papers published a paragraph with the "sensational" heading, "Death from simple over-work." It dealt with the death of the milliner, Mary Anne Walkley, 20 years of age, employed in a highly-respectable dressmaking establishment, exploited by a lady with the pleasant name of Elise. The old, often-told story, was once more recounted. This girl worked, on an average, 16½ hours, during the season often 30 hours, without a break, whilst her failing labour-power was revived by occasional supplies of sherry, port, or coffee. It was just now the height of the season. It was necessary to conjure up in the twinkling of an eye the gorgeous dresses for the noble ladies bidden to the ball in honour of the newly-imported Princess of Wales. Mary Anne Walkley had worked without intermission for 26½ hours, with 60 other girls, 30 in one room, that only afforded 1/3 of the cubic feet of air required for them. At night, they slept in pairs in one of the stifling holes into which the bedroom was divided by partitions of board. And this was one of the best millinery establishments in London. Mary Anne Walkley fell ill on the Friday, died on Sunday, without, to the astonishment of Madame Elise, having previously completed the work in hand. The doctor, Mr. Keys, called too late to the death-bed, duly bore witness before the coroner's jury that "Mary Anne Walkley had died from long hours of work in an over-crowded work-room, and a too small and badly ventilated bedroom."

In order to give the doctor a lesson in good manners, the coroner's jury thereupon brought in a verdict that "the deceased had died of apoplexy, but there was reason to fear that her death had been accelerated by over-work in an overcrowded work-room, etc." (Marx 1990, 364).

to read it, she is there, she is not just a name, she is a human being, and how she worked sixteen-and-a-half hours a day to make a gown for the Duchess's ball and died very young. This is the scientific Marx talking about exploitation. His illustrations are concrete.

The short point is, you can have narratives of alienated understanding of exploitation as a form of structural violence. And you can have a dialogical understanding of the forms of structural violence. You don't need to go far: we think about it in India. You just have to look at Babasaheb Ambedkar, particularly the great *What Congress and Gandhi have done to the Untouchables* (Ambedkar 1979). There is no book in my esteem that is more worthy of repeated reading than that. He provided embodied, erudite, and organic narratives of structural injustice. All are relevant. I am not privileging one over the other. But you have to combine them. Judgment and description, an esoteric versus organic understanding of whatever you call violence, and finally, the way out—the problem of redress or the problem of justice.

Expropriation and Re-appropriation

UB (*contd*): I used to tell my Warwick class, learn to think in pairs. What is the other of colonisation? What is the other of globalisation, that is, colonisation without colonisers? What is the other of exploitation? If you think exploitation has no other, then virtually the struggle for justice ends. This I learnt from my Rangpur folks (see Chapter 5). When I first went there, everyone, the young and the old, the women and the men, they called me *Ujjaliyat*, which means white man. I was stunned; they said, you are *Ujjaliyat*, and we (whom you call Adivasis) are non-*Ujjaliyat*.

After a long process, I understood them to mean that anybody who comes from the outside is an imperialist exploiter. Who comes from the outside in their lives: the moneylender, revenue officer, the police, and the district judge. They are white people. Who are the white people? Those who deny us our rights. So I had great difficulty persuading them that I am not a blasted *Ujjaliyat*, but one of them.

How could I say I was one of them? That was a fake positioning. I knew that. They knew that. They collectively said to me, tell us in four simple sentences what you think are our problems. No one had the temerity to make such a request to the constitutional law and human rights expert that I was!

In the end, it took me three days to speak four sentences, which I have cited in *The Future of Human Rights*. My first sentence was, a man called Mohandas Gandhi invented India. The second was, a man called Jawaharlal Nehru then discovered what the Mahatma had invented. Those who have venerated Gandhi and Nehru, Mohandas and Jawaharlal, then appropriated what Mohandas invented and Jawaharlal discovered. Then, in the fourth and final sentence, I said, the task for all of us is to recover what Mohandas invented and Jawaharlal discovered. These four sentences deal with the dialectics of expropriation and re-appropriation. That is the uncomfortable truth that emerged. Once you get there, the question is: How do you redress it? How do you get out of it?

Ludwig Wittgenstein once said that the task of philosophy is to show the way out to a fly in a fly-bottle and Ved Mehta, a visually challenged British India-born writer, made this image the title of his autobiography (Mehta, *Fly and the Fly-Bottle: Encounters with British Intellectuals*, 1962). Studying how the fly was caught in the fly-bottle is important, but equally, even more crucial is to show it a way out. I think that one may extend this acute identification of the tasks of philosophy to the philosophy of violence. But we should also be attentive to Sir Karl Popper's Criticism. He wrote:

> Wittgenstein very fittingly compares a certain type of philosopher with a fly in a bottle, going on and on, buzzing about. And he says it is the task of his philosophy to show the fly the way out of the bottle. But I think it is Wittgenstein himself who is in the bottle and never finds his way out of it; and I certainly don't think he has shown anybody else the way out. (Magee 1971, 136)

Is this so for everyone? I wonder!

Collective Political Violence

UB (*contd*): Now I am denying, Arvind, the wider discourse of liberal violence, justification of liberal violence, alternatives of revolutionary violence, socialist violence, and I have a long article, for which I was called antinational, called 'Violence, Dissent and Development' (Baxi 1988a).[12] I presented it at the University of Tufts, Justice Yashwant Chandrachud was presiding, and a young Member of Parliament, who was the member of an Indo-US sub-commission, was also present in the gathering. I said, there is a collective political violence of the State (CPV-1), this is structural violence, and you cannot understand the idea of Constitution, rights, justice, or development outside of this.

I was a baby then, this was during my ILI days. I worked very hard, and I discovered a lot of literature on justifications for CPV-1, State-oriented justifications, and I didn't judge them. I said, this is what they are. In that paper, I described the Home Ministry's accounts of arson, rape, burning, and loot, particularly that affecting the Scheduled Castes and Tribes and minority communities, and I posed the question: What is this 'development' if it perpetuates CPV-1? And are we able to understand the other CPV, insurgent collective political violence (let us call it CPV-2)?

At which point this young MP, I did not know who he was, raised a patriotic slogan that I was not to defame India! I said, I do not know who you are, why you are at an international colloquium—the theme was a bi-national comparison of India and America—I urge you to remain silent when you do not quite follow the logic of a seminar. I politely requested Justice Chandrachud, who was chairing the session, to protect free discussion at an academic event. I was stunned! Habermas has a notion of constitutional patriotism, but I don't think this guy had any! And this young MP later became a powerful minister and noted on file that I was an antinational! Although he dealt with me with gestures so respectful that no one could think that he would ever do so!

---

[12] Paper presented at a conference titled 'Indo-American Seminar on Law and Social Change', organised jointly by the Indian Law Institute, Fletcher School of Law and Diplomacy, and Tufts University in 1983; see Baxi 1988a.

Coming back to the point, we can talk about violence on the side of State actors and on the side of insurgency (CPV-1 and CPV-2), and on the side of bystanders, of the bulk of educated citizens. The discourse of description and justification of violence remains almost a taboo discourse. Or, when it is allowed to happen, one has to take sides, for violence, for equality versus violence, horror or insecurity. No matter what your authorial intention is when you write—Ram should know this more than I do from his experiences with the Andhra Pradesh Civil Liberties Union, and so on—no matter what your intention, the leadership and security agencies of the State determine what the intention is. It is the label that sticks, no matter how innocent one is.

Do not peoples' movements that create a discourse of State and social violence against the subaltern offer justifications of violence for equality? Do not anti-systemic forces need, as much as the system, to produce 'loyal subjects'? Is not the watchword 'discipline' in both? Is it wrong to say that repression of dissent is wrong wherever it found, whether in the movement as well as the State? And is normative insurgency to be kept apart from 'political' insurgency ('armed opposition groups')? How long and at whose cost? Mohandas was admirably clear on this aspect; should we be any less?

Do you recall a related conversation with Gayatri Spivak (see Chapter 6), where I said that an activist is one regarded as worthy of suppression by the State? Gayatri disagreed, saying anyone who works with people's or social groups and ameliorates their plight is an activist. She gave a warming account of the educational work she was doing in Bankura, West Bengal, where media publicity also helped. Is the message here that we would be better off using the earlier term 'social reform' rather than 'social activism'?

Making Sense/Making Meaning

AN: I think that is the point you make in the *Social Scientist* article, of how social theory is totally complicit in structures of power because of the fact that it never seems to see repression by the State. You say that the 'pervasiveness of collective political violence in India since 1950 is matched only by slenderness of theoretical reflections' (Baxi 1991, 22).

UB: Social theory does not care about the effects of power/power effects, something like that, right, though it would be rather wild to say this!

AN: What you say is: 'Administering philosophical, theoretical, scientific silence, by not talking about these issues itself is a form of complicity with power.'

UB: There are some things you need to say again and again, in a situation of non-communication. This is my grouse, even till today. We do not understand CPV-1 and CPV-2, we have a stake in peace and order, but most of us do not spend much time in understanding—description, analysis, explanation, and evaluation of—violence. I am particularly referring to work in the university. There is, of course, some work on CPV-2.

On this theme, have you read Ranajit Guha's inestimable work, *The Elementary Aspects of Peasant Insurgency in Colonial India* (1999)? The works of other Subaltern Studies scholars are equally worthy. So is the genre of magical realist fiction and poignant Partition studies. When I wrote that article, I didn't have all that before me. But now I can derive comfort from the fact that a different kind of scholarship exists. My only caveat would be that institutionalised social and political science scholarship does not figure in this prominently. A different kind of scholarship concerns mass atrocities of the Partition which does not figure prominently in social and legal studies. Reasons for this abound, but chiefly the lack of interest in the theory and reality of violence matters—niche studies, like modern history, subaltern studies, feminist studies, humanities, cultivate this memory. This general lack affects legal pedagogy. How may we know whether, and what do students think about these problems if we don't bring this material into the classroom? What do you tell them, then, about legitimacy, obligation, the Constitution? What difference would it make, for example, to tracing the patterns of human rights violations in criminal law administration?

What can you tell them that makes sense? There is a very important distinction, like I said last night over dinner, there is a difference between making sense and making meaning. You can make sense of many things without making meaning of them. Teaching beyond the classroom is the art of making meaning out of that which you sense. That is my personal feeling. You can make sense of a hundred thousand things at once: all of us do, of things on the cutting edge, of postmodernism, we can make sense of a large number of things; the question is, is it making sense *enough*? Of course, the question arises: What does one mean by making meaning, as opposed to making sense? Sense is the sensuous, the sensory, the sensorium, there are different ways of learning with the body and with the mind, analytically, for pedagogy and for research, the art of making meaning is what do you say after you say hello. I have skipped your anxiety about liberal, postliberal, Marxian, post-Marxian, globalising theories or approaches to violence. That awaits a separate discourse.

A Word on Populism

UB: Allow me to add something that bears on the turn to populism during commissariat dictatorship. Most of us tend to associate populism with constitutional dictatorship or authoritarian (despotic) governance. I had to invent a concept of judicial populism to explain what the Supreme Court of India was doing by way of a newly founded epistolary jurisdiction in social action litigation. But Ernesto Laclau, a distinguished political philosopher of our times, has maintained that populism 'is the royal road to understanding something about the ontological constitution of the political as such' (Laclau 2005a, 67). He argues that the logic of populism is based on 'a plurality of demands which, through their equivalential articulation, constitute a broader social subjectivity we will call popular demands' (ibid., 74). And a 'social situation in which demands tend to reaggregate themselves on the negative basis that they all remain unsatisfied is the first precondition—but by no means the only one—of that mode of political articulation that we call populism' (2005b, 37). Put differently, 'Equivalential popular discourses divide ... the social into two camps: power and the underdog. This transforms the nature of the demands: they cease to be simple requests and become fighting demands...' (ibid., 38), and the

> more social demands tend to be differentially absorbed within a successful institutional system, the weaker the equivalential links will be and the more unlikely the constitution of a popular subjectivity; conversely, a situation in which a plurality of unsatisfied demands and an increasing inability of the institutional system to absorb them differentially co-exist, creates the conditions leading to a populist logic. (ibid., 37)

Laclau certainly offers a distinctive enunciation of populism, but does this overcome the two kinds of emergencies on which Schmitt bases the edifice of his thought? Or does his analysis of populism, as being integral to doing politics as such, offer an alternate way of grasping constitutional emergencies that arise from popular demands always in excess of what political institutions may deliver? In any event, it would seem that populism is not a special way of doing politics in times of commissariat dictatorship. Many questions, no? However, the important takeaway is: populism is integral and central to doing politics, rather than being a super addition or suppression of politics.

Between Reformism and Revolutionary Violence: Balagopal's Thought

AN: You have indicated a very important distinction between the two forms of collective political violence. I think the person who has done the most on this is our friend, Mr Balagopal.[13] We had invited him to

[13] Kandalla Balagopal (1952–2009), human rights activist and lawyer. Formerly associated with the Andhra Pradesh Civil Liberties Committee (APCLC), breaking away from it over the issue of the legitimacy of violence perpetrated by the erstwhile CPI-ML Peoples War, he later founded the

speak at a conference in Bangalore on 'State Violence and Democracy'. He offered a strong critique of State violence and, when talking about violence by the Naxal grouping, his entire point was that there should be some sense of accountability. If you are going to kill someone, at least try and be transparent about it. Tell us why you are killing him. He was, of course, being slightly ironic, but the audience was scandalised and wondered how one could even talk about accountability or transparency in killing. In a sense, he is grappling with a very similar issue: 'how do you evaluate violence by a Naxal grouping?'

UB: If you say there is a state of grace and a state of fall, violence is an aside. It becomes a problem only when the state of grace itself is viewed as, or indeed is, a state of fall.

SRK: Let me add to what Arvind is saying with reference to the debate between PUCL and the Andhra Pradesh Civil Liberties Committee (APCLC). When PUCL took a position on Naxal violence with the claim that all violence is problematic, that State violence is a result of Naxal violence, it became politically contentious. And Balagopal wrote a response on private violence and State violence, or State violence and non-State group violence, which became central to the turmoil in the civil liberties movement as well as the national movement. I was wondering if we can frame the larger question in this manner: from your conversations, as well as from your writing, we can trace the triad of humiliation, suffering, and violence, perhaps as the epistemic core of your explorations and conceptualisations of justice and rights. But at the same time, you have painstakingly complicated—as in your conversations, like the one we had in Christ College, for instance—each of this triad of terms in its own respect. I was wondering whether, from the vantage point of your preceding remarks on violence, you could provide us a handle on the relationship between suffering, humiliation, and violence in order to understand your jurisprudence of justice.

Human Rights Forum. His English writings, mainly in the *Economic and Political Weekly*, are assembled in Balagopal (1988, 2011). Also see www.balagopal.org (accessed March 2022).

UB: Thank you, Arvind and Ram, for these comments. They are exceedingly important. Accountability in violence ushers in normative considerations of considerable variety. First, these raise the issue of agency: it cannot be that either State or rebel killing is perfectly self-justifying; each must bear the burdens of justification.

State violence is justified only when it is just or constitutional in the sense of being proportionate and reasonable. This norm extends equally to 'private' (non-State) violence. In neither does the end justify the means employed. Both need to be just. Second, Ram's idea of a 'handle on the relationship between suffering, humiliation, and violence in order to understand ... jurisprudence of justice' is, I believe, a good step further to elaborate the idea of just violence. We need to develop that 'handle'. I think the later Balgopal found it through normativity mediating both 'reform' and non-violent 'revolution'. Perhaps there emerges, in the rambling remarks that follow, some further understanding of agency and types of violence!

First, I think we have to study Balagopal very carefully. He deserves to be theorised, he deserves to be written up. He is among the foremost contemporary Indian thinkers and activists concerned with the history of political violence. There are many stages in his development. We really should engage with Balagopal to develop an understanding of the epistemology of violence. He deserves to be really codified and written up. Not fossilised.

Having said that, the point is: How does one revisit the distinction between 'reformist' and 'revolutionary' acts of violence? I have quoted Foucault, the other day; if the other of politics is revolution, then if there is no revolution, how can there be politics? In contrast, prior to this heavy remark of Foucault's, there was at one time the sense that violence, or collective political violence, was not the best pedagogy of reform of State or society. Most consider that violence is *not* the best pedagogy of reform of State or society. The message of the national independence movement and the Constitution of India is that the path should not be violence, but processual reform. It is a harmony ideology which does not deny identity or conflict, but regards recourse to violence as always an ethically extravagant means. Non-violence—*ahimsa*—is a deeply ingrained ideal of Indian culture and civilisation and the constitutional morality, in all its forms, is deeply dialogical. A fundamental duty is cast by the Constitution on every citizen to abjure violence and develop compassion for every living being. Social change reform or reform of State rationality or social change does not come from the barrel of a gun—you wouldn't want your students to come with swords or bullets to achieve changes in the curriculum! The logic of reformism says all differences and demands are best met through dialogue. True, sometimes the dialogue may be protracted. And often the outcome is of a moral or political majority (such as the results of a referendum or a constitutional enactment or amendment); but even here, the substantial minority is expected to sustain the outcome.

There is a broad consensus now in India, however, that symbolic violence is okay. Even in reform. Burn buses and public property, throw stones at police, burn police jeeps. Over fifty years of Indian governance shows you that burning, defacing, routinely damaging public property, injuring police is considered a species of symbolic violence, fully justified in reforming agendas. Elsewhere, it is not so. Despite the Damage to Public Property Act, 1984, and many a Supreme Court guideline and the Court adoption in 2008 of the sensible recommendations of committee (comprising Justice K. T. Thomas and Fali Nariman), which has been reiterated in later decades, there has been a concerted rise' in symbolic violence!

So broadly, the question is, reform of what? State and society are big words. A trade-off between change agents and society and those in power and those who speak for power and those who speak with power. You can have a leader-led reformist discourse, like the New Deal in the US, or, to take a wholly different example, the Twenty-Point Programme during the Emergency. You can have participatory reformist discourse. In both, to some extent, the legitimacy of violent action is foreclosed. I think reformism has a long history, in India and elsewhere. How to decipher this history in terms of co-equal engagement with symbolic protests and negotiations? Look at the movement for the reorganisation of states along linguistic lines, a live example in Nehru's time. This led to the Justice Gajendragadkar Commission on boundaries and the reorganisation of states without violence. On the other hand, look at the Punjab agitation led by Sant

Plate 1 **Early life.** Prem Mandir: The house at Rajkot (1922)

Plate 2 Upendra Baxi's grandmother, Kashibahen Venilal Baxi, the 'storyteller', in centre, at Prem Mandir

Plate 3 Upendra Baxi's father, Vishnuprasad Baxi

Plate 4 Upendra Baxi's mother, Muktaben, on the left

Plate 5 Upendra Baxi on the right with his brother, Madhusudhan Baxi

Plate 6 From left: Madhusudhan Baxi, Upendra Baxi, Kirit Swadia, Asghar Ali Jasdanwala, Jayant Swadia

PLATE 7 **Learning the law.** Senior L.L.M., Branch 1, 1962–1963, Government Law College, University of Bombay. Upendra Baxi is in the second row, second from the right

PLATE 8 At the National House, University of California—Berkeley, 1964

Plate 9 Hans Kelsen Inscription, reads 'to Mr. Upendra Baxi, with kindest regards, Hans Kelsen, Berkeley, 19 October 1964'

Plate 10 Berkeley student protests (from Upendra Baxi's Berkeley album)

Plate 11 **The Australian interlude.** Teaching at the Sydney Law School, from left: Garth Nettheim, Upendra Baxi, Julius Stone

Plate 12 In front of the New South Wales Supreme Court

Head tax on Jews: an appeal

SIR, — Allow us to express warm agreement with your cogent editorial of September 11 on the deplorable new Soviet taxes on freedom of movement of Soviet intellectuals.

You correctly perceive in these massive imposts not only an immediate oppression of Jewish intellectuals but a more long-term pressure against other Soviet intellectuals who may wish to leave the Soviet Union.

They are thus of a piece with patterns of persecution, dismissal from employment, political prosecutions and relegation to psychiatric wards, exile or labour camps, which continue to mar the post-Stalinist Soviet Government, and against which Nobel Prize-winner Solzhenitsyn has heroically raised his voice.

We venture to write to you about certain wider aspects of the despotic Kremlin Decree No 572/3 of August 3, 1972, which imposes these novel burdens.

(1) The Soviet ban on citizens who wish to leave the Soviet Union is a long-standing violation of Article 13 of the United Nations Declaration of Human Rights of 1948.

This invasion of basic liberties takes an additional menace when applied to ethnic or religious groups within the Soviet Union, who are there deprived of the right to maintain their cultural, traditional or religious identity, whether directly, or indirectly by denial of the requisite books, meeting places or other essential facilities of group existence.

(2) In the case of Jewish intellectuals, the wrong has been compounded further by the growth of Soviet practices since the notorious "Jewish doctors" case under Stalin, whereby they have been kept under constant fear of arbitrary measures of loss of employment, demotions, detention, prosecution, and committal to "psychiatric wards" and labour camps, for themselves or their families.

The current case of Veniamin Levich, a 55-year-old Soviet theoretical physicist and theoretical electro-chemist, circumstantially related in "Newsweek" on August 28, is typical. Demoted from his job, harassed by the KGB, denied access to international conferences, ostracised by his colleagues, this leading scientist faces threats also against his family. Latest reports indicate that his son, Yevgeny, 28, himself an astrophysicist in his own right, has "disappeared" — presumably kidnapped.

(3) Whether for Jews or non-Jews, this Soviet so-called "exit fee" (rising for PhDs to more than $US26,000) introduces a practice which is in outrageous conflict not only with the freedom of movement sanctified by the Declaration of Human Rights, but also invades the inner sanctum of human personality and intellect of each individual. It asserts that the State, by virtue merely of performing its responsibilities to educate its citizens, acquires a property right in every individual's mind and body. Even putting the best complexion on it, this is a demand for monstrous ransom before the Soviet Government will release a captive human mind and body.

(4) As your editoral indicated, it is a gross fiction to defend this ransom as a case of debt-collection. In any case, the civilised world has come, after thousands of years, to see imprisonment for civil debt as inhuman. Yet this new Soviet decree also threatens a grand revival of barbarism by automatically burdening every boy and girl who receives an education with a vast personal debt, which most individuals cannot meet and which then, at the whim of the State, makes them liable to life-long restraint of movement.

(5) There are some differences between these Soviet measures and the practices of the Nazis in stripping persecuted Jews of all their assets before driving them out or even (during World War II) demanding massive ransoms in money or capital goods for allowing them to escape the genocidal death camps. But these still leave the policy morally revolting.

For instance, Soviet policy not only strips the victims of their external assets but requires, as a condition of release, the further payment of a massive fine on each human being under cover of a "debt" imputed to the individual without his consent.

All this differs from the Nazi blood-ransom by a gross hypocrisy which pretends that a ransom is an "educational debt," and because the Soviet oppressions from which Jewish intellectuals are trying to escape take subtler forms of employment and promotion discrimination, administrative and KGB hounding, and political prosecutions and detentions. Yet such oppressions are no less repugnant to civilised standards merely because they stop short of the Nazi horrors of physical genocide.

(6) This leads to a wider point of personal importance to intellectuals in every part of the world. We must reject out of hand the precedent sought to be created by the Soviet Government whereby other Governments, too, may be tempted to assert a kind of property right in the mind and body of each of its citizens merely because these Governments have fulfilled their educational responsibilities to their citizens.

We may recognise that poorly endowed developing States may sometimes have "brain drain" problems which require temporary controls of movement of trained personnel. But, strictly, even such practices violate principles of individual freedom. In the case of a Soviet Union, which has for years poured billions of dollars of its equipment and expertise into supporting their external policies, pleas of national poverty and brain drain mock the intelligence.

Decree No 572/3 of the Soviet Council of Ministers must thus be condemned also as a vicious precedent which may tempt other Governments into similar courses. It is thus vital for the civilised world to reject, at the very outset and with the utmost vigour, the Soviet precedent for States claiming that, because they help to educate their citizens, they therefore acquire some dominion over the intellectual talents and integrity of each of their citizens.

(7) In the interests of its own citizens, of men and women everywhere, and also of continued intellectual and scientific co-operation between the Soviet Union and other countries, we wish to appeal to the Soviet Government to withdraw Decree No 572/3 immediately.

Representations of like tenor on the Levich case are, we understand, already being made in England by eminent scientists, including more than 100 Fellows of the Royal Society and others. Levich's scientific work is widely known to physicists, engineers and chemists in Australia as well, many of whom have already protested to the Soviet authorities. We hope that any of our colleagues in tertiary institutions throughout Australia who would wish to be associated with the present appeal will write to one of us as soon as possible.

UPENDRA BAXI,
Senior Lecturer in Law.
NOEL SYDNEY HUSH,
Professor of Theoretical Chemistry.
JULIUS STONE,
Challis Professor of International Law and [illegible]
University of Sydney.

Plate 13 Letter to the Editor, *Sydney Morning Herald*, 14 September 1971. 'Head tax on Jews: an appeal', signed by Upendra Baxi, Noel Sydney Hush, and Julius Stone

Plate 14 **Return to Delhi.** Upendra Baxi with Professor Sarup Singh, former Vice-Chancellor, University of Delhi

Plate 15 First Curriculum Development Committee, UGC: includes (facing camera) Lotika Sarkar, B. S. Sivarammayya, Upendra Baxi

Plate 16 **Indian Legal Theory.** Participants at a seminar on Judicial Process and the Law (Vizag), includes (seated) B. S. Sivarammaya, T. S. Rama Rao, Alice Jacob, Lotika Sarkar, S. N. Jain, D. K. Singh, M. L. Upadhyaya, V. S. Murthy. Upendra Baxi is centre, second row

Plate 17 Upendra Baxi, on the right, with Justice Krishna Iyer, centre

Plate 18 Conference of the International Political Science Association (IPSA) study group on political philosophy meeting at Vadodara, 1984. Upendra Baxi is in the second row, second from the left

Plate 19 **What indigenous law can teach us.** The Lok Adalat at Rangpur, with Harivallabh Bhai Parekh

Plate 20 The Bellagio Declaration, 1993. Includes Peter Jasszi and Rosemary Coombs (third and fourth from left, seated). Upendra Baxi is third from left (standing)

Plate 21 Gwyer Hall, 1996: From left: Upendra Baxi, André Béteille, and Justice Ranganath Misra

Plate 22 Asian Coalition of Human Rights Organization workshop on Effective Human Rights in Asia, October 1988. From left: Upendra Baxi, Clarence Dias

PLATE 23 Workshop on Gender Justice: Role of the Law Commission, from left: Lotika Sarkar, Justice D. A. Desai, Upendra Baxi

PLATE 24 University of Warwick: From left: Upendra Baxi, Abdul Paliwala, Issa G. Shivji, and William Twining, at a conference held in the memory of Dwijen Rangnekar

PLATE 25 Giorgio Agamben, Università IUAV di Venezia & Collège International de Philosophie Paris on *What is a Dispositif?*, 16 January 2007, Centre for the Study of Law and Governance, Jawaharlal Nehru University. From left: Upendra Baxi, Niraja Gopal Jayal, Giorgio Agamben

Bhindranwale.[14] So, somewhere the reformist agenda comes unstuck. In strange ways, in uncanny ways, it comes unstuck. Or it does not deliver the outcomes it promised to all groups at the table, or delivers in ways which are staggered, unanticipated, or ineffective. I am making very large generalisations. If we look at the history of reformism, this will emerge in richer detail, but its contours will be the same. The short point is, in the genre of reformist discourse, violence is restricted to the threshold of symbolic violence. And the category of symbolic violence gets enlarged. If I use too frequently the terms 'symbolic' and 'real', I will sound like a poor person's Lacan, but you know what I mean!

Then comes reformism, which does not accomplish its goal or accomplishes it in ways which are not acceptable. If you look at liberal feminism, what does it say? More of the same, more gender parity, more equality, more equal rights for women, more State action on violence against women, stricter rape law, stricter priorities. Liberal legal feminism is a paradigm, I am not criticising it, a paradigm case of endless reformism. You never cease to tread the path. Have you read Lawrence Sanders, *The Passion of Molly T*? It is a fantastic novel, and I have suggested to Indian feminist colleagues that they read it. The trouble with me is that people cannot make me out—when I am actually joking, they take me seriously, and when I say something serious, they think I am joking!

Lawrence Sanders (1984) has a marvellous account in this book of militant feminism, the whole idea and programme of which is the violent destruction of sex industries, especially of *Playboy*. They are not asking for anti-pornography legislation like Catherine Mackinnon, they just blow up the headquarters of *Playboy*, and there are all kinds of violent insurrections by women for equality. It is a marvellous story. Then the question arises, why doesn't one of us contest the US Presidency and bring about change from the top, rather than from

[14]The literature is vast and growing, but see, for example, Gill (2005); Kaur (2011); Mitta and Phoolka (2008); Singh (2011); and Tully and Jacob (2006), who show how a marginalisation of a whole conflict entails a narrative confiscation of stories of 'faith, feminist action, and the power of citizen-activists'.

below? I won't tell you the second part of the story. Anticlimactic! Obviously, the system captures you more often than you capture the system. In a first step towards justifying recourse to more than symbolic violence, one begins to say, let us employ real or material violence. And it takes many shapes. We all know that cross-border terrorism is a very different category. Are not the acts of terror, whether national or cross-border, political statements? It all depends on where you hitch your wagon, it is all a matter of interpretation or the hermeneutics of terror.

What Balagopal seems to be saying is, this disenchantment with reformism and recourse to revolutionary violence may be felt as necessary moments in the development of peoples' liberation movements, or of movements against injustice, suffering, and humiliation. But the more enduring moment, a historic moment, is when revolutionary violence takes an enlightened path, a different kind of reformism. This is how I read it. It was neither reformism nor revolutionary action from which emancipation (*swaraj*) was fully promised. Freedom must come, as Mohandas insisted, from 'militant nonviolence' (see Erikson 1969). There is, of course, a distinction and difference between those who espouse it and those who expect to benefit from it. Balagopal was at a very fascinating stage, in my view, when I last heard him in Patna.[15] But it is rarely the case that 'benefits' (or 'costs') are instant. Are these intra-generational or inter-generational? And who may do the counting?

Balagopal is not just a name, or just a civil rights activist, he is not just a thinker; he embodies these multiple contradictions between the exhaustion point of reformism and the exhaustion point of revolutionary violence, and he is still trying to negotiate a passage which does not betray the inspiration of total social change. This is the reason I respect him so much. There are not too many Balagopals in the Third World, honestly. I think it is right to capture him discursively, to engage him in this kind of discussion: it will have lasting value. Theorising suffering and deprivation, perhaps he is not bothered about humiliation. In class analysis, humiliation is not

[15]'Use of Fatal Force by the State: Transparency and Accountability Issues', symposium at Chanakya National Law University, Patna, 30 March 2008.

a moral concept. Class warfare or class contradictions predominate. Humiliation relates to honour, honour relates to feudalism, and in the transition to post-feudalism, honour is not a virtue. Humiliation is my category for ancient injustices based on birth. Not so much of race or gender, but of belonging to primordial communities. And that might seem to many people as historically irrelevant. But is this ever really so?

It is interesting to me that Balagopal is intensely local, not in his mind, but in his praxis. That is his strength. From my memory of Patna, his renewed faith in the judicial system, his return to civil liberties, to the judicial protection of civil liberties, is quite an interesting narrative shift, because he says revolutionary movements need this support in a historic conjuncture in India. This revolutionary reformist moment is a worthy engagement.

Ram, I have not really responded to you. You say or feel that my triad—suffering, violence/violation, and humiliation—are further complicated by me. Probably, but with a purpose. And that is summed up in terms of visibility. Some violence, humiliation, or suffering is not perceived as such by the perpetrators, and even the violated/victims take these as justified to a point that those subject to it cannot or will not protest the injustice of it all. To some extent, then, what happens is not perceived as violence, but rather, as a part of the discipline of normal, the routine, or the way of things, or the order of nature. Thinking and feeling are but another name for trying to break this conspiracy of silence around suffering, and to fully expose the inner order of violence resplendent with all sorts of justifications.

How to make visible that which is made invisible? This is the problem, both for thought and action. It was Jean Baudrillard who, in his *The Mirror of Production* (I think), famously drew a contrast between production (to make manifest that which could not be seen) and seduction (to make invisible what was previously visible) (Baudrillard 1975). Aside from offering a devastating critique of the notion of 'production' in Marx, and among Marxians, my interest lies in the notion (dangerously close, in present contexts, to the idea of 'fake or 'alternate' news) of *theory-fiction* that Baudrillard draws from the distinction. Philosophy can be either truth or fiction; it is the *indeterminacy* that puzzles. He calls it 'pataphysics'—the 'science of imaginary solutions' (as distinct from metaphysics of truth and morals).

In this sense, both State and subaltern violence (CPV-1 and CPV-2) produce their own contingent and relative truths. The difference one draws between 'reform' and 'revolutions' produce and seduce the reality of suffering and humiliation. The important thing is to acknowledge that the experience of these twin phenomena is real, and at times abiding, for individuals as well as the communities of hurt, and to make it socially and politically visible at all times. The politics against seduction of power is another name for the possibility of rights and justice. If truth fictions are all we have, Balgopal would have agreed, it is worth making dignity rather than humiliation, ontological robustness rather than fragility, and human rights over sheer rightlessness the sites of peaceful resistance and human emancipation.

Nine

Marx, Law, and Justice

Experience of Reading Marx

AN: It was really fascinating reading *Marx, Law and Justice* (Baxi 1993b). It is a text which not too many of us have read because it is not easy to get. In fact, there was only one copy of it in the National Law School. From the point of view of an introduction to Marx, the way you have introduced Marx's relevance to ideas of justice makes you want to go back to Marx and, in that sense, it was a fantastic invitation. It is what you once called in class a gift of love, that is, a recommendation of a book which was an invitation to explore a thinker. I was curious about the difficulty of reading Marx—Marx himself, in his Preface to *Das Kapital*, Vol. I, says, 'there is no royal road to science'. What is your experience of reading Marx?

UB: Arvind, it is really difficult to read Marx's own works. For one thing, numerous translations exist, despite some authoritative versions in English. Second, there are many ways of reading Marx: Alvin Gouldner (1980), for example, made a very helpful distinction between the 'scientific' and the 'ideological' works of Marx; he also spoke about what he called 'Nightmare Marxism' and about deep ambivalences concerning 'property' as the locus of all social relations (mode of production). Third, there is my own distinction between Marx, Marxians, and Marxism.[1] Marxians now include both Euro-Marxians and post-Marxians. Fourth, contexts do matter and our reception changes with shaping or formative contexts (for example, reading Marx during the first industrial revolution and in the times now of the fourth industrial revolution, and reading in the twenty-first-century contexts of the Anthropocene, the accelerating anthropogenic effects). Fifth, there is the disciplinary context (both uni- and interdisciplinary) of law and literature, and of the intersections between social theory and movements and the geopolitical context (decolonisation, Cold War, globalisation, neoliberalism, digitalisation, for example). Sixth, there is the context of political and social violence and suffering in each period and the kinds of 'justifications' offered. Undoubtedly, these features afflict or surround all practices of reading and reception, but it seems that the case of Marx and Marxians is different as offering a total alternative to the capitalistic mode of production.

Reading original texts of Marx is very difficult; indeed. I came to the verge of having a nervous breakdown, particularly when reading Vol. 2 of *Das Kapital.* I was at Duke then preparing for a set of lectures, and I wanted to read Marx in the original. The second Marx, the ideological Marx, is relatively easy. The theoretical Marx is more difficult. Maybe it was because I had no background in David Ricardo and Adam Smith, with whom he was conversant, or rather, whom he was reconstructing. So, I had to read those guys.

There is a particular chapter in Vol. 2 that I was trying to read and re-read, and I could not make sense of it for well over six weeks. This was in English, not in German. The language did not make it any easier for me. I actually banged my head several times against the wall and

[1]'Marx' refers to Marx's own corpus (including works of joint authorship). 'Marxians' refers to those who sought to develop Marx's insights: the preeminent names, of course, are Engels, Lenin, Trotsky, Luxemburg, Mao, Lukacs, and Gramsci; in recent times, one would have to include among these, notably, Althusser, Poulantzas, E. P. Thompson, P. Anderson. I reserve the term 'Marxist' more for the practitioners (party members, regime leaders, and ideological workers) of Marxism (Baxi 1993b, 11–12).

I had a wound for which I had to be treated. I was so unhappy with myself. I was miserable. I could not understand what I was reading. It was painful, but that was the real call of Marx.

How do you understand surplus becoming profit, the mode of primitive accumulation... all of this was fascinating stuff. I went back to it again and I felt I was beginning to understand him, but those six or seven weeks were the worst period of my life, I could have committed suicide. I was so unhappy that I neglected my teaching, because I could not say I was a teacher when, in the privacy of my own room, I could not understand a book. It was that bad. So, reading is difficult. But I also don't believe one can ever fully understand Marx.

I began to understand the mystery of the second volume by going to *Grundrisse*, which is also difficult to read, but it somehow opened the doors for me. In the last 150 pages of *Grundrisse*, there is the prophecy of what we today call globalisation. Marx had a prophetic vision, and we cannot ever fully understand him. We can only ever *attempt* to understand him. In my book, I have attempted to avoid what I thought to be awful misunderstandings. There is a great philosopher from whom I have learnt a lot, named Jon Elster. He has written some fantastic books on game theory, and he has also written a book called *Making Sense of Marx* (Elster 1985), in which he treats Marx and Engels as if they are submitting a series of Ph.D. dissertations, and he goes on to say, this presentation is below standard, this is first rate, this could have been done better! The book itself is very elusive, but the underlying spirit is of a pedagogic evaluation. Rather than being a student of Marx, you make Marx a student of yours. This, to me, is a very wrong way of going about it.

The other approach I was trying to avoid was a vulgar Marxism (different from a scholarly post-Marxian manner of understanding Marxism), in which you attribute things to him that he never said. You pick up certain things he said, words and phrases like 'the withering away of the state'. Then you have the post-Marxist critique, which attempts to be a critique of Marx, but which is nothing more than a very generic reading of Marx. For example, in the gendered critique of Marx, Marx is said to be wrong because his analysis is not gender-specific. In my opinion, Marx was an ethical thinker, and you can ask all kinds of questions of him, from race to sexual orientation. Post-Marxists are then thinkers who see Marx from the vantage point of the contemporary they occupy, and they engage in a critique of Marx which is legitimate, but which cannot be the entire story.

There is a Sanskrit word called *manthan*, which means churning. The Devas and Asuras churned the oceans in search of elixir.[2] Reading must be a churning. It cannot be an apology, that is, finding gaps in a classic thinker and proceeding to fill them. I am not saying that mine is the accurate method. I am merely describing how I began to read him. I made a big distinction in my mind between Marx, Marxians, and Marxists, which helped me. By Marx, I mean the actual Marx and his writings, whether scientific, polemical, or ideological. Marxians are people like, for example, Engels, Trotsky, Benjamin, Rosa Luxemburg, and Antonio Gramsci, who, in Marx's lifetime or soon thereafter, began to make sense of him, after the great October Revolution, and so on. Lenin was the greatest figure among them. Marxists are those who may never have read Marx. Marxism then becomes a political construction around a name called Marx, for acquiring power, prominence, prestige, whatever. This differentiation was a heuristic device, a tool that helped me in my approach. It was important for me to state that these are things that I have to avoid, and that these are things I have to bear in mind. That's what makes my book a little talkative on the whole. It is a book I want to revive. However, I am in a different place now. Since then, I have read a whole lot of literature which I had not read at the time.

---

[2] Upendra Baxi note: This great story is differently narrated in the *Mahabharata*, *Visnu Purana*, and *Ramayana*: they all deal with the *sagarmanthana* (the churning of the ocean by the Gods and Demons), which produced varieties of violence and many other things in addition to *amrit* (the elixir that conferred immortality). However, the elixir was wanted both by the demons (Asura) and the Gods, because both were earlier accursed by Sage Durvasa and had subsequently lost all their power, valour, and fortune. Finally, the Devas (Gods) succeeded in outwitting the Asuras and began to enjoy the gift of immortality. The leitmotif of the story is the churning of the ocean for the amrit. As to how this tradition was related to the Kumbh Mela, see Maclean (2003).

These were six lectures I gave as part of the Krishna Menon lecture series in Trivandrum on the topic of Marx, Law, and Justice (Baxi 1983a). To digress a bit, when I went to deliver the lecture, I found that it was a large room, but only a few standing spaces were available. I was surprised. Now, I am not a natural-born entertainer, although some of you may now begin to think so! In my first lecture, I said, I am going to talk to you about Hidayatullah and Marx. I said, I am going to tell you a joke first, a poor joke, but a joke nevertheless. In north India, a speaker like me was giving a talk on some subject. When he looked up from his notes, he saw only one person left in the auditorium. He said, you have been attentive for a long time, it is quality versus quantity, even if one person is listening to me, that is enough. And that person says, sir, I am sorry to disappoint you, but I am the person who has to take the mics and the carpets! I was worried that I would be similarly reduced to an audience of one, but to my astonishment, all the lectures were over-attended. They were trying to assess what I was saying, and to link it to their life situation under Parliamentary Marxism.

It is unusual in India for academic discussions to attract vast audiences. I was warmed by this, and I put in more work into the *Marx, Law and Justice* text because I wanted to pay tribute to the hundreds of people who came for these sessions on six working days. It was a kind of proletarian assemblage, and the work is also similar. But I don't think I have got to the point. So let me ask you: What did you find the most contestable portion of the book, what did you most enormously disagree with?

AN: I did not find anything hugely contestable, but what I would have liked to explore a bit more is the idea of terror inside and outside the law. This is related to the question of what Marx means for a Third World legal thinker. You discuss Marx's notion of reckless terrorism and the links between terror inside the law and terror outside the law. We had a discussion on the Karnataka Control of Organised Crime Act, 2000 (KCOCA),[3] and the question that came up was: When

[3]Public discussion hosted at the Alternative Law Forum on the implications of departing from conventional safeguards of the ordinary

does the State use terror inside the law and when does it use terror outside the law? I had no answer to this. So I thought I would come back and ask you.

Force of Phrases and Force without Phrases

UB: This is a very complex terrain. You invoke a term, 'terror outside of law'. I was struck by Marx's formulation, the 'force of phrases' and 'force without phrases' (Baxi 1993b, 85–94). This is a most germinal distinction. (I hope you never use the word 'seminal'; I would be very unhappy if you did, I think it is a sexist word. I always use the word 'germinal'.) Now 'force of phrases' and 'force without phrases' is actually what constitutes legal violence, the legitimate monopoly of force by the State. Marx was describing the innate violence of the 'enclosures' in Britain.

Any nonviolent analysis of violence has to be carefully responsible—if only because some others have to bear the costs of violence. The most important thing is to use terms carefully: if violence is considered a 'necessary evil', an ethical stance that takes nonviolence as a postulate of civilised life has to consider the scope of that 'necessary evil'. How much of evil is necessary? And are the measures that are considered 'necessary evil' also, by the same token, fair and just?

How may we distinguish between a few allied notions, such as 'coercion', 'force', 'violence', 'terror', and 'horror'?

I do not define this state of affairs and relation/affinities between or among them, but merely offer a snapshot picture. Coercion is writ large in law-making within a generalised consent at the hustings, which is often termed as a political mandate. In private law, it connotes lack of, or faulty, consent. Perhaps the best articulation of force in the whole world is in the Indian Penal Code drafted by Macaulay, where

criminal law in extraordinary laws like the Karnataka Control of Organised Crime Act, 2000.

there is a range of force that is classified.[4] Force does not have to be physical, of course.

I am a curious animal because I, though attracted by the theoretical Marx, am also a Weberian. (Incidentally, animals—NHAP, non-human animal persons, as I call them—may find clause three in the definition quite interesting.) Weber gave the most outstanding understanding of force (Weber 1965). He said, force is a social relation. The one example he gave is, when two opposing armies are confronting one another, there may not be a shot that is fired, but the way they are positioned is such that it sociologically explains force as the reduction of alternatives—the power of the other and their ability to choose. That is the meaning of force. So you have force, coercion, violence, and you have terror. This is a family of words whose distinction is more important than their kinship. One can say that they form a continuum because, in each, power is present, and in each, counter-power can also be present. However, we do not necessarily object to force in social relationships, such as friendship, love, and worship. You object to force

---

[4] Section 349: A person is said to use force to another if he causes motion, change of motion, or cessation of motion to that other, or if he causes to any substance such motion, or change of motion, or cessation of motion as brings that substance into contact with that other's body, or with anything which that other is wearing or carrying, or with anything so situated that such contact affects that other's sense of feeling: Provided that the person causing the motion, or change of motion, or cessation of motion, causes that motion, change of motion, or cessation of motion in one of the three ways hereinafter described.

First, by his own bodily power.

Secondly, by disposing any substance in such a manner that the motion or change or cessation of motion takes place without any further act on his part, or on the part of any other person.

Thirdly, by inducing any animal to move, to change its motion, or to cease to move.

Section 350: Whoever intentionally uses force to any person, without that person's consent, in order to the committing of any offence, or intending by the use of such force to cause, or knowing it to be likely that by the use of such force he will cause injury, fear or annoyance to the person to whom the force is used, is said to use criminal force to that other (Indian Penal Code 1860).

when it becomes violence, unmerited, totally arbitrary, and results in irremediable physical, mental, or cultural harm.

Ultimately, force reduces the scope of my action or my ability to engage in action. If you are against all force, then you cannot accept the legitimacy of any power. Power is not operative between the citizen and the State alone, power is diffused within the family, among friends, etc. All these are power relationships. Friendships and love are all shot through with power. Sociologically, force is a way of defining power and relationships with others, because you are constantly exercising force in relation to others. Our relationships are marked by force, even in the here and now. Can I willingly consent to force being used against me by friends? The structure of friendship means loyalty, it means fidelity, and it means you cannot do some things to one another. Terror, on the other hand, is an asymmetric arrangement between or across social agents. Some have more power to hurt than others have. But these relationships are constantly changing. Terror consists in surprise. It does not take place in a preordained rhythm, and it occurs when you least expect it. 'Force without phrases' is one way of describing terror. There are many others. And towards the end of the spectrum, there is the phenomenon of pure horror, which has been well annotated by Agamben and Butler (Agamben 1998, 2002; Butler 2004b, 2009; Coleman 2007; Debrix 2011; Gregory 2006; Minca 2005, 2006).

I realise that I am going much beyond your question, but I am getting excited by this topic. So, you cannot say force is inherently bad or evil, but it is widespread. Depending on what accent you give to that word 'force'. That's how Kelsen defined law, and so did Weber. Weber asked the question, what is law, what is the difference between law and custom. He said, in law, some entity called 'State' monopolises the legitimate use of force. This, anybody can say. Weber went on, further, to say that it is not just a legitimate monopoly over the use of violence that defines the State, but rather, the State is different from other social groups in that it reveals at work a distinct sociological structure of violence.

The State employs skilled and professionalised people whose business it is to administer violence. Judges, jailers, police, paramilitary, and security forces, all form part of a bureaucracy. But they differ in their social methods and in the missions, in the ends, and cultures of law. So if you want to study the violence of the State, you have to study the bureaucratic organisation across the various institutions of the State. This is very important. This second dimension has stayed with me all my life. So, while everybody knows that the State has a monopoly over force, the question is: How is that force exercised—conserved, circulated, deployed, distributed, and consumed—that is, held back in reserve and often openly flaunted?

You cannot have a bureaucracy without recruitment, you cannot have recruitment without rules, you cannot have rules and recruitment that do not entail selection. The bureaucratic organisation is a rule-bound structure, and only the top echelon is entitled to the use of the privilege of discretion. So when you ask this question, you have to answer it by finding out what this social structure of violence is that the State has appropriated and developed?

I think it is a major failing that we never talk about the military and the paramilitary forces in particular. I think one has to be kidding if one thinks one can understand law, society, and the idea of justice without understanding how these security forces are organised; I had studied the police and paramilitary in my *The Crisis of the Indian Legal System* (Baxi 1982a). But this theme seems to have little or no resonance in legal studies. Now if you go further down this line, we have to cut closer to the bone, and we have to see how they are organised, how they are recruited, trained, and disciplined. We would have to understand the nature of the power of armed forces: is it capillary power, or is it juridical power? We have to understand that the operations, even the very being of the armed forces, is gestated within secrecy. Everything is a military secret, including the way defence production is organised. There cannot be an army without armaments, and there cannot be an army without the constant development of technologies of destruction. The normal social-scientific or constitutional understanding does not look at this. What we look at, then, is another text. The image of somebody being beaten up or in imminent apprehension of death or serious injury—these necrophiliac aspects of law is what we focus on.

These are undoubtedly terrible things, but the core of State power in modern times is the military, and defence production and procurement.

Two conceptions are pertinent here. For Deleuze and Guattari (1987), the 'war machine' is both outside (and is 'directed against the formation of the State; as "another justice"') and is appropriated by the State, such that one may even speak of 'an "ideological," scientific, or artistic movement' as a 'potential war machine' (ibid., 357, 422). E. P. Thompson (1970) addresses the 'secret State', underlying a constitutional state-industrial-military-security complex, which operates in peace as well as war. Militarisation of governance occurs when the policymaker thinks like a 'warrior' (in managing crowds, in organising law and order, and treating peaceful protests as 'riots' or as entailing serious crimes against the State). However, thought carefully, militarisation in a good sense entails respect to a social organisation of citizen-soldiers, as it pursues, even with their lives, wars of self-defence and just wars following just means prescribed by norms and standards governing armed conflicts in international humanitarian law. It was recognised as early as the works of Plato and Aristotle. The values of discipline, loyalty, valour, and sacrifice are built into military forces and demand courage 'more than the virtue of courage for the citizen'. We ought to respect (1) an ethics central to military ethics, (2) the connection between 'military ethics and the fundamental issues of justice and the value of human life', and (3) the life of a 'good' military professional (see Hittinger 2010). Of course, when there is a clear violation of laws of armed conflict even a just war becomes unjust, especially when the crimes of aggression, crimes against humanity, and war crimes are proven. Levinas put it well when he said that war is a situation of the suspension of the ethical (Levinas 1979, 21).

We hear of terror through the prism of international law. We think of war crimes. We think of crimes against humanity. We think of crimes of aggression which States, singly or in concert, commit. May a nation-State acting within its jurisdiction use terror when it is at war with another nation-State? When is the use of force against a non-uniformed non-combatant an act of collateral damage, and when is it an unlawful act of impunity and terror? How do we address the killing and wounding of civilians in internal armed conflict?

The secret State develops justifications for the use of violence, which eventually proliferate in governance. This cannot but happen. The phrase that emerged during the Cold War, a phrase used by J. K. Galbraith, was the military-industrial complex. A lot of the industrial benefits that we enjoy today, a lot of technological advancements—the computer, telecommunications, the Internet—they come from military technology. You name a major invention that has been put to use in civilian medicine, information and communication, and engineering, and there is a 99 per cent chance it emerged from military production. There is a close connection. The war technology is constantly in the process of development; the study of these technology developments as integral to the idea of law and justice is writ large on military hardware. The connection between the modern State and law is very close. In an unconscious irony, the US defence establishment abbreviates the drones which are recognised as (l)ethal (a)utomatic (w)eapons (s)ystems as LAWS!

May this war machine turn inwards—that is, not against an enemy alien as defined in the law of warfare, but in peacetime, within its own territory and against its own citizens? The first move to describe this phenomenon is to maintain that whatever you may think of the justification for resorting to the use of force against other people, the State ought not to go to war against its own people. If it does so, it is terror. Terror is not constituted in one mode only (like genocide, concentration camp, or the use of food as a weapon); you can further apply it to inflation by 4,000 per cent (as recently in Zimbabwe, or now runaway inflation in Venezuela), or Apartheid South Africa—the State at war against its own people.

Second, this position looks untenable to many as far as internal armed opposition groups or cross-border terrorism is concerned; when such groups defy State authority as unjust and anti-people and take recourse to violent means, can the State be justified in using terror as an integral aspect of counter-terrorism policy? One must here distinguish cross-border terrorist acts and domestic militant violence by separatists or secessionists.

If actions aim at the dismemberment of India into different countries, then here is a *de facto* act of war by some people against the constitutional idea of India, and this, according to some people, justifies when necessary the exercise of extra-legal terror or undue force. This argument has been constantly made since the 1950s, in the context of insurgency and acts of terror imbricated in cross-border geopolitics.

Third, if the State is defined by legitimate monopoly over the use of violence, it raises two or three issues. Is the State legitimate in the eyes of the people? Here, lurks the question: Do we just mean the particular regime, or the very idea of the State? Then, the use of force is only legitimate when it is proportionate and reasonable, and when the decision to use force is justified in advance by recourse to certain principles that guide it. Finally, the use of force must remain untouched or uncontaminated by logics of impunity. There must be expeditious and equitable accountability for force, and even violence used, and a regime of fair and full compensation (rather than any patchwork of compensatory measures) for the violated or the next of kin, in case of death. There is an abundance of the UN and other networks specifying 'soft' and 'hard' laws, for example, the UN Draft Code for Law Enforcement Officials, 1979 (known as the Singhvi Code). So these three aspects have to be fulfilled if one is to say that the State ought to have a monopoly over violence.

When these conditions are broken individually or cumulatively, you can speak of the law's terror. One should also note that a big distinction can be made between immunity and impunity (Baxi 2013). We speak, for example, of sovereign immunity in tort, we talk about immunity in the Bhopal settlement. Impunity is the cousin of immunity, but a big cousin nonetheless. What I am saying is that you can speak about State terror under certain approaches to a constitutionally legitimated monopoly of force. If you take terms such as reasonableness and proportionality, unaccompanied by impunity, these are good enough to start with. If you do not have this normative structure, then you say, yes, here is a system of State terror in which deliberate use of force by the State is beyond the bounds of the exercise of reasonable force, and hence, it fosters impunity.

What form does a protest against the secret State take? If, like the philosophical anarchists, you say that there is no right to use force against the people, then the State, as a form of collective organisation, disappears! Philosophical anarchists have always said that State power to use force is never legitimate, and Jayaprakash Narayan almost reached that point in 1973. This was when he asked the army and the police to disobey unjust orders of the executive. It was then that Emergency was declared. Emergency was not declared only because of all the protests or political processions. The act of asking the armed forces and police to disobey unjust orders was perceived as an act to destabilise the regime, it was a request to the agents of the secret State to act autonomously.

Justice K. K. Mathew, who was the one-man commission on the Samastipur bomb blast,[5] asked me if I could lend him any material on this idea of the unjust State, on the disobeying of manifestly unjust and unlawful orders, and so on. There is a marvellous chapter in his report that examines whether Jayaprakash's call is situationally, constitutionally, and ethically justified. It is worth going back to. My point is, it is fine to talk about Robert Cover, Benjamin, Derrida, Agamben, and so on, I do it myself, and I continue doing it. However, we also have indigenous materials that speak to these questions. I may be wrong here, but I don't think Benjamin or Derrida go into strategies of de-legitimation of the monopoly of the State in the way that Gandhi, Ambedkar, or Jayaprakash did.

There is, of course, a very strong point that can be maintained in defence of the State's counter-insurgency operations. And unsurprisingly, it relates to the *collective human right to a social order and to peace and tranquillity*. The justifications actually offered speak of security, law, and order as matters merely of policy or statecraft. But if one were instead to say that there is a human right to collective security that guarantees a minimum or a modicum of integration of (a term of Talcott Parsons, refined by Julius Stone) 'pattern expectations', then counter-insurgency operations would be justified in the very name of human rights. It is another matter that human rights logics and paralogics may also demand that the collective human right may

[5]'Report of the One-Man Commission of Inquiry Headed by the Hon'ble Mr Justice K. K. Mathew to Enquire into the Incidents of Explosion that Took Place on 2–1–1975 at Samastipur', 1977.

be thus preserved only by reasonable and proportionate means, open always to the gaze of impartial adjudication. A civilised and just State will always endeavour to maintain a sense of proportionality and a wise balance; the right and interests in collective security is at the same moment an individual interest in security that is maintained by, and is consistent with, basic rights and freedoms, both under the Constitution and international human rights norms and standards. The State, in the name of national security, is expected to prevent and punish acts of violence and terror (and this obligation is writ large in the Genocide Convention); it has also to look after the victims, but it is wrong to say that these duties are inconsistent with minimum obligations to protect, promote, and fulfil human rights, and it unnecessarily and unwisely flouts the Declaration on the Right and Responsibility of Individuals, Groups and Organs of Society to Promote and Protect Universally Recognized Human Rights and Fundamental Freedoms (adopted by General Assembly Resolution 53/144 of 9 December 998).[6]

Idea of Rule of Law

LL: To follow up on Arvind's question and to bring together Thompson and the Warwick school debate and your own position on

[6] Article 5 of the Declaration states:

> For the purpose of promoting and protecting human rights and fundamental freedoms, everyone has the right, individually and in association with others, at the national and international levels: (a) To meet or assemble peacefully; (b) To form, join and participate in non-governmental organizations, associations or groups; (c) To communicate with non-governmental or intergovernmental organizations.

And Article 10 declares that: 'No one shall participate, by act or by failure to act where required, in violating human rights and fundamental freedoms and no one shall be subjected to punishment or adverse action of any kind for refusing to do so'. For a critique, see Fernandez and Patel (2015), Mutua (2007).

it. In Thompson, there is the tension of trying to reconcile between the idea of law as a larger universal good after seeing the terror of the law. This produces an ambiguous relationship to the rule of law, in contrast to Douglas Hay (Hay, et al. 2011) or Peter Linebaugh (1991), for whom there is no rule of law outside terror. In your own work, there is this tension as well. There is an acknowledgment of the secret State and the terror of law, yet at the same time, you will not abandon the idea of the rule of law.

AN: To add to that point by Lawrence, I want to quote from *Marx, Law and Justice*:

> And there is no gainsaying of the 'massive evidence' of colonial law's appropriation of subjects, bodies, lives, honour and property. But even Ranajit Guha elsewhere in *Subaltern Studies* had to refer to [the] Raj's 'hegemonic judicature', suggesting that British law in India is not wholly reducible to sheer force of domination without hegemony. We shall have to contend after all with reiteration of E.P. Thompson's stirring observation:
>
>> In a context of gross class inequalities, the equity of the law must always be in some part sham. Transplanted as it were to even more inequitable contexts, this law could become an instrument of imperialism. For this law has found its way to a good many parts of the globe. But even here the rules and rhetoric have imposed some inhibitions upon the imperial power. If the rhetoric was a mask, it was a mask which Gandhi and Nehru were to borrow at the head of a million masked supporters.
>
> The puzzle remains! (Baxi 1993b, 183)

UB: Was I speaking tongue in cheek? When Thompson says that the rule of law is an unqualified human good, I would ask, what is the rule of law? One can say that the most general formulation is the sweeping idea that we should all try to make power increasingly accountable, governance incrementally just, and State progressively ethical. This is the key idea, that is, *making power accountable and governance just*. But this is an activist understanding of the notion of the rule of law. As against this, there are all other kinds of legal and juridical understandings of the rule of law. If you look at Chapter Ten of Vol. 1 of *Das Kapital,* on the sixty-year struggle to ameliorate the Factories Act, the last sentence of this great chapter is that the changes to the Factories Act was the *magna carta* of workers' rights. What one calls the bourgeois understanding of the rule of law is not to be understood only as an ensemble of instruments of domination. They are also notions that provide the means and materials for resistance. You cannot understand capitalism without contradictions. On the one hand, Marx scoffs at bourgeois notions of the rule of law, and on the other, he calls it the *magna carta* of the workers movement. How do we understand this contradiction?

Thompson came much later. My understanding is that Marx is not looking only at the potential of the rule of law for domination; he also saw in it the potential for emancipatory politics. There will always be contradictions in the mode of production. It is the strange stupidity of some contemporary writing on globalisation and neoliberalism which refuses to understand this. They see it as a smooth surface with no contradictions, as if the days of contradiction are over. It is this class and gender-impervious understanding that induces the feeling that there is no alternative. This idea of the world as a smooth surface without contradictions would be unintelligible to a Marxian. So, returning to Thompson and the rule of law, the first thing to understand is the bounded and wounded nature of the rule of law as the source of resistance to this very nature. This is a kind of dialectical understanding.

The same is true of socialist notions of law. There were indeed socialist notions of law. Who has bothered to read the Soviet Constitution? If you take Marxism as a political doctrine, as opposed to the Marxians, then you gloss over structures through words like bourgeois constitutionalism, but these are words that don't mean anything, leading to a nihilistic approach. Take Lenin on nationalism. Or the experience of Uzbekistan and Kazakhstan, where women reformed Islam to make it more equitable and accessible without renouncing their faith. If you look at the struggle of factory workers in socialist States, such as in Tito's Yugoslavia, there are contradictions within the socialist idea of the rule of law.

Here, I am focusing more on the visible State, and not on the secret State which resulted in the Gulag, the so-called 'cultural revolution', the re-education camps, etc. There were immense contradictions. For me, the rule of law is not necessarily all or nothing, as the liberals have it. Bourgeois and socialist understandings do not exhaust the possibilities of the rule of law. Even the Indian variant is extraordinary in itself (Baxi 2007b).

So, one could say that there are two ways of thinking about the rule of law. One is a thin conception, and the other is a thick conception. The thin conception sets out certain basic minimum ethical requirements to make law legitimate. It is called human rights minimalism. The right to free speech, the right of assembly, the right to practice religion, these are basic rights, and *baaki sab chalta rahega* [the rest will go on]. Thompson had the thin idea of the rule of law. You also have Gandhi and his million supporters exercising their right to protest, their right to form assemblies, and that is the rule of law in action. There is a lot in favour of saying that the rule of law should be as thin as possible, and that it becomes difficult to achieve if you make it too thick and crowd it with too many notions. Or even make it a ground of criticism or critique of all forms and structures of power. Nevertheless, there are also thick notions of the rule of law, which you will find if you go back to Mohandas, Jayaprakash, Vinoba, and Lohia. They rarely use the phrase 'the rule of law', but they fought for just governance and an ethical State. You can go even further back to the concept of *raja dharma*.

What did Jayaprakash say? Jayaprakash asked for the right to recall elected representatives who were corrupt and who had a proven reputation, not necessarily even conduct, just reputation. Even mid-term, anytime during the five years, the right to recall could be exercised. Jayaprakash also spoke of proportional representation. Now you put these two ideas together, and you have the idea of participatory governance or *janta sarkar* and *janta* police stations. This is a thick conception of the rule of law. How you come to power is dependent on what electoral system you have, and he said, the form of electoral system you have should be subject to questioning. That is at the heart of legitimate government. It is not just the right to assemble, the right to move, etc. You can do whatever you like, but the same class of people is elected again. The system is geared everywhere towards undemocratic governance and unresponsive government because of the structural impossibility of access by the people to sources of power. Whether proportional representation could have achieved that task is another question. That was JP and Mohandas' idea in 1947. JP had also written a little book called the *Alternative Constitution of India*, elaborating the idea of *Panchayati Raj*. However, it took many movements, right from 1947, to set up the *Panchayati Raj* system.

So thick conceptions always invite disagreement. Thick conceptions do not say that minimalism is justice, or that minimalism is the rule of law. Thick conceptions do not undermine the importance of liberal rights, but they do not stop there. Rights are what they do. Rights are not only what they say you have. That is the thick conception. Doing things with rights—such as raising questions about the morality of power and ethics of good governance, the constitutionality of laws and the reasonability of policies—demosprudental co-governance of the nation involving the legislatures, executive, and judiciary. Otherwise, a right is merely a civic entitlement, like the right to property, by which you have the right to buy a house, a car, etc. But these rights have social consequences. You need to have a conception of just governance, as opposed to good governance. Good governance is what we are doing to facilitate multinationals, globalisation, etc. How does that relate to thick or thin conceptions of justice? That is my second take on this.

My third take is on the mediation by the Constitution, or mediation by constitutional language, of the thick and the thin conception of rights. Part III of the Constitution was thin, and Part IV was thick. Over the years, the Supreme Court of India has tended to blur the distinction between Parts III and IV. While they did not make Part IV justiciable, they said they are as much rights as the other rights. Constitutional mediation occurs within what Derrida describes as the impossibility of justice, or what Lenin described as the 'one step forward and two steps backward' approach. Judicial process is like that. It is like a see-saw. It does not achieve what it tells you it seeks to achieve, but it is always open to a good start.

Human rights is another kind of mediation of thick and thin notions of the rule of law. One needs to understand how contemporary human rights and international human rights discursively impact constitutional operation, as well as how this impacts movements and activism.

I have not looked at a third sort of mediation. I have been accused of having very little faith in representational institutions. Is it a fair indictment? But I do not mean that it is not a worthy field of enquiry. One should look at mediation by the legislative and political processes of thick and thin notions of the rule of law. I am all for a study of legisprudence. Fortunately, we have studies of legislatures at work: see, for example, the recent studies by Shirin Rai and Carol Spray, *Performing Representation: Women Members in the Indian Parliament* (2019), and *The Grammar of Politics and Performance* (Rai and Reinelt 2015). But by and large, we have a lot of judgmental literature which says that for over seventy years, there have been no changes in legislative processes that matter. But do we ask any questions of these processes? How representative is political representation? In what way are reservations for Scheduled Castes (SCs) and Scheduled Tribes (STs) renewed every ten years, in what way have they worked to empower SCs and STs, not just outside but within the legislature? How many people from the SCs and STs have asked difficult questions about atrocity/terror? Have demands and violent agitations increased? Have they decreased? Or have they just emerged as puppets of political parties? I fully accept the criticism that I am a court-centred human rights activist, but I have not been unmindful of demosprudential legisprudence, and the wisdom of resilient social movements that impact on this.

So how does mediation occur? How, for example, was Part IV amended? How did the right to workers' participation come in?[7]

[7] Article 43A of the Constitution reads as follows:

> Participation of workers in management of industries
> The State shall take steps, by suitable legislation or in any other way, to secure the participation of workers in the management of undertakings, establishments or other organisation engaged in any industry.

Was it merely an Indira Gandhi/Emergency legislation? All these are vulgar and superficial explanations. This is not how one reads changes in Constitutions. Any fool can say, yes, the regime was stripped of legitimacy. However, that is not the only story in town. If you go back to the struggles of the workers' movements and the trade-union movements, if you go back to party manifestoes, which party manifesto, at what point in time, talked about workers' participation? This is a rich field that requires to be studied.

I think there is mediation at several levels of legislative processes, in judicial discourse, etc., between thick and thin conceptions of the rule of law. I think Thompson has an elegant phrase for it, the 'unqualified human good', but I think we should read Thompson with a little less alacrity and a lot of generosity. He was not a warrior of the Cold War, espousing an ideology, he was a serious Marxian historian. A lot of criticisms or attempts at criticism have been levelled at this phrase, 'unqualified human good'. Why pick one phrase and nitpick on it all your life? You should show a little intellectual generosity in understanding the context in which he is writing, and that is how I read him.

In an article I wrote on colonial legality for a volume on comparative law traditions (Baxi 2003b), I read Thompson differently, to say that he was perhaps insufficiently aware of how this may have been a mechanism for colonial legality by which to respect some procedural rights of people while denying substantive rights to others. Despite millions of people protesting, if the Empire had not become too costly to maintain after World War II, it might well have continued. The internal contradictions of the British Empire were also part of the objective cause for the decline of Empire. This is not to take away from the freedom movement in which millions of ordinary Indians took part. And indeed, who may at all claim this?

Then there is the whole area of mediation by the nationalist movement of the ideas of rule of law. The Karachi Resolution, and the work of women like Sarojini Naidu, who were the home-spun pre-feminist subjects, come to mind. Some work has been done on this, but only in the context of the Uniform Civil Code, etc. How did this pan-Indian structure of postponement relate to the women's movement?

How did the constant refrain of 'let us first come to power, then we shall meet all your demands' relate to the women's movement? This is a structure of postponement, as against a structure of engagement in which you say, we pre-commit ourselves, we draft hereby a constitution which will fulfil these demands. If you approve of it, you support us. But what we had instead was a structure of postponement. Let us first get the enemy out, and then we will do something. It is important to understand how this negotiation between the thick and the thin occurred in the nationalist movement, because that is the pre-history of the Constitution. The structure of postponement, or deferred outcomes, continues, and it never becomes a structure of engagement, except through movements and struggles.

It is that kind of discourse that I am interested in. I love some of the people you mentioned and their writing. I have yet to read Linebaugh, I have not studied *The London Hanged* (1991) yet, but that whole discourse looks at the contradiction between the rule of law in books and the rule of law in action. That is, the criminal justice system is presented as a massive field negating the absolute commitment to the rule of law. The power to punish and the sovereign dispensation of punishment, whether or not judicially mediated, is inherently the rule of law challenged. How can the criminal justice system be justified? Hundreds of people who have been hung turn out to be innocent. This has been shown through empirical research. Does all this make sense in terms of modern biopolitics? I wonder.

This is a special aspect of power, what Benjamin called the police—he never used the word 'law', he used the word 'police'; he said 'law-police', he reduced in one stroke all law to police power. That is a rich tradition, and really in India, we would benefit a great deal from it. However, I don't know many people who would read it. I think criminal law teaching and research needs to be based on these germinal texts, and on many others of this school of critical criminology. The concept of the rule of law is considered a sublime concept, a constitutional concept, a justice concept. But there will always be this tension between the idea and reality. So you cannot use the weight of the criminal law system in operation to deflate its value, you just rearrange those values adequately, for example, to say that the State will not detain anybody unjustly and arbitrarily, or capital punishment is progressively abolished.

People argue, saying, don't give us empirical studies of the criminal justice system, let us go up and rearrange the values, and make it less thin. A thin conception of the rule of law is a procedural matter, and it requires as many procedural safeguards as possible. A thick conception of the rule of law is substantive. It involves putting rights to work. You rearrange your thin and thick conceptions, and much of the debate between Thompson and his critics can be reworked in a different light. Part of the key is the bag of tools and concepts with which we rethink our notions of the rule of law, rethink with and beyond Thompson.

Poulantzas and a Theory of the State

AN: How are conceptions of rule of law mediated by popular struggle? In *Marx, Law and Justice*, you draw inspiration from Poulantzas to make the point that, 'historiography of legal institutions has, barring notable exceptions, still to respond to the issue of how law was shaped by popular struggles against patterns of domination' (Baxi 1993b). Could you comment?

UB: Poulantzas had a lot of things to say. In his book on law and Marx (Poulantzas 2000), he talks about the norm and the exception. He was concerned with Marxism and the Constitution. Much before all this talk about Carl Schmitt became fashionable, he had a rich concept of the absolute State or the fascist State or the corporatist State. He committed suicide at a very young age. Through his suicide, he was making a statement about what he valued, and since he could not put his thoughts into practice, the act of living was an inauthentic one. That's a kind of testimony which I obviously cannot provide for you, as I am still around! But he is among my moral heroes.

Poulantzas was an analyst of State and regime forms, and of the instability of State forms. Marx started understanding capital as a social relation of domination, exploitation, hegemony, etc. Contrary to the Marxists, the scientific Marx did not articulate the notion of a class. There are only one-and-a-half pages in *Das Kapital,* Vol. I where he tries to articulate the concept of class in broken sentences. But the other Marx, the activist Marx, he could not speak without reference to class struggle. The scientific Marx had the elements of class, but he could not provide you with a full theory. Therefore, a number of people have tried to reimagine the idea of class in Marx. They try to imagine what Marx meant to say.

Poulantzas draws from Marx and says, there are many kinds of capital, there is merchant capital, banking capital, finance capital, industrial capital, and these forms of capital are in constant tension or in contradiction with each other. There is no such thing as homogenous capital, which is opposed to a homogenous mass of the exploited. There are all kinds of interests within capital, capital is often at war with itself, and there are always strategic interests in particular sections of owners of that capital. That is why, for Poulantzas, Marx's idea of State is as a manager of the *whole bourgeoisie,* as opposed to the vulgar Marxists, who claim that the State is the manager of the bourgeoisie. That makes a world of difference. The entire bourgeoisie means all of these people in conflict with each other.

Poulantzas asks: Why is it that owners of capital do not directly run the State? In response to this question, Poulantzas developed a theory of the State following Marx. So, his first question was: Why does the bourgeois class not run the government? Why do they prefer an arrangement where government is run by political parties? It is totally absurd and inefficient, and he found the answer in Marx that these capital formations are constantly colliding because they have different interests, and therefore they need a neutral space which would iron out these differences so that they could all work together in different periods of time. That is the concept of the State as a managing committee of the entire bourgeoisie.

Poulantzas goes further and identifies different forms of State. One is the monopoly capitalist State, which is the source of fascism, and so on. It is called the Bonapartist theory of State (Martin 2008). Poulantzas believed you cannot understand Marx without a theory of the State and of State formations. State formation is not a superstructure. Vulgar Marxism says that State, law, and religion are superstructures. That is totally absurd because, according to them, capitalism is the ownership of the means of production. But what is ownership? It is a juridical category, and law is at the heart of it. If you read Marx, you know that the jural is already present at the site of production. Law and State are material factors of production. The brilliance of Poulantzas was in bringing this into his theory of articulation of the State. Then, of course, comes the problem—where does the rule of law figure? Just as there are factions of capital, the working class itself is not homogenous. Organised and disorganised labour, men and women, vulnerable sections like child workers, there is a whole range of tensions among the working classes themselves.

So, can the State ever be a neutral player? Can it ever be a neutral player between competing factions of capital *inter se*, and between competing factions of the working class? That's the question of the autonomy of the State. The State should be relatively autonomous of capital, market, and labour. Only then can it function as a useful arbiter. They all need some agency to help them sort out problems without necessarily appropriating them. Poulantzas speaks about struggle and the rule of law in that context. The State, thus, is not an entity. It is a form in which various classes attempt to capture the ultimate power for their own ends. It is in the process of capturing the State or appropriating the State that the State reinvents itself.

There is always an invisible State that Marxians don't talk about. The first need in any capitalist form is security, that is, security of persons and of property. How do you provide this security? It is through criminal law, law and order, police, paramilitary forces. That is at the base. Who says this is the superstructure? It is very annoying for me to hear the description of this as the superstructure.

In short, Poulantzas says that the State is not an entity or an essence. It is a condensation of forces or interests. In this context, struggle is very important. It is because the State is constituted by struggles and contestations on all sides that its autonomy is perilous. It is respected only to the extent of the maintenance of interests of different classes.

Poulantzas therefore had a very fine understanding of the rule of law, and he says, you cannot understand the nature of justice, the nature of law, without an understanding of the State. When you understand the nature of the beast—and depending on how you understand the idea of the State as a field of forces—you come to the second level of questions. You then understand struggle as the necessary outcome of contradictions. This may seem abstract, but you can see it everywhere in the law.

We only need to apply these abstract formulations. But Marx himself was never abstract. He lived amongst contradictions. You have to learn to live amidst the contradictions of suffering to make the abstract real. It is abstract only for those who think it is lying in the books. But it is not. Marx's book is an open book. Poulantzas gives you example after example of how the State becomes a regulatory force, how State pathologies occur. If the State captures power absolutely, then it is a fascist State. If it assists particular forms, it can be a corporatist State. If it denies autonomy to others, he describes it as a State of exception. It is in his reflections on the exceptional State that some of his best writings on struggle have emerged. Poulantzas's book, *State, Power, Socialism* (2000), is relevant even now.

AN: You referred to Vol. I and the discussions of Committees on the Factories Act and the contradictions of people who should, if they were loyal to their class, not support any kind of reform at all. In fact, speaking of the role of labour law reformers, Marx approvingly calls them 'knowledgeable, impartial and relentless men'. You note that Marx regarded them as 'articulators of subaltern consciousness in the theatre of bourgeoisie law, administration and politics' (Baxi 1993b). How does this happen?

UB: This happens because Marx also speaks about moral economy, and not just about political economy. He said that certain forms of common moral sentiment, for example, led to the movement for the abolition of slavery in Britain. This could have emerged from Christian sentiments of brotherhood, or from the moral sentiment of community against the denial of humanity. When does it get triggered, and when does it becomes the basis of action for change, is a very difficult question to answer.

On the one side, you have the bourgeoisie and what Marx called the petit bourgeoisie. My poor joke is that I don't like the petit bourgeoisie, but I am all for the pretty bourgeoisie! The petty bourgeoisie are those who are not directly implicated in the ownership of the means of production. They are ancillary—teachers, journalists, etc. The petit bourgeoisie perform several roles. Sometimes, they perform extraordinary roles. A cartoonist or a satirist can cause the most serious disruptions to the legitimacy of the State. It is a very complex formulation.

On the other side, you have the terribly un-Marxian notion of the *lumpen proletariat*. That is more of an Engels-ian conception. So, you have the bourgeoisie, the petit bourgeoisie, and the lumpen. And the petit and the bourgeoisie are always united against what they call the lumpen. Those of the poor who beg are the lumpen. They are not involved in production, nor do they support production. They are cancerous people. They put out their hand and beg for money. This disrupts our moral economy. It is said even now that poor people beg because they are lazy and affected by cultures of poverty! So we can see the usefulness of these distinctions. The lumpen disrupt the progress of the State, and when seen that way, it is a useful category. But lumpen as a category of judgement is awful. I would say, if there are any lumpen elements to be found, they are in our classes and not outside them. The kind of corruption in politics, as well as in academia, is simply unbelievable. The pretty bourgeois is perhaps the foremost lumpen class globally today!

So, returning to the Factories Act, how does the working cross-class coalition take place? Marx describes it in great detail. But if you ask me today, I will try and put it in slightly different terms. One is the idea of the relative autonomy of the State. This is a terribly important idea. This means that the State, in order to perform a certain function of mediation between the working classes and the property-owning classes, has to have a certain autonomy of action. It may come out at the end of the day in favour of the property-owning classes. Politics is the art of mystification. In the name of acting for the working classes, it ultimately seeks to benefit the propertiat.

You know the story of the Twenty Point Programme in India. Some people would even say that one can analyse the NREGA in terms of the mystification of power relations.[8] You can ask the question: Why did it take until 2008 to enact the Domestic Workers Act?[9] Why was it not done earlier? Is it because of the present need to produce an idea of the State as inclusive and of globalisation as fair? Is it to produce the idea that we are not merely neoliberal, we are for a progressive constitutional governance? What is mystified is enormous. These have been the demands of a whole range of movements and struggles from the 1950s. So, however you may read its *telos*, whether to say that the State is systematically biased in favour of the working classes or in favour of the capitalists, intuitively we can say that the State can be a managing committee of the entire bourgeoisie when it also protects and promotes certain emancipatory interests. The only condition is that it should be autonomous.

Therefore, it sets up the Factory Law Reform Committee. Factories were self-sufficient in the nineteenth century. It was then that doctors were made to go and report on the working conditions of factories. This is the internal differentiation of the State. The State is not one thing. It is a bureaucracy. It consists of its officers, its experts (now of course dignified by the name 'epistocracy'), as well as of those who are called in to testify. It is this autonomy that enables a whole range of other voices to come in. Of course, there is the fact of struggle outside—what in liberal language you call public opinion, and what

---

[8]NREGA, National Rural Employment Guarantee Act 2005 (later renamed as the Mahatma Gandhi National Rural Employment Guarantee Act, MGNREGA): labour law and social security measure that aims to guarantee the right to work, and to enhance livelihood security in rural areas, by providing at least 100 days of wage employment in a financial year to every household whose adult members volunteers to do unskilled manual work.

[9]Domestic Workers (Registration, Social Security and Welfare) Act, 2008, introduced to regulate payment and working conditions and check exploitation of domestic workers (Domestic Workers Act 2008).

you now call policymaking. In order to justify the functioning of the State, you must at times remedy the most radical evil to which property owners subject the working class. The time dimension is very important. It is not a process that takes place in one sweep. I would read this in terms of State differentiation and State autonomy.

State and Regime

UB (***contd***): The requirement of the liberal State is to manage the appearance of being *of* all people, if not *for* all people. The question of legitimacy, of being elected, is important. The way the party system develops is through the competition for power, be it as a multi-party system or a two-party system. Each party claims to be more representative of the plight of the working classes and of the industrial classes. Here, you have to be very careful about this distinction between State and regime.

Take Foucault's distinction between governmentality and government. Foucault is not a materialist thinker. That is my difficulty with him. He is not a rigorously Marxian thinker. He is highly influenced by Marx, but Marx is not his problem. That does not take away anything from Foucault. But we need to marry Foucault with Marxians like Poulantzas. There was a Polish economist (Kalecki 1972; Raj 2014) who spoke about India as an intermediate regime, as neither capitalist nor socialist. There is, of course, our friend Utsa Patnaik among the foremost Marxian economists we have produced. She worked on exploitative relationships in agricultural production, on the idea of unfree labour. In Utsa Patnaik's work, the regime may be a historic formulation which stands in contrast to the State (Patnaik 1986). The State is in the business of managing contradictions, including contradictions of its own, while seeming autonomous and neutral. This is very difficult. So what happens is that struggle consists almost always of efforts to change the regime, not the State. A change of State requires a change of the rules, not of the players.

This particular seventy-year formation (India) was a regime-building formation in which certain elements of State autonomy, certain elements of liberal society, certain elements of struggle all came together over many generations.

I mentioned the implications of Panchayati Raj for bonded labour, though it is superficial to say that it all comes down to the legitimacy of one leader. It is a work of regime change and of regime collisions. And now we are talking also of regime collisions in international law. There are regime collisions in global governance. You cannot speak of globalisation just like that. If you look at how many institutions exist today, the International Monetary Fund (IMF), the World Bank, the World Trade Organization (WTO), the International Court of Justice, they are all not just one thing. It is not just the WTO, it is a whole series of things. Within that is the distinction of public and private. There are various notions of law under each. You have institutional law. You also have something called project law. Each project generates a private legal system of its own. The project grantor, the investor, the institute, the relationship between the project director and the worker are all subject to private legislations. Project law is a kind of legal pluralism in its most astonishing form, and is very important to the process of knowledge production today. (I can't recall it, but there was a colleague from Switzerland who presented a paper on 'project law' at a legal pluralism seminar at Edinburgh in early 2000).

So, you have to walk with both feet simultaneously—the State, on the one side, and the regime on the other. This is the contribution of Poulantzas. A regime is constituted by several interests, not only of the bourgeois and the working class alone, but also of the petty bourgeoisie who have no power, but only influence. One of the great distinctions made by Weber is that power is my ability to impose my will on others, but influence is not power. As Lewis Coser (1956) long ago demonstrated, Marx had influence, but no power. Einstein had influence, but no power. We may add similarly that Gandhi had influence, but no power. Influence is sometimes a higher form of power. It is a different form. You are not trying to overpower the will of the other. You are instantiating alternative ways of thinking. Indian

Administrative Service (IAS) officers seek power, but intellectuals seek influence. The significance of the other, and of the alternative, cannot be undermined. Take JP. He had no power, even though he was articulating the alternative of a Total Revolution. He is still here with us in activist movements. Every single activist in India is a residual legatee of the influence of JP, as is every single activist lawyer, and every radical judge. Power is contested, it is ever changing, always fragile. The paradox of power is that the stronger your power, the more vulnerable you are to counter-power. The more concentrated you think is the power in you, the more secure you think your power is, the more vulnerable you are. But when power is thought more as a structure and less in terms of power relations (a distinction that Julius Stone memorably made while discussing Talcott Parsons in Chapter 13 of the *Social Dimensions of Law and Justice* [Stone 1966b]), what we have is a more stable vector of power. Structures are thought of as more enduring and resilient, though never impervious to change. Put another way, a soft (rhetorical/persuasive) form of power begins to assume the visages of absolute power.

The Scientific Marx and the Activist Marx

AN: You have used the phrase 'vulgar criticism' often. And you have stated that 'a truly philosophic criticism of the present state constitution not only shows up contradictions as existing, it explains them, it comprehends their genesis, their special significance' (Baxi 1993b, 10). Could you expand on this?

UB: I thought you were quoting somebody else! If that was me, that is very good. Collars up for me! It looks somewhat like my prose, but I have no monopoly over that style. *Vulgaris* is a Latin term. Vulgarity lies in ostentatious displays of wealth, for example. Driving a Ferrari on the streets of Bangalore is vulgar. Driving a scooter causes no raised eyebrows and may even be considered responsible. What is vulgar and what is not vulgar is a very difficult issue, and in contemporary politics it acquires the form of political correctness. If, for example, the challenge of humour as a mode of expression in these days of political correctness is to distinguish between forms of humour and hate speech, speech must not be vulgar, it must be responsible and responsive. It is that notion of civility. Are forms of civility inherently repressive or emancipatory?

So, how can you be responsible and responsive to Marx? If you are speed-reading him, if speed-reading were to constitute reading in the first place, it cannot be responsive, because Marx acknowledged meticulously every author he cited, the logic they presented, arguments on their behalf, and then he criticised them. He was a responsive thinker as well as a responsible thinker. He did not just present a digest or a chronology of thought, but he exerted himself to thinking another worldview. Vulgarising is a cash-and-carry discourse. Like in a shop, where you can pick up anything, take it to the counter, and pay for it.

The other form of vulgar Marxism is a political appropriation, the appropriation of Marx's textuality and intertextuality and legacy for engaging in competitive politics. This is very different from Marxian notions of politics. The question is not whether he is a political philosopher or not. The question is that bourgeois politics created conditions of exploitation and conditions of misery, even as it created conditions of material progress. One is a descriptive form of politics, and even though he despised bourgeois politics, the question is whether he had an alternative form. The question is not of what is, but of what does one do to take it beyond? There is no use telling me, this is wrong, that is wrong. The question is whether all of this is raw material for an alternative politics. Do we have an alternative way of arriving at the idea of politics? Marx, of course, had such an alternative vision. He had a whole socialist utopia of human liberation. This, of course, opens out the realm of what you can call emancipatory politics, or what some people call redemptive politics. Redemptive politics sounds good and rolls off our tongues rather smoothly, but the question always is, redemption from what and to what? *And at whose cost, for how long?*

In an interview with Foucault (1966) a week before his death, the interviewer asked: What do you think about politics? Foucault paused for a long while. The interviewer repeated his question. Foucault said, I know what your question is, I have been told that, objectively, the conditions for revolution have ceased to exist. So I am asking myself, what is the other of politics? If the other of politics is revolution, and revolution is no longer a possibility, then how can politics survive?

So what is the other of politics? Now we cannot speak of revolution. You lose your audience when you use that word. You cannot communicate. Revolution has a terrible history, and you know that. But there are also honourable histories. The postcolonial revolution, it is a revolution that we must learn to honour for its overthrowing of imperialism. We now talk about non-revolutionary politics that is redemptive, transformative, emancipatory. I wondered whether Boaventura de Sousa Santos had any thoughts on setting up a worldwide centre on emancipatory politics, and he has now come up with the notion that we must re-do the idea of the State (Santos 1995). He looked at the Zapatistas in Mexico, the World Social Forum in Brazil, and he says we should think about the Third World State not as a State in the conventional sense, but as a social movement in itself.

I take this very seriously, but I find it astonishing for being indicted of making the mistake of stating (in 'Taking Suffering Seriously', Baxi 1985c) that the Supreme Court of India has become the Supreme Court for Indians in partnership with professionals, teachers, journalists, that it has assumed the visages of a social movement. But I clearly talked both about enchantment and disenchantment with creative judicial process. Likewise, Boaventura de Sousa Santos talks later of the emancipatory and the repressive pillars of law, but also entertains the notion of the State as a social movement. The State and law as a normative frame consist of an ideational frame for domination, but also provides scope for subaltern elements for struggle. Materialism does not merely mean the material production of goods and services, but also the production of desires and symbols. If we were to forget that, we become vulgar Marxists who look at just one ideal imaginary of the State.

Now the question that arises is whether the second Marx is a vulgar Marxist. The first Marx, the scientific Marx, is a thinker. It was recently the [sesqui] centenary of the *Communist Manifesto*. Read the *Manifesto* for yourself and decide. The *Manifesto* has summoning prose, vivid prose, with phrases like, 'Workers of the World, Unite. You have nothing to lose but your chains.' The polemical Marx, the activist Marx, the street-smart Marx, are they examples of vulgar Marxism? I don't know. Does he carry over his scientific understanding into his activism? If he does, then he would not be a vulgar Marxist.

The question is, how do we put together the two Marx-es? The activist Marx is very important. However, we are now fed on a diet that theory is no good for praxis. That theory disables solidarity. That theory causes paralysis by analysis—what I described in *Human Rights in a Post-Human World* (Baxi 2007a) as a theory aversion. An allergy to theory. I have shown why it is wrong and counterproductive. I distinguish this from another form called resistance to theory, which can be very productive. It is about asking questions to theory about what it is good for. If theory is no good, then what are other ways of understanding? Resistance to theory can be emancipatory. The theory that women are inferior to men was a whole discourse for two centuries or more. So there can be regressive or emancipatory theories.

And the task of resistance to theory is to bring this distinction alive. How can you say that a certain form of theory is a regressive form of theorising, while another is emancipatory? That demands serious work. I do not agree with the approach which simply says that all theory is jargon. I don't like theory, I don't understand theory, theory is so boring that it reminds me of what Eliot said (in a misogynist mood and disparagingly) in *The Wasteland*, 'women come and go talking of Michelangelo'. This is as though people who engage in theory come and go talking of Michelangelo. It is, on the other hand, very important to ask: Can you be effective, create an effective imaginary through theory?

Is the power of the second Marx—the ideologue—with a summoning imaginary ever possible without the existence of the first Marx? My criticism of vulgar Marxism raises a set of wider questions. In modern times, we call this a form of reflexivity. Reflexivity is a learning from the crisis of action—the crisis of institutional action, of moral action, and of systemic action. Reflexivity is considered very important. It is an important virtue. Some people say that reflexivity consists not of our self-serving interests, but of our capacity to take interest in our interests. Everybody has interests. A reflexive mind is an entity which retains an *interest in interests.* The second Marx retained an interest in reflexive activism. He transmuted his enormous scientific interests without necessarily weakening or vulgarising these. You can say this about Engels' work on the origins of family and property.

Without damaging your capacity to think through contradictions, you have to cultivate an ability to understand contradictions. Ambedkar (1949) said that on 26 January 1950, we shall enter into a life of contradictions with the grant of equal votes for every person and continuing inequality in social and economic life. The question that I tried to raise is: What is the understanding of contradictions in Ambedkar and in Marx? I tried to understand five kinds of contradictions. One is normative contradiction, when norms don't cohere and you have to make sense of them. There is institutional contradiction, when institutions don't cohere, for instance, the fundamental disagreement over judicial activism (excepting when it suits specific party-political interests) in the Indian political class and the Supreme Court. Then there are material contradictions. Marx wrote about material contradictions, which arise out of the ownership of means of production and ownership over means of labour. And that is the contradiction that drives history, that drives resistance, and that drives change. Ambedkar was talking about normative contradictions, and possibly about institutional contradictions.

Chairman Mao tried to supersede Marx, and whatever you think of Mao, you cannot ignore the fact—I certainly don't—that he was the first Third World or Asian Marxian in theory and in practice. One of the great self-imposed limitations of Marx was that he himself stated that he was dealing only with the laws of industrial capital in industrially developed nations. He mentioned several times the Asiatic mode of production, but he never developed it because that was not within his scope. Those who criticise Marx for not talking about the Asiatic mode of production are like people who say the computer chap who repairs your computer is bad because he does not know how to carve a turkey. This is absurd. He deliberately excluded the Asiatic mode of production from his analysis. But Mao developed it. For Mao, there can only be two types of contradictions: antagonistic and non-antagonistic contradictions. You can have more. You can have a typology of contradictions. I am only illustrating it.

Marx and Re-enchanting the World

AN: I was thinking of the quotation from Marx: 'Religion is the heart of a heartless world, the sigh of an oppressed world. Religion is the opium of the masses.' The last part of it we remember. The first part is quite poetic and invokes the notion of religion as enchantment.

UB: Yes! He says religion is the *sigh of the oppressed* and the *heart of a heartless world*. It is true, everybody remembers the opium part. Marx says, sigh of the oppressed. He does not say curse. Now that is interesting. Because *sigh* is very different from *curse*. Both sigh and curse entail human collective agency, of course. But curse differs because, instead of narrating this vast exploitation as the sigh does, it is an active power, a counter-power, that the accursed will not enjoy what they think they have 'got' or gained.

I think it is vital to stay with the power of the sigh and the counter-power of the curse. The sigh is far from effete—it creates a trans-human power of religion, of a wrathful or a benign Being of which we are mere creatures. Religion as a sigh of the oppressed enchants as well as disenchants, there is an imagination of the omnipotent non-human which is at work in all religions. When the sigh mocks the sovereign, the latter is quick to take on the attributes of being Divine, in origin and function. Marx says a lot about histories of sovereignty when he writes about a sigh that has no history.

When does the sigh become an addiction, the opium of the masses? Marx believed genuinely that a natural response (sigh) becomes a habit (addiction) in and with religiosity. The sense of wonder or astonishment that is at the root of the experience of religion is dulled into the catechesis of routine: the robes, the liturgy, the chanting, the incense, the altar, or the *avatar*, and the worship itself becomes prayer.

Marx did not offer any social or ethical views about addiction in general, although he was aware that it can be viciously organised to promote capitalist colonialism through the exploitation of workers and consumers. Aggressive promotion of such exploitation leads to such phenomena as drug wars and retaliatory State wars on drugs (narcotic drugs and other psychotropic substances) at all levels (global, regional, national, and local). But his reference to opium suggests that even as measured addiction does escalate the powers of the mind, a mass-level addiction presents a public danger. The general addiction to something—the rationalist to 'reason', the militia to 'discipline', the historian to 'facts', the mass media to news and views, the Marxian intellectual to 'critique', or a judge to 'justice'—seems unproblematic.

In comparing religion to opium, Marx used addiction in a pejorative sense, where one loses the sense of acting responsibly and responsively. 'Opium' heightens both responsibility and responsiveness in the short run; in the long haul, it leads to self-destruction. Real power, then, lies not in deaddiction, but in measured addiction. Is this what Marx meant to say?

The description you prefer—whether sigh, curse, or opium—is a matter of one's choice and judgement (whether this is conditioned or even determined), but it is also about the powers of self-control and of controlling others (domination in Weber, exploitation and alienation in Marx).

I have written somewhere about Justice Y. V. Chandrachud uttering an explicit curse in *Kesavananda* (Baxi 1974). He decides to give Parliament total power to amend the Constitution, to even repeal it. In so doing, he utters, for the first time in Indian, even modern, judicial history, a curse—we have given you vast powers for the welfare of the country, but woe betide you (it is delicious, this phrase!), woe betide you if you misuse these powers.[10] Judicial curse is a pre-modern

[10]'*Kesavananda* has also produced (or rather revived) the institution of *judicial curse* which Chandrachud, J., utters towards the end of his opinion. He says: "But, if despite the large powers now conceded to the Parliament, the

phenomenon; its evocation in opposing the basic structure (itself a judicial innovation) is at once judicial self-abnegation.

AN: You quite enjoy Justice Chandrachud's language, one can make out—from 'two swallows do not a summer make', to the soaring rhetoric in Minerva Mills and your statement about the pilgrim's progress. One can't make out if you are making fun of Justice Chandrachud or admiring him. Is it a fine balance between both?[11]

UB: The answer to this lies with you, Arvind, or with each reader! Yes, I do enjoy critiquing the judges: they are critical of all institutions except of the office of a judge or of the institution of a court. Even as they see the beam in other eyes and seek to control or cure it, they scarcely seek to remove the mote in their own.[12] They also tie themselves into several knots as they move from bench to bench (the discretion of the Chief Justice in composing the bench is untrammelled), from court to court (ours is probably the only country where they can be transferred from one high court to another in the name of national integration), and from case to case (as there is now precious little of institutional memory). I consciously engage my works in a process of, as I name it, 'pickling' the judges, of making them more edible, preserving their good and bad work for future memory, and assessing them individually and collectively (as actors and as institutions) with a view to rendering their workings more transparent and hopefully more democratically accountable. This work is serious because it does not come easily to academics, and to others, to understand the ways of 'thinking like a judge'. There is a strange alchemy going on here, and one seeks, as best

---

social objectives are going to be a dustbin of sentiments, then *woe betide those in whom the country has placed such massive faith*'" (Baxi 1974).

[11] See 'The Fair Name of Justice' (Baxi 1985f).

[12] Upendra Baxi note: 'This passage is from Matthew 7:3–5, King James Version (KJV): '3 And why beholdest thou the mote that is in thy brother's eye, but considerest not the beam that is in thine own eye?/4 Or how wilt thou say to thy brother, Let me pull out the mote out of thine eye; and, behold, a beam is in thine own eye?/5 Thou hypocrite, first cast out the beam out of thine own eye; and then shalt thou see clearly to cast out the mote out of thy brother's eye.'

as one can, to lay bare a glimpse of the working of the judicial mind. I was also conscious of the privilege that some judges accorded me of calling me 'Brother Baxi'. (I also know that the epithet occasionally changes to 'Blighter Baxi'!)

To come specifically to your question, Justice Chandrachud was a friend of mine as well as a favourite judge. Like all Indian appellate judges, he had a problem with adjudicative consistency, but the way in which he addressed or resolved it was his very own. He is a pragmatic judge, in the best sense of that term. This he shared with Justice P. N. Bhagwati.[13] This is not to say that either adjusted their judicial principles to the political exigencies of the day, but they did not let principles *alone* decide every case before them. The social and political context mattered to them certainly in cataclysmic situations. The situation of Emergency and post-Emergency was one of them, and how they dealt with them is fully explained in *The Indian Supreme Court and Politics* (Baxi 1980), in *Courage, Craft, and Contention* (Baxi 1985b), and in some other writings of mine. These works commented upon them and even critiqued them, but they never attributed to Justices or the Court any sinister political motivation, unlike most grapevine criticism of our judges today. All acts of reading, as Jacques Derrida has taught us in recent times, and as Marx said a long while ago, are complex and difficult, especially when tracing the *unsaid in what gets said*.

Coming back to Marx, the activist Marx is the Marx who is seeking to re-enchant the world with ideas of ultimate human liberation and emancipation. It is in this utopia that the State will wither away on its own. Among a lot of vulgar Marxists, illiterate people, this has been reduced to a meaningless slogan. Some people say, ho! ho! ho! Marx said the State will wither away, it has withered away in Bihar! It's only a poor joke. It has nothing to do with Marx. Some people today even

[13] Prafullachandra Natwarlal Bhagwati (1921–2017), seventeenth Chief Justice of India (1985–1986), pioneer of judicial activism, known as one of the initiators of public interest litigation. See 'Uprooting Injustice, Organizing Negation: The Enduring Contribution of Justice P. N. Bhagwati' (Baxi 2019c).

cannot differentiate between Karl Marx and the screen comedians Groucho, Chico, Harpo, and Zeppo! Utopia is best understood as a context in which domination is not a natural condition for human existence. It is a spiritual notion. I have worked on the notion of utopia, I have written a paper on the notion of Constitutional utopia (Baxi 2009a). Alan Norrie and others are working on the notion of utopia.[14] This has nothing to do with actually existing liberalism or communism—they are announced as theories of utopia, but they are ideologies that mask the reality of oppression.

We must take care, of course, when we talk about 'destruction'. One may ask, what is creative about the Holocaust? Or about apartheid? Or about the cultural revolution in Mao's People's Republic of China? Or about Stalinism, which was considered creative destruction by leading Euro-Marxians? On the other side, the question is posed not in political terms at all, but rather, in economic terms. For the non-slave mode of production to arise, the slave mode had to be destroyed; for the industrial mode to thrive, the pre-industrial or feudal mode had to be destroyed; the Asiatic mode of production had to be likewise destroyed if the colonial mode was to be established. Judged from the standpoint of pure economic growth, such destruction is creative.

The law also destroys, even as it creates. Robert Cover was among the first thinkers of this. In his famous article *Nomos and Narrative* (1983), he draws a distinction between jurisgenerative and jurispathic violence of law. He showed that when the State kills in the name of law or justice, regardless of whether you are an abolitionist or retentionist, '...legal interpretation occurs on the field of pain and death'. Walter Benjamin, whom Jacques Derrida followed in this respect (not to worry in this context about any Derridean play on the meaning of the word 'followed'!), also emphasised the centrality of police and of the force of law. Marx summated all this well in his analysis of 'force without phrases' and the 'force of phrases'.

[14]'Utopian Legalities': Workshop at Kings College London, 19 November 2005. Upendra Baxi presented a paper, 'Constitutional Utopias', and Alan Norrie on 'Law Discloses the Utopian: Justice and the Nation State'.

LL: There is a wonderful encyclopaedia put together by Alberto Manguel which is an encyclopaedia of imaginary places (Manguel and Guadalpi 1980). And a lot of it is on the various utopias people have imagined.

UB: Wonderful! I will surely look at it. But it is curious to provide a list of imaginary places, places which were not in existence. A topography of places which did not, yet may exist seems like a wonderful idea, doesn't it? One does not ask of the Utopic questions about the Real. Even so, one hears a lot of talk about 'rational utopias'. This is, for example, the favourite of post-Marxists, who imagine that something like 'coupon socialism' may yet possibly reform, or even overcome, capitalism.

The Utopic as an imaginary ideal is often contrasted with this notion of 'rational utopia'; earlier, folks talked about not just 'alternative development', but alternatives to development; today, the idea of 'degrowth' seems to confront the paradigm of 'sustainable development'.

I have only looked at Leibniz, at some Arabian philosophers of the twelfth or thirteenth centuries. The contrast is between a book-based vision of the utopia of millennialism and a philosophical tradition of considering utopia.

LL: The former Ford Foundation head, Sumathi Ramaswamy (2004), has a beautiful book. Her background is in cartography, and she writes about Lemuria, the imaginary land between Tamil Nadu and Africa. It is a fabulous geography.

UB: Oh! So Utopia is another non-contaminable place (or is it space?). We can talk about utopia because enchantment comes from the possibility of transcendence from all that we know, that is said to be necessary and inevitable. TINA—There is No Alternative. Against this, the act of imagination, needs to develop the utopic. It is a marvellous, marvellous idea, though there are many questions and problems, as with any notion. I think Chhatrapati Singh (1985) was the first and only Indian legal philosopher who went to Leibniz, and I acknowledge him. Leibniz's idea of utopia was of the compossibility of all possible worlds. That's where the World Social Forum gets its slogan from, 'Another World Is Possible'. There are, of course, socialist utopias.

Scientific Marx had little use for the romantic imagination. He said it up front. Nobody reads the Preface to the first volume of *Das Kapital*. Two sentences. When I write my prefaces, I always wonder when I will learn to write like this man. Although in *Crisis*, I did try to emulate him. The Preface should summarise the theme of the book in one sentence. I quoted Marx in my very brief Preface, 'Justice can never rise beyond the necessities of the time' (Baxi 1982a). Marx said, I am offering only a study of early industrial capitalism and its flaws. So he has to say that all feudal bonds, like master-servant, must dissolve in capitalism. Is it a good thing or a bad thing?

In *Das Kapital*, there is so much poetry. My God! It's fantastic, especially the first volume. He says, in the change from feudalism to industrial capitalism, workers move from being tied by iron chains to being tied by silken fetters. He would incessantly say, you cannot have movement without destruction. The understanding of destruction is the key to Marx. You cannot create without destruction, you have to destroy pre-capitalist forms if you want to create capitalist forms. Although not explicitly stated by arch-globalisers of contemporary India, the perspective was that a good deal of the Constitution needed destruction to achieve a global India, with its uneasy model of rights, justice, development, and governance; if you want to follow a different model, you need to change it totally, say in the direction of neoliberalism and its many Ds: denationalisation, deregulation, disinvestment, de-constitutionalisation, de-solidarisation, and depoliticisation.

So, the notion of destruction and creation is not wholly sacred. It is not the privilege of the gods alone. Like Brahma–Vishnu–Mahesh, one creates, the other preserves, the third destroys. What forms of destruction are necessary for creation, and what forms of destruction are unjust and impermissible, is the important question. What is written in my heart and what guides me is what Marx wrote somewhere in 1850: The classical saint of Christianity mortified his body for the sake of the redemption of the masses. The modern educated saint mortifies the body of the masses for his own redemption. There is no better epitaph on scholarship. It cannot be written. It cannot be re-written.

LL: Activists always have this bookmark Marx: 'Philosophers have merely interpreted the world, now is the time to change it.' But in *The Eighteenth Brumaire*, there is also the other famous line: 'Philosophy cannot actualize itself without the transcendence of the proletariat. The proletariat cannot actualize itself without the actualization of philosophy.'

AN: We had a chance to read *Marx, Law and Justice* for the first time in Warwick University. As an introduction to Marx, it makes you want to visit Marx or revisit Marx. Because you have really gone into all these texts in detail: 'The Law of Theft', *The Eighteenth Brumaire*, *Das Kapital*, Vol. 1, *Grundrisse*, and 'The German Ideology'.

LL: To read him, is to learn how to write. 'On the Jewish Question' is so beautifully written.

UB: Absolutely! And he is an exemplary scholar. Look at Marx's footnotes and the conditions in which he wrote; there was no dictaphone, no computer, nothing like that. And he wrote this three-volume manuscript. He used to sit in the British Museum from nine o'clock every morning until he was thrown out by the guards when it closed at 10 or 10.30 PM. Regularly, for ten or twelve years. When you look at his footnotes, you see cited *The London Star*, *The Pall Mall Gazette*, etc. Anything that was written on the working conditions of women and children and factory workers in that period is footnoted and commented upon. Not a single thinker, or a journalist escapes his attention. He builds on some of them, demolishes others, and re-builds anew. Whatever one may think of him as an ideologue or as a scientist, he is a model of how to pursue an enquiry. The great loss to the human world after the fall of the Berlin Wall was the complete works of Marx. This is because Progress Publishers in Moscow had planned a Collected Works of Marx in thirty-seven volumes. They had come up to twenty-six volumes when the Berlin Wall collapsed.

Someone from the London School of Economics wrote to me and said, why are you citing Progress Publishers? I said, why not? They said, there are distortions. I said, there are plenty of distortions in the more heavily priced versions available in England. Besides, I could not afford those. The great thing about Progress Publishers is that you would go to their bookshops and you would get an astonishing range in Gujarati, Marathi, Tamil, you name it. It was absolutely brilliant.

One of the books I bought is a beautiful study by a Soviet scholar in around the late 1960s on Modern Indian Thinkers—lovely!—Tagore, Nehru, Gandhi, and Aurobindo. The author was an ideologue, but one who was clearly bound to the discipline of loyal exposition before he began his critique. The more loyal the exposition is, the more cogent the critique is. They don't take short cuts in narrating the enemy they are going to attack. Now, this is remarkable, is it not? ... this ability to describe fully what the other had good grounds for saying, before demolishing the argument. Demolition only follows after a full exposition. Can that become the task of critique, as distinct from mere criticism?

Why Should We Engage with Marx Today?

UB (*contd*): What a question! Why should we engage with Marx today? Well, as we always ought to with the founders of inaugural discursivity. 'Utopian legalities' surely flow over the embankments and enclosures of both progressive and regressive lineages of Eurocentric thought. It inverts the grammar of a 'universal' utopic 'Imperialism of Same (*per* Levinas), the Eternal Return of mimetic, and fecund, sameness'. The task is two-fold: one, to provide an alternative politics by whatever name you call it, and two, to relate erudite understanding with local movement and action. To convert your understanding of economy and society to everyday action, to the sites of production, distribution, exchange, consumption, and reproduction. To purse the utopic is at the same time understand the dystopic and even heterotopic.

Marx does not allow you to read him half-heartedly. You cannot read him and play tricks. You cannot read him starting from the middle or beginning with the end. You cannot also speed-read him.

You have to engage with him. You have to do *manthan*—reading as an act of churning. I am yet to find a comparable thinker to Marx. You then have to read all the others in light of our understanding of Marx. You have to resituate Foucault or, as Agamben said, you have 'to complete Foucault'. You should resituate Agamben through an original reading of Marx.

In this context, I also think of Negri. I don't mean Negri and Hardt. I like my Negri neat! I am talking here of the Negri not of *Multitude* but of *Marx Beyond Marx*, where he tried to present the possibility of contradictions within Marx's own thought in the *Grundrisse*. Then he wrote *Insurgencies*, which is about popular and legal sovereignty, in which he explored this through the concepts of constituted power and constitutive power (Hardt and Negri 2004; Negri 1991, 1999). Another book I have learnt a lot from is *A Grammar of the Multitude* by Paolo Virno (2004). But one is outdated as soon as one completes a book because more are already added to one's reading list by then! The bibliophiles amongst us may warm up to John Stuart Mill's dictum that it is always better to be human being dissatisfied than a pig satisfied! Of course, those who (like me) assail speciesism in thinking will object to the unkind violence in reference to pigs.[15]

Oh, but I have not fully responded to many of your posers. I would agree, Lawrence, that we do not merely learn to read, but to write with him. And, Arvind, the bookmark quote you mentioned entails a robust understating of the world and tasks of change, very hard work, isn't it?

[15] The full quote from his *Utilitarianism* (1863) is as follows: 'It is better to be a human being dissatisfied than a pig satisfied; better to be Socrates dissatisfied than a fool satisfied. And if the fool, or the pig, is of a different opinion, it is only because they only know their own side of the question.'

Ten

Constitutionalism, Human Rights Activism, and Their Futures

Essentialising the 'Human' in Human Rights

AN: You spoke about strategic essentialism earlier. Does not the idea of a strategic essentialism seem a little too instrumental? Isn't there something to essentialism that may be precious? I recently read Judith Butler's essays post 9/11, *Precarious Life* (2006), and I get the sense that she seems to be returning to some idea of the universal in the context of Guantanamo Bay, where there is a denial of the humanity of certain sections of people. In such a context, what can you come back to? You can come back to the language of the human, which seems to be the only way to critique the process of de-humanisation, based on the idea of what it means to be human. So I am a little curious, because this idea of *strategic* seems to be putting it in an instrumental manner, which might be ducking the real question. And so I am wondering whether there is a value in the idea of a commonality that people may share. If there is something to be said for what is common between you and me, why do we focus only on what is different?

UB: I do not think strategic essentialism is necessarily a bad phrase or strategy. What we call praxis is an instance of this notion. For example, this entire idea of an unnatural course of conduct, that's an essentialisation: saying that same sex is unethical or bestial denies the human right to difference and plurality in the name of a universal essence called 'human'. Some essentialisations are exploitative or negative, which are constitutive of domination; in contrast, you may have a widely shared agreement of what it means to be human that respects the dignity of difference as an aspect of equality. You can thus have the idea of a benign or creative essentialism, as against the idea of a negative essentialism. That's exactly what the talk of strategic essentialism is about. To call it instrumental is not necessarily bad or ethically questionable.

AN: Strategic essentialism seems to imply that there is something fundamentally wrong with essentialism, but we recognise its value and hence will use it. To take it one step further, maybe there are points of commonality between people. Using the word 'strategic' may not capture the fact of stressing commonality.

UB: 'Strategic' is an unfortunate term. There are other kinds, for example, narrative essentialism. We may think of action-based essentialism. But I am sure that given where it comes from, which is, 'Can the Subaltern Speak' (Gayatri Spivak's famous essay), it is more likely the former. They are narrative strategies. How do we speak about that for which we want a common frame of action?

For example, I spoke earlier about the reform of the British Factories Act (see Marx, *Das Kapital* Vol. 1, Chapter 7), about how trade unionists were not the only actors, how government officials, factory inspectors, the clergy, etc., came together too to bring it about—that's a kind of strategic essentialism. Workers are human beings with far fewer rights, and what distinguishes human beings from others is that all human beings have some minimum rights. The right to live, the right to limited working hours. They are doing what they are saying. They are reconstructing the human with a certain thinness, a certain minimum. You recognise hierarchy and social exploitation and inequality within that minimum. You use the term 'human' to say that there are minimum and inherent human rights. It is a deeply puzzling philosophical concept.

Essence is defined by central qualities. If you have x, y, z in you, then you are entity A. If you do not have them, you are not entity A. So it is a marker, a semantic marker. That is how, for a long time, slaves were not considered human. Women were not considered fully human. Because they lacked certain essential properties.

What would be a good example of strategic essentialism? I spoke of CEDAW, for example (see Chapter 6). The idea of women as human beings and women's rights as human rights. What follows the abstract universal 'human'? By using the term 'human', you are already speaking about certain essential properties, a certain sameness, a commonality, as you say, Arvind. Anti-essentialism is the fight against established markers of essential features. A catalogue of essential features that represses other people is what is morally wrong with essentialism. Now, there may be a morally responsible kind of essentialism. For example, the Torture Convention [UNCAT, or Convention against Torture and Other Cruel, Inhuman or Degrading Treatment or Punishment] says that no human being shall be subjected to degrading or cruel treatment by State officials. Why? Why should human beings not be tortured? One answer is that they should not be tortured by state officials because it is an abuse of public power. How about torture by civil society? All this genital cutting, dowry, that's not torture in the international law sense. Now you could say this is wrong, you essentialise torture as State torture, whereas you could argue that human rights standards should apply to all agents, not just to the State.

You have new technologies coming up in the post-human era, and you can say, all right, you do not have to use human beings for torture, you can have robots which are programmed to torture people. What happens then? These fourth-generation robots are thinking beings. Earlier, they were programmed to do x or y, now they think on their own, they rectify the course of their behaviour. They solve problems for which there was no programming done. For example, space flights. So what happens when you use robots to inflict torture? Then you say, this is not about who inflicts torture, it is about saying that torture itself is wrong.

Animal rights people say this 'human' does not mean human at all, you cannot be human unless you are a part of the great chain of being, and you are linked to other kinds of entities like animals, flowers, etc. As Agamben says in *Potentialities* (1999), potentiality is the unfolding of being. The mistake is to think of potentiality as the potentiality to be or to do something. It is also the potentiality *not* to be or *not* to do something. It works both ways. And that is where the problem is.

You constantly reposition the idea of the 'human' in a particular context. That is my understanding of strategic essentialism. It is obviously instrumental, but I have no problems with instrumentalism. I am not a pragmatist, but I am also not a purist who thinks that you must always be at the level of ends and not means, that ends determine the means. This is a very dialectical relationship, sometimes you use means to reach the ends, and sometimes the ends may be used to disrupt the means. It is not the end that always structures everything you do, so I would pose a counter question: What is wrong with instrumentalism? Or, when is instrumentalism morally problematic?

AN: My point would be that the charge of essentialism may disguise the fact that there are commonalities between human beings, and instead only focus on the differences. These commonalities may be difficult to talk about, but they are there.

UB: You are right, strategic essentialism can be ethically informed social intervention or practice or praxis. It is tinged with a certain notion of evil to be contained or combated or named. Unnameable evil is the very name for terror, and I do not mean terror in the current sense. Or, in some ways what Kant called the sublime, the experience of social life. So there are kinds and kinds of instrumentalism.

The other day, at the convocation,[1] I read this passage from Nietzsche in which he says that a healthy aristocracy is one whose dharma and duty it is to torment the masses for their own gain. Now that is one kind of instrumentalism. Gandhi used another kind of instrumentalism against the British when he used his body and converted it into an instrument of national liberation. Buddhist monks

[1] XVI Annual Convocation, National Law School of India University, 31 August 2008.

commit suicide through self-immolation. The question is, what kind of ethics should surround our use of instrumentalism? You can say there is never a right to use any human being as a means to your end.

Kant says every human being has a moral agency and autonomy. That's a very demanding proposition. Outside of this, if you speak of using people—networking is using people, training sessions are using people, tea-making is using people. We do not think in all contexts that I am being used. Oh Sruti, where is my telephone, please find my telephone. That is not using Sruti, that is a certain friendliness. If she took a position saying, I feel I am being used—I hope she never feels that way—that I am an instrument of comfort, now that would be unethical. So, we all make decisions when we begin to consider ourselves as being used, and when it is something we would like to do without feeling we are being used.

It's a very phenomenological experience. What does it mean for someone to be the means to your ends? Of course, this conversation would not be possible without my being a means to your ends, or rather, our ends. You guys want to do something by way of a conversation, I am the perfect means to your ends, and there is an implicit assumption that I probably share the same idea. So for my part, I am not, and I ought not to feel that I am, being used. It is a call of friendship and affection, I should make myself available for a conversation with you. When this kaleidoscope changes is a very important question. Today I may feel like this, tomorrow I may feel, oh God, these people are detaining me, they are harassing me. But when will I be justified? It is not a question of my own subjectivity. The question is, by what standards can I say that I am being used? I have never spoken about this with such summoning clarity. In the intersubjective world, we place ourselves at the service of the other, and that is what love is. Love is that. It is the sharing of subjectivities, there is no question of being used. That is my notion of love, perhaps a very romantic one.

Very often people say, oh you know, my body was used, my labour was used, I was exploited as a woman, as a womb. Mary Joe Frug has, in her 'A Postmodern Feminist Legal Manifesto', a bitter statement that all women are wives, whores, or mothers (Frug 1992). That is all that women are—either wombs, or sexual objects, or they are reproductive agents that sustain family and society. From this point of view, there cannot be any love between men and women, it is always an exploitative relationship. There is a reading of all relationships between men and women as abuse and subjugation. In that case, a call to intersubjectivity is a call to exploitation. But can you really say that every woman's subjectivity can be reduced to that of a whore, mother, or wife? I am not saying that women are not conscious of their exploitation or of their subordinate positions. Women are still capable of relating freely and wholly in spite of this position, and when that happens, this statement is not true. But I understand Frug's work as creating a platform for countering vicious forms of brutality and patriarchy. As such, it is a very powerful statement, and that is strategic essentialism. We know it is not true as a whole.

I quote in *Crisis* from Anne Summers, who has penned perhaps one of the best dedications I have read. It reads thus,

> The traditional two-line acknowledgement: 'To my wife, without whom etc. ...' is a nauseatingly jejune recompense which disguises what is often the absolute truth, as would become readily apparent if the slaves upon whose supportive psyches these books are written were to withdraw their services. The wives (and children) of writers contribute more than is ever acknowledged to the getting out of a book. (Quoted in Baxi 1982a, xiii)

Strategic essentialisation is a positioning, it is a gesture of a particular kind. Essentialisation posits the possibility of a universal truth. Take the idea that sexual intercourse between people of the same sex is beastly and unnatural. Strategic essentialisms create attributes in certain kinds of ethical struggle over what you are faced with. I do not think we are differing, but we differ in our emphasis. We differ in our notion of what is instrumental, and what the morality of the instrumental is.

AN: To quote you on crude instrumentalism, when drawing our attention to this issue, you nonetheless alert us to the importance of instrumental analysis, 'so overlaid is the social consciousness with the idea of the law as the medium for the pursuit of public interest that the reiteration of the instrumentalist thesis itself becomes a radical act'.... You also note that the instrumentalist view 'directs attention to the law as a central figure in the concrete history of domination' (Baxi 1993b, 20–21).

UB: There I was concerned with the idea of the tool. Vulgar Marxism says that the law is a tool of oppression. So, what is a tool? Fountain pens, cars, etc., are tools, and the law is not that kind of tool. That was my main concern. One was trying to understand the difference between the different kinds of tools, non-normative and normative tools, animate and inanimate tools, different kinds of uses, and the non-instrumental as such or for itself. Are all things best described as tools? Does one say that certain states of affairs, certain configurations, are/should never be used as tools or instruments?

AN: There might be an element of difficulty in speaking in an activist language and in a more philosophical language. The difficulty may be of which one you choose. You point it out even in *Marx, Law and Justice*, where you speak of an activist Marx and a philosophical Marx. Sometimes, it is tough to see which language he speaks in.

LL: You see this in activist circles all the time, where you have the general disavowal of the law as a tool of oppression, but at the same time, a debate around what kind of legal strategies we should adopt. In one particular workshop there was a reference by Ram Guha to Ambedkar being a constitutionalist, and a number of people objected, saying how dare he say Ambedkar was a constitutionalist when he was a radical. They had to be reminded that Ambedkar was the Chairman of the drafting committee of the Constitution!

UB: Yes, I see the difficulties. These relate to habits of reading. Marxism is a habit of reading, in which one appropriates his corpus for purposes of power. Here, selections are made according to what one considers appropriate to the given ends of power. Marxian ways of reading arise when one reads the corpus for the ends of understanding what he was actually saying, or trying to say; it is a search for meanings, not acts of appropriation. So one may speak, as Alvin Gouldner (1980) does, of 'two Marxisms'—the ideological and the scientific. For example, *The Communist Manifesto* or *Das Kapital*. The activist Marx has much to say about 'classes'; however, there are only a few portions in his scientific works, and they are inconclusive fragments about 'class', whereas his activist writings more elaborately and explicitly speak about class warfare or struggles.

There is a great essay in a book on Ambedkar (Zelliot 1992) where the author says, when the Constitution was adopted, everybody said, Mahatma Gandhi *ki jai*! But Gandhi does not feature in the Constitution. The Constitution was a repudiation of Gandhi's approach to power, which was based on trust, on moral concepts. Nonetheless, Ambedkar is called the modern Manu. This is about a man who symbolically burnt the *Manusmriti*. How is one to read this highly symbolic statement and its various aftermaths?

So I say that this is wicked in a moral sense, because it shows a surprising ability to assimilate, it is python-like. It embraces everybody. From the point of view of the depressed, there can be no greater insult than to call Babasaheb a Manu. Whatever radical legacy there is of Ambedkar's contributions is thus cancelled.

The system invents untouchability and justifies violence, and when there comes a moment in history when this is threatened, the system seeks to invert this threat. The radical consciousness of the untouchables is almost gone in parliamentary politics. This radical consciousness might be there in literature, it might be there in movements, or in diasporic movements.

In the UN Durban conference, some claimed that untouchability equals racism.[2] The Indian Constitution also rejects assimilationist aspirations and logics. Discrimination and denial of dignity is a structural trait, characteristic, or cultural propensity, almost a collective consciousness which has persisted, and every time its logic or arrangement is perturbed or disturbed at the foundation, the challenge is assimilated. One may even think with Giorgio Agamben about how social exclusion becomes a form of inclusion. There has always been controversy about 'racism'. Many people, including people who govern 'nations', repudiate this indictment. They do deny discrimination and point to new normativities of egalitarianism crystallised in law and the

[2] World Conference Against Racism, Racial Discrimination, Xenophobia, and Related Intolerance, Durban, 31 August–7 September 2001.

Constitution. One may well draw a distinction between 'race' and 'caste', but may not deny the everyday tale of atrocities and subordination, and it is clear that Dalits are victims of structural social prejudice. Even granting that this may be so, the violated, these subjects of everyday violence, call for protection of rights to life and liberty, and protection against discrimination—it does not matter, whether ethnic or not. Arvind, don't they appeal to commonalties of the human or recourse to strategic essentialisms? And does either make any difference on the ground? In what precisely may that difference lie?

Gandhi and the Indian Constitution

Sruti Chaganti: In 'The Little Done, The Vast Undone', you speak of the alternative to parliamentary democracy proposed at the time of the drafting of the Constitution by the Gandhian Plan, with its emphasis on revitalising village life and decentralised government, and you say that Gandhi could not possibly have meant it, that there were perhaps political reasons for why he deployed it: 'It is doubtful ... that Gandhi himself proposed [the Gandhian Plan] as a meaningful alternative ... was [Gandhi] so naïve as to project this as an institutional alternative to parliamentary democracy? ... Was Gandhi really a *passéiste*? (Baxi 1967a, 342).

I was wondering about this in terms of your later reflections on the Gandhian Plan, and on the absence of its consideration within the law and society movement in India.

UB: I espy at least three trends in your comment. The first concerns, Sruti, the approaches that Mohandas developed regarding the Constituion and constitutionalism in general. Second, the impact of his ideas in the making of constitutionalism; and third, his impact on adjudicative interpreation (demosprudence, as I now call it).

On the first, one must carefully distinguish between his pre-Independence writings and/thought, and eve-of-Independence thought. As we should know, in *Hind Swaraj and Otter Writings or*

Indian Home Rule (1909)—and the book was banned in 1910 by the then British government in India as a 'seditious' text, even though he advocated empire ('moral empire'). The monograph expresses his views on varied related themes, *inter alia*: Swaraj, modern civilisation, mechanisation.[3]

I think that the question you raise is important. The context of this was his plea to the Congress Party to dissolve itself, and my later research has shown that in many countries in Africa, a similar argument was made. In the African context, it was a more violent movement through which independence was won. Amilcar Cabral, in particular, had said (like Gandhi) that the party or the formation that led to independence must not become the hegemonic formation. This was some kind of a collective suicide pact, because these were people who understood what power was all about.

Gandhi's advice was addressed to what was (as Granville Austin shows) the largest party, in fact, an umbrella party, encompassing a multiplicity of views. This could mean that there would be a lack of competitive party politics. I argue that Mohandas could not have meant this. In my articles on Nehru, I found materials where Nehru was saying in 1949 that we have tolerated this old man and his vagaries for too long, now is the time to act (Baxi 1978b). Mohandas knew that this was not going to happen, but he wanted to leave some bequest or legacy. He knew that what he stood for was not there in the Constitution.

The only places where his ideas come in the Constitution are on prohibition and on cowslaughter in the Directive Principles, and those not as moral virtues, but as matters of policy—prohibition of intoxicating drinks is not based on the idea that drinking is a moral vice, but rather measured in terms of public health; similarly, cow slaughter stands linked to injunctions about animal husbandry and reorganisation of agriculture. There, too, the prohibition is only of the slaughter of milch cattle. Cow slaughter is increasingly being construed as a Hindu sentiment. This is a problem, if it assumes that

[3]The most recent text being the Centenary Edition of *Hind Swaraj and Other Writings*; see also Parel (2009).

there are no other sacred animals in India. If you read that Article in the Constitution[4] as a protection of Hindu majority sentiment, then the question of secularism comes in at the threshold.

Sacred animals and birds are everywhere, and it really depends on which indigenous community you are talking about. Even the prohibition of liquor, which was a key Gandhian programme, was conceptualised as a measure for the protection of public health. The third idea of Gandhi's, *Ram Rajya*, with the village being a unit of self-governance, was shot down by Ambedkar. Ambedkar, as you know, famously said, '*What is the village but a sink of localism, a den of ignorance, narrow-mindedness and communalism?*'[5] Ambedkar didn't want to go local, the local was a site of untouchability and intergenerational violence. He wanted national or pan-local. So I think that in that context, I was not too far wrong.

Second, Mohandas never formulated any alternative draft or principles for the Constitution.[6] That was formulated by Jayaprakash Narayan around 1978 in *Socialist Polity of India*. But Gandhi did not do so. It was not a winning proposition, and everybody knew it was going to be a Nehruvian Constitution. Not that Nehru would repudiate the values of Mohandas, but that he would rearticulate them in a very different context. Why do I then say: revert to the Mohandasian form? I consistently ask the question, what is constitutionalism?, and I believe it is a relationship between four ideas: rights, justice, governance, and development. That is my idea of constitutionalism. If you look at the text of the Indian Constitution, and you simply count the words in Part Three, the Preamble, the Directive Principles of State Policy, and now the Fundamental Duties—how many hundred thousand words

[4] Article 48. Organisation of agriculture and animal husbandry. 'The State shall endeavour to organize agriculture and animal husbandry on modern and scientific lines and shall, in particular, take steps for preserving and improving the breeds, and prohibiting the slaughter, of cows and calves and other milch and draught cattle.'

[5] Constituent Assembly Debates, Vol. VII, 4 November 1948, 39 (emphasis added).

[6] See Baxi (1967a).

do these comprise? And compare this with the verbiage of governance and development. What you find is an overwhelming number of words comprising the governance and development text, compared with the slender texts of rights and justice. But take governance, the whole text is about governance—the union executive, union legislature, state legislature and executive, the public service commission, the electoral commission, everything. The bulk of the text is about governance.

The Constitution does not even provide a thin notion of development, it relegates the task of silhouetting a desired social order to the Directive Principles of State Policy, to which now is appended Part IVA that lays out the duties of those who are ruled—the development of a scientific temper, cultivation of excellence in all walks of life, etc. Both these parts have to be read as a whole; in fact, the entire Constitution needs to be read as a whole because the State is everywhere and so are basic rights-oriented constraints on power.

So development is an affair between a virtuous citizen and a good State with just governance. I look at constitutionalism as this dynamic, as the complex and contradictory relationship between these key aspects. If you conceptualise constitutionalism in this fashion, then a return to Mohandas is absolutely indispensable. In the area of governance, in the area of development, in the area of what is just, and of what rights human beings have, the metaphysical or spiritual ethic of Mohandas returns to haunt Indian constitutionalism.

I have often been asked, in the interior parts of India, for a definition of development. I once went (together with Kishen Mahajan) as a Supreme Court Commissioner to Sarsaul block, Kanpur district, Uttar Pradesh in the Gulshan Kallu case.[7] There was an ordinance passed by

---

[7] *Gulshan Kallu & Ors. vs. Zilla Parishad, Etawah, U.P. & Ors.*, AIR 1981 SC 1668: 'Since there was a dispute between the parties as to what is the correct position in regard to the work of carrying out skinning of dead animals in the Kanpur district, we made an order on 1st May, 1981 appointing a Commission of Dr. Upendra Baxi and Mr. Krishan Mahajan to visit two specific areas in Sarsol block of Kanpur district with a view to ascertaining as to what is the manner in which skinning of dead animals is being carried out in those specific areas and who carry out this work and whether they receive any payment for the work carried out by them and from whom and what

the UP government, at the behest of the contractor lobby, that the state would be the owner of the bodies of dead animals. And the state would auction licences for skinning carcasses to the highest bidder. So, on the one hand, the Chamars will be deprived of a livelihood, and on the other, they will be performing unpaid labour. When animals die, you have to remove them immediately, you cannot wait. The Chamars were forced to do something that both state and society had now made illegal for them to do. We were two Commissioners appointed by the Supreme Court, Mr Kishen Mahajan and I, and we went to all the districts, and all the blocks, and at the end, we met the District Collector. In one of the Chamar *bastis* I went to, I asked some of them, do you know your BDO (Block Development Officer), does he not do anything about these conditions? One of those present there said, yes, I know the BDO, he is an officer who blocks development!

In this horrible situation, they could laugh. They then asked me, what is your idea of development? This is my one sentence encapsulation of the relation between Indian constitutionalism and development—'development is a set of policies and actions which disproportionately benefits the impoverished'. Development should disproportionately benefit the constitutional have-nots as compared to the haves. This is one simple sentence. This idea is Mohandasian unto the last, that nobody should be left behind—this is the heart of inclusive development.

Mohandas is also very relevant in our understanding of the right to freedom of speech and expression. Ashish Rajadhyaksha (2009) has spoken about the idea of spectatorial rights embedded in the very structure of basic rights of Article 19 (1). The idea that spectators have basic rights under Article 19 is a very important notion, because reasonable restrictions then cannot go so far as to abrogate this right. Indeed, the idea can be read as confronting the whole notion and structures of censorship, whether imposed by State or non-State actors.

would be the impact of giving out this work to contractors on the livelihood of those who have been originally carrying out this work and also how the contract system has operated and with what effect.'

Similarly, Gandhi's whole approach to the question of rights and responsibilities is that there cannot be rights without responsibilities, whether one is talking about a corporate right or a minority right. So the ethics of rights are Mohandasian, which is virtually unscripted. In the '(Im)possibility of Constitutional Justice', I have listed out six different types of constitutionalisms: indigenous constitutionalism, Mohandasian, INC, BJP, Jayaprakash Narayan, and ultra-left, etc. (Baxi 2005c). If you turn to the exemplary followers of Mohandas, like Vinoba Bhave or Jayaprakash Narayan, how did these Mohandasians rework all these ideas?

There is a fantastic book by B. N. Ganguli (1973), one of the finest Vice-Chancellors of Delhi University, in which he compares the early Mao's theory of development with Gandhi's theory of development. When I was studying in Rajkot, the standard economic textbook always taught us that resources are scarce, and that wants and needs are infinite. But what is Gandhian economics about? Mohandas has written that Western economic theory takes a wrong turn, and a morally problematic turn, by these two ideas that wants are unlimited and resources are finite. He says, it is the other way around, resources are infinite if you only knew how to minimise your needs. He critiques the very foundations of bourgeois economics in a way that Marx could not. This is a very rich heritage, and it encompasses ideas such as village decentralisation, khadi, the whole movement for small-scale industry, bringing industry to the doorstep of the villager, eradicating the middlemen who exploit the returns from it, the idea of self-reliance, etc. One should thus widen this concept of constitutionalism as a relationship between these four factors, and make governance and development constantly converse with rights and justice.

Further, I have tried to understand the idea of constitutionalism in my article on 'Constitutionalism as a Site of State Formative Practices', in which I have said:

> Perhaps one way of conceptualizing constitutions is to differentiate the idea of constitution at three interlocking planes, which I name as C1, C2, and C3. C1 stands for the word as the world, the site of initially formulated historic constitutional texts. C2 represents constitutional hermeneutics,

> the site of what is understood in the dominant discourse as constitutional interpretation or constitutional law. C3 signifies 'constitutionalism,' a set of ideological sites that provide justification/mystification for constitutional theory and practice. These three forming practices may constitute the idea, in complex and contradictory mode, of a constitution. (Baxi 1999)

To me, C2 is not merely constitutional law as produced by courts and legislatures. I always say that C2 is another kind of activity. It is citizen interpretation, which does not necessarily produce law, but produces movements. Martin Luther King Jr. changed the US Constitution on voting rights. The US Supreme Court judges had earlier said, it is a political thicket, we do not enter this domain. But Martin Luther King Jr., when he declared that 'I have a dream', began a process of interpreting the Constitution that is both normatively and experientially truly colour-blind. Citizen interpretation in India begins with Mohandas. Using the technology of self-reliant communitarian interpretation of the law and the text of the Constitution, I have looked at the collected works of Mohandas, and I have not found a coherent blueprint for the future Constitution of India. I found a lot of ideas that relate to constitutionalism, and I think that is good enough to start with.

Similarly, if you look at the texts of the Constituent Assembly Debates, you will find that Gandhi's principles were not allowed to be pushed through. You have the Lohiaites and others who say that the profit motive should be abolished. They are socialists. But that is not a programme, that is a mere statement, and it sounds ridiculous. How can the Constitution abolish the profit motive? Or any motive, for that matter? There is no care taken to formulate even the propositional sense of what is being said. Supposing the Indian Constitution had abolished the profit motive, we would have been the laughing stock of the world. If there was a Gandhian strategy to put in something that was distinctly Gandhian, either it did not succeed, or my guess is they did not even try!

Of course, one can wish for the structures of desire to be normatively transformed by a Constitution which socialises the entire mode of production in the pursuit of revolutionary equality. But one may not incorporate this as a Directive Principle of State Policy while leaving intact the colonial mode of production, adding to it forms and features of (what has been called) 'modern slavery'.

But perhaps, Sruti, in this rambling, I have sidestepped your comments.

Governance, Legality, and Constitutionalism

SC: It is interesting the way you construct constitutionalism with these four ideas. There is a tension between the idea of constitutionalism and legality in the manner in which you unfold the history of the Indian Constitution. You speak about how, for Nehru, the modern State, armed with modern science, would be the way ahead, but modern law would always be a hindrance to that process. And you speak about how the idea of legality is always compromised for political legitimacy, and how Nehru manages it through tradition and charisma. Now with their decline, where would you locate the ethical impulse of constitutionalism today?

UB: There are many aspects of Nehru which have still to be understood. Rajeev Dhavan valuably edited for the Indian Law Institute an anthology (which carried two articles by me). Dr Subhas Kashyap has edited a very important collection, entitled *Nehru and the Constitution* (1982). Unfortunately, the law schools pay little attention to these works. I simply do not know how this deficiency may be remedied. Some of the Nehruvian ideals found their way into *Kesavananda Bharati* discourses; some presided over the judicial interpretation, and not just that of Fundamental Rights and Directive Principles of State Policy.

Nehru started a tradition, which says that governance and development are affairs for the supreme political executive. He created a hegemonic executive. He said, no courts should come in, no lawyers should come in, the executive is supreme, because it is the elected representative of the people. The legislature is an instrument of the supreme executive when it comes to development. What Nehru did right from the beginning was to say, trust us, the executive, and he was right in a sense because, as a founder of the Indian republic, his cabinet had to be seen to be believed! Everyone had suffered in prison and had fought for Swaraj. So when he said trust me, he had a platform to say that.

But ideas about development change with time. Now, the days of neoliberalism and globalisation mean that governance and development are technocratic concepts in which ideas of rights and justice at best take a back seat or at worst, may not even appear. Development as a technopolitics cannot, it is said, be made the subject of legality. You can raise questions of legitimacy, but not of legality because most development occurs outside the frame of law. You cannot question a lot of policy on the grounds of rights. You cannot question the legality of it. Policies may give rise to laws, but policies are not laws. Since they are not laws, the Supreme Court has consistently said that they cannot arbitrate on these issues.

The Dunkel Draft, which eventually facilitated the emergence of a World Trade Organization (WTO), illustrates this, as do many aspects of trade and investment policies. The Indian accession to the WTO was taken to the Bombay High Court, and so it was in the Philippines. The decisions of both the Courts are still worth reading. They said, in effect, that the Court will act upon a showing of fundamental rights violation. One could show them, at best, clear and present danger. There is an autonomy of developmental policy from the realm of legality, making it completely discretionary. This is why I have been arguing that major projects should come under the framework of legislation. If the costs overshoot the budget, if the dam bursts, who is responsible? The challenge is: How do you bring the policy regime under strict constitutional scrutiny?

I have evaded your other question. In 'The Recovery of Fire' (Baxi 1990b), I argue that in India, there is a culture of oral governance which operates through telephonic conversations and orders. There is this idea that you can suspend laws because you think that something good may come out of the suspension of this law. The idea of the sovereign executive impairs the very idea of legality. It really means the suspension of the rule of law. It gives rise to oral governance rather than to a culture of written governance.

This reached its pinnacle in the internal Emergency of 1975–1977. My point was not to either exonerate the architects and the managers of the 1975 Emergency or to insulate them, as some of my critics thought I was doing. All I was saying in that article was that it is short-sighted to say that the culture of oral governance started with a person called Indira Gandhi or Sanjay Gandhi, because it has a longer and larger history. There is a simple denial of the connection between governance and legality.

Seven Types of Constitutions and Three Forms of Constitutionalism

UB: In 'The (Im)possibility of Constitutional Justice' (2005c), I said that there are seven kinds of Constitutions, although we think there is only one. This constitutional 'monism' is problematic. You have the original Constitution of 1949–1950, the Nehru Constitution (with its bulging Ninth Schedule), the State finance capitalist Constitution of Indira Gandhi (State ownership of insurance and banking), the 1973 Constitution (of basic structure, which still continues), the Emergency Constitution, the populist and activist Supreme Court Constitution, and the globalising one (in which, via the Bhopal settlement, we notice a structural adjustment of constitutionalism). Each needs a careful study, and none disappears entirely. The text remains the same, but the underlying spirit or content and ethical context undergoes a transformation. So C1 remains the same, but C2 (interpretation) and C3 (normative theory or ideological discourse) undergo a fundamental change.

C3 is what we might call the ideology or ethic of Constitutions. C3 can be Hitlerite, fascist, socialist, feminist, post-apartheid, transformative, and so on. C1 is the constitutional text, C2 is constitutional interpretation. Broadly, we have a liberal bourgeois Constitution. C2 and C1, instead of being wholly shaped by C3, have shaped C3. You have the addition of socialism to the Preamble, and the laying down of the basic structure doctrine. It breaks my heart when I hear people write about the legitimacy of the basic structure, about whether it is proper for the judiciary to go so far. You cannot forget the context in which it emerged, when the overwhelming claim was that the true sovereign of India is the supreme executive, and that it could treat the Constitution like toilet tissue. The basic structure doctrine is a response to this claim.

It is pathetic that this questioning of its legitimacy still goes on and is called progressive, even when the political machines have accepted this. I have such a sense of personal scholarly pain that, after thirty-five years, I have not been able to convince senior teachers and young scholars about understanding constitutional development, and the development of C3 and C2, as an insurrection against the unbridled power of the executive. But that is what limited government is all about. It includes the practice of restraining constitutional amendment and the ascendancy of judicial review, leading to the expansion of the basic structure doctrine. One may say that further extensions of the doctrine are ill-justified. Basic structure is not only concerned with changes *in* the Constitution, but it is also concerned with limiting changes *of* the Constitution.

I have spoken about insensitive students and teachers. How about Justices? That is a fair, democratic question. Nowadays, judges liberate themselves from any degree of anxiety or discipline. In *S.R. Bommai vs. Union of India*,[8] the power exercised under Article 356 to impose President's Rule was held to be violative of the basic structure. In other judgments, they say that the doctrine of basic structure can also extend to an interpretation of legislations. What we have now is an enormously creative response to the sovereignty of executive power. But may it still be maintained that the doctrine of basic structure, by their own saying, was limited to policing amendments, and only those amendments that destroyed the basic personality of the Constitution?

[8] 1994 SCC (3).

So C3 is a magnificent edifice. It is a response to a particular kind of governance. So was Social Action Litigation. Its ethicality comes from C3. You can find a number of areas radicalising C3. You can find it in realms of privacy, women's rights as human rights, freedoms of sexual minorities, identity/dignity, jurisprudence, and environment rights. The formation of Indian C3 is an astonishing realm with all its contradictions and controversies, particularly of the routinisation of the charisma of the basic structure. I now call it demosprudence—adjudicatory leadership of the nation.

Is C3 a kind of dharma which goes beyond the language of political theory and other *isms*, and which leads to a spiritual fulfilment of all human beings in India, generating collective energies to a point where you do not need a Constitution! When you reach a particular state of being, you do not need law. That's what Mother Teresa did. All your notions of sovereignty, rights, justice get imbued and charged with dharma where the collective energies are fully developed.

Invention of C3: Mathura Open Letter

LL: Pratiksha said the moment Upen starts talking about C3, ask him this from my side. She wanted to know about the presence of your personal voice in C3. That's the only place where it is animated by more than an analytical concern as opposed to the way you write about C1 and C2. You have a very different form of writing.

UB: I do not know, since I am not a student of my own writing! But yes, C3 is the place where I am primarily talking about justice. It is also the place of passion. It is a political, but also a moral and ethical, question. It is the logic of sentiment, not just an assembly of disembodied ideas. Finally, it is a site of struggle. It takes a reinvention of yourself. The two C3 moments which were very important were the Mathura Open Letter and the beginning of Social Action Litigation.

When I read the Mathura judgment,[9] I could not for days together eat, drink, or even sleep. As your good friend Robert Cover tells you, legal interpretation takes place in a field of pain and death (Cover 1986). I was not in a place where I could embody my pain in the larger universe, but I was very hurt and upset because the High Court convicts the policemen, but the Supreme Court says there are no marks of resistance on this tribal girl, and therefore it must be deemed that she consented. I had never heard of this kind of injustice. So I said, what should I do, write a monograph, write an essay, a newspaper or a learned journal article? Will any of this work? As my friend Professor Oliver Mendelsohn (of La Trobe University, Melbourne) often irately used to say about my activist interventions, Upen-san, you are not merely pissing in the wind but, as the Americans say, just 'pissing into a tornado'.

And, after a week of anguishing about this after my classes every day, I hit on the idea of an open letter to the Chief Justice of India, which I actually drafted.[10] Then I said, if I do it myself, it is not good enough for me to individually sign it, I must persuade my colleagues to sign as well. It must be a collective statement, and I could find only three in the whole of India to sign. They were Lotika Sarkar, Vasudha Dhagamwar, and Raghunath Kelkar. Each one of them had profound reservations, not to the text, but to the form. It was a sheer hands-folded request to them to put their names to it, sheer emotional insistence that overcame their resistance. As a form, it worked. It is an imagination of intervention, writing an Open Letter to the CJI. It was certainly not an academic work, as was conceived thus far. The

[9] *Tukaram And Anr vs. State Of Maharashtra*, (1979) 2 SCC 143. Also see Dutta (2018, 181–202).

[10] Upendra Baxi note: First published by the intrepid Surendra Malik of the *Supreme Court Cases*, (1979) 4 SCC (Journal) 17, this had the valuable use that it reached all Justices, the Bar, law teachers, and students. The letter has also been archived by the Partners for Law in Development, especially in the amiable person of their founder, Ms. Madhu Mehra, have for decades worked indefatigably for gender justice. See also http://pldindia.org/wp-content/uploads/2013/03/Open-Letter-to-CJI-in-the-Mathura-Rape-Case.pdf (accessed April 2022). See also Kanjilal (2022).

Open Letter ends by attributing to the Supreme Court a universal bias of patriarchy, and asks the Court to correct the error of its ways of interpreting the Constitution and the law.

Now, why did I write the draft of the Open Letter in that manner? The first thing to see about C3 is what animates it. In my case, it was a deep and profound hurt, and discontentment with forums for the articulation of that hurt and for seeking redressal of that injustice. There was therefore the compulsion to invent a new form of intervention, and that is what happened in the Open Letter. Of course, we were sniggered at.

We were told by our colleagues that we were publicity hungry. We sent it to Chief Justice Y. V. Chandrachud and his entire Court, but nobody in the press was interested. The National Conference of Women was not interested. The Left lawyers, the United Lawyers Association led by Jitendra Sharma, published a journal called *Progress*. They asked me to write for it, and I said, I cannot write anything new. This is the only thing I have written, and they said no, they could not publish that. When Chief Justice Chandrachud inaugurated the journal, he asked, why is the Open Letter not a part of the inaugural issue—a good question for a journal entitled *Progress*! Officially, however, I had no response from the CJI. The first thing about C3 is creativity and passion of commitment to a cause. One also needs to be able to cope with intimidation, as I got constant threat calls warning me that my children would not return from school. There is a whole range of consequences that follow from attempting changes in C3, and the ability to cope with these consequences is absolutely essential to developing C3.

We were totally stunned by the silence that the Open Letter met with, until two things happened. You see how these things work by contingency. Some newspapers overseas carried aspects of the Open Letter. It was after this that Indian journalists began their demand for it. They said, we do not have a copy. The women's movement was initially not concerned about the Open Letter, but they suddenly became very interested in this. Around this time, I was called to Ahmedabad for an event organised by the Consumer Research Group. There was a beautiful Gandhian organisation there called the Jyoti

Sangh. They were a Gandhian women's organisation, weaving khadi and practising a simple lifestyle. In Jyoti Sangh, a woman was called a warrior—Yodha. Charumati Bahen Yodha was their leader. She said, Baxi, come and speak to our group.

I spoke very bad Gujarati then, I didn't even know how to translate certain words which are very technical, words like penetration. So I spoke in Hindi. She said, do not worry about the language, I will take care of it—*tum khali bolo* (you just speak), *aur bolte jao* (and keep on talking). I took her advice and *bolta gaya* (talked endlessly)! Once Jyoti Sangh took the issue up, it gained momentum. This was a very powerful grassroots movement, they had a history of abducting women from their husbands and then making the women self-reliant. They had no compunctions in breaking up homes because, according to them, homes were vicious places where women were beaten up. They are the only NGO I know with the largest number of criminal cases filed against them. They were not bothered. They never hired a lawyer. They simply marched before the magistrate and 'terrorised' him narratively by the details of the sordid and sad matrimonial plight and spousal violence. It was fantastic. It was a different kind of movement. They didn't even go to a lawyer's office earlier, now they have a legal advisor.

Once it became known that the Jyoti Sangh was espousing this cause, something happened within the national women's movement. The issue then started gaining a certain momentum. Pramila Dandavate of the Mahila Dakshata Samiti[11] and many others got very involved and engaged. Then they said to me, we want to file a review petition, and I said, sorry, we cannot entertain the idea, because we (here, Lotika Sarkar and myself) do not believe that convictions or acquittals should be overruled by popular protest. I am a very strong believer in the fact that popular protest (despite Jessica Lal)[12] is not

[11]The Mahila Dakshata Samiti: mainstream social service NGO set up in 1976 by Suman Krishankant (wife of the former Vice-President of India), Pramila Dandavate, Mrudula Sinha, and Sushila Nayyar, primarily to address dowry deaths and other violence against women.

[12]Jessica Lal: a model in New Delhi who was shot dead on 30 April 1999 by Manu Sharma, son of a Congress-nominated Member of Parliament

the best form of public action. It can be corrupted, it can be bought, it can be hired. We can hire civil disobedience, renting a crowd is very easy in politics. So, for a variety of reasons, I said, I cannot associate with this. What is more, they were going to do a *dharna* outside the Chief Justice's chambers. This did not grasp the real issue: Would you want to decide the guilt or innocence of the accused by public sentiment or protest? The objective of the Open Letter was to ensure that their lordships would realise the error of their ways and proceed *suo motu*. The women's groups did not appreciate this point and even thought we were insensitive to women's suffering!

Of course, they lost the review petition because it went up before the same Bench—A. D. Kaushal, Jaswant Singh, and P. S. Kailasam. The women's groups then upped the demonstrations and protests. The review order that was passed was very terse, and it simply could have ended all subsequent developments even before they began. However, one thing led to another, and calls were made for law reform. We submitted a memorandum which said that certain forms of rape should be included, such as matrimonial rape and power rape. It is now in the Penal Code, though not in those terms.[13] However, matrimonial rape was not included as the Marxist feminist activist, Susheela Gopalan

---

from Haryana, while working as a celebrity bartender at a party. Sharma was acquitted in the trial, but the Delhi High Court overruled the judgment.

[13]See Section 376(2) of the IPC. (2): Whoever (a) being a police officer commits rape (i) within the limits of the police station to which he is appointed; or (ii) in the premises of any station house whether or not situated in the police station to which he is appointed; or (iii) on a woman in his custody or in the custody of a police officer subordinate to him; or (b) being a public servant, takes advantage of his official position and commits rape on a woman in his custody as such public servant or in the custody of a public servant subordinate to him; or (c) being on the management or on the staff of a jail, remand home or other place of custody established by or under any law for the time being in force or of a woman's or children's institution takes advantage of his official position and commits rape on any inmate of such jail, remand home, place or institution; or (d) being on the management or on the staff of a hospital, takes advantage of his official position and commits rape on a woman in that hospital.

and Geeta Mukherjee, among others,[14] said that the time had not yet come to include matrimonial rape as an offence. Many in the women's movement at that time was clear that they could not support it. They felt that women would lose their security, they would get turned out of their houses, and that they would lose the custody of their children.

So we learnt through this model of law reform. In *Human Rights and Inhuman Wrongs*, I have an article called 'Women and the Labyrinth of Law' (Baxi 1994b), in which I describe my experiments in the companionship of Lotika Sarkar in presenting the memorandum to the MPs and how difficult it was. I narrate there a conversation with a senior Congress leader in Gujarat who said, this is not how you lobby, you should carry briefcases, you will not get anywhere at this rate. I said, I cannot do this, and he said, I thought you are concerned with tribal women? He was from a tribal area, and I said, yes, I am, but not with helping in any way possible, but in a manner that promises deeper change, not merely an episodic engagement with a top leader.

It was a great disappointment. One of our colleagues even parted company from us that day because she had reservations about the memorandum. We had begun an engagement which got lost in the nitty gritty. It had no destiny, no point of arrival, but in retrospect, we realised that there were ideas that had not been thought about and forms that had not been experimented with, which came into being at that time. Thereafter, a few people thought of writing open letters. With respect to the Abhyankar murder case, S. P. Sathe felt deeply and wanted to write an open letter in Pune, and he asked me to sign it.[15] I said, Sathe *saab*, I cannot sign this. He said, why, you can write

[14] Key figures among the women leadership of the Communist movement. Geeta Mukherjee (1924–2000) represented the Communist Party of India as a Member of Parliament from West Bengal, and was President of the National Federation of Indian Women. Susheela Gopalan (1929–2001), member of the CPI(M), Member of Parliament and Minister in the Government of Kerala.

[15] Joshi-Abhyankar serial murders: ten murders committed by four commercial art students of Pune between January 1976 and March 1977. The murderers were hanged on 27 November 1983. Originally sentenced by the Pune Sessions Court on 28 September 1978, their appeal was rejected

open letters and I cannot? It was very difficult to explain to him my viewpoint, which was really about the role of public opinion when it came to the question of the quantum of sentence. I felt that public opinion should, as far as possible, be kept out of sentencing. Of course, due regard should be given to victim presentations. But should the judicial sentencing be moved by public protest or movement?

Invention of C3: Social Action Litigation

UB: Then comes the second interesting C3 moment with the invention of Social Action Litigation. We were concerned about what was happening in the Agra Women's Home.[16] We got to know that there were hundreds of women living in a space the size of a small room, some of them suffering from STD and other physical ailments. I read about this in a letter written by Dr R. S. Sodhi, whom I then met.

---

by the Bombay High Court, a special leave petition was dismissed by the Supreme Court on 17 November 1980, and a review petition dismissed on 11 February 1981. The accused then filed writ petitions against their prolonged detentions, which were rejected by the Supreme Court on 5 March 1982. They eventually submitted mercy petitions to the President of India, which were rejected on 23 March 1983. Among those who publicly protested what he considered the 'dilatory tactics' of the accused was the principal of the Pune Law College, S. P. Sathe, who wrote a public letter to Chief Justice Chandrachud. Sathe contended that the ruling of Justice Chinnappa Reddy and Justice Mishra (in the matter of R. V. Vatheeswaran), that 'delay exceeding two years in the execution of a death sentence should entitle a condemned prisoner to claim reprieve and conversion of his sentence into one of life imprisonment', was leading to these dilatory tactics.

[16] Upendra Baxi note: Lotika Sarkar was a co-petitioner, but she always wanted me to argue; and though our job was to produce lawyers and eventually judges, neither of us had the experience or skills to argue a case before the Courts. What we lacked in terms of courtcraft, we made up in our pedagogic convictions for justice. It was magnanimous of Justices to allow the new development of petitioners in person (*Dr. Upendra Baxi (I) vs. State of Uttar Pradesh and Anr.*, [1983] 2 SCC 308).

This was the second moment of invention, and I derived the inspiration from Justice P. N. Bhagwati, who had written a vivid letter, with phrases such as 'the golden rays of the rising sun' and whatnot, to the Prime Minister, asking for legal aid authorities to be established, although I did not have to invoke this letter, after all! Lotika Sarkar asked me to handle all the oral arguments. The Court was not used to requests that the letters be regarded as a writ petition. It had a major problem concerning our *locus standi* as no rights of ours as citizen petitioners were violated. In my response to this question was where the Social Action Litigation was born. It did not come out of the classroom, it did not come out of the books. I took some time answering, and when the Justices insisted on a quick response, I apologised and said I was thumbing through the Constitution for the term *locus standi*, but it was nowhere to be found! I also realised how quick-witted the lawyers had to be—thinking on the feet is a necessary cognitive skill and craft of senior counsel!

I said, standing is a bourgeois concept, a common law concept. We have a socialist Constitution, I said, why cannot I come to you on behalf of other citizens? The Justices reiterated: You may do so only when your own interest is also affected. I said, why cannot I come before you in the interest of another? What conception of democracy is this? What conception of C3 is this? I went on to explain to the Court that under Article 32, the court has the power to issue writs not just of *mandamus* or *certiorari*. It says writs 'in the nature of'. So, we come before you via this letter, treat it as a writ petition, nobody can question it.

Then I read out the fundamental duties, and it is one of the fundamental duties to renounce practices which are derogatory (exploitative) of women. I said, when you interpret the doctrine of standing, you should interpret it in the light of Part IVA (on Fundamental Duties of the Citizen), and not like Denning and all those common law judges. I argued that the common law world had no conception of duties. I got carried away and said that no Indian middle-class person can fulfil these qualifications, because it is deeply schizophrenic [between Mall and Mandir, East and West], and I deserved a sharp reprimand, which I got, saying that I was bordering on contempt. In retrospect, this ability to produce results was not a result of instant exchange, but rather, through engagement in a dialogical terrain that nobody had thought of travelling. This was a direct result of the thorough immersion in the immiseration of the Agra Home women's lives. It is not a question of my brilliance or anything. So, citizen interpretation is a passionate engagement with the suffering of the other. This is the key to the whole thing. And when you are really immersed, it is unlikely that you will be impoverished in your imagination or your articulation. That has been my experience. If you sit back and think of the consequences, what will I say, I have never been before a judge, if he dismisses me what will I do, it will never happen.

I argued that the State had made rules directing the Director of Social Welfare, the Ministry of Social Welfare, UP, to undertake schemes for the welfare of the inhabitants of the reform home. However, everyone knows that the money is not being used for the purpose for which it has been given, and this is the condition of women not just in Agra, but throughout the state of Uttar Pradesh. To which one of the judges said, Baxi, we are a court of appeal, we do not deal with facts. After some dialogue, we found the way: socio-legal commissions. Justice Bhagwati said, there is a District Collector in Agra, we can direct him to submit monthly reports. There were also AIDS patients among the women, and we literally brought them to AIIMS. The Supreme Court directed the AIIMS staff to be members of the socio-legal commission.

Much later, when I was asked how long conditions in the home should be monitored by the court, I said, for as long as it takes for the state of UP to lisp the alphabet of the rule of law and comply with constitutional guarantees! I said, if this does not happen in my lifetime, somebody else will inherit this litigation. It is a heritable litigation, not an infinite litigation. The struggle is not just about the home, but about the legality of state action or inaction. I do not believe in what Lord Krishna says in the Gita, that you must do your duty without aspiring for results or desiring any fruits of your action (*nishkama karma*). Of course, when you are trying to help people who have been wounded and tormented, you want the fruits of action for them. It is a *non sequitur* to say that you can be a public activist and not desire results.

C3 and Judicial Innovation in the Doctrine of Standing

UB: Then the question immediately came to me about the theorisation of this experience. What does it mean to do these things? My article, 'Taking Suffering Seriously' (Baxi 1985c), has been published and translated many times. I raised the question about whether SAL was merely an 'establishment revolution' (to use my friend Rajeev Dhavan's insightful words), that is, reinstating the legitimacy of the court. Or, on the contrary, was it really enriching the quality of administration of justice? Is it possible to ever reform a state administration that is deeply inegalitarian? Does it depoliticise the issue? (In this case, though, it was never politicised, so there was no question of depoliticisation.) Does it lead to alienation and all of that?

There was no precedent in the whole wide world to the phenomenon of SAL. There were anxieties—of the petitioner, of the respondent, and also of some judges who were very new to the field. They didn't want to look foolish before their brethren. So I had to understand their constraints and raise the contention of the adequacy of what they were doing. This was a back and forth dialogue.

Where do I get this idea that the Constitution is about these four things: governance, development, rights, and justice? Why do I think of this? It was because of my activism in one sense, a small-scale activism with the courts, that I began to theorise the Constitution as an enterprise of bringing closer performances of social justice through the law. It is not just law, it is also movements—or the uncertain yet evolving relationship of law and social movements. So I began 'Taking Suffering Seriously' by saying that the Supreme Court *of* India has become the Supreme Court *for* Indians. It was crazy at that time to state that an organ of the State could become a part of social movements, and I knew it. But it was an exceptional conjuncture in which this did begin to happen.

The court played ball; it took to this new role. Of course, there was a master craftsman in Justice Bhagwati. He never addressed the issue of standing in the *Agra Home* case, he waited for the *Judges* case in which advocates, both at the national and the state level, fought against the transfer of some judges (*S.P. Gupta vs. President*

Of India And Ors[17]). It was in this case that he expounded on public interest standing. He makes the point that the rule of standing must be expanded in the interest of the dispossessed, disadvantaged, and deprived people of India, and not for political purposes. The articulation of the democratisation of standing, the radical broadening of *locus standi,* was an inaugural feat. In order to minimise resistance from the bar, he waited for the right context. Some people may say that it was very slow, but it was a strategy. He carried the bar with him and found a context in which there was a great deal of legitimacy for the finding on standing. If he had done it in the *Agra Home* case, it would have had less legitimacy. In this case, he had the support of the entire bar. Somehow the judge, and later the whole court, felt that there was something wrong in confining standing only to persons whose rights were affected adversely. Someone whose rights were not directly affected now had the right to appear in matters of constitutional importance.

Whose rights were violated by the transfer of judges? Nobody's rights, unless you say people's rights. Which right of the bar is violated by elevation to the Supreme Court and the High Courts or by the transfer of High Court judges? There are no rights, strictly speaking, that are violated when judges are transferred.

The genius of Justice Bhagwati lies in giving them standing in a structural way. There is a legitimate public interest in preserving judicial independence. Judicial independence is an instrument for furthering the protection of the Constitution. So, a connection is established. That is an enormous contribution. Some people say, Baxi is a suffering-monger, but I am enormously happy when this connection is drawn. It was my happiest moment, because the court was rewriting the Constitution of India, re-engaging in C3. Without a total immersion in a cause, one cannot make any of these kinds of connections and begin thinking *for* the other and *with* the other. It is this engagement with the idea and theory of constitutionalism [C3] that gives you the strength, which you do not otherwise have as a teacher of law.

[17] AIR 1982 SC 149.

Blasphemy and Constitutional Love

LL: There are various places in your writings on constitutional law on the link between the Constitution and memory, and I tried to characterise your relationship to the Constitution as a relationship of genuine blasphemy. As T. S. Eliot puts it, genuine blasphemy is the product of a partial belief; it is as unavailable to the complete believer as it is to the absolute atheist. Would you agree with this characterisation?

UB: Well, it is very nice! One day I am told I am scandalous, the other that I am blasphemous! That is wonderful! Is Baxi the same fellow?

The notion of blasphemy is a very deep one. I have some kind of a non-instrumental affection or regard and solicitude for what emerges as judicial activism, and a certain degree of enchantment with it. I have described this in several papers as the site for re-democratisation and the larger possibilities for the realisation of democracy. So yes, in a sense, it is a kind of passionate engagement with, or commitment to, re-imagining the Constitution and to re-crafting it for the constitutional have-nots. However, it does not always work the way you want it to. Therefore, there comes the constant recognition in my writing and in my speeches, in all my work, that you must never forget that the court is a part of the State. If you forget that, you cannot love your Constitution. SAL always lies between judicial activism and the judiciary as an apparatus of the State. That is where the germination of the relationship between courts and social movements occurs, but only within this contradiction, never outside of it.

I have been very pained by certain criticisms of judges, complaints of this or that case. What can you expect? It is a structural contradiction. You have to remember that there is the Supreme Court and there are the judges, but the latter do not sit together, they sit in benches. Is there a court? Are there as many Supreme Courts as there are judges? So one takes the judicial process as a conflict with the system of distribution, exchange, and maintenance of constitutional political power. And one attempts to steer it towards the protection of the Constitution—especially the expectation of the have-nots or, as John Rawls would have it, the 'worst-off'.

My favourite quote is from Justice Dwivedi in *Kesavananda Bharati*, 'the constitution is not intended to be the arena of legal quibbling for men with long purses' (*Kesavananda* at 947 para 1947, also cited in Baxi 1985c, 107). It is a heritage or a possession, and it should be the object of your love. The idea that Constitutions can be considered worthy of citizens' affection is very strong with me now. You would never have guessed it on the basis of my Marx book. This is not how Marx or Marxians think of courts or Constitutions. But they do so in the sense that there cannot be any sense of struggle outside of a sense of contradiction. So blasphemy, yes, if it is used in a strict sense. I neither engage in Constitution worship, nor do I believe in the idea that every human being is potentially divine. I am not that kind of deist, although Granville Austin speaks of an oligarchy in the Constituent Assembly, composed of God-like people such as Nehru, Patel, Prasad, and Ambedkar.

But if you mean by blasphemy what Eliot said, then it is not a theological notion, it is a different kind of notion. When you are talking about belief in relation to Constitutions, you are talking of a constitutional faith. My good friend Sanford Levinson has written a book called *Constitutional Faith*, in which he calls constitutionalism a civic religion, with its congregation, its church, its followers, its canon, its popes, and so on (Levinson 2011). The second chapter of the book shows that you cannot understand the Supreme Court of the United States and its jurisprudence unless you grasp the similarity and difference between two kinds of constitutional (interpretive) practices—one which he calls Catholic and the other, Protestant. In his understanding, civic religion is already enwombed in some sense into the constitutional traditions of interpretation. So, to broaden this point, you are only secular within the religious tradition, and it is the religious tradition that gives you your meaning to travel into and arrive at secularity in a constitutional sense.

However, a political heresy lies in resisting the practices of de-subjectification. It does not recognise State sovereignty as constituting you. The Constitution in which you have faith is the one you make for yourself. It is not an entity or an object that is outside you. C2 or citizen interpretation is so precious because it begins in the modern language of 'ownership'. Now I do not know what ownership means, but I have in mind here owning the Constitution in terms of caring for it, of living within it. Things that you do not own, you do not care for. I do not like this owning metaphor, but never mind. It is the field or the path, it is the meadow or the road, that you create for yourself. It is an ecology of the self as an activist with other people, for other people, who are suffering, of making enclaves of justice.

Enclaves of justice—that's a Julius Stone metaphor—is what we struggle to establish, and these are very fragile spaces. They represent numerous sites of struggle, sacrifice, tragedies, exuberance, partnerships, and they have to be constantly protected and nourished. They are fragile spaces which are created by the loving labour of many minds and hands. I like to think of C3 this way, that it is not out there. C1 is out there, part of C2 is out there, but C3 is inside us because we also have to rebuild the Constitution and reinterpret what constitutional law is for. That's a kind of constitutional love because it is irredeemably related to justice. It is permeated by the struggle for justice, and it is a place where there is no one meaning for justice that is shared by all, but each one of these meanings somehow relate to the suffering of humanity in one way or the other. That's what makes it beautiful, and that's what enthrals me, engages me, makes me a kind of perpetual labourer. In many ways, whatever I talk about or write about, it is the Constitution that I am laying for myself that I am in love with. I think that these enclaves of justice have shown the capacity for people like me and others to take the responsibility for suffering others in a public way that matters to me. That is the only way I can relate to the Constitution. That is a wonderful feeling. Despite all this, it is not a solid edifice, it is not always certain that it will be productive of justice and variety, but it is a field of forces of struggle and that is where the partial belief comes in.

J. M. Coetzee has a marvellous book where he says there is a germ of doubt gnawing at the heart of conviction.[18] This is where you are, you

[18]'And standing in the doorway I would turn my bleakest stare in upon myself, seeking by the last means I knew to detect the germ of dishonesty at the heart of the conviction…' (Coetzee 2004, 165).

cannot avoid the germ of doubt. You cannot avoid its nibbling away at your convictions, of justice, of suffering, even beauty in struggles. Your relationship with your convictions is a torrid affair. Partial belief—yes, that is what constitutional faith really means. But then, is not all faith after all partial?

But there is also a renewal of spirit in the struggle, and that's what matters. The ability to respond instead of to retreat. Perhaps I am making it very mystical, but you asked me for my experience. It cannot be put down in words totally.

Working with Bhopal victims, I re-learnt how much virtue there is in total self-effacement. There were several groups: some wanted to pursue the multinational corporation, some wanted only the Union of India to fully be answerable at the bar of civil and criminal liability, some others wanted both. And all wanted, and expected, urgent and long-term medical care, and catastrophe-specific relief and rehabilitation, including regional economic planning. The needs, interests, and even ideologies of the victims themselves and the next of kin (as it were) of the urban social and human rights activists were different, although all converged on the accountability and responsibility of the perpetrators.

I took the view that one should lay one's knowledge and skills at the service of the groups concerned. One has to be at the tap, not the top: one has to co-suffer and learn. But in the process lie new struggles, fresh hopes, and uncertain futures. Strewn are the hopes about what law and adjudication could have done and despair at what it failed to, or would not, do. Yes, this is parlous positioning when emotions run very high, and a demand is made that you ally publicly with one. At one meeting, I was even called a Carbide Stooge! One risks the name-calling and even being misunderstood when activism consists in respecting the different wishes of the violated groups, when different routes are available to obtain some succour. One risks many misperceptions, many misunderstandings, but one should realise oneself the reasons for and emotions underlying why one offers to help. I still recall Ralph Waldo Emerson, who in one of his essays said axiomatically: 'To be understood is a luxury'. One must draw a distinction between narcissistic engagement with a social cause and an other-directed one.

In the first year of the catastrophic disaster and the first anniversary, I published my speech in *Mainstream* on the lethal lineal descendant of the East India Company, which maintains a toxic continuity with the Green Revolution. It is something that wrote itself.

This one time, late evening, I was asked if I would join the lighting of the effigy of Warren Anderson. The effigy proved to be stronger than all of us put together! But do you know what the demand of the protest was? They did not want compensation. *Hum log ko muhaf ja nahi, Union Carbide ko phaansi do.* Look at this notion. Hang a multinational unto death. So I came up with five different strategies for five different needs and said that I would begin working on all of them if it was so required.

While some people said only this must be done and not that, I think that while working in such a catastrophe with a range of groups and people, it is important to efface oneself, to rule out a sense that you possess the right answer to a problem. Lots of people were cross with me. That happens. I did research worldwide on corporations being hanged for manslaughter and I found this case in Cook County, Iowa. This was not Internet-era research. I had to go to so many places to find material, I read American law reports, so much work went into it.

Many years later when I was at Warwick, David Bergman,[19] who was with us in the International Coalition for Justice in Bhopal (which Ward Morehouse[20] had founded), wanted to set up an alternative law practice. He ended up setting up a centre for corporate accountability. The first thing to work on was corporate crime, and he said there must be a separate category called corporate manslaughter.

---

[19] David Bergman: British human rights activist and journalist, actively involved in relief work in the context of the Bhopal disaster, who also worked in the UK (see the Hatfield rail crash incident, Chapter 12). Bergman is especially well-known for his work in Bangladesh.

[20] Ward Morehouse (1929–2012), major activist in the context of the Bhopal disaster. Founder of the Center for International and Comparative Studies, the Council on International and Public Affairs (CIPA), the International Campaign for Justice on Bhopal (ICJB), and co-founder of Programs on Corporations, Law and Democracy (POCLAD).

The battle against Methyl Isocyanate (MIC) is something that does not leave you, it is something that enters your genes. It is not something that you can leave behind because something did not work out, it is something that goes on and recreates itself wherever you are. The East India Company was a charter company, the charter could be renewed and revoked. We argued that there should be a similar thing for UCC, that we should be able to revoke its status. Ward Morehouse and others (we all chipped in) took out an expensive ad appeal in the American dailies on the East and West coasts asking for withdrawal of the charter and extradition of Warren Anderson to India, an appeal that was signed by artists and thinkers among a lot of people, including Toni Morrison, Noam Chomsky, etc. Some things you can never learn even if you get a Ph.D. or you get a post-doctorate. I ask myself where did I learn my law from and the answer is: from public struggles for justice and personal reflexivity. From reading and doing things with what you read. Reading the face of the suffering Other and bending law towards justice. And of course the struggle to find the twenty-fifth hour of the day!

It is the constant re-creation of self and the imagination of what constitutes justice in whatever dimension that matters. So C3 is what each one makes. That is the heart of the matter.

The Future of Human Rights

AN: Would a similar notion be applicable to the notion of human rights as well? Your relationship to the idea of human rights is similar to your relationship to the idea of C3. In my reading of *The Future of Human Rights* (Baxi 2013c), your notion of human rights is based on faith, but there is doubt gnawing at the faith. *The Future of Human Rights* seems to forecast the 'end' of human rights. However, the notion of constitutional love or faith appears quite powerfully in your report on Human Rights Education, because that conveyed the sense of faith far more powerfully than *The Future* did. You say of human rights that

> It is, in a true sense, a continual collective search for the plenitude of life, for meaning that confirms individual and collective dignity, and for the resources for human coexistence. In this sense, HRE symbolizes a secular, or multi religious equivalent of liberation theology.[21]

UB: This is mighty strange! This was work that I did for about ten years, human rights education with a dear friend of mine named Shulamith Koenig.[22] She is not an academic or activist, but she knows everything about human rights learning. She introduced me to many friends: Walther Lichem,[23] Steve Marks,[24] and Ivanka Corti. Walther is a bureaucrat who, unlike most of that special species, *actually* thinks, and is very committed to human rights education. And for Steve Marks, a former Ford Foundation Chief in Delhi, then Harvard Chair in Human Right to Health, there is little concerning the UN and human rights that escapes him. Ivanka Corti is from Italy, she is very fond of Gramsci, she goes to Gramsci's grave even now. She was the chair of CEDAW. All of us got together. They would make fun of me, calling me Professor Praxis! And some did not like my use of big words. It was an extraordinary group. It (the human rights education

[21] https://www.pdhre.org/report/(accessed April 2022).

[22] Shulamith Koenig: President of the People's Movement for Human Rights Learning (formerly known as People's Decade for Human Rights Education), which she founded in 1988. Worked to have the UN declare a Decade for Human Rights Educations (1995–2004) and international public policy to enhance inclusive learning worldwide. See Chapter 13 for more on Koenig.

[23] Walther Lichem worked in the field of international water resources with development cooperation missions to Ethiopia (1971), Argentina (1971–1974) and to the Senegal River Development Organisation (1980), as Rapporteur on international river basins at the International Conference on Water Law (Caracas, 1976), and at the IVth World Water Conference (Buenos Aires, 1982). Later, he was Consul General in the SR Slovenia (1976–1980) and Ambassador to Chile (1980–1984) and Canada (1993–2000).

[24] Stephen P. Marks, Professor of Health and Human Rights at the Harvard School of Public Health and Director of the Program on Human Rights in Development.

group) was a non-academic group with different kinds of people who were interested in carrying this forward.

The idea that appealed to Shulamith was to write a book on the legends of human rights. Take human rights learning away from law and jurisprudence, take it away from relativism and absolutism, and all these stupid controversies that we talk about. My idea was to look at early classics, epics, folklore throughout the world, and to read the legends in such a way as to see what the word 'human', the word 'rights', meant in different faiths, in millennia of history. It was going to be a cultural story. Whether or not it would be useful to lawyers was not our prime concern. But it did not take off, although many people were interested. It was too big a project for a small NGO called Human Rights Education Incorporated. There were no resources, many world institutions who should have been were not interested.

It was then that the idea of a People's Report on Human Rights Education was born. This is the one you are referring to. I have also written a paper on the UDHR website on the impossibility of human rights education (Baxi 1994d). I believe in what I have said there. I ask the question: What is the meaning of human rights education? The primary authors of human rights are people in struggle and communities in resistance. How can there be human rights education? We created human rights, so obviously the rights we created by struggle are appropriated by somebody else. Human rights now have to be re-appropriated from them. It's the analysis of the politics *of* and politics *for* human rights which I have elaborated in my *The Future of Human Rights*. My colleagues said this is important, it is a fragile movement. So I put it in, and they said Baxi is cheating the world, he is speaking in two voices. It is not that, actually. One is a movement document, and I do think that each phrase here is important. I think it has to be seen in the light of the second piece. Therefore, my answer was that human rights education is needed not for the first authors of human rights, but for those who have appropriated it, for presidents, politicians, multinationals, etc. You do not go to villages, communities, etc., and tell them what human rights are. You go up!

The second piece was about globalisation and human rights. You know what Marx wrote. Capitalism is about the generalised commodity production of goods and services. But it is not only about that. Capitalism is primarily about the production of desire. The idea that to be human, to be efficient, or to do things better, you must have a variety of objects to choose from. Endless desire. In Moscow, when I used to go there before the Berlin Wall fell, there were only two brands of toothpaste. Their dental health was the best in the world. After the fall of the Berlin Wall, there were 150 brands of toothpaste and the dental health index actually came down. It is so bizarre. So I said, if we are saying life within capitalism is enjoyable, actually existing capitalism, then enjoyment should be extended to all human beings, so much so that life after capitalism is also enjoyable. Washing machines, *chappati*-making machines, dishwashers liberate women who are working or are at home, or even domestic help, but the production of desire in itself is regarded as an emancipatory force. Now, when more and more people believe in it, what role does human rights education have? What can it do? The obscenity of capitalism is at its culminating point. The only rights that will remain are residual civil and political rights, and the human rights of investors, that kind of human rights.

What is dialogue? How can you do dialogue in human rights? It is in *The Future of Human Rights* that you find the distillation of my thought and language about the human. In one of my first chapters, I talk about human rights as languages. I speak there of six types of languages.[25] Each type of language creates an image of human rights. Human rights as language of governance, human rights as juridical production, human rights as a language of resistance, human rights as syndrome of shared sovereignty, human rights as an insurrectionary practice, and so on. The six languages of human rights necessarily produce a diversity of conceptions, united, however, only by two words: human and rights. If there were no rights, would there be any human left? It is a necessary correlation, it is a continuing thing. The answer to this is found in six different languages. What constitutes the distinctively human? Then I complicate my life and everybody else's by asking a third question: What is the relationship between being human and having rights on the one hand, and both put together and

[25] See the third edition of *The Future of Human Rights* (Baxi 2013c, 14–25).

suffering on the other? That's where the plot thickens. I thought I was clear on the six languages—I could have developed it more, maybe it needs more labour of explanation. But it is a whole way of looking at what is human, and what may it mean to say one has rights.

AN: I think the notion of an enchantment was what I missed in *The Future of Human Rights*. There, you spoke about the end of human rights. The notion of the future (that's a powerful notion), it did not seem to emerge in *The Future* in the way you had articulated it in the conversations.

UB: Yes, in *The Future* I tucked it into the Preface in the second edition. There are many futures, there is no single future. One may imagine a future as continuity with the past or as a series of 'breaks' or discontinuities. Now, I am very clear that as far as human rights can be thought of as moral or ethical languages, they are on their way to extinction. Just as a whole history of concepts emerging from the Soviet Union is over. The struggle is now over recognition, status, honour, not over material redistribution. You see it everywhere, except perhaps in the struggles against impoverishment. Rights are the products of struggle, they are not given. One has won the right of recognition of oneself as a desiring being who is liberated from some extraordinary laws. But when it comes to the redistribution of material resources, how do you do that without dispossessing those who have an abundance or surfeit? As against redistribution, the politics of recognition has taken over. Does post-Marxism mean redistribution is now a matter of luck, enterprise, and the free market? The importance of redistribution in the service of being human and having rights, it seems, has been forgotten.

So what happens when a moral language is lost? Not everything is lost. Another moral language will replace it.

The question, then, is: What new moral language is in emergence, and how do we relate it to our preferred languages of human rights? Do you recognise that some of these languages have lost their valence? But imagine what languages will come back! I think the candidate is already there: justice. Global justice—reparation for Black slavery in Africa, reparations for colonialism, the Cold War. Reparation is justice.

I have written on Rawls and global reparative justice.[26] Somehow, we are moving either backwards or forwards through the language of justice. We need to unpack this. Justice has a global dimension. Where Rawls stops his theory of justice, we begin. Is justice merely a moribund concept? Can you speak of justice in international relations between States, between States and citizens, between States and diasporic citizens? Is justice only forward-looking or backward-looking? That is, can you ask for restorative justice for past violations? This is a whole new field.

I base myself on these straws in the wind. The question, then, is partly: How do we retrieve the good parts or the survivable parts of the language of human rights? That is a work of enormous magnitude. A lot of this will be in the Tagore Law Lectures on approaches to global justice. I have bits and pieces written here and there. I want to go beyond them and put the question in the very way in which you helped me to formulate it now.

This is an important clarification for me. Languages of justice are coming in now, human rights languages are going out. There is an active connection I am now making between the new languages and the active residue of the past. I am a great follower of Raymond Williams. There is always a dominant culture, an emergent culture, and a residual culture.[27] And these three always coalesce into each other. The residual culture is one of human rights and the emergent one, that of justice. What laws of residual culture still persist in the emergent is a question.

Hospitality and Human Rights

AN: As you were saying, *The Future of Human Rights* comes at a much later point in time, and maybe the notion of C3 is an earlier notion. Is there also a darkening pessimism in that sense? Obviously, if you look at *Crisis*, or your earlier work, or even *Taking Suffering Seriously*, there is a certain kind of exuberance. *The Future* does not seem to have the spirit of resistance.

[26] Baxi, 'Some Notes on John Rawls,' *The Law of Peoples* (n.d.).

[27] See 'Dominant, Residual and Emergent' (Williams 1977, 121–127).

UB: No, it does not. Local and global are always interconnected, and part of the same reality. We know that there are no binaries, but struggles are intensely local. They present themselves very differently to the challenges of imagination and action. We use this expression, 'space', and talk about 'creating spaces' without knowing how tremendously geographers have worked with it. You need to ask yourself the question: What does this dimension called space mean? I have read some Deleuze and Guattari and geosophical—not geographic, but geo-philosophic, or geosophical—works. They say that, for example, there are three types of Western human rights epistemes—spaces—France, England, America. The study of space is very important to the study of time.

You can think of the question, 'How can we peacefully use the law of the oppressor on behalf of the oppressed?' surely in relation to many issues. This is a different geographical space, and in India, you have to insinuate human rights in a different way in the struggle for land rights, water rights, forest rights, etc. I am not defending myself, I am just trying to say that the geosophical spatiality of human rights in its global distribution is a very difficult and different terrain. For example, there cannot be SAL, nothing compared to that can ever happen in the same way in which it happened here, in Africa, Europe, Scandinavia, or Eastern Europe. The best you can hope for is an amicus filing in which you are not allowed to present the case as a petitioner in person; in the international arena, legislatures are more open to human rights activism than the judiciary, for example, the EU Parliament. Then there is the issue of corporate governance and multinationals, for example, the entire question of the regulation of sweatshops. Chapter 9 of *The Future* is based on the UN norms regarding multinational business entities and their human rights responsibilities.[28] John Ruggie[29] has led a missionary crusade against these draft norms, saying they do

[28]'Norms on the Responsibilities of Transnational Corporations and Other Business Enterprises with Regard to Human Rights', UN Doc. E/CN.4/Sub.2/2003/12/Rev.2 (2003); see also *The Future of Human Rights* (Baxi 2013c, Chapter 9).

[29]John Gerard Ruggie (b. 1944), Professor in Human Rights and International Affairs at Harvard's Kennedy School of Government. From

not even deserve the dignity of a third-class funeral! I am against this kind of polemical thinking. Struggles in the international arena often have to respect disagreement among activists and pave future paths of consensual thought.

What we have to do here is worry not so much about optimism, but to look instead at the emerging history of human rights movements. The World Social Forum, the Permanent People's Tribunal, specific sectoral movements like the anti-Nike movement against child labour, consumer boycotts (industrial strikes are not possible, but consumer boycotts will work), the anti-globalisation mass protests in Seattle, the Arab Spring, global consumer movements, the 99% movement,[30] Occupy Now campaigns, etc.—all these, taken together, present a scenario of the future of human rights at an international or global level. I am aware of the possibilities, of the importance of it.

Neither time nor space is a homogenous notion. It is what Deleuze calls deterritorialisation. Swami Agnivesh[31] goes to the UN and says, India has slave-like practices. Bonded labour is a slave-like practice. Gail Omvedt[32] goes to the IMF and to the World Bank to make sure that labour laws are properly enforced as conditionalities. Now, how do you speak this language?

On the one hand, we are positioned against international finance capital and on the other hand, the demands of nation-worship—patriotism. Is going international necessarily anti-patriotic? At the

---

2005–2011, he served as the UN Secretary-General's Special Representative for Business and Human Rights.

[30] Refers to the Occupy Wall Street movement, with its slogan, 'We are the 99%'.

[31] Swami Agnivesh (1939–2020) was a political activist, Arya Samaj member, former Haryana MLA, founder of the Bonded Labour Liberation Front, and Chair of the UN Voluntary Trust Fund on Contemporary Forms of Slavery between 1994–2004.

[32] Gail Omvedt (1941–2021): sociologist, human rights activist, and renowned writer on anti-caste movements, Dalit politics, and women's struggles. Author of *We Will Smash This Prison!: Indian Women in Struggle* (1980), *Buddhism in India: Challenging Brahmanism and Caste* (2003), *Understanding Caste: From Buddha to Ambedkar and Beyond* (2011).

Singapore WTO meeting, a lot of us insisted that there should be incorporation of social clauses in trade agreements. Social clauses are clauses that prevent the exploitation of labour in production, and that insist on minimum wages. There was a big debate on whether we should go to the WTO or oppose it. The question was: Are you inviting them to discipline national governments in the guise of human rights? Spaces are not given, they are constructed or created. They merge in a really strange form or shape. I really have to control very vigorously any harsh word that I might say about some of these people. But it creates the same dilemma of collaboration versus resistance. What are the broad human rights dilemmas? Working with or against power. Working with the system or going against it. That is the same problem in both local and international spaces. How do you turn around the international agencies? No matter how liberally I criticise them, calling them Northern, even authoritarian, all those things, how do you turn all States and people to a *new commonwealth of core rights?*

You talk of the strategy of human rights action. One strategy is of working with so that it works against itself. Another is to disorganise, replace, ambush that system as a whole. That's the talk of reform of the UN, ways of participatory democracy, protests, etc. There are many other strategies—direct action, for example. Ward Morehouse and other people have developed this strategy of citizen arrests. A world citizen's arrest warrant for G8 leaders. They actually go and try to serve the summons, but are often prevented from acting by the police and are instead put in jail. There is a dilemma between the choice of direct action and policy advocacy. It should be the same in the national sphere. I can list out the choices of dilemmas or strategies. They are broadly similar.

If you are asking me whether my international work does not have the same quality of lyricism which my more local work has, then you are right. I don't have that same relation to international human rights movements. You got me by the jugular, as it were.

AN: Is it to do with the birth of each of these terms? You are from (what you would call) the 'Mohandasian' heritage, whereas for international human rights, the birthplace of rights is different. Would that be your understanding?

UB: No, it is a question, in one sense, of the limits of all that one can do as a finite individual. One makes certain personal strategic choices on what normativity to foster, what normativity to critique, on what partnerships to develop, that kind of thing. There, the Mohandasian heritage is guiding us well, especially with respect to the question of *swaraj*/self-determination. What Mohandas called *swaraj* is a difficult notion to translate. It means total emancipation from superior powers within and without. This is like the great *jihad* and the little jihad. The little jihad is fighting one's enemies outside, and the great jihad is fighting enemies within. For example, the idea of *ahimsa* suffuses human rights. In fact, the best writing on the 'animal' rights movement starts with Mohandas. My own reading is that he never went beyond the justification of vegetarianism as dietary reform. But other people like Peter Singer have read into him a great wealth of insight.[33]

Take the notion of planetary citizenship. We are trustees, not owners. Trustees have a certain fiduciary loyalty not to destroy what is given to them. Look at the biodiversity convention, at climate change, there are cutting-edge developments in international law. It is not just a question of State obligations, obligations of corporations, etc. It is a new idea of planetary loyalty, multispecies solidarity, and not territorially based, not value-added. That is why it is difficult to materialise. But if we do not have loyalties to where we belong, so where is the

[33] Upendra Baxi, 'Animal Rights as Companion Human Rights', 19th IP Desai Memorial Lecture, Centre for Social Studies, South Gujarat University, 12 August 2008 (unpublished lecture on file with the editors):

> While we have some animal rights movements, contemporary Indian political and social theory may not claim to have made any serious contribution to animal rights discourse. Even today, many Euroamerican philosophers and champions of animal rights find in the works of Mohandas some extraordinary richness, providing the bases for animal rights talk. True, as far as we can read his corpus, even Mohandas, while speaking of 'vegetarianism as a moral choice', never fully went beyond an advocacy of diet-reform; no doubt he concluded that we should all emphasise the 'moral consequences of vegetarianism', but he did not quite address the cause. I here address the Euroamerican discourse because it is there that the full entailments of Mohandasian concerns remain fully at work.

question of planetary loyalty? Barbara Ward (Ward 1966) wrote about this very evocatively. Take the example of the international peace movement. In Mary Kaldor's book (2003), she talks about the peace movement as being the essence of global civil society. This is not the kind of activism that we talk about today. The question is, why so? How is planetary multispecies survival to be ensured by world peace though the law?

Mohandas' heritage is there, although it is different. The symbolisation of 2 October as World Peace Day is not unimportant. There is that heritage as well. We should study this, either directly or indirectly—the impact of Mohandasian thought on world governance. He referred to the duties of the citizens of the world in connection with the UDHR, which was then being drafted (Goodale 2018). The reference to citizens of the world is usually missed, but is even more important in these days of spiralling anthropogenic harm to the planet.

So, yes, this is the answer to your question.

For example, I keep asking myself the question—reflexivity is very difficult—can there be an ethical immigration policy? My first major article before 'The Little Done, The Vast Undone' was a review article on White Australia Policy, published in a journal for LAWASIA. Is immigration a matter of choice? Is there a case for open borders? Global capital does not need a visa, capital is not population, it is something else. Capitalists do not migrate. We have to be very careful in seeking a human right to migration. There is obviously a case to be made for open borders, against the case usually made for border control. Yet open borders are taken to mean that restrictions on the free movement of capital and the sale of currency are relatively unburdened by regulations. But that is not what one is talking about in immigration. We are talking of the movement of bodies. Not of capital or material and symbolic capital. Now, how do you address that? India has a relatively, and most surprisingly, ethical immigration policy. In fact, the influx of East Pakistani people was ultimately taken as a ground to authorise military intervention in what has now become Bangladesh. India is a remarkably hospitable place. It does not throw people out in a big way.

Reading the Indian State is very difficult, though, and I do not mean to be hypercritical, although it is the duty of every citizen to develop the scientific temper, the spirit of enquiry, and of critical reform under Article 51A of the Constitution. Taslima Nasreen illustrated the dilemmas of governance when confronted with the claims of justice.[34] I would not instance this as a symbol of India's hospitality in terms of its semi-open borders. But the latter is not to be found elsewhere. What are the factors? If you were a human rights-oriented immigration minister or Head of State, what kind of immigration policy would you put in place? Obviously, it cannot be a barbarian equivalent where you put them in camps, and so on. There is a difference between asylum and refuge-seekers in international law. Immanuel Kant, who was a cosmopolitan, created this thinking of *jus cosmopoliticum*. He advocated the right of a stranger to enter your country. A right to hospitality. A right to reside amicably, but not a right to settle. Yes, within India, within anybody's country, questions about ethical immigration policies arise.

What ought to be the commandment of global justice of all human rights? Then you get into Hardin's 'The Tragedy of the Commons' (Hardin 1968) and the question of the carrying capacity of national entities. The related question of controlling civil society attitudes to migrants, interethnic violence, taking jobs away, etc., is also as important as it is difficult. What happened in South Africa, in Johannesburg, was that all the Zimbabweans and Malawians were beaten up. They are now a marked community. So, it is not a question of letting as many people as you want come in, as the fact that after they come in, you have to look after them, create and sustain the conditions for multi-ethnic peace, and so on.

[34]In 2007, a mob, led by legislators from the Majlis-e-Ittehadul Muslimeen, violently protested the extension of visa to Bangladeshi writer Taslima Nasreen, who had been residing in India. Although she applied for permanent residency, the Indian government only extended her visa for six months. Since then, the government has been extending Nasreen's visa, while not granting her request for permanent residency. See https://timesofindia.indiatimes.com/india/taslima-nasreens-visa-extended-for-six-months/articleshow/2290465.cms (accessed June 2022).

It is a tough world. I do not think human rights are immaterial. They come as an inset into the wider question of global justice. Take, for example, a citizen of a rich country in the North who can be justly said to have obligations towards co-nationals. But how about similar obligations to non-nationals, say in the Sudan? What if my resources are limited? What if investing these resources in the Sudan would aggravate the plight of the poor co-nationals? What would justice require? Tough question. This is what I have addressed in my Tagore Law Lectures. I have been looking at these problems and writing on them. Iraq, etc., are clear cases where you manipulate resources to invade somebody because it is politically expedient, and it is very difficult to justify. Or take, for instance, the Millennium Development Goals (MDG) versus internationally recognised socioeconomic rights. On the one hand, there is a right to nutrition in Article 11 of the International Covenant on Economic, Social, and Cultural Rights. On the other hand, you have a global social policy called the MDG, which says we will halve the number of absolutely starving people in the world by 2015. Are social, economic, and cultural rights trumped [no reference to President Trump intended!] here by policy enunciations?

Global governance is developing a new policy regime through international institutions which is not wholly conversant with human rights. All I can say is, yes, there is a difference in my approach in dealing with these spheres. I am reading now an article on regime collisions in world governance. We are not talking only about the State or multinational corporations, we are talking of all kinds of things, of private arbitration, dispute settlement agencies, mediation, and the conflicting spaces they create. The question, in short, is of plurality. One might object to this long harangue by stating that working from below for cross-border justice is a more grounded strategy than working with people in Strasbourg, in New York, in Vienna. Which is the better thing? The thing to do is, as far as possible, to merge your actions.

LL: One thing which seems to be missing here: taking from Leela Gandhi's work on *Affective Communities* (Gandhi 2006), where she talks about Gandhi's friendship with the vegetarians, we see very different kinds of cosmopolitanism. This is what I think Upen is referring to when he speaks about the international peace movement, where it is a solidarity, or a kind of a move which is *affective*, whereas the international human rights movement in the Strasbourg or New York sense seems to be devoid of that. This is a linguistic movement, almost brought about by *a* particular language of human rights.

UB: I do not know as much as I should about peace movements in India. In my writings, I have talked about the human right to the de-nuclearisation of the world.[35] Should not Hiroshima and Nagasaki be impetus enough? It is very important to talk about de-nuclearisation. I do not think the languages of human rights are necessarily relevant here, although one can stretch the point by speaking of a human right to a de-nuclearised world.

Take UN peacekeeping—the human right to humanitarian relief. Take peace as a prism—the human right to world peace. Increasingly, global civil society movements are very different. Even in the World Social Forum, there are sector-specific movements—the rights of habitat/housing, rights of migrant workers, environmental movements, etc. They are all important. The WHO Council fortunately agreed with some distinguished scholars and activists and decided to refer the matter of the legality of nuclear weapons for the opinion of the International Court of Justice (ICJ). The US opposed it, and the ICJ did not give them standing. It is worth looking at. The strategy was to argue that its fallouts on the environment are considerable, that it is a violation of the right to peace, and so on. It produced a very interesting discourse. Once you are hooked on to the pursuit of peace in the international space, you have a fundamental ground on which to define what global civil society is. War is not civil. The women's movement has played a key role in the peace movement. There was this example of women chaining themselves to the fence of a military base in the UK in protest against nuclear weapons.[36] Women are the

[35] Fischer-Lescano and Teubner (2004).

[36] Reference to the Greenham Common Women's Peace Camp (started in September 1981) to protest against the decision of the British government

worst sufferers of war, of whatever kind. It is all very well to talk about compensation, rehabilitation, restoration, etc., and it is important, I am not denying it, but peace is hard work. Much harder work than waging conflict or even war.

This does not respond to Lawrence's comment entirely, but the concerns he validly raises are a part of these conversations.

Justice without Borders?

LL: I'll read out a bit from Peter Linebaugh's *The Many-headed Hydra* (2002), which has a beautiful section. He is here documenting subaltern histories of cosmopolitanism.

> It was landless, exploited. It lost the integument of the commons to cover and protect its needs. It was poor, lacking property, money or material riches of any kind. It was often unwaged, forced to perform the paid labors of capitalism. It was often hungry, with uncertain means of survival. It was mobile, transatlantic. It powered industries of worldwide transportation. It left the land, migrating from country to town, from region to region, across the oceans, and from one island to another. It was terrorized, subject to coercion. Its hide was calloused by indentured labour, galley slavery, plantation slavery, convict transportation, the workhouse, the house of correction. Its origins were often traumatic: enclosure, capture, and imprisonment left lasting marks. It was female and male, of all ages. (Indeed, the very term proletarian originally referred to poor women who served the state by bearing children.) It included everyone from youth to old folks, from ship's boys to old salts, from apprentices to savvy old masters, from young prostitutes to old 'witches.' It was multitudinous, numerous, and growing. Whether in a square, at a market, on a common, in a

to allow cruise missiles to be stored there. The first blockade of the base occurred in May 1982 with 250 women protesting, during which thirty-four arrests were made. The camp was active for nineteen years, and was disbanded in 2000.

> regiment, or on a man-of-war with banners flying and drums beating, its gatherings were wondrous to contemporaries. It was numbered, weighed, and measured. Unknown as individuals or by name, it was objectified and counted for purposes of taxation, production, and reproduction. It was cooperative and laboring. The collective power of the many rather than the skilled labor of the one produced its most forceful energy. It moved burdens, shifted earth, and transformed the landscape. It was motley, both dressed in rags and multi-ethnic in appearance. Like Caliban, it originated in Europe, Africa, and America. It included clowns, or cloons (i.e., country people). It was without genealogical unity. It was vulgar. It spoke its own speech, with a distinctive pronunciation, lexicon, and grammar made up of slang, cant, jargon, and pidgin—talk from work, the street, the prison, the gang, and the dock. It was planetary, in its origins, its motions, and its consciousness. Finally, the proletariat was self-active, creative; it was—and is—alive; it is on a move. (Linebaugh and Rediker 2002, 332)

UB: This is a beautiful and vivid evocation indeed! I did not know till now that the term proletariat referred originally to child-bearing women and their labour and effort. And there is a great deal here, for example, 'proletarian' being very diverse and *on the move always*. I will, if I may, focus only on one aspect of it, now celebrated in high social theory.

Cosmopolitanism lays the foundations of a simple idea that is very powerful, that national boundaries are ethically arbitrary. The mere fact that you have special rights to the resources of a territory by virtue of being born there is a deeply feudal idea. The mere fact that because you are born in Saudi Arabia or in the OPEC countries, you have a right to oil, of which you have unsuspected reserves, and that you owe no duty to others in the world, is morally wrong. Some recognition of this is available in the international legal conception of 'common heritage of (hu)mankind', and to add another example, for the right of access to other territories when a country is landlocked (the UN Convention on the Law of the Seas have rectified this position somewhat). Because birth, the fact of being born in a particular place, is not morally relevant. From this simple idea arises the notion of distributive justice across the globe. You are not entitled to these resources just because you are born in the territory. Justice without borders and across borders is the claim that the new proletariat is going to be making, and is in fact already making in Doha Round and elsewhere. Most pharmaceutical MNCs have shut down the production of vaccines necessary for Third World diseases because it does not fetch them any profit. They concentrate on small niche markets for very expensive medicines. The movement around the Doha Round in a sense marks a beginning.

Iris Marion Young says, to raise questions about inequity, you first have to learn to name it (Young 2001). The best way to name it is as global structural injustice. She goes on to say that naming is not enough. Then comes the task of saying what duties of justice we owe each other across countries. Since all of us have only one life and it is already pre-committed to certain priorities, agendas, practicalities, each individual may have some *influence*, but very little *power*. How best do we discharge our responsibilities for justice? It is a very good analysis, which was done just before she died. It is not enough to say that boundaries are arbitrary, that citizenship is a feudal concept, that there are certain things which are unjust and which should be called structural injustice. To respond to this is our responsibility. Responsibility is not all or nothing. Situated in a particular location, you can discharge a global responsibility. There is only so much one can do, and one should appreciate one's limits. Appreciating one's limits, for me, is an ethical situation full of promise, not an alibi for doing nothing.

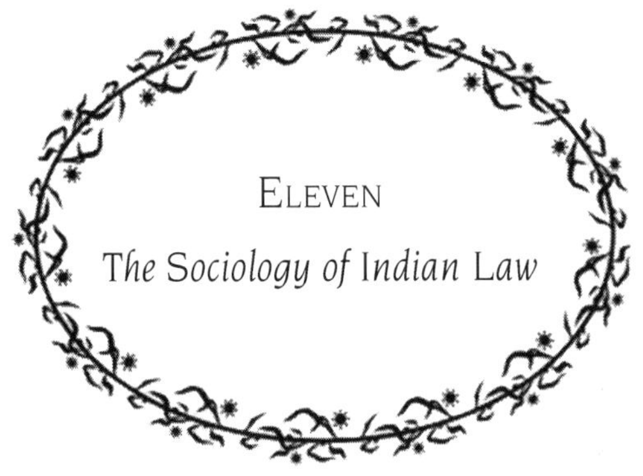

ELEVEN
The Sociology of Indian Law

Indian Legal Theory

LL: Is there an Indian Legal Theory?

UB: This is a difficult question. Not every common law country has something called 'legal theory', although they all have 'jurisprudence'. The latter is what law students, law teachers, lawyers, and judges have time for. Jurisprudence does contain some large questions about the nature of law and judicial process. But only a handful in common law societies pursue abstract thought, philosophy (epistemology and ontology), and meta-ethics (questions about the nature of ethics and morality). This is understandable, but it is not justifiable.

That is why Ambedkar scholarship matters so much to me. At last people have woken up to the fact that there are different ways of reading him. He was amongst the first truly postcolonial thinkers in South Asia. I am a student of Ambedkar. Every time I read him, I discover something new. I gave a lecture once on Agamben and Ambedkar (Baxi 2013b). The notion of *Homo Sacer* as a person who can neither be killed nor sacrificed is central to untouchability. For many, discrimination on the grounds of untouchability is neither a sin nor a crime, neither is arson, assault, everyday humiliation, and discrimination a sin or a crime, but Article 17 outlaws this conduct as a crime against the basic human/fundamental right.

When I met Giorgio Agamben, he asked me this: Where can I go in search of Indian legal theory? I said, go to Ambedkar if you want to understand the link between biopolitics and the *nomos*. Ambedkar was among the first theorists of biopolitics. What did Ambedkar talk about in relation to *Atisudras* excepting biopower and biopolitics? And even about macro-politics of the 'lawless law'? True, these words, labels, or theories, were not then specifically available. But should that deter us today from comparing today's Western thinkers with Indian thinkers who first envisioned ancient truths about biopower? Much the same can be said concerning Ambedkar as a theorist of contradiction, representation, emancipation, and justice.

LL: One of the genuine problems I have is, how does one find one's voice when there is an inheritance of scholarship that one has, and we are relatively untrained within Indian philosophical traditions.

UB: You are right, Lawrence, there is a problem here of our own resources. The philosophic traditions we learn or are schooled in are wholly the development of the Western metaphysics. There are courses in Indian metaphysical theory, but only a few students learn it. Which does not mean that later in life one may not learn it, particularly if one regards teaching and research as an opportunity for learning and formation/reformation of oneself, rather than as a bureaucratic burden.

But political philosophy, a close cousin of legal theory, should come easy to us. If you do not want to go so far as Mohandas Gandhi or his contemporaries, one can at least study JP, who singlehandedly sought deliberative democracy in India. I often write that every single activist judge is indebted to JP, almost as a residuary legatee attempted. Power as public trust, as public participation, as anti-corruption—these were all manifestos for the Total Revolution. You also have to go to the Buddha and to the moderns, among them Swami Vivekananda, Ram Manohar Lohia, M. N. Roy, Rabindranath Tagore, Iqbal, Subramania Bharathi, Narayana Guru, Acharya Vinoba Bhave, Jawaharlal Nehru, Maulana Abul Kalam Azad, and others.

There is a body of Indian thinkers who may not be regarded as erudite intellectuals or professional thinkers, but as organic thinkers. Actually, this very distinction may also be questioned in the Indian, and the Third World, contexts, but that remains a different theme. But this much may be safely said: We (most of us) talk a lot about non-Western thinkers, but we study only Western theories and texts.

LL: Going back to the 1960s, there emerged from that period, apart from very few exceptions like yourself, no body of scholarship. Why is there only an isolated Rajeev Dhavan and Baxi? Of course, there is J. Duncan M. Derrett (1963, 1968, 1970, 1976, 1978) and Robert Lingat (1973).

UB: This is a bit unfair, historically. We do not trace the intellectual traditions of reading law in India. But there were many jurisprudence teachers and jurisprudentially inclined scholars before Baxi and Dhavan! And they taught law and jurisprudence to generations of would-be lawyers and justices. Some of them published textbooks in jurisprudence, some unconventionally thought about ancient Indian and medieval jurisprudence, going beyond the-then leading texts (such as John Salmond), some combined teaching of jurisprudence with one or two domains, normally public law and international law. In fact, at the Masters' level, some departments were called departments of jurisprudence and international law. Teaching of Roman law was also considered essential to doing jurisprudence; so was studying the principles of legislation. I had the occasion to meet most of the senior teachers in jurisprudence at Dharwad (1979), where Professors G. S. Sharma and Ajjapa were the core faculty (with some other senior colleagues like S. Dhyani and S. K. Agarwala), and the regional workshops were on 'Towards Socially Relevant Legal Education' (1973–1975) and 'Curricular Development in Law' (1981–1983). Even a bare look at the names of participants in these three events will disclose how many good teachers of jurisprudence there were, both as teachers and textbook writers. Lord Ajjapa is still active in Mysore, catching up with new books on Roman law and jurisprudence!

It is true that scientific writing in jurisprudence is new: its beginnings are somewhat difficult to trace and, barring a few names, it is not widespread. But there are encouraging trends, too. Traditional teaching in jurisprudence has been gradually transformed by greater emphasis on legal theory and philosophy; there exist feminist, ecological, ethnographical, and anthropological trends. Writings on ways of doing legal history have also transformed the landscape (Baxi 2007c, 2018a; P. Baxi 2014).

One must look at early and contemporary social scientists' work entailing the significance of law. There was Dharma Kumar,[1] an economist, she worked on property, and Andre Beteille,[2] who gave a lot of attention to reservations in the context of the Constitution and law. There were a lot of people, but you are right, we were not interconnected. We tried to breach this non-communication, along with Veena Das and some others. Three kinds of groups emerged. The first was focused on behavioural political science, psephology, voting behaviour, etc. The second re-fertilised caste studies. M. N. Srinivas and others were concerned with equality and hierarchy in a big way. The main problem that emerged was justification of inequalities; thinking had to occur within 'social exclusion' because there was a historical body of thought that *justified* violent social exclusion. The third phenomenon was the rise of economics. This was an independent domain unconcerned with the other two domains that I mentioned. We did not produce a similar body of political and social philosophers.

With respect to law studies, it was inundated by people who came along with the Ford Foundation. The end result was, without being unfair to friends like (N. R.) Madhava Menon,[3] a cloning of liberal

---

[1] Dharma Kumar (1928–2001), economic historian, author of *Land and Caste in South India* (Kumar 1965).

[2] Andre Beteille (b. 1934), sociologist and author, among others, of *Caste, Class and Power: Changing Patterns of Stratification in a Tanjore Village* (1965), *Castes: Old and New, Essays in Social Structure and Social Stratification* (1969), *Inequality and Social Change* (1972), and *The Backward Classes in Contemporary India* (1992).

[3] Neelakanta Ramakrishna Madhava Menon (1935–2019), Founder-Director of the National Law School of India University (NLSIU), Bangalore, the National Judicial Academy, Bhopal, and the founder Vice-Chancellor of the West Bengal National University of Juridical Sciences (NUJS).

American legal education with some professionalism thrown into it. So, you had the liberal agenda to push legal aid, clinical teaching, curricular reform, etc. Dr R. U. Singh, Dean Lucknow, was personally responsible for ensuring that A. T. Markose, P. K. Tripathi, and Gyan Swaroop Sharma went on to study at Yale. In more favourable times, and as a part of faculty development plan, Dean Anandjee and P. K. Tripathi facilitated many teachers to go to the USA for higher studies. These people became the carriers of the first wave of modernisation of legal education.

LL: In a number of places, you have described the phenomenon of the modernisation of legal education.

UB: Modernisation is a Cold War term, which replaced offensive terms such as 'Westernisation' or 'Stalinisation'; it was later to be replaced by the term 'development', partly sculpted by the Third World (Baxi 2012). G. S. Sharma was concerned with the questions of a distinctive Indian philosophy of law, and why the law of tort is not developed in India; A. T. Markose was the first author of a treatise on administrative law. He wrote *Judicial Control of Administrative Action in India* (Markose 1956) long before Wade and Phillips wrote their book on the same subject. If you look at the level of his scholarship, it is better than Wade and Phillips in some respects. We had several Hindu and Islamic law teachers. There was a whole framework which was relatively independent of decolonised Indian legal theory. This was then confronted by the project of 'modernising legal education', and it was marginalised. How to redefine 'modernisation' was an agenda that remained; some were to fight from within or to mercilessly promote this modernising agenda. The struggles were mainly fought on the terrain of family law and Hindu law and jurisprudence perspectives, and here, the corpus of Jonathan Duncan Derrett, Werner Menski, Marc Galanter, and Masaji Chiba remains the most illuminating.

Many reformers of law and legal education chose the latter. The result is what we see, a package of pedagogic methods such as the case method, better evaluation systems, and curricular interventions such as the inclusion of legal aid in clinical education, etc. But it did not happen the way it could have happened had we followed some sort of indigenous leadership.

What emerged in India was extremely sophisticated scholarship in constitutional and international law. Right from the 1960s till today, very few developing countries had this kind of advanced scholarship, where we produced brilliant international lawyers under the stewardship of people like R. P. Anand, Charles Alexandrowicz, T. S. Rama Rao, Rahmatullah Khan, B. S Murthy, and M. K. Nawaz, here only to mention the forerunners and in some ways early founders.

It did not happen outside these two fields of law—in, for instance, criminal law or banking or tax law. I don't know the reasons for this. Perhaps it is because the best students and teachers went to those two fields. But later criminological writing: Raghunath Kelkar contributed a fantastic work on teaching criminal law, so did Bhavan Pande with his radical criminology, Chandrasekhar Pillai, K. D. Gaur, K. I. Vibhute, Ahmad Siddique, and others.

I tried to influence people to study other fields of law with a new kind of approach. This battle still continues. Take disciplines like contract law, for instance. With the exception of I. C. Saxena in Jaipur, we have not produced any figure who thinks about the theory of contract (Saxena 1967, 1969, 1970, 1971, 1972, 1980, 1981, 1982, 1983, 1984, 1985, 1986, 1987, 1988, 1989, 1990, 1996). B. B. Pande came along a little later with his work on the law of torts (Pande 2004, 2009), though everyone regards his work well as a famous criminologist. With respect to intellectual property rights, there was nobody till the 1980s, but now we have an impressive body of work.

Nurul Hasan, the then Union education minister—this was the early 1970s, and these were happy days, for it wasn't yet termed 'human resources'—telephoned me one day and said, Baxi-ji, our reputation is in your hands, this agency called WIPO in Geneva wants an academic piece on copyright law in India. I consulted my colleagues at Delhi University who were teaching the subject (indeed, a portmanteau course called copyright, patent, and trademarks) to see if they were interested in writing it, but they declined. It was a question of honour, so I burnt the midnight oil. I did a critical survey of the evolution of Indian copyright law (Baxi 1983b, 1986c). Later, I decided that, whenever I would be able to, I would set up a chair on intellectual property law. In time, I did it. Today, intellectual property has grown into a niche specialty.

I have over the years critiqued the conventional model of legal scholarship. I still recall the first attack at a moribund forum called the Association of Indian Law Teachers. At its meeting in Hyderabad, I presented a keynote titled *What Can the Convicts of Rajahmundry Teach Us?* This was regarding the prison revolt in Andhra. In this keynote, I talked about two kinds of consciousness. One, I called an AIR [All India Reporter] consciousness, in which the entire world of 'law' consisted of the pages of the AIR. In the second, we learn the law not from the imagination of lawpersons but from the experience of law by 'common' people, the subjects of law. The latter was to be about everyday legal consciousness. It became quite an event, I was much applauded. And then, when the time came to pass resolutions, the two were: first, law teachers and members of the association must get railway concessions, and the second was something about grades!

After four or five such meetings, I finally gave up. I think we should continue this work by having an association of teachers from the so-called pre-law subjects. My friends Jawahar Kaul and Manoj Kumar Sinha now maintain a very different Indian Council of Law Teachers; and Manoj maintains a specialist dialogue among law teachers and policymakers regarding international humanitarian law and human rights responsibilities of corporate entities (areas much ignored in law teaching and research in India).

There are professional associations of economists, historians, scientists. The real bane was, I think, money. A lot of good law teachers spent their time grading answer scripts. They used to send teachers at the law faculty huge bundles of scripts to grade. With the UPSC exams, grading has become a huge industry, and not just in Delhi. I used to say, you are a researcher first, you are not supposed to grade scripts during the day. Drink tea, chat, do anything you like, just don't visibly kill the idea of a learning and research institution!

I did some LLM grading and got into trouble with my friend G. S. Sharma. I always write comments, even in the exam scripts. Otherwise, there is no check on my arbitrariness. It shows that I have read the paper. I worked very hard and gave my grades. GS came up to me and in exasperation asked me: What have you done? I asked, what is the problem? He said, you have brought me again to great distress. It turns out, GS was the other grader, and he had given this one student less marks than I had because he knew the student, he was a useless fellow, he said, he never attended class; he also knew his family well, and nobody in his family could write sensible legal essays. I said, Gyani-ji, this is not fair, you cannot apply generational grounds to grading! GS said that the student will never make a career in law, that I was committing a sin, and he insisted I give him the same marks he had. I asked him to show me his comments. He said, what comments? I said, I have so many comments on his paper. He said, did I not tell you that once you come to India, you should not waste your time on these things? I said, I don't know what the appropriate standards are to have, I only know how to work scrupulously. He was very angry. He said, I will report this to the Vice-Chancellor, but ultimately, I prevailed. But I decided that I will not mark any other students than those at Delhi, which had an internal assessment system.

I have always felt that we need to have more discussions between law teachers, a kind of talk shop, where we can discuss how to teach better, and not just for law teachers. Noam Chomsky is an extraordinary figure in my mind because he managed to overcome his marginalised status in MIT to produce a new pedagogy, to the point where he began to matter. But not everyone can be Chomsky. There is no use saying law schools are going down. We need a countervailing collective force. All my life I have supported teachers' unions. This is not fashionable, of course, in these postmodern, poststructural days, when there is no central subject who can be the figure of emancipation. New collectivities must appear and old ways of association ought to pursue academic directions, not just trade-union tactics. What a didactic tone! Just as well, I say!

LL: Tell us more about the efforts at breaching the non-communication with the social sciences you talked about earlier.

UB: ICSSR had a several-volume survey of anthropology and sociology in India.[4] My *Sociology of Indian Law* arose as a part of this enterprise (Baxi 1986b). Veena Das (1974) had done the first survey. I became aware of this when I was teaching in Sydney. I did not know her then, but I wrote to her, and she was kind enough to send me a typed copy of the whole text. It is a very good survey which needs to be redeemed and excavated. Above all, it should be taught in law and social science courses; also, someone should do a fuller study of Veena Das' views on law and jurisprudence in search of an adequate social theory.

I did the second survey. I realised that law teachers and colleagues are very special, you not only have to bring them something on a platter, but you also have to actually put it in their mouths. It is a very special kind of transmission! So, I asked ICSSR for a separate publication. It was already a monograph, about the size of 'The Little Done, The Vast Undone', maybe a little longer. They agreed and gave the book to this press, Satvahan, which was owned by a Hindi playwright, a very good author. He was a gifted mind, but not a commercial genius. He ran into debt and later died. So that was that. I have the copyright, so I can reproduce it with my own permission.

If the whole idea was to survey the field, how do you do that? Veena did it in a very distinctive way, starting with the *Dharmasastras*, with culture and civilisation. I did it to nourish my movement for empirical studies in the sociology of law. Now, a survey needs a framework, a mission, and a method, and I invented all this on my own as I went along. I made a survey not of the literature, which is what the ICSSR really wants, but also of themes and issues. They gave me a little room for my own type of conceptualisation. I don't

[4]A collection of twenty-five studies was published in a three-volume series entitled 'A Survey of Research in Sociology and Social Anthropology' by the Indian Council of Social Science Research (ICSSR). The studies were carried out by a variety of distinguished scholars, invited by the ICSSR as part of their programme to identify the trends of development in various social disciplines in India. The studies are concerned broadly and primarily with Indian Sociology, Social and Cultural Anthropology, and Social Work.

know how much it is used in India, but it is most widely used overseas, I am told, by my friends. It has almost attained the status of an indispensable text, it surveys so much—classical law, legal profession, tribal law and justice, all kinds of things. In the Postscript to the book, I review Ranajit Guha's *Elementary Aspects of Peasant Insurgency* (1999) alongside Marc Galanter's *Competing Equalities* (1984). It doesn't quite fit in, but it enables me to say that a standard work on compensatory discrimination does not breathe a word about violence, which is associated either with the demand for greater equity or is in opposition to such a demand. There is hardly anything in sociological studies of equality about the politics of violence, or about the violence of ethnicity. But a second's thought reveals that *willed inequality* in social relations is the inner order of violence.

I saw my function in *Sociology of Indian Law* as that of building bridges. One of the things I discovered was that, at that point in time, not many historians/social theorists, even when they had taken into account law and legal theory or legal process, directly addressed law or even jurisprudence. Historians, for example, deal with the category of law, but it is not a fully-fledged narrative presence; rather, it is a lurking presence. I re-read some of these things I had read carefully, and asked, what would happen if the concern and engagement with law in a broad sense was made more explicit or grounded? The *Sociology of Indian Law* is the result.

There is, for instance, a longish meditation on Ravinder Kumar's classic work (Kumar 1968) on the Deccan Debt Riots. A historian by definition must deal with power/resistance, and the operations of the legal system and its ideology are necessarily integrated into such an inquiry. A historian does not normally read case law and legislations. It was considered a part of legal history, not a part of social history.

There were these distinctions being made between social history and legal history. The legal history that was being taught in the law schools was the history of legal institutions (such as the *Sadr Diwani Adalat*, etc.) simpliciter. I taught legal history, it was an absolutely soul-destroying experience. It typically combined elements of the legal system with a potpourri of institutional history thrown in. Legal historians, then, did not take care of the issues that historians assumed they would take care of. Till the subaltern historians came onto the scene, historians had perhaps only a remote concern with the history of law as seen from below. That is the gap I was trying to bridge.

For example, I sought to completely transform the teaching of legal history in the three years I taught the course in Delhi. I said, this rote learning of jurisdictions, of the types of courts, and so on, is not history. It does not tell me the history of power: why there is, for instance, differentiation between civil and criminal jurisdictions. Why could the colonial powers not just rule by combined jurisdiction?

Why did they provide this formula of justice, equity, and good conscience? That became the formula that would be the basis of the rule of law in India. What lies behind all the effort at codification? What is the big difference between—which nobody looked at—the Company Raj and the imperial takeover? Nobody had looked at the Proclamation of Queen Victoria. I am very weak on dynasties, but even I saw that it was an extraordinary document. One has to look at its text to see how law can be deployed to mystify the total domination of the Empire; and to continue with the tasks of producing loyal subjects in the face of an incipient new decolonial stateness. In doing legal history, nobody asks the question of why certain institutions did not develop. For example, I have still not found an answer to why the jury system never took off in India. These questions are rarely asked; therefore, they are little researched. This is because of the taught tradition of legal history. It has done us great harm. Lawrence, you have done a cameo study of the last (Nanavati) jury trial, but it has not been followed up; it is a pity that this study has not been taught in legal history courses in most law colleges.

The only admirable exception among the various kinds of books on Indian Legal History that flourish is the one by Professor M. P. Jain (1966). After great harassment from me, he did develop an interest in the social history of Indian law in the later editions—he even read Susan and Lloyd Rudolph—although he kept the main body and his general pragmatic approach of institutional study. You will find, for example, in his later editions a chapter on the jury system, on how the jury was racialised, on how the fact that no non-European could be a member of the jury in a matter dealing with an accused who was

British left a deep adverse impression on the minds and hearts of even Anglophone nationalist leaders.

This was one of the little pleasures/privileges of knowing a bit of the other social disciplines. I had to do a lot of work. But the at times grudging, at times affectionate, reception of my criticism and questions by very senior and established scholars and persons who took them into account in their writing was a very nourishing thing, and I really was very pleased that I could form a sensible question worthy of their attention. I also learnt a lot from students, who specialised in irreverence.

One time, we were discussing ideas of purity and pollution, and we were reading Veena Das's (1974) article in the first report on the sociology of law. I brought Kautilya into the discussion. I am kind of an arrested Kautilyan scholar: some of my early writing on Kautilya concerns his theory of *Mandala* and international law as we know it today (Baxi 1967d). For me, the distinction between the *Dharmasastra* and *Arthasastra* traditions matters, so I focused in the discussion on the power to punish, and on the definitions of forbidden conduct the Dandaniti.

You can see the creativity that is waiting in the classroom. The classroom was full of that. It is only the notion that the knowledge provider, in the form of the teacher, is an authority figure and necessarily knows more that kills creativity. Or the banking conception that Paulo Freire mentions in the *Pedagogy of the Oppressed* (Freire 1968), which I popularised in my report on legal education (Baxi 1975). But that is a different story.

This was, at the time, a broad and rough division of labour. By and large, historians would not enter into, leave alone taking over, the burdens of explanation that belonged to a sub-branch of history called legal history. And legal historians, such as they were, were stuck in institutional history. They still are, by and large, stuck there. I don't know why this information on the differentiation of the judiciary is so important. Colonial legality is a big phrase that means nothing. What needs to be tracked are the specific and diverse itineraries of accumulation of jurisdictions by colonial legality during the Company Raj and after the takeover by the Crown.

That's why, when Mathew John sent me a project statement on history (arguing that we had virtually no legal history and we should begin afresh), I couldn't cope with the total discontinuity proposed there. Shraddha Chigateri was then at Warwick and she told me Mathew was very upset that I had not responded to his email. I wrote him a detailed note, to which he never responded. Though I don't now have the text, it was, I thought, a very useful exchange. I said, yes, it is wonderful to want to engage Foucault, but if you are going to plan a new journey in legal history, you should look at how a new consciousness has come into the practice of writing history in India. I had surveyed some part of that in the *Sociology*.

There have been other developments also in the literature and in my later writing, after the publication of the *Sociology*. Radhika Singha (2000) has, for example, brought out *A Despotism of Law*. Colonial history cannot be understood outside legal history. Subaltern history cannot be understood outside legal history. There is now a sustained stream of contributions to this (so-called) sub-discipline. While the framework of Foucault for all this is very important, and I am not criticising anyone when I say this, to say that there is no legal history in India is wrong.

This is the same syndrome I saw at the *Enculturing Law* conference.[5] That was the reason why I was so polemical there, because you guys are so precious that reminders are necessary if you begin to think that there is nothing before you. There is a great danger of reinventing the wheel, that much of what you wanted to do has already been done differently, and much better. In short, to say that there is no legal history in India is wrong, but it is another thing to say that such history, as it exists, is problematic and needs to be resituated.

---

[5] *Enculturing Law*: Conference organised by the Centre for the Study of Culture & Society, Bangalore, in collaboration with the Alternative Law Forum and the National Law School of India University, in Bangalore, August 2005. Proceedings published in John and Kakarala (2007).

Indian Legal Historiography: A History of the Writing of Legal History

UB: The general point is: What is Indian legal historiography and how did it emerge? This is the question we have to pose before we say that we want to do alternative history in India. What does Indian legal historiography consist of? What is its craft? And to go further, what is legal historiography in general in the common law world?

I am not a close student of British legal history. I have not cultivated that field, so maybe you will find that there is continuity here, that we have just borrowed the colonial craft of doing legal history in a certain way. We couldn't, however, have done this consciously, because our legal history has a much wider range than that of the colonising power. If you were to go to the Buddhist theory of law and justice and Buddhist institutions, to Hindu jurisprudence, or to indigenous traditions, for instance, in none of these would you find any source of inspiration from the colonial way of history writing. This question has not, I think, yet been posed. I tried to pose it in several scattered ways. I didn't want to adopt a confrontationist posture, but I raised these issues subtly. In my estimation, one of the issues is the *history of history writing* in India—or the lack thereof.

We do not, for example, have a history of law publishing in India. I worked very hard with the *All India Reporter* (AIR). I went to Nagpur especially for this, and I spent days with Dada Chitale and his colleagues, encouraging them to commission somebody to write a history of law publishing in India. It would be a wonderful story to tell. At the time, they told me that none of the persons who prepared the head notes for AIR was a matriculate, let alone a law graduate. This might still be the case. It is very interesting to know what part non-lawyers played in the evolution of law: the way eminent lawyers and justices learnt from head notes in AIR is a fascinating story (with lots of implications for law itself), but it has never been told. This is just one little glimpse of the many rich conversations I had there.

So the questions to ask are: What was the conception of legal reporting? Of accuracy? The conception of a synoptic approach to judicial decisions? And it is very egalitarian: if a non-lawyer can write a head note, it is a very democratic gesture, and if lawyers actually use it—whatever happens to development of the law and the understanding of judgment is a different matter—it is a very radical gesture. The AIR head notes mostly consist, of course, of verbatim quotations from the judgment itself, and the head notes provide mainly a classification by statute, issue, etc., but the questions to ask are: How far was that manner of writing head notes peculiar to India; was it a reflection of early English law reporting, or did its inspiration lie elsewhere? These are very interesting questions, but not found very exciting. Or so it seems when you look at the state of research in legal history. So I gave up. What to do, I didn't have the time to do it all!

AIR Nagpur was prepared, in fact, to hire a professor who had written books on legal history, and to draw up a plan for such a book, but it didn't work out. All was not lost, though. What is it that explains the extraordinary diffusion of law reporters: for instance, the *Madras Law Times*, *Kerala Law Times*, *Calcutta Weekly Notes*, etc.? AIR was of course the main reporter, but it was not the only one. Who were these people who were bringing these reporters out? We know the journal sections of these reports were extremely powerful. So, I said to them, first do a survey for an analysis of who writes in the AIR journal section, and a content analysis of the concerns expressed in a given time period. Not the authorities, but the anxieties. It would transform our understanding of Indian law.

It was only the late Professor Duncan Derrett, and now Professor Werner Menski following him, who has looked at every single article in the journals of the *Kerala Law Times*, *Calcutta Weekly Notes*, *Nagpur Law Journal*, *Madras Law Journal*, etc., not least because that's where most people wrote. It is not a question of publishing, it is a question of juridical writing in a period when there were no law reviews. For instance, where did this chap Upendra Baxi write his first article? Straight after the LLM exams, he sent the only answer he wrote in his jurisprudence exam (Bombay University then had a system for LLM exams where you were expected to answer a minimum of one question and a maximum of four questions) to the *Bombay Law Reporter*, and it was published there. The article was titled 'Relativism in Classical Indian Legal Thought', and in it I compared Sage Parashara with Gustav Radbruch. These reporters were the only outlets.

In a sense, the story of my life is really the story of a series of failures as far as legal education is concerned. I tried so hard to generate wider interest in these kinds of issues, but it has never fully taken off, never. And it was my aspiration to integrate what the Bar basically called '"pre"-law' with 'law' education, that is partly why I accepted the National Law School (NLSIU) mandate, in the hope that if it succeeded, there would be a nucleus of people who would be interested in taking this further, but that also did not happen. These are accidents of biography, but it is still a serious concern for me, and I will be happy to support anyone who wants to do this. Now is probably a better time than my time was, because now there is access to information. Now we also have a different kind of access/approach to work.

What, then, is the history of the writing of history? By writing, I mean also the history of publication. What sense of periodisation, for example, affects legal history writing? Periodisation is the most vexing thing with any history: how do you periodise? How do you decide that you will break units of time into different zones of interest? I am not sure whether this problem has been consciously addressed or not. Again, if you go to *Towards a Sociology of Indian Law* (Baxi 1986b), you will find the anxieties expressed there in a gentle way, not upfront.

Moving Beyond Legal History as Institutional History

Then, of course, there is the question of institutional history, and it is a minefield. The question is: Can there be any history without an analytic? The understanding of words, the clarification of concepts is important, especially in the law. Lawyers always quibble about words and their meanings. When you try to read history, of whatever kind, you must have an analytical approach. Say, when I am doing institutional history, the question to ask is, why are *courts* the only institution treated? Why can religious, cultural civilisations and their interaction with the legal institutions not be researched? How do these institutions relate to each other, why and how do they conflict—in sum, their interaction is the real history of institutions, no matter how specific jurisdictions are accumulated, appropriated, or articulated.

The question then arises: What is an institution? You must have some idea of what an institution is. Courts are a State institution, marriage is a private institution. You must have the notion of private and public lurking in your head somewhere. This is how I taught legal history then, so I remember—taught or shared, whatever it was. Roscoe Pound used to say that taught law is tough law. The way you teach law or the way you are taught law is very difficult to overcome later. It stays with you, it's a tough tradition. Taught law is tough law, you cannot unlearn it. It requires a real superhuman effort to unlearn it. Whatever the ways of perceiving law, you are stuck with what you learn for the rest of your life, unless you are extremely precocious as a student.

So, what is an institution? In my sense, it is (as most sociologists say) a sustained pattern of behaviours and is oriented to certain values. We are all dedicated to the law, so we must ask, of what institutions does it consist? Are these just? What are the values of judicial institutions? Is it order, is it justice, is it fairness, is it domination, what is it? These kinds of issues have not been raised by legal history. Mere narratives are offered instead, this was the jurisdiction, this was the hierarchy, not even the names of judges are given. In fact, if you ask any one of us in India today, including retired Chief Justices of India and living legends of law, who were the fifteen leading Indian justices and lawyers from the period 1857–1947, and who were the leading English justices, we will have unsatisfactory responses! Why?

The idea of an institution as a slot machine, a robotic idea, a post-human idea is erroneous. Even if you are an institutional historian, you must at the very minimum stray into some good names and bad names, but it does not happen. There is something basically weird about this institutional history. Everybody quotes Holmes—judges quote Holmes, jurists quote Holmes, historians quote Holmes. My favourite question—my single question questionnaire—particularly to people who wax eloquent on Holmes is: Do you mean Oliver Wendell Holmes Jr. or Sherlock Holmes? And some people get confused, it is that bad!

I read a lot of history, though legal history was not my strong forte. I came into it partly through David Daube at Berkeley, who was discussing the notion of impossibility in Roman and Greek law (Daube 1956, 1967). These are the *samskaras* of teaching, the *samskaras* of learning. *Samskara* is that configuration which emerges when you need it the most. It is not an abstract thing.

My other inspiration was, and still is, my favourite thinker, a man called James Willard Hurst from Wisconsin. Hurst wrote a huge book of over 1,000 pages on *Law and Economic Growth,* and its subtitle was the real history bit: *The Legal History of the Lumber Industry in Wisconsin, 1836–1915* (Hurst 1964). While one may not be interested in Wisconsin, or in the lumber industry of Wisconsin, one should read that book to learn how institutional history is done. In fact, when Julius Stone and I were parting ways, Julius asked me what he could give me as a gift, and I said, if you can spare it, I want Willard Hurst's book. He gave it to me. He said he had read it, but didn't find it very interesting. I said, don't worry, I find it very exciting. It is still lying with me somewhere.

What does Hurst do? You can't study law and its development and industrial growth without understanding two things, contract and property: they are legal institutions. And when you put both of them together, you come to the market. You cannot think of the market outside transaction. Now transaction is contract. You cannot think of contract without freedom. You must be free to contract in various ways. It is not always free, but one could think in terms of degrees of freedom. You must have some choice. Property is a background institution of the market. Probably there cannot be transaction without the market, there cannot be a market without property as its basis, and so on. Lovely book. I used this in my classes, and I still do. Later, I learnt from some moral philosophers about market and non-market values. How do the dominant doctrines such as 'separation of powers', 'the rule of law', or even unconstitutional constitutional amendments serve these types of values at different times?

The point, however, is not what I read or did not read! The point is that if you want to do institutional history, law people can do this because they know what a court is, what is the hierarchy of pecuniary jurisdictions, what are the kinds of punishment, etc. There is a special language, which inhibits historians from looking at the law, but we law people are supposed to know it. But we have to step back and be self-conscious, we cannot say that anything we do as legal historians is history. That is not on.

There is a lot of work that needs to be done. Even if you look at the titles of the chapters of *Sociology*, there is a progression of themes to which a legal history ought to extend its concerns. When we narrate legal history as institutional history of the *Sadr Diwani Adalat—jahaan se shuru, wahan khatam. Ajeeb dastaan hain.* This is an extraordinary story, just to reverse the words of the song!

Sociology of Indian Law

UB: Then comes the question, how to do a sociology of law? I had a huge difference of opinion with Julius Stone. Stone used to say, you can have a study of law and social change, you can have a study of law and power, but you cannot have a science called sociology of law. Law is not a science, law is a technique: we produce law as an instrument, and to add further, perhaps are also produced by it. The study of law can be a science, but law itself cannot be a science. I think he was right, and I am grateful to him.

While jurisprudence or legal theory can be science, law itself cannot be science. I said, that is what I mean by the sociology of law, it is a field which scientifically studies the social dimensions of law. Then the question was, what is the net gain of calling it sociology of law? One may as well term it law and society, or law and anthropology, or law and power, or whatever else one may want to call it. Why develop a master field called sociology of law? Now this title, 'Sociology of Indian Law', was in my mind since 1968; in fact, you will find it in 'The Little Done, The Vast Undone', which was my attempt to do a sociology of Indian constitutional law, and I refer there to the sociology of law, so there is a method in this madness.

The real difference between Stone and me arose when he said, all right, if you want sociology of law as a field of scientific study, you cannot have a sociology of *Indian* law. Can you have an Indian chemistry, physics, botany? Incidentally—although, as I used to say to my trade union leaders in the academic council in DU when I got cross with them (very rarely did I explode, but when I did explode, everyone would be stunned), you are very silly if you think there can be a BJP Botany or a CPI(M) Chemistry or a Congress whatever—knowledges are not produced by political parties. That was Stone's point—you cannot have a sociology of Indian law and of Australian law. Sociology of law is a meta-discipline, a comparative science, a universal master frame.

I won't go into the theoretical quarrel, but I was determined, notwithstanding the objection, to create or contribute to a field called Sociology of Indian Law. And this is what I sought to do in that book. Had it been studied in India properly and carefully, there would have been a deluge of criticism, but nothing has happened. It is used like a telephone directory or a reference book for research, to find relevant citations for appropriate readings, I have no problem with that! But there has been no sustained discussion of the underlying thesis of the work, either on the part of social scientists or on the part of lawpersons. This is only a resource for what I call the Genghis Khan manner of reading. Like Genghis Khan, one comes to raid, conquer, and lay to waste. It is reading as an act of plunder. It is not the best kind of reading, it is in fact the most atrocious. I again failed to communicate—there must obviously be something wrong with the way I collected material sources, I should have been more explicit, or something. But again, the story is not about whether I failed or not, it is of the issues involved.

In the Wake of the Sociology *of Indian Law*

LL: A lot has happened since then, particularly in other disciplines. So we should talk about that, but also maybe chart out all those concerns, some of which clearly haven't been addressed yet, despite the newer work that has been done. What would it mean to chart an agenda of research for the future, given the developments that have taken place?

UB: I don't know, it should collectively emerge. Agenda-setting is a hegemonic task. But I can say what has happened since, some of it was incipient at the time, some non-existent, some a fresh start. What was incipient then, the anthropology of law, has now come into being as a very serious discipline. Ethnography of law is now an important discipline. Since my monograph came out in 1986, there has been a considerable number of books and articles that deal with an anthropological understanding of law. That is one very rich development. Anthropology of law and ethnography have changed in many ways, and have gone beyond empirical studies of law. For example, Pratiksha (Baxi) has pioneered the feminist ethnography of law, and encouraged students to take seriously ethnographies of courtroom talk and visual anthropology of law; Janaki Nair has continually drawn our attention to local dispute-handling in religious settings and to ways in which law relates to urban history; Kalpana Kannabiran has, among other things, studied whether, and how, feminist methods and ways of looking at the world make a difference. And Arvind and your joint courses, especially on law and literature, additional to some pioneering studies by Alternative Law Forum are 'considerable contributions'. One must also fully take note of Professor Ranbir Samaddar and his colleagues at the Calcutta Research Group (CRG).

The second growth has been in empirical studies: is a particular law working or not, and if not, what can be done with it? Is the world better without it? Empirical studies in law were the hallmark for a particular period from around 1975 to the early 1990s: the early studies were Kumari (juvenile justice), Amita Dhanda (mental health), Vijay Gupta (jurimetrics), Rose Varghese (rape), but now they have ably extended to local/micro-histories of imperial legality, especially to criminal and family law. Renewing these was my minor success, I encouraged people everywhere, in social methods courses, workshops, to work on empirical studies. It still continues its scattered itineraries.

Then, of course, a completely new dimension of writing has emerged in what is called feminist historiography of law. It wasn't there at the time of my monograph. Look, for instance, at Ritu Menon's and Urvashi Butalia's work on Partition (Menon and Bhasin 1998; Butalia 2000). Where was Partition in Indian legal studies? H. M. Seervai, before he died, included a long discussion on it in his last edition of *Constitutional Law of India*, because he disagreed with Ayesha Jalal and decided to write about it (Seervai 1989, 1991). Lawyers, however, tended to behave as if Partition never happened. So did most social theorists. The only narratives of Partition were from literary people: Manohar Malgonkar's *A Bend in the Ganges* (1965), Khushwant Singh's *Train to Pakistan* (2012), Manto's stories about Partition (1989, 1993, 2011), Amrita Pritam's writings (1982, 1984, 1989, 1995), and so on. There was a trace of it in literature. Nearly fifty years after that come the feminists who write on the Partition. Now, for Partition, law is a crucial event.

This is, then, a very major breach. Did it affect law teaching and research in any significant ways.? A polite answer is that I don't know, but the impolite reality is that it did not! It may well be the case that it is taught now, what with professionally trained sociologists, political scientists, etc., teaching these subjects, rather than law teachers. I do not know for sure, it will be interesting to find out. The feminist studies did not relate only to Partition, they looked at the question of writing history as a woman. That was the methodological question: Does it make a difference? This is an epistemological question of great importance, of whether women also think differently from men. And if they do, then there are at least two epistemologies—two ways of knowing—as men and as women. There is some very interesting writing on that. There are more categories—exploitation, oppression, or modern slavery, concerning which Asha Bajpai (2003) and Prabha Kotiswaran (2017) have made valuable beginnings—that are defined very differently by feminist thinkers. I am very excited about feminist historiography based on the law, and if you are doing a second edition of the *Sociology*, that is something that needs to be surveyed.

The fourth dimension that has opened up in a major way since I wrote is ecological history. Ram Guha and Madhav Gadgil (Guha and Gadgil 1992) are the pioneers, but there are many others. If you transform this idea of how one does legal history and look at what the law has done or not done to the environment—drainage, agricultural reform, groundwater, deforestation, you name it—you discover how central the law is to this conversation. Now I do not know whether ecological historians—I have read some of them, they do not necessarily bring in the law in a big way, but they cannot help being concerned with the law. Vandana Shiva, although not an ecological historian, clearly belongs here and is an inspiring figure (Shiva 1993; Mies and Shiva 1993).

And then there have been chronicles/narratives arising from subaltern studies; the subaltern historians were already at work when I was writing. They placed a very specific emphasis on the problem of narrating insurrection. There are, however, few historical studies on Naxalism in India. I know of hardly two or three in English, I do not know what the case may be in the vernacular languages. Even purely as a security concern, one needs to understand the histories and futures of militant and violent armed opposition groups. Histories of counter-insurgencies should provide valuable correctives to the deployment of force, bearing the modified international humanitarian law and human rights futures in view. But histories of the growth and development of violence as a means for solving social conflicts should interest us all in terms of the futures of constitutionalism and law, even granting that security and integrity of the nation are important goals and that there is a collective human right to peace and security.

But, in a sense, the Tebhaga movement transformed our understanding of movement histories. Women were involved in shaping them. There has been a lot of good work done on this kind of understanding of the Santhal and the Ho rebellions, for example. Vasudha Dhagamwar (1992, 2006) has a book now on this topic. There is some landscape here to be visited, that is, micro/meta-narratives of insurrection and militancy, and what this may do to our understanding of law and constitutionalism.

Is it possible to do constitutional studies without understanding the Partition, without an actual understanding of the history of insurgency? Can you understand Articles 21 and 22 of the Indian Constitution outside the struggles in the Northeast and in Kashmir? The simple answer is, you cannot. I know we have a lot of work to do in the classroom, and we cannot do everything together. So I reiterated to the Socio-Legal Studies group in NLS, Bangalore, the other day that you prepare one module, one lecture, one topic in this way—these are the leading decisions on X or Y area, these are the socio-political contexts at the time these judgments were passed. Now you have to teach law, so you teach law, but you can at least make some people aware that this was the period when Naxalism was very active, or the period when talks broke down with Sheikh Abdullah—even these names are not known now, so what can you do?

And there is, of course, a massive shift in the writing of the history of colonial law in India; colonial India, generally, but colonial law in particular. There is Radhika Singha's work, and many other works. Certainly, there is a whole new range of studies that is coming to my attention on labour histories. Labour history now is of a very different kind. I speak not of the kind of New Labour as appropriated by Tony Blair, but of the new labour of macro- and micro-histories by labour historians. Beverly Silver (2003) has done a global study of the prospects of working-class movements in the world. Hers is a very thorough and welcome optimistic account of what the future of the renewal of labour movements is, transnational and otherwise.

There are also some important histories being written of policy and law reform, and what you now call governance. My friend Navroz Dubash, for instance, has worked on the history of electricity regulation in India (Dubash and Rao 2007). There is some writing on the origins of models of regulatory law, and now, in particular, Adithya Chintapanti has made a rigorous theoretical contribution in the context of the regulatory framework for the supply of electricity and power in the state of Andhra Pradesh.

There is this notion that administrative law is only judge-made law. I considered this point in my Massey Introduction to say that this is *primarily* the case, but not *wholly* so (Baxi 2017b). Legislative regulation or policy regulation of certain public utilities had encoded administrative law standards into itself in a different way, which rarely came before the courts. This is exciting, and I think this is policy history. I don't know how else to name it. History of regulation and policies? There are whole fields poorly explored: climate change now provides whole new arenas and domains calling for new types of regulation and law. We will find a rubric for it—one can say histories of global governance, or histories of new domination and injustices, or of the travails of regulation.

One can also talk about specific accounts of histories of religion and of religious movements. It is a slice of contemporary history, but it goes back to other movements that have been well-studied, like the Bhakti movement, Chaitanya movement, Satnami movement. Dalit histories must, of course, be mentioned as a separate category. Very useful work is being done in that area, albeit a little scattered, with a part of it in subaltern studies. It is very difficult to label these histories, but these are just some of the discoveries I have made since I wrote that monograph.

All this is off the cuff. Obviously, I must have thought about it, it comes so clearly to me. I have, off and on, toyed with the idea of doing a second edition of *Towards a Sociology of Indian Law*. I find the task beyond me, even by way of a mere literature survey. If I was doing it solo, it requires at least several years of total seclusion and catching up with a lot of reading and meditating upon it.

LL: One of the tragedies that I think I have seen is there is some really valuable work that is done as Ph.D.s in the US, which have never found their way as publications in India. Vinay Lal's history of Committees of Enquiry in law and order problems in colonial India (Lal 1992) has never been published here.

UB: Those are the real institutional tasks. That is why you have the Centre for Study of Culture and Society, that is why you have the Alternative Law Forum. Somebody has to begin to archive them—it could be a funded project—and establish a team of good people for four or five years.

LL: Even the meagre law and society reader that we began with is exactly for this reason, to try and get these things together.[6]

UB: It is important to retrieve these archives. It is not resources only from the US or the UK, it is also about all these dissertations that are written in Third World countries, somebody in Jamaica writing on Indian plantation labour, or colonial labour histories in Malaysia. These were all related—the forms of labour that were invented by colonialism. Take the lovely book by Amitav Ghosh on Malaysia and plantation labour, *The Glass Palace* (2000). David Ludden (1999) has also been doing a lot of work on Indian labour practices.

LL: In the case of the US and the UK, you have a starting point with the databases. All the Ph.D.s have been digitised.

UB: Yes, you start with what you have, but I think once you do that, all of us have friends or young colleagues, we can then make a general plea that if you have any materials, we will share ours and you share yours, it is possible. I tried to do it some years ago. I said, let us collect expatriate writings on Indian constitutional law and publish it in a volume. Oxford was ready to publish it. I tried to get several Indian-origin teachers interested in the project. I said, you do it, I am not involved, I do not even want editorship or ownership of this idea, this is the concept, but you can have a free hand with the selection of material.

They all agreed. Nothing came of it, though, except that I collated a file of writings from young scholars, including a pungent piece by a young scholar called Sara Ahmad (1996) on the Ayodhya decision. She is most anxious about the 'communalisation' of the judicial process in India. We do not write like that. There is a certain detachment and a certain engagement, a passion about India, in their writing. They want to preserve Indian secularity. Therefore, it is a very precious thing for them, and they are sharper than some of us are. This is just one kind of archive one can put together, there are so many other possibilities also.

I mentioned the Third World because the point about hegemony in knowledge production is important to keep in mind. I think we

[6]On file with the Alternative Law Forum.

should be interested in somebody in Brazil, in South Africa, in Cuba, or Estonia. We should look at the period in which socialist States invested a great deal of talent, time, and resources to create a body of socialist literature about India. It is an immense, exciting programme.

LL: The BISA (Brazil, India, South Africa) project should mutate into something like this.[7]

UB: Yes, that is the attraction of the project, as it were. The point is not just to look at the work done on colonial legal history, but also to retrieve some material from social historians. By the minute, the idea grows vaster and vaster.

LL: We started a process, in some sense, of trying to create a bibliography of the social sciences wherever they have written about the law in a kind of direct manner. We started it because it was feeding into some of the courses and stuff that we were doing. But yes, it needs to be a much more concerted effort. The reason why this account is so useful is our starting point: the starting point of a certain kind of lack, when you are trying to look at places which have put together the material and you don't find them, then you are doing it at a very individual level. But the account that you have given, from the sociology to the survey to the developments that have happened, you suddenly realise the immensity of what is possible.

UB: One needs a perspective or framework to orient oneself, otherwise one can go adrift in such an ocean of material. When I was writing in the 1980s, mine was then only a pedagogic concern, namely how to make friends of lawpersons and social scientists, and how to mainstream this into teaching and research on both sides. This was the idea at a modest level. It was the schema in which I proceeded to write: there was no framework, but the immediate aim was very modest.

---

[7]See Baxi (2013e). This edited volume focusses on the role of the highest ('apex') courts in Brazil, India, and South Africa. It is the result of a collaborative research project between researchers in the three countries and aims to provide starting points for a horizontal South-South-South 'trialogue' about transformative constitutionalism.

Now, however, so much has changed, new fields like environmental jurisprudence and climate change have emerged, so have some new histories of regulation. And within the history of regulation, the element of mimesis and innovation, of emulation and originality, has to be looked at afresh. It is very complex. If you are retrieving materials on the history of the legal profession, you suddenly find that history is not a continuous linear narrative. You will find now an explosive disruption. Because if 'the darlings of the globalised legal profession' is the only phrase that sticks in the media, it just shows that the legal profession has become, or is in the way of becoming, something very different from anything that India has ever known, in its culture, in its outlook, in its hegemonic disposition. So, you will find in many areas a sudden rupture, a colossal rupture. There is a multilinearity here, there are different stories to be told in different times, but there is also a judicial globalisation or a juridical globalisation that is taking place now. It will affect some of the narratives in a very big way.

The Names of History

UB: I use the word 'histories' too loosely, of course. Implicit there is a notion of history with a small 'h', and it is so diverse and so fragmented that it raises the question of the point at which disciplinary burdens and boundaries have to be respected. Gayatri Spivak challenged me on this once. I was speaking at an event (organised by the Subaltern Studies collective in Delhi—this was the first time I met Gayatri, and by way of obiter, I said, subaltern studies has dissipated now after the great Ranajit Guha's six volumes. Gayatri said, dissipation is a very important notion, but you should remember that there are disciplinary burdens and responsibilities, and disciplinary boundaries do exist. There is a virtue in preserving these, even as you try to cross them.

There are so many histories; is there any such thing, then, that you can still refer to as the discipline of history? Or is one just mapping out fields of historical enquiry? If one is mapping out fields of enquiry, fine, but in what way is it distinctly *historical*, as against legal or sociological or anthropological? There are beings who call themselves historians and by that they mean something quite important. They are not merely protecting their turf or policing their boundaries. There is a particular way of *being in the world* that we call anthropological or ethnographic, or that we call juridical, or feminist, or activist for that matter. Each such positioning has its gravitational field: take this away, and you have nothing. We have emerging fields of historical enquiry rather than histories as such. They are histories because they are informed, they share a common way of being, dealing, of narrativising, all of which is very distinct from other ways of doing so. It turns out there is something called meta-history which is unchanging, but that is not the idea.

There are various ways of doing history, there is no one specific way. Each way matters for the other, but not decisively. I can name here a very few:

First, there is a history of history itself, a meta-narrative about all meta-narratives. Here, a principal question is: What is history?

Second, there is the idea of universal history. Hegel, Rousseau, enlightenment thinkers, all promoted thought about the history of humankind; it is species history, but the history of one species.

Third, the history or histories of 'nature' or the transition from the Holocene ('Recent Whole'), a name given to the post-glacial geological epoch of the past 10,000–12,000 years as agreed upon by the International Geological Congress in Bologna in 1885, to the Anthropocene era (now recognised as an era in which harm, often irreversible, has been done by humans to nature, and science/technology-based means are adopted to reverse it). We live in the Anthropocene era, but especially with climate change (and the infinite possibility for global warming), we need a global, inter-species, planetary history, the history not just of the world and its peoples, but a history of all species and objects in nature.

Fourth, if (and when) we imbue history with a *telos* (teleological history), history with an end. The word 'end' is taken literally as the end of history. Take Francis Fukuyama and his idea that liberalism is one thing on which all of humankind may converge. *End of man*, what is now called post-history. We live amidst ends, almost every day the 'end' of something is proclaimed—the end of science, capitalism, peasant[ry], religion, human rights, and so on, excepting the end of those who say everything is ended. I have described in *The Future of Human Rights* (2013c) the various forms of what I call *endology*, *endomania*, and even *endolatry*!

Fifth, another form of endology is really a different teleology; the 'end' is here thought of as *ends*. Ends are purposes. Understanding the 'everyday', distinct from the exotic, is one form of history; here, and in terms of subaltern history at least, we study the life as lived by the 'victims' in contrast to 'dynasties' or hierarchies of power. Understanding history as *her story*, the various stories of the subject position of woman. Varieties of understanding history as subaltern—the insurgent subject, the 'dangerous' subject, the 'dissenting' subject, 'history from below', eco-history, and so on—also exist.

Sixth, the history or histories of disciplines, of law, politics, economics, medicine, civil professions, etc.

Seventh, as the French say, we have history of only three things—imagination, reason, and science. May one add also the dimension of faith?

Eighth, imaginative, virtual, or counterfactual history, which asks the question: What if a particular event had not happened, or had happened differently?

I think that we need to state at the outset in which sense we are referring to 'history'. I also think that if 'history' is all stories/narratives, we are still left with the question, what narrative becomes compelling and why? Is this a matter of method, and are all methods in the end narratives whose truth or validity cannot be determined? What, then, is the difference and convergence between historiography and narratology?

Now, granted there are all these ways of doing histories, yet if one were to put all the fields of enquiry in order, there is something that enables us to say—ha!—she is not an anthropologist, she is a historian. What is that? What sets her apart? The distinction cannot be only that the historian goes to the archives, whereas the anthropologist goes to the field. If you remember, Foucault said in *The Order of Things* (1966) something to the effect that earlier, we studied monuments and now we study documents. Monuments are the documents of yesterday, documents are the monuments of today, he said. I am taking a lot of liberty here, but what are the breaks in the tradition of doing history is also a very important question. What epistemic breaks, what paradigm shifts—like subaltern studies, for instance—have occurred in the doing of history? It is also a question of method.

The Types of History

UB (***contd***): We also cannot think of history without a subject, the question of agency is important. There are two kinds of history: one is universal history and the other is contingent or particular histories. Now, universal histories imply a teleology. Fukuyama says that every society in the world must end up as a liberal society. That is the end of history. History is not an unseen accumulation of events, happenings, trends, but everything is directed towards a goal. So, one kind of universal history is a teleological history. The history of capitalism is a universal teleological history, because in teleological history, ends are given either by the divine or they are moral goods which admit of no moral ambiguity, that is, ends are ethically positive. If you look at Amartya Sen's *Development as Freedom* (1999a), there is a consciously foregrounded teleology and there is a teleology that is politically unconscious. This is the political unconsciousness of thinkers. We all have our political unconsciousness and more explicitly worked out notions. If the political unconsciousness is that history is not the accumulation of contingent events and happenings, the question is: What salience does this have in the more explicitly worked out thought of the thinker? For most Western thinkers, that unconscious is European history; for Badiou (2013), for example, there were only three events that were worthy of being named political events, and they occurred in Western history. History, in this view, is less a matter of chance and more a matter of necessity. As against speech, however, the silent spaces in this view are more momentous. And then there is the other view, that history is contingent, with its focus on the random ebb and flow of events. Both views have their problems.

If you want to make new beginnings in legal history, you have to think of what traditions of thinking of history you share consciously or unconsciously, the consciousness of what you consider history to be or what it ought to be. It is the same with respect to histories of human rights. If you ask me how I dealt with it in my *Future* book, the notion of contemporary trade-related, market-friendly human rights—that is one way of organising the chaotic flow of events that we call human rights. In the idea of history as an accumulation of contingencies, the question is, how do you make narratives that make sense? That is the art of history. True, everything is without a purpose, without an end. In this second view of history, you have to tell a story. History is stories. In fact, *her* story. Telling a story about the past, or about what happened, or about *is-ness* in Lata Mani's sense, requires a narrative strategy. Those narrative strategies can vary. They can be micro-, meso- or macro-histories.

The trouble is: Can there be laws of history? Evolutionary laws, that you grow from simple to complex, complex to more complex, and so on. Evolutionary history is a dominant theme in legal history. Weber postulated a charismatic law: traditional legal authority evolves into the modern legal State, custom into modern law. So, when we do legal history, we do it within an evolutionary master frame in making sense of this contingency. There are laws of social evolution that operate through simple chance into a culmination of notions of flux. There is no final end or telos of history. You can still explain history as contingency or particularity by reference to some kind of idea of progress. It is never the idea of progress with a capital P, it is a question of change, and the issue is whether you can tell stories of it in a sensible way. Teleological history, on the other hand, says that there are certain universal laws. Is Marxian history evolutionary in the sense that you move from the slave mode of production to feudal to capitalist to post-capitalist modes of production? Problems of narrative strategy are also present in teleological history. I think the temptation to reject or dismiss universal history is now very common. This temptation must be closely examined, particularly in the context of post-socialist States. What sense do we make, in this light, of human rights, freedom, etc.?

Law and Technology

UB: I discuss anthropology and history in *Sociology*, but there is a third dimension rather absent there, and that is technology (except in the chapters on agrarian conditions and reforms). This is not absent in my monograph on Marx, though it is not explicit there. I discuss it most directly in the last chapter of my post-human book, *Human Rights in a Posthuman World: Critical Essays* (Baxi 2007a), where I take up the question of the relationship between human beings, other sentient creatures, and intelligent life forms, including machines. In Berkeley, I read this very nice book called *Medieval Technology and Social Change* (White 1962). It dealt with the history of the invention of stirrups for climbing horses—you know, that steel thing you put your foot in to climb a horse—and how that little invention spread into a whole web of social relations, how it became a marker of distinction and led to the germination of class distinctions, how the horse and rider became an instrument of warfare with the whole unit technologised for defence. This calls attention to, and is very important in understanding, human consciousness and social organisation. These cannot be understood outside of *techne*.

William Baumol, a noted economic historian, said of the handshake that it is one of the greatest human inventions, it is an initiation of peace processes, of cooperative processes, of overcoming distances, of sealing contracts, of greeting each other, determining or shaping social relationships. We may ask how the *namaskar*, by contrast, must seem like a repudiation of this, and somewhat alienating by marking a distance and articulating different hegemonies of social distances. How does all this compare with hugs and kissing on the cheeks? How do we think through all that? There is so much to think about here.

Bruno Latour, J. Katherine Hayles, and Donna Haraway are all engaged in thinking aspects of the techno-social. I have very often spoken of law as a social technology, as normative technology. In the second edition of *Sociology*, there must be some way in which we can look at this. In my Family Planning Foundational Lectures, and my two essays on population planning in India,[8] I said technology and freedom are related, and the reproductive rights of women become possible with dreadful contraceptive inventions, from the loop to Norplant. Norplant is an implant that regulates your sexuality/sexual desires. The whole agenda of women owning their bodies is a moral invention, but it requires technological innovation to fulfil that. There is also the story to be told of surgical interventions for abortions, etc. This is a facilitation of freedom, capabilities, and so on. You cannot have reproductive rights outside of technological change, particularly of diagnostic tools, therapies, and techniques.

I did a whole class in the Washington D. C. College of Law on this: on how diagnostic therapies, which are mostly technological, remain key to the protection of the human right to health, and how at the same time they are unequally distributed and are monopolised. There is a contradiction between the general promise of technology as liberating and the actual working of the laws of property, bolstered as it is by the idea of an eventual proliferation of benefits. This is the conflict between the granting of patents on anti-retroviral drugs and the need for the generic production of these drugs. At stake is the so-called trickle-down effect: technology in a particular historical moment becomes the monopoly of certain powerful corporations in order that it may become, over time, more widespread and more equitably distributed. That should be obvious: patents do not go on forever. They last for twenty/forty years, and then they become part of the prior state of art. But of course they can be renewed frequently, to the point of contention about evergreen patents!

One knows at a reflexive level that all of us expire, and so do patents! There is no universal monopolisation: patents are superseded

[8]'Sense and Sensibility' (Baxi 2002c), and 'Gender and Reproductive Rights in India' (Baxi 2001b).

once their legal life is over and they come into the public domain. We know, however, that this is not how things actually are. The effect of the expiry of patents for the public domain is nullified through the monopolisation of know-how, which is treated as a commercial secret. And like Novartis, pharmaceutical MNCs even talk of 'evergreen' patents. The relationship between technology and violence bears scrutiny while talking about liberalisation, market construction, warfare.

Julius Stone has written a marvellous book, *Legal Controls of International Conflict* (Stone 1954). Writing in 1949–1950 after Hiroshima–Nagasaki, he said a new problematic was emerging: international humanitarian law and the laws of war now stood threatened by the *de-personalisation of the means of violence*. You do not, you cannot, act as an ethical agent when all that you are trained to do is pressing the button. That is exactly what happened when you had an American pilot (I think in his early twenties) pressing a button, and there was an exclamation of joy and wonder, but he did not know anything about what it unleashed. Julius Stone, in his classic work, talks about modern warfare and 'de-personalisation' of the means of conflict. Technology is de-personalised, the human element of choice, of understanding, of grasping the impact, of evaluating consequences is not there. Destruction often begins to take on a very different kind of form, it becomes commoditised, de-personalised, and ethically corrosive.

The question arises: Can we apply the discourse of ethics to technologies? It is a difficult domain. How to link the use of drones to kill with ethics? One view is that the technological and ethical are different domains; the other that since all such decisions are socially embedded (and have adverse human rights impacts, especially anthropogenic harm), ethical considerations enter at the very threshold. Interestingly, in an unconscious irony, drones are now renamed (by the American war machine) as LAWS—Lethal Autonomous Weapons Systems! But aside from peaceniks, most people regard weaponry and even war as a necessary evil. At any rate, we must increasingly think through our love of technological artefacts (as Latour names it). The most profound work, or a most profound work, is by the French thinker Jacques Ellul, called *The Technological Society* (1964); it is really worth reading, worth its weight in gold. Bruno Latour and others have written a lot on these questions, too, but this book has a much wider social import and is a tremendous work.

Genetic Activism and the Second Open Letter

UB: There is another open letter that I ought to mention. In a sense, it has produced many textual children. It was addressed to the Food and Agriculture Organization (FAO) around the time of the adoption of the plant genetic resources undertaking, and was co-authored with Dr Clarence Dias, President of the International Centre for Law in Development, New York.[9]

At that time, there was very little genetic activism. It started with this letter. It was translated into seven Indian languages. A big national meeting was held in Benares, and they asked me to speak in Hindi. Now, how do you translate germplasm into Telugu, Gujarati, or Sanskrit? So we worked it out, and we called it *biyaran*. Out of this arose the movement with Vandana Shiva, and much later, our friend Suman Sahai.[10] Suman came to Delhi from Heidelberg and asked for a copy of the letter, it was published in *Mainstream*. She took up the gene campaign and it has become a huge discourse now. It is just as well. The activist discourse on technology is an important

[9] The International Undertaking on Plant Genetic Resources was adopted by the Food and Agriculture Organization in November 1983. Baxi and Dias wrote a letter titled 'An Open Letter to Non-Governmental Organisations and Non-Government Individuals on the Problem of Plant Genetic Resources' in December 1983.

[10] Suman Sahai, activist and the founder of Gene Campaign, a grassroots-level non-profit NGO in India, works in the field of bioresources, farmers' and community rights, intellectual property rights and indigenous knowledge, biopiracy, regulations of GMOs, and impact of climate change on agriculture and food.

one, it is rights and justice-related. Technology is socially embedded, it originates somewhere in time and place. But it is interesting to ask why we have not developed bioethics as a major field of legal studies. Although we have developed a social action movement on genetics, and now earth ethics, we seem not to have developed genethics. There are very important questions here.

Unfortunately, I did not exercise enough care. I trusted Clarence Dias, a friend of long standing. He must have cut and pasted something and put it in the text that became the Second Open Letter. I have always acknowledged the author in full details. But in this case, Pat Roy Mooney,[11] a towering activist figure at the time, an activist fighting early biotechnology, was not sufficiently acknowledged. My friend Ward Morehouse tells me that he is still concerned about 'plagiarism', which is a very sad story.

A second edition of *Sociology* would need to take in so much more, particularly geoethics or earth ethics now, but given that there is so much demand, maybe the simplest solution would be to reprint it as is and to find different approaches for incorporating all these other themes. But perhaps Generation Z may have different reading habits!

[11]Pat Roy Mooney: worked with civil society organisations on international trade and development issues related to agriculture, biodiversity etc. With Cary Fowler and Hope Shand, founded RAFI (Rural Advancement Foundation International) in 1984, and ETC Group in 2001, addressing the impact of new technologies on vulnerable communities. Author of *Seeds of the Earth: A Private or Public Resource?* (1980) and *Shattering: Food, Politics, and the Loss of Genetic Diversity* (1990).

Twelve
Social Action Litigation, Judicial Accountability, and Bhopal

Teachers, Students, Activists

LL: I think the other thing that we should also try and talk about, since you mentioned children of the open letter, are all your students. You have also mentored a generation of law teachers, law practitioners in various ways.

UB: I have referred warmly to students earlier, and I have no hesitation in saying that they have contributed more than can ever be imagined to forming me as teacher, researcher, and public activist. And I am grateful that I had the opportunity to engage different generations of students at various sites—India, Australia, Canada, the UK, and the USA. In the last two countries, I had students from South America and Africa. In India, I had lots of students from Nepal, and many of them came after studying in the Soviet Union.

The relationship with students is a difficult one, of course! I maintained no hierarchy (even in Delhi, most called me by my first name as I insisted), to the point of my senior colleagues maintaining that I fraternised with students overmuch. Fraternisation carried some costs, no doubt: some wanted to know all about my life, some came in to say 'hi' as a matter of right, some regarded me as a psychotherapist and solvent to all problems of adolescence and youth, and some thought of me as a bosom friend!

You had to fill many roles, for which you were ill-equipped, and educate yourself and your students that the teacher has not the answers to all problems in life. One maintained a dialogical *presence*, not *authority*, in class; life outside class was full of problems, as problematic as all forms of living and of being alive are.

But yes, it really is a question of creating a gravitational field of concern, whatever that concern is. And certainly, it operated in various different ways. The law-teaching bit was, of course, the fact that doing things with law in new ways challenged certain conventional ways of thinking and doing law. One initial reaction which proved fairly persistent was simply that this is not law, this is not how you do it. Only a person weakly grounded in law, it was said, would do such transgressive things.

Gestures of denial, gestures of dismissal, were common. With some people, that was the end of the conversation. People placed differently in different positions in life reacted differently to this call to unlearn, or to think differently, about doing things with law.

Another response was to say, you can do it, but we cannot. That changed rapidly. After we filed the *Agra Home* petition,[1] Nandita Haksar filed a petition about a women's remand home in Delhi.[2] Many students followed suit and young lawyers now go straight to the High Court and Supreme Court to seek directions against injustice.

Some of our students who had gone into journalism started filing petitions, and I said, well, anyone can do it, that is the whole point of it, it is not necessarily a new game to play, but it is a new field of force. As long as you did not claim ownership of a particular mode of intervention, did not necessarily call it your own, and set the parameters of how it was to be done, it was easy. Those who wanted to

---

[1] *Dr. Upendra Baxi vs. State of U.P.*, (1983) 2 SCC 308.

[2] *People's Union for Democratic Rights & Anr vs. Ministry of Home Affairs*, AIR 1985 Delhi 268.

do it found that they could do it, and did it. There was the occasional dithering as to what the issue is in social action litigation or in whether it signified genuine commitment. I am not saying anyone did it part-time, but doing it part-time, doing it as a one-shot affair, doing it as some kind of a conscience massage, teaches one that the practice of law is the unintended consequence of aggravating the plight of the rightless.

I always say the most important thing is to ask the question: To whom are you answerable? The question is, who are you accountable to for when you get into social action litigation? If you are not able to answer that question, or it is personal interest that motivates you, clearly it is something else that takes you there. Then it is a fling with social justice, it is making of social justice a high-class conversational commodity. The world is a large place, and as Justice Oliver Wendell Holmes would say when he had differences with his brethren on the US Supreme Court and got really angry about it, dash it all, I learnt a long time ago that I am not God and I cannot set everything right!

People are doing it with my hands, in Hidayatullah's story (narrated earlier), but what can I do? I always conveyed this notion without being so supererogatory, that this is the threshold, ask yourself to whom are you accountable, ask whether you are acting responsibly. Some of the tragedies of social action litigation are precisely that people have failed to act responsibly. (Of course, I have now learnt from Jacques Derrida how we should even abandon the word 'responsibility' and deploy the term 'response-ability' [Baxi 2016b].)

Responsible and Self-Reflexive Activism

UB (*contd*): Now, what does acting responsibly mean? I have written about it. Acting responsibly means many things. There are at least two ways of intervening: you can engage in episodic activism, or you can practice structural activism. I have spoken about that (Baxi 1985c). These are not neatly divided categories. There is too much coming and going in between the two. Either way, you have to have a fully planned strategy of action. Strategy is not just researching the way in which you draft your petition or letter. Research is about understanding the existence or situation of the people you are trying to help. That is the whole heart of SAL. So, what is the strategy? Strategy is not just about your legal competence and your legal ability and prowess, but it is about linking it to the suffering of the people whom you say you are representing. I have already spoken about speaking *for* and speaking *with* others.

SAL is not about speaking *to* others—an art best left to competitive politics. SAL is a strategy of politics for human rights. Whose human rights? For the utterly deprived, whom Ambedkar calls the *ati*-Shudras. *Ati* means the lowest of the low or, in Marxian vocabulary, the social and economic proletariat. This is perhaps what the word 'Dalit' ought to mean. That is very difficult because the communities out there are not one body, they are a series of tormented bodies. In the *Agra Home* case, did I practice the responsibility which I preach? Did I do so in *Narmada*? I always ask myself this question, and I put it to my colleagues and to my critics. That is called ethical reflexivity. If you do not have ethical reflexivity, one ends up almost exploiting the suffering of the other. As I said, it is an open question, I wish I knew what the dos and don'ts are, but I do not.

In order to get elected, for instance, you have to follow a particular code of ethics, howsoever minimal. The Election Commission can hold you accountable for its violation. If you are guilty of corrupt practices, you can be thrown out by the courts. Those who enter politics at least have some degree of accountability. There are an awful number of things wrong with power, we all know that, but there are some threshold conditions for forming a party. If you are not secular, you cannot form a party, said Justice Jeevan Reddy in *Bommai*. No elected government can be dismissed and President's Rule imposed, unless certain conditions exist, and the Supreme Court is the best and last resort to ascertain that those conditions are satisfied. Whether it is an extreme right-wing government, left-wing, or of a variety of centrist hues, so far as it is validly elected, it is constitutionally legal and cannot be dismissed, unless it acts unconstitutionally. Article 356 used the exact phrase 'in accordance with the provisions of this Constitution'.

Election codes, symbols, anti-defection laws—there are a whole lot of ethical constraints. The fact that they are constantly said to be violated does not mean there are no normative thresholds. If you look at the legal profession, again there are a certain number of minimum ethical standards that are stipulated. In the medical profession, you have to take a modern version of the Oath to care adequately for the sick. In Indian English, of course, it is hard to pronounce 'Hippocratic', it sounds like 'hypocratic', but it is not the same thing! There are these thresholds of normativity which are important, and they begin to provide some standards of responsibility. This is the case with the Press Council also.

But as activists, we simply say: I have decided to be an activist, and therefore I am an activist. I do not need to have any qualification, degrees, representative choice-making by others on whether I should be an activist or not, no code of conduct, no certification of knowledges, nothing. The activist is like a *swayambhu*, a self-manifesting being, or what the Buddhists call independent origination! I am not asking for the regulation of activists. I am just pointing out a social fact.

Today, we have what I call Article 311 citizens,[3] civil servants who, on superannuation, become activist citizens, though they did not do the very things that they now say they will do while they were in power. This is not a criticism, it is just a description. We also have people who resigned from the services and have become activists. Professors, journalists, all kinds of people call themselves activists. No problem, they have the right. The question, however, is: How do we talk about their accountability or responsibility for the suffering other? If this is not a live question, then activism is a kind of an upper-class game. It is a commodity for conversation and a resource for symbolic capital. That is what it is. I am sorry to speak so strongly, but this is my opinion. I do not want to sound dogmatic, but I speak from the heart and often think with my blood on this issue.

---

[3]Article 311. (1) No person who is a member of a civil service of the Union or an all-India service or a civil service of a State or holds a civil post under the Union or a State shall be dismissed or removed by an authority subordinate to that by which he was appointed.

Being Accountable

UB (*contd*): This does not answer the question, to whom are we accountable? One way of answering the question is what I said about character the other day at the NLSIU Convocation.[4] Character is not a notion by which you judge others, it is a notion by which you judge yourself. You have to have a constitutional character as an activist. Whether anybody else in society has a character or not is not our concern. Why? Because we are presenting ourselves as representatives of the voices of suffering.

As I was saying earlier, this is what my role in Bhopal was (Baxi and Dhanda 1990). It was to say, look, you want this strategy, these are the pluses and the minuses, if you want it, I will get it done for you. It is not a position of hegemony, or the possession of a single emancipative truth. It is a dialogic position of mutual respect. Accountability lies in dialogical performance, it lies in understanding the diversity of social suffering. One has to try and elucidate the distinctions between accountability and responsibility. It is well-known, isn't it, that one may be held accountable but not held responsible for action or conduct?

Take any social action litigation regarding land acquisition, for instance. One must surely ask the question, what superior moral right do I have to judge those fellows who want to take their compensation? In which ways are they being exploited? And which among the strategies that I counsel as effective involve more existential suffering and less effective delivery of services to the concerned peoples? You must, at the very minimum, ask these questions. That is something that has been very difficult for me to communicate to my students, colleagues, social action groups, and activists. I have criticised, privately and publicly, some social action litigation petitions as not being responsible in my terms. I do not know whether the silence that has greeted me is a tribute to me or a gesture of denial! I could not quite understand how folks who call themselves activists think. For example, when I

[4] XVI Annual Convocation, 31 August 2008, National Law School of India University. Incidentally, this is a rare convocation address replete with footnotes!

wondered aloud why they do not distinguish between episodic and structural activism, they insisted: 'But, Upen, we do think this way'. What may this mean? If they do not, what may be good reasons for this? Reading silence is more difficult than reading speech!

So far, the point I have made is that responsibility is a process of learning. My idea of the learning curve is simple. I only ask, at whose cost do activists learn? When they learn at their own cost, from their own suffering, that is their privilege. However, if they learn at the cost of aggravating the suffering of suffering people, then I have a problem with that. Very big problem. Here is where you come to a wider understanding of walking with both the feet. The episodic can, at the same moment, become a gateway for the structural moment; it is not that the event is episodic (for example, the Mathura case) and law reform is structural, one can make one flow into the other. It has to flow into the other.

Take a SAL, or what people call PIL (it is very important to use the right language[5]): you can say custodial deaths in detention are a violation of Article 21, and you can get compensation. That is episodic. Then, if you fail to participate in a movement for reform of law on custodial deaths, I have a problem. Your obligation is to resist certain kinds of states of terror which are exemplified in a particular writ petition or letter petition. If your concern is overwhelmingly moral, it cannot end there. It is demanding, it is a constant call. As Levinas says, it is the call of 'the face of the suffering other'. It puts a non-negotiable moral responsibility on you.

So how do you do it? You study law reform reports, comparative reports, if there is a call for action you join it, you organise voter education, it is very important to study party manifestos and see what is and what needs to be included. There are a whole range of

[5]As Upen (Baxi 2017c) notes, 'The conflation between SAL and PIL has caused much scholarly and judicial confusion and mischief: it is my firm belief that not every 'PIL' is a 'SAL'.. While PIL could become about the name of the petitioners, the impulse of SAL is to 'anonymise and collectivise'. SAL speaks to the suffering other, while PIL need not.' Upen goes on to elaborate below what the essential features of SAL are.

techniques, but all this is a part of responsible action. I have tried this all the time. Walking with two feet is the answer.

We failed in Bhopal on so many fronts, but we got the principle of absolute corporate liability written into the Oleum Gas Leak case (*M.C. Mehta vs. Union of India*[6]). It became a part of Indian jurisprudence. When we were fighting Bhopal, we played a role in drafting the Public Insurance Liability Act (1991). In the event of an industrial disaster, the victims will be paid interim compensation pending the sorting out of legal responsibility. A rider was added, however, that this will be deducted from the final compensation. This was not charity, but a right. There were difficulties, but a principle of law was enacted.

We worked with the Consumer Education and Research Society in seven states to carry out studies on the chemical industry, on applicable laws and regulations, and on what needed to be changed after Bhopal. We worked for the amendment of the Factories Act to include sections relating to hazardous industries. This is a combination of strategies, you cannot have single-shot activism. That is not activism, that is play, that is *leela*. If you are out on a publicity lark, that is another matter, *naam aa gaya akhbaaro mein, charchaa mein aa gaya* (my name has come in the papers and in public discussion), I would not call that activism.

Is this too arduous a responsibility that one is asking for? Are those people who have actually borne this responsibility a different kind of people? Superhuman? Do they not have the same constraints as other human beings have, do they not have family, do they not raise children, feel pain, experience pleasure, face intimidation or threats, etc.? Obviously, they do. To say, oh! you are gifted, sir, is a slap in my face! This is individualising what is a collective responsibility, this is running away from the fact that everybody who takes the first step has to walk a few steps longer. I am saying that, overall, we seem content with episodic activism, we do not move to structural activism. I say, let us find ways to make the episodic *as* structural. We have to reconstruct the binary.

How did the activism on Bhopal happen? How does any activism on any such mass industrial disaster happen? Is it because of a

---

[6] [1987] 1 SCC 395.

biographical accident of a moral agent calling herself a social activist taking notice of it, or of a judge telling activists, come along, I will hear your letter petition, that it becomes an event? Episodic activism is an actor-oriented way of thinking about things. That way of thinking about things would not have happened if it were understood that the structures were violative of human rights. This is a problem of communication and techniques of how to redo, recast, retool, re-imagine—the four 'R's of law and rights.

I am happy to say, looking at my life, that I have been instrumental in spreading the four Rs wide across the country through a variety of tricks: teaching, writing, being present in seminars, all kinds of ways. Seen strictly as a personal matter, I should be satisfied. But in communicating or working together to create an ethic, I have not moved forward. It would seem that one has a right to free speech and to form an association, not the right to be an activist. You can, of course, say that my right to free speech involves my right to be an activist. But when you see activism as your citizenship right, as your personal property, private property to act or not to act, then the ethical platform collapses.

Judges call some petitions vexatious, saying it is not public interest but political interest that is represented, or they term it private interest litigation. They dismiss these and impose fines. Sure, that is a different kind of discussion about the motives and rewards of being a public citizen. You can say certain motives are illegitimate. But as responsive agencies, courts expanded their jurisdiction and legitimacy—their credentials for activism—through letter petitions to reinforce their democratic legitimacy after the Emergency. This is an institutional response, not necessarily a well-considered institutional ethical response. The question is of ethical preference. In any event, social activism must be activism at a long haul—being in constant dialogue with courts and justices about the suffering other and discovering constitutional ways of amelioration. Then, it is a constitutional (re)-enchantment which is intoxicating.

Activism is a coat of many colours, obviously. Activism is not always in the aid of the suffering other. Should the judicial retirement age be revised upwards? Should some judges be transferred from one

High Court to another? How should allegations of corruption against judges be heard? Who should be appointed as judges? Hundreds of questions like these come before the Court. They are not speaking to the suffering other. That is the diet of SAL today. SAL here emerges as a form of countervailing political power. Will you all go along with me, to describe it as a form of inter-class warfare?

All this has nothing to do, some people say, at least directly with the suffering other. But is SAL therefore appropriated for other political ends? What then could be the ethical platform here? It is about the politics *of* human rights, that is all. (I variously distinguish the politics *of* and *for* human rights in my *Future of Human Rights* [Baxi 2013c].) It is not *of* SAL, it is *for* SAL. I do not want to press this distinction too much, but it is one way of expressing the shock. Part of the reason why my concerns have not been heard, or have not made sense, is that the river has changed its course. The best argument here would be, look, these intra-ruling class, intra-elite tensions and contradictions ultimately benefit the poor. But in no sense is all this directly addressed to the suffering other, or to the suffering of the have-nots. My concern properly addresses those kinds of activists who initiate SAL on behalf of, if not at the behest of, the constitutional have-nots. And that is where it becomes relevant and poignant.

I told you my Narmada story; the question I raised with Medha Patkar and other friends is what accountability the activists owe to each other, and to people at large for whom we are acting. The response may be simpler when most of the suffering other (often the victims or, more appropriately, violated peoples; I have difficulty with replacing both usages by naming them 'vulnerable', when the question of who caused this vulnerability is not even posed) are themselves engaged in a constant dialogue with the people. That is indeed the case with the Narmada Bachao Andolan or Mazdoor Kisan Shakti Sangathan [MKSS]; both Medha Patkar and Aruna Roy engage in constant dialogue with the suffering people. But when you are at one remove from the suffering other, one is more tormented by this question.

It torments me even now. One would say, tormenting yourself is not the most efficient way of handling the situation. It is not sufficiently rational. But I do not know any other way. If I am not tormented by deep ethical anxieties, then I am not an activist. I cannot lay down standards for others, but I can judge myself: and that is good enough for me, I know where I am lapsing. Maybe this kind of torment has over the years been so severe as to actually limit my presence directly as a social action petitioner, and has led me to re-emerge as a kind of helping hand to those who want my help. I have sort of taken an invisible—or at least less visible—public role, where I can assist people who want to act more responsibly. I have ceased to be a prominent actor myself. When my name was cited in the *Agra Home* case as Dr Upendra Baxi, I was very upset. I did not like it. The thing to do is to anonymise or collectivise SAL or generally all social action.

Raising this tormenting question does not allow any easy ways out. For example, one response is that the activists must remain accountable to the State. They should, in a trivial sense, comply with the conditions that the law or authorised administration lays down. I call these conditions 'trivial' in the sense that if activists want to form a group or association under an existing law, the expectation that they will comply with statutory regulation forms a legitimate State expectation of NGO conduct. But in a non-trivial sense, it is often maintained that activism of any sort that amounts to questioning the State and regimes deserves moral opprobrium and State action. This overlooks the fact that activist action is legitimate only when the State and the regime does not implement its laws and policies and remains non-compliant with the letter and the spirit of the Constitution. Activism by people is not always oppositional; often, it helps the State in implementation of laws and policies, and compliance with the constitutional spirit, values, and goals.

Often it is alleged that the mere fact of foreign funding is a ground for suspicion of the bona fides of activism. But the modern State always has regulations in place for receiving such funding, and overseas philanthropic funding is always under State vigil. With the rise of global terrorism, the State everywhere has acquired extraordinary powers of invigilation, but the imperatives of security always need to be balanced with freedom of dissent and social action in a democratic republic. The same consideration has to be borne in view: no criticism of governance and development should be regarded as dissent which slanders the State or the regime, no free speech should be criminalised as sedition unless it has the intention or tendency to incite violence.

It is important in levelling or investigating, or in the trial of the offence of sedition to understand that the Indian Supreme Court had held in 1962 in *Kedar Nath Singh vs. State of Bihar*[7] that:

> read as a whole, along with the explanations, make it reasonably clear that the sections aim at rendering penal only such activities as would be intended, or have a tendency, to create disorder or disturbance of public peace by resort to violence. As already pointed out, the explanations appended to the main body of the section make it clear that criticism of public measures or comment on Government action, however strongly worded, would be within reasonable limits and would be consistent with the fundamental right of freedom of speech and expression. It is only when the words, written or spoken, etc. which have *the pernicious tendency or intention of creating public disorder or disturbance of law and order that the law steps in to prevent such activities in the interest of public order*. So construed, the section, in our opinion, strikes the correct balance between individual fundamental rights and the interest of public order. It is also well settled that *in interpreting an enactment the Court should have regard not merely to the literal meaning of the words used, but also take into consideration the antecedent history of the legislation, its purpose and the mischief it seeks to suppress*. (emphases added)

This decision rendered Section 124-A of the Indian Penal Code constitutional, but given the ways of the history of criminal law administration in India, the time has come for its replacement with the incorporation of this test, if not for its total abolition. The arsenal of State powers is very vast, and restriction or outright abolition ought not to be considered an unreasonable limitation upon it. Certainly, what has been called its 'chilling effect' on free speech and expression should indeed be fully borne in view. I do enter here the complex arena of 'social media', but the crime of sedition need not be there to regulate conduct when the Information Technology Act and other administrative means are available to the State.

---

[7] AIR 1962 SC 955.

Epistolary and Bibliophilic Litigation

In South Gujarat University, a student wrote an MPhil thesis on the terribly exploitative conditions of migrant workers from Odisha and Bihar who are working in powerlooms. The student and his supervisor responded to my urging and filed the entire thesis as a social action litigation. This was a different form—not epistolary, but bibliophilic. Similarly, I have helped the filing of an entire report and books (the entire report of the Twenty-Eighth Scheduled Castes and Scheduled Tribes Commission by Dr B. D. Sharma, the Chair of the Commission, on his retirement from it), or the book on the re-promulgation of ordinances as a fraud on the Constitution (by Dr D. C. Wahwa of the Gokhale Institute, Pune).

The Constitution of India, *A Fine Balance*, the Twenty-Eighth Report, and *Kesavananda Bharathi*—these are compulsory reading for any understanding of Indian constitutionalism. These are four texts. So, allow me to distinguish the bibliophilic form from the epistolary form. Scholarship has travelled to the courts this way. Of course, I had to write the petition, but I wrote it in the name of the University as a public institution (*Lok Adhikar Sangh vs. State of Gujarat and Ors.*[8]). We called a meeting, everyone was excited—science professors, social science faculty, humanities faculty, everybody wanted to examine the conditions of these people. The Court said, we direct the South Gujarat University, the collective petitioner, to present a report on the working conditions. All these people came together to prepare a questionnaire. They had orientation sessions for those not familiar with the questionnaire, got some people living in the area to identify the study sites broadly, and the students wanted to conduct the study. The student union, the teachers union, and everyone wanted to be involved.

It was a *Shivji ka mela*, a wedding party for Lord Shiva—gods, angels, ghosts, spirits, everybody was there. It was great fun! We had a problem of limiting the range of people who wanted to participate!

[8] AIR 2002 Guj 59.

What we did was to divide all the areas where the empirical study would be undertaken, and we said, each committee will be led by a student, and will consist of three faculty members and three students. The students will write the report with the help of the faculty. We had twenty such committees. It took us six or seven months to prepare the report.

Surat is a cash culture. Everything is measured by money, but people paid their way when I said, I cannot commit university funds. We paid our own money and we wrote a report which was published. We made several suggestions, both episodic and structural. We said, certain kinds of practices must stop. We asked for the expansion of rights education programme over the next five years to ensure self-empowerment. The High Court asked us to do all these things and report to it periodically. This was an institutional SAL, not an NGO one. It was a campus-wide SAL. So much so, that when I left at the end of three years, it continued through the terms of two successive Vice-Chancellors. They could not disown it as a Baxi phenomenon, as an aberration. On the ground, there were people who were constantly engaging with it. Contingency of tenure was not a problem here, at least in the short run.

A question that I have asked myself often is, did we harm these powerloom workers? In a job blackmail situation, for every 100 who were complaining to the Court, there were many who were willing to take the job. How does the Court or SAL petitioner cope with this situation in a labour-surplus economy? We tried our utmost: we said, legal aid must be provided, a roster must be kept of workers. We put several things in place. This is what I meant by strategy. We have to anticipate how the system will react. If you do not, you are acting wrongly and are morally responsible. I learned all this earlier on as well, I learned it from the people themselves.

Somebody had filed a petition about contract workers at an industrial plant in Hazira, near Surat, and they were all thrown out the moment the petition was filed. So one fine morning, about fifty to seventy people came to my home in Surat when I was VC. They said, *aapke saathi ne* petition *file kiya*, your colleagues filed the petition alongside with you, and we are jobless from today. Help us find one. This was a concrete situation, you cannot allow exploitation to be un-redressed, but an individual cannot give them jobs at the same time. When you file a petition, you have got to talk to them and tell them what the consequences might be. You have to think of how to help them raise resources—instead of taking money from this or that foundation, we must see if we can get them support payment. We cannot pay them all the time. Do we have enough of a material base in that location to provide their women some earning jobs? This is the micro-level concern that has to be there. I could not go to the textile industry which was their largest employer, because I was fighting them.

They were startled that the VC of a university would lead a movement. Surat is the most vibrant capitalist city in the country. So they said, well, you asked for it, it is your problem. I lost considerable goodwill. It was only my standing, or my funny Gujarati accent, which got the crowds to listen to me and ultimately allowed me to prevail over some of them. They said, what does the university have to do with it? I set up a council of south Gujarat citizens to advise the VC, in which there were MLAs, MPs, trade union leaders, social workers, cultural workers, and I said, this is what I am doing, this is what I have done, this is what I have to do, if you do not support it, if you have criticisms, tell me what they are. What is your idea of a university?

Our first meeting was focused on a single question: Why did we need this university? They said, sir, nobody else has asked this question. I said, I am asking this question, you are citizens, you have fought for this university. I had done my homework. I had gone through the Gujarat legislative debates and obtained stacks of photocopies, as I knew they would not have the answer. The legislative debates revealed that leading people in south Gujarat, some of whom were present at these meetings, had said this is a backward, destitute tribal area where there was a lot of exploitation, and that there was need for a university to assist and empower them. I said, this is what you and your predecessors said. Am I doing something wrong, or were my predecessors, who knew nothing about these people, doing something right? That is the kind of labour you have to do, name and shame! This is very hard work, when you move from a mere judgment on others to a collective action.

I was teaching in the law college. Teaching is often a resource for the movement, as strategy, for articulating your moral concerns, when you move from a mere judgment on others to a collective action. The idea that you can do these things by yourself because you are gifted is irresponsible. So, how to collectivise forms of SAL is a very important question. And I made sure that, outside of the accident of the *Agra Home* case, not a single one of the cases bear my name. That was my first concern. I said, I will not put my petition that way at all, not in the first person singular. How to anonymise, collectivise, de-individualise is the question. Social action cannot be yours. Public interest, yes, you can embody a public interest. Social action is the very idea of an emergent collectivity—a social collective strength, a collective responsibility. Short question, long answers!

The Phases of SAL: From the Charismatic to the Routine

AN: How would you look back at the history of SAL?

UB: When I was speaking about personalisation or collectivisation of SAL, the period I had in mind was the three or four years from *Agra Home* in the 1980s. After that, it was the associational actors who pursued SAL, such as PUDR, PUCL, the Indian Federation of Working Journalists, and many others. The only major exception was M. C. Mehta,[9] who filed a large number of environmental SALs in his own name. SAL diversifies. I will get into the kinds of diversification that we need to study.

One is the letter petition for down-and-out citizens, for the invisible, those rendered inarticulate, the tortured and tormented—these were the people we were speaking for before the court in the first

[9]Mahesh Chandra Mehta, public interest attorney, who was responsible for numerous landmark judgments from the Supreme Court since 1984. These include the introduction of lead-free gasoline, reducing industrial pollution in the Ganges, and protecting the Taj Mahal from the effects of environmental pollution.

flush of SAL, or in the charismatic moment of its founding. These were the people who educated the judges about democratising standing, and who gave the gift of activism to Indian judges. Their sufferings were converted into gifts of judicial activism, of constitutional policing of the State. This was the first marker, the birthing moment of SAL. Here, it was not always possible to distinguish the individual petitioner from the people who were represented. People were amorphous, there was often no association on the ground representing them.

Then comes the second stage when institutional players come onto the scene, such as Bandhua Mukti Morcha (a voluntary association), PUCL, PUDR, etc. The third moment is the diversification of SAL, primarily with the environmental SAL, which creates itself into a related but distinct genre of judicial activism. In the fourth moment, the attempt is to convert Directive Principles into Fundamental Rights. In the migration from Part IV to Part III, education, health, shelter all become Fundamental Rights. After this comes the movement against the corrupt sovereign. The two Antulay cases *Abdul Rehman Antulay and Ors. vs. R.S. Nayak and Ors.*,[10] *A.R. Antulay vs. R.S. Nayak and Ors.*,[11] for instance, or the Vineet Narain case,[12] in which the Supreme Court conscripted the senior advocate Anil Divan as amicus.

From long-haired, pipe-smoking professors in dishevelled clothes taking matters to the Chief Justice and the companion Justices, this is now a professionalised discourse between senior counsel and judges. It becomes completely de-individualised and structural. The purity and integrity of elections, the debate between the Election Commission and political parties, and such like, these become the province of SAL momentarily. Alongside with it also appear (although this is not easy to identify) attempts to engender SAL.

An interesting story is of when we did a series of essays in honour of my colleague Lotika Sarkar, called *Engendering Law* (Dhanda and Parashar 1999). The then CJI was releasing it and, in speaking about the book and its importance, he kept calling the book *Endangering the*

[10] AIR 1988 SC 1531.

[11] AIR 1992 SC 1701.

[12] *Vineet Narain and Ors. vs. Union of India*, [1997] 1 SCC 226.

Constitution. It is a very interesting slip of tongue because engendering does endanger. It is the political unconscious that translates *engendering into endangering*! You can plot Vishakha (*Vishakha and Ors. vs. State of Rajasthan and Ors.*[13]), Mathura ... there is no linear time of actual events and of law reform, it is a criss-cross of time, the time of crime, the (long) time of convictions and punishments, the time of protest and change, the time of reform and its very long aftermath, and this is only legal/juridical time, plotting on one timeline different registers of concerns.

Then comes the appropriation of SAL by the newly globalising middle classes of India. You have SAL appearing as a function of judicially mandated investigation. It is very interesting: gated communities with twenty-four-hour supply of water and electricity do not want their properties to be blighted by slums nearby, and SAL is pressed into service for the ideology of urbanisation, of the global city, or the mega-city. Aditya Nigam and Nivedita Menon (2007) have done a beautiful book on the politics of dispossession. SAL is used as a way of consolidating interests in property in upper-class Delhi, and there is a resort to urban planning in litigation. This is the story of SAL in the hyper-globalising moment of India's development.

Within all this comes the phase of judicial management of SAL. SAL gets initially bureaucratised. We have a Joint Registrar of PIL. A charismatic form of judicial activism becomes—as Weber would say—routinised, bureaucratised. It is the Joint Registrar who decides what letters are to be placed before the Court, not the judge. Earlier, it was the Chief Justice who used to decide. In the High Court, the decision to hear a letter petition is perhaps still a judicial function. The trend of bureaucratisation has on the whole proceeded along with the rise of human rights commissions, commissions for women and children's rights, etc. There is a judicial tendency now emerging to farm out the load, with some letters referred to legal aid and Lok Adalat boards, or to the NHRC, for instance. What was at one point a visible social intervention becomes relatively invisible to scholarship and to public commentary through bureaucratisation. We still don't know

[13] *Vishakha and Ors. vs. State of Rajasthan and Ors.*, AIR 1997 SC 3011.

what percentage is farmed out to state human rights commissions and other human rights institutions, and to what effect.

Farming out of SAL is an inevitable development, because commissions are specialised bodies for the protection of human rights, and the Court thinks it is best to refer the matter to the functionally autonomous body. Judges retain some oversight over this, and this depends in part on how far activist-lawyers are satisfied. Some activist-lawyers are happy with such farming out, because it is not a Court atmosphere in these commissions, and there are greater possibilities for manoeuvrability of the litigant. Visibility is less, but manoeuvrability is more. Some social action litigants and beneficiaries are, however, very upset with this farming out. We need a mapping, a description of what is actually happening.

So, the first moment was of a charismatic law-giving. I was a party and witness to it, a minor pioneer! Then comes routinisation or traditionalisation. If you follow Weber, the third condition in any legal development is transformation into a legal-rational authority, by which he means that you need a body of rules: matters must be presented and argued in a certain way, it becomes a part of modern legality, drifting away from its original lofty heroic purposes. Legal rationality for Weber, as is well-known, was a conflict between the formal rationality of law and the substantive rationality of law.

What was charismatic about SAL? That it foregrounded substantive rationality with its focus on the impoverished, on equality, justice, care, concern, commitment. This is diluted in the legal rational mode, where formal rationality takes root. Process over substance.[14]

The question that has been repeatedly raised is: How do you set limits to SAL? In my time, in the first phase, Brother Venkataramiah posed ten questions in the Sudipto Mazumdar case,[15] the firing range case in which tribal villagers were killed in army test firing. Sudipto was a correspondent for *The Indian Express* and a friend of Nandita Haksar's. Justice Venkataramiah raised ten difficult questions, which were referred to a constitutional bench. It was too much; SAL had just

[14]'Uprooting Injustice, Organizing Negation' (Baxi 2019c).

[15]*Sudipto Mazumdar vs. State of MP*, (1983) 2 SCC 258.

begun. I was in Surat when this judgment came out, and I decided to do something about it.

I think that about 100 intervener petitions, all with the same text, saying these questions that have been raised are very important, not just to judges and lawyers, but to all poor people, the impoverished people in the country, the constitutional have-nots. These petitions in effect said, we are the representatives of this class of have-nots, we are very far from Delhi, we do not have resources, we are not legally trained, but if the Court is supposed to consider these questions, it should send us the entire history of the case. We pray to your lordships to send us complimentary copies of the paperbooks of the entire case on which the Sudipto Mazumdar reference to the larger bench is made. These petitions, all of them properly done letter petitions, said, we want the paperbook of the case, so that we can file proper responses to these questions.

And the whole thing sank. Later on, I was authoritatively told that this is neither a load that the Supreme Court can ever discharge, nor an expense which it could bear in this or in future cases. Most intervener petitions were filed from obscure places, from the smallest district towns. These groups never, as far as I know, heard from the Court. But the matter never came up for a hearing. I was a mere facilitator. Even so, the hegemonic impression of me was quite strong!

So there comes a moment of premature judicial closure, of self-disciplining judicial activism. It is a legitimate concern not always, legitimate as warranted by facts. Even today, I am prepared to say that, although I have not studied the so-called PIL, SAL constitutes a very tiny percentage of filings. Normatively, it is a small percentage which gives birth to activism on the High Bench. Judicial activism is authored by suffering people, those who bring the plight of bonded labour, people in solitary confinement, wounded and persecuted sexualities, people living with disabilities, and all kinds of marginalised groups and the pathology of State power live into the Court. This creates activist jurisprudence. We need to study these reflexive or pre-reflexive moments of judicial self-awareness triggered by some kinds of SAL. The point I am making is that the question of anonymisation, of collectivisation, of reflexivity, of ethical introspection into my representation of the suffering other appears in different forms in its different phases. We need to study this: there is nothing more important.

More recently, the Supreme Court (via Justice Katju) said, we do not know the impact of what we are doing: there are no studies documenting the impact.[16] That can mean two things. Either judges want to know the impact of what they are doing, or they can mean, enough is enough, we have ventured far enough, we must close shop and limit ourselves to what we may effectively achieve, to jurisprudence and not practice any more of this demosprudence, do just the 'law jobs' (Llewellyn 1939; Llewellyn and Hoebel 1941) that are our proper function. This is the time when there must be serious writing on the subject, on constitutional intentions, on processes, on the aftermath of the impact of people-judiciary partnerships, at least in the Supreme Court and High Courts.

On many questions that earlier went to the Supreme Court, people are now making choices as to which the proper forum is to start with. This is another phase of litigation that I should mention: it uses SAL as a process of law reform, to strike down a statute or provision of law as unconstitutional or otherwise by actually asking judges to perform tasks that law commissions and legislatures have to perform. In *Vishakha*, the judges said, this is the law on sexual harassment at the workplace under Article 141, until Parliament passes a law to the contrary. So we are triggering off legislative law-making functions of the Court, of which there are quite a few examples. There is the way SAL itself takes over day-to-day governance, like in the *Agra Home* case, for example. Even now, the district judge files a monthly report! Now, the district judge is not a functionary under the immoral trafficking act; this is the granting of a supervisory, monitoring authority by the Supreme Court. The Court functions to amend a statute *de facto* for good or bad reasons. A number of amazing SALs thus function as a vehicle of law reform.

In fact, take the recent travails of the Supreme Court in the case of Prakash Singh.[17] The demand there was for the Court to re-enact

[16] *Common Cause vs. Union of India and Ors.*, AIR 2008 SC 2116.

[17] *Prakash Singh and Ors. vs. Union of India*, (2006) 8 SCC 1.

the Police Act of 1861. The Court asked the states as to what their suggestions were, and a committee headed by Soli Sorabjee was appointed to draft a revised Police Act. Then the Court passes on the draft Police Act to all the states for their comments, with a timeline. The Court might say, if you are not going to do anything, this is the Police Act. Nowhere else in the world is this possible. It is happening: whether you think it should happen or not is a matter of whether you are an Anglophile or Americophile. The limits to the nature of judicial power, moral wisdom, the question of the legitimacy of the juristocracy, these are all big questions.

What I have been saying in these rather rambling remarks is that we need, first of all, to *periodise* and to *classify* the SAL. I have offered the following moments or, if you like, phases: the charismatic founding moment, routinisation, appropriation, impact, the post-SAL moment. The routinisation moment includes the practice of farming out SAL, the judicial institutionalisation of SAL in the Supreme Court and the High Courts, and its overall bureaucratisation. The post-SAL moment is still occurring through the typically Indian ways of affecting as well as managing hyper-globalisation and, in particular, the structural adjustment of judicial activism, often court-induced.

The Impact of SAL

AN: By impact, do you mean impact at the ground level? What has changed?

UB: Impact is a very notorious word. You may have read this article by me in the *JILI* called 'Who Bothers about the Supreme Court?' (Baxi 1982c). That was about the question of the impact of judicial decisions. So yes, there can be many kinds of impact, including the actual result on the ground. Determining what the actual result is, is a question of method. It is an analytical question. There are two ways of thinking about it: one is to say, this is a symbolic result, and the other is to say, this is an instrumental result in the here and the now, an actual result. Now, the distinction is quite tricky and technical, but it is still important.

Very often, symbolic change is designed to affect social attitudes, to change the way people think. Look at the Dowry Prohibition Act (1961), for instance: it simply says ban dowry, we do not approve of it. But the way it was drafted, it was never likely to be enforced. It was, in fact, rarely enforced. Legislations like these are designed to dispose citizens towards certain values and virtues. They are educational legislations, nothing follows from them on the ground. Over generations, the idea of the Dowry Prohibition Act is to make people think that dowry is criminal and illegal, and to bring about change in the long run.

An instrumental result is one that hits people on the head and says, accomplish this here and now. Instrumental results are intended not for changing attitudes and dispositions, but for changing behaviour and conduct; what you think in your mind, what is your concept or ideology, does not matter here. Take the subsequent amendments to the Dowry Prohibition Act. The Dowry Prohibition (Amendment) Act of 1984 prescribes a minimum punishment of two years imprisonment and fine to anyone demanding dowry. And a person who gives, takes, or helps in the giving or taking of dowry can be sentenced to jail for five years and fined Rs 15,000 or the amount of the value of dowry, whichever is more. It is prohibited to give or to agree to give, directly or indirectly, any property or valuable security in connection with a marriage. The giving of, or agreeing to the giving of, any amount, either in cash or kind, jewellery, articles, properties, etc., in respect of a marriage is absolutely prohibited by the Act. Even the making of a demand for dowry is also now prohibited, and it is punishable with imprisonment of five years and a fine of Rs 10,000. The Dowry Prohibition (Maintenance of List of Presents to the Bride and Bridegroom) Rules 1985 require that the list of gifts, in the form of a sworn affidavit, has to be notarised, signed by a protection officer or a dowry prohibition officer, and kept by both the parties. Non-observance with this can invite heavy penalty, including a three-year term in jail for not only the bride and groom, but also their parents.

To stop the offences of cruelty by the husband or his relatives on the wife, Section 498-A has been added in the Indian Penal Code, and Section 198-A has been added in the Criminal Procedure Code since the year 1983. In the case of suicide by a married woman within seven years from the date of her marriage, the Court may presume that such suicide has been abetted, encouraged by her husband or his relatives (the Indian Evidence Act has been amended to this effect by adding Section 113-A). Section 304-B of the Indian Penal Code in 1983 deals with dowry deaths. It states that where the death of a woman is caused by any burns or bodily injury, or occurs otherwise than under normal circumstances within seven years of her marriage, and it is shown that soon before her death she was subjected to cruelty or harassment by her husband or any relative of her husband for, or in connection with, any demand for dowry, such death shall be called 'dowry death', and such a husband or relative shall be deemed to have caused her death. Clause (2) of Section 304-B states that whoever commits dowry death shall be punished with imprisonment for a term which shall not be less than seven years, but which may extend to imprisonment for life. The Domestic Violence Act 2005 aims at domestic violence against women and to provide protection to women from domestic violence. The various amendments lead to a more effective normative system to combat violence against women.

The Untouchability Offences Act, 1955 becomes the Protection of Civil Rights Act, 1976, which then becomes the Scheduled Castes and Tribes (Prevention of Atrocities) Act, 1989. These are instrumental, in a manner of speaking; here, the power of the State is invested in making things happen on the ground.

Yes, impact could be symbolic. Are State lawyers persuaded by the importance of attending to certain kinds of situations more seriously? Is the bureaucracy more disposed towards looking at these as problems? Is the political system better as a result of SAL? Are they thinking about these problems more seriously? SAL, as symbolic judicial action, has a pedagogic role. That is one dimension of measuring impact. That is a difficult one to track empirically; attitude changes take place over a long period of time, and you need to find out and study how these changes take place. The instrumental impact of SAL, on the other hand, is relatively easier to track. One could ask, for example, how often the contempt power has been used, how often are chief secretaries and ministers summoned before the Court while hearings are on? They are not punished, just asked to be present like petitioners.

Many bureaucrats have told me this is a pain, you have to come and sit in Court, the case goes on interminably, they are treated like ordinary people, without all the accoutrements of office, sometimes they have to stand, there is no space. One could read these as non-penal inducements to gain compliance. In both symbolic and instrumental judicial action, the question of communication is very important. I used to criticise, and I still do, the delay in bringing acts into force. In *Crisis*, I identify some seven or eight major amendment acts which were enacted by Parliament, but were never brought into force (Baxi 1982a). Our Constitution does not provide for executive veto of legislations. You have a duty to bring legislations into force.

A State can kill a statute by not taking constructive steps to appoint officers. I was always critical of delays which vetoed a legislation. I met Sujaya, who was then the Secretary of the Department of Women and Child Welfare, with regard to a law relating to the age of marriage. I said, madam, it has been two years and you have not brought the statute into force. She took me by hand and led me to a huge godown at the end of the corridor and said, Professor, do you see what this is? She said that the Act and its provisions have to be translated into all the Indian languages. If you do not translate a bill, only lawyers who are privileged are capable of understanding it. Then we have to devise audio-visual packets for Doordarshan. She said, unless I do all this, how do I notify the Act? Notification is nothing, people have no idea what is involved in this. Officers have no idea what it is. This is the reason why I have to prepare toolkits for the officers. I have to hold conferences and seminars for which I have to struggle with the finance ministry to get grants, because it costs enormous money. No social legislation is cost-free. The more serious you are, the more financial investment you will have to make. So, I learnt from Secretary Sujaya that sometimes we academics criticise governments, but there are some people in the government who mean business, who take their time and fight some tough battles. What was she trying to do? She was trying to focus on communication. Communication of a legislative principle, its design and detail, is vital for impact. You cannot have any impact if you do not know what the thing is, if you have never heard of the law.

Take the Bonded Labour Abolition Act 1976: the fanfare with which it was enacted during the Emergency was indeed notable. But long years after the enactment of the Act, in our struggles in participation with the Rural Litigation and Entitlement Kendra in Dehradun, we realised that district magistrates, who are burdened with the statutory duties of enforcement under it, claimed to never even have heard of it! The Rural Litigation Kendra actually made copies and got them notarised, as we did not have the copies of the government gazette notification. Gazettes are the most difficult to get. The activists got notarised copies and gave them to the district magistrates. This is the law passed in 1975–1976, now do your duty, they were told. There is no communication of the contents of the legislation to those who are meant to implement it. Or the quality of communication of the law is poor. I refer to this in my article on the question of the impact of judicial decisions. How do you convey a Shah Bano,[18] a Bandua Mukti Morcha,[19] an Unnikrishnan,[20] or any major decision to those beyond the ones who may be immediately involved in the litigation?

How do you communicate with the ruling classes, with the government, with the bureaucracy, within government departments, with beneficiaries, between various groups, with the media? How do you become a legal correspondent? By long years of practice, and gaining some independence from the sub-editor? Or is it by going to a school, is there a school for training legal correspondents? With Chanchal Sarkar (the founder-director of the Press Institute of India), we organised five years of developmental training for grassroots

[18] *Mohd Ahmed Khan vs. Shah Bano Begum and Ors*, AIR 1985 SC 945.

[19] *Bandhua Mukti Morcha vs. Union of India*, AIR 1984 SC 802.

[20] *Unnikrishnan P.J. and Ors. vs. State of A.P. and Ors.*, AIR 1993 SC 2178.

journalists, in which I accentuated the role of legal literacy and it produced some effects in the vernacular press.

Today, you have the 24/7 press, and now social media. How is a judicial decision communicated? How is its quality, its redemptive image communicated? It is commoditised, it becomes a news commodity. Again, I gave up, how much can one do? After Chanchal Sarkar left the Press Institute, I spoke to many media departments, including in Jawaharlal Nehru University, in Jamia Millia, etc. I said, please set aside a small component in your training for legal journalism. In Surat, I tried it with a new department in mass media. Wherever I could, I tried, and I failed; you cannot do it as a solo affair. There is a greater need for communication, for visualisation, for understanding. It is a long story, but over a short span of time, the impact has been on the ground, it has changed the life situation of people. Apart from SAL, there are other preliminary steps that you need to take, both with respect to symbolic and instrumental judicial decisions and legislations. You cannot study impact, only the opinion of people. Everybody has opinions on social disaffectedness; sometimes these opinions are useful, sometimes they are abominable and useless. The only indicator of impact which we currently have is the anguish of disappointed SAL litigants.

You may also wish to study the impact of SAL from the standpoint of the petitioners. Increasingly, petitioners are not petitioners-in-person, but are social movement and NGO actors. There are two kinds of petitioners in SAL: celebrity petitioners and the 'also ran' kind of people. When celebrity-petitioners articulate despair with the eventual outcome, it provides one indicator. Celebrities are not celebrities in the sense of inauthentic people. They are grounded in their own realities, struggling with the many options they have when they come to court. If they do not want to come to court, they settle the matter elsewhere. Properly called just celebrities, when they criticise the courts, at least that is one indicator of impact. And they are live communicators, live transmitters of social meanings of the Constitution, of what justice does or does not or will not do.

Courts in SAL make the most important contribution to the growth of new social movements. They provide them with the political time and space never available before. Take Narmada, for instance. There was a stay order in effect for four-and-a-half years: it was in this time that the Narmada Bachao Andolan became a nation-wide movement. Delay is very critical to creating the social space and political time in which to create linkages among suffering people. Delay is a very important resource for people's movements. If you say, judges have taken ten years to give a judgment, therefore there has been no impact, this is stupid. When you have this political time and social space, you cannot be repressed. It is a non-repressive space. When you are before the Court, you are protected. Even the *thanedar* knows what the Supreme Court is.

When I went to Sarsaul block in Kanpur district (along with Krishan Mahajan as court commissioners), everyone knew that we had come from a court (see Chapter 10). Even my friends, the Chamars I worked with, they did not know the Supreme Court, they did not know the daily courts, but they said, *aap kutchery se aaye?* (You have come from a court?). They knew what a court was, even if they did not know the judicial hierarchy. There is the sense of a different kind of authority prevailing than if you came from a political party. Very often this is a great contribution, creating a non-repressive space before the Court. Although people get beaten up—I was nearly beaten up in Sarsaul block—the fact that one is before the Supreme Court of India still remains of some importance in social life.

But celebrity-petitioners sometimes miss this. They fail to acknowledge the contribution that courts have made, when their only expectation from the court is of content, not process. Take the question of preventing the raising of the height of the Narmada dam. We are probably among a handful of countries where the Court has said, wait till you rehabilitate the displaced, no raising the height of the dam until then. Later, they evolved a *pari passu* principle that says both have to be taken up together. After seven or eight years of litigation, when the dam height is raised, we say, this is terrible, the Court has failed the people, ignoring the half-a-dozen-plus years when the Court did other things. This is not a fair assessment. You have to scientifically take into account what the process of going to court meant for the growth of the movement, apart from the eventual outcomes alone.

In the Gulshan Kallu case, for instance, the immediate question was that Chamars were being deprived of their livelihood.[21] But in our report to the Supreme Court, we had a chapter called 'Follow the Vultures'. We found that the Chamars were not the only persons affected. The carcasses of the cattle were traditionally skinned by the Chamars. After that, there is still some blood on the bones, and the vultures would come. The Qureshis were a group of people whose whole livelihood depended on following the vultures. When a flock of vultures went by, they followed them, and took up the bones and skulls of the dead cattle which had been cleaned up by the vultures. These bones were then crushed in a rough mill and were sold in two major markets: pharmaceuticals and beauty products. So, the leather workers bought the skin of the dead cattle from the Chamars, and the bone powder provided the livelihood of the Qureshis.

We did a full follow-up research on what the Supreme Court ought to do. We found that in Agra, there was a leather corporation, and looked into the question of how the leather corporation might assist these communities by helping them get around the middlemen. The case was about the legality of the ordinance. But to study the impact of that, one had to take into account the role of the leather corporation in boosting the livelihood of the Chamars, whether the pharmaceutical industry or the beauty industry were paying the Qureshis fair wages and prices for their commodities, etc. This kind of litigation is different from putting an end to solitary confinement, custodial torture, deaths in custody. In such cases, you stop increments to officials, dismiss or suspend them, etc. These are cases in which impact is easy to assess; institutional change is made, abuse is stopped, etc. However, in the Gulshan Kallu case, the question of impact was a long-term issue. How does one guardedly chase up the CEO of the leather corporation and speak with Dalit MPs, or write letters to the prime minister? After five years, I moved on. This is all you can do, there comes a time when you cannot do any more. You have to know so much when you assist the Court, the question of impact comes later.

[21] *Gulshan Kallu & Ors. vs. Zilla Parishad, Etawah, U.P. & Ors.*, AIR 1981 SC 1668.

But it is not only a question of the impact on livelihood, it is also a question of culture. As Uncle Marx told us, goods are alienated labour. We do not ask, where was this good produced, under what circumstances? How much blood is there on this commodity? The worker who produces these things is also consumed by the objects produced. And these objects are something that the labouring class can never enjoy. Take construction workers, for instance. Several generations of them are never going to have the remotest chance of living in the types of palatial houses they help build. Objects you create under exploitative conditions confront you with a reality that colonises.

Impact is a function of the times. There is symbolic and instrumental impact, short-term, medium-, and long-term impacts, you cannot study them all at once. What renders itself as a measurable impact in the short term? Bhopal is an example of long-term impact. Long-term impact includes things other than immediate results, things like the widening of social solidarity and empathy. You get this Section 377 read down in the Naz Foundation case. It is an instrumental result, but how do you make sure that certain kinds of people are actually respected in life, regardless of their sexual orientation, except continuing movements/struggles of people to enforce and, where necessary, amend the law? How are you going to prevent discrimination over the long term?

The classic case is the Criminal Tribes Act repealed by Nehru. Even now, you go to any city and, in the SHO's [Station House Officer] drawer, you will find a schedule enumerating the various criminal tribes. The Act is repealed, the concept is abhorrent, but policing says, when there is a crime wave, you have to produce arrests and these are the marked communities, you know where they are. Each time a new police commissioner is appointed, chain-snatching incidents are said to have been stopped forever. All the menacing culprits have been nabbed in a wide swoop. Those who are nabbed are invariably those who belong to the erstwhile criminal tribes.

Symbolic impact is difficult to measure in the long term. In short, the question of impact is not only about results, but is also about what forms of new social cooperation have been fostered by this judicial stance among activists, civil servants, people affected, media, etc. This is long-term, it is not instantaneous. The Court is not a slot machine which always gives you the right result. It is the pattern of civic cooperation fostered by a decision, it is the partnership among professionals that this brings about. In the *Agra Home* case, psychiatric professionals, the women's movement, medical people, and social workers were knit into acting together. Activism is a form of social investment in change. Responsible activism is an agency of transformation, it is not a fashion. There cannot be such investments without costs. How do you measure the costs of activism? One kind of cost is where activists flourish at the cost of the suffering people. Pratap Bhanu Mehta once said that the eclipse of the institutions of representative governance is the cost to pay for judicial activism. Resource cost, legitimacy cost, costs of creating a hierarchy of programmes of change. The latter you see in the environmental judgments of the Supreme Court. Take the Ganges Tannery case, for example.[22] The Court directed the shutting down of tanneries right across Uttar Pradesh. The livelihoods of hundreds of thousands of people depended on these tanneries. You have here the logic of livelihood rights competing with environmental rights. Costs have to be conceptualised beyond a conventional cost-benefit analysis.

Judicial Accountability

LL: What we seem to have is the competing idea of sovereignty itself. Partha Chatterjee's notion of civil and political society would squarely place the courts as part of rationalising, modernising civil society, which does not have any place for political negotiation as such. In your conceptualisation, it is the illegitimacy of political parties in particular which had led to the corruption of the parliamentary form of democracy. And hence a move towards a reliance on the judiciary to fill in democratic spaces. But is there not an equal danger of the

[22] *M.C. Mehta vs. Union of India*, AIR 1988 SC 1115.

corruption of the judiciary? So, in that case, what happens? That is a strategic question and a political question.

UB: I think you are using the term 'corruption' in its widest import. In a spiritual sense, one talks of 'corruption of the flesh' and 'corruption of the Soul', namely the struggle against vices like greed, egotism, envy, lust, which negate just social cooperation and the ethics of the inner self. In a different way, Dr Ambedkar described it (in his observation while piloting the Constitution on 4 November 1947) by saying: 'I feel that the Constitution is strong and flexible to hold the country together, ... both in peace and war, Indeed, if I may say so, if things go wrong under the new Constitution, the reason would not be it was a bad Constitution. What we would have to say is that *Man was vile*' (emphasis added).

Thinking deeply about the word 'vile' is essential everywhere. The thesaurus lists several synonyms for 'vile', as 'bad, dark, evil, immoral, iniquitous, nefarious, rotten, sinful, unethical, unlawful, unrighteous, unsavoury, vicious, villainous, wicked, wrong', and its near antonyms include 'decent, ethical, good, honest, honourable, just, moral, right, righteous, sublime, upright, virtuous'. The binary will naturally draw a complete contrast between the ethically good and bad qualities of a person. I am sure every Indian language has words which are equivalent to 'vile' and Sanskrit words for 'vile' persons may suggest synonyms as '*dusta*' (morally wicked), or '*duracahri*', one who engages in evil practices or ways). Significantly missing (as far as I can tell) is the absence of demonisation of the other, showing a theory of reformation of a 'vile' man—reformation of the total self, not just of the actual conduct but of character and moral will. The Constitution thus carries some important messages for criminologists and law reformers.

True, often the same lapses in the virtues of an individual leads to individuals being described as corrupt when they behave in radical contradiction with institutional manifest roles or goals. Some examples of role deviation stand provided when individual judges lapse in their role, responsibility, or rectitude, or when media persons themselves indulge in fake news. But people also talk about the failures of societal and constitutional institutions as a whole in terms of moral corruption or levels of political corruptibility.

However, many a social theorist has pointed out the difficulties/complexities of such a description. First, institutions are remarkably heterogeneous; a demographic inventory is here not possible; but we all know that we may illustrate this heterogeneity—for example, political institutions (the legislative/administrative complex differ from market-based institutions), and these in turn from the institutions of learning and research, security agencies such as the armed forces, police and military, and para-military organisations. Second, even when they coalesce and function in concert to form hegemonies, the kinds of, and even motives for, institutional corruption vary greatly from one kind of institution to another. Third, expectations of their roles and function markedly differ within the institutions, across them, and relevant and even general publics.

This is not to say that institutional erosion does not occur, but one must study the extent of norm-deviation from a total collapse of all 'major' institutions. Some deviations from institutional norms (ethics or morality) are not necessarily corruption in a broad sense—say, legislative judicial activism or populism—but some are. Not all conflicts and disagreements are intrinsically disruptive of democracy or constitutional order, but some manifestly are. The hard work lies in understanding the nature and types, the causes, careers, and consequences, and costs and impacts of corruption on constitutional and social selves. Mere armchair judgments do not help very much!

Your comments remind me of Justice Venkataramiah's dissent in the Ramkrishnan decision. He says, if the executive conducts itself unworthily, people may turn to the legislature; if both the executive and the legislature transgress their limits, then people go to courts. What if this court itself begins to behave unlawfully, where would you go? Justice Venkataramiah also formulated ten questions on SAL.[23] Now, he is not just taking pot-shots at Justices Bhagwati or Krishna Iyer, he is genuinely worried. You must take judges seriously, they have a difficult job. In *Ramakrishnan's* case, justice according to the law is served well by accepting the statutory provision—the Company law provides only that when a company is wound up, the first charge is of

[23] *Sudipto Mazumdar vs. State of MP*, 1988 [2] SCALE 25.

secured creditors, then of unsecured creditors, workers do not figure in this. The Court, however, took a wider substantive view, holding that[24] workers have a right to be heard. The company, outside of its workers, is unimaginable. Therefore, in winding up, their interests also must be considered (Baxi 1983c).

Brother Venkataramiah asks, in effect, who guards the guardians?

Many answers are possible. One, that Justices must hold themselves bound by the law they declare and create. An allied answer it that they must uphold the constitutions established by law (the form of oath to decide without fear or favour and uphold the supremacy of the Constitution stands inscribed in the Third Schedule). A third answer is that Justices are bound by legal traditions which, *inter alia*, furnish canons of constitutional construction and a regime of internal judicial discipline. And when the law here fail people, social movements are justified in holding the judiciary accountable.

When law students and teachers, and the organised Bar and its leaders in India do not do this, they contribute to judicial domination. The law lords in England are said to tremble when they open the latest issue of the *Law Quarterly Review*. Why tremble? LQR has thirty to forty pages of scholarly comments on judicial decisions, and they look eagerly lest their names appear in those pages. But the power of the academic mind in ensuring judicial accountability is a relatively unknown cultural commodity in India. Very few people have developed the sustained hobby of interrogating judges. Then comes the media, especially those not beholden to State and market, which by and large spotlight spectacular injustices yet follow up their own stories and reinforce the demand for structural social change.

So, really, the cultural resource which would answer the question Venkataramiah poses is scarcely available in India. Only a couple of names have made it their life pursuit—that is what a jurist is—to study the accountability of judges. Venkataramiah did not have in mind what you have in mind, namely corruptibility or corruption. As I said in my *Antulay* book (Baxi 1989b), the problem of political

[24] Upendra Baxi note: The Bench comprised P. N. Bhagwati, O. Chinnappa Reddy, E. S. Venkataramiah, Baharul Islam, and Amarendra Nath Sen.

corruption is made difficult by the fact that we have very few means of establishing the act of corruption. When people lack the means to establish the fact of corruption, we think everybody to be corrupt. We think all politicians, parties, judges are corrupt, this is the mindset. If you seriously consider corruption structurally and not episodically, in what ways does our legal system enable articulation and action against corruption?

There are very few studies on the Prevention of Corruption Act, 1988. Impeachment of judges is another mechanism. Even during the Total Revolution Movement and after, no major national movement proposed a workable alternative law on corruption. Corruption is defined as monetary inducement for the performance of one's duty. Somebody has to sanction prosecution under the PCA. In the case of bureaucrats, the sanction comes from the Chief Secretary. Who can sanction prosecution when the chief minister is accused of violating the PCA? It is the Governor. It was President Venkataraman who asked me this question, he read the Antulay book and he said, who would be the competent authority in the case of the chief minister, you have not addressed this in your book. I was so damn pleased—somebody so exalted had read the book! We have not bothered much about this law, nor to define or understand the concept of corruption.

The only National Commission on corruption we had was in Nehru's time, which was led by K. Santhanam.[25] A past member of the Constituent Assembly, he produced the only national report on corruption in 1964. The kind of corruption he dealt with was bribery—one paid money to expedite processes. But there was hard evidence that people did not consider paying speed money as bribery. It occurred only when the payment of speed money did not result in getting the work done! Apparently, few people in law have read Munshi Premchand's classic short story set in colonial India, called *Namak ka Daroga*. The upright young man is appointed as a salt inspector, whose duties include prohibiting or punishing salt manufacturers who pay no excise duties. He is bewildered by his father's counsel that he should begin *uppar ki kamai* (earning income additionally by violating the law).

[25]'Report of the Committee on Prevention of Corruption', 1964.

Civility and Protest

LL: Earlier, you had mentioned that you would be against people doing a *dharna* outside the courts. Why do you take the judiciary outside the practices of democracy which are available to discipline other institutions?

UB: *Gherao* and *dharna* are Indian equivalents of what is now known internationally as the 'Occupy Now' resistance or social movements. In Indian public life, they were used first in the labour union movements and then in the classic Chipko movement, which may be regarded as a pioneering environment movement or women's movement, or both. These are traditional ways of articulation of political or social dissent in India, now somewhat modernised. We must also note that practices of enclosure also began fairly early against these forms, culminating in reasonable restrictions on the right of freedom of expression, even to the point of outlawing the gherao.

These practices do not necessarily constitute the best practices of democracy, anyway. Some political operatives are specialists in these techniques. These are techniques of coercion. I had a student leader whose main objective was to gherao me as the Vice-Chancellor of Delhi University for four-and-a-half years. She did not succeed. Not because I had protection, but because I was me! If you say gherao and dharna are coercive political processes, that can only mean that they are the articulation of responsible acts of freedom of speech and association, not that they are coercive processes that produce the immediate outcomes that a group desires.

In real life, of course, it is very difficult to make this distinction. Judges can be subjected to more severe criticism, look at my books, they should be! I have been told that *The Indian Supreme Court and Politics* (Baxi 1980) made many of them feel accountable in a way that they did not think they were. What is absolutely necessary is disciplined study and a reasonable (almost judicious) evaluation based on such a study, not merely personal opinion, allegation, or insinuations.

To each institution of governance, there might be corresponding modes of public influence and articulation. Dharna was initially considered inappropriate for the deliberative atmosphere of Parliament. Gherao, if directed at a business (say, the CEO of a company) is considered appropriate because it is the manifestation of a charter of demand, of making sure it is heard. Gherao does not take place suddenly. It takes place because of manifest acts of indifference. These are non-violent modes of drawing attention to a valid demand. Now the Supreme Court has declared coercive acts in ghearo as illegal.

If you can show that the judiciary or certain types of judges are behaving in a despotic way and are not heeding the demands voiced by different litigants and lawyers, then the convention is to approach the leaders of the Bar, the Bar Association, the Bar Council of India, and the Chief Justice, but to do a dharna on a random judicial decision is not considered a responsible way of relating to the court. These practices go against the very idea of public reason or deliberation that the court is supposed to embody. Courts may not be reduced to political parties.

What is the institutionally appropriate form of collective public protest is a very important question. Every year, in the midst of horrible snowfall in Washington, D.C., there is a pro-life protest against *Roe vs. Wade*.[26] The moral sentiment of this protest is the right to life. There is a certain moral technology of protest, of the ethics of protest. For example, a disappointed litigant can go on a fast unto death. The floor is open, but I would still say that deliberative institutions of democracy require situationally apt modes of protest. Lawyers' protests have sometimes breached this requirement, weakening the frame of deliberative democracy. Some lawyers have engaged in ill-mannered and unseemly behaviour, ostensibly in the name of protest. In the case of Justice Sunanda Bhandari, for instance, some lawyers jumped and squatted on her table and called her unseemly names. In the Allahabad High Court, some lawyers stormed the chamber of the Chief Justice and threw things around. There is, of course, a contempt of scandalising courts, which has been held as a reasonable restriction on the right to free speech.

[26] *Roe vs. Wade*, 410 U.S. 113 [1973].

Judges have to reason in public, they have to publish their judgments, they cannot answer back when they are criticised. They cannot use contempt powers to articulate their sense of hurt. If this is the kind of institution it is meant to be, you have to have appropriate modes of accountability in appraising the judicial role.

The 'Deep Mystery' of Bhopal Settlement?

AN: As far as the Bhopal settlement is concerned, you have been harshly critical of it. The most charitable interpretation that could be given is that the justices thought that a settlement now is better than no settlement at all. When we read your work on Bhopal, there is a sense of a little mystery.

> But it takes two to arrive at a settlement and the February settlement also involved a third entity: the Supreme Court of India, in many respects among the most admired and respected judicial institution in the contemporary world. And it is the co-optation of the Union of India and the Supreme Court which makes the February settlement a deep mystery. (Baxi and Dhanda 1990, xxxvi)

You also say that, 'MIC has entered the soul of Indian jurisprudence'. What is one trying to say? Is it the question of corruption that is being raised? A settlement has never been done before, it goes against all canons of judicial response. The rumours which swirl around it. Justice Pathak was elevated to the ICJ after the settlement.

UB: I have no means of verifying the stories which all of us have heard. Some believe what the bar says about the judges, but if one relies on such grapevine, there would be no Indian judge who is not corrupt. It is very easy for me to go the other route, to give authority to these rumours and allege a direct transactional connectivity between some judge and the settlement. But I would never have been able to live it down. They say all is fair in love and war, but I do not think this is fair. Indeed, it is quite unworthy.

I was asked to write about this, I did not. The whole national press was waiting for anything I would write on the Bhopal settlement. I was even given some *prima facie* evidence. I said, I do not want that, that is not the route I travel by. I travelled instead with the textuality and contextuality of the judgment. I assumed the *bona fides* of the judgment, that it was not a corrupt judicial decision. It was a bad judicial decision, but not one which was coerced or purchased. It was clear that it was an unfortunate settlement and my anger and criticism were directed at the fact that the Court did not take into account the Bhopal violated, who were properly before them arguing the case. There was no pre-decisional hearing before the settlement. We were there as parties to this litigation right from the district court upwards. If you had to have a settlement, it ought to have been a settlement in which every party participated, not just some select entities. That was the first ground of criticism.

The second ground of criticism was that the terms of settlement were extraordinary. Third, the settlement order itself mentions the ground of urgency for doing something for the victims. That was not persuasive at all, because we had managed to obtain interim relief. I had myself gone to V. P. Singh's durbar! As a citizen, I went there with three or four people from Bhopal. I said, Mr Prime Minster, give us interim relief as otherwise it will take a long time, how long can we wait? Singh said, go back to Bhopal. This was a big compliment he paid me. He thought I was living in Bhopal. He made me an honorary citizen of Bhopal! An ordinance was passed to grant interim relief. Even otherwise, there is a judgment of Justice Seth of Jabalpur High Court, who gave Rs 250 crore as interim allowance.[27] The Supreme Court stayed this. The Court could easily have said, we are concerned with the victims, the GOI and UCC must pay interim compensation. Then there would have been no urgency for settlement. So that was rhetoric, and bad rhetoric at that.

Even if there was urgency, there was no urgency to settle in such a horrendous way, granting criminal immunity to UCC, India undertaking to defend UCC worldwide on civil compensation claims.

---

[27] *Union Carbide Corp. vs. Union of India*, cf. Baxi 1990c.

The sovereign plaintiff would defend the defendant. It was clearly not a judicious settlement. Then your question comes: Why? I heard worse things than you heard, but I dismissed the rumours, I wouldn't even hear them. It is unworthy to say that the entire Bench was fixed or was directed to settle. It is not real. I had it conveyed to Rajiv Gandhi, the then Prime Minister (Bofors was going on), that the UOI had to pay a damage of three billion US dollars as per the Government of India's plaint before Judge Keenan[28] if, for any reason, this case is settled for any lower amount; Bofors would be peanuts compared to that. We had made whatever political communication was necessary.[29]

---

[28] See Baxi (1985g) for all documents filed by both the Union of India and Union Carbide before the United States District Court presided over by Judge John F. Keenan. The decision by Justice Keenan was in effect to send the case back to India on grounds of *forum non conveniens*. The proceedings before Justice Keenan are documented and the decision is analysed in Baxi (1986g). Also see Baxi (1990c) for an analytical introduction to key documents which were filed before the Indian courts, and which tell the story of the litigation before the Indian courts, from the district court to the Supreme Court.

[29] The correctness of the settlement was challenged through a curative petition filed in December 2010, which sought additional compensation of Rs 7,413 crore and a re-examination of the Apex Court's order dated 14 February 1989, where the compensation was fixed at US$ 470 million (INR 750 crore). The Union Government also claimed that the settlement was based on an incorrect assumption of the total number of deaths, injuries, and losses, and did not factor in the subsequent environmental degradation. As per the curative plea, the earlier figure for deaths was 3,000 and that for injury cases was 70,000. However, the actual number of deaths is 5,295 and the injury figure stands at 527,894. But the Supreme Court dismissed the curative petition, observing that, 'We are unsatisfied with the Union of India for not furnishing any rationale for raking up this issue more than two decades after the incident.' The Court went on to observe that the 'Union of India's claim for a "top up" has no foundations in any known legal principle. Either a settlement is valid or it is to be set aside in cases where it is vitiated by fraud. No such fraud has been pleaded by the Union, and their only contention relates to a of victims, injuries, and costs that were not contemplated at the time the number was effected' (see *Union of India vs. Union Carbide Corporation*, 2023 LiveLaw (SC) 200).

It is unlikely that Mr Gandhi and his government would have dared to talk to each one of these five judges and said: settle on the most favourable terms. Then the question is: Why? I have an answer which I have not published, but it makes sense. We worked on the Bhopal Ordinance by which India became the sovereign plaintiff surrogate for the victims. I was very much misunderstood for my limited role in doing this. Most people said that this is a violation of the legal profession and its rights. How do you trust the GOI, all these questions were raised. The technical problem was that Union Carbide Company was outside India's jurisdiction. All we could get was the Union Carbide India Limited (UCIL). But all actions were perpetrated by the main corporation and that was in Danbury. The essential bargain which was struck was that UCC would accept the jurisdiction of Indian courts in this case willingly. Then Judge Keenan directed that, despite it being a non-convenient forum, UCC must submit itself to India's jurisdiction and that India would ensure due process.

Now my guess is that Mr Fali Nariman and Mr K. Parasaran both played up the apprehensions of the Court. Any award the Supreme Court gave would have to go back to the garnishee court in the US for its enforcement. The garnishee court is akin to what we would here call the small causes court, and a judge of this court is in the hierarchy like a judge in the beggars' court in Delhi. It is my hunch that both the gentlemen conveyed to the judges that if they did not settle, no matter what order they gave, it would be subject to whatever the garnishee court judge decided. Now if this judge, on the ground that the 'due process' mandated by Judge Keenan was not adequately observed, knocked down your order, the Supreme Court of India would suffer an indignity which should not be permitted, they would have said. Therefore, the settlement was brought about.

I think it was collective institutional ego and a lack of judgment and a lack of appreciation of the enormity of injustice which led them to this point. I had done some research on the garnishee court and I was thinking I would argue it when it came up, but the time never came, they did not allow it to come up. If we had lost, we could have gone back to Keenan again, so the second element used to persuade the judges to settle must have been that this will lead to endless litigation. Even if the court passed an order on merits, and the garnishee court quibbled about due process, the rest of us would go back to Keenan, and the litigation could potentially go on endlessly, they might have argued. It is entirely conceivable that in that process of persuasion, Attorney General may have said the government was anxious to settle this matter. But we have to await better information.

For these institutional reasons, the Supreme Court of India may have decided to settle. Even so, the terms of settlement do not justify any of this. There is a hiatus between the decision to settle and the terms on which the settlement was arrived at. I have not given credence to many rumours that were floating around. No way was I going to enter that thicket. Just about anything can be said about anybody in this country, it is no holds barred. In your personal life it is hurtful, and it is hurtful when it comes to nourishing democratic institutions. I have been gossiped about endlessly and I find it terrifying. I do not know how to understand this as a social dimension of Indian life. The question still remains, why these unconscionable terms of settlement. The only answer is that the judges must have been presented with it by the lawyers as an agreed upon settlement between the GOI and UCC. The parties present were agreed on the terms of the settlement and the Court adopted it. They did not realise how unconscionable these terms were. True, the government is the party, it is the surrogate for the Bhopal victims. Whether these were good terms, who was going to decide?

The judges were shocked when I wrote an article in a newspaper, calling it 'The Second Bhopal Catastrophe' (Baxi 1989d). The first catastrophe was the MIC and the second catastrophe was the settlement. I quit the directorship of the ILI, I went to the CJI and said, I am leaving the Institute. He asked why, and I said this is what has happened. What you have done is unconscionable and I have to fight the court from outside. I cannot be the honorary director of a place of which the CJI is the ex-officio head. This issue has hurt me so deeply that I am going to fight this globally. And many Justices, including Justice Venkataramiah and Justice Ranganath Misra, made specific statements about me, though neither named me. Justice

Venkataramiah said, we are under great harassment by critics of the Bhopal judgment. Then Justice Ranganath Misra, in the final review judgment, had a long paragraph about me, once again without naming me. Eminent teachers of law and jurisprudence must know better than to criticise us on the Bhopal judgment, he wrote.

Then enters Justice Venkatachaliah as the pacifier of communities of dissent! The learned Justice partially admitted how wrong they were, but said, I cannot help the settlement, I will give you a post-decisional hearing. The court then said, criminal immunity is struck down.[30] We said, we demand three billion dollars, the people of Bhopal are not interested where the money comes from, this is the money we consider to be just compensation, order the GOI/Government of Madhya Pradesh to make good the remaining amount. They would not do that. This time around, UCC did not appear as the case had been settled. So we said, re-establish continuing mandamus over UCC. And if they do not play ball, confiscate their assets. To answer the question of why we were not given a hearing, they quoted *The Merchant of Venice*. They said: 'To do a great right, sometimes a little wrong is justified'. End of the story!

If this is a little wrong—a great deal more than one lakh people gassed and suffering, nearly 2,000 people killed, for which peanuts of compensation were to be distributed to the people of Bhopal. Seventeen wards in Jayaprakash Nagar and other innumerable folks suffered. They said, now all kinds of people are appearing from the woodwork, claiming to be affected.

I went to Bhopal on the third or fourth day after the catastrophe. I was in South Gujarat University at the time; I just took a plane and went to Bhopal. I saw contingency-fee lawyers right on the roadside. I saw bodies piled over each other in hospital or being taken in public trucks for mass cremation. I saw nobody was drinking water; nobody I thought I knew in Bhopal was in town. Until I located Professor Shyama Charan Dubey. He asked me if I had been eating and drinking there. He said, you should not have done that. That was the fear. The fear that you will be contaminated, even if you were not at the site.

[30] *Charanlal Sahu and Others vs. Union of India*, [1990] 1 SCC 613.

Maybe I was, in a manner of speaking, considering all the unexplained illnesses I struggled with later on. I went to the seventeen wards. I paid a special tribute to the station master who vacated the trains, but died himself. I stayed there two or three nights talking to people, they did not know me, I did not know them. I just had to do it, I had to go. It is kind of a strange happening, you would say.

After the judgment was delivered, I went to meet the Chair of the Tribunal, and said to him that what I had heard the officers were doing was simply unbelievable, it is so inhuman. I know that there were some exaggerated claims, but how would you produce a death certificate if you were staying in a basti? And people just perished on the streets as they choked with MIC. Then the compensation tribunals said, if you do not have a death certificate, it is okay, tell us how many people attended the funeral. Some of them had no family because they were porters moving around from here to there. They were out of breath and they were asked to come the next day, and then the day after, and they knew that whatever little work they could find, they would lose by having to keep up with these proceedings. I requested the Chairman, who was presiding over all the tribunals, that if you are having difficulties, technical ones, in fear of 'bogus' claims, if you need the assistance of the Supreme Court, we will file an interim order to expedite this relief.

I was so frustrated at the failures of the Chairman that I thought one could start proceedings against him for revocation of the degree he had got from an American university. It was a light-hearted thought, never executed! But revocation of degree has always interested me. In DU, I had actually moved for revocation of the degrees of certain kinds of people. I wanted to issue a show cause notice on the ground that every university has a right to withdraw the degree it confers. In DU, for example, in the Convocation, we say, 'Be you worthy in your conduct and speech of this degree.' So the ground of withdrawal is that in your speech and conduct, you have made yourself unworthy to retain this degree. The idea was to use this power in a symbolic manner of disapproving certain conduct, not to actually act instrumentally. Revocation of degrees is not a small matter; it actually involves individuals, families, social networks, and more. The idea of a university is to educate, not to punish, people.

An Excess of Love

AN: You were referring to newspaper articles. Were you always writing regularly in the papers right from the Delhi years?

UB: Oh yes. I was a prolific writer for several national newspapers and journals, including *The Hindu*, sometimes for *The Pioneer*, and always for *The Indian Express*. I wrote for *Mainstream* almost every second week; Nikhilda (Nikhil Chakravarty) would publish almost anything I wrote, and anything that he thought was worthy of publication: for instance, my Capital Foundation Lectures on social action litigation, legal education and research (Baxi 1996a). If I gave a speech somewhere, he would find out and publish it. Sometime ago, I met a group of Dalit scholars in Chennai who asked me why I stopped writing in *Mainstream*. They had clippings from the 1970s. Pratiksha has always been saying I should revive my newspaper writing—I say, it is too much work to write within a severe word limit of 1,000/1,100 words, and then to retrieve it all after so many years.

I always tried to beat the sub-editor. The whole job of sub-editors is to manage space and to take out offensive material. At that time, there was no word count on the computer, so I used to count the words and, of course, I cannot count beyond ten. I would request Prema, Pratiksha, and Viplav to count the words! It was hard work, you had to go over it again and again.

In a recent centre-page article in *The Indian Express* (Baxi 2008b), I took serious issue with the Supreme Court's denial of bail in the Jessica Lal murder case. I said, while no tears could be shed for the man who murdered Jessica Lal, judicial discretion ought not to be exercised to deny bail without good (rights-respecting) reasons. I would have had no problem if they had denied bail by giving reasons such as the heinousness of the murder, etc. But instead, the court denied bail because the trial court had convicted the accused and therefore the accused could not claim any longer the presumption of innocence, despite the fact that his appeal was pending. But is this fair? Once you are convicted—you know how it is—it takes ages in the High Court/Supreme Court to finally decide the case. There is no priority hearing because one is incarcerated. People detained during trial do not get out for long years, and in many cases even for decades, and then imagine being detained for all the time the appeal takes as well.

I wrote about it. Two district judges and one retired High Court judge (amongst others) wrote to me that they were very happy with the analysis! I only wanted to write in *Mainstream* about decisions that were not likely to be noticed, but needed to be highlighted. I wrote a lot of polemics; I fought with Bunker Roy in *Mainstream*, for instance, because he seemed to advocate a Code of Conduct to be legislated for NGOs. I had my differences with Nikhilda also. SAHMAT (Safdar Hashmi Memorial Trust) had put up a poster on the Ramayana which was considered offensive. I wrote an article in *Mainstream* about it with which Nikhilda disagreed, and yet published it. A professor of architecture from Harvard wanted to re-publish it on the twenty-fifth anniversary of SAHMAT, and wanted my permission.

I enjoyed writing for newspapers. I also appeared frequently on Doordarshan. I have done hundreds of shows. I interviewed, on a live show, Archibald Cox on the Watergate scandal. It was lots and lots of fun; and I remember how Cox was amazed that the intricacies of what was then called 'midnight massacre' in the White House were known to an Indian Professor of Law! I interviewed R. V. S. Peri Sastri, the then Chief Election Commissioner. I began my discussion with him by saying, when Shakuntala was beginning to worry about whether Dushyanta would come back to her or not, she said an excess of love makes you always fear the worst (*ati sneha paap shanki*). *Paap* literally means sin, but here we are better off using Foucault's phrase, 'the fear of fear'. Being afraid of certain consequences is one thing; being afraid of fear itself is another. Perhaps real (effective) power lies in producing a general, abstract, state of being permanently in fear. Or accepting fatalism as generated by domination—politics/governance as *prarabdha* (fate or destiny): I have sounded this theme differently in *Human Rights and Inhuman Wrongs* (Baxi 1994b).

So, I asked the Election Commissioner, are you in that state of nervous rationality? That was a way of starting, because you have to engage the viewer's attention—or interest—in the first two minutes. It was a very good interview, but it was my undoing! For six months, I received very nasty calls. Somebody thought the programme was party politically motivated. There are such rabid minds here. Every time I entered my house on campus, the phone would ring, and a man would start abusing and threatening me. It abated later, when I finally informed the police.

Not knowing abuses was my undoing in Surat, when Khushwant Singh came there. He said, I have come to Surat, tell me some Surati abuses! Then he asked me if he could use my car. I said, go ahead. In the evening, I had to introduce him to a big crowd. He said to them, this man Baxi, whom I know very well over long years, he does not deserve to be your VC. The audience did not know whether to applaud or not, but I guess internally some of them did applaud! He said, I came this morning and I asked him what the newly fashionable abuses in Surat are. He did not know any. So, I asked for his car and I went to the Surat railway station and stood there for half-an-hour. The coolies and the passengers hurled freshly minted slangs at each other, and I learnt these from them. And he took out his notebook and started reciting *gaalis*! I thought to myself, why am I here with him? Amazing guy, amazing, except for his sexism, which I do not like.

LL: Shahid Amin has a lovely paper, that very often we complain there is too much bad language. He says the problem is that it is not true, we have too little. Everything we have now is a limited repertoire, limited to consanguine relationships. He went through women's Urdu journals of the late nineteenth/early twentieth century and uncovered an entire range of *gaalis* that are imaginatively rich. They have a whole range of states of being which they express.

UB: I think the agenda for CSCS is building up! I have considerable respect for Shahid Amin (though the reverse may not be true), and I must accept as fact what he says about history! Maybe we need more abuse than what we have, but my problem is not with less or more, rather it is with civility, dignity, and the avoidance of sexism in public conversation. That is a normative question, not a historical one. But one may put it differently: one may say transgression is a virtue of the oppressed, not civility or the dignity of the other (the oppressor). If this is so, *gaalis* are means of resistance, an insignia of liberation, a protest against domination. Indeed, Ranajit Guha developed the notion of inversion of civility (an extension of the theory of) as subaltern, or even rebel, action (in the context of the 'Mutiny', or the First War of Independence) (Guha 1999). I may have said this earlier, but it bears reiteration. *The Elementary Aspects of Peasant Insurgency* is a great book, one that should be read many a time. No doubt, protest/ rebellion/emancipation may begin by a process of inversion, where a right to insult is equated with the right to free speech. But should it also end with this?

Of course, we may debate conceptions of 'political correctness'. Some even doubt the very concept itself. Indeed, some loathe this as a code of new censorship! I will not go into that debate now. But I know about cultural stereotypes that make certain racial, misogynist, anti-LGBTQI, and even about entire cultural groups which the dominant cultures wish to deride and degrade. I think that reasonable restrictions on free speech are necessary to uproot the experience of discrimination and internalisation of humiliation by the dominated or politically subordinated peoples. I agree that 'free speech' can be toxic when subordination or domination, or even hate speech aimed at or actually causing violence, is the sole aim or effect.

As against this, the votaries of an absolute right to freedom of speech say that no restriction on it can be justified; for them, the right to free speech includes the right to insult, offend, and to scandalise and shock. They are against any prior restraint and censorship, and especially emphasise the chilling effect on free speech and the shrinking of the space for dissent, and have a dim view of the State claiming to act in public interest.

Faced with fierce contentions on either side, constitutional courts in democratic societies tend to adopt a strict constitutional scrutiny of restrictions and under the proportionality doctrine of judicial review powers the State has to demonstrate a compelling State interest in regulation. Whether, how and what they do is good enough, remains a constant source of dialogue and discontent in any given place and circumstance, and the issue gets even more complex when one looks at blasphemy and free speech and faith versus law. When free speech is considered a 'weapon of the weak'—insult, abuse, and offence as a strategy of inversion—it is often considered an unqualified good in itself, and any restriction of it as a signature of uncivility that invites the repression of the State or society! These sorts of interrogations relate not so much to the value of unrestricted speech, but concern the power to impose censorship and the inner order of the violence inherent to the administration of the law.

LL: Do you have your newspaper articles with you?

UB: Nikhilda used to send me copies from *Mainstream*. Newspapers I do not have, because I used to pass it around. A few years ago, I destroyed a mountain of reprints! It was too much to keep. Perishable stuff. In one of my periodic visits to Warwick, upon superannuation, a student from India gave me a scanned collection of *Lex et juris*, which Mahesh Jethmalani produced from Bombay, saying this was with the compliments of his father, a lawyer, who had maintained a few of the articles. How touching! I will send these to you, if any use. I also worked with Rani Jethmalani, an astonishing warrior against all forms of violence against women, in the formation of what I named as WARLAW (Women's Action for Law and Legal Action for Women)—she did not agree with the term 'lawfare' after 'warfare', and we published for many years a journal named *Kali's Yuga*, it also has a number of my articles.

LL: Contrast this with Rajeev Dhavan's office—anything he has written is there in bound volumes. Thirty-six volumes.

UB: Rajeev is legendary in many ways! Yes, I have seen the first few volumes, now there must be many more. It is a good way of record-keeping and keeping together all one writes. A quick check is thus provided by devices such as innovated by Rajeev. A kind of early digital-era archive.

But if I may venture into pop psychology: to refer to what you have written requires a sense of self, or continuity of self. If you do not have a high sense of self-esteem and if you think what you are doing is perishable anyway, then it is hard to keep track of your writing. In oral conversations, sometimes you repeat yourself. I hate to repeat myself in my writing. I really get very angry with myself. But I rarely read what I have written. Now I realise that some of what I have said earlier is not too bad, it might be relevant. The Marx book, for instance. I had to revise it, for which I read it again, and I liked what I read. It is a book I really am proud of, despite the many typos and textual glitches!

This is the only time when I find particular delight in going back to Althusser, Poulantzas, Lukacs, Gramsci, etc. These names are hardly used, so I look back and insert some of the literature. If I find sentences which are repeated in my writing, I get most upset. I never even kept class notes. As a result, every time I was made to read afresh. It is very good training. If you ever want to teach, never keep class notes. Make it a point to discard them.

Julius (Stone) used to teach using half-slips of paper, which he kept in stacks. He used to go back to them, though he prepared fresh notes for each class. I would go to his office before class and he would be a nervous heap. I asked him once, you are a giant in your field, and you are nervous in class? He said it was because it was a new audience each time. I asked him why he went back to his own notes, and he said he did not want to deprive his students of whatever might have been of some significance when he studied this thing earlier on. He said, in order to give my best, I have to recall what I did earlier. And if I cannot have vivid physical recall, I must have my notes. Amazing chap. Some of us just go and fire in the air! For example, every time we did *Delgamuukw* in class, I found something which I had never noticed before. It is amazing. You can never read a text once and for all. You grow with it. Other things happen to you, you grow up, you bring new meanings to it. But it is labour-intensive. Teaching/learning are manifestations of continuity with the past, but everyone has to learn the art of speaking to the future also. Julius Stone used to call legal education the high art of speaking to the future. How today, and for many generations to come, artificial intelligence will reshape our memory and this high art of speaking to the future is probably worth some understanding. Will freedom as such survive the onslaughts of AI?

THIRTEEN

Vice-Chancellorship and the Mandal Years

Warwick Activism

LL: From the time you went to Warwick, one sees a certain kind of international engagement which happens in your writing as well as in your activism. There is also a certain density that comes into your writing in the Warwick years.

UB: How nice! So earlier, I was lucid!

One of the reasons I decided to go to Warwick was that I had a long innings in Delhi University administration: also, a long innings in activist work, and I wanted to put myself together, to put on a reflective hat. I began to see the complexity of things, which you cannot always afford to see even in struggle. If you are working with people, you cannot always draw fine distinctions, it disturbs solidarity. When you work with the civil liberties movement, it is one kind of thing; when you sit back, you are free to raise questions. So, my real engagement began! I was not considered a human rights scholar, I had never taught a human rights course before. I was never allocated constitutional law to teach in Delhi University! The only thing I had written was 'The

Little Done, The Vast Undone' (Baxi 1967a), and *The Indian Supreme Court and Politics* (Baxi 1980), which my colleagues said were not *about* constitutional law! I did not have a textbook on the subject in multiple editions like M. P. Jain (2018), etc.

Then I wrote a huge introduction to Justice K. K. Mathew's book of essays and excerpts from judgments, but that was not considered constitutional law either. I could have got my way, but everybody wanted to teach constitutional law, so I ended up teaching evidence, sales tax, administrative law, etc. I learnt a lot of law. I am grateful I taught these subjects. Otherwise, you cannot do any significant legal theory in India.

I never sought to teach human rights, I did not understand the entire framework. International law was also over-subscribed, so I rarely got to teach it. So, when Burns Weston and Stephen Marks were editing the Special Issue on human rights in *Iowa Law Review*, they said, we have not heard you say anything important about the future of human rights. *The Future of Human Rights* was thus born. It appeared first as an article in *Iowa Law Review* (Baxi 1998). It was that article which became a book. I thought I should bring back that article and make an Honest Reader's Guide to *The Future of Human Rights*. Many people say it is too complex. It got a lot of attention. Some people said, you should enlarge it. And I have done so, in large ways, but the basic structure remains! Now, a fourth edition is in press, expected in 2023.

In between, I also became very interested in the Permanent Peoples' Tribunal,[1] based on Bertrand Russell's Stockholm Tribunal

[1]The Permanent Peoples' Tribunal (PPT) was established on 24 June 1979 in Bologna, on the basis of the framework defined in the Universal Declaration of the Rights of Peoples proclaimed in Algiers on 4 July 1976, to be: 'a tribune of visibility, of the right to speak, of the affirmation of the rights of peoples exposed to severe and systematic violations by public and private actors, at national and international levels, who have no possibility of referring and having access to competent organs of the organised international community; an instrument of explicitation and verification of the existence, the severity, the responsibilities, and impunity of the concrete violations, as well as of the due measures of justice and reparation; a witness and promoter

(Russell and Sartre 1968). I was very interested in this Tribunal doing a series of hearings on mass industrial disasters. We organised one in Bhopal, in which Shabana Azmi, Swami Agnivesh, and others participated.[2] We organised a second one in London.[3] That was my extension of the Bhopal social action, because it needed to be reiterated in the British context.

A student of Indian origin, Himanshu Raj Sharma, was somewhat active already re Bhopal, and I requested him to work on commerce, justice, and mass torts. Then a student at Washington College of Law, he later worked as a lawyer in the New York Bar, and took Bhopal litigation to a new height by claiming UCC and their successors' liability to clean-up of toxic wastes, air and water pollution, and its acute health effects. Raj is still working on some of this. Bhopal is always, in one way or the other, with me wherever I go. So, activism in my Warwick days was in a sense a continuation of what had gone before.

The other big change was the Iraq war, the Second Gulf War. We held a tribunal on war crimes committed by the British government (Shiner and Williams 2008). This was partly due to the effort of an organisation called Peacerights, along with a brilliant barrister named Phil Shiner. We decided to do a tribunal with eight colleagues from Europe and America. Christine Chinkin of LSE, William Schwabas, and other very eminent people were involved;[4] I was the relatively

---

of research aimed at filling the institutional and doctrinal gaps in existing international law' (Permanent People's Tribunal Statute 1979).

[2]Twentieth Permanent Peoples' Tribunal on Industrial risks and human rights I (Bhopal, 19–23 October 1992).

[3]Twenty-first Permanent Peoples' Tribunal on Industrial risks and human rights II (London, 28 November–2 December 1992). Judgment available at http://permanentpeoplestribunal.org/21-industrial-hazards-and-human-rights-bhopal-ii-london-28-november-2-december-1994/?lang=en (accessed May 2022).

[4]The other members of the Tribunal were Dr Andrew Williams of Warwick University's law department; William Schabas, Professor of human rights law at the National University of Ireland, Galway; Christine Chinkin, Professor of international law at the London School of Economics;

unknown commodity. I had vacated the field of international law a long time ago in terms of writing. But people knew me, and I also lent it a kind of colour! We met at the LSE for a day-and-a-half, and people agreed that we should keep it tightly focused on technical international law regarding the violation of the international law of war, on war crimes, and on crimes against humanity as defined by ICC. We were not going to go into the question of the legality of invasion. We wanted to file the evidence before an ICC prosecutor in The Hague under the statute of the Rome Convention. The prosecutor is under a duty to receive such submissions and make investigations, either by asking the concerned State to report investigations, or by going to the judges in chamber and seeking their permission to proceed independently, regardless of the particular State's cooperation. Of course, this is only possible if the State is a member party.

Very few of us thought the ICC would act on this. It was a lot of work. It took us about eleven months to compile the dossier. Evidence which was available, from the internet and otherwise—there were five volumes of that. We started in 2003 alongside the invasion. It was a very poignant experience. There was an organisation of young students and doctors named Iraq Body Count.[5] Many other NGOs from Iraq and elsewhere testified. It was heartrending. The use of cluster bombs because the war office had to get rid of them—there was no market for them, no major war, and they were occupying space in the godown. When cluster bombs explode, they fragment human bodies into several pieces. If you survive, you are in a terrible state.

We (mainly Professor Andrew Williams and Dr Solange Mouthaan) worked for six to eight months on this report and we filed it before the ICC. Nothing happened. Then the Prosecutor, Luis

---

Bill Bowring, Professor of human rights and international law at London Metropolitan University; René Provost, Associate Professor, Faculty of Law, McGill University, Canada; Paul Tavernier, Professor at the Faculté Jean Monnet; Nick Grief, Steele Raymond Professor of law and Head of the School of Finance and Law at the University of Bournemouth; and Guy Goodwin-Gill, barrister, senior research fellow, All Souls College Oxford.

[5] https://www.iraqbodycount.org/(accessed May 2022).

Moreno Ocampo, for the first time, gave reasons on why he could open prosecution, in effect entrusting the report to the British government, which was not going to do anything about it. We received good press, and we kept pressing them, we did not give up. I am not as intensely involved in the pursuit as I am not there now. Since the USA was not a party to the Rome Treaty, we worked out a notion of constructive and joint responsibility, trying to use customary international law. It was really good work. All my international law came back. Taught law is tough law, as Dean Roscoe Pound used to say. If you teach it well, it never goes out of the hard drive of your memory.

I also worked with David Bergman, who organised a public movement against a train crash where some people died, and lots were injured.[6] His Centre for Corporate Accountability repudiated the claim that in this public-private arrangement, nobody was responsible. Bergman questioned that kind of privatisation model in Britain. Somebody is responsible for infrastructure, somebody for operations, somebody for planning routes. The CEOs were paid several hundred thousand pounds in salaries in each of these companies. Yet accidents continued to occur.

At the Centre for Corporate Accountability, we worked on making corporate manslaughter an offence under British law. He carried out a lot of lobbying work, conducted seminars, and so on. Tony Blair promised to do something, but like all good politicians, did not follow it up. The Bill has now almost become a law (Corporate Manslaughter and Corporate Homicide Act 2007). I decided that I do not want to be an activist of the sort I was not in India in Britain. It was not a society I fully understood. It was not a society on which I could speak about countering injustice with as much assurance as I could in India. I soon realised that in some ways, it was the most extraordinary society in the world. It has found ways of containing and managing

[6]The Hatfield rail crash was a railway accident that occurred on 17 October 2000 at Hatfield, Hertfordshire, UK. Caused by a metal fatigue-induced derailment, it killed four people and injured more than seventy others. Railtrack was found guilty of breaching health and safety laws in 2005. On Bergman's Bhopal work, see Chapter 11.

radical dissent in a way no other country has. Radical dissent is not a real possibility. They manage it through a variety of mechanisms, the Oxbridge connection (civil service), monarchy, enormous creation of entertainment industry-reality shows, etc. Intra-system protest and resistance is allowed, but this is subject to some well-maintained red lines that no one should cross and raise questions about the political and economic structuring of society.

You will all have your stories about Warwick. It would be interesting if there is a forum which deals with how Warwick experiences transformed us as we tried to change the institutional system. Our Law and Development programme attracted some gifted and bright minds. I learnt a very great deal from the LLM class at Warwick. Also, from several Ph.D. scholars, who somehow flocked to me. To talk about this experience will take another set of conversations. But perhaps some aspects appear later.

Oversleeping is a Crime against Humanity

LL: How many hours do you sleep a day?

UB: Does it really matter, Lawrence! But yes, my sleeping hours vary. When I was younger, when I had no medicines to take, I used to work till 4–4.15 in the morning, and would be up again by 7.30–7.45. If it was a minute later, my day would be disoriented, I would think I had overslept. But these last few years, with the hundreds of medicines I take, I get to bed by around 11.30–11.45—this used to be unusual for me—and wake up around 3.15–3.30 or a quarter to four.

LL: Three hours?

UB: I think oversleeping is a crime. What matters is sound sleep, not long sleep! Sleeping long hours is a crime against humanity. Present company included!

I must also add that the Indian Supreme Court has, in 2012, held in the Baba Ramdev case that there is a fundamental right to sleep—this may be music to some ears! This right emanates from Article 21.

As an individual right, it emerges as an anti-torture right as in sleep deprivation, where an individual is punished for drooping eyes or has to compulsorily stay awake under all circumstances; as a collective right, it is uncertain whether it extends to sleeping in public places! Also, is it not frivolous or vexatious to wonder whether the Court ruled that Article 21 contemplates a component right to snore! The human right to dream, and perhaps to have nightmares, is a very important question in this Guantanamo and post-liberal world; important also remains the question of how the 'right' to hallucinate in public, if it were to exist, is compatible with the right to sleep.

Feudalism and Academic Power

LL: The VC years and leading up to the Mandal experience. And South Gujarat.

UB: I keep trying to distract you, but you keep coming back to the point! Delhi was my first major experience after Sydney of teaching and of campus life. It was a very different experience. Sydney was not a political society. The University was not an overtly political system. There were no trade unions from different parties with teachers and students and members and so on. So, for me, Delhi was my first experience of a University as a sub-political system. This is a mighty one, because by the time I left Delhi, the University had 250,000 students and ninety colleges. By the time I left the office of Vice-Chancellor, we had enlarged some forty-five departments into ninety departments. Of course, as VC, I was burdened by the sheer size of, and the distance between the locations of, the different institutions; and by the politics—student unions, *karmachari* unions, teachers' unions, whatnot. There was a professors' forum, which I tried to revive.

I was burdened by the scale and political complexity of this system. When I was in office, I had to receive all kinds of people, visiting academic dignitaries, among others. One day, after the first one-and-a-half years of Vice-Chancellorship, I felt truly liberated when I met a person who was associated with the University of Iran. It turned out that he was the VC of all the Iranian universities. He said he must have 600,000 students. I made the mistake of asking him, do you have any leisure time and what do you do in your leisure time? He said, the Iranian revolutionary council has entrusted me with the job of Islamising science and technology. I had no problems compared to that. DU's problems did not exist, compared to the kinds of problems he had to face! So, after that, like Bertie Wooster, I had a song on my lips, *tra-la-la,* without a care in the world. It's all relative!

What struck me, apart from the political complexity, was the semi-feudal nature of university systems. By semi-feudal, I mean the kind of distinctive hierarchy—a professor who is a Head of Department is head for life. There is an enormous accumulation of impunity. This was my experience in Bombay and in Surat; in fact, most state universities have permanent heads of department. In Delhi, fortunately, K. N. Raj[7] carried out some fundamental reforms. One of them was to rotate headships. You take it by turn, according to seniority. Rotating headships often creates its own quota of problems, but the removal of the sole discretion of the Dean and Head offsets these and associated problems.

People have their own followers. The Dean would have some teachers always in his office, whether they worked or not, carrying tales about other colleagues, a kind of durbar. You cannot imagine a feudal system without a royal court. Holding court with people sitting around. Whether they were doing any work, academic, administrative, scientific, was not the question. There were all kinds of trade-offs with these retainers. It struck me that you should have no hierarchy except in a functional way, in which certain people are charged with taking decisions, maybe even charged with taking decisions by turn. But most Indian Universities are feudal; there is no difference of kind but

[7]Kakkadan Nandanath Raj (1924–2010), economist, associated with some of India's early Five-Year Plans, later advisor to several prime ministers. Vice-Chancellor of Delhi University (1969–1970), instrumental in setting up the Delhi School of Economics and the Centre for Development Studies, Kerala.

of degree, and that difference does matter, even when disciplining of discretion remains the goal. In such a milieu, what we know today as a culture of principled dissent and difference does not grow.

I was puzzled by this. But I made a conscious decision to de-feudalise the university and its administration. During my first and second years as Dean of the Law Faculty—I was third in terms of seniority in the law school—I decided to be ruggedly democratic: everything was transparent, no retainers, no kitchen cabinet, I was not a king. The only rule was, you want to criticise me, criticise me upfront. Do not hesitate, I am not superhuman, I may be hurt, but that is all right. So I will also speak to you straight, no quarters given. It worked. Not with all people. I used to bring out a monthly newsletter called *Outlaw* (see Chapter 7). I said, if anyone wants to criticise me in writing, I will print it. I insisted on using first names in my classes and with my colleagues. The marker of our relationships cannot be titles such as Dr, Prof., etc. I practised small steps of communicative courtesy. It worked.

An alternative culture was created. When I became VC, the press asked me what my priorities were. When I reached my Delhi University campus home from the Indian Law Institute when the TV had apparently beamed my appointment, the whole area was crowded with reporters, etc. It was a big event in a town like Delhi. They asked me what my priorities were, and I said I wanted to de-feudalise the university administration. When they asked, do you have any other priorities, I said, I have seen many people with long faces and misery inscribed on their foreheads, so I want more smiling faces on campus. Tension-free complexions. Campuses must be happy communities, not conspiratorial ones!

While I was still new in the Law Faculty, Margaret Mead came to DU. Professor Mead had expressed a desire to meet with me, to everybody's surprise, so Sarup Singh invited me to a lawn tea meeting with very senior professors. The reason Margaret wanted to meet me was because her informant in Papua-New Guinea was my student, Bernard Narokobi—I mentioned him earlier (see Chapter 4). She was an elderly person with a walking stick, a brilliant person, but in conversation, it turned out she was very unhappy because each departmental head wanted her to come to their department. She said, you know what these various heads of department are trying to do to me? She said, they continue to talk about me in my presence and they are fighting over my time. Whom I will have tea with first, which building I shall go to, treating me not as a colleague, but as a piece of real estate. She got angry and then she said, Baxi, I do not remember which of my husbands used to tell me this, but one of them used to tell me that if you want money, you do not go to the university, if you want power, you do not go to the university, the only reason you go to the university is if you like thinking and reading and writing. Money and power are not consistent with a university career.

I was struck by this line. I used to repeat it. What power do you have in a university? To recruit somebody, to raise somebody's marks, to give jobs, to make somebody from temporary to permanent employee. I would say, you are kidding yourself if you think this is power. This is the lowest form of power. You ask anybody, they will laugh at you. I said to my colleagues, if you are power hungry, you should be elsewhere. As Vladimir Lenin used to say, serious politics does not begin with thousands, or ten thousand, but with hundreds of thousands of people. With the captive audience of a maximum of 100 in a classroom, one does not capture or exercise sovereign power of a State or peoples. Of course, there are some minor powers—disciplinary and investigative powers (police power)—and such powers are often vertically connected with the State or sovereign powers. But such powers are not always easy to exercise, and when exercised they can be questioned in courts, which may not always endorse university action. There are other ways to convert disciplinary power into, at best, a soft power—the power of persuasion, rather than power as a hammer.

One can be a person of influence, though not a person of power. Lewis Coser, one of the major protagonists of conflict theory, talking about the manifest and latent functions of social conflict, differentiated between power and influence. He instanced Einstein and Marx as having great influence, but no power. We can expand the list in Third World terms referring, for example, to Nelson Mandela (in Robben Island prison for a little over two decades) and Mahatma Gandhi.

Good and great scholars can provide leadership through influence, though not through power.

The paradoxes of power are endless. Power goes with the insecurity of those at the helm of governance; the more power one has, the more paranoid about the security of that power one becomes. At its very height, power also becomes vulnerability, whereas influence is in the long run more abiding.

For example, if a senior person (senior, but not productive) has a younger colleague who is productive and gets invited to another place, or does a Ph.D. in the Sorbonne and comes and teaches in the university, then your power as the senior person lies in preventing the younger person from joining your university or presenting in a conference. When younger colleagues came to me with stories such as this, I talked to the principal, I talked to the governing body, I said, I will never interfere with what you do, but if you do not allow space for bright young people to grow, I will come down on you very hard. I had sufficient dialogical legitimacy, I never had to invoke the residual emergency power which the VC had. So, when I came to office these were my two priorities, and when I left office, to a large extent the feudal culture was mitigated.

Emergency Powers

UB (***contd***): Emergency powers have been the very being of a Vice-Chancellor. I announced in the academic council that there would be no use of emergency powers in my tenure because a University is the life of many minds where matters should be decided upon by dialogue, and where necessary, by voting. A calendar of monthly meetings of the Academic and Executive Council was set up. I never used my emergency powers as Vice-Chancellor except to approve Ph.D.s and results, for there it was a question of careers.

I resisted using emergency powers, though there were occasions when it was urged. That was my moral strength, which was sought to be converted into all kinds of politics. May I here only recall one incident. Endless discussions were held on the demands of DUTA for readership in colleges. Ultimately the University had created a new category called Lecturer in Reader's grade before my time. There was a revised salary, but the designation of Readership was withheld. The pressure for a full Reader's designation and grade was revived and I requested Professor Abad Ahmed to be a one-person committee to talk with teachers, and I was glad that he agreed with my view that it was an act of academic injustice. After some time, we passed an ordinance and said, all Lecturers of Readers' grade will appear for an interview before a newly constituted committee and then will be given, based on the interview outcome, the status of a Reader. And the princes at DU felt betrayed! There was great opposition from Heads of Departments and Professoriate, overlooking the fact that a little over half the departments comprised former college teachers, and in appointments to colleges, it was customary for the Dean to appoint (other things being equal) their own students. In the UGC merit promotion scheme for University teachers, the process was that from Lecturer, you can become Reader, from Reader you can become Professor, all by way of interviews, of course, but it was your right to be interviewed for a promotion. If you were not promoted in one year, the next year you had to promote the person. The ordinance was approved by the Visitor, the President, but before he did that, an HRD Jt Secretary came to my house to ascertain my own position: If the Visitor did not approve it, what would be my position? I said, I want to remove academic injustice. If the Visitor does not approve it, I go out of this job. It was passed. The result was different internally: many took to calling me a DUTA Vice-Chancellor. A myth was created by those opposed to this move that it would cause an additional financial burden, whereas there was no change in the salary!

Mandal

UB (*contd*): I took office as Vice-Chancellor of DU in May. In September came the Mandal decision.[8] Obviously it was a bombshell. The students were worried. The newspaper announcement stunned everybody. Then the anti-reservation movement started on campus. From the third day or so, from one end of the road called the University Road up to 2.5 kilometres on, there was an ocean of student faces, all part of the university. Police came and said, give us permission to disperse them. I said, nothing doing. They said, they want you to address them. I said, fine.

I climbed atop the roof of the police car (as the mass of students could not see me, nor I them) and used their loudspeaker and spoke into the mike. I said, if you are unhappy about this—this is a national policy decision—I can do very little as Vice-Chancellor of the university. But I can at least convey your protest in a dignified way to the government and ask them to enter into negotiations with you. I can facilitate an interview with whoever you want. I said, if you want to continue on the path of protest, that is your right. But it has to be the right of everybody, including people who want these reservations, and you shall not intimidate them as long as I am Vice-Chancellor of this university.

I said, I want to make this very clear: I will respect your rights as long as you respect others' rights. There was a huge thunderous applause when everything was over. After that, during the entire Mandal agitation, the police called me to address the crowds: whether it was in Hauz Khas, South Delhi, or East Delhi. I drove my own official car and spoke to them, the same thing, more or less. The crowds did behave as far as I could see. It was then a wholly politically

[8]This refers to the decision of the V.P. Singh-led administration to implement the recommendations of the Mandal Commission, which argued for a reservation of 27 per cent only for other backward castes (OBC) in higher education and employment (Report of the Backward Classes Commission 1980).

appropriated issue—campus teachers' unions, students' unions, all were involved. The movement grew and grew. They started a *dharna* and *chakajam*. *Chakajam* means road blocks, and they put up several in the city, including near AIIMS. I addressed a huge crowd and said, move back a few feet because you have a duty to those in medical emergency. And they did. In a sense, there was a feeling that I was supporting them. For whatever reason, they listened to me.

This was the time that everybody seemed to have sent their minds on sabbatical! Long sabbatical! Either you were pro- or anti-reservation. In one of my articles, I said I was neither pro- nor anti-, I said, this is an emptiness of the mind which means the university ceases to exist and minds cease to function (Baxi 1986d). Then I said, the Mandal report came out ten years ago, there were six people in India (including myself) who had read it: if, by reading the report, you mean writing about it. I said, you have not read the Mandal Commission Report and you are taking pro- and anti-positions. This turned out to be an invitation to commercial publishers to violate GOI copyright and, after that appeared, everybody had a copy of the Mandal report. There was, of course, a lot of orchestrated violence, so people came and complained that backward-class students were being harassed. On the other side, they said they are beating us up. It was terrible.

The movement became nation-wide. There was Rajiv Goswami,[9] who was supposed to have self-immolated. Everybody knows he was made to set himself on fire. So, I made a number of trips to Safdarjung hospital (which was India's leading burns treatment hospital), his father was a postmaster and he had a large number of brothers and sisters, they were in a piteous condition, they could not afford medical care. There was no provision for the university to provide medical assistance. I said, nothing doing, the university shall bear the expenses. The man had 80 per cent burns. He deserves a better future. He later became DUSU President.

[9] Rajiv Goswami was a commerce student from Deshbandhu College, who the media reported as attempting self-immolation as a mark of protest against the decision to implement the Mandal Commision Recommendations.

The political parties during Mandal were quite fully engaged. Once the *chota* Minister for Education, Chimanbhai Mehta, a Gandhian, asked me to meet him. He said, I hear all kinds of intelligence reports, the situation is getting out of hand, it is becoming explosive. One of the crazy ideas in circulation was that there were terrorists getting into the hostels. I said, this is too much, this scare scenario. Violence was everywhere, emotions were charged. Once, at one o'clock, the police came and said, students are burning a jeep and throwing stones, so I went, and I harangued them publicly. I said, are you not ashamed? They went back. They could have thrown a stone at me, I am not a hero, but I was just so angry. The situation was getting very tense.

To cut a long story short, there came a time when some plot was afoot. The Police Commissioner and some other people who respected me alerted me that a crowd of 4,000–5,000 people would come on campus on Sunday with the intention of burning the library down. I was told two ministers might be a part of the group. I was terrified. Who was I to go to? I took my Fiat and went to V. P. Singh's secretary and, subsequently, to the Prime Minister's home. They would not let me in. I said, I will stay here all night until I can meet him, this is a crisis situation. Atal Bihari Vajpayee came just then to meet V. P. Singh, and he said: *Chaliye Baxi saab, chaliye chaliye*. Everybody knows everybody in Delhi, it is an overblown village! V. P. Singh was saying, what Professor Baxi, we have not met at all since I took office. I said, this is not the time to talk about it. I have the following information. He said, what are your sources? I said, I will not tell you, the intention is to do damage to the library. I said, you have to do something, put the fire brigade on alert, and so on. This is not the time for further talk. Check it out with your colleagues. So far, this conversation is confidential between the two of us, but this is an important matter concerning the well-being of the university and, Mr Prime Minister, the first thing I will do when I go back to the university is to put this down in writing and swear to it before a notary (I always do this when I have a meeting with somebody, I said). If something happens to the university tomorrow, it will become public knowledge that I had come to you. I normally do not go to meet politicians, but this time I had to relax my own scruples, as I did not want to go down in history as the man who stood by and watched while his precious library burned.

He talked to one of the ministers and I could see his face change. He said, go write your minutes. I wrote the minutes, but there was no time for a notary and all that. That whole night, I had my heart in my mouth. I had to tell Prema. The burden the family had to bear because of the pressures of this office was terrible. Pratiksha and Viplav were there, they were college-going kids. Viplav had suffered a huge personal loss of a lovely friend because of the Mandal agitation, he lost his life in an accident. Viplav was very upset. He said, why are you not doing something? It was tough for everyone. For decision-makers, it was particularly tough.

The next day, I kept up with the relevant information networks, and I knew that a crowd had assembled near Kamla Nagar, 2 kilometres from the campus, and that they were marching. At twelve o'clock, they were stopped by the police. Five MPs were arrested and taken to the Civil Lines police station. The crowd was not allowed to proceed. I said, *bach gaye baba, bach gaye*. At six o'clock, I received a call on my direct line. I said, who is this, and a person said, *mein Vishwanath bol rahan hoon*. He said, sensing my disorientation, I am Vishwanath Pratap Singh speaking. He asked: is everything all right, is your library safe? I said, I am very grateful to you for saving the university from a disaster. He said, I was only doing my duty, but I would not have been able to do it if you had not gatecrashed my house. I said, I will not apologise for that, because it was a matter of life and death. That is the only conversation I had with him as the Head of the University.

I was taking public positions. *The Indian Express*, rightly, carried a short article by me saying the Court should issue a stay order—contrary to their earlier order declining judicial intervention, they constituted a larger bench. It was publicly known that my article did the trick! But I do not think that my arguments at all impacted on the learned Justices; they acted in their own wisdom, as they always do and should do. Then Inder (Kumar) Gujral called me and said I should see him, 'off the record', he added, because he knew that I met, as a matter of principle, with no ministers. I met him one afternoon and he straightway said, 'the Prime Minister is extremely unhappy with you and I do not like any such discord or misunderstanding'. I asked him to tell me, what can I do? He said, DU is the epicentre of the anti-Mandal movement. And you have been responsible in part for this happening. Out of the goodness of his heart, he had offered mediation—to 'speak to Vishwanath-*ji*', whom he had tried to persuade to talk to me, but obviously the Prime Minister had been angry. I could see Inder's face fall. He said, I tried my best, but the Prime Minister is so angry, he doesn't want to see you. But later, he did meet with me when I gatecrashed: and he telephoned me the next day to enquire whether everything had been all right with the University.

Pressures were growing on me from political parties, leaders, all quarters. Earlier, I had written an account of what was happening in DU and sent it to the Visitor and Chancellor—R. Venkataraman and Shankar Dayal Sharma. This letter had reached the Education Minister and the Prime Minister! That is why he was so angry. I must have talked in it about political interference, and so on. It was seen as a letter of grievance to the President of India. The Visitor and the Chancellor called me to see them after they got my letter. They both communicated to me in different ways that I was not to bother to write to them as they knew what I was doing, and they wished there were more Vice-Chancellors like me in India! But to the political mind, it was seen as me seeking support from other sources. This was utter drivel!

Whenever I met V. P. Singh later, he would tell me (with a twinkle in the eye) that I was responsible for the downfall of his government! His point was that he was trying to do social justice and that people like me ought to have supported him. I did: I welcomed the report as a scholar and a teacher, I studied Mandal and I had written about it six years prior to all this (Baxi 1985d, 1985e, 1986d, 1990c), but that got drowned in the fact that I was respecting the freedom of dissent of the students. As long as they were non-violent, non-sexist, not anti-backward class, fine, have a dialogue, go on *dharna*, have a carnival of protest. It is my job to protect the campus. Universities are the only sites in India where you can speak freely, it is the function of the university. My job as ringmaster was to manage that space. A number of people were arrested, and I personally went and got them released. I was called a political Vice-Chancellor, destabilising the government. I was not popular, either with the ruling party, or with the opposition party, or with the progressive teachers. Everybody thought I should be on one side or the other. My positions were far more nuanced, my mind was not on sabbatical, I had to think all the time. It was a baptism by fire. Nothing in my life had prepared me, and no other Vice-Chancellor of DU had been subjected to this in their first six months of office. It was a national crisis, but it got sorted out through the court and I got a lot of flak for it. I remember the particular circumstance and context for its poignancy, that is about all.

LL: That is about all? Remember we were in our tenth standard then.

UB: That is about all, children! I once said, at a seminar in Hong Kong, that I was President of the Society for the Prevention of Flogging Dead Horses! Seriously, you need to study, with the objectivity that distance is said to bring, the Mandal-Kamandal developments and their impact on India's future.

Sarfaroshi ki Tamanna

LL: Why did you eventually resign, then?

UB: I was stymied for resources. I came into office at a time when the overall university budget was some Rs 17 crore. I tried to raise the deficit from alumni, but they were only interested in getting a seat on the Executive Council or on the senate. There was no alumni spirit like we have elsewhere. So, I decided to raise some internal resources. I talked to the student union and raised the issue of a fee hike. Nobody had done that before. The fees then were very low by any standards—they were, I recall, far short of Rs 1,000 per semester.

How could I provide a library or any other facilities on this? They did not agree; reluctantly, they agreed in principle to negotiate a campus development fee. I spoke to my executive council and I set up a university industry council. They said, how can we contribute when you are cash-strapped, when you impose such a burden on us? When your students come to us, we have to make them unlearn what they have learnt and invest two years of re-learning because of the campus syllabus, which has not been revised for fifteen to twenty years. That became another process.

The process started. Then the problem arose with the UGC rule that if you earned anything, the grant would correspondingly be reduced. I fought my way through.

Manmohan Singh was the minister then. My treasurer was a student, Dr Gupta, and he said, we will fight it together. It took me a year-and-a-half, I appealed to all the Vice-Chancellors. The rule was relaxed by the UGC in my case and then everybody jumped on it. That period was complex and got more complicated by my newspaper writing. Dr Manmohan Singh presented his first budget, it was a good speech, he quoted Bismil saab's beautiful Urdu verse, *dekhna hai ... sarfaroshi ki tamanna*. He ended his speech by saying: 'I want to see how much strength my adversary has. As far as I am concerned, I am enveloped by *sarfaroshi*.' At the heart of it, of course, was the early globalising agenda. He constantly referred in his speech to the founding fathers of the Constitution.

So, I wrote an article in *The Times of India* applauding the poetry in his speech, but a key point of my article was that neither Manmohan Singh nor I had English as our mother tongue. So, when he referred to founding fathers of the Constitution, being a teacher of law, I went to Part IV and Part III, but nothing of that appears in the budget. Then I realised that, not being trained in the English language, we all make some confusion between these animals called vowels and these other animals called consonants. Perhaps the real thing here, when he said *founding* fathers, was that he meant *funding* fathers! It was, of course, said with greater finesse, but this was the substance.

This article, I was later told, was translated into several Indian languages. Then an artist produced a calendar called Vowels and Consonants of India. I always used to sign these articles as Professor of Law, and would put in a rider that I did not write in my official capacity. This article must have had some reverberations in the government, although it is difficult to piece the whole story being outside of the corridors of power! At this time, I wrote a lot of letters to ministers. It was, in a Churchillian phrase, 'a gathering storm'. There was a growing crisis of accountability, etc. I wrote several letters asking why the UGC was not relaxing the rule I referred to earlier. I got no reply. I wrote a monograph on the question of crisis of governance and accountability in DU, half-a-dozen ideas were implemented in my time. I was satisfied. We got some experts in to make estimates: if this is the population of Delhi, and this is the demand for commerce, arts education, then what will be our requirements in 2010? I also requested all the Vice-Chancellors to produce similar perspective plans. I also requested UGC to do a similar thing so as to have a rational approach. Five universities did produce perspective plans. But it took considerable time for the idea to grow and endure. Now, I am told, it is the done thing.

I had decided that the manner of my leaving the university should serve the university better in terms of release of funds from the Central government. I decided on a date in August 1994 to leave. I told Prema, but on an obligation of confidentiality. I went to Shankar Dayal Sharma, he was the Chancellor. He had the memory of an elephant. I went to Sharma-ji and said, I have a small favour to ask you, I want to resign on 23 August. I told him, the government is putting the screws on me, I do not have manoeuvrability, I need Rs 25 crore which is legitimately due to me, I have written letters, nothing has happened. He asked me, why 23 August, have you consulted an astrologer? I said no, it just came to me, I am going to stick to it. I wanted to go back to teaching, but I could not make that public. I said, Sharma-ji, if the matter becomes public for any reason, I will become a lame duck officer. You have to keep it a closely guarded secret. He said, are you asking me for an oath of secrecy? He asked me, what will satisfy you? I said, just your word. He said, let me give you something better. He took my letter from me, removed his Gandhi cap, put the letter in it, placed the cap back on his head and said, are you satisfied? This will not go out of my cap or my head! It was a very dramatic gesture, and a stunning one, but I thanked him profusely. I said, see you as a citizen, not as an officer of the university, in late August.

When it was time, and I sought another appointment to meet with him, his secretary said, can you tell me what it is about? I said, it is a secret. He said, if it is a secret from me, how can I arrange a meeting? I said, just tell him it is a secret. In the evening, when I called him, with such a fine memory, he could not recall what all this was about! On the midnight of the 22nd, I called in my team, they came in bleary-eyed and said, tell us what is the matter. I said, at the stroke of twelve, I have demitted my office. They said, you cannot demit, there is no provision for that, resignation goes through a process, the letter goes to the Chancellor, and then the minister announces it. There was great consternation, but Prema was very happy, so she came in with *jalebis*. These people said, nothing doing Ms. Baxi, this is no way to leave us in the middle of everything, they were very unhappy. Next morning, the reporters asked the HRD Minister, have you heard Professor Baxi has demitted office? He said, ask Professor Baxi. A legal correspondent asked me, under what provision was I demitting office? I said, I have spent my whole life studying law. If you want me to find a provision, I will find a provision, but it is the inherent power of the VC to demit office.

I got calls from many people overseas. Peter Jaszi asked me to take up a visiting professorship at the American College of Law at American University, Washington, D.C. I said, it is too soon, people will say that I planned my exit, that I went after dollars, and so on. Prema said, nothing doing, the money is welcome! So, from October, I went on leave without pay and started teaching at the Law Faculty. Then I learnt that, a few weeks after my resignation, a hefty payment arrived from the GOI to the University. Obviously, the implication was that as long as I was there, there would be no release of monies legitimately due.

A Russian Toast

UB (***contd***): It was an interesting tenure, all said. This one time, when Boris Yeltsin was visiting India, I was asked to confer an honorary degree on him. DU has a tradition of awarding academic degrees, not political degrees, generally speaking. The proposal was discussed, everybody said fine, but those from the Left said, we will protest. I said, politics should be kept outside the convocation. Mani Shankar Dixit was then the foreign secretary; I thought it was only courtesy to tell him about the likely protests by some teachers. He said he got the message and in the end, Yeltsin got the honorary doctorate from Benares University. You know what Shankar Dayal Sharma toasts with? *Lassi*! Poor Yeltsin, I guess, also received the same treatment! He went back, and within two weeks, he had stormed the Duma. I think it was a direct result of our toasting him with lassi! There is a funny side to everything.

Then one time, the head of WIPO visited India. He asked me whom he should meet. With a great deal of hesitancy, I said, I can arrange a meeting with the President. We met the President. Mid-conversation, SD's mind suddenly turned to the making of *ghee*. He went on and on about the many varieties of ghee and the many ways of making ghee in India. I was delighted; sometimes, it is so necessary to puncture this diplomatic ego! After some time, the conversation ended. I told our visiting dignitary that what the President had in mind was that indigenous products like this can be made the subject matter of patent or other kinds of intellectual property protection. He was very confused, and he looked daggers at me. I think I totally ruined his sojourn!

One time, the Hungarian President conveyed to me that he would like to give the gift of a radio station to DU. I was always keen on campus radio. It is common elsewhere, in America particularly. But how was I to receive this gift without paying duty? I came across such a stone wall of opposition. Radio frequency was under State monopoly. The reasons given were virtually paranoid. No doubt it was post-Khalistan paranoia. I said, the university will use this to do some *Vividh Bharti* or we will have some talks on duty and patriotism. Young people, particularly some musical and performing arts groups, were thrilled with the idea. But the reasons given by top officials were unbelievable—the fear of misuse, foreign propaganda, extremism, what not.

There was one time when Yash Pal (the Chair of the UGC) just walked into my office, and after some time, he said, let us go for a quick lunch. There was then really no good restaurant on the campus; and the only place nearby was the Hotel Imperial, about fifteen minutes away by car. We both then decided to walk to the nearby coffee house where south Indian food was served. There was consternation when we walked into the canteen and many teachers got up and offered their seats, but we declined, deciding to wait till a table became available. We both were pipe smokers and lit our pipes outside, and a small group joined our conversation. Then we went for a quick lunch of *idli dosa*. I insisted on paying, only to realise that I had left all the money home in the shirt that I changed! Jokingly, I said to Yash: 'This is the dire state of the University of Delhi.' He offered to pay, but I said, I can't have that happen, and the manager of the canteen said not to worry about this, as he was proud to host us. The next day, of course, I sent the money.

The culture of total informality was reinforced by Yash's visit, and of course we worked for a year on the 'crazy' idea we had of closing all universities in India for a year when students, teachers, *karmacharis*, will go to the interior and launch a literacy mission. Anil Sadgopal, Yash, and I indeed had some cross-party meetings with Parliamentarians and related political actors, and it was agreed that it should be done. But nothing at all survived that endorsement. It was a great failure of ours, as we often reminisced, but worth the effort at raising social consciousness; with us, it was much more—a plan of action to transform India. Someday, the idea, we hope, will be resurrected.

Concluding Thoughts on University Systems

There are many matters of which I have not spoken of here, for various reasons, mostly because they are still sensitive and some may remain so, even at this distance, to persons and families involved. But I have tried to illustrate, as best I could, that a university is a live social system that encourages vibrant dissent, whether expressed in public or private.

But it is also at the same time a live gossipy place, in which many kind and unkind things are said, against the university officials, including sometimes chiefly against the Vice-Chancellor, Principals, Deans of Faculties, Heads of Departments, the Registrar, and other units within the system, often unprintable. However, it is also not directed to them. Usually, the more autocratic the style and functioning of the units, the more destructive is the grapevine! However, the networks of gossip can also be constructive. Very often, as generally remarked of rumors and gossip, what is said today may come to pass tomorrow—here gossiping takes a predictive role!

As Professor Andre Beteille used to say, in neighbourly exchanges, the urban campuses are little more than 'overgrown villages', at least in this respect! He should certainly know the truth of this as a renowned anthropologist. At the same time, the diversity of the university systems is indeed staggering. May we not draw distinctions between residential campuses and far-flung university systems with a federal structure, with affiliated colleges on the one hand and university departments on the other? And in what ways do the special institutions of national excellence (the IIM and IIT, for example) present a different picture? And do not these days of neoliberal educational hierarchies and control, aiming at 'world class' (whatever it may mean) education elevating corporatisation of universities, offer some radically different ways of understanding?

As concerns dissent—whether cultural, social, economic, or religious—the University system has (as I have said with some anecdotal but substantial evidence) a basic duty to promote free and frank constitutional discussion and debate. The Supreme Court of India has often described the importance of judicial dissent as both 'historic' and 'prophetic'. Recently, it has also emphasised dissent as the 'lifeblood of democracy'. This is equally true of universities (and all education institutions, if I may say so).

But as a lawperson, I believe that this dissent must be, like the very education system itself, disciplined by the Constitution—especially by the values enunciated and declared in the Preamble, the

Fundamental Rights (to which respect is owed by the executive and legislative powers and all constituted public authorities and agencies), and duties of the citizen and civil society, plus the authoritative decisions of the constitutional courts. The very idea of a university education represents a social compact between the learners and the learned, a key feature of it being the freedom of speech, expression, and disciplined opinion (judgment) which is open to scientific verification or invalidation. Collegiate and civil conduct and conversation is a sine qua non of educational institutional culture and processes.

The life of the mind (that I have stressed constantly) welcomes disciplined disagreement but abhors what in logic, and reason, is named as *argumentum ad baculum* ('argument to the cudgel' or 'appeal to the stick'), or more generally put, the fallacy of an appeal, or recourse, to force to compel a morally or politically 'right 'conclusion. This kind of argumentation comes to the fore when the very means of compulsion are controlled or used by a protagonist. It is, I believe, an ethical obligation of a campus community to maintain peace and harmony while critically exploring all the justifications for uses or threat of force offered by the State, society, and the economy within nations as well across borders.

How I wish that those who had the good fortune to serve the nation as the heads of the university systems would publicly reminisce about their experiences! That will, surely, enhance the social memory of educational institutions and culture. Their role in national and constitutional development remains inestimable.

But let this 'homily' end now! And I can find no better way of ending than contesting the view that the end of all education is a suitable degree that serves the State and economy, and that the main social function of education is to impart sets of skills and competences. An associated concern is one that relates to a return on investment in schools, colleges, and other institutions of learning. True, receiving university education has, especially in 'world class' university systems, become quite costly and it is but normal that parents or guardians expect good returns from such investment. The expectation that the wards will settle down well in life is considered a reasonable one.

However, there is no reason to think that 'settling down well in life' should be indifferent to the suffering of others and reinforce an inclination which is detrimental to the plight of disadvantaged, disabled, and disenfranchised co-citizens and persons; this is deeply unconstitutional. We wrote, at the lamented Chhatrapati Singh's persuasion, in our first UGC Curriculum Development Centre in Law (in the early 1980s) that a principal function of legal education is to produce 'soldiers of constitutional justice', and I have always added, not the 'shoulders' for State or the Market. I think that all the citizens of India ought to recall every day the fundamental duties of citizens (and persons, as crystallised in Part IV-A of the Constitution) as an approach to education and learning.

Fourteen

Human Rights

Teaching, Education, and Theory

Curricularisation of Human Rights

SRK: You spoke briefly earlier of human rights education. Human rights curricularisation and education has been an abiding concern in your work and writing. How important do you think curricularisation of human rights is in law teaching?

UB: Human Rights Education (HRE, hereafter) includes processes of learning what human rights are and how they could be lived every day by all—individuals, groups, institutions, community, markets, State: human beings living as such and together everywhere. In my friend Shulamith Koenig's voice, HRE is a 'way of life' for some peoples and cultures, but should inform all and everywhere (also see Chapter 10). I have called Shulamith the 'Mother of Human Rights Education'; she won a coveted UN Human Rights Award. She calls HRE the 'ownership' by people of States' solemn treaty commitments. The organisation she has founded, called The People's Movement for Human Rights Learning, has embarked on many imaginative projects, including Human Rights Learning Cities, and putting out a manifesto of Human Rights Education. Today, as I have analysed it elsewhere, if

Human Rights Education is enshrined as a basic human right by the United Nations, it owes a great deal to Shulamith's voice, vision, and vocation. In this work, we had many eminent friends and movements that helped by invaluable contributions. CLADEM, a movement for women's human rights in Latin America, was a powerful voice. So were individuals, and I mention only a few: Stephen P. Marks, Lorretta Ross, Kathleen Murkowski, Ivanka Corti, Walter Litchem, Danilo Turk, Clarence Dias, Miloon Kothari, Jerry Koning, Susana Chiarotti, and other valued colleagues (see Chapter 12).

Clearly, HRE is broadly conceived as education in human rights. But what are human rights? One way to think about HRE is to think about the norms and standards that already exist in law (whether local/regional/national/supranational and international levels), and in their mutual dynamic interaction. This is how law schools conceive of HRE.

I think that the doctrinal teaching of human rights as a discipline within law schools has its place and will always continue to do so. It is (if well-taught) a set of techniques by which one can interrogate power in all its places, particularly in its hiding places. It is a very important legalistic limb of working with human rights, but this is one form of curricular engagement with human rights, and it should be recognised as a part of law school syllabi in many places. (Teaching and research in constitutional and administrative law, affirmative action, gender justice, law, poverty, disability, sexual orientation and conduct, natural resources, environmental law and jurisprudence, statutory interpretation, tax interpretation, and jurisprudence, comparative law, among others.)

But HRE, as an assemblage of pedagogic and juristic practices, occurs at many places: primary, secondary, tertiary, and lifelong (adult and continuing); there are also in-service professional courses which should impart HRE. In framing a national HRE policy, these and many levels have to be fully kept in view.

Fundamentally, there is also a wider meaning, of values and goals, of basic rights (such as liberty, equality, sorority, fraternity, and dignity), such that we must think of more broad-based HRE education or learning. The two other ways in which to conceive human rights education comprise history and philosophy. In the latter, we pursue human rights as a set of above-mentioned metanorms—their Being (ontology), ways of knowing (epistemologies), and the pursuit of human/social good (moral/ethical philosophy). Here, one is dealing with the ethics and philosophy (metaphysics) of the very idea of human rights. Not so much as human rights which exist in the life of States, in domestic, comparative, and international law, but as they *ought to* exist.

When I was in office at DU, I set up a committee comprising social scientists, linguists, historians, etc. I insisted that we should take human rights out of its legal niche and provide for a more general education, perspectives that matter by way of critique. I thought we could introduce a B.A. in Human Rights. This took everybody by surprise: the law faculty was simply in shock because they thought it was their disciplinary domain. Now, in several colleges we have a B.A. in Human Rights. They are taught human rights history, the meaning of human rights, history of colonial struggles—essentially, this is a wider frame of looking at human rights.

The third experiment was human rights education at a global level, which was conceived of in two ways. One was geared towards activist workers, how they should come to own human rights, etc. The second was intended for violators of human rights, potential violators, for people in power. The latter occurred to me very early on.

When I was teaching International Humanitarian Law at Sydney, I asked my colleagues to see how far the Australian military manuals had incorporated the Nuremberg principles. We found there was hardly much included. This line of enquiry caused some consternation, of course, because I was an outsider and these were very hard realms of State power, and there was also the question of the intrusion of an Asian academic into security concerns. But I realised that human rights education for potential violators of human rights is very important. This did not fly (though I thought this was important) because activists can also be potential human rights violators, even if inadvertently.

Who is an activist, is indeed a difficult question, Ram. Anyone who services a transformative task or mission can be entitled to call herself an activist; but not all entities and agencies become thereby activists, if that term is used only for those who foster transformation with the purpose of serving human rights. Here, the difference in being active and being activists assumes a teleological edge. Business NGOs, those engaging in unfair labour practices, for example, also claim to represent human rights cultures. Call them B-NGOs. There are also what I call E-NGOs or the environmental activists; at the Kyoto Conference, there were more B-NGOs representing environmental causes than E-NGOs. Now climate change is increasingly owned by multinational corporations who say they best represent environmental justice. The UN system thus becomes increasingly privatised. This is now known to environmental activists as 'greenwashing' by corporations.

I've had the privilege of knowing Susana Chiarotti somewhat while working with CLADEM (Committee for Latin America and the Caribbean for the Defense of Women's Rights). They were very keen to take CEDAW to Latin American women, to ensure accountability of the government and of elected representatives. An activist HRE says that any solemn commitments a State has entered into must be fulfilled. This is also a way of pursuing accountability of rulers. It is an implementation strategy of international human rights. In the process of doing HRE, particularly in Africa, people started searching for past precedents of justice, equality, and dignity in their own cultures and histories. Thus, they find a blend of the historical with the now proclaimed universal human rights. We can go to other cultures for important anticipations and preformed enunciations of what we now call human rights.

That excited me greatly, because it meant a partial realisation of my big project of compiling the stories of human rights in legends and folklore, which never took off. HRE for activists means: implementing international human rights principles on the ground and at the State level; empowering people to use human rights in sites other than the State; connecting communities of human rights educators; overcoming the grand diversion of the dichotomy between universality and relativism. None of these activities can be called anti-governmental, anti-political, or anti-national because these are programmes of pacific human rights obligations which States have undertaken through custom, treaties, policies, and pronouncements; these also include the national Constitutions, laws, and legal traditions.

HRE is complex and contradictory. It is eminently possible, while at the same time impossible (Baxi 1996c). To illustrate: I had raised some basic questions concerning the setting up of women's studies departments in colleges and universities when I was chair of the ICSSR committee. There were a lot of outstanding people who were friends, like Lotika Sarkar, Veena Mazumdar, etc. I told them, let's send a memo to each other on why we need to set up women's studies departments, centres, or cells, whether it is a good or bad thing. I wrote a paper, titled 'Liberation from Women's Studies' (Baxi 1987a). I was severely disowned by my Committee colleagues. They said, the women's movement is a fragile movement, this form of critique is untimely. I have never believed that honest critique disables solidarity, in fact, it should reinforce solidarity. My point was simply that we cannot develop women's studies by seeing the world exclusively from a female point of view; and an authentic voice of women can only be acquired by taking part in their lives and social existence. Many women do research the same way as males do; nor should there be a male epistemology that predominates. How do we introduce the difference that changes the field of pedagogy and research as a whole?

I still believe that doing HRE with activists is very difficult, because they resent, and most often rightly so, any note of expertise. You get attacked as speaking jargon and are asked to speak simply. This is a good thing, but it can be carried a bit far, especially when one ignores the many linguistic codes that academic languages (as well as activist ones) contain and carry within them. The constant refrain of an Afro-American woman activist who is doing good work in HRE was, 'Upen, if it's a practice, why should you use the word praxis?' The person who attacked me was a strong person, with a booming voice. We had great fun. Even now, she calls me Professor Praxis!

If one's style is complex, it may be because one doesn't know how to communicate, or because one is trying to communicate complex ideas. I don't think one can do HRE for activists without being immersed oneself in activism. It cannot be done at one remove. One can teach human rights, or political science in colleges, without having any experience of a mass struggle or a social movement. You cannot do it in the activist world.

How does one do HRE for people in power who are potential violators of human rights? Put all the law ministers together and give them an elementary test on human rights, they won't pass! I have evidence. I publicly asked three law ministers of India, one after the other, about the ILO Convention, to which India is a party, which grants unorganised rural workers the right to organise and imposes an obligation on governments which are parties to it to facilitate this right. None of the three knew about this convention.

Illiteracy begins at the top with the literate, not with the illiterate. In fact, I have often said that the illiteracy of the literate is far more dangerous than the illiteracy of the illiterate.

The Jurisprudence of Human Rights

SRK: Do you therefore think it is a futile exercise to curricularise human rights?

UB: I don't think anything is futile. It's like the controversy about jurisprudence, whether it should be taught in the first or the second year, or taught at all. What is jurisprudence, but thinking about law? If it is thinking about law, then whether you are teaching property law or tort law or whatever else, if it is law you are teaching, thinking about law should come into it. So those who say jurisprudence should not be a separate course must be said to mean that every course should be a course in jurisprudence!

It's not a separate topic, it's an approach, a state of mind. It's not 'practical'. In India, we have this theory and practice divide. In the US, there are hardly any courses on jurisprudence. This is because they do law as a policy science. They open up every judgment and question it. To question it, you must have some background theory. People never take the law as it is for what it is. You must have some idea of what it ought to be—that is jurisprudence. The function of jurisprudence is to elaborate the difference between what is and what ought to be.

Human rights, likewise, should be a state of mind in the teaching of law. After Bhopal, how can you teach the law of torts outside the question of human rights violations by multinational corporations? Or the question of whether non-State actors owe an obligation to people whom they hurt? Or when you teach contract and the freedom of consent, must you not ask whether those who are economically weaker are capable of giving authentic consent? Whether such a contract would even be valid? Of course, there is a need for curricularisation, but every law teacher, just as s/he ought to know jurisprudence, ought to know the jurisprudence of human rights.

Human rights are a part of jurisprudence. It involves more than theoretical quibbling over questions such as: What does it mean to say 'human', what does it mean to say 'rights', where do they come from, are they absolute? It also means putting human rights to work, taking risks to produce a wealth of new meanings, and learning from struggles. All this is a part of jurisprudence.

So, I would say, walk with both feet at once. It would never work if human rights curricularisation becomes a ghettoised field within the law school. Tax law, criminal law, family law, everything is a part of human rights today, this may not have been so fifty years ago. I used to teach sessions in so-called refresher courses conducted by the UGC for law teachers, and I would say, give me one statute from any field of law, and I will tell you how to teach it with a human rights orientation.

But let me tell you how, in practice, this works in India. We have a system of refresher courses; I have conducted several in jurisprudence. Once, they wanted me to lecture on Dworkin, and when I asked them why, they said that the teachers had only read Austin and Hart. So, a refresher course to this mindset means getting to the next Englishman you haven't yet read! That's not what refresher courses are about. Particularly after the professionalisation of law with the so-called national law schools, I strongly believe it is even more important to have human rights perspectives in all courses of law. It is possible, it can be done. It does not disturb the integrity of the field of knowledge. But then, who bothers?

SRK: We all know that the teaching of a particular subject depends on the teacher's orientation. A teacher of criminal law who is inclined to go over it section by section obviously focuses on the nitty-gritties of procedure, as opposed to a more substantive approach.

UB: Of course, they should look at the nitty-gritty, because that is what criminal law is all about, but they should at least ask some general jurisprudential questions: for example, concerning the classification of crimes—the question of why the criminal code has three parts, crimes against person, property, and State. Where shall we place crimes against environment (eco-crimes), crimes against health (CAH), human rights crimes (crimes against humanity, crimes of aggression, cross-border crimes in situations of ethnic wars or other conflicts)? Why should the State have sole monopoly over prosecution? The prosecutor is State-appointed, because many crimes are offences against the sociopolitical order. Although it says crime against *persons*, why is it that the *State* has a monopoly over prosecution? Police officers acting in the course of duty are not criminally liable, where does that notion come from? It's a hard penal code, but you can't explain it on the terms given by the code.

As Foucault pointed out long ago, freedom only makes sense within codes of constraint. In the first volume of the *History of Sexuality*, he says, you cannot understand freedom of speech outside the code of censorship, you cannot understand the incessant chatter around sexuality outside of the early canon law interdicts on sexuality. Today also, in the Indian Constitution, you cannot have freedom of speech outside of its 'reasonable' restrictions. To understand Section 153A of the Indian Penal Code,[1] or obscenity,[2] or defamation,[3] it is

[1] 153A. Promoting enmity between different groups on grounds of religion, race, place of birth, residence, language, etc., and doing acts prejudicial to maintenance of harmony.

[2] 292. Sale, etc., of obscene books. 293. Sale, etc., of obscene objects to young person. 294. Obscene acts and songs.

[3] 499. Defamation—Whoever, by words either spoken or intended to be read, or by signs or by visible representations, makes or publishes any imputation concerning any person intending to harm, or knowing or having reason to believe that such imputation will harm, the reputation of such person, is said, except in the cases hereinafter expected, to defame that person.

very necessary to understand reasonable restrictions of speech in the Constitution.

But you introduce a serious problem: How do you incorporate this sensibility into the curriculum without undermining the autonomy of the teacher? That is the hardest task of all. Certain cuts in academic autonomy are introduced by the syllabi and the curriculum; certain others are insinuated by the need for concurrence among colleagues when it is being taught by two or more colleagues (it is only in cases of teachers doing a solo course that pure autonomy may be said to exist). So, the autonomy is always relative, never absolute, yet further, it is surrounded by the calls for 'accountability', a concept that needs to be re-thought not merely as responsibility, but (to here adapt Jacques Derrida's phrase) as 'response-ability'. Curricular reform needs to be an ongoing conversation; it is not easy, but it is important to continuously engage with it.

Pedagogic Experiments

SRK: What pedagogic experiments do you recollect from your Delhi and Warwick days?

UB: I've never taught a human rights course in Delhi or other Indian cities. But have offered several human rights jurisprudence courses. Of experiments, there are many; all teaching is an experimentation. I talked earlier of the UGC refresher courses of which I was a part.

One of those was in Bhavnagar, near Rajkot. At that time, in Saurashtra, the big problem was the crisis in groundnut oil. I asked the participants in the course to bring the daily newspaper for twenty days and to look at what the issues were. It could become a course in sociological jurisprudence—I set assignments in which they had to find out who the producers of groundnuts were, who the consumers were, what the law regulating the same was, etc.

For about three years in Delhi, in the jurisprudence course, the focus of our discussions in class were the new-wave films like

Ankur, Aakrosh (a film about the complexities of legal aid), and other post-Mathura movies on questions of social justice, corruption, etc. Everybody had seen these movies. The course was about the popular representations of law and ideas of justice in current cinema. The question was: How far did the popular representations of justice tally, or not tally, with official ideas of law, governance, development, rights, and justice? In *Ankur*, as the film ends, a little boy is shown expressing his outrage by throwing a stone at the house of the aristocrat, the village landlord. The principal character in *Ankur* is a disabled person, he is almost flogged to death, and the little boy was watching all this. Just picture for yourself the various states of deep subalterneity entailed!

How do you understand the symbolism in this movie? Is throwing a small stone a sign of future incipient resistance? Or is it just the outrage of a single young person? I also lectured extensively on a movie called *Shahenshah*. Amitabh Bachchan is by day a very venal and corrupt police inspector. By night, he attacks the very same people who are corrupt. It is equally important to recall that Amitabh Bachchan was then also a nominated member of the Rajya Sabha. It was a wonderful way of encoding a whole variety of themes of law and justice, including what it means to achieve even a modicum of justice for the rightless.

In Warwick, we did a lot around the Delgamuukw case (*Delgamuukw vs. British Columbia*[4]). The question we focussed on was how 'development' related to human rights. Every teacher, I suppose, needs to be able to look at her/himself in the mirror. Not only to look at one's reflection, but one also looks in the mirror in a search for moral perfection, and if you cannot bear to look at your face because it makes visible the agonies of millions, then you have not arrived as a teacher. Teaching is to do justice to yourself—not to a body of knowledge—and justice to some congregation that you call the class. What matters is whether you have been true to your chosen vocation. It is to come back to the simple principle that justice is openness to the suffering of the other. These are no major pedagogic experiments, but merely incidents in my teaching life.

[4] [1997] 3 SCR 1010.

For example, in many Indian languages, instead of saying 'state', one says 'estate'. Many people, and not just from Haryana, say 'estate' instead of 'state.' Hegel has a theory where he says that the State emerges from estates. So, I used to say that many folks thought of that distinction, thus bringing Hegel down from his high pedestal. So misspellings, mispronunciations can be resources for teaching law and human rights. Different styles of spoken Indian English are gateways to jurisprudence. These are just minor things, but it gets the class interested.

The point is to not let them ever feel that this is theory. Everything is practice, and theory is also a kind of practice. And there cannot be practice as such without theory. That has to be constantly articulated.

At Warwick, the curricular experimentation turned out to be contextually different, though the general aim was for students and teachers alike to learn afresh. In the Masters Law and Development programme, there was a foundation course which underwent many pedagogic transitions. Some colleagues and students felt it was too theoretically and analytically demanding. I suspect I aggravated this impression somewhat by prescribing required, recommended, and advanced readings, and by further elongating the seminars that followed the class presentations by three hours. All of which meant that, at the very minimum, it was a six-hour class on its scheduled day. But we ensured that students participated throughout by general questions, and also by structured and team-based voluntary class presentations in seminars.

Listening closely to generations of students, colleagues decided that a time had come for a change in the total programme. Some vast fluctuations in enrolment were also considered a problem, aggravated by the view that there should be higher and consistent enrolment. We (Abdul Paliwala, Ann Stewart, Shaheen Ali, Samuel Adelman, Jayan Nayyar, Andrew Williams, and George Mészáros) deliberated for about two years. By this time, contemporary globalisation and market fundamentalisms were being furthered and consolidated, and university administrators were demanding better linkages with industry, the EU, and generally self-financing courses. Some colleagues felt that incoming students who had to make some difficult and hard choices viewed the discourse on 'development' as having now a musty air, and even a bad odour in these globalising days. But colleagues were divided on this: While all felt that something new should be done, it was also felt that the old emphasis on critical discourse concerning development should be retained and that the foundational (or the core) course should continue; on the other hand, some felt that students of the future would be more keen on obtaining practical, not theoretic, skills, and they were demanding means of formulating manageable problems and methods of solving them, and for learning geared to decisional, rather than structural and ideological, concerns.

A dialogue on curriculum transformation (as distinct, of course, from syllabi change) invariably brings out in the open some hidden ideological concerns and cultural conflicts. These emerged rather fully in closed group discussions and wider debates in the faculty meetings. Warwick was no exception in the intensity of discussions. What was novel was the fashioning of continuity amidst change.

This was achieved finally by retaining the core course, but with equal emphasis on skills; and providing four optional clusters from which students must choose to obtain a specialisation mentioned in the degree (such as gender and feminism, human rights, governance, and global justice). Each cluster would have at least six courses, out of which students would have to elect four. The programme itself was renamed as International Development and Human Rights Law, which sought to re-emphasise the role of law and the rule of law in attaining the processes and objectives of governance, rights, development, and justice. It continues even today with notable continuity, though with some redistribution of emphases and changes, and the general perception is that it is more satisfying to new generations of students.

A Disposition or Discipline Towards Human Rights Learning?

SRK: Looking at human rights from the vantage point you are suggesting, would you say it is more important to treat it as an approach rather than as a specialisation?

UB: Particularly in the days of globalisation, it is very important to charge or inflect every subject of law with the vibrations, intonations, pulsations of human rights. In any five-year law course, there is no justification for pre-law subjects to be taught without a human rights orientation. Political science, history, literature and language, economics, sociology—teaching these subjects in law school means that these disciplines should be reoriented to certain values that the law seeks to serve. Professor R. K. Misra and I prepared the first draft curriculum for the National Law School [of India University, Bangalore], along with a long note which explained why I included history, literature, and language in the pre-law curriculum. It is there in the Bar Council of India archives. It was a struggle because other people said that the purpose of the National Law School was to produce good lawyers. I also insistently raised the question: what is a good lawyer? Even the admission test that we designed, the objective questions, were already socially oriented, not just information or skill-oriented. You want the kind of student to come in who would combine information with a certain trigger of sensitivity. One wants them also to be 'indignation entrepreneurs', to now borrow the words of Cass Sunstein and Ullmann-Margalit (2002).

Both an approach and a specialisation—of course, a Masters' degree in human rights is very necessary. There is a need for human rights-trained cadre for government services. Like the IAS, IPS, IRS, IFS, etc., there should be the IHRS (Indian Human Rights Service). You need to prepare cadres to serve the NHRIs (National—and regional—Human Rights Institutions). There is a value to specialisation. But only certain people who walk that career path will go there. There is a value in specialisation to promote advanced research and writing in human rights. You need specific degrees on women's rights as human rights. Specialisation doesn't just mean knowing the international human rights norms and standards, but it also means being able to devise litigation strategies, campaigns, etc.

One of the battles in Warwick with respect to the core course concerned a skill development component. The core course in the new programme we developed was called 'Theory and Practice in Development', and students were asked not only to write papers, but also to prepare press notes, briefing statements, etc. I absented myself from that part of the course because I am not capable of doing that. Sometimes skill-set competence can distract from real concerns. It is not tactics but strategies of human rights that interest me. Tactics are things like press notes, lobbying, etc. Strategies are different from tactics. This is a battle that I lost, but that's all right, so long as efforts at curricularisation do not lose their focus on the human rights needs of a particular society and how they can be best addressed. A major war has been won!

Theoretical Labours as Source Material for Curricular Reform

AN: Is the lack of materials the reason why collective political violence or caste-based violence (which are key to understanding Indian society) rarely figure in human rights teaching in India, with the focus being instead on international human rights norms? Thinking of collective political violence or caste violence, and the lack of materials which have been compiled on the point, if one would base a course on human rights on material within Indian society as compared to international human rights norms alone, would such an effort have been possible?

UB: Lack of materials, Arvind? My view is that we have abundant material and we should start using what we have! Akshay R. Desai has put together an excellent compilation for his time, and it's an excellent sourcebook even now (Desai 1986). There is an abundance of material, including government reports on atrocities and inquiries into communal riots, starting with the Justice Jaganmohan Reddy Inquiry Commission's report on the Ahmedabad riots in 1969. The landscape has vastly expanded since Akshay Bhai wrote that book, and there are agencies and processes by which CPV (collective political violence) is exposed. There are judicial decisions/recommendations of the National Human Rights Commission (NHRC), particularly on the Gujarat riots in 2002, which show a new kind of engagement with these gross violations, some already authoritatively handled by courts and others still in the pipeline. But this can be said about many instances of CPV, such as the 1984 massacres in Delhi. There are also quite a few micronarratives emerging through blogs and the expansion of the internet. This allows us to access, for example, the events in Singur. However, what we don't have, of course, is a history of CPV.

I must add that I have only marginal access to regional literature. There is hardly anything on Partition outside the work of feminist historians and literary theorists. So we don't even have a textbook including material which would be relevant to many fields of knowledge—not just to human rights, but also to philosophy, literature, history, etc. We need to organise some reading material and a narrative in the form of a textbook, but beyond this, we need to ask if we have any moral theories about violence. Violence evokes very strong visceral responses. It's always bad, evil, but can violence ever be jurisgenerative? Social theory, history, ethics, and philosophy tend to adopt different perspectives here, which we ought to study diligently.

An example is the French Revolution. I have said this in my essay in *The Right to be Human* (Baxi 1987b), that organised political violence can also be regenerative. History shows it. Decolonisation meant that there is no definition of terrorism in the United Nations because Third World nations maintain that one person's terrorist is another person's freedom fighter. This statement points to the difficulty in theorising CPV. One of the last colonies to be liberated was East Timor in 2002. There are still places which are colonised. Assuming CPV is justified in some historical context, the question is, if the ends are justified, are the means also justified?

It's a big question. When are the means so radically disjointed from the ends? Assume that the best way to hit the underbelly of the imperialistic power is to target non-combatant civilians and its women. Or to kill all new-born infants of the imperialist settlers. Or one may say the same about the colonial CPV targeting. So, violence is often thought to be regenerative when it is directed against certain specific political targets. Fortunately, such violence is rendered contrary to discourses of international humanitarian law, the Hague and Geneva Conventions in particular.

In the monograph by Bhagat Singh,[5] he says, some people are called terrorists because they hurt innocent persons, and he says, terrorism is propaganda by deed, not by words, and therefore targeting innocents is the most efficient way of doing propaganda by deed, as there is a universal revulsion produced, both against terrorists and against the structures which they are trying to oppose. There was a great demand on Mohandas that, when he met the Viceroy, he should ask for the release of Bhagat Singh. He did not. We have here a contradiction between the saint and the politician in Mohandas, who was concerned with dominion status at that time. This is of great importance now, because we believe there is something called terror which needs to be rooted out and is the greatest evil. It is also the case that you cannot root these things out without addressing the structural conditions that cause them. It is recognised by political leaders all round that it will not work to simply nab people with dragnet legislation, etc. You have to see what are the political injustices against which acts of terror also constitute a statement.

The big question, as you know, in today's world is whether recourse to terror is justified as organised political violence. Should CPV include terror? For example, Chauri Chaura included burning police stations, killing policemen, etc. Policemen were as much enslaved by colonisation, but were seen as symbols of the British Raj, and Mohandas' protest against Chauri Chaura is an instructive one. Partly he was saying violence is not justified and partly that killing your own people in the pursuit of national liberation is not justified, even if they are employed in the army, police, or government of the enemy. The question of terror as CPV is a complex one, and people are afraid to talk about it directly. That is the only conclusion I can draw, for otherwise we should have had an extremely articulate non-partisan discourse. We had only fifty-sixty universities at Independence, now we have around 300–400, yet there is no theory of CPV. Is it the case

[5]See Lal (2019). See, in particular, the Manifestos of the Naujawan Bharat Sabha and Hindustan Socialist Republican Association, drafted in consultation with Bhagat Singh, according to Lal.

that the more academic minds we have, the more remote becomes the prospect of studying CPV?

Now, of course, people are afraid, post 9/11, for the fear of being misunderstood. Of course you will be misunderstood. Anytime you raise the issue of CPV and say that the question of justification is of some importance, under some law or the other, you are seen as conniving or encouraging terrorism. There is a plethora of anti-terror legislation—POTA[6] made the justification of certain kinds of terror itself an offence. Thinking about it is an offence. So we are worried. I am worried too, but after 9/11, I have written profusely on the wars and other related forms of terror and the wars on terror.

I have an essay, 'Translating Terror', in the volume *Globalization, Political Violence and Translation* (Baxi 2009b), and the publisher and the editors said they salute me for my exceptional courage. I was quite puzzled until I realised they were complimenting themselves and their courage in publishing the volume! It is crazy, but this is how knowledge production is. Alternative law must confront this. It must be alternative to the existing indifference to certain central problems of law and State, and to be alternative is to draw the curtain, not down but up, on things that are taboo, like sexuality, terror, CPV, systemic violence against Dalits, violence against the disabled, etc.

That's why it is important to engage with Balagopal and Kannabiran's thinking (also see Chapter 8 on Balagopal). Kannabiran's position is very clear. Overtly, he will support only the rule of law-based struggles. This is entirely okay because he had a mediating role, somebody had to go to the courts, meet the CM, etc., and you cannot play such a role and justify violent struggles. However, the question to ask is if this was a strategy or a conviction. If it is a conviction,

[6]The Prevention of Terrorism Act was passed by the Parliament of India with the objective of strengthening anti-terrorism operations. The Act was enacted in the aftermath of the attack on the Parliament of India. It replaced the Prevention of Terrorism Ordinance and the Terrorist and Disruptive Activities Act. Once in force, reports surfaced of the gross abuse of the law, leading to its repeal in 2004 (The Prevention of Terrorism Act 2002).

then perhaps that was a conviction towards which Balagopal too was moving towards the end of his life.

I do not think that Balagopal, when he goes Gandhian, is just making a strategic move. In retrospect, he is saying, this is something that is simply not right morally. There are other, morally better ways of doing it. I am only saying that the actual people intimately involved with this question have moved from one kind of thinking about CPV to another kind of thinking. One has to begin to understand and classify and decode and translate CPV, not in biographical terms, but in philosophical terms. It is unlikely to happen directly, I'm afraid. In the meantime, you read some pre-theoretical writings by a man called Upendra Baxi, which occupy the field, and that is unfortunate.

SRK: Why unfortunate?

UB: Because it is pre-theoretical. I don't offer a theory. I look at various bodies of Western discourse which have considered these issues. Virginia Held (my favourite feminist philosopher), for example, says that in certain cases CPV is morally justified, even if it causes harm to innocents (Held 2008). The key question is: Who is innocent when everyone is implicated in the system? They say about the Third Reich that no German of that time period was innocent. People had to have known that so many Jews were being taken away from Berlin, Hamburg, etc. So it's a question of German guilt. Karl Jaspers said that every German is complicit with the Third Reich (Jaspers 1961). We've not said that every Indian is guilty of the Partition, or is complicit with it. There is also the work of a Kantian philosopher I've looked at, whose name I forget, who says that CPV is justified when all channels of political communication are closed.[7] So an act of violence is a way to open up the channels of political communication. I examine this discourse in my essay in *The Right to be Human* (Baxi 1987b) and in 'Violence, Dissent and Development' (Baxi 1988a). In these two articles, I find an Indian position on CPV. I look at new literature and open up new questions. I suppose it is better than doing nothing. Modesty is not my virtue!

[7] Refers to Honderich (1980).

Theories are not Pies in the Sky

SRK: Why do you privilege theorisations with a European location in some ways?

UB: That is a very crucial question to raise in Mahatma Gandhi's India. That apostle of non-violence showed how even a national liberation struggle should be waged without violence. He mortified his body for acts of collective political violence. He did not agree that violence is a necessary evil, not even collective political violence. It is overwhelmingly apparent that society, as well as the State in India, has refused to walk on his well-trodden path of peace and non-violence, though both Nelson Mandela and Martin Luther King Jr, followed that path in the movement for civil liberties. What renewed global attention will be accorded to Gandhiji's principles on the occasion of his 150th birth anniversary yet remains to be seen.

There is an alternate approach that insists that violence as a means of last resort is a necessary evil. It also attends to ethical questions with a great sense of urgency. According to this position, to say violence is evil *per se* does not quite work because that makes every act of State against other States or geopolitical entities acts of aggression. This ignores the theory of just war, in which going to war might be a necessary evil. There is so much discourse from Kautilya onwards on the theory of the *dharmayuddha* (just war). The Confucian tradition refers as well to the notion of just war. If violence was *per se* evil, then war would be the worst form of CPV. War has always been considered morally problematic, but not *per se* evil. Or you will not have doctrines of just war which tell you what are the just means to pursue just causes. Just war can also become unjust by the means you adopt to pursue it. You have to privilege theory, which means careful thinking about the problem. Careful thinking cannot be done when you're actually fighting.

You have to acknowledge previous lines of enquiry. Theory doesn't happen because one wants to theorise. Ordinary people don't have the time to think about these things. Some people don't have the time because they are doing worthwhile things, but they need a backup, and that backup I call theory. If people ask, why the hell are you doing all these things about sexual orientation or conduct, violence for equality, etc., when they call you an enemy of State, an enemy of society, you have to say, wait a minute, there is something else that can explain why you are doing this.

Theory is an alternate explanation, an alternate reality. Theories are not pies in the sky! They are accounts that either problematise or justify courses of action in relation to human rights. I am talking about moral theories, not causal theories.

Theory is an attempt to resolve unresolved questions in practice. It's not unresolved because people in practice do not have the ability to resolve them, but because they do not have the time or the temperament to resolve them. Take Mohandas Gandhi—he could never produce a theory of nonviolence, even though he preached and practised nonviolence. He did not have the time, he had to move from place to place. If he was thinking of producing a theory of violence, we would have achieved independence much later. Theorising Gandhi is as important as understanding Gandhian action.

What were the questions he would have ideally liked to think through, systematically and clearly, and could not because the higher end for him was the liberation of India? Privileging theory is very important because you are only taking off from what the action leaves outside of itself: what praxis does not attend to. Marx says ideas are material forces and theories are weapons of class struggle. I think we should never forget that theory is not abstract. Theories are material forces which shape the world and react upon the world. He showed how understanding the nature of capitalism and exploitation, the tendency of profits to decline, the contradictions of capitalism, etc. might benefit the workers' struggle. The struggle is based upon an exploitation of the contradictions of the system. Struggle is always system-bound, although often brimming with global solidarity.

As Foucault said, struggle or resistance is always situated within the very field of power to which resistance is directed. Resistance is a kind of renewal/reinforcement of the system in some ways. That is a question that activists have to face—whether to go before the Supreme Court, or to continue to struggle only on the ground, or whether (and when) to do both together. I shamelessly privilege theory for these reasons. To theorise is to work on, work with, re-tool, and re-craft dilemmas of action and to take responsibility in struggle.

May I add a word or two concerning the typology of CPV? The situation of war declared (or undeclared) on another State or States is no doubt a paradigm situation. But there are also other types of CPV situations, often described in security theory as 'low intensity conflicts'. From the standpoint of the violated, of course, there is no such thing, but it is considered by theorists as less catastrophic than acts of war. Other situations involve: (*i*) a civil war; (*ii*) states of armed insurgency; (*iii*) collective acts of violence falling short of states of civil war or insurgency; (*iv*) cross-border acts of terrorism; (*v*) group acts of violence against fellow citizens, which may or may not be punished by law; (*vi*) multinational and national acts complicit with the States or terrorists; (*vii*) ethnic and ecological CPV; and finally, here (*viii*) CPV acts committed by multinational corporations. I do not take into account here (*ix*) CPV symbolic acts of violence that comprise defacement or destruction of public property. Nor do I include here acts that are already described as criminal violence, distinguished from CPV. Of course, there are situations in which the drawing of such bright lines is rather difficult....

More Bricklayer than Architect

SRK: Then the question is, why don't you consider your work as also a work in theory?

UB: I am not the best person to speak to about my work, but I would say it is implicitly theoretical, yes. Theories can be hegemonic or subaltern. My work would come under the latter rubric and also within social theory. I speak specifically of the empirical and comparative social theory of human rights. I am a labourer in the sphere of theory construction, more like a bricklayer than an architect.

If you distinguish theoretical labours in its different forms, I am certainly not a meta-theorist.

However, I have not worked out theory in such a way that it would answer some of the practical questions. I have also used the counter-theory genre to deflate some stories about the origins of traditions of thinking about human rights. Very early on I had (alongside with Professor R. P. Anand) the privilege of waging a war against Eurocentrism in thinking about law and justice, and also in starting a wave of critique for Third World-ism in international law, which goes now by the name of TWAIL (Third World Approaches to International Law). I have relied on some secondary material, but have not systematically developed my own worldview on radical evil. I have been doing comparative sociological theory of human rights with hints of a moral theory. Some would say it is very daring of me to say so, but that has been my conscious effort!

Mimesis and Originality in Human Rights Thinking

SRK: When you start looking at human rights critically, you realise the Euro- of the discourse. It is a political question, because there is no representation of nationalist movements, of anti-colonial struggles, or of the questions of justice that anti-colonial struggles have raised. This is completely absent from the historical account. There is also the epistemic question that *Future* raises, for instance: Is equality necessarily Western?

This is an epistemic question. Do we need to take it for granted that equality is a Western value, or do we need to look at different social theories of equality in different social contexts? I think the epistemic question is more important than the political one. Not that I am hierarchising the issues, but I would like to hear your reflections on this.

UB: I have a huge digression here to offer. But I will first take your point about equality. First, some people say that stratification is inherent to any social order, they further say that hierarchy is not necessarily anti-equality. Second, then some people say that equality is a 'complex virtue' and in that sense one talks, as John Rawls did in his *Law of Peoples*, of a 'decent hierarchical society'. What makes hierarchies decent is that some respect is accorded to some core human rights.

Third, equality itself is considered a basic human right—as both a horizontal and a vertical right, both the right of all individuals and a group—differentiated vertical right (Will Kymlicka maintains this position, and the vertical rights are group differentiated rights, as is the case, for example, with special provisions or affirmative action for the Scheduled Castes and Scheduled Tribes, and reservations for Other Backward Classes). In polyethnic rights situations, an individual has a horizontal equality right as well as group-differentiated human rights.

Is equality a Western virtue or notion? I do not think so. Every midnight's child knows that political and social inferiority of the colonised was considered a justified state of affairs. So was State apartheid, even the genocide of peoples. My favourite phrase, which comes from Robert J. C. Young's magisterial *Postcolonialism: An Historical Introduction* (2001), is that human rights were merely a 'whites-only affair'. One may maintain this, despite the fact that even after the normative justification of inequality became problematic with the French Revolution, and the elimination of chattel slavery marked the beginning of modern human rights, large swathes of non-Euro others were considered outside the sway of the equality principle. In terms of the history of ideas, too, the claim that ideas about equality originated in Europe is too Eurocentric a claim. In fact, it is my claim that to the tasks of equality as a human right, all societies come to it as equal strangers, and progress in egalitarian sentiment has been historically slow and tardy.

Changing the lens, let us look at controls over sexuality imposed by the dominant institutions of the State and society. Oscar Wilde came out of Reading jail and went to France, never to return to England. He died there, not as a broken spirit, but as a bitter man. He felt betrayed by his lover, Alfred Douglas. He was an epicure, a man who liked to live the good life. He enjoyed the best wines and music, and for him, to be in jail was a deprivation of the greatest magnitude. I signed a petition on the centenary of Wilde's conviction for 'gross indecency' to the Queen seeking the pardon of Oscar Wilde. I was much moved.

It is one of the very few online petitions that I have signed. I don't sign online petitions as long as I can help it because it's a completely alienated mode of expressing solidarity. You go to petitions.com and add your name and comments. It is very easy to do. It takes one minute to put your name, one minute to put your comments. Petitions.com is the universal brainchild of global social activism. But this is one of the most memorable petitions I have put my name to. The whole idea of saying that after 100 years, you must atone for the injustice done to one of the finest human beings in the world, one of the most creative spirits, is very moving.

It was not a question of the violation of Oscar Wilde's rights, because there were no rights in place then. It was a time that was a stranger to the language of contemporary human rights. It was the violation of the human spirit that was in issue. Therefore, to say that the criminal proceedings were misconceived, and the sentence was wrong, was a way to somewhat redress the violation of the human spirit. That was the understanding with which this was done.

We should do that in relation to oppressed sexualities in India and memorialise those who were tried and punished for no wrongdoing on their part. We should name them and, at appropriate times, ask the State to absolve itself for the guilt of having punished them. It is a moral gesture which should not be limited to the Oscar Wilde example, but should be a generalisable way of memorialising.

There are different ways of memorialisation. This is all there is to human rights, actually. To remember how the spirit and being of the human stands violated with immunity and impunity is the inauguration of the struggle for human rights. This involves the construction of a future memory, as Benjamin would say. He doesn't speak only to past events. You address future memory by recalling the past.

The question Ram is raising is about the colonisation of memory. Colonisation is just a word. It can be of territory, of people, of resources. But colonisation of images, notions of self, constructions of the past—that begins with an erasure. That is why I cited Milan Kundera at the first anniversary of Bhopal to say that the struggle of men (and women, I add) for rights and justice is the struggle of memory against forgetting. That is why the Wilde petition was so touching to me. It is not a truth and reconciliation commission, a truth finding commission, etc. These are all important things. But this is also a means of human rights education, asking the powerful to realise the error of their ways, as we sought to do in the Open Letter to the Chief Justice of India in the Mathura Case a while ago.

The act of reform has always to be imaginative. The very idea of doing something about the violation of the human spirit cannot just be reiterative, it has to break out of existing moulds. I would say it has to be an act of imaginative memory, of commemoration. Take, for example, the candlelight protest seen in *Rang De Basanti*. Solidarity and struggle can also be seen in the Jessica Lal protests at India Gate. Now, you see it everywhere. It is touching and moving, but it is reiterative. It doesn't differentiate between the contexts which give rise to solidarity, between the acts protested. The mode of showing solidarity is the same, everyone marching hand in hand, singing 'we shall overcome'. This is an important symbolisation, but it does not break the mould of protest. Solidarity is contextual, it has a particular poignancy, it has a particular moment, and it cannot culminate in widely common symbolisations which run across continents.

I put it this way, it is a distinction between mimesis and originality. That's a terribly important distinction, which I use in my work on constitutional law. Granville Austin says history had done the work for India's Constitution. The Constituent Assembly had only to extend and expand the Government of India Act of 1935. Mimesis is not about the elements of originality or creativity or of radical breaks, it is about the art of emulation. When gestures of protest and solidarity are deeply mimetic, they sometimes lose their historical edge.

On the other hand, originality is not given; it is sometimes spontaneous, and sometimes a work of infinite imaginative labour.

In human rights, the question is not whether all human rights are Western in origin or Eastern. That is mimetic. It is the Zapatistas, Ken Saro-Wiwa,[8] and others like that, who have authored declarations of

[8] Kenule Beeson 'Ken' Saro-Wiwa (1941–1995): Nigerian writer, television producer, environmental activist, member of the Ogoni people, whose homeland was targeted for the extraction of oil. Later, President of the Movement for the Survival of the Ogoni People (MOSOP). He was tried by a military tribunal and executed, leading to international outrage.

human rights which are indigenous, in the sense that they are beyond original. These transcend the petty debates about universalism and relativism in such a magnificent way. I would always say to my class, put the UDHR aside. Look at Ken Saro-Wiwa, Ogoniland, and the Zapatistas instead. These historical examples are so powerful. Where did their indigeneity come from? They have a memory of the earth before it became land, and thus a commodity. Land is a system of rights and relations. Earth is a spiritual entity. We have lost the notion of earth, we only have the notion of land. The indigenous person goes beyond the dichotomy between mimesis and originality [see Chapters 4 and 5 for more].

The important challenge for those who would colonise or globalise the world is to destroy plurality and to not have any worldviews other than the industrial or post-industrial one. You must destroy as pre-rational and dysfunctional all prior civilisations, because they all stand in the way of rationality and science. This is modernity as perceived and installed by world conquerors. Human rights education should also go aboriginal. Historically, the first postmodernists to mount a critique of civilisation, to de-centre and deconstruct, to propose alternatives in a real way, were the First Nations' peoples. Obviously, they have not read Derrida or Foucault, but they know that when earth becomes land, the world becomes an evil place.

Epistemic Humility in Promoting Human Rights Cultures

SRK: Your position on the epistemic question of human rights is very different from the position of postcolonial theory. Take Spivak's distinction between rights-based cultures and responsibility-based cultures and the American Anthropological Association's essentialist position, which took culture as constitutive of the subject, thereby denying any possibility of dialogue between cultures, or at least challenging universalism (Spivak 2005). Your position seems to be engaging with both in trying to present a different picture of those categories of universal ambition, reworking them by asking how these concepts could be understood in a non-Western cultural context like the notion of equality in the way you talk about it in *Future*.

UB: Ram, do you always go for the jugular? I don't know about unique! Why do I make a distinction between politics *of* and *for* human rights? That is one way of cutting through these thickets. I make several moves, I ask who the primary authors of human rights are. Wherever there is struggle against injustice or domination or rightlessness, that is the birthplace of human rights. There cannot be one single geographical place in the world that is such a birthplace, as if there are no injustices or struggles elsewhere.

Second, I look at the relationship between what Foucault calls technologies of the self and human rights. Can we talk about an individual or collective human rights self? I think we live in a world where it is possible to speak about human rights selfhood as against human rights agency. So if you think of Mohandas Gandhi, Martin Luther King Jr, the early Nelson Mandela in Robben Island, the monks who immolated themselves in Vietnam, and many others: they are people impregnated with the notion of human emancipation. I know that Mohandas has a very different reading of rights. When he talks of Swaraj, he certainly includes the formation of the human rights self. Of course, human rights selves are formed not only by notions of rights, but also by an ethic of responsibility. It is not that some cultures are responsibility-based and some are rights-based; all are intersectional, based both on rights and duties, whether secular or God-based. If we can say that the consciousness of human rights as a set of values helps, enables, and foments the formation of selves, then again it cannot be bound by history or geography or accident to some one place.

Third, it is true that certain kinds of consciousness of rights emerge only with the rise of industrial capitalism. They do not rise prior to it. Therefore, it is said that since it is in the Occident that capitalism arose and not in the Orient, there can be no notion of rights in the Orient. That is one way of looking at things, but it is curious because industrial capitalism, as Uncle Marx says, cannot be country-bound, it has to go global. It is so inbuilt into the dynamic of the industrial revolution that it becomes cross-border or worldwide. Therefore, colonisation is also justified in the march towards equality. If that is the case, the growth of industrial capitalism in the West means a denial of similar growth in the colonies. The story of India shows you how systemic de-industrialisation was pursued by the British. India had lots of natural resources, etc., but the colonial policy was to ensure that India did not develop. And then to say that these people had no capacity for industrial capitalism, and therefore no sense of rights, is only a part of the story, because you made sure that capitalism would not develop in the colonies, that they would remain a purely export-oriented market. The labour and capital of the colonies were pressed into the service of the Empire.

To say that capitalism would never arise in Asia and Africa is self-serving. The counterfactual is important—if colonialism had not happened, would there have been no development or industrialisation in the ex-colonies? It is true that industrial capitalism foregrounded respect for certain kinds of rights with respect to property. As I have said in *The Right to be Human* (Baxi, et al. 1987a), the essence of a bourgeois right is the right to lawfully harm others. That's what free competition is.

I used to tell my students in Delhi: imagine the impossible, that I run a boutique in Karol Bagh! I'm quite prosperous, I send my children to school. Then Madhava Menon comes to Karol Bagh and opens up a boutique. He has the gift of organisational entrepreneurship. In the ensuing competition, I go broke. I then go to the bankruptcy court as my family and I are rendered destitute. The question I ask is: Has Madhava Menon done me any wrong? It is the case of the market being based on free and fair competition. If somebody drives me out of business, what does it mean in terms of human rights? I have the human right to lawfully harm others. What is lawful harm and unlawful harm is something that the law will decide.

Who will decide the law? The ruling bourgeoisie. Who are they? The owners of the means of production or their agents. How will they define what is lawful harm? By minimising the identification of unlawful harms. If they are saying that this kind of right did not emerge elsewhere, just as well. This paradigm did not emerge in Korea or Japan or China. Instead, the notion that emerged in those places was that rights ought to know certain moral and ethical limits. Rights are relational propositions, a part of social relations, not just a factor of production. Human rights imply a sense of respect for the other. Thinkers like Immanuel Kant have also said this, with greater finesse.

I went through this controversy about the uniqueness of the Western notion and so on, and I found it not merely wanting, but a huge distraction. I decided to make my book a statement about how distracting and unproductive this specific claim of Eurocentric authorship is, and then I begin to distinguish between progressive and regressive Eurocentric authorship. As far as the recognition and realisation of human rights are concerned, all countries come to it as equal strangers to the task of realising human rights. There is no such distinction as developed country/developing country/least developed country in this context.

Epistemic humility is something which I believe is very important for promoting human rights cultures. Therefore, we must not make the same mistake in the reverse direction by saying that India is a source of all human values. There is no source of all human values—there are only different sources, and this does not take us to relativism, it takes us to the understanding of civilisations, of cultures, of how they flourish. Now the question is, what to do with these kinds of ideas? If civilisations and cultures do not merely disrespect human dignity but actually justify the violation of human dignity, what do you do? The position of women in culture, be it sati or devadasi, child marriage or hijab, whatever your favourite example is, what do you do? Therefore, some universal standards are necessary. Now these universal standards can come from two or more sources. One source is from some kind of international declaration, another is by way of cross-civilisational dialogue. What Raimon Panikkar (1979) calls *diatopical hermeneutics*.

Advocating a return to the Mecca School in which the Prophet [PBUH] emphasised the inherent dignity of all human beings, regardless of gender, religious belief, race, Professor Abdullahi An-Naim stressed that dialogue among the Believers is the most enduring path of social stability and change. A return to the more progressive and egalitarian version of traditions entails the rejection of repressive or dominant interpretation that favours a few. Thus, one also seeks to reconstruct the world by multicultural dialogue towards understanding the role of religion, law, and understandings of society. An internal rediscovery of more egalitarian trends in your own traditions liberates us from any borrowal of values from outside.

My favourite example is the verse in the Qu'ran on polygamy. It says, marry ye four wives, if ye can treat them equally. The first half of the verse authorises polygamy. The second half reigns it in, by imposing a condition almost impossible to fulfil. Now, which do you privilege, the first half of the verse or the second half? This is juristic interpretation. One of the greatest things about Hindu, Islamic, and Rabbinic law is that they are jurist-made laws. The State is not the authority. The duty of interpretation lies with Maulanas, Pandits, and Rabbis. To me, a jurist is someone who makes law, not just studies law. As pious interpreters, we should take every word of God seriously.

So, coming back to this verse, you cannot ignore its last half. How can you treat all four wives equally? What does it mean? Conjugal equality? Is it equality of esteem? How do you have equality of esteem, affection, conjugality if one person is young, another is old; if one cooks well, one doesn't, etc.? Many bearded Maulanas completely unintroduced to feminist thought said that such equality is not possible. A deadlock arose. They got out of this by saying, Allah does not command the impossible of his followers. If it is not possible to treat four wives equally, he could not have commanded that you marry four wives. Therefore, polygamy is against the will of Allah.

Take Madhavacharya from south India. In Manu, cross-cousin marriage is forbidden. Madhavacharya said Dharma is *deshakala*, region and time-specific. Natural law, in the sense of eternal law, applies everywhere, but its content changes according to time, manner, and circumstance. The distinction between Dharma and Vyavahara, to take another great example, expresses natural law with a changing content. These are interpretations that favour human rights. The Shastras often impose contradictory restrictions. Madhavacharya brought in the notion of *sadachara*, custom or knowledge of the wise as a guide to action. The short point is, it is possible to find answers to the oppressive aspects of a civilisational tradition, human wrongs of a tradition, by rediscovering that tradition and removing the corruptions it has undergone.

For every single major human rights enunciation, non-European culture has a similar standard. Whether it is torture, discrimination, rights of specific communities, sex workers, or sexual orientation, you will find comparable articulations. In fact, you will find specific gods in the Hindu pantheon who are worshipped because they embody the idea of people with differential abilities and tastes and dispositions. For example, Lord Jagannath of Puri, who is disabled and is worshipped.

Relativism of human rights is thus an intracultural affair. The relativism debate has taken up so much of our energy for no good reason because the American Anthropological Association of 2001 now speaks of the right to culture. What is the right to culture? Is it the right of belonging? Is it tradition? What is culture? Is it that which gives ultimate meaning to experience, thereby creating unbridgeable divides across cultures? These are absolutely self-serving discourses which should never have been taken seriously by anybody but unfortunately have been, such as Lee Kuan Yew's theory of Asian values. I would give dignity of discourse to everyone, but this is not to say that all discourses are ethically equal. How can dictators who violate everybody's humanity be taken seriously? The idea that we must give the voice of the South some standing, to bend over backwards after having claimed that human rights are Eurocentric, to condescend now to give some respect, only to end up giving respect to the voice of dictators. The voices thus given a hearing are not those of the Zapatistas or of Ken Saro-Wiwa, nor is it the statement of Dalit activists, nor is it the voices of LGBTQI at world fora. Instead emerge some voices of the far right, of signifying a democratic dictator, or 'democratorship', as it is now called![9]

[9]This is a new coinage recently adopted by some political theorists to describe the hybrid passage between democracy and dictatorship, especially in Hungary and Poland, but it can used globally to describe authoritarian legality which is also democratic. The recent election results in Italy provide an instance.

Amartya Sen (1999b) has an article on Asian values saying much the same thing. If you are interested in transformative politics, you don't generate facile distinctions such as rights cultures, responsibility cultures, Asian values, and so on. Uncle Marx said it a long time ago in *On the Jewish Question*—we must distinguish between values and interests. Interests are the desires that we have. Values are the desires that we ought to have. Very often, interests are rationalised as values. Like the idea of an India without the diversity represented by 'composite culture' (as Part IV-A of the Constitution of India describes it) may be said to be unethical in the sense that it doesn't regard other people as worthy of respect. I am very impatient with these protean versions of the values debate. For example, Robert Mugabe's anti-imperialist position means that many Africans are reluctant to speak against him, because he's the spokesperson for all Africans who take up a position against the imperialist West.[10] But does anti-imperialism confer a total impunity for human rights violations and catastrophes?

Against Epistemic Racism

SRK: I see two aspects emerging from your thought. One aspect is your politics of and for modern and contemporary human rights, which is very important for the postcolonial context. The other is asking us to rework concepts such as equality and dignity.

UB: We have to criticise epistemic racism. It is a strong word, but it is the word that has to be used. When the claim is that only certain people can have access to certain forms of knowledge and not others, that only the heirs of European enlightenment know what liberty is

[10] Robert Gabriel Mugabe (21 February 1924–6 September 2019) was a Zimbabwean revolutionary hero who came to prominence as a guerrilla leader in the 1970s and led his country to independence. He then proceeded to rule Zimbabwe for thirty-seven years. His record as a leader was both as the 'public face of a hopeful experiment in African independence' as well as 'freedom fighter turned tyrant'. See Chan (2003).

and the rest of the world is not capable of understanding what it is, we have to criticise that claim. During colonisation, one of the court of appeal judges said about the African people that they are at so inferior a stage of civilisation that we should not 'impose' rights on them (Baxi 2013c, Ch 2). This is epistemic racism, in which the people of manifest destiny are the only ones who can have true knowledge of dignity, equality, etc. This is exactly what was called priesthood, what Ambedkar denounces as the Brahmanical conception of Varna. Ambedkar is very relevant to this discussion. He exposed the epistemic racism of the way the Shastras are constructed. I have been criticised by various scholars for having used the word 'racism', as they feel that it is a thing of the past. But is it? Not every discrimination amounts to racism, but perhaps, we may begin to distinguish (with Slavoj Zizek) between its 'modern' and 'postmodern' forms.

What is the opposite of epistemic racism? It is epistemic egalitarianism. When you say all human beings, singly or collectively, remain capable of ethical knowledge, the claim of specially constituted morally gifted people is undone. Look at the period between the two international covenants on human rights, on the one hand, and the emergence of the right to development and the new international economic order, on the other. It was the period of the Cold War, between 1950 and 1985–1986, but it was also the period of radical epistemic egalitarianism. Human rights enunciations are formulated by those people whose civilisations were thought to be incapable of moral sensibility. Look at the African Charter of Human Rights—the Banjul Charter[11]—and compare it with the UDHR, you can see the difference. John Rawls and Jürgen Habermas probably never read the African Declaration, but you will find such resonances in their thought of the principles enunciated in the Charter. The Banjul Charter talks of participation as a basic human right, of development as a human right. Yet the creativity of the non-European peoples in the field of human rights still continues to be disciplined and tamed. They have expanded the meaning of human rights at the level of

[11] African Charter on Human and Peoples' Rights, also known as the Banjul Charter (1981).

normativity. Indeed, as shown by Miloon Kothari in an article on the Indian contribution to the making of UDHR,[12] it was Ms. Hansa Mehta's forceful intervention that brought an end to the Christian invocation of 'God' in the final version and made the UDHR a secular document, and interventions by Piloo Mody brought about the added prohibition of discrimination on the basis of race. Very often, thus, the epistemic arrogance is brought about by total ignorance of the drafting history of a human rights enunciation; it is always a work of many minds.

Normativity is very important, as is institutionality. Now epistemic egalitarianism has moved to a third phase where you say, it is not only the state elites and the constitutional elite who write standards of human rights, it is also the struggling people, NGOs, etc., who do so. If you ask why the Declaration on the Rights of Indigenous Peoples (2007) comes so late—after declarations on the rights of women, children, migrant workers—part of the problem was, how should the indigenous peoples define that category?

In the definitional quarrel, indigenous people were saying that we do not give an essentialist definition by birth, by family, etc., we say an indigenous person is one who is recognised by the group that is now found in the definition. That is indigenous thinking. Your membership is not decided by your choice or accident of birth, but by collective recognition of you as belonging to us. In a sense, radical egalitarianism comes from other directions, non-State directions, non-expert directions, so little groups can make big human rights statements. Hierarchies within human rights groups are thus also being questioned on the ground of what entitles them to speak for us all. Sometimes, in my human rights courses, I have said, let nobody talk about Asian values, African values, universalism, relativism. My students would be aghast, because those are the easiest, and surely essential, things to do!

---

[12] Miloon Kothari, 'India's Contribution to the Universal Declaration of Human Rights', *Journal of the National Human Rights Commission* 17, 2018, 65–98.

Normative Expectations and the Struggle against Injustice

AN: You were referring to this notion of normativity, and the role that normativity plays in human rights thinking. You say in the J. P. Naik memorial lecture,

> The experience of injustice always involves normative expectations. Take these away and you lose the very possibility of experience of injustice. The other may not be said to violate the self, which has no expectation of how the other ought to regard it, no basis for articulating this expectation, no memory for its narrative history. Domination and exploitation becomes naturalized. (Baxi 2003c)

UB: It was Bentham, who first drew our attention to the dynamics of relations between law and expectations, and much later Niklas Luhmann, drew a contrast between two kinds of expectations: existential expectations and normative expectations. Existential expectations are what we hope will happen as a result of certain actions of others. For example, Bentham said that law, society, and economics must be so organised that the expectations of the maximum number of people are fulfilled. These are existential expectations. As against this, you have normative expectations. Existential expectations perish when they are not fulfilled. If you are hungry and you don't get food, the expectation dies. In case of normative expectations, the more you are disappointed, the stronger they become! This is what Luhmann guides us to with respect to his analysis of the rule of law.

Every time the rule of law is said to be violated, the greater becomes the demand for conduct that follows the rule of law. Every time human rights are violated, the greater becomes the demand that human rights should be observed. With each violation, the normative expectation grows stronger, but each existential expectation perishes with its disappointment, the expectation collapses, nothing more happens. It remains a memory, an ache, a void, but does not always result in compelling action.

So, if you make the distinction between normative and existential, then human rights expectations create all the things I have stated—memory, futures, action, struggle. Every time the normative expectation is violated, the impulse is to do something to prevent the violation from recurring. If human rights expectations were only existential expectations, then every time somebody is tortured or encountered, the expectation would perish. Therefore, normativity is important to make the point that State power is not exercised barbarically. It enables one to read what I call the hardcore pornography of power—read, decode, and attack. Pornography of power is a voyeuristic and sadistic interest in imposing suffering on the other. Harassing people, putting them in prison, these are forms of State sexuality/eroticism, in which this power is a source of joy. If you have to study this hardcore pornography, you can only do this by using certain normative standards. If you say that power is the standard for itself, it goes nowhere. If you say counter-power sets the standard, then it becomes the object of a gaze, critique, struggle. But you also need norms by which to continually re-evaluate existing norms. Different kinds of normativity of law, ethics, spirit are necessary for this reason.

Legal normativity is often ethically fractured. We need human rights to question legal normativity. Some people say that human rights normativity is itself ethically fractured. CEDAW, for example, does not care about the right to sexual orientation. I have asked many CEDAW activists why the word 'family' appears in it. There are a number of reasons given from the point of view of human rights diplomacy—activists want to get certain statements internationally approved, so of necessity they have to make certain compromises. Human rights ethicality is fractured because of the necessity of agreement. Everybody knows that the family is the most important site for human rights violations. I said to these activists, why not recognise the sexual orientation of women as a human right? Why take heterosexuality as a norm? They told me, first, let us get the rights of women recognised as human rights, if we speak now of the rights of women of different sexualities, we will not even get recognition in CEDAW as women. When we were fighting for making marital rape an offence, the

Communist leaders, Susheela Gopalan and Geeta Mukherjee, told us the time for that has not yet come. This is strategy, diplomacy, but it is ethically wrong if this is not how inclusivity is constructed otherwise in terms of a human right to be different.

One might say there are four normativities—legal, human rights, ethical, and spiritual. Kelsen said every moral and normative system entails a grundnorm because otherwise, we invite infinite regress.

Aakrosh ends with a young lawyer being told by a senior lawyer how to behave in courts; when he asks why, he is told, if you keep asking why, you will never be a good lawyer. Every system must have a cut-off point of asking why. In *Aakrosh*, the senior lawyer says, you are asking the cause of every cause. It can result in infinite regress until we come to the point where there can be no more conversation, only force. No logical or social system is conceivable unless there is a cut-off point to avoid infinite regress. So, if legal normativity is fractured, turn to human rights normativity. If human rights normativity is fractured, turn to ethical normativity. If ethical normativity is fractured, turn to spiritual normativity. If you ask what if spiritual normativity is also fractured, then the only recourse is to appropriate therapies, or to pray. Or is there any better response?

References

Works by Upendra Baxi

Baxi, Upendra. 1967a. 'The Little Done, The Vast Undone: Reflections on Reading Granville Austin's The Indian Constitution'. *Journal of the Indian Law Institute* 9: 323–430.

_____. 1967b. 'Kautilyan Principles and the Law of Nations—A Comment'. In *Indian Yearbook of International Affairs*, Indian Study Group of International Law and Affairs, 230–255. Madras: Madras University.

_____. 1967c. 'Validity of Professio Juris Stipulations in Maritime Passage Contracts—A Study in American Conflicts Law'. *Houston Law Review* 6 (4): 657–684.

_____. 1967d. 'Kautilyan Principles and the Law of Nations—A Comment'. In *Indian Yearbook of International Affairs*, Indian Study Group of International Law and Affairs, 230–255. Madras: Madras University.

_____. 1968a. 'Contract Law in India: When Will Rip Van Winkle Awake?' Discussion Meet on Contract Law in India at Nainital, Indian Law Institute, New Delhi.

_____. 1968b. 'Allepey Turmeric Fingers and Arbitral Awards: Spices in the Conflict of Laws'. *Journal of the Indian Law Institute* 9: 149–170.

_____. 1969a. 'Directive Principles and Sociology of Indian Law: A Reply to Dr Jagat Narain'. *Journal of the Indian Law Institute* 11 (3): 245–272.

_____. 1969b. 'The Travails of Land Use Planning: Compensation and Urbanization'. In N. M. Tripathi (ed.), *Law and Urbanization in India*, 153–172. New Delhi: Indian Law Institute.

_____. 1969c. 'State of Gujarat vs. Shantilal: A Requiem for "Just Compensation"?' *Jaipur L.J.* 9: 29–97.

_____. 1972a. 'Some Remarks on Eurocentricism and the Law of Nations'. In R. P. Anand (ed.), *Asian States and the Development of Universal International Law*, 3–9. Delhi: Vikas Publications.

_____. 1972b. 'The Lost Dreamtime: Now Forever Lost. A Critique of the Gove Land Rights Decision'. Australian Universities Law Schools Association Annual Conference, University of Tasmania.

Baxi, Upendra. 1974. 'The Constitutional Quicksands of *Kesavananda Bharati* and the Twenty-Fifth Amendment'. *Supreme Court Cases Journal* 1 (45).

———. 1975a. 'Notes Towards Socially Relevant Legal Education: A Working Paper for the UGC Regional Workshop in Law'. *Journal of the Bar Council of India* 51: 23–55.

———. 1975b. 'Legal Assistance to the Poor: A Critique of the Expert Committee Report'. *Economic and Political Weekly* 10 (27): 1005–1013.

———. 1976a. 'Constitutional Changes: An Analysis of the Swaran Singh Committee Report'. *Supreme Court Cases Journal* 2 (17).

———. 1976b. 'From Takrar to Karar: The Lok Adalat—A Preliminary Study'. *Journal of Constitutional and Parliamentary Studies* 10: 53.

——— (ed.). 1978a. *K.K. Mathew on Democracy, Equality and Freedom*. Lucknow: Eastern Book Company.

———. 1978b. 'Some Reflections on the Nature of Constituent Power'. In Rajeev Dhavan and Alice Jacob (eds), *Indian Constitution: Trends and Issues*. New Delhi: Indian Law Institute.

———. 1980. *The Indian Supreme Court and Politics*. Lucknow: Eastern Book Company.

———. 1982a. *The Crisis of the Indian Legal System*. New Delhi: Vikas Publishing House.

———. 1982b. 'Socio-Legal Research in India—A Programschrift'. *Journal of the Indian Law Institute* 24 (2&3): 416–449.

———. 1982c. 'Who Bothers about the Supreme Court? The Problem of Impact of Judicial Decisions'. *Journal of the Indian Law Institute* 24 (4): 848–862.

———. 1983a. 'Marx, Law and Justice'. Third V. K. Krishna Menon Law Lecture, Kerala Law Academy, Trivandrum.

———. 1983b. 'Letter from India: The Law of Copyright in India'. *Copyright* 19: 91–109.

———. 1983c. 'Pre-Marxist Socialism and the Supreme Court of India'. *Supreme Court Cases Journal* 4: 3–9.

———. 1985a. 'Popular Justice, Participatory Development and Power Politics: The Lok Adalat in Turmoil'. In Antony Allott and Gordon R. Goodman (eds), *People's Law and State Law: The Bellagio Papers*, 171–186. Dordrecht: Foris Publications.

———. 1985b. *Courage, Craft and Contention: The Indian Supreme Court in the Eighties*. Bombay: N.M. Tripathi.

———. 1985c. 'Taking Suffering Seriously: Social Action Litigation in the Supreme Court of India'. *Third World Legal Studies* 4 (6): 107–132.

Baxi, Upendra. 1985d. 'Reflections on Reservation Crisis in Gujarat'. *Mainstream*, June.

_____. 1985e. 'Caste, Class and Reservations (In Memoriam: IP Desai)'. *Economic and Political Weekly* 20 (10): 426–428.

_____. 1985f. 'The Fair Name of Justice: The Memorable Voyage of Chief Justice Chandrachud'. In Y. V. Chandrachud, and Vasant Shamrao Deshpande, *A Chandrachud Reader: Collection of Judgements With Annotations*. New Delhi: Documentation Centre for Corporate & Business Policy Research/Universal Book Traders.

_____. 1986a. 'People's Law in India, the Hindu Society'. In Masaji Chiba (ed.), *Asian Indigenous Law: In Interaction With Received Law*. London/ New York: Routledge and Kegan Paul.

_____. 1986b. *Towards a Sociology of Indian Law*. New Delhi: Satvahan Publications.

_____. 1986c. 'Copyright Law and Justice in India'. *Journal of the Indian Law Institute* 28 (4): 497–540.

_____. 1986d. 'Redeeming the University'. *Economic and Political Weekly* 21 (17): 742–744.

_____ (ed.). 1986e. *Bentham's Theory of Legislation*. Bombay: N. M. Tripathi.

_____. 1986f. 'The Pathology of the Indian Legal Professions'. *Indian Bar Review* 13 (3/4): 455–484.

_____. 1986g. *Inconvenient Forum and Convenient Catastrophe*. New Delhi: Indian Law Institute.

_____. 1987a. 'Towards the Liberation of Women's Studies'. *ICSSR Newsletter* 18 (3): 6.

_____. 1987b. 'From Human Rights to the Right to be Human'. In Upendra Baxi, et al. (eds), *The Right to be Human*, 185–200.

_____. 1988a. 'Violence, Dissent and Development'. In Robert F. Meagher (ed.), *Law and Social Change: Indo-American Reflections*, 72–93. Bombay: N. M. Tripathi.

_____ (ed.). 1988b. *Law and Poverty: Critical Essays*. Bombay: N. M. Tripathi.

_____. 1989a. 'Historic New Law: Protecting SCs/SLs Human Rights'. *The Times of India*, Bombay, 15 September.

_____. 1989b. *Liberty and Corruption: The Antulay Case and Beyond*. Lucknow: Eastern Book Co.

_____. 1989c. 'Revictimizing the Bhopal Victims'. *Mainstream*, 5 March: 5.

_____. 1989d. 'The Second Bhopal Catastrophe'. *The Indian Express*, 19 December.

_____. 1990a. 'Teaching as Provocation'. In Amrik Singh (ed.), *On Being a Teacher*, 150–158. New Delhi: Konarak Publishers.

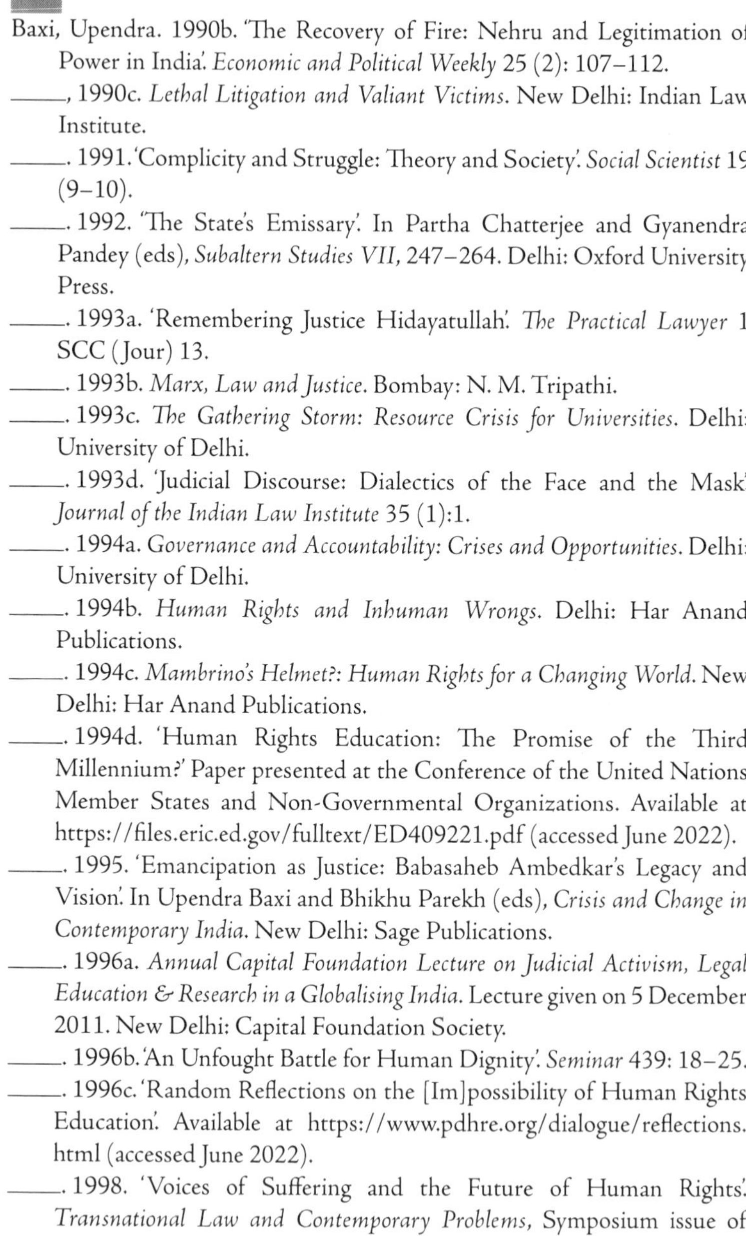

Baxi, Upendra. 1990b. 'The Recovery of Fire: Nehru and Legitimation of Power in India'. *Economic and Political Weekly* 25 (2): 107–112.

———, 1990c. *Lethal Litigation and Valiant Victims*. New Delhi: Indian Law Institute.

———. 1991. 'Complicity and Struggle: Theory and Society'. *Social Scientist* 19 (9–10).

———. 1992. 'The State's Emissary'. In Partha Chatterjee and Gyanendra Pandey (eds), *Subaltern Studies VII*, 247–264. Delhi: Oxford University Press.

———. 1993a. 'Remembering Justice Hidayatullah'. *The Practical Lawyer* 1 SCC (Jour) 13.

———. 1993b. *Marx, Law and Justice*. Bombay: N. M. Tripathi.

———. 1993c. *The Gathering Storm: Resource Crisis for Universities*. Delhi: University of Delhi.

———. 1993d. 'Judicial Discourse: Dialectics of the Face and the Mask'. *Journal of the Indian Law Institute* 35 (1):1.

———. 1994a. *Governance and Accountability: Crises and Opportunities*. Delhi: University of Delhi.

———. 1994b. *Human Rights and Inhuman Wrongs*. Delhi: Har Anand Publications.

———. 1994c. *Mambrino's Helmet?: Human Rights for a Changing World*. New Delhi: Har Anand Publications.

———. 1994d. 'Human Rights Education: The Promise of the Third Millennium?' Paper presented at the Conference of the United Nations Member States and Non-Governmental Organizations. Available at https://files.eric.ed.gov/fulltext/ED409221.pdf (accessed June 2022).

———. 1995. 'Emancipation as Justice: Babasaheb Ambedkar's Legacy and Vision'. In Upendra Baxi and Bhikhu Parekh (eds), *Crisis and Change in Contemporary India*. New Delhi: Sage Publications.

———. 1996a. *Annual Capital Foundation Lecture on Judicial Activism, Legal Education & Research in a Globalising India*. Lecture given on 5 December 2011. New Delhi: Capital Foundation Society.

———. 1996b. 'An Unfought Battle for Human Dignity'. *Seminar* 439: 18–25.

———. 1996c. 'Random Reflections on the [Im]possibility of Human Rights Education'. Available at https://www.pdhre.org/dialogue/reflections.html (accessed June 2022).

———. 1998. 'Voices of Suffering and the Future of Human Rights'. *Transnational Law and Contemporary Problems*, Symposium issue of 'International Human Rights at Fifty' 5 (2): 125–170.

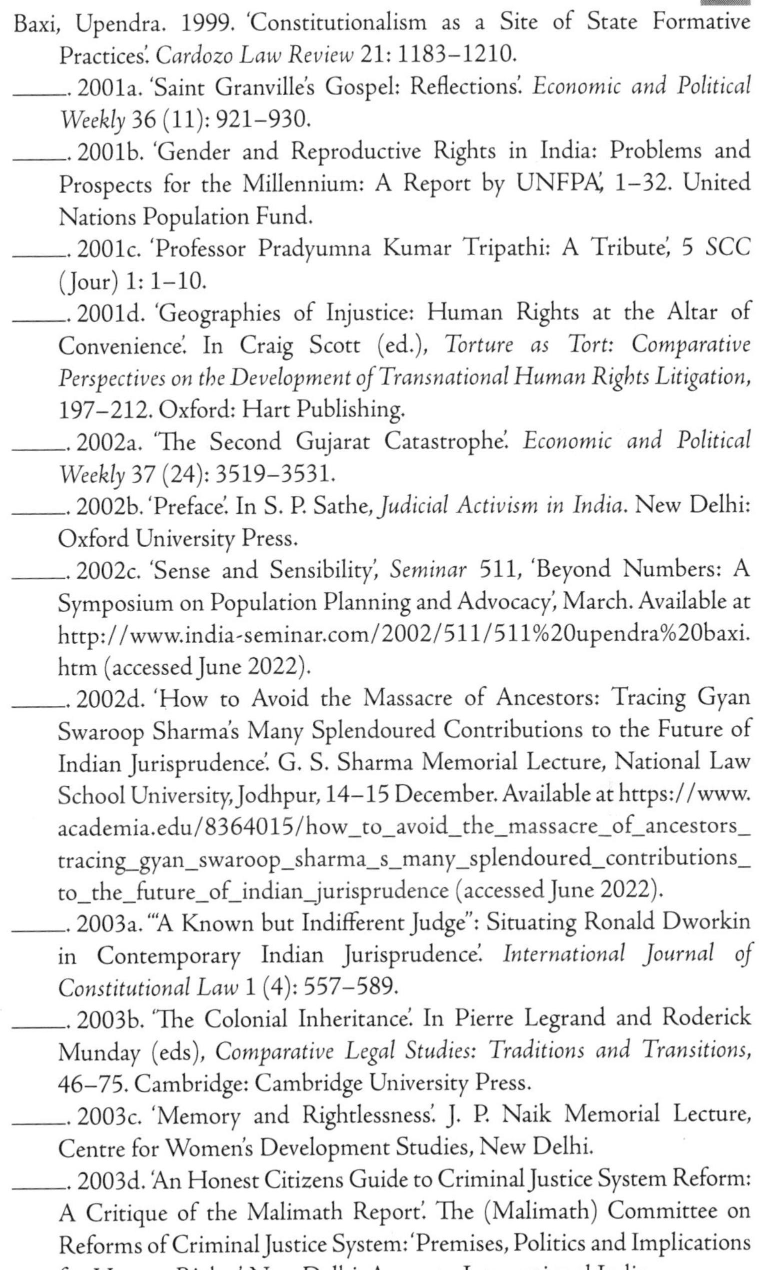

Baxi, Upendra. 1999. 'Constitutionalism as a Site of State Formative Practices'. *Cardozo Law Review* 21: 1183–1210.

———. 2001a. 'Saint Granville's Gospel: Reflections'. *Economic and Political Weekly* 36 (11): 921–930.

———. 2001b. 'Gender and Reproductive Rights in India: Problems and Prospects for the Millennium: A Report by UNFPA', 1–32. United Nations Population Fund.

———. 2001c. 'Professor Pradyumna Kumar Tripathi: A Tribute', 5 SCC (Jour) 1: 1–10.

———. 2001d. 'Geographies of Injustice: Human Rights at the Altar of Convenience'. In Craig Scott (ed.), *Torture as Tort: Comparative Perspectives on the Development of Transnational Human Rights Litigation*, 197–212. Oxford: Hart Publishing.

———. 2002a. 'The Second Gujarat Catastrophe'. *Economic and Political Weekly* 37 (24): 3519–3531.

———. 2002b. 'Preface'. In S. P. Sathe, *Judicial Activism in India*. New Delhi: Oxford University Press.

———. 2002c. 'Sense and Sensibility', *Seminar* 511, 'Beyond Numbers: A Symposium on Population Planning and Advocacy', March. Available at http://www.india-seminar.com/2002/511/511%20upendra%20baxi.htm (accessed June 2022).

———. 2002d. 'How to Avoid the Massacre of Ancestors: Tracing Gyan Swaroop Sharma's Many Splendoured Contributions to the Future of Indian Jurisprudence'. G. S. Sharma Memorial Lecture, National Law School University, Jodhpur, 14–15 December. Available at https://www.academia.edu/8364015/how_to_avoid_the_massacre_of_ancestors_tracing_gyan_swaroop_sharma_s_many_splendoured_contributions_to_the_future_of_indian_jurisprudence (accessed June 2022).

———. 2003a. '"A Known but Indifferent Judge": Situating Ronald Dworkin in Contemporary Indian Jurisprudence'. *International Journal of Constitutional Law* 1 (4): 557–589.

———. 2003b. 'The Colonial Inheritance'. In Pierre Legrand and Roderick Munday (eds), *Comparative Legal Studies: Traditions and Transitions*, 46–75. Cambridge: Cambridge University Press.

———. 2003c. 'Memory and Rightlessness'. J. P. Naik Memorial Lecture, Centre for Women's Development Studies, New Delhi.

———. 2003d. 'An Honest Citizens Guide to Criminal Justice System Reform: A Critique of the Malimath Report'. The (Malimath) Committee on Reforms of Criminal Justice System: 'Premises, Politics and Implications for Human Rights'. New Delhi: Amnesty International India.

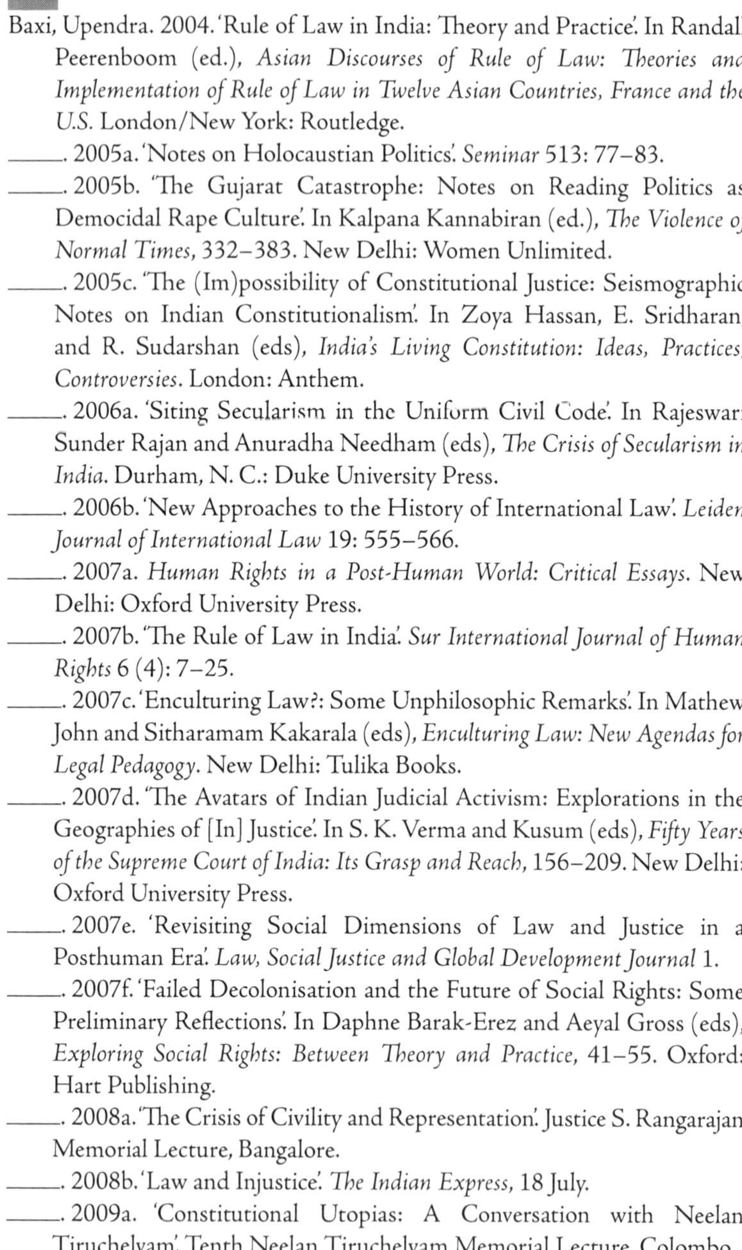

Baxi, Upendra. 2004. 'Rule of Law in India: Theory and Practice'. In Randall Peerenboom (ed.), *Asian Discourses of Rule of Law: Theories and Implementation of Rule of Law in Twelve Asian Countries, France and the U.S.* London/New York: Routledge.

———. 2005a. 'Notes on Holocaustian Politics'. *Seminar* 513: 77–83.

———. 2005b. 'The Gujarat Catastrophe: Notes on Reading Politics as Democidal Rape Culture'. In Kalpana Kannabiran (ed.), *The Violence of Normal Times*, 332–383. New Delhi: Women Unlimited.

———. 2005c. 'The (Im)possibility of Constitutional Justice: Seismographic Notes on Indian Constitutionalism'. In Zoya Hassan, E. Sridharan, and R. Sudarshan (eds), *India's Living Constitution: Ideas, Practices, Controversies*. London: Anthem.

———. 2006a. 'Siting Secularism in the Uniform Civil Code'. In Rajeswari Sunder Rajan and Anuradha Needham (eds), *The Crisis of Secularism in India*. Durham, N. C.: Duke University Press.

———. 2006b. 'New Approaches to the History of International Law'. *Leiden Journal of International Law* 19: 555–566.

———. 2007a. *Human Rights in a Post-Human World: Critical Essays*. New Delhi: Oxford University Press.

———. 2007b. 'The Rule of Law in India'. *Sur International Journal of Human Rights* 6 (4): 7–25.

———. 2007c. 'Enculturing Law?: Some Unphilosophic Remarks'. In Mathew John and Sitharamam Kakarala (eds), *Enculturing Law: New Agendas for Legal Pedagogy*. New Delhi: Tulika Books.

———. 2007d. 'The Avatars of Indian Judicial Activism: Explorations in the Geographies of [In] Justice'. In S. K. Verma and Kusum (eds), *Fifty Years of the Supreme Court of India: Its Grasp and Reach*, 156–209. New Delhi: Oxford University Press.

———. 2007e. 'Revisiting Social Dimensions of Law and Justice in a Posthuman Era'. *Law, Social Justice and Global Development Journal* 1.

———. 2007f. 'Failed Decolonisation and the Future of Social Rights: Some Preliminary Reflections'. In Daphne Barak-Erez and Aeyal Gross (eds), *Exploring Social Rights: Between Theory and Practice*, 41–55. Oxford: Hart Publishing.

———. 2008a. 'The Crisis of Civility and Representation'. Justice S. Rangarajan Memorial Lecture, Bangalore.

———. 2008b. 'Law and Injustice'. *The Indian Express*, 18 July.

———. 2009a. 'Constitutional Utopias: A Conversation with Neelan Tiruchelvam'. Tenth Neelan Tiruchelvam Memorial Lecture, Colombo.

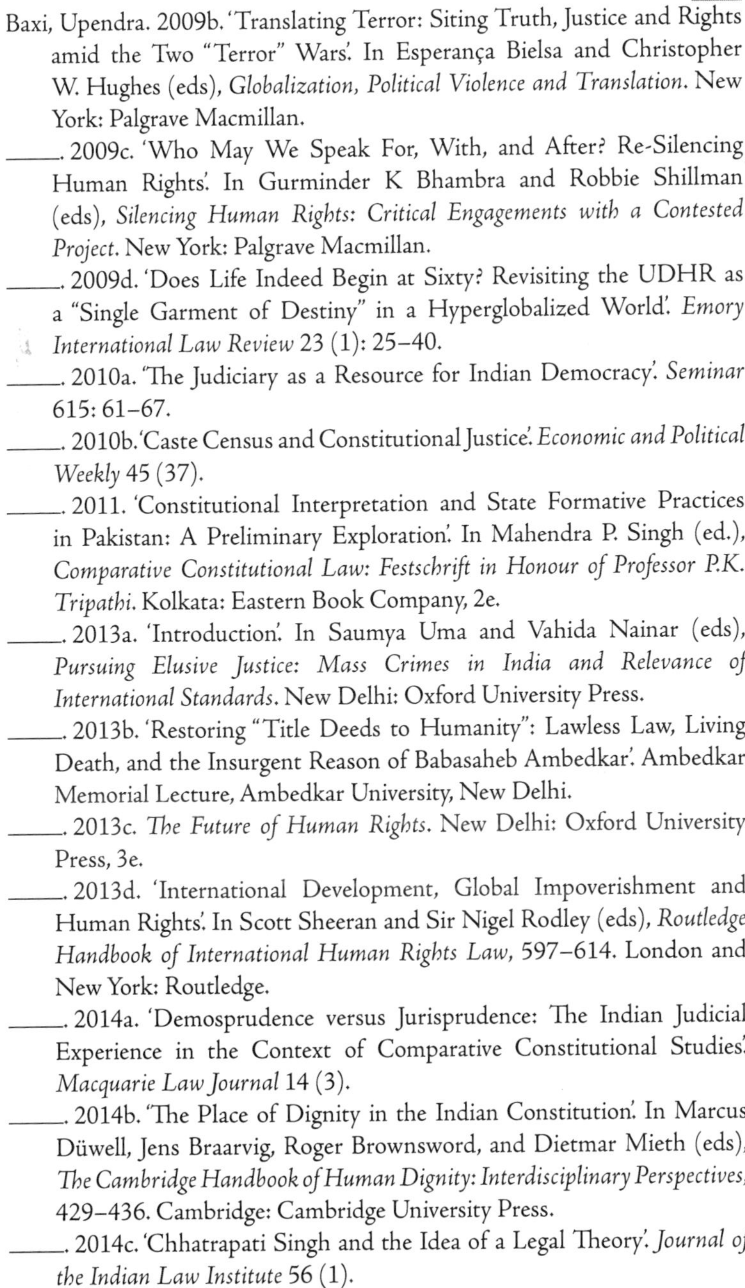

Baxi, Upendra. 2009b. 'Translating Terror: Siting Truth, Justice and Rights amid the Two "Terror" Wars'. In Esperança Bielsa and Christopher W. Hughes (eds), *Globalization, Political Violence and Translation*. New York: Palgrave Macmillan.

_____. 2009c. 'Who May We Speak For, With, and After? Re-Silencing Human Rights'. In Gurminder K Bhambra and Robbie Shillman (eds), *Silencing Human Rights: Critical Engagements with a Contested Project*. New York: Palgrave Macmillan.

_____. 2009d. 'Does Life Indeed Begin at Sixty? Revisiting the UDHR as a "Single Garment of Destiny" in a Hyperglobalized World'. *Emory International Law Review* 23 (1): 25–40.

_____. 2010a. 'The Judiciary as a Resource for Indian Democracy'. *Seminar* 615: 61–67.

_____. 2010b. 'Caste Census and Constitutional Justice'. *Economic and Political Weekly* 45 (37).

_____. 2011. 'Constitutional Interpretation and State Formative Practices in Pakistan: A Preliminary Exploration'. In Mahendra P. Singh (ed.), *Comparative Constitutional Law: Festschrift in Honour of Professor P.K. Tripathi*. Kolkata: Eastern Book Company, 2e.

_____. 2013a. 'Introduction'. In Saumya Uma and Vahida Nainar (eds), *Pursuing Elusive Justice: Mass Crimes in India and Relevance of International Standards*. New Delhi: Oxford University Press.

_____. 2013b. 'Restoring "Title Deeds to Humanity": Lawless Law, Living Death, and the Insurgent Reason of Babasaheb Ambedkar'. Ambedkar Memorial Lecture, Ambedkar University, New Delhi.

_____. 2013c. *The Future of Human Rights*. New Delhi: Oxford University Press, 3e.

_____. 2013d. 'International Development, Global Impoverishment and Human Rights'. In Scott Sheeran and Sir Nigel Rodley (eds), *Routledge Handbook of International Human Rights Law*, 597–614. London and New York: Routledge.

_____. 2014a. 'Demosprudence versus Jurisprudence: The Indian Judicial Experience in the Context of Comparative Constitutional Studies'. *Macquarie Law Journal* 14 (3).

_____. 2014b. 'The Place of Dignity in the Indian Constitution'. In Marcus Düwell, Jens Braarvig, Roger Brownsword, and Dietmar Mieth (eds), *The Cambridge Handbook of Human Dignity: Interdisciplinary Perspectives*, 429–436. Cambridge: Cambridge University Press.

_____. 2014c. 'Chhatrapati Singh and the Idea of a Legal Theory'. *Journal of the Indian Law Institute* 56 (1).

Baxi, Upendra. 2016a. 'Law, Politics, and Constitutional Hegemony: The Supreme Court, Jurisprudence, and Demosprudence'. In Sujit Choudhury, Madhav Khosla, and Pratap Bhanu Mehta (eds), *The Oxford Handbook of the Indian Constitution*. Oxford: Oxford University Press.

———. 2016b. 'Demosprudence and Socially Responsible/Response-Able Criticism: The NJAC Decision and Beyond'. *NUJS Law Review* 9 (3–4): 153–172.

———. 2016c. 'Human Rights Responsibility of Multinational Corporations, Political Ecology of Injustice: Learning from Bhopal Thirty Plus?'. *Business and Human Rights Journal* 1(1): 21–40.

———. 2016d. 'Some Newly Emergent Geographies of Injustice: Boundaries and Borders in International Law'. *Indiana Journal of Global Legal Studies* 23 (1): 15–37.

———. 2016e. 'The Aesthetics of Human Rights: Law, Language and Performatives'. *Journal of the Indian Law Institute* 58 (1).

———. 2016f. 'Reversing Gramsci: Notes on Optimism of the Intellect and Pessimism of the Will'. LASSNET, 10–12 December.

———. 2017a. 'Human Rights to do a Moral Wrong'. *Nirma University Law Journal* 6 (2): 7–13.

———. 2017b. 'Introduction'. In I. P. Massey, *Administrative Law*. Lucknow: Eastern Book Company.

———. 2017c. 'Farewell to Adjudicatory Leadership?: Some Thoughts on Dr Anuj Bhuwania's *Courting The People: Public Interest Litigation In Postemergency India*. In Memoriam: Justice Prafulchandra Natwarlal Bhagwati'. *NLUD Student Journal*: 1–19. New Delhi: National Law University.

———. 2018a. '"Touch it Not, If You Are Not a Historian": Toward a New Historiography of Colonial Indian Law: Recrafting Clio'. *Comparative Studies of South Asia, Africa and the Middle East* 38 (3): 375–384.

———. 2018b. 'Heard Melodies are Sweet but those Unheard are Sweeter': An Unfinished Response';'Letters to Kaka: Postcard-images of Upendra Baxi'; 'Upendra Baxi in our Times: Law, Life, Liminality', Debolina Dutta, Adil Hasan Khan, Oishik Sircar (eds). *Jindal Global Law Review* 9 (2): 223–230.

———. 2019a. 'Emergency's Useful Scars'. *The Indian Express*, 27 April.

———. 2019b. 'Uprooting Injustice, Organizing Negation: The Enduring Contribution of Justice P.N. Bhagwati'. In Mool Chand Sharma (ed.), *Law, Justice and Judicial Power: Justice P.N. Bhagwati's Judicial Approach*, 112–132. Haryana: Oakbridge Publishing.

Baxi, Upendra. 2019c. 'Kautilyan Principles and the Law of Nations: A Comment'. *Tamil Nadu National Law University Law Review* 2 TNNLU LR 1.

_____. 2020b.'Lawless Law, Living Death, and the Insurgent Moral Reason of Babasaheb Ambedkar'. In Aakash Singh Rathore (ed.), *B. R. Ambedkar: The Quest for Justice*, Vol. III. New Delhi: Penguin.

_____. 2023. *Aspects of Justice: A Tale of Three Cities*. Tagore Law Lectures, Calcutta. New Delhi: Oxford University Press.

Baxi, Upendra. n.d. 'Some Notes on John Rawls'. In *The Law of Peoples*. Institut D'études Avancées De Nantes. Available at https://www.iea-nantes.fr/rtefiles/File/Ateliers/20140619-Huri/baxi-some-notes-on-john-rawls-lop.pdf (accessed June 2022).

Baxi, Upendra, Noel Sydney Hush, and Julius Stone. 1971. 'Letter to the Editor: Head Tax on Jews: An Appeal'. *Sydney Morning Herald*, 14 September.

Baxi, Upendra, et al. (eds). 1985. *Mass Disasters and Multinational Liability: The Bhopal Case*. New Delhi: Indian Law Institute.

Baxi, Upendra, Geeti Sen, and Jeanette Fernandes (eds). 1987. *The Right to be Human*. New Delhi: Lancer International, in association with India International Centre.

Baxi, Upendra, and Amita Dhanda. 1990. *Valiant Victims and Lethal Litigation: The Bhopal Case*. Bombay: N. M. Tripathi.

Baxi, Upendra, and Bhikhu Parekh (eds). 1995. *Crisis and Change in Contemporary India*. New Delhi: Sage.

Baxi, Upendra, and Oliver Mendelsohn (eds). 1997. *The Rights of Subordinated Peoples*. New Delhi: Oxford University Press.

Baxi, Upendra, Vijay K. Nagaraj, et al. 2005. 'Communication'. *Seminar* 546 (February). Available at http://www.india-seminar.com/2005/546.htm (accessed June 2022).

Baxi, Upendra, et al. (eds). 2013. 'Transformative Constitutionalism: Comparing the Apex Courts of Brazil, India and South Africa'. Pretoria: University of Pretoria Press.

Books, Journal Articles, Edited Chapters

Abdullahi, Ahmed An-Na'im. 2008. *Islam and the Secular State: Negotiating the Future of Shari'a*. Cambridge, MA, and London, England: Harvard University Press.

Adavi, Lekha. Forthcoming. 'Jurisprudence of the Slums'. Alternative Law Forum.

Agamben, Giorgio. 1998. *Homo Sacer: Sovereign Power and Bare Life*. Stanford: Stanford University Press.

———. 1999. *Potentialities: Collected Essays in Philosophy*. Stanford, California: Stanford University Press.

———. 2002. *Remnants of Auschwitz: The Witness and the Archive*. New York: Zone Books.

Ahmad, Sara. 1996. 'Judicial Complicity with Communal Violence in India'. *Northwestern Journal of International Law and Business* 17 (1): 320–350.

Alexandrowicz, Charles Henry, David Armitage, and Jennifer Pitts. 2017. *The Law of Nations in Global History*. Oxford: Oxford University Press.

Allen, Paula Gun. 1986. *The Sacred Hoop: Recovering the Feminine in American Indian Traditions*. Boston: Beacon Press.

Ambedkar, B. R. 1949. 'Final Speech Delivered in the Indian Constituent Assembly'. *Constituent Assembly Debates* XI (25): 972–981.

———. 1994. 'What Congress and Gandhi have done to the Untouchables: Mr. Gandhi and the Emancipation of the Untouchables'. In Vasant Moon (ed.), *Dr. Babasaheb Ambedkar: Writings and Speeches*, Vol. 9. Bombay: Education Department, Government of Maharashtra.

Amnesty International. 1974. 'Detention Conditions in West Bengal—Text of Report by Amnesty International'. *Economic and Political Weekly* 9 (38).

Anderson, Perry. 2012. 'After Nehru'. *London Review of Books* 34 (15): 21–23.

Arendt, Hannah. 1961. *Between Past and Future: Six Exercises in Political Thought*. New York: Viking Press.

———. 1968. *Men in Dark Times*. California: Harcourt, Brace & World, Inc.

Asad, Talal. 2003. *Formations of the Secular: Christianity, Islam, Modernity*. Stanford: Stanford University Press.

Austin, Granville Seward. 1966. *The Indian Constitution: Cornerstone of a Nation*. Oxford: Clarendon Press.

———. 1999. *Working a Democratic Constitution: The Indian Experience*. New Delhi/New York: Oxford University Press.

Ayyangar, N. Rajagopala J. 1959. 'Report on the Revision of the Patents Law'. Ministry of Commerce and Industry, Government of India.

Badiou, Alain. 2013. *Being and Event*. New York: Bloomsbury Academic.

Bajpai, Asha. 2003. *Child Rights in India: Law, Policy, and Practice*. New Delhi, New York: Oxford University Press.

Balagopal, K. 1988. *Probings in the Political Economy of Agrarian Classes and Conflicts*. Hyderabad: Perspectives.

Balagopal, K. 2009. 'Ideology and Adjudication: The Supreme Court and OBC Reservations'. *Economic and Political Weekly* 44 (43): 16–19.

_____. 2011. *Ear to the Ground: Selected Writings on Class and Caste*. New Delhi: Navayana.

Barthes, Roland. 1975. *Mythologies*. New York: Hill and Wang.

Baudrillard, Jean. 1975. *The Mirror of Production*, Mark Poster (trans.). St. Louis: Telos Press.

Baxi, Pratiksha. 2014. *Public Secrets of Law: Rape Trials in India*. New Delhi: Oxford University Press.

Baxi, Pratiksha, and Viplav Baxi. 2018. 'Letters to Kaka: Postcard-images of Upendra Baxi', 'Upendra Baxi in our Times: Law, Life, Liminality'. In Debolina Dutta, Adil Hasan Khan, and Oishik Sircar (eds), *Jindal Global Law Review* 9 (2): 239–255.

Baxi, Prema. 2013. *My Spiritual Journey with Swami Satyananda*. Munger: Yoga Publications Trust.

_____. 2019. *Uma Tuli: Lighting Many Lives*. New Delhi: Amber Books.

Bell, Diane. 1997. 'Representing Aboriginal Women: Who Speaks for Whom?'. In Oliver Mendelsohn and Upendra Baxi (eds), *The Rights of Subordinated Peoples*, 221–250. New Delhi: Oxford University Press.

Bell, Diane, and Renate Kline. 1996. *Radically Speaking: Feminism Reclaimed*. Melbourne: Spinifex Press.

Benedict, R. 1946. *The Chrysanthemum and the Sword: Patterns of Japanese Culture*. Boston: Houghton Mifflin.

Benegal, Shyam. 1974. *Ankur*. Blaze Film Enterprises.

Benjamin, Walter. 2003. 'On the Concept of History', H. Zohn (trans.). In H. Eiland and M. W. Jennings (eds), *Walter Benjamin: Selected Writings*, 4: 1938–1940. Cambridge: Harvard University Press.

_____. 2021 [1921]. *Toward the Critique of Violence: A Critical Edition*, Peter Fenves and Julia Ng (eds). Stanford: Stanford University Press.

Bentham, Jeremy. 1907 [1789]. *An Introduction to the Principles of Morals and Legislation*. Oxford: Clarendon Press.

Berman, Marshall. 1983. *All That is Solid Melts into Air: The Experience of Modernity*. London: Verso.

Bernstein, J. M. 1984. *The Philosophy of the Novel: Lukács, Marxism, and the Dialectics of Form*. Minneapolis: University of Minnesota Press.

Beteille, Andre. 1965. *Caste, Class and Power: Changing Patterns of Stratification in a Tanjore Village*. Berkeley and Los Angeles: University of California Press.

_____. 1969. *Castes: Old and New, Essays in Social Structure and Social Stratification*. New York: Asia Publishing House.

Beteille, Andre. 1972. *Inequality and Social Change*. Delhi: Oxford University Press.

———. 1992. *The Backward Classes in Contemporary India*. Delhi: Oxford University Press.

Bhuwania, Anuj. 2017. *Courting the People*. New Delhi: Cambridge University Press.

Blackshield, Anthony. 2012. 'Stone, Julius'. *Australian Dictionary of Biography* 18.

Blackshield, Anthony, George Williams, Sean Brennan, and Andrew Lynch (eds). 2010. *Blackshield and Williams: Australian Constitutional Law and Theory, Commentary and Materials*. Sydney: The Federation Press, 7e.

Blake, Cassels, and Graydon. 1998. 'Paper: Delgamuukw v. British Columbia (SSC)—Summary of the Reasons for Judgment of Chief Justice Lamer—1998'. *Aboriginal Mapping Network*. Available at http://nativemaps.org/node/2151 (accessed June 2022).

Bobb, Dilip. 2005. 'India is Indira, and Indira is India. Who lives if Indira dies?' *India Today*, 26 December.

Bose, Brinda. 2018. 'Teacher Provocateur: Hedonism and the Humanities'. In 'Upendra Baxi in our Times: Law, Life, Liminality', Debolina Dutta, Adil Hasan Khan, Oishik Sircar (eds). *Jindal Global Law Review* 9 (2): 279–285.

Bourdieu, Pierre, and Alain Accardo. 1999. *The Weight of the World: Social Suffering in Contemporary Society*. Stanford, California: Stanford University Press.

Brecher, Michael. 1959. *Nehru: A Political Biography*. Delhi: Oxford University Press.

Breman, Jan. 1974. *Patronage and Exploitation: Changing Agrarian Relations in South Gujarat, India*. Berkeley, Los Angeles, London: University of California Press.

———. 1978. 'Seasonal Migration and Co-operative Capitalism: The Crushing of Cane and of Labour by the Sugar Factories of Bardoli, South Gujarat—Part 1'. *The Journal of Peasant Studies* 6 (1): 41–70.

———. 1979. 'Seasonal Migration and co-operative Capitalism: The Crushing of Cane and of Labour by the Sugar Factories of Bardoli, South Gujarat—Part 2'. *The Journal of Peasant Studies* 6 (2): 168–209.

———. 1990. '"Even dogs are better off": The Ongoing Battle between Capital and Labor in the Cane-fields of Gujarat'. *The Journal of Peasant Studies* 17 (4): 546–608.

———. 1994. *Wage Hunters and Gatherers: Search for Work in the Urban and Rural Economy of Southern Gujarat*. Delhi: Oxford University Press.

Brown, Elsa Barkley. 1992. '"What has Happened Here": The Politics of Difference in Women's History and Feminist Politics'. *Feminist Studies* 18 (2): 295–312.

Buffett, Peter. 2013. 'The Charitable-Industrial Complex'. *New York Times*, 26 July.

Butalia, Urvashi. 2000. *The Other Side of Silence: Voices from the Partition of India*. Durham, NC: Duke University Press.

Butler, Judith. 1993. *Bodies that Matter: On the Discursive Limits of Sex*. New York: Routledge.

_____. 2004. *Undoing Gender*. New York: Routledge.

_____. 2006. *Precarious Life: The Powers of Mourning and Violence*. London, New York: Verso.

_____. 2009. *Frames of War: When is Life Grievable?* London: Verso.

Calman, Leslie J. 1985. *Protest in Democratic India: Authority's Response to Challenge*. New York: Routledge.

Calvino, Italo. 2016. *Six Memos for the Next Millennium*. London: Vintage, Penguin.

Castoriadis, Cornelius. 1998 [1987]. *The Imaginary Institution of Society*. Boston, Mass.: MIT University Press.

Cavell, Stanley. 1994. *A Pitch of Philosophy: Autobiographical Exercises*. Cambridge, Mass.: Harvard University Press.

_____. 1999. *The Claim of Reason: Wittgenstein, Skepticism, Morality, and Tragedy*. New York: Oxford University Press.

_____. 2010. *Little Did I Know: Excerpts From Memory*. Stanford: Stanford University Press.

Chan, Stephen. 2003. *Robert Mugabe: A Life of Power and Violence*. Ann Arbor: University of Michigan Press.

Chandrasekhar, S. 1976. *Population and Law in India*. Bombay: Blackie & Son.

Coetzee, J. M. 2004. *Life and Times of Michael K*. London: Vintage Books.

Coleman, Mathew. 2007. 'Review: State of Exception'. *Environment and Planning D: Society and Space* 25 (1): 187–190.

Coser, L. 1956. *The Functions of Social Conflict*. Glencoe, Il: Free Press.

Cover, Robert. 1983. 'The Supreme Court, 1982 Term—Foreword: Nomos and Narrative'. *Yale Law School Faculty Scholarship Series*, Paper 2705.

_____. 1986. 'Violence and the Word'. *The Yale Law Journal* 95 (8): 1601–1629.

Crawford, James. 1997. 'Legal Pluralism and the Indigenous Peoples of Australia'. In Oliver Mendelsohn and Upendra Baxi, *The Rights of Subordinated Peoples*. New Delhi: Oxford University Press.

Crenshaw, Kimberle. 1991. 'Mapping the Margins: Intersectionality, Identity Politics and Violence Against Women of Colour'. *Stanford Law Review* 43 (6): 1241–1299.

Croce, Mariano, and Andrea Salvatore. 2014. *The Legal Theory of Carl Schmitt*. London: Routledge.

Das, Veena. 1974. 'Sociology of Law'. In *ICSSR: A Survey of Research in Sociology and Social Anthropology*, Vol. 2. Bombay: Popular Prakashan.

———. 2007. 'Language and Body: Transactions in the Construction of Pain'. In *Life and Words: Violence and the Descent Into the Ordinary*. Berkeley: University of California Press.

———. 2011. 'State, Citizenship, and the Urban Poor'. *Citizenship Studies* 1 (3–4): 319–333.

———. 2016. 'The Boundaries of the "We:" Cruelty, Responsibility and Forms of Life'. *Critical Horizons* 17 (2): 168–185.

Daube, David. 1956. *Forms of Roman Legislation*. Oxford: Clarendon Press.

———. 1967. 'Greek and Roman Reflections on Impossible Laws'. *The American Journal of Jurisprudence* 12 (1): 1–84.

De, Rohit. 2018. *A People's Constitution*. Princeton: Princeton University Press.

Debrix, Francois. 2011. 'The Virtual Nomos?'. In Stephen Legg (ed.), *Spatiality, Sovereignty, and Carl Schmitt*. London: Routledge.

Deleuze, Gilles and Félix Guattari. 1987. *A Thousand Plateaus: Capitalism and Schizophrenia*. Minneapolis: University of Minnesota Press.

Derrett, J. D. M. 1970 [1957]. *Hindu Law—Past and Present*. Calcutta: Mukherjee.

———. 1963. *Introduction to Modern Hindu Law*. Bombay: Oxford.

———. 1968. *Religion, Law and State in India*. London: Faber & Faber.

———. 1970. *A Critique of Modern Hindu Law*. Bombay: Tripathi.

———. 1976. *Essays in Classical and Modern Law*, 4 vols. Delhi: Vikas.

———. 1978. *Death of a Marriage Law: Epitaph for the Rishis*. Durham: University of Carolina Press.

Desai, Akshay Ramanlal. 1986. *Violation of Democratic Rights in India*. Bombay: Popular Prakashan.

Dhagamwar, Vasudha. 1992. *Law, Power and Justice: The Protection of Personal Rights in the Indian Penal Code*. London: Sage Publications.

———. 2006. *Role and Image of Law in India: The Tribal Experience*. New Delhi: Sage.

Dhanda, Amita. 2018. 'Teaching Baxi and Learning from Him: The Symbiotic Relationship between Learning and Teaching'. In 'Upendra Baxi in our Times: Law, Life, Liminality', Debolina Dutta, Adil Hasan Khan, and Oishik Sircar (eds), *Jindal Global Law Review* 9 (2): 259–265.

Dhanda, Amita, and Archana Parashar. 1999. *Engendering Law: Essays in Honour of Lotika Sarkar*. Lucknow: Eastern Book Company.

Dicey, Albert Venn. 1919 [1905]. *Lectures on the Relation between Law and Opinion during the 19th Century*. London: Macmillan and Co. Limited.

Drost, Pieter N. 1959. *International Law: The Crime of State (Vol. 1, Humanicide; Vol. 2, Genocide)*. Leyden: A. W. Sythoff.

Dubash, Navroz K. and D. Narasimha Rao. 2007. *The Practice and Politics of Regulation: Regulatory Governance in Indian Electricity*. New Delhi: Macmillan India.

Dutta, Debolina. 2018. 'Another Story of the Open Letter: An Inheritance of Relationship Making'. In 'Upendra Baxi in Our Times: Law, Life, Liminality', Debolina Dutta, Adil Hasan Khan, and Oishik Sircar (eds). *Jindal Global Law Review* 9 (2): 181–202.

Ehrenzweig, Albert A. 1971. *Psychoanalytic Jurisprudence: On Ethics, Aesthetics, and 'Law'—On Crime, Tort, and Procedure*. Leiden/Dobbs Ferry: N.Y./Sijthoff: Oceana Publications.

Eliade, Mircea. 2009 [1958]. *Yoga: Immortality and Freedom*. Princeton: Princeton University Press.

Ellul, Jacques. 1964. *The Technological Society*. New York: Knopf.

Elster, Jon. 1985. *Making Sense of Marx*. Cambridge: Cambridge University Press.

Emerson, Ralph Waldo. 2003. *Nature and Selected Essays*. New York: Penguin Books.

Erikson, Erik. 1969. *Gandhi's Truth: On the Origins of Militant Nonviolence*. New York: Norton.

Estlund, David. 2008. *Democratic Authority: A Philosophical Framework*. Princeton, N.J.: Princeton University Press.

Farge, Arlette. 2013. *The Allure of the Archives*, Thomas Scott-Railton (trans.). New Haven: Yale University Press.

Fernandez, Luis Enrique Eguren, and Champa Patel. 2015. 'Towards Developing a Critical and Ethical Approach for Better Recognising and Protecting Human Rights Defenders'. *The International Journal of Human Rights* 19 (7): 896–907.

Fischer-Lescano, Andreas, and Gunther Teubner. 2004. 'Regime-Collisions: The Vain Search for Legal Unity in the Fragmentation of Global Law'. 25 *Mich. J. Int'l. L.* 999.

Fitzpatrick, Peter. 1992. *The Mythology of Modern Law*. London, New York: Routledge.

Fleming, John G. 1971. *The Law of Torts*. Sydney: Law Book Co.

Foucault, Michel. 1994 [1966]. *The Order of Things: An Archaeology of the Human Sciences*. New York: Random House.

———. 1978. *The History of Sexuality*. New York: Pantheon Books.

Foucault, Michel, and Sylvère Lotringer. 1966. *Foucault Live: (Interviews, 1961–1984)*. New York, N.Y.: Semiotext(e).

Freire, Paulo. 1968. *Pedagogy of the Oppressed*. New York: Seabury Press.

Frug, Mary Joe. 1992. 'A Postmodern Feminist Legal Manifesto (An Unfinished Draft)'. *Harvard Law Review* 105 (5): 1045–1075.

Furer-Haimendorf, Christoph-Von. 1967. *Morals and Merit: A Study of Values and Social Control in South Asian Societies*. Chicago: University of Chicago Press.

Gadamer, H.-G, 1989 [1975]. *Truth and Method*, J. Weinsheimer and D. G. Marshall (trans.). London: Sheed and Ward, 2e.

Galanter, Marc. 1984. *Competing Equalities: Law and the Backward Classes in India*. Berkeley: University of California Press.

Gandhi, Leela. 2006. *Affective Communities: Anticolonial Thought, Fin-De-Siècle Radicalism, and the Politics of Friendship*. Durham: Duke University Press.

Gandhi, M. K. 1921. 'Notes—Cobblers vs. Lawyers'. *Young India* 3 (39).

———. 2013 [1927]. *My Experiments with Truth*. Mumbai: Jaico Publishing House.

Ganguli, B. N. 1973. *Gandhi's Social Philosophy: Perspective and Relevance*. Delhi: Vikas.

Ghosh, Amitav. 2000. *The Glass Palace*. London: HarperCollins.

———. 2016. *The Great Derangement: Climate Change and the Unthinkable*. Chicago: The University of Chicago Press.

Gill, K. P. S. 2005. *The Punjab Story*. New Delhi: Roli Books.

Goodale, Mark. 2018. *Letters to the Contrary: A Curated History of the UNESCO Human Rights Survey*. Stanford, California: Stanford University Press.

Gopal, Sarvepalli. 1976. *Jawaharlal Nehru: A Biography*. Cambridge, Mass: Harvard University Press.

———. 1989. *Radhakrishnan, a Biography*. Delhi, New York: Oxford University Press.

Gouldner, Alvin W. 1980. *The Two Marxisms: Contradictions and Anomalies in the Development of Theory*. London: Macmillan.

Grear, Anna. 2010. *Redirecting Human Rights: Facing the Challenge of Corporate Legal Humanity*. Houndsmills, Basingstoke, Hampshire: Palgrave Macmillan.

Gregory, Derek. 2006. 'The black flag: Guantánamo Bay and the space of exception'. *Geografiska Annaler: Series B, Human Geography* 88 (4): 405–427.

Guha, Ramachandra. 1999. *Savaging the Civilized: Verrier Elwin, His Tribals, and India*. Chicago: University of Chicago Press.

Guha, Ramachandra, and Madhav Gadgil. 1992. *This Fissured Land: An Ecological History of India*. Delhi: Oxford University Press.

Guha, Ranajit. 1999. *Elementary Aspects of Peasant Insurgency in Colonial India*. Durham: Duke University Press.

Gündoğdu, Ayten. 2014. 'Statelessness and the Right to have Rights'. In Patrick Hayden (ed.), *Hannah Arendt: Key Concepts*. Durham: Acumen Publishing.

_____. 2015. *Rightlessness in an Age of Rights: Hannah Arendt and the Contemporary Struggles of Migrants*. New York: Oxford University Press.

Guru, Gopal, and Sunder Sarukkai. 2020. *Experience, Caste, and the Everyday Social*, New Delhi: Oxford University Press.

Haksar, Nandita. 1986. *Demystification of Law for Women*. New Delhi: Lancer Press.

_____. 2007. *Framing Geelani, Hanging Afzal: Patriotism in the Time of Terror*. New Delhi: Promilla & Co., Publishers, in association with Bibliophile South Asia.

_____. 2009. *Rogue Agent: How India's Military Intelligence Betrayed the Burmese Resistance*. New Delhi: Penguin Books.

Hardin, Garrett. 1968. 'The Tragedy of the Commons'. *Science* 162 (3859): 1243–1248.

Hardt, Michael, and Antonio Negri. 2004. *Multitude: War and Democracy in the Age of Empire*. New York: Penguin Press.

Harrison, Selig. 1960. *India: The Most Dangerous Decades*. New Jersey: Princeton University Press.

Hay, Douglas, Peter Linebaugh, John G. Rule, E. P. Thompson, et al. 2011. *Albion's Fatal Tree: Crime and Society in Eighteenth-Century England*. London: Verso, revised edn.

Heidegger, Martin. 2001 [1962]. *Being and Time*, John Macquarrie and Edward Robinson (trans.). London: Blackwell Press.

Held, Virginia. 2008. *How Terrorism is Wrong: Morality and Political Violence*. Oxford: Oxford University Press.

Hittinger, John P. 2010. 'The Soldier and The Citizen: Lessons From Plato and Aristotle'. *International Society for Military Ethics* 95.

Honderich, Ted. 1980. *Violence for Equality: Inquiries in Political Philosophy: Incorporating Three Essays on Political Violence*. London: Penguin.

Huntington, Samuel P. 1996. *The Clash of Civilizations and the Remaking of World Order*. New York: Simon and Schuster.

Hurst, James Willard. 1964. *Law and Economic Growth: The Legal History of the Lumber Industry in Wisconsin, 1836–1915*. Cambridge, MA: Belknap Press of Harvard University Press.

Hussain, Nasser. 2003. *The Jurisprudence of Emergency: Colonialism and the Rule of Law*. Ann Arbor: University of Michigan Press.

Indian Law Institute. 1966. *All India Seminar on Educational Planning in India: Its Legal and Constitutional Implications*. New Delhi: Indian Law Institute.

______. 1969a. *Seminar on Government Regulation of Private Enterprises*. New Delhi: Indian Law Institute.

______. 1969b. *Seminar on Law of Torts*. New Delhi: Indian Law Institute.

______. 1970. *Seminar on Company Law*. New Delhi: Indian Law Institute.

______. 1973a. *Seminar on Constitutional Development since Independence*. New Delhi: Indian Law Institute.

______. 1973b. *Seminar on Administrative Law*. New Delhi: Indian Law Institute.

______. 1978a. *Seminar on Indian Constitution: Trends and Developments*. New Delhi: Indian Law Institute.

______. 1978b. *Seminar on Criminal Law*. New Delhi: Indian Law Institute.

______. 1983. *Seminar on Company Law*. New Delhi: Indian Law Institute.

Ingole, Kishore D. (ed.). 2021. *Dalit Discourse: Critical Perspectives in Indian Literature*. Singapore: Notion Press.

Ivison, Duncan. 1997. 'Decolonizing the Rule of Law: Mabo's Case and Postcolonial Constitutionalism'. *Oxford Journal of Legal Studies* Summer, 17 (2), 253–279.

Jain, Mahabir Prashad. 1966. *Outlines of Indian Legal History*. Bombay: N. M. Tripathi.

______. 2018. *Indian Constitutional Law*. Gurgaon: LexisNexis.

Jaspers, Karl. 1961. *The Question of German Guilt*. New York: Capricorn Books.

Jodhka, Surinder S. 2002. 'Review of *Dalit Identity and Politics*', *Economic and Political Weekly* 30 March, 1255–1257.

Jog, Narayan Gopal. 1969. *Saga of Scindia: Struggle for the Revival of Indian Shipping and Shipbuilding [1919–1969]*. Bomay: The Scindia Steam Navigation Company.

Johansen, Bruce E. 1982. *Forgotten Founders: Benjamin Franklin, the Iroquois, and the Rationale for the American Revolution*. Ipswich, Massachusetts: Gambit.

John, Mathew. 2018. 'Reading Upendra Baxi as a Guide to the Study of Indian Constitutionalism: A Comment'. In 'Upendra Baxi in our Times: Law, Life, Liminality', Debolina Dutta, Adil Hasan Khan, and Oishik Sircar (eds). *Jindal Global Law Review* 9 (2): 327–333.

John, Mathew, and Kakarala Sitharamam (eds). 2007. *Enculturing Law: New Agendas for Legal Pedagogy*. New Delhi: Tulika Books.

Kaldor, Mary. 2003. *Global Civil Society: An Answer to War*. Cambridge, UK/Malden, MA: Polity Press.

Kalecki, Michal. 1972. *Selected Essays on the Economic Growth of the Socialist and the Mixed Economy*. Cambridge: Cambridge University Press.

Kanjilal, Amaraya. 2022. 'Narrating Legal Reform: The Open Letter and the Anti-rape Movement in Perspective'. *Indian Journal of Gender Studies* 29 (2), 1–23.

Kannabiran, K. G. 2004. *The Wages of Impunity: Power, Justice and Human Rights*. Hyderabad: Orient Longman.

_____. 2022. *The Speaking Constitution: A Sisyphean Life in Law*. New Delhi: HarperCollins India.

Kashyap, Subhash C., and Jawaharlal Nehru. 1982. *Jawaharlal Nehru and the Constitution*. New Delhi: Metropolitan.

Kaufmann, Walter. 2013. *Nietzsche: Philosopher, Psychologist, Antichrist*. Princeton: Princeton University Press.

Kaur, Mallika. 2011. *Faith, Gender, and Activism in the Punjab Conflict: The Wheat Fields Still Whisper*. New Delhi: Palgrave McMillan.

Kelsen, Hans. 1964. 'Professor Stone and the Pure Theory of Law'. *Stanford Law Review* 17: 1128.

_____. 1967. *Pure Theory of Law*. Berkeley: University of California Press.

Khan, Adil Hasan. 2018. 'For "...those who ... lost their Utopias...but...still rebel...": Taking up Upendra Baxi's Bequixotements in Times of Crisis'. In 'Upendra Baxi in our Times: Law, Life, Liminality', Debolina Dutta, Adil Hasan Khan, and Oishik Sircar (eds), *Jindal Global Law Review* 9 (2): 155–180.

Kirby, Michael. 2013. 'A.R. Blackshield and Realism in Australian Constitutional Law'. *Macquarie Law Journal* 11: 7.

Kishwar, Madhu Purnima. 2006. 'Cycle Rickshaw: A Post Modern Vehicle Challenging Government's Warfare against Citizen Friendly, Eco-Friendly Rickshaws'. *Manushi* 156 (November–December).

Klinsky, Sonja, Timmons Roberts, Saleemul Haq, et al. 2016. 'Why Equity is Fundamental in Climate Change Policy Research'. *Global Environmental Change* 44 (May), 170–173. Available at http://dx.doi.org/10.1016/j.gloenvcha.2016.08.002 (accessed July 2023).

Kochanek, Stanley A. 1974. *Business and Politics in India*. Berkeley: University of California Press.

Kothari, Miloon. n.d. 'India's Contribution to the Universal Declaration of Human Rights'. UDHR, Chapter 12.

Kothari, Rajni. 1970. *Politics in India*. Hyderabad: Orient Longman.

———. 2002. *Memoirs: Uneasy is the Life of the Mind*. New Delhi: Rupa & Co.

Kotiswaran, Prabha. 2017. *Revisiting the Law and Governance of Trafficking, Forced Labor and Modern Slavery*. Cambridge, UK: Cambridge University Press.

Krishna, Daya. 1955. *The Nature of Philosophy*. Calcutta: Prachi Prakashan.

Kumar, Dharma. 1965. *Land and Caste in South India: Agricultural Labour in the Madras Presidency During the Nineteenth Century*. Cambridge: Cambridge University Press.

Kumar, Ravinder. 1968. *Western India in the Nineteenth Century: A Study in the Social History of Maharashtra*. London: Routledge and Kegan Paul.

Lacan, Jacques, and James B. Swenson. 1989. 'Kant with Sade'. *October* 51: 55–75.

Lacey, Nicola. 2006. *A Life of H.L.A. Hart: The Nightmare and the Noble Dream*. Oxford: Oxford University Press.

Laclau, Ernesto. 2005a. *On Populist Reason*. London: Verso.

———. 2005b. 'Populism: What's in a Name'. In Francisco Panizza (ed.), *Populism and the Mirror of Democracy*. London: Verso.

Lal, Chaman (ed.). 2019. *The Bhagat Singh Reader*, 545–553. New Delhi: HarperCollins.

Lal, Hardwari. 1979. *Myth and Law of Parliamentary Privileges*. New Delhi: Allied Publishers Private Limited.

Lal, Vinay. 1992. 'Committees of Inquiry and Discourses of "Law and Order" in Twentieth-Century British India'. Unpublished Ph.D. Dissertation, The University of Chicago.

Landis, Elizabeth S. 1964. 'South West Africa in the International Court of Justice'. *Africa Today* 11 (4): 10–12.

Lavie, Smadar. 1990. *The Poetics of Military Occupation: Mzeina Allegories of Bedouin Identity under Israeli and Egyptian Rule*. Berkeley and Los Angeles: University of California Press.

Lee, Alexander. 2015. 'How (and How Not) to Use Archival Sources in Political Science', 16 January. Available at https://www.rochester.edu/college/faculty/alexander_lee/wp-content/uploads/2014/07/archives.pdf (accessed November 2023).

Levinas, Emmanuel, 1979. *Totality and Infinity: An Essay on Exteriority*. London: Martinus Nijhoff Publishers.

Levinson, Sanford. 2011. *Constitutional Faith*. Princeton, N.J.: Princeton University Press.

Linarelli, John, Margot E. Salomon, and M. Sornarajah. 2018. *The Misery of International Law: Confrontations with Injustice in the Global Economy*. Oxford: Oxford University Press.

Lindall, Ryan. 2008. 'List of Multiple Killings of Aborigines in Tasmania: 1804–1835'. *Violence de mass et Résistance—Réseau de Recherche*. Available on https://www.sciencespo.fr/mass-violence-war-massacre-resistance/fr/document/list-multiple-killings-aborigines-tasmania-1804-1835 (accessed June 2022).

Linebaugh, Peter. 1991. *The London Hanged: Crime and Civil Society in the Eighteenth Century*. London: Allen Lane.

Linebaugh, Peter, and Marcus Rediker. 2002. *The Many-headed Hydra: Sailors, Slaves, Commoners, and the Hidden History of the Revolutionary Atlantic*. Boston: Beacon Press.

Lingat, Robert. 1973. *The Classical Law of India*, J. D. M. Derrett (trans.). New Delhi: Thomson Press.

Llewellyn, Karl. 1939. 'The Normative, the Legal, and the Law-jobs: The Problem of the Juristic Method'. *Yale Law Journal* 49: 1355.

Llewellyn, Karl, and E. Adamson Hoebel. 1941. *The Cheyenne Way; Conflict and Case Law in Primitive Jurisprudence*. Norman, Oklahoma: University of Oklahoma Press.

Ludden, David E. 1999. *An Agrarian History of South Asia*. Cambridge, UK, New York: Cambridge University Press.

Maclean, Kama. 2003. 'Making the Colonial State Work for You: The Modern Beginnings of the Ancient Kumbh Mela in Allahabad'. *The Journal of Asian Studies* 62 (3): 873–905.

Magee, Bryan (ed.). 1971. *Modern British Philosophy*. New York: St. Martin's Press.

Mahida, U. N. 1980. *Water Pollution and Disposal of Waste Water on Land*. New Delhi: Tata McGraw-Hill.

Malgonkar, Manohar. 1965. *A Bend in the Ganges: A Novel*. New York: Viking Press.

Manguel, Alberto, and Gianni Guadalpi. 1980. *The Dictionary of Imaginary Places*. New York: Macmillan.

Mani, Lata. 2013a. 'Human Dignity and Suffering: Some Considerations'. *Economic and Political Weekly* 46 (36): 23–26.

_____. 2013b. 'Reconjugating Law and Dharma'. In Lata Mani, *The Integral Nature of Things: Critical Reflections on the Present*, 101–108. New Delhi, London: Routledge.

Manto, Saadat Hasan. 1989. *The Best of Manto: A Collection of his Short Stories*. New Delhi: Sterling Publishers.

_____. 1993. *Thanda Gosht*. Lahore: Sang e Mil.

_____. 2011. *Toba Tek Singh: Stories*. New Delhi: Penguin.

Markose, A. T. 1956. *Judicial Control of Administrative Action in India: A Study of Methods*. Madras: Madras Law Journal Office.

Markovits, Claude. 2009. *Indian Business and Nationalist Politics, 1931–1939*. Cambridge: Cambridge University Press.

Martin, James. 2008. *The Poulantzas Reader: Marxism, Law and the State*. London: Verso.

Marx, Karl. 1909. *Capital: A Critique of Political Economy/Vol. 2, The Process of Circulation of Capital*. Chicago: Charles H. Kerr.

_____. 1973. *Grundrisse: Foundations of the Critique of Political Economy*. New York: Random House.

_____. 1990. *Capital*, Vol. I. London: Penguin Books.

May, Erskine. 2011. *Parliamentary Practice*. London: LexisNexis.

Maybury-Lewis, David. 1965. *The Savage and the Innocent*. London: Evans Brothers.

_____. 1992. *Millennium: Tribal Wisdom and the Modern World*. New York: Viking.

_____. 1997. *Indigenous Peoples, Ethnic Groups, and the State*. Boston: Allyn and Bacon.

Maybury-Lewis, David, and Uri Almagor. 1989. *The Attraction of Opposites: Thought and Society in the Dualistic Mode*. Ann Arbor: University of Michigan Press.

Mehra, Rakesh Omprakash. 2006. *Rang De Basanti*. UTV Motion Pictures.

Mehta, Pratap Bhanu. 2016. 'Prof Baxi Vs. St. Baxi'. *The Indian Express*, 14 December. Available at https://indianexpress.com/article/opinion/columns/supreme-court-national-anthem-cinema-halls-indian-judiciary-4425814/ (accessed June 2022).

Mehta, Ved. 1962. *Fly and the Fly-bottle: Encounters with British Intellectuals*. Boston: Little, Brown and Company.

Mendelsohn, Oliver, and Upendra Baxi (eds). 1997. *The Rights of Subordinated Peoples*. New Delhi: Oxford University Press.

Menon, Ritu, and Kamla Bhasin. 1998. *Borders & Boundaries: Women in India's Partition*. New Brunswick, N.J.: Rutgers University Press.

Mies, Maria, and Vandana Shiva. 1993. *Ecofeminism*. New Delhi: Kali for Women.

Milsom, Stroud Francis Charles. 1969. *Historical Foundations of the Common Law*. London: Butterworths.

Milsom, Stroud Francis Charles. 1976. *The Legal Framework of English Feudalism*. Cambridge: Cambridge University Press.

Minca, Claudio. 2005.'The Return of the Camp'. *Progress in Human Geography* 29 (4): 405–412.

_____. 2006. 'Giorgio Agamben and the new biopolitical nomos'. *Geografiska Annaler: Series B, Human Geography* 88 (4): 387–403.

Misra, R. K. 1965. 'Judicial Process'. Annual Survey of Indian Law, *Journal of the Indian Law Institute* 5–36.

Mitta, Manoj, and H. S. Phoolka. 2008. *When a Tree Shook Delhi: The 1984 Carnage and its Aftermath*. New Delhi: Lotus.

Monk, Ray. 1991. *Ludwig Wittgenstein*. London: Vintage.

Montes, Manuel F. 2018. 'Six Development Paths in Southeast Asia: Three plus Three'. UNU-WIDER.

Moon, Vasant (ed.). 1979. *Dr. Babasaheb Ambedkar: Writings and Speeches*, Vol. 12, 733–736. Bombay: Education Department, Government of Maharashtra.

Mooney, Patrick Roy. 1980. *Seeds of the Earth: A Private or Public Resource?* Ottawa: Inter Pares.

_____. 1990. *Shattering: Food, Politics, and the Loss of Genetic Diversity*. Tucson, AZ: The University of Arizona Press.

Morris, Lulu. 2017. 'The Last Indigenous Tasmanian'. *National Geographic*. Available at https://www.nationalgeographic.com.au/australia/the-last-indigenous-tasmanian.aspx (accessed June 2022).

Mushi, K. M. 2016. *Somanatha: The Shrine Eternal*. Bombay: Baratya Vudya Bhavan, 3d edition.

Mutua, Makau. 2007. 'Standard Setting in Human Rights: Critique and Prognosis'. *Human Rights Quarterly* 29 (3): 547–630.

Myrdal, Gunnar. 1968. *Asian Drama: An Inquiry into the Poverty of Nations*, Vols I, II, and III. New York: Pantheon.

Naik, T. B. 1956. *The Bhils*. Delhi: Bharatiya Adimjati Sevak Sangh.

Narain, Jagat. 1966. 'Equal Protection Guarantee and the Right of Property Under the Indian Constitution'. *International and Comparative Law Quarterly* 15 (1): 199–230.

Narrain, Arvind. 2004. *Queer: Despised Sexuality, Law and Social Change*. Bangalore: Books For Change.

_____. 2013. 'My Experiments with Law: Gandhi's Exploration of Law's Potential', 6 *NUJS L. Rev*. 273.

Narrain, Arvind, and Saumya Uma. 2016. *Breathing life into the Constitution*. Bangalore: Alternative Law Forum.

Narrain, Siddharth. 2018. 'A Co-traveller in the Long Road to Decriminalisation: Upendra Baxi's Engagement with the Queer Movement in India'. In 'Upendra Baxi in Our Times: Law, Life, Liminality', Debolina Dutta, Adil Hasan Khan, and Oishik Sircar (eds). *Jindal Global Law Review* 9 (2): 299–305.

Negri, Antonio. 1991. *Marx beyond Marx: Lessons on the Grundrisse*. Brooklyn, N.Y.: Autonomedia.

———. 1999. *Insurgencies: Constituent Power and the Modern State*. Minneapolis: University of Minnesota Press.

Nehru, Jawaharlal. 1964. *Selected Speeches: Vol. 4*. New Delhi: Publications Division, Ministry of Information & Broadcasting.

Nehru, Jawaharlal, et al. 1972. *Selected Works of Jawaharlal Nehru*. New Delhi: Orient Longman.

Nietzsche, Friedrich Wilhelm. 1982. *The Portable Nietzsche*. New York: Penguin Books.

Nigam, Aditya, and Nivedita Menon. 2007. *Power and Contestation: India Since 1989*. Halifax, N.S.: Fernwood Publishing.

Nigam, Sanjay. 1990. 'Disciplining and policing the "criminals by birth", Part 1: The making of a colonial stereotype—The criminal tribes and castes of North India'. *The Indian Economic and Social History Review* 27 (2): 131–164.

Nihalani, Govind. 1980. *Aakrosh*. National Film Development Corporation of India.

Nikolakaki, Maria, Henry A. Giroux, and Ana-Maria Friere. 2012. *Critical Pedagogy in the New Dark Ages: Challenges and Possibilities*, Counterpoints, 32–44. New York: Peter Lang.

Nilekani, Rohini. 2011. 'Land: Anand Mahindra and Medha Patkar'. In *Uncommon Ground: Dialogues between Business and Social Leaders*, 109–147. New Delhi: Penguin Viking. [Book based on the television series, *Uncommon Ground*, broadcast on NDTV in 2008.]

Nussbaum, Martha C. 2006. *Frontiers of Justice: Disability, Nationality, and Species Membership*. Cambridge: The Belknap Press.

O'Hara, John. 1972a. 'Law school move raises storm'. *Sydney Morning Herald*, 14 September.

———. 1972b. 'Law Dept: Call by Wran for review'. *Sydney Morning Herald*, 26 September.

Pande, B. B. 2004. 'Torts Law'. *Annual Survey of Indian Law* 40: 563–574.

———. 2009. 'Why Indian Patients do not Deserve the Highest Expert Skills from Doctors?' *Supreme Court Cases Journal* 4: 21.

Panikkar, Raimondo. 1979. *Myth, Faith and Hermeneutics*. New York: Paulist Press.

Parekh, Bhikhu C. 1988. *Gandhi's Political Philosophy: A Critical Examination*. Notre Dame, Ind.: University of Notre Dame Press.

______. 1989. *Colonialism, Tradition, and Reform: An Analysis of Gandhi's Political Discourse*. Newbury Park, California: Sage.

______. 2006 [2000]. *Rethinking Multiculturalism: Cultural Diversity and Political Theory*. Basingstoke, New York: Palgrave Macmillan, 2e.

______. 2008. *A New Politics of Identity: Political Principles for an Interdependent World*. New York: Palgrave Macmillan.

Parsons, Talcott. 1970. *The Social System*. London: Routledge & Kegan Paul Ltd.

Patnaik, Utsa. 1986. *The Agrarian Question and the Development of Capitalism in India*. Delhi/New York: Oxford University Press.

PDHRE. n.d. 'Human Rights Learning: A Peoples' Report'. People's Movement for Human Rights Learning. Available at https://www.pdhre.org/report (accessed June 2022).

Peoples Union for Civil Liberties—Karnataka. 2003. *Human Rights Violations Against the Transgender Community*. Bangalore: PUCL-K.

______. 2019. *A Millennial Struggle for Dignity*. Bangalore: PUCL-K.

Poulantzas, Nicos. 2000. *State, Power, Socialism*. New York: Verso.

Prakash, Gyan. 2019. *Emergency Chronicles*. Princeton: Princeton University Press.

Pritam, Amrita. 1982. *Selected Poems*. Delhi: Bhartiya Jananpith Publications.

______. 1984. *Kagaz Aur Canvas*. New Delhi: Rajkamal.

______. 1989. *Life and Times*. New Delhi: Vikas Publishing House.

______. 1995. *Aksharon Ki Chhaya Mein*. New Delhi: Aman Publication.

Purnell, John. 1972. 'Letters to the Editor: Studying the law in action'. *Sydney Morning Herald*, 10 October.

Rai, Shirin, and Carol Spray. 2019. *Performing Representation: Women Members in the Indian Parliament*. New Delhi: Oxford University Press.

Rai, Shirin, and Janelle Reinelt (eds). 2015. *The Grammer of Politics and Performance*. London: Routledge.

Raj, K. N. 2014. 'The Politics and Economics of "Immediate Regimes"'. *Economic and Political Weekly* 49 (37): 1189–1198.

Rajadhyaksha, Ashish. 2009. '"You Can See Without Looking": The Cinematic Author and Freedom of Expression in Cinema'. In *Indian Cinema in the Time of Celluloid: From Bollywood to the Emergency*. New Delhi: Tulika Books.

Ramaswamy, Sumathi. 2004. *The Lost Land of Lemuria: Fabulous Geographies, Catastrophic Histories*. Berkeley: University of California Press.

Rancière, Jacques. 2012. *Proletarian Nights: The Workers' Dream in Nineteenth-Century France*, John Drury (trans). Brooklyn: Verso.

Rawls, John. 1999. *The Law of the Peoples*. Cambridge, Mass.: Harvard University Press.

Report of the Committee on Prevention of Corruption. 1963. Ministry of Home Affairs, Government of India. Available at https://cvc.gov.in/sites/default/files/scr_rpt_cvc.pdf (accessed August 2022).

Report of the One-Man Commission of Inquiry Headed by the Hon'ble Mr Justice K.K. Mathew to Enquire into the Incidents of Explosion that Took Place on 2–1–1975 at Samastipur. 1977. New Delhi: Government of India Press.

Rorty, Richard. 2000. *Philosophy and Social Hope*. London: Penguin.

Russell, Bertrand. 1994. *Autobiography*. London: Routledge.

Russell, Bertrand, and Jean-Paul Sartre. 1968. *International War Crimes Tribunal*. Toronto: Canadian Committee for the International War Crimes Tribunal.

Said, Edward W., and Gauri Viswanathan. 2001. *Power, Politics, and Culture: Interviews with Edward W. Said*. New York: Pantheon Books.

Salmond, John W., and Glanville Llewelyn Williams. 1957. *Salmond On Jurisprudence*, by Glanville Williams. London: Sweet & Maxwell, 11e.

Sanders, Lawrence. 1984. *The Passion of Molly T*. New York: Putnam.

Santos, Boaventura de Sousa. 1995. *Toward a New Common Sense: Law, Science and Politics in the Paradigmatic Transition*. London: Routledge.

Saxena, I. C. 1967. 'Law of Contract'. *Annual Survey of Indian Law* 3&4: 165–192.

———. 1969. 'Law of Contract'. *Annual Survey of Indian Law* 5: 1–41.

———. 1970. 'Law of Contract'. *Annual Survey of Indian Law* 6: 320–357.

———. 1971. 'Law of Contract'. *Annual Survey of Indian Law* 7: 48–76.

———. 1972. 'Offer and Acceptance—A Centennial Survey'. *Journal of the Indian Law Institute* 14: 116–131.

———. 1980. 'Law of Contract'. *Annual Survey of Indian Law* 16: 1–31.

———. 1981. 'Law of Contract'. *Annual Survey of Indian Law* 17: 16–45.

———. 1982. 'Law of Contract'. *Annual Survey of Indian Law* 18: 57–81.

———. 1983. 'Law of Contract'. *Annual Survey of Indian Law* 19: 104–125.

———. 1984. 'Law of Contract'. *Annual Survey of Indian Law* 20: 108–133.

———. 1985. 'Law of Contract'. *Annual Survey of Indian Law* 21: 185–208.

———. 1986. 'Law of Contract'. *Annual Survey of Indian Law* 22: 72–107.

———. 1987. 'Law of Contract'. *Annual Survey of Indian Law* 23: 53–75.

———. 1988. 'Law of Contract'. *Annual Survey of Indian Law* 24: 64–77.

Saxena, I. C. 1989. 'Law of Contract'. *Annual Survey of Indian Law* 25: 115–132.

———. 1990. 'Law of Contract'. *Annual Survey of Indian Law* 26: 261–278.

———. 1996. 'Contract Law'. *Annual Survey of Indian Law* 32: 165–180.

Scarry, Elaine. 1985. *The Body in Pain: The Making and Unmaking of the World*. New York: Oxford University Press.

Scheuermann, William E. 2019. *The End of Law: Carl Schmitt in the 21st Century*. New York: Rowfield & Littlefield International, 2nd edn.

Schmitt, Carl. 1985. *Political Theology: Four Chapters on the Concept of Sovereignty*, G. Schwab (trans). Chicago: University of Chicago Press.

———. 1986. *Political Romanticism*. Cambridge, Mass.: MIT Press.

Seervai, H. M. 1989. *Partition of India: Legend and Reality*. Bombay: Emmenem Publications.

———. 1991. *Constitutional Law of India: A Critical Commentary*. Bombay: N. M. Tripathi.

Sen, Amartya. 1999a. *Development as Freedom*. New York: Knopf.

———. 1999b. 'Democracy as a Universal Value'. *Journal of Democracy* 10 (3): 3–17.

Sen, Geeti. 2012. *Your History Gets in the Way of My Memory: Essays on Indian Artists*. New Delhi: Collins India.

Sethna, M. J. 1962. *Contributions to Synthetic Jurisprudence*. Dobbs Ferry, N.Y.: Oceana Publications.

Shah, Ghansyam (ed,). 2001. *Dalit Identity and Politics*, New Delhi: Sage.

Shankar, Shylashri. 2009. *Scaling Justice: India's Supreme Court, Anti-Terror Laws and Social Rights*. New Delhi: Oxford University Press.

Sharma, Mool Chand. 2018. *Law, Justice and Judicial Power: Justice P.N. Bhagwati's Approach*. Gurugram: OakBridge Publishing.

Sharp, Nonie. 1996. *No Ordinary Judgment: Mabo, the Murray Islanders Land Case*. Canberra, Australia: Aboriginal Studies Press.

Shiner, Philip, and Andrew Williams (eds). 2008. *The Iraq War and International Law*. Oxford: Hart Publishing.

Shiva, Vandana. 1993. *Monocultures of the Mind: Perspectives on Biodiversity and Biotechnology*. London: Atlantic Highlands.

Shklar, Judith N. 1964. *Legalism*. Cambridge: Harvard University Press.

Schmitt, Carl. 1985. *Political Theology: Four Chapters on the Concept of Sovereignty*, G. Schwab (trans). Chicago: University of Chicago Press.

Silva, G. V. S. de, N. Mehta, M. A. Rahman, and P. Wignaraja. 1979. 'Bhoomi Sena: A Struggle for People's Power'. *Development Dialogue* 2, 3–70.

Silver, Beverly J. 2003. *Forces of Labour: Workers' Movements and Globalization since 1870*. Cambridge, New York: Cambridge University Press.

Singer, Peter. 1990. *Animal Liberation*. New York: New York Review of Books, 2e.

Singh, Bhrigupati. 2015. *Poverty and the Quest for Life: Spiritual and Material Striving in Rural India*. Chicago: University of Chicago Press.

Singh, Chhatrapati. 1985. *Law from Anarchy to Utopia*. Delhi: Oxford University Press.

Singh, Jarnail. 2011. *I Accuse: The Anti-Sikh Violence of 1994*. New Delhi: Penguin India.

Singh, Khushwant. 2012. *Train to Pakistan*. New Delhi: Ravi Dayal.

Singh, Mahendra Pal. 2011. *Comparative Constitutional Law: Festschrift in Honour of Professor P.K. Tripathi*. Lucknow: Eastern Book Co., 2e.

Singha, Radhika. 2000. *A Despotism of Law: Crime and Justice in Early Colonial India*. New Delhi: Oxford University Press.

Sircar, Oishik. 2018. 'Professor of Pathos: Upendra Baxi's Minor Jurisprudence'. In 'Upendra Baxi in our Times: Law, Life, Liminality', Debolina Dutta, Adil Hasan Khan, and Oishik Sircar (eds). *Jindal Global Law Review* 9 (2): 203–222.

Sontag, Susan. 2009. *Notes on Camp*. In *Against Interpretation and Other Essays*. New York: Penguin Books.

Sontag, Susan, Paolo Dilonardo, and Anne Jump. 2007. *At the Same Time: Essays and Speeches*. New York: Farrar, Straus, and Giroux.

Spivak, Gayatri Chakravorty. 1988. 'Can the Subaltern Speak?'. In Cary Nelson and Lawrence Grossberg (eds), *Marxism and the Interpretation of Culture*, 271–313. Urbana: University of Illinois Press.

———. 2005. 'Use and Abuse of Human Rights'. *Boundary* 2 (32): 131–189.

Stone, Julius. 1954. *Legal Controls of International Conflict: A Treatise on the Dynamics of Disputes and War-Law*. New York: Rinehart.

———. 1963. 'Mystery and Mystique in the Basic Norm'. *The Modern Law Review* 26 (2): 34–50.

———. 1964. *The Legal System and Lawyers' Reasonings*. Stanford: Stanford University Press.

———. 1965. *Human Law and Human Justice*. Stanford, California: Stanford University Press.

———. 1966a. 'Reflections on Apartheid after the South West Africa Cases'. *Washington Law Review* 42: 1069–1082.

———. 1966b. *Social Dimensions of Law and Justice*. Sydney: Maitland Publications.

Sunstein, Cass, and Edna Ullman-Margalit. 2002. 'Inequality and Indignation'. John M. Olin Program in Law and Economics Working Paper No. 141. The University of Chicago Law School.

Tambiah, Stanley J. 1976. *World Conqueror and World Renouncer: A Study of Buddhism and Polity in Thailand against a Historical Background*. Cambridge, UK, New York: Cambridge University Press.

Tarlo, Emma. 2003. *Unsettling Memories: Narratives of the Emergency in Delhi*. London: C. Hurst.

Tatz, Colin. 1997. 'A Question of Rights and Wrongs'. In Oliver Mendelsohn and Upendra Baxi (eds), *The Rights of Subordinated Peoples*, 159–177. New Delhi: Oxford University Press.

Teubner, Gunther. 1993. *Law As an Autopoietic System*. Oxford, UK, Cambridge, Mass.: Blackwell Publishers.

Thapar, Romila. 2005. *Somantha: Many Voices of History*. London: Verso.

Thompson, E. P. 1980 [1970]. *The Secret State*. London: Merlin.

_____. 1991a [1966]. *The Making of the English Working Class*. New York: Vintage Books.

_____. 1991b. *Customs in Common*. London: Merlin Press.

_____. 2013 [1975]. *Whigs and Hunters*. London: Breviary Stuff Publications.

Tigar, Michael E. 1977. *Law and the Rise of Capitalism*. New York: Monthly Review Press.

Tiwari, G. S. 2001. 'Conversation of Biodiversity and techniques of People's Activism'. *Journal of Indian Law Institute* 43 (2): 191–220.

_____. 2002. 'The Equality-Liberty Axis: A Socio-Political Paradigm of Human Development'. *Journal of Indian Law Institute* 44 (4): 534–554.

_____. 2003. 'Drugs, Trade and Terrorism: An Assault on Human Rights'. *Journal of Indian Law Institute* 45 (1): 25–37.

_____. 2010. 'Sustainable Development as a Socio-Economic Growth Strategy: Expanding Horizons of Environmental Law in India'. *Journal of Indian Law Institute* 52 (3&4): 435–452.

Tully, Mark, and Satish Jacob. 2006. *Amritsar, Mrs. Gandhi's Last Battle*. New Delhi: Rupa.

Twining, William (ed.). 2009. *Human Rights: Southern Voices*. New York: Cambridge University Press.

Uma, Saumya, and Arvind Narrain. 2018. 'Human Rights and Its Future: Some Reflections'. In 'Upendra Baxi in our Times: Law, Life, Liminality', Debolina Dutta, Adil Hasan Khan, and Oishik Sircar (eds). *Jindal Global Law Review* 9 (2): 287–297.

United States Senate, Special Committee on National Emergencies. 1974. *A Brief History of Emergency Powers in the United States*, vi. Washington, DC: US Government.

Vanderheiden, Elisabeth, and Claude-Helene Mayer. 2017. *The Value of Shame: Exploring a Health Resource in Cultural Contexts*. New York: Springer International Publishing.

Virno, Paolo. 2004. *A Grammar of the Multitude: For an Analysis of Contemporary Forms of Life*. Los Angeles, CA: Semiotext(e).

Wade, Robert. 1982.'The System of Administrative and Political Corruption: Canal Irrigation in South India'. *The Journal of Development Studies* 18 (3): 287–328.

Walzer, Michael. 2008. *Spheres of Justice: A Defense of Pluralism and Equality*. New York: Perseus Books, LLC: Basic Books.

Ward, Barbara. 1966. *Spaceship Earth*. New York: Columbia University Press.

Weber, Max. 1965. *Politics as a Vocation*. Philadelphia: Fortress Press.

Welles, Orson. 1941. *Citizen Kane*. Mercury Pictures.

White, Lynn. 1962. *Medieval Technology and Social Change*. London: Oxford University Press.

Williams, Raymond. 1977. *Marxism and Literature*. Oxford, New York: Oxford University Press.

Winch, Peter. 1958. *The Idea of a Social Science and its Relation to Philosophy*. London: Routledge & Kegan Paul.

Young, Iris Marion. 2001. 'Equality of whom? Social groups and judgments of injustice'. *Journal of Political Philosophy* 9 (1): 1–18.

Young, Robert J. C. 2001. *Postcolonialism: An Historical Introduction*. London: Wiley.

Zelliot, Eleanor. 1992. *From Untouchable to Dalit: Essays on the Ambedkar Movement*. New Delhi: Manohar Publications.

Zizek, Slavoj. 2010. 'A Permanent Economic Emergency'. *New Left Review* 64 (July–August): 85–95.

———. 2012.'Living in the Time of Monsters'. *Counterpoints* 422.

Zorn, Jean. 2010.'In Memory of Bernard Narokobi'. *eJournal of the Australian Association for the Advancement of Pacific Studies* 2 (1).

Zweig, Stefan. 2009. *The World of Yesterday*. London: Pushkin Press.

List of Cases

A.R. Antulay vs. R.S. Nayak and Ors, AIR 1988 SC 1531.

Abdul Rehman Antulay and Ors. vs. R.S. Nayak and Ors, AIR 1992 SC 1701.

Ashoka Kumar Thakur vs. Union of India & Ors, (2007) 4 SCC 361.

Azad Rickshaw Pullers Union vs. State of Punjab and Others, AIR 1981 SC 14.

Banco Nacional de Cuba vs. Sabbatino, 376 U.S. 398 (1964).

Bandhua Mukti Morcha vs. Union of India (UOI) and Ors, AIR 1984 SC 802.
Chandra Lal Sahu and Others vs. Union of India, (1990) 1 SCC 613.
Common Cause (A Regd. Society) vs. Union of India (UOI) and Ors, AIR 2008 SC 2116.
Delgamuukw vs. British Columbia, (1997) 3 SCR 1010.
Dr S.C. Bhatia vs. University of Delhi, 2009 ILR (2009) Supp. (3) Delhi 307.
Dr Upendra Baxi vs. State of U.P., (1981) 3 Scale 1137.
Dr Upendra Baxi (I) vs. State of Uttar Pradesh and Anr., (1983) 2 SCC 308.
D.S. Nakara vs. Union of India, AIR 1983 SC 130.
Gulshan Kallu & Ors. vs. Zilla Parishad, Etawah, U.P. & Ors, AIR 1981 SC 1668.
Hardwari Lal vs Election Commission of India, LAWS(P&H)-1977-4-19.
I.C. Golaknath & Ors vs. State Of Punjab & Anrs, AIR 1967 SC 1643.
Indira Nehru Gandhi vs. Raj Narain & Anr, AIR 1975 SC 1590.
K. Veeraswami vs. Union of India & Ors, (1991) 3 SCC 655.
Kedar Nath Singh vs. State of Bihar, AIR 1962 SC 955.
Kesavananda Bharathi vs. State of Kerala, (1973) 4 S.C.C. 225.
Lok Adhikar Sangh vs. State of Gujarat and Ors, AIR 2002 Guj 59.
M.C. Mehta vs. Union of India, (1987) 1 SCC 395.
M.C. Mehta vs. Union of India, AIR 1988 SC 1115.
Mabo vs. Queensland (no. 2), (1992) HCA 23.
Maneka Gandhi vs. Union Of India, AIR 1978 SC 597.
Milirrpum vs. Nabalco Pty Ltd, (1971) 17 FLR 141.
Mohd Ahmed Khan vs. Shah Bano Begum and Ors, AIR 1985 SC 945.
Mohd. Hanif Quareshi vs. The State of Bihar, AIR 1958 SC 731.
National Textile Workers vs. P.R. Ramakrishnan & Ors, AIR 1983 SC 75.
Narmada Bachao Andolan v. Union of India, (2000) 10 S.C.C. 664.
National Textile Workers vs. P.R. Ramakrishnan & Ors, AIR 1983 SC 750.
Navtej Singh Johar vs. Union of India, (2018) 10 SCC 1.
Naz Foundation vs. Government of NCT and Ors, 160 (2009) DLT 277.
Olga Tellis and Ors vs. Bombay Municipal Corporation and Ors, AIR 1986 SC 180.
People's Union for Democratic Rights & Anr vs. Ministry of Home Affairs, AIR 1985 Delhi 268.
Prakash Singh and Ors vs. Union of India (UOI), (2006) 8 SCC 1.
Raja Ram Pal vs. Hon'ble Speaker, Lok Sabha and Others, (2007) 3 SCC 184.
Raj Narain vs. Smt Indira Nehru Gandhi and Another, AIR 1972 SC 1302.
Ranjit D. Udeshi vs. State Of Maharashtra, AIR 1965 SC 881.
Roe vs. Wade, 410 U.S. 113 (1973).
Rustom Cavasjee Cooper vs. Union of India, AIR 1970 SC 564.

S.P. Gupta vs. President Of India And Ors, AIR 1982 SC 149.
S.R. Bommai vs. Union of India, AIR 1994 SC 1918.
State of Uttar Pradesh vs. Raj Narain, AIR 1975 SC 865.
Sudipto Mazumdar vs. State of MP, (1983) 2 SCC 258.
Surat (Hazira) Kamdar Karmachari Union vs. State of Gujarat, (1999) 2 GLR 826, (2000) ILLJ 823 Guj.
Tukaram And Anr vs. State Of Maharashtra, (1979) 2 SCC 143.
Union Carbide Corporation vs. Union of India and Ors, 1989 SCALE (1) 380.
United States vs. Seeger, 380 US 163 (1965).
Unnikrishnan P.J. and Ors vs. State of A.P. and Ors, AIR 1993 SC 2178.
Vineet Narain and Ors vs. Union of India, (1997) 1 SCC 226.
Vishakha and Ors vs. State of Rajasthan and Ors, AIR 1997 SC 3011.

List of Acts/Reports/Declarations/Treaties

African Charter on Human and Peoples' Rights, also known as the Banjul Charter, 1981.
Ordinance XV-D: Prohibition of and Punishment for Sexual Harassment, University of Delhi, 2003.
Report of the Backward Classes Commission, National Commission for Backward Classes, Government of India, 1980.
The Bonded Labour System (Abolition) Act, 1976.
The Corporate Manslaughter and Corporate Homicide Act, 2007.
The Criminal Tribes Act, 1871.
The Domestic Workers (Registration, Social Security and Welfare) Act, 2008.
The Dowry Prohibition Act, 1961.
The Indian Penal Code, 1860.
The Legal Services Authority Act, 1987.
The Mahatma Gandhi National Rural Employment Guarantee Act, 2005.
Permanent Peoples' Tribunal Statute, 1979.
The Prevention of Terrorism Act, 2002.
The Public Insurance Liability Act, 1991.
The Scheduled Castes and Tribes (Prevention of Atrocities) Act, 1989.
The Transfer of Property Act, 1882.
The United Nations Declaration on the Rights of Indigenous Peoples, 2007.

Index

GLOBALIZATION AND LOCAL DEVELOPMENT IN INDIA

Examining the Spatial Dimension

Centre de Sciences Humaines (Centre for Social Sciences and Humanities): Created in New Delhi in 1989, the CSH is part of the network of research centres of the French Ministry of Foreign Affairs. The Centre's research work is primarily oriented towards the study of issues concerning the contemporary dynamics of development in India and South Asia. The activities of the Centre are focused on four main themes, namely: Economic transition and sustainable development, political dynamics, institutional set-up and social transformations, regional dynamics in South Asia and international relations and urban dynamics.

Centre de Sciences Humaines, 2, Aurangzeb Road, New Delhi 110011, India, Tel: (91) 11 2301 62 59, Fax: (91) 11 2301 84 80
E-mail: public@csh-delhi.com
Website: http://www.csh-delhi.com

Institut Français de Pondichéry (French Institute of Pondicherry): Created in 1955, the IFP is a multidisciplinary research and advanced educational institute. Major research works are focusing on Sanskrit and Tamil Languages and literatures-in close collaboration with the Ecole Française d'Extrême-Orient-ecosystems, biodiversity and sustainability, dynamics of population and socio-economic development.

Institut Français de Pondichéry, 11 Saint Louis Street, PB 33, Pondicherry 605001, Tel: (91) 413 2334 168/2334 170, Fax: (91) 413 2339 534
E-mail: ifpdir@ifpindia.org
Website: http://www.ifpindia.org

Globalization and Local Development in India

Examining the Spatial Dimension

Edited by
Frédéric Landy and Basudeb Chaudhuri

MANOHAR

CENTRE DE SCIENCES HIMAINES
2004

This volume is, except for one chapter, a translation of *De la mondialisation au développement local en Inde. Questions d'échelles*, éditions CNRS, Paris 2002, published for an academic readership in the francophone countries. The bibliography, the methodological questions and the issues raised were inspired by current debates in French social sciences and humanities. This English version aims to give the Indian and anglophone audience some specifically French perspectives, in order to reduce barriers and to create a more fruitful academic dialogue between these two worlds.

The book results from a monthly seminar *From the global to the local: economic liberalization and development,* held between 1997 and 2000 in the Centre d'Etudes de l'Inde et de l'Asie du Sud (CEIAS), Paris, a joint research unit, Centre National de la Recherche Scientifique—Ecole des Hautes Etudes en Sciences Sociales. This is a multidisciplinary centre bringing together Indologists, Islamicists, and social scientists.

CEIAS: 54 bd Raspail, 75006 Paris.
Internet site: www.ehess.fr/centres/ceias

First published 2004

ISBN 81-7304-540-2

Published by

Ajay Kumar Jain for
Manohar Publishers & Distributors
4753/23 Ansari Road, Daryaganj
New Delhi 110 002

Typeset at

Digigrafics
New Delhi 110 049

Printed at

Lordson Publishers Pvt. Ltd.
Delhi 110 007

Contents

Introduction

Frédéric Landy and Basudeb Chaudhuri

Everything seems to indicate that the nation-states of the world are opening up both from above and from below. On the one hand, 'globalization' is the progressive extension to the entire planet of exchanges of all kinds, which is more than anything else an economic phenomenon, and on the other hand, 'localization' (is a political phenomenon by which local populations express their rights to a say in government, a process which can serve as an aid to economic transformation).[1] It is this complex process that we examine in this volume, in order to evaluate how economic transformations, social mutations, cultural changes, and all that affects or involves as players the one billion inhabitants of India, 'the largest democracy in the world', are interacting with one another at local, regional, national and global levels.

THE RETREAT OF THE 'NATIONAL'?

The fact of continuing poverty in the countries of the South often goes against a teleological concept of 'development' as a linear process engendered by a strong state within borders often defined by the colonial power. For many, the liberal reforms marking the failure of the policies deployed at the time of independence provide proof of this. Moreover, the awareness of ecological issues worldwide, and the numerous world summits on this subject are a sign of a certain amount of erosion of the state as an entity capable of handling problems. Global warming takes no heed of international borders. Concepts of territoriality and national sovereignty are consequently called into question in what is, somewhat inappropriately, called the 'post-colonial era' (A. Gupta 1998).

But the state falls apart also at the other end, since concerns over identity and regionalist demands bring about an even greater separation between state and nation. The 'nation-state', a happy combination of these two entities, appears then as no more than an accident of history, born in the sixteenth century and finding itself in a state of decline right from the end of the twentieth. On the whole, the classical approach of the world system with states as the constitutive entities becomes more and more a matter for reappraisal in the face of the upsurge of *regions* in the geopolitics of the planet.

There are 'regions' made up of several nations, of the ASEAN type, but this regionalization on the continental scale is itself a very imperfect one and each grouping remains very heterogeneous. Since its inception in 1985 SAARC (South Asian Association for Regional Cooperation), undermined by bilateral quarrels and rivalry between India and Pakistan, finds reconciliation amongst its seven members particularly difficult. Thus continental assemblages are not regions in the true sense, which we would define as 'territories' forming the basis of social, economic and cultural identity.

It is more the actual regions, in the conventional meaning of the term, on the local scale, within the national units, that could be viewed as threats to the states. As capital gets concentrated in certain metropolitan areas, these function as hubs whose geo-economic and geo-political powers give shape to what some unhesitatingly call an 'inter-regional planet', meaning thereby a world dominated by some regions that are so powerful that they conduct more and more dealings between themselves, bypassing the framework of the state (*Revue française de géoéconomie* 1998).

It is not however certain that nation-states are in too bad a shape. Those who see in the way the wars in Yugoslavia were managed as a sign of their undermining and of a challenge to the principle of sovereignty forget that these wars led to the creation of several nation-states within the borders of the former Yugoslavia. In fact, the Yugoslav crises testify more to threats to federations, and generally speaking to all states made up of a plurality of nations. This is not reassuring for India which is much more a 'civilization-state' than a 'nation-state'. In India as in all other federal states, this is all the more complex a question as the national level would progressively be losing its importance not only with relation to the 'global' and to the 'local' defined in terms of small region or of city. An intermediary rung is indeed vital, that of the states of the Union. It should be remembered in fact that the 1950 Constitution has defined a list of sectors that come within the competence of the states (agriculture, health, certain industries) over which, theoretically, the central government has no control. That in actual fact this is not so, does not preclude the existence of a whole series of filters between New Delhi and the citizen, the states, as also districts, *taluks/tehsils,* blocks and *panchayats*, all these being institutions which can accelerate, slow down, modify or even block the application of measures taken by the centre. India is one of the few countries of the South which is fully democratic, where the current economic liberalization, accelerated by the 1991 structural adjustment programme, can therefore suffer a halt if a general disapproval were to decide so at the time of elections to the Lok Sabha, the State Assemblies, or the local bodies. The importance of not favouring any of these levels at the cost of the others is obvious.

GLOBALIZATION IS NOT GLOBALITY

The term 'globalization' has been used so often since the mid-1990s that one often forgets to define it.[2] The notion characterizes the progressive extension to the entire world of exchanges of all kinds through two modalities of very unequal force. These are, on the one hand, the strategies adopted by enterprises to fan out over a planet dominated largely by the ideology of free exchange ('Globalization is the devaluation of space and the increase in value of time'),[3] and on the other hand a realization of the importance of ecology, this also on the planetary scale, an awareness of the solidarity of environments, be they natural or anthropized.

Let us not disregard the suffix in the word 'globalization', which implies an incomplete process. Those who believe in 'globality' as its final stage, the putting to an end of Geography, are probably the very same who believe in the end of History.[4] There will however always be some heterogeneities and some spatial inequalities, even if only because they are essential to the working of a global market economy.

Discreetly known as 'comparative advantages' they will undoubtedly get dislodged. Krugman and Venables (1995) have shown that as globalization advances and transportation costs come down, countries less endowed with economic resources can develop thanks to economies of scale and spatial concentration. But rich countries are the first to benefit. In 1998 the 'developing' countries received only 25 per cent of the world's foreign investments, one-fourth of which went to China alone. In India, investments have been made by foreign firms far more in Gujarat and Maharashtra, the richest states, than in impoverished Bihar. Even the 'multinational firms', hence, remain anchored to 'territorial moorings' (Savy and Veltz eds. 1995). Moreover, there will always be some upsurges of identity crises and some reactions, sometimes violent ones, against the so-called homogenizing effect of globalization, in a kind of 'revenge of geography' (Raison 1999).

That the world is hereafter becoming a single system does not mean that it is one.[5] There still remain some blind spots, some neglected areas or individuals, so that 'international integration can lead to national disintegration' (Streeten 1998). This is all the more evident in two processes which have picked up speed at the end of the 1980s, the 'just in time' development in the matter of strategies adopted by firms, and the end of blocs in the matter of international geopolitics. Both have had the same effect, that of an increased awareness of space. Poland has once again come closer to France than Indonesia. This being so, the world system remains polarized around three centres (United States, Europe, Japan) and we witness the strengthening of this 'triad' rather than true 'globalization', to borrow two words popularized by K. Ohmae.

Consequently, to confuse globalization which is a process, with 'globality' which is a state that has been achieved, is at best to be naïve. It is more often a matter of a political discourse of liberal inspiration aimed at giving rise to the belief in the birth of an ideal world. Besides, the speed of the process is as exaggerated as its omnipresence. International (rather than 'global') institutions have not advanced at the same speed as has the development and integration of global markets, and neither the WTO, nor the UNO, nor the IMF avail of powers enabling them to completely control this evolution. Even international agreements on the environment, however 'global' they may be, are then to be put into application by the states and therefore function in a framework which is at least as international as it is planetary. Signed in December 1977, the Kyoto protocol on the greenhouse effect had not yet been ratified by any developed country till September 2000. 'Global governance' is far from being effective.

SPACE AND GLOBALIZATION

What perspective does a spatial framework bring to research on globalization and its bonds with things local?

1. *Geography continues to exist.* Globalization does not mean the disappearance of places, a homogenization which would make world space 'isotropic', submerged in a monotonous uniformity synonymous with equality. What is the percentage of world space occupied by what Marc Augé has called 'non-places', such as international airports or motorways? When we assert that New York is a 'global city' (Sassen 1991), do we mean New York, the financial and commercial marketplace, or New York as a geographic entity, a city made up of the poor and the rich, of Bronx as of Wall Street?

Equality in space is not something that will come about in the near future. There will always be 'spatial advantages' in the form of proximity to an airport or a foothill easier to irrigate, a tax haven or a coastal land. Even if distance, on account of the improvement in transport and communications, does matter less than before, the number of places on the planet where production, processing and dispatch can be effected on a large scale, remains limited (O. Dollfus 1994). Mumbai avails of certain services which connect it directly to the networks of developed countries (finance, trade, information technology) and simultaneously depends less on its hinterland. The regional framework, which ensured a certain degree of harmony between the city and the surrounding periurban and rural space, is losing its importance. The poles belonging to this world-economy are integrated into a process of growth and development while the neighbouring underprivileged spaces and individuals, once *dominated* (through exploitative relations), are now in the process of becoming *excluded* (as they have become useless), which is perhaps worse.

2. *The depreciation of nesting dolls.* Globalization breaks up traditional perspectives of geography based on the 'zoom effect' or the changing of scales. The same area in India may well be selling vegetables to the neighbouring town and opium to an international drug cartel. In the so-called 'glocalization' such channels branching out from the local

level to the global scale are used by entrepreneurs in globalization for profits. 'We are living in the era of manipulators of scales' (Raison 1999).

'All players, very unequally, it is true, influence the world system like the fluttering of the wings of social butterflies' (Dollfus et al. 1999: 2). This is questionable, and one may ask in what way a Dalit labourer in a remote area in Madhya Pradesh could influence the global system; it would be committing an intellectual fraud prompted by a certain neo-conservative way of thinking less which leads us to believe that all is well in this best of possible ultra-liberal worlds. Nonetheless, the statement rings true, as the hierarchies of scales are blurred. The Indian government conducts negotiations with the Coca Cola company. The World Bank defines a programme of structural adjustment for just one state, Andhra Pradesh.[6] American rating agencies make an evaluation of the states of the Indian Union, assigning marks to them for their financial standing and their budgetary allocations. India's Export Processing Zones, and the new Special Economic Zones, granting even further benefits to capital, are places where imports are not liable to taxes, and where production remains outside the circuit of the domestic market. These are veritable 'embassies' of international capital and they enjoy an almost extraterritorial status. These few square kilometres are as much a part of the world system as they are of the Indian state. This blurring of scales has led to the suggestion that 'networks' have gained a victory over 'territories', spaces whose boundaries are marked out. 'The continuity and the exhaustivity of the territory of states come into conflict with the discontinuities and the lacunae of the networks of enterprises', of professional associations or of diasporas (Levy 1999), and the way things work, it would seem that the state level is being skipped over more and more to directly connect the local to the international. 'The archipelago economy' of the world cities that Veltz (1997) talks of, is made up of 'islets' (metropolises, but also stock exchanges, airports, computer terminals) that are so small that what matters is less their place than the links which connect them.

Time and space thus acquire new dimensions. Not that there is anything new in this. In his rehabilitation of the dynamics of the ancient East, Goody (1996) shows that even before British colonization, the *jajmani* system in the village could be linked to regional or even international trade. Already the local was interwoven into the international. For centuries the Marwari and the Chettiar diasporas had carved out trade networks, extending from Malaysia to Canada, on the basis of family or caste. The phenomenon of 'globalization' is definitely much older than the concept. But the acceleration of the processes made possible by the new means of communication leads to a growing complexity. The world is now more and more 'multimetric' (Dollfus et al. 1999). For long, the only choices available for transport were between walking, horseback and the wind in the sailboat. The motor car, the plane and fibre optics have come. Nevertheless they have not always supplanted existing modes of transport and communication: India uses both the Internet and the bullock cart.

3. *New relationships between homogeneities and disparities*. An indirect consequence of the decline of territories is the reduction in certain spatial disparities. Tamil Nadu now resembles Uttar Pradesh more than it did a century ago. Rural and urban landscapes, like cultural values and practices, testify to a relative decline in regional peculiarities. The sari is now worn by most Indian women. In 1990, almost the whole of India watched the *Mahabharata* being enacted on television on Sunday mornings. But this homogenization concerns only spaces at similar levels. When we separate the scales, and we consider an urban area and a village, or compare Nariman Point (in south Mumbai) and a small town in the interior of Maharashtra, or a senior executive and a small farmer, the distance has undoubtedly grown. In short, the differences are less related to a distance in space (in kilometres) than to an economic and social distance (in kilorupees).

One can thus conciliate two *a priori* contradictory points of view. The first lays stress on the break-up of the local in favour of a 'new nomadism' (de Gournay 1994). Formerly Michelin in Clermont-Ferrand, or Godrej in Mumbai, or Tata in Jamshedpur had to get the workers to entrench themselves deeply in a specific place in order to generate a spirit of enterprise, for which purpose they had to install a self-contained township in which everything, from the living quarters to the stadium, bore the mark of the firm. The modern firm, on the contrary, allows for shifting of locations, for the geographic mobility of staff, investments, and production units, as well as a rapid rotation in hierarchies. The local then loses its identity. It is no longer a territory but a simple place of production with hardly any bonds of identity, a space that has become neutral, an element in a network that has overpowered it.

Other perspectives however show that the 'revenge of the networks' is far from total. The circulation of goods (and people) still takes place largely on a national or an international basis. The case of 'industrial districts', and particularly the two examples mentioned here by L. Kennedy and P. Lachaier, does indeed show that the networks can in fact very well be part of 'territories' with a strong local identity, which nevertheless does not prevent them from working within international export circuits. 'There is no network without a paving of territories offering amenities, security and benefits' (Dollfus 1994: 62). In the race for innovation and quality, the enterprise has to mobilize all the motivations permitted by local society, history and culture. The economy becomes basically relational.

TOWARDS A VERTICAL APPROACH

Rather than laying stress on the horizontal nature and mobility of the network as opposed to the fixed nature of the territory, it is undoubtedly more credible to see things in terms of superimposed levels, extending from the local to the global. We will then be able to understand how the network is nurtured by the territory and vice versa, how globalization and local inequalities proceed in symbiosis and not in conflict. It is a known fact that a Lorenz curve depicting the concentration of the French population will sketch a very different path depending on whether the statistics are on the level of the *commune* (the French equivalent of the Indian revenue village), the *canton* (*tehsil*) or the *département* (district) (Le Bras 1997). Perhaps more basically, it is the relations of causality which change with the scale of study (Landy returns to this in his conclusion). That is how the spatial variations with regard to fertility in India give rise to very divergent interpretations depending on the levels of analysis (Guilmoto 2000). On the level of the states we see a contrast between the north and the south, the latter having made greater progress towards the demographic transition. On the scale of the districts, however, there appears the inshore factor and the role of the opening out towards the world (Kerala). Finally, on the local level, the contrast between the rural and the urban areas is obvious. It is understandable therefore that it is important to undertake a 'multi-scalar' and many-layered analysis.

This book does not deal with any one sector, social group, or region of India. The range of subjects tackled extends from food policy to foreign investments, power stations to diesel engines. The issue debated through the pages is the interplay between the 'local' and the 'global'. Not all the chapters deal with the links between these levels. Some concentrate, for instance, on global-regional links, others on national-local links. Underlying all these, however, is the omnipresent question of the relations between several levels, showing in this way that a certain contemporary reality of India can be demonstrated by matters of scales.[7] Finally, this book will be a way of reflecting over the content of the now hackneyed terms, 'global' and 'local'. G. Heuzé and F. Landy in their respective chapters testify to the fact that behind these two notions are hidden a certain haziness of concept, an immense complexity and a great deal of vested interest.

Let us add three reasons specific to India for invoking the matter of scale.

1. From the global to the local via the national, the issue at debate in this book is, as one might say in a somewhat cavalier fashion, that of India's entire policy of development. Already the swadeshi ('Buy Indian') movement had played a major role in the struggle for independence. Once independence had been achieved, planning turned progressively towards one objective, that of no longer being dependent on foreign aid and becoming self-reliant, by way of a more and more deliberate policy of import substitution (Ahluwalia 1998). Finally, the notion of self-reliance (which appeared explicitly only in the 1961 Third Five-Year Plan) became identified with self-sufficiency. For India, independence thereafter meant falling back on everything national and not opening up to the world (cf. the chapter by B. Dorin).

Moreover, planning was marked by what one would call in France a 'town and country planning' policy (*aménagement du territoire*). However, rather than taking note of local interests, this attempted, through regional development, to develop the nation itself. Indeed, planning was formulated with the objective of achieving self-reliance, considering that it had aims that were productive (integrating into the mainstream of the national economy those regions which till then had remained underprivileged) and even strategic (taking note of dangers to the borders by the inception of some ventures in endangered zones, strengthening the policy of national integration by curbing regionalist movements). The local served the interests of the national.

Liberalization, which quickened its pace after 1991, brought about a profound paradigmatic change. As F. Landy shows in his conclusion, there was a progressive transition from the concept of self-sufficiency in cereals (focused on the national level) to that of food security (directed both towards global trade exchanges as well as towards meeting the nutritional needs on the local and even the individual plane). More generally, the opening up of India to the world grew in proportion to the reduction in its protectionist measures. G. Boquérat shows here the growth of trade exchanges and of foreign investments, small as compared to many other 'emerging' countries but impressive nonetheless considering the initial situation. But the objective still remains, at least in the official discourse held by the Indian government, that of not sacrificing self-reliance to economic growth. Foreign investments are meant to further exports much more than to penetrate the domestic market, for instance.

As for local development, officially it is now structured around a democracy based on the decentralization of power and is no longer subservient to the policy of national growth. The constitutional amendments of 1992-3 have defined the village *panchayats* (village councils) and the urban municipalities as 'institutions of self-government', whose members are elected by the public. They are the first rung of a three-layered local democracy, from the village to the block/*taluk*/*tehsil*, then on to the district. These institutions are responsible for economic development and for social justice, and funds are allotted to provide them with a certain degree of financial autonomy. This is at least the situation postulated by the constitutional amendments which, for the time being, have been implemented only in some states. The chapter by G. Heuzé on Singrauli shows that there is a considerable distance between the laws enacted and the ground reality.

2. Depicting India as a land of contrasts has now become a cliché, for this country is capable of launching satellites, and yet not able to bring literacy to more than 65 per cent of its population. It exports software but cannot make the budget on food expenses of households come down below 46 per cent. It is a country where the wealth of some city-centres contrasts sharply with the poverty in the slums or in many villages. It would be too simple to present this situation in a Manichean light, to attribute the effects of the growth arising out of the integration of India into international economic currents to globalization, and under-development and poverty to the fallback on the local. In fact, in many cases globalization thrives on local poverty. The petty cotton planter of Andhra Pradesh supplies through his production the material for the clothing industry abroad; the computer engineers of Mumbai draw a part of their competitiveness from the small salaries made possible on account of a rate of exchange of the rupee largely dictated by the economic problems of the country. One of the wagers of this

book is to assess the extent to which globalization could mitigate these economic, social and spatial contrasts, or else accentuate them.

3. 'India is made up of 26 governments, one at the Centre and the rest in the 25 states' (Guhan 1995: 73).[8] While the scope for action by the states of the Union should not be exaggerated, it should not be underestimated either. In the early 1990s, the American multinational Enron had obtained the agreement of the federal government to invest a billion dollars in the production of electricity in Maharashtra. The construction of the power station had already begun when, in 1995, this agreement was called into question by the BJP government in Maharashtra (opposed to the federal government) for reasons both political as well as economic. A great deal of time and money was wasted in renegotiating the contract in such a way that none of the parties involved should lose face. This incident brought an awareness that it is no longer through the central government alone that access can be had to India's economy. The governments of the states also have their say, as is testified moreover by the numerous trips abroad undertaken by chief ministers to seek foreign direct investments. The future of the federal structure of India, and the powers of the different states (or regions), whose autonomy, it is often asserted, is constantly growing, are hence investigated in this book. Ruet has shown, in the matter of the State Electricity Boards, that this assertion needs, to say the least, to be qualified.

The first part of this volume deals with recent dynamics at the upper levels, namely, the world, nation, and the states of the Union. Boquérat deals with the economic opening up of India which became more marked at the turn of the year 1991, giving up, it would seem, once and for all, the old principles of priority to the domestic market and protection of internal trade, which had been progressively set up after independence. Import-export therefore made progress as also the entry of external private investments of capital, while the national framework remained predominant. Domestic savings continue to play a crucial role and the role of trade remains, all in all, limited. Is this an advantage or a drawback? So progressive an evolution testifies to 'some difficulties in the integration of the Indian economy within the mainstream of globalization', but it also makes it possible for it to put up a greater resistance to upheavals in the international economic arena. This was obvious during the 'Asian crisis' of 1997 which hardly affected India at all.

Alain Vaguet deals with a specific sector. He portrays the

'globalization of the health system' in India as being marked by the flow of capital and of doctors originating in the diaspora, as well as by the boom experienced by multinational pharmaceutical companies. It is not however a one-way process, thanks to the spread of Indian, more particularly ayurvedic, pharmacopeia, and of yoga, which have drawn towards them an international clientele. The penetration of foreign capital into the economy is being matched by a certain cultural expansion of India's healthcare systems in the world. However, it is private hospitals which are mushrooming in the large cities, in contrast to the discredited public dispensaries and the overcrowded public hospitals. Social and regional inequalities are growing in the field of health even if there is a general improvement on the pan-Indian scale due undoubtedly to the development of the private sector. The 'globalizing' context does not therefore prevent the continuance of local or regional specificities. On the one hand, we note the maintenance of non-Western systems of medicine even though their high cost hardly brings them within the reach of the common man. And on the other hand, there are the private hospitals financed by large industrial groups, sometimes on charitable bases, which fit into 'a discourse not very distant from that of public service, and which is not foreign to a sentiment of cohesion of identity of the region . . .' . Finally, on the micro-local scale, it is noted that the staff in hospitals continues to be recruited on the basis of religion and caste; the patients also go on the same basis to these hospitals which are more generally used as devices for acquiring status and recognition through patron-client relationships.

Some types of liberalization are smokescreens which end up in effects that are, to say the least, unexpected, as the reader can see from the chapter by Ruet on the power sector. The regional State Electricity Boards used to control, till not long ago, two-thirds of the production and the near-totality of the distribution of power, and the states enjoyed great freedom with regard to fixing of rates, within the framework of a local policy which, more often than not, was hardly bothered with efficiency. Since then, reforms have been undertaken in the power sector, but what has been called 'liberalization' has neither brought in private capital nor the release of the states from the fetters tying them to the centre. The 'opening-up' has in fact enabled New Delhi to tighten its grip over matters which were earlier within the competence of the states. The latter have moreover not been necessarily unhappy as these steps have enabled them to avoid bankruptcy. And in the matter of globalization, foreign capital is conspicuously rare. At any rate, one is led to question the possibility of the success of these reforms when reading this study which has been the outcome of long investigations conducted within the administrative departments and which paints a distressing picture of the strategies adopted by officials.

The second part of our book deals with two processes of industrialization which are the antithesis of each other. The first, from below, corresponds to a development based on local resources. The second, from above, is a type of technocratic industrialization which pays no heed to local needs and characteristics in the name of national interest. The former is presented here through the example of two 'industrial districts', those of the Palar Valley and of the Kolhapur region. Veltz (1997: 82) had, it is true, been able to describe the effects of globalization in space as an 'archipelago-network of large poles', in which 'horizontal relationships, apparently, got the better, to an increasingly greater degree, of the traditional vertical relationships with the hinterlands'. But the industrial districts bring out one of the limitations of this process. While intensifying their relationships with the other levels on account of their growing integration within worldwide circuits, they keep a strong local base since the greater part of their economic dynamism arises out of their territorial entrenchment and social networks based on proximity, trust and a common culture.

The case of the Palar Valley in Tamil Nadu, where almost half the leather of India is produced, enables Loraine Kennedy to bring out the peculiarities of the industrial district, a symbol of the victories of 'flexible specialization' over the Fordist model. The 'spatial concentration of specialized enterprises in a single sector gives rise to external economies' based on trust and on social institutions deeply rooted within a territory. The 'local' factor is therefore essential: the water from the coastal river, the proximity to Madras, as also the presence of Muslim tanners in the five towns investigated. The existing social structures make effective cooperation possible, testimony of which is found in the setting up of collective units for waste water treatment in response to the new legislation for environmental protection.

One cannot, however, restrict oneself to an 'ideal' view of the local situation. Kennedy shows the force of social and religious segmentation. This is undoubtedly peculiar to India when one makes a comparison with the industrial districts usually described by scholars in the rest of the world. Obviously, the district cannot function without the numerous relationships which bind it to the higher levels and which are necessary for its development and for innovation (national or international legislations and markets). The 'pollution crisis' here appears highly symptomatic, since it shows how the global ecological norms directly interfere, sometimes in a dramatic fashion, by forcing retrenchments, on the local level albeit through the medium of the national level. Thus it was in New Delhi that the Supreme Court passed a ruling ordering the closure of factories not equipped with anti-pollution devices, just as it was in New Delhi that it had been decided, on an earlier occasion, to ban the export of semi-finished leather, a decision that had a strong impact on the Palar Valley. The State of Tamil Nadu, for its part, appeared to have played only a secondary role.

Pierre Lachaier highlights the same ambiguity by recounting for us a saga of diesel engines played out in the region of Kolhapur in Maharashtra. Here is a local industry, based originally on resourcefulness, which, in a century, has succeeded in evolving on the regional, then the national, and finally the international scale. The role played by the local factors is brought out: the importance of the cultivation of sugar-cane for capturing market outlets and capital, as also that of networks in which the bonds of kinship, friendship, and community are involved. The impact of the state of Maharashtra and the centre appears to be secondary to the enlightened monarchy of the pioneering era, the creation of a local industrial zone, and subsidized loans. The role of this industry on the global scale, finally, is quite clear. Confined to the imitation of foreign technologies to begin with, it developed thereafter on account of the growing importance of trade and financial dealings with foreign countries. All this was not devoid of its share of problems and profound mutations. The process of expansion does indeed have technological implications (more and more sophisticated and capital intensive technology, more and more rigid quality norms), as also economic implications, with the setting in of a dependence (inflow of funds, transfer of technologies, but also a situation of inferiority as sub-contractors), and finally, the social implications of anonymity and more strained relationships. This saga in the shape of a pyramid, from the local to the global, is not devoid of fragility. Besides, the reader will note that among the major enterprises found in Kolhapur today are those founded by Ram Menon and 'R', natives of Kerala and of Gujarat. Need one say more about the narrowness of the local bases of this industrial district?

Gérard Heuzé gives an account of the blurring of scales in his virulent analysis of the large industrial and technocratic project of Singrauli, testimony to an authoritarianism that has survived the Nehru and Indira Gandhi eras. In the casting of the actors involved, one would expect to see the local in the role of the good person (the tribal people displaced by large development projects), the national in that of the villain (New Delhi's technocratic power), assisted by the global (the international geo-economic powers). But the next thing we know, certain global institutions (EDF International, some American NGOs) rush to the help of the tribal people against the national. Then, all of a sudden, another global entity (the World Bank) supports the national interest against the local self-interests. And then, on the local and regional scales, social groups, regional authorities, businessmen of a more or less dubious character, and political leaders of the more or less mafia variety, all enter the fray, pulling in different directions. It is indeed, a 'complexification of the stage' that comes into being. This rough and ready mode of development shows that it is not globalization by itself that is responsible for scandals. The reader could even consider, from a certain point of view, that the opening-up of India has enabled foreign pressure groups to serve as a chamber for echoing the protests of local victims.

The last part of this book deals with a matter critical to India's development, namely, agriculture and food. Bruno Dorin chooses the level of the central government to examine the formulation of an agricultural policy, relating to the development of oilseeds. He starts with the old question, how to achieve self-reliance. Is this to be by insulation within the national network, by self-sufficiency? Or by opening up, allowing foreign intercourse to develop and therefore play a role in the world, which itself could become a source of independence? To these theoretical questions, which Dorin sets out within an entire epistemological field, comes a concrete answer from the history of the 'yellow revolution' of oilseeds. An inter-ministerial mission, set up in 1985, enabled India to become self-sufficient in edible oils within a period of five years. This was achieved by means somewhat different from those deployed at the time of the 'green revolution' in cereals. Until then, enormous imports of edible oils had been profitable to the central government as they had brought in tariff revenues. They were profitable also to the states and to industrialists, but not so to consumers and even less so to the farmers who produced oilseeds. This was the situation that Rajiv Gandhi did away with by appointing, in 1987, the dynamic and media-conscious Sam Pitroda, at the head of the Technology Missions. His mode of action was to short-circuit the bureaucracy by putting information to advantage, thanks to a flow chart based on the cooperation and the commitment of civil society in order to give rise to *auto-nomous* actors, that is to say, participants capable of adapting themselves to an environment of growing complexity. The trade balance went over to the plus side. But the rise in agricultural prices prevented any great increase in the consumption of oil, and today, in an internal and external context that has been remodelled, the import situation is once again a cause for concern.

While B. Dorin describes the inception of the yellow revolution in New Delhi, it is, on the contrary, 'from below' that the 'white revolution' is perceived by Véronique Alary, Anne-Claire Degail and Rachel Rivière. They analyse the factors which determine the production and the marketing of milk in Gujarat and Haryana, and attempt to uncover those arising from choice and those from constraints, by studying the farmers within their local or regional environment. The choice of the scale of study appears to be fundamental, insofar as it can lead to the appearance or the dis-appearance of certain factors. The authors therefore take recourse to a regional break-up which transcends the antithesis between arid and semi-arid in the official agro-climatic classifications of the Planning Commission. Villages were selected for study in accordance with the extent of their irrigation and their landlocked status. A sampling of households took account of the internal factors differentiating the farms from one another. These factors are brought out notably by a statistical analysis keeping in mind the connections between capital and land ownership, caste, and investment in irrigation. The factors peculiar to the region are also highlighted, the institutional ones with the importance or otherwise of cooperatives, and the more agricultural ones with the type of commercial crops grown. Generally, irrigation, making cash crops possible, allows the farmer to keep his milk for consumption within the household. The poorest farms, on the contrary, are often those that sell the most milk, as they need the money it brings. On the whole, the official agro-climatic break-up is a functional one, since the conditions of aridity appear on the third axis of the factor analysis.

In his concluding chapter Frédéric Landy reflects over the definition of the different scales of approach. He notes the vague nature of the all-purpose concepts of 'local' and 'global', a vagueness which is all the more detrimental as the post-modern analyses of 'complexity' might well conceal many a vested interest. The local/regional/global dialectic is then applied to the study of India's policy in the matter of food. It demonstrates the voluntarist nature of this policy of the centre, as also the great fragility of the entire structure undermined by costs, limited effectiveness and the disagreements between the different players at the different levels. It confirms also the necessity for approaches on several levels showing concern for the micro-scale in order to avoid the excesses of the past generalizing visions, but which refuse to confine themselves within it. For it is true indeed that causalities and factors of explanation vary in accordance with scale, and we must therefore attempt to comprehend all of them.

NOTES

1. From out of an overabundant bibliography concerning globalization and its relationship with local development, special mention should be made to Benko and Lipietz (2000), Chesnais (1997), Demazière ed. (1996), *Mondes en développement* (1998). The reflections of Featherstone (1995) or Robertson (1992) on the cultural impact of globalization appear to us to be quite abstract. For a general appraisal of such perceptions see the penetrating article by Assayag (1998) on Appadurai (1996).
2. The misuse should be noted of the adjective 'global' employed sometimes to indicate what is 'foreign'. Gardner (1995), for instance, when showing that the local culture of Sylhet (Bangladesh) is influenced by emigration, asserts that '*global processes are transformed into local idioms*'. Assimilating the 'local/ global' dialectics to 'my country/foreign land', *desh/bidesh* would imply that there exists just a single worldwide culture, as if immigrants in London were steeped in the same culture as those of the Gulf.
3. B. Antheaume, in 'La mondialisation', a discussion published in *L'espace géographique*, 1999, 1, pp. 36-48.
4. R. O'Brien, *Global Financial Integration: The End of Geography*, London: Pinter Publishers, quoted by R. Knafou in the debate 'La mondialisation', op. cit.
5. 'Systemic approaches give a view of a global system which is included in the method itself while an analytical examination leads to a contrary reality' (Ph. Hugon, 'L'évolution de la pensée économique et la mondialisation', in GEMDEV, 1999, p. 21).
6. *Frontline*, 18 June 1999.
7. This vertical dimension undoubtedly does not work in some cases, such as in the remote regions of India like the forests of Madhya Pradesh where even now villages are being 'discovered' (*India Today*, 15 April 1992). The involvement of higher, national and global, levels is extremely limited on account of the exclusion of these zones. That the matter we are debating has

no relevance here highlights sufficiently the terrible situation of these regions.

8. With the demarcation of 3 new states in 2000, it can be considered that there are now 28 states in India.

REFERENCES

Ahluwalia, I.J., 'The Contribution of Planning to Indian Industrialisation', in T.J. Byres (ed.), *The State, Development Planning and Liberalisation in India*, Delhi: Oxford University Press, 1998, pp. 254-97.

Appadurai, A., *Modernity at Large. Cultural Dimensions of Globalization*, Minneapolis: University of Minnesota Press, 1996.

Assayag, J., 'La culture comme fait social global? Anthropologie et (post)modernité', *L'Homme*, 148, (1998): 201-24.

Benko, G. and Lipietz, A. (eds.), *La richesse des régions. La nouvelle géographie socio-économique*, Paris, PUF, 2000.

Chandrasekhar, C.P. and Ghosh, J., The Poverty Puzzle, www.macroscan.com, 2000.

Chesnais, F., *La mondialisation du capital*, Paris: Syros, 1997.

Datt, G., 'Has Poverty in India Declined since the Economic Reforms?', *Economic and Political Weekly*, 34, (11-17 December, 1999): 3516-18.

De Gournay, Ch., 'En attendant les nomades', *Réseaux,* (May-June 1994), 5-13.

Demazière, C. (ed.), *Du local au global. Les intiatives locales pour le développement économique en Europe et en Amérique*, Paris: L'Harmattan, 1996.

Dollfus, O., *L'espace Monde*, Paris: Economica, 1994.

Dollfus, O., Grataloup, C. and Levy, J., 'Trois ou quatre choses que la mondialisation dit à la géographie', *L'espace géographique*, 1 (1999):1-11.

Dupont, L. and Lemarchand, N., 'Culture et commerce. Du système national américain au système-monde: le cas-type de McDonald's', *Géographie et cultures*, 32 (1999): 51-66.

Featherstone, M., *Undoing Culture. Globalization, Postmodernism and Identity*, London: Sage, 1995.

Gardner, K., *Global Migrants, Local Lives. Travel and Transformation in Rural Bangladesh*, Oxford: Clarendon, 1995.

GEMDEV, *Mondialisation. Les mots et les choses*, Paris: Karthala, 1999.

Goody, J., *The East in the West*, Cambridge University Press, 1996.

Guhan, S., 'Centre and States in the Reform Process', in Cassen, R.and Joshi, V. (ed.), *India. The Future of Economic Reform*, Delhi: Oxford University Press, 1995, pp. 71-111.

Guilmoto, C.Z., 'The Geography of Fertility in India (1981-1991)', in C.Z. Guilmoto and A. Vaguet (eds.), *Essays on Population and Space in India*, Pondicherry: French Institute of Pondicherry, 2000, pp. 37-56.

Gupta, A., *Postcolonial Developments. Agriculture in the Making of Modern India*, Durham: Duke University Press, 1998.

Krugman, P., *Geography and Trade*, Boston: MIT Press, 1991.

Krugman P. and Venables, A.J., 'Globalization and the Inequality of Nations', *Quarterly Journal of Economics*, November 1995: 857-80.

Le Bras, H., *La planète au village*, La Tour d'Aigues: DATAR-Editions de l'Aube, 1997.

Levy, J., 'Une géographie visitée par le Monde', *L'espace géographique*, 1 (1999): 23-8.

Mondes En Développement, 1998, t. 26, no. 103 'Développement Local et Mondialisation'.

Raison, J.P., 'La géographie du mondial au local . . . et retour. Mondialisation et différentiations spatiales et sociales des territoires dans les pays du Tiers-Monde', *Géotropiques*, University of Paris X-Nanterre, 1999.

Revue Française de Géoéconomie, 'Les régions dans la nouvelle donne économique mondiale', 5, (1998).

Robertson, R., *Globalization. Social Theory and Global Culture*, London: Sage, 1992.

Sassen, S., *The Global City. New York, London, Tokyo*, Princeton: Princeton University Press, 1991.

Savy, M. and Veltz, P. (eds.), *Economie globale et réinvention du local*, La Tour d'Aigues: DATAR-Editions de l'Aube, 1995.

Streeten, P., 1998, 'La mondialisation: intégration et désintégration', *Mondes en développement*, vol. 26, no.103 (1998): 29-36.

Veltz, P., *Mondialisation, villes et territoires. L'économie d'archipel*, Paris: PUF, 1997.

Swadeshi in the Throes of Liberalization[1]

Gilles Boquérat

By moving in the early 1990s towards economic liberalization and opening up to international trade and foreign capital, India was casting aside certain principles that had governed its economic policy since independence. First and foremost was the priority given to the development of a self-reliant economy through an import-substitution policy and high customs duty. International capital flows and trade exchanges had been suspected of promoting a neo-colonialism that exploited the resources of the Third World as a supplier of raw materials and primary products, and of instituting an economic hegemony in which these countries were kept closely dependent on the industrialized nations. In the mind of leaders like Nehru, politics and economics were inter-linked, and too great an integration by India's economy into world trade would mean the undermining of independence.

The effect of these beliefs were reflected notably in India's decline in world trade. Its share dipped from 1.78 per cent in 1950 to 0.53 per cent in 1991, and has marginally recovered at 0.7 per cent in 2001 (*Economic Survey 1996-97:* 88; *Economic Survey 2002-2003:* 102).[2] Industrial policy was such that domestic production came to constitute around 95 per cent of the supply of manufactured goods and all of consumer goods (World Bank 1989: 7). As regards foreign direct investment, the industrial policy resolution of 1948 and successive decisions had resulted in making foreign investors turn to greener pastures offering more attractive conditions. Thus the Foreign Exchange Regulation Act of 1973 restricted the participation, on a case-by-case basis, of foreign enterprises in joint ventures with Indian partners to 40 per cent of total equity capital, except for a few exceptions in priority industries if technology was not available in the country or if the venture was largely export-oriented. India had not, for all that, renounced to external financing for its development. It could not afford to do so in view of the structural deficit of its trade balance. However, this had taken the form basically of foreign aid.

In the early 1980s, nonetheless, it came to be acknowledged that international trade functioned as a catalyst for economic dynamism, since it involved the modernization of a production machinery that the protectionism of earlier years had largely rendered obsolete. It had been vitiated with low productivity and consequently poor international competitiveness. The transition from a self-reliant development to an outward-looking economy has been brought up on several occasions by Rajiv Gandhi, as prime minister, stressing, for instance, that 'the biggest challenge that we are going to face is that of exports really earning enough money to import items that we are forced to import' (Gandhi 1989: 69). The mobilization of foreign direct investments fitted into this process, involving as it did transfers of technology and managerial expertise, the growth of exports, associated with an integration into global production chains, and supporting investment needs for higher growth without burdening the debt position. The leadership had yet no intention to sacrifice the national sovereignty to a higher degree of engagement with the international economy. Quite the contrary, the latter policy was conducted with the desire to regain room for manoeuvre in the face of a deterioration in external finances that took the country to the verge of default on its international obligations (reserves had come down to about one month's imports in the spring of 1991).

THE REHABILITATION OF TRADE EXCHANGES

Over and above the constraints imposed by international financial organizations to rescue India in the spring of 1991, the rapid export-driven growth of the South-East and East Asian economies served as an incentive to do away with an inward-looking economic model. Until the end of the Cold War, the faster pace of development in this region had not drawn special attention, tainted as it was by political alignment with the United States. Once the Cold War had ended, there was no longer the same reticence towards showing keen interest at the economic progress achieved in a part of Asia which had since long been viewed with a certain condescension. For instance, Y.D. Gundevia, a senior ICS officer who was then Commonwealth Secretary, has narrated that during a conference of India's ambassadors to the South-East Asian countries in the summer of 1963, Nehru, in response to the Indian envoy in Bangkok extolling the virtues of Indo-Thai cooperation, protested: 'Great deal in common between Thailand and India! What is there in common? The Prime Minister of Thailand is an important personality in the Coca-Cola Company!' (M.J. Akbar 1988: 498-9). It was now recalled that South Korea and India had been, in the early 1950s, in a comparable state of underdevelopment and that forty years later, the overall outcome hardly went in favour of the latter. What is more, the high growth rate recorded by the People's Republic of China, yet another country which in its time had laid stress on the necessity of being self-reliant, went to prove that opening up an economy was not synonymous with political dependence.

The necessity of sustained growth in exports through the liberalization of imports and a more conciliatory attitude towards foreign direct investment was not a new idea. It had already been suggested by different commissions entrusted with the study of trade policy reforms, for instance, the Alexander Committee (1978), the P. Tandon Committee (1982), and the Abid Hussain Committee (1984). The trend however took practical form only in the 1990s, particularly with the announcement in April 1992 of a new import-export policy for the next five years. Exports had already been made easier by the two-stage devaluation of the rupee in July 1991. Thereafter the financial authorities intervened relatively little, preferring to allow the currency to float freely. The value of the rupee moved from 21 to 47 to the dollar between June 1991 and June 2001. The decision to devalue was accompanied by structural reforms in trade and industrial policies, aimed at liberalizing an inhibiting system of administrative authorizations and tariff and non-tariff barriers, and at improving the penetration of Indian enterprises into the sphere of international exchange. By means of a deliberate policy of lowering of customs duty, the simple mean tariff came down, between 1990 to 1999, from 79.1 per cent to 32.2 per cent, a significant decline even though it still remains higher than in East and South-East Asia (World Bank 2001: 336-7). Non-tariff barriers (goods whose import is restricted, canalized through state agencies or simply prohibited) were reduced during the 1990s.[3] Since 1 April 2001, in conformity with World Trade Organization rules, quantitative restrictions have been phased out and most products have moved to the Open General License. The state can yet replace quantitative restrictions by high import duties, by compliance with quality standards or point-of-entry limitations for some 'sensitive items'. High local taxes can also blur the picture when it comes to the access of foreign products to the Indian market.

Here is a sign of the times. The negligible dependence of the country on foreign trade, for long considered a factor providing freedom from the upheavals of international exchange, is being perceived henceforth as an outmoded idea calling for introspection. Initially, the dominant position in both policy-making and academic circles in India rested on the notion that export earnings were determined primarily by exogenous factors and that it was therefore more sensible to give preference to a deliberate import-substitution policy. In effect this circumscribed the export capabilities of the country as it ended up with an ageing production machinery and low productivity. It took some time before it began to be admitted that an endogenous policy, mainly the liberalization of capital goods imports, was possible and necessary to a certain extent. Further, the lack of competitiveness of Indian industry could not be overcome without a flexibility of employment and a reduction of the public deficit enabling a lowering of the interest rate for firms. In both cases, the social cost paralyses a risk-averse political class, and it often remained desirous of ensuring the survival of unprofitable public undertakings rather than facilitating the cause of exporters whose main asset has been in the nineties exchange rates variations and some government incentives. There is nevertheless a vague consensus, more crisis-driven than resulting from a long-term strategy, on the necessity of adapting India's production system by opening it to international competition. This requires, notably at the ground level, addressing the inadequacy of the transport and communications infrastructure which does not provide for a satisfactory mobility of goods and services, both within India and abroad.

A distinct increase has been observed in the growth of export of goods and services, from an average annual growth of 5.9 per cent in

1980-90, to an average of 11.3 per cent in 1990-9. The propensity to export still remains relatively low—the exports of goods and services accounted for only 11 per cent of the gross domestic product in 1999. This puts India far behind China (22 per cent), South Korea (42 per cent) or Thailand (57 per cent) (World Bank 2001: 294, 298-9). India continues, therefore, to produce mostly for the domestic market. Export performance has been characterized by unevenness, witnessing a respectable growth between 1993-4 and 1995-6, with an average annual growth of around 20 per cent (in dollar terms), and then distinctly slowing down during the Ninth Plan period (1997-2002) with an actual growth per annum of 5.6 per cent, against an envisaged growth of 11.8 per cent. The export-import ratio nevertheless improved considerably during the 1990s, jumping from an average of 66 per cent between 1980-1 to 1990-1, to 86.2 per cent between 1991-2 to 2001-2. Undoubtedly the fact that the oil prices have not excessively soared over the decade has contributed towards this result considering the growing imbalance between domestic production and consumption: their share in total imports increased from 25 per cent at the beginning of the 1990s to 30 per cent in 2000-1 (*Economic Survey 2002-2003:* S-82).[4] Another positive development has been the fact that India has been consistent with the global trend favouring demand for more value-added product categories. Its share of technology and knowledge-intensive exports has increased, from 18.5 per cent of total exports in 1991-2 to 23.7 per cent in 1997-8, whereas the share of labour-intensive exports has gone down from 31.8 per cent of total exports in 1991-2 to 24.7 per cent in 1997-8. The share of resource-intensive exports remained more or less the same for the same period (B. Bhattacharyya 2001: 9-11). Exportations have to acquire the consistency that would ensure a sustainable balance in the current account and have the range of tradable goods and services that would soften unforeseen external shocks.

India has had to overcome the consequences of the dismemberment of the Soviet Union, the largest trading customer for Indian products in 1990-1, accounting for 16.1 per cent of India's total exports. Two years later, the share of the former USSR in goods exported by India had fallen to 3.2 per cent (*Economic Survey 1993-94:* S-84-5). Meanwhile, India and Russia had signed in May 1992 an agreement on trade and economic cooperation providing that transactions between the two countries be calculated thereafter in hard currency, and no longer in rupees. An exception was however made to this new regime for political reasons with the arrangement made in 1993 relating to the repayment of loans given to India by the former USSR, after the delicate issue of the rupee-rouble parity had been settled. It was agreed that debt-servicing would—as before—take the form of exports of goods and services to Russia and that, for this purpose, the reimbursement made by India would be deposited in a special rupee account opened in the Reserve Bank of India. This measure did not succeed in stemming the decline in Indian exports, as the value of these remained less than the balance in rupees put at Russia's disposal.[5] It was then suggested that part of the amount coming from debt-servicing could be used to establish joint ventures in the two countries. As for imports of Russian products, they account for less than 2 per cent of India's total imports in 2001-2.

With the fall in exports to Russia, the United States has not only become the largest client but has also seen its share continuously grow in India's total exports. Only the European Union, taken as a whole, can claim larger trade exchanges. These two entities accounted, throughout the 1990s, for about 45 per cent of India's total exports. As for the share of the emerging countries of Asia, despite the financial crisis which affected them in 1997-8, it has distinctly increased, and forms part and parcel of a policy of coming closer by way of the 'Look East Policy' launched in 1991.

TABLE 1: INDIA'S TRADING PARTNERS—EXPORTS

(*percentage share*)

	1987-8	1990-1	1995-6	2000-1
United States of America	18.6	14.7	17.4	20.9
European Union	25.1	27.5	27.4	23.4
Japan	10.3	9.3	7.0	4.0
OPEC	6.1	5.6	9.7	10.9
Russia	12.5	16.1	3.3	2.0
Developing Countries*—Asia	11.9	14.4	23.0	22.5
of which SAARC	2.6	2.9	5.4	4.3
Others	9.3	11.5	17.6	18.2
Developing Countries—Africa	2.0	2.2	4.8	4.4
Developing Countries—Latin America	0.3	0.5	1.2	2.3
Others	13.2	9.7	6.2	9.6

NOTE: * Excluding members of OPEC.

SOURCE: Directorate General of Commercial Intelligence and Statistics, Calcutta. Percentage based on Table 123: Direction of Foreign Trade, *www.rbi.org.in.*

TABLE 2 : INDIA'S TRADING PARTNERS—IMPORTS

(percentage share)

	1987-8	1990-1	1995-6	2000-1
United States of America	9.0	12.1	10.5	6.0
European Union	33.3	29.4	28.1	20.8
Japan	9.6	7.5	6.7	3.6
OPEC	13.3	16.3	20.9	5.4
Russia	7.2	5.9	3.3	1.0
Developing Countries—Asia	112.1	14.0	17.5	16.7
of which: SAARC	0.4	0.5	0.7	0.9
Others	11.7	13.5	16.8	15.8
Developing Countries—Africa	2.9	2.4	3.1	3.9
Developing Countries—Latin America	2.3	2.3	1.6	1.4
Others	10.3	10.1	8.3	31.2

SOURCE : As for Table 1.

THE CHANGE IN THE STRUCTURE OF EXTERNAL CAPITAL

Until about 1980, mention of external financial resources almost always implied external assistance from foreign creditors. The increase in trade and fiscal deficits thereafter modified this order of things. India had become greedy for credit, which foreign aid could not always meet: utilization of foreign aid can take long, and the international financial institutions had become more stingy and offered loans on less favourable terms than before. China had also entered the fray and was in a position to borrow from the International Development Association, thereby competing with India for cheap loans (Asian Development Bank 1993: 128-9).[6] What was particularly worrisome was the growing share in the external debt, from the mid-1980s, of commercial borrowing (often requiring short-term reimbursement and carrying high interest rates) which had more than tripled and which constituted in March 1990 almost 30 per cent of the external debt (*India Today* 15 February 1991: 42; *Economic and Political Weekly* 9 February 1991: 264-5). A year later, debt-servicing accounted for 35 per cent of the export of goods and services. With globalization, external assistance, suspected in some aid-giving countries and international organizations of having too often served to bring economies under 'outdated' state control, took a back seat, giving precedence to foreign private capital. Proof of this is seen in the fact that the total amount of aid authorized reached a ceiling during the Seventh Five-Year Plan (1985-6 to 1989-90) and has since then been continuously declining (*Economic Survey 1999-2000:* S-99). By the end of the nineties aid accounted for less than 10 per cent of the net inflow of capital as against 30 per cent in 1990-1.

As regards the donor nations, the two superpowers of the Cold War had already become outstripped by Japan, which is today the first aid-giving country on the bilateral level. If the United States continue to maintain a not negligible influence in the aid negotiations, it is more through a leading role in international financial organizations (IBRD, IDA, ADB) which came to account in 2001-2 for two-thirds of the aid utilized by India. India's smaller dependence on aid can be seen in the fact that its share in central government expenditure has declined from 5.9 per cent in 1991 to 1.9 per cent in 2000 and also that on this latter date, it accounted for just 1.8 per cent of imports of goods and services as against 9.3 per cent in 1991 (World Bank 1998, 2002: 343, 361). In fact, a substantial part of the external assistance (about 81 per cent in 1999-2000) is channelled into the states and the Union Territories as additional central assistance. Foreign aid plays a useful role in the social sector, such as primary education and health, as well as in the energy and the infrastructure sectors (*Financial Express* 8 and 9 March 2001).

With decreasing foreign aid, the increasing place of private external capital has taken essentially three forms: commercial borrowings, NRI (Non-Resident Indian) deposits, and foreign investments, direct

TABLE 3 : UTILIZATION OF EXTERNAL ASSISTANCE

(in US $ million)

	1980-1	1985-6	1990-1	1995-6	2000-1
1. Aid-India Consortium members	2527.8	2085.7	3230.5	2671.0	2588.9
of which: Germany (former FRG)	181.4	120.0	235.6	186.1	84.9
United States	104.2	57.5	31.7	11.3	17.8
Japan	114.1	143.1	498.7	841.4	598.8
IBRD	175.5	322.5	1217.5	597.6	712.2
IDA	684.1	979.2	773.9	731.5	1065.6
2. Russia (former USSR)	41.6	131.8	174.3	—	28.5
3. Others	164.3	182.2	331.6	635.4	509.2
Of which: *Asian Development Bank*	—	—	212.4	572.3	470.9
Total	2733.7	2399.7	3736.5	3306.5	3126.7

NOTE: The member countries of the Aid-India Consortium are: Austria, Belgium, Canada, Denmark, France, Germany, Italy, Japan, Netherlands, Sweden, United Kingdom, United States, IBRD and IDA.

SOURCE: *Economic Survey 2001-2002*, Ministry of Finance, Government of India, S-103-104.

TABLE 4 : NET INFLOWS OF CAPITAL

(*in US $ million*)

	1990-1	1992-3	1994-5	1996-7	1998-9	2000-1	2001-2
Foreign investment	103	557	4807	5963	2312	4588	5286
FDI	*97*	*315*	*1228*	*2651*	*2380*	*1828*	*3266*
portfolio	*6*	*242*	*3579*	*3312*	*-68*	*2760*	*2020*
External assistance	2210	1859	1526	1109	820	427	1204
Commercial borrowings	2248	-358	1030	2848	4362	4011	-2034
IMF	1214	1288	-1143	-975	-393	- 26	—
NRI deposits	1536	2001	172	3350	960	2317	2754

SOURCE: *Economic Survey 1998-99*, p. 76 and *Economic Survey 2002-2003*, p. 100, Ministry of Finance, Government of India.

and portfolio. The first option is often costly and the second source of capital is considered with some ambivalence as, while they can reflect the concern of the Indian community abroad in propitious times, NRI deposits are volatile and can leave the country at short notice, as was observed during the Gulf War. Measures have incidentally been taken to stabilize these deposits, and NRIs are also expected to have larger role in FDI inflows as happens with the Chinese expatriate community. Foreign investments have grown rapidly in the early 1990s, going up from US $ 133 million in 1991-2 to reach $ 6.1 billion in 1996-7, before coming down to less than $ 5 billion in 2000-1. The evolution points to a greater circumspection by foreign investors after the slackening of the economic reforms, the permanence of a large fiscal deficit and to the impact of the East Asian crisis. The international economic sanctions imposed after the nuclear tests of May 1998 have led to a further constriction and foreign investments experienced a distinct slowdown during the financial year 1998-9 (risk-averse portfolio investments even recorded a negative balance as compared to the previous year). Signs of recovery, brought by foreign institutional investors and by deposits from NRIs attracted by high interest rates and easier convertibility and followed by a spurt in FDI inflows, have been noticeable at the turn of the millennium.

Until 1990, the restrictive policy followed by the government was such that foreign direct investments in 1990-1 had hardly reached the level of US $ 100 million, an insignificant amount as compared with funds from external assistance. Nothing had better symbolized the government's will, under Rajiv Gandhi, for a more flexible interpretation of the rules governing foreign direct investment than the entry by Pepsi into the Indian market in 1988, a decade after the equally symbolic departure of Coca Cola and IBM. The American company entered into a partnership with Voltas Limited, a firm belonging to the Tata group, and with the Punjab Agro-Industries Corporation, a public sector undertaking controlled by the Punjab government. It is an irony of history that Parle, the main Indian manufacturer of carbonated drinks, which had, at the time, opposed the entry of Pepsi by giving vent vehemently to a nationalist discourse, was subsequently to 'sell itself' to Coca Cola in 1993. The CEOs of Indian enterprises have mostly been hesitant over an unrestrained opening up of the market to foreign multinationals. The most well-known case is that of the 'Bombay Club' which, at the instigation of Rahul Bajaj, demanded in 1993 that the national industry should not be put at a disadvantage in the face of foreign groups better accustomed to the ways of competition.

Despite these reservations on the part of businessmen, there has been at the government level no question of reconsidering the new industrial policy adopted in July 1991. This provided, if certain norms were satisfied, for automatic approval of FDI up to 51 per cent foreign equity holding in 34 specified high-priority, capital-intensive, high technology industries. 100 per cent foreign equity was permitted in power generation in a bid to attract large international companies and for projects in export-processing zones. Foreign companies have taken advantage of new rules to increase their stake in their existing affiliates in the country. In this way, a third of FDI approvals accounted for by wholly foreign owned subsidiaries (*EPW* 30 May 1998: 1323). On an aggregate, over the period extending from 1991-2 to 2001-2, the flow of foreign direct investments attained $ 21.7 billion.[7] This figure remains less than the total amount of $ 23.3 billion of portfolio investments recorded during the same period (*Economic Survey 2002-2003:* 119). The emphasis on FDI has therefore given only partial results. India's share in the flow of direct investments made in developing economies has increased from 0.5 per cent in 1992 to 1.0 per cent in 2000, after reaching a peak of 1.9 per cent in 1997, thanks particularly to the faster pace of approvals to invest, and in spite of the continued and still very real bureaucratic hurdles. Yet FDI has not fulfilled the somewhat irrational expectations in this matter (*Economic Survey 1998-99:* 87; *Economic Survey 2002-2003:* 120). Even when the approval is given by the central government, FDI has been slow in materializing because of a maze of clearances at the local and central levels. Between 1991 and 2000, the actual inflows of FDI represented 36 per cent of the value of the approvals given by the government over the same period. One can nevertheless observe that the actual FDI inflow ratio has improved substantially since 1998 and that a significant amount of FDI is now on the automatic route and does not require prior approval. The general growth of FDI is a significant fact since, in absolute terms, it has increased from $ 1.03 billion between 1991-2 and 1993-4 to $ 8.4 billion between 1999-2000 and 2001-2 (*Economic Survey 2002-2003:* 119, 132).[8]

While the government of Inder Kumar Gujral (April 1997-March 1998) had pinned its hopes on a net inflow of direct investments of the order of $ 10 billion, India had to remain content with $ 3.6 billion in 1997, $ 2.6 billion in 1998, and $ 2.3 billion in 2000. This makes India a moderately attractive investment destination among developing countries. In 2000, China received $ 40.8 billion, Brazil $ 33.5 billion, South Korea $ 10.2 billion, and Malaysia $ 5.5 billion (UNCTAD, 2001, 294). Equally optimistic, the National Democratic Alliance (NDA), led by the Bharatiya Janata Party (BJP), reiterated, in its electoral manifesto of September 1999, the hope of acceding to FDI of the order of at least $ 10 billion per year, an amount commensurate with an annual 7-8 per cent growth rate (after the economic crisis of 1990-2, India has maintained an annual average growth rate of 6.8 per cent during the Eighth Plan (1992-7) and 5.6 during the Ninth Plan).[9] That the BJP should have rallied to such a correlation was, to say the least, unexpected from a party whose nationalist agenda has for long called for treading the path of 'swadeshi' and 'self-reliance' in development and production by encouraging import substitution and by adhering to a regime of strict austerity. Before coming to power in March 1998, the BJP had moreover severely criticised the policy of 'opening up' adopted by the Congress party, denouncing the 'crony capitalism' and the 'phony liberalization' which had been the outcome of the self-seeking collusion between politicians and bureaucrats and which had supposedly benefited the foreign companies more than anyone else.[10] The fear was that market mechanisms alone had encouraged foreign investors to seek out a niche with an easy return on investments (notably consumer goods) but no positive impact on development. The Hindu nationalists felt it would be necessary to restrict these by taking recourse to appropriate procedures of approval. However, in the electoral manifesto of the NDA in 1999, the concept of swadeshi aimed not at reviving the spinning wheel but at facilitating the national industry 'to gain enough muscles to compete with the multinationals in the local and global markets'. As for FDI, it is now considered indispensable in terms of transfer of technologies, new market practices and employment (NDA Election Manifesto, 1999: 4).

Actual government practice tends to show that the pursuit of growth is taking precedence over ideological reservations. The Union Cabinet decided in early 2000 to widen the list of products for which FDI would be permitted without prior approval of the Foreign Investment Promotion Board (FIPB). Ultimately, security clearance would be needed only on a negative list comprising the defence sector and some goods such as alcohol, cigarettes, medicines, and dangerous chemicals. Drawing inspiration from the Chinese model, it was recommended that Special Economic Zones (encompassing in fact the already existing export-processing zones, the older ones like Kandla, created in 1965, and Santa Cruz (1972) or the more recent one in Cochin) should be developed as competitive destinations for export-oriented FDI by granting tax exemptions and relaxing bureaucratic procedures. With the passing months, the government has decided to raise ceilings on FDI in the energy sector for projects related to generation, transportation and marketing, as well as in the telecom sector. The energy sector attracted the largest share—27.4 per cent—of FDI approved between August 1991 and October 2002, but inflows were just 9.7 per cent of approvals. Telecommunications came second with 20 per cent of FDI approved, but inflows were only 16.5 per cent of approvals. Approvals turned into inflows more consistently (more than one-third of approvals) in the electrical equipment sector (incl. computer software and electronics), in the transportation industry and in the chemical sector (*Economic Survey 2002-2003:* 135).

Foreign equity participation up to 26 per cent had also been allowed in the insurance sector, much to the dismay of the Sangh Parivar. The liberalization process has not found favour with the Rashtriya Swayamsevak Sangh (RSS) which, as the guarantor of the ideological purity of the Hindu nationalist right, enjoined the BJP to return to a conservative swadeshi model and protect national industry. An affiliated organization, the Swadeshi Jagran Manch (SJM), came forward to condemn globalization and allegiance to MNCs. These arguments, however, find little receptivity among the ruling class and an upper middle class newly converted to consumerism. The will of the Chief Ministers, irrespective of political affiliation, to mobilize foreign capital should not be underestimated either. However, they have not all displayed the same ardour in implementing reforms for setting up a proper legal and industrial framework. With the sole exception of the Union Territory of Delhi, FDI approved during 1991-2002 were to be located above all in the coastal states of western and southern India (except Kerala) whereas northern states have been largely ignored (Map 1). This imbalance could widen, particularly on account of the heavy fiscal deficit in the latter which restricts their capacity to undertake expenditure on infrastructure that is absolutely necessary for attracting capital.

As regards the country-wise break up of FDI inflows, between August 1991 and October 2002, Mauritius comes first, thanks to the special tax treatment given to investments routed through the island, with an amount of US $ 6.8 billion, i.e. 38.7 per cent of total FDI inflows. The United States follow with $ 3.2 billion (17.1 per cent), far ahead of Japan ($ 1.3 billion, 6.8 per cent), the United Kingdom (5.2 per cent), Germany (5 per cent), and in decreasing order: Netherlands, South Korea, France, Italy, Singapore (*Economic Survey 2002-2003:* 134).

In absolute terms, the fact remains however that the expenditure on development still depends mostly on domestic savings. During the past decade, the overall saving–investment gap has averaged 1.3 per cent of GDP. Gross investment during the Tenth Plan (2002-7),

TABLE 5 : OPENNESS AND SUSTAINABILITY

(*in percentage*)

	1990-1	1992-3	1994-5	1996-7	1998-9	2000-1
1. Indicators of integration and openness						
Export to GDPmp (at current market prices)	5.8	7.1	8.3	8.9	8.3	9.8
Import to GDPmp	8.8	9.4	11.1	12.7	11.5	13.0
Foreign investments to GDP	0.04	0.3	1.6	1.7	0.6	1.1
Foreign investments to exports	0.6	3.0	17.9	17.5	6.7	10.2
2. Indicators of sustainability						
Export growth rate	9.2	3.8	18.4	5.3	- 5.1	21.0
Import growth rate	13.4	12.7	22.9	6.7	2.2	1.7
Export to import	75.4	84.7	91.9	85.5	78.4	88.2
Debt service to current receipts	35.3	27.5	26.2	22.5	18.0	15.4
Import to foreign currency assets (no. of months)	1.1	3.5	8.7	6.9	8.4	9.4
Short-term debt to foreign currency assets	382.1	98.5	20.5	30.1	14.5	9.2

SOURCE: Based on different *Economic Surveys*.

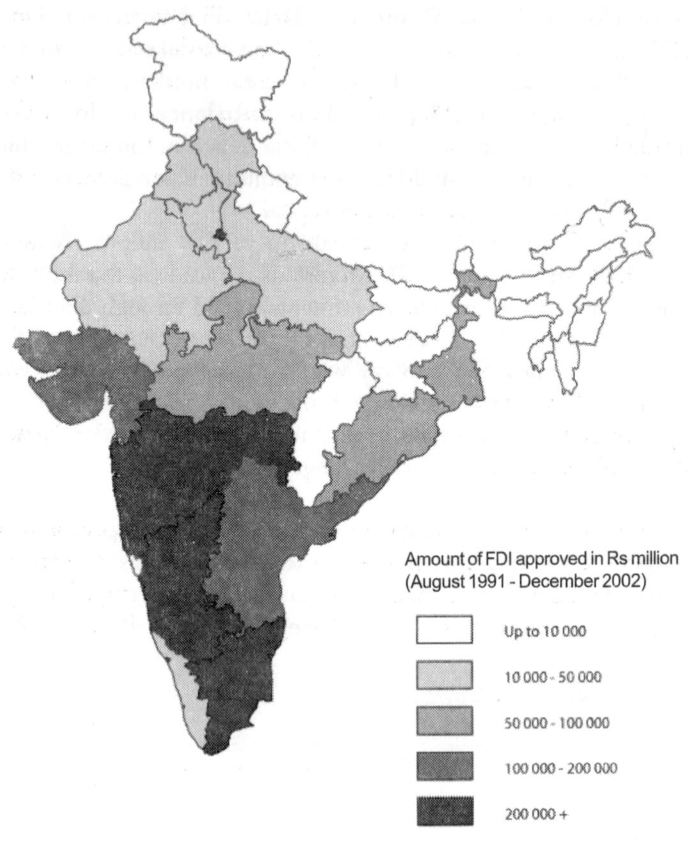

SOURCE: SIA Newsletter, Ministry of Commerce and Industry (GOI): http://www.indmin.nic.in

MAP 1: STATEWISE BREAK-UP FOR FOREIGN DIRECT INVESTMENT APPROVED DURING 1991-1992

estimated at 28.41 per cent of the GDP, is to be financed by domestic savings for 26.84 per cent and by external source for 1.57 per cent (Tenth Five Year Plan 2002: 34). The relatively small recourse to foreign capital which, what is more, aims at securing those resources which are the most stable, has enabled India to escape relatively unhurt from the East Asian financial crisis. In March 1991, the external debt was of the order of US $ 83.8 billion. Ten years later, it had risen to $ 101.1 billion. Despite this increase, the key debt indicators have improved over time. With respect to the GDP, the external debt, after having touched the 40 per cent mark in 1992 and 1993, was brought down from 30.4 per cent in 1990-1 to 22.4. per cent in 2000-1. Moreover, the structure of the debt has been modified. While the proportion of concessional debt to the total external debt has shown a decline (from 45 per cent in March 1992 to 36 per cent in March 2002), India's indebtedness position has improved, in absolute terms, from third largest debtor after Brazil and Mexico in 1991 to ninth in 2000. India can also take comfort in the fact that short-term debt (debt with original maturity of up to one year) has steadily declined, since in March 2001 it was confined to US $ 3.6 billion, i.e. 3.6 per cent of the total external debt, thus mitigating the risk of a severe financial crisis. Short-term debt to foreign currency assets ratio has also significantly declined to 5.4 per cent in March 2002, compare to 19.4 in March 1998 *(Economic Survey 2002-2003:* 125). The relatively comfortable foreign exchange position provides a margin of safety (foreign currency assets, excluding gold and SDRs, cover one year's imports), even though a wider opening up to the world involves a greater vulnerability to external shocks.

The desirability of a bolder outlook towards international economic exchanges is widely recognized. The pace at which this should be accomplished is, on the other hand, still a matter of debate. In this respect, during the East Asian crisis, India expressed itself fortunate at having chosen the middle path of integrating with the outside world making a transition through the cautious management of foreign capital inflow and a partial convertibility of the rupee (since it was restricted to the current account and it favours a measured approach towards capital account convertibility). This spared it from being caught in the financial turmoil that erupted.[11] This attitude fitted into a stance of inferred wisdom but it also masked the difficulties of integration into the mainstream of globalization.

NOTES

1. During the fight for independence, swadeshi was part and parcel of a call for economic emancipation from the colonial power. Later, it took on the enunciation of an economic nationalism, whose expression is found in the slogans 'Be Indian, Buy Indian' during Indira Gandhi's days or 'India shall be built by Indians' of the Bharatiya Janata Party.
2. It is significantly less than the export-driven economies of East and South-East Asia. By comparison, China's share is 4.3 per cent, Korea: 2.4 per cent, Malaysia: 1.4 per cent, Thailand: 1.1 per cent, and Indonesia: 0.9 per cent.

3. 66.1 per cent of India's imports (in value) in 1998-9 were undertaken under the Open General License, while 14.6 per cent were subjected to restrictions and 17.3 per cent were channelled.
4. In 1991, India imported less than one-third of its requirements of crude oil and petroleum products. During 2002-03, an estimated 73 per cent of the total value of crude oil consumed in the country was imported.
5. The tea industry, especially the low-value bulk tea segment, had availed for a long time in the USSR, then in the CIS, of a wide market. Consequently, the search for new clients in a very competitive market was neglected. With the depreciation of the ruble in 1998, this industry found itself weakened with painful consequences, notably for the plantations in the south of the country. Furthermore, the Russian market has eroded due to an image problem created out of export of substandard tea. Russia buying has been at its lowest in 2002.
6. While in 1975, the average rate of interest on new loans obtained by India was 2.5 per cent, it went up to 6.2 per cent in 1988. At the same time, the period of maturity and the grace period had, on an average, been shortened.
7. FDI inflows amounted to an annual average of $ 394 millions during 1989-1994 (0.6 per cent of gross fixed capital formation). In 1999, the figure was $ 2.15 billion (2.4 per cent of GFCF), after reaching an unequalled level of $ 3.61 billion in 1997 (3.8 per cent of GFCF) (UNCTAD, *World Investment Report 2001: Promoting Linkages*, New York: United Nations, pp. 294, 320).
8. The case of the US firm Cogentrix Energy is revealing as it brings out the distance separating promises from reality. In the first phase of the economic reforms of 1991-3, the proposal of Cogentrix for the construction of a power station in Karnataka had formed part of eight projects in the energy sector that the Indian government had promised to facilitate. In end 1999, Cogentrix; faced with legal obstacles and an uncooperative bureaucracy, threaten to throw in the towel and to pull out of the country.
9. If the $ 10 billion figure was nearly reached in 2001, it was by Indian workers' remittances. In this regard, India is the top recipient country in the world of this relatively stable source of foreign exchange, much less affected by political and financial crisis than FDI or official flows. The challenge is to direct these overseas remittances towards productive investment.
10. When Arun Shourie, the BJP Minister for Disinvestment announced the privatization of BALCO (Bharat Aluminium Company Limited), it was the turn of Manmohan Singh, the architect of the 1991 liberalization process, to accuse the government of 'crony capitalism', with charges of non-transparency regarding the evaluation process done by the US financial firm, Jardine Fleming (*India Today*, 12 March 2001, p. 28).
11. The Reserve Bank of India cites as a proof of this cautious approach the fact that the current account deficits went on an average a little over 1 per cent of the GDP during the 1990s, whereas in Thailand and Malaysia, it exceeded 6 per cent (*Report on Currency and Finance 1998-99*, op. cit., p. X-4).

REFERENCES

Akbar, M.J., *Nehru—The Making of India*, New Delhi: Viking, 1988.

Asian Development Bank, *Key Indicators of Developing Asian and Pacific Countries*, vol. 24, Manila: ADB, 1993.

Bhattacharyya, B., *Increasing Competitiveness through New Sources of Productivity Growth*, 2001, Indian Institute of Foreign Trade, *www.iift.edu*

Gandhi, Rajiv, *Selected Speeches and Writings*, vol. 2, New Delhi: Government of India, Publications Division, 1989.

Ghosh, Arun, 'Eighth Plan: Challenges and Possibilities—IV: Balance of Payments', *Economic and Political Weekly*, vol. 26, no. 6, 9 February 1991.

Kumar, Nagesh, 'Liberalisation and Changing Patterns of Foreign Direct Investments', *Economic and Political Weekly*, vol. 33, no. 22, May 30, 1998.

Mehta, Rajesh, *Tariff and Non-Tariff Barriers of Indian Economy: A Profile*, New Delhi: RIS, 1999.

Ministry of Finance, Economic Division, *Economic Survey 1993-94*, New Delhi: Government of India Press, 1994.

——, *Economic Survey 1996-97*, New Delhi: Government of India Press, 1997.

——, *Economic Survey 1998-99*, New Delhi: Government of India Press, 1999.

——, *Economic Survey 1999-2000*, New Delhi, Government of India Press, 2000.

——, *Economic Survey 2000-2001*, New Delhi: Government of India Press, 2001.

Ministry of Finance and Company Affairs, Economic Division, *Economic Survey 2002-2003*, New Delhi: Government of India Press, 2003.

The National Democratic Alliance, *Election Manifesto, Lok Saha Election, 1999*, New Delhi, 1999.

Reserve Bank of India, *Report on Currency and Finance 1998-99*, Mumbai: RBI Press, 1999.

UNCTAD, *World Investment Report 2001: Promoting Linkages*, New York: United Nations, 2001.

World Bank, *India: An Industrializing Economy in Transition*, Washington: World Bank, 1989.

——, *World Development Indicators 1998*, Washington: World Bank, 1998.

——, *World Development Report 2000/2001*, New York: World Bank, 2001.

——, *World Development Indicators 2002*, Washington: World Bank, 2002.

Healthcare Systems Caught in the Twists and Turns of Globalization

Alain Vaguet

It would seem that since Greek antiquity, the way the West perceives India is doomed to alternate between wonder and horror. Consequently, the clichés associated in the imagination of Europeans concerning the healthcare situation in India are not far from verging on the spectacular. They picture in their mind either homes for the dying in Calcutta or the extraordinary control that practitioners of yoga have over their body. Be it adulation for an idealistic model or loathing for an idolatrous religion, they find it difficult to escape from preconceived notions. Now, all Indians are not gymnosophists, and all their hospitals are not places where people are doomed to die.

This paper does not describe in detail the reality of India's health systems but seeks to underscore its recent developments. After presenting some elements that combine to show the forms of internationalization taking place in the allopathic health system, stress will be laid on the trends within the internal systems in such a way as to qualify some complex ground realities. The relatively sudden emergence of new modes of treatment is bringing about an inequality of access to medical practices. This is perhaps resulting, above all, in the diversification of the modes of treatment in consonance with the expectations of an emerging middle class, a category of population leading a lifestyle close to that of the rich countries, its socio-spatial networks distinctly apart from those of the most impoverished.

Is this mutation exogenous, forcibly thrust from the outside? Or is it more a manifestation of the kind of endogenous evolution found in all societies? Numerous scholars express their alarm today at the neo-liberal strategies that are being propagated over the entire planet. China itself does not seem to be able to resist a serious move towards privatization. India's health systems, themselves complex legacies of a multiplicity of contacts, find themselves confronted with this world-wide logic. Are they, for all that, losing their identity?

It needs to be asserted at the outset that the state of health of India's population has improved considerably during the course of the twentieth century. Life expectancy has soared from 32 years at the time of independence to nearly 63 in 1997. A considerable transformation in living conditions and the vaccination programmes of the Universal Immunization Programme, the spearhead of public policy, are the two main factors that have contributed towards this result. The battle has however not been completely won, the threshold of efficiency targeted at 85 per cent of children to be immunized is far from having been achieved, and it is the children of the poorest who have gained the least from these initiatives.[1] Contrary to the period of the 1980s, infant mortality is declining at a slower pace than general mortality.[2] It is lower in the cities and studies show that the children of the slums of Calcutta die in smaller numbers than those in the rural areas. Nevertheless, it is the smaller Indian towns that enjoy the more advantageous situation, as they are less deeply affected by the serious environmental problems than the metropolises (Gupta and Bagel 1999: 353-66).

The pathologies of overloading, degeneration (diabetes, cancer, cardio-vascular disease, etc.) and sociopathies such as addiction to alcohol, have come to be added on to the infectious diseases which have not yet been fully controlled. Thus, Japanese encephalitis breaks out sporadically in the poorer areas of the towns of Maharashtra during the season when water stagnates (Thakare 1999). The resurgence of malaria has been accompanied by a change in its pathological profile, as the common manifestations are decreasing and giving way to unusual ones (Patkar et al. 1995). One million new cases of tuberculosis are declared every year, of which half are fatal and the rates of resistance to the major commonly used medicines are becoming a cause of anxiety. AIDS, with an at least equal annual incidence, has been making its presence felt since 1986. Even though it arrived here late, India is already the nation worst affected by it in terms of number (Patkar et al. 1995).[3] It had been felt in the country that the outbreak of this disease was a manifestation of the depravation of the West which would never find a place in India. This perception has had necessarily to be modified in view of the enormity of the epidemic. Thus pathogenic systems also are good indicators of globalization.

GLOBALIZATION IS NOT A ONE-WAY PROCESS

In India probably more than elsewhere, there are multiple ways of treatment arising out of several health care systems. The storehouse of learning used as a guide by those individuals who practise these systems, is the product of a complex mixture of a more or less scientific traditional knowledge, and of information having its source in modern medicine.

Although it does not cover the entire medical realm, the Western system of medicine dominates the scene very largely in economic terms. The strength of this market is well brought out when we consider that there are 20,000 licensed pharmaceutical companies in India, which is a larger total than the number of primary health centres (17,000). In some states such as Kerala, their number has doubled in 1990s alone. The poor control over the sale of medicines gives rise to a great deal of self-medication, particularly in the matter of antibiotics. Around half of these are bought without prescription, at the risk of developing multi-resistant microbes (Saradamma et al. 2000).

After independence, the 'non-Western' (Craig 1999)[4] systems of medicine began to regain popularity. They play a large role in the conduct and rules of day-to-day life by which the people abide. Ayurveda, and in the south the Siddha systems of galenical medicine, probably date back to very early centuries (Filiozat 1949). We also find Unani medicine, practised mostly by Muslims. Homeopathy, founded two centuries ago by a German, is also popular. Hence, a multiplicity of absolutely cosmopolitan medical systems coexist in India. The government recognizes them by institutionalizing the training of doctors in 'traditional' medicine (Registered Medical Practitioners or RMP). They are trained to use allopathic medicines also (Zimmermann 1989).

There are 42 doctors for every 100,000 inhabitants in India, as against 160 in Japan and 230 in the United States (*The Economist* 1999).

Considered nevertheless as being too numerous (Baru 1998), and above all ill distributed over the land, Indian doctors, like their colleagues all over the world, do not set up practice in accordance with the needs of the people, but converge in the areas where the demand is of a profitable nature. In the rural areas, 'the RMP is more commonly found (Carrière 1983) and asks for smaller fees, but some of the medicines based on rare components, prepared by reputed masters, can turn out to be very expensive. The prices vary considerably and it is not always easy to decide if traditional medicine really is the least expensive. It should not be imagined that modern medicine is confined to the more well-off among the social categories while traditional medicine constitutes a cheaper palliative. Slum dwellers are commonly found consulting a liberal doctor or going for free consultation to a public hospital, while it is prevalent in wealthy families to consult a renowned practitioner of traditional medicine. Naturally the hospital with its interminable queues is shunned by those who have the means to do without it. On the whole, research confirms that the recourse to non-Western medical systems remains small and confined to specific health problems (Khanna et al. 1991: 893). It is therefore constituted in accordance with the perception of the individuals and their means, within a galaxy of available choices.

The endeavour to rationalize non-Western medical systems undertaken with the help of the state has reduced them to a state where they are equated with treatment through herbal medicines, whereas their major characteristic lies actually in their capacity to deal with the disease within the context of a specific cultural field. This rationalizing 'legitimization' (Janes 1999: 805) has led anthropologists to talk of a crisis. This body of learning is in fact being partially incorporated into bio-medicine at a time precisely when the multiplicity of chronic pathologies is giving credibility to healthcare systems which keep the psychological dimension in mind.

The success of Western pharmacopoeia does not mean that the globalized modern medical system has won a decisive victory. Ayurvedic medicines continue to remain popularly utilized. R.D. Saradamma found 16 per cent of such remedies being used in a sampling of 400 households in Kerala (Saradamma 2000: 893). Moreover, competition is intensifying between Ayurvedic medicine, for instance, representing the north Indian tradition and its languages, and the Siddha medicine emanating from south India and in particular from the Tamil culture (Jules 2000). Major seminars on Siddha medicine have been organized outside Tamil Nadu. In keeping with the linguistic

Babel that India represents, what one could call medical identities remain alive and contribute also to its diversity. Some medicines of these non-Western pharmacopoeia, which on the whole are not very different from each other when reduced to their active principles, are already selling in such great numbers the world over that the Indian government is beginning to become apprehensive over the biodiversity of the places where the herbs are picked if their collection is not regulated. A consumerist attitude is indeed leading some Westerners, perplexed over the onset of certain iatrogenic diseases or nosocomial infections, to use these preparations as they would any other drugs, whereas they cannot be separated from the civilization in which they need to be taken. Should we conclude that a new fascination for India has set in? Is it the effect of a passing fancy? Is it new evidence of an unequal flow of influences on the scale of the planet?

It would not be correct to put on the same footing the economic globalization which has manifested itself in the inflow of foreign capital into India's health system, and the cultural dissemination which is popularizing values and learning of Indian origin in the world. The two currents are flowing in opposite directions, but they far from overrule each other. That the use of Ayurvedic medicine is expanding cannot be a matter of satisfaction for those who support India's geo-economic independence if it is the multinationals who will become its vectors and reap its fruits. The case of yoga is an illustration of this complexity. A study conducted in Coimbatore, tenth largest city of India, has brought out the existence of three meditation centres (Hoyez 1999). This activity, considered among others as a non-medical recourse to good health, is based on the seventh level of yoga practice. Two of these centres are local branches of international groups, and their main preoccupation seems to be to spread a body of Hindu knowledge outside India. There are more centres of the 'Integral Yoga Centre' in the United States than in India, and as many in France as in India. The headquarters, where the guru lives, is situated in Yogaville, Virginia. The Pranic Healing Centre, for its part, is based in the Philippines. Only the Ysa Centre happens to be of local origin, and even there, the wife of the guru is an American. It does not seem to be exaggerated to speak of a 'canvasser guru' when the latter organizes annual promotional trips across many continents. The difference in perspective is obvious when, in the same study, we read that out of 128 inhabitants questioned in the city, one-fourth said they practised meditation but alone and at home. While Indian society is indeed steeped in this course of action of religious origin, the fact remains that it is only a cultural and financial elite which has the means, if it so desires, to attend lessons for which fees are charged.

THE PRIVATIZATION OF THE RECOURSE TO ALLOPATHY: A MISDOING OF GLOBALIZATION?

The methods and strategies of the supply of healthcare as required by the WHO for poorer countries are being adopted in India. There are free primary healthcare centres in the countryside and a multiplicity of variously financed dispensaries function in the cities. A study of the clientele of these public institutions shows that it is only the very poor who take recourse to them (Bazin 1996). The people are acutely aware of this and know well the limits of what is being offered to them. They lament the absenteeism of the employees, as well as the system of bribery which alone can give them access to the more expensive medicines. But, a closer look shows that the real economic challenges lie elsewhere.

The evolution of the availability in India of allopathic care can be properly understood only if we set it in perspective by viewing the international political choices and the macro-economic decisions which have made investment in the field of health more productive. The indebtedness of the country and the worldwide recession of the 1980s had forced the government to liberalize a public sector which, it must be admitted, did not satisfy the aspirations of the people. The Indian healthcare system, inspired initially by the commendable British model, follows even today the same logic. Relatively speaking and with a time lag of a few years, the notion shared by both countries of undertaking a mixed public/private discharge of responsibilities, has gone in favour of the latter, in the face of the mediocre results shown by the public sector, and as a result of the upsurge of American pharmaceutical companies. Indeed the latter, in order to escape the intense competition in their own country as well as the onslaught of legal proceedings by consumer associations, are conducting a market-cornering strategy on a planetary scale. Oriented towards profit, their investments are contributing towards the development of high quality services in the form of exclusive private hospitals. Though small in number, they constitute nonetheless the pinnacle of a range of particularly extensive healthcare availability which is often unequally distributed over the country.

The Indian diaspora represents a vector of change. There are a larger number of persons of Indian origin in America (2.7 million) than in Europe (1.3 million), which is probably one of the reasons for the Americanization of the Indian healthcare system. Numerous doctors trained in India were attracted by United States at a time (the 1960s) when there was a great demand for health professionals following the setting up of the Medicare and Medicaid insurance systems. 227,000 Indian immigrants entered the United States between 1981 and 1989 and another 190,000 between 1990 and 1994. In 1990, three-fourths of these new arrivals of over 25 years of age had university degrees, as against less than one-third for other immigrants in this age group (Visaria and Visaria 1995). One of the driving forces leading to emigration was the decision in some states to ban private practice by doctors of the public sector (1968 then 1983 in Andhra Pradesh) (Baru 1998: 140). Today, however, saturation in the American healthcare market and a rise in creditworthy demand in India have combined to make investment in India and a return to the home country an attractive option.

If the availability of private practitioners is soaring since these last few years, it is undoubtedly less as a response to healthcare needs than to provide employment opportunities for the plethora of trained doctors who, moreover, are now coming up against American immigration quotas. The increase in the load being borne by the private sector does not however fulfil the demand from all segments and even less all places. Perceptible since the mid-1970s, it is noticeable in the cities of dynamic regions. Conversely, the rural areas and 'low-speed India'[5] (Chapman 1992) are suffering with the health services offered by a public sector of mediocre quality. From all points of view, inequalities of access are widening between social groups and between regions.

For the time being, privatization is increasing the cost of treatment without bringing some harmony into medical practices, which explains the great increase in complaints by patients. Indian doctors themselves admit that it is common practice to favour an inordinate prescription of medicines and tests. They explain this attitude by their desire to pay off the debts incurred on setting themselves up in practice. It should be borne in mind that they depend on the international market and its high prices for their high technology equipment, while their consultation fees remain relatively low in consonance with the pockets of their clientele. Inevitably, the length of time they require for a return on their investment remains necessarily longer than elsewhere in the world (Bhat 1999).

For long, industrial groups in India have been organizing the availability of alternative healthcare arrangements. But as this was mostly with a view to obtaining tax reductions, they remained small in number. The idea of massive investing has come from doctors living sometimes abroad. . . . The Indian government is allowing this to happen, and is even encouraging this trend in an attempt to compensate for the mediocrity of the healthcare facilities available in the public sector. This situation arises out of the reduction in the outlay in this sector, itself induced since 1991 by the structural adjustment which seeks to reduce budget deficits and regulate the balance of payments situation.

An initial consequence on healthcare financing has been that the share of funds allotted by the centre to the states has come down (Tulasidhar 1993). Thus, the expenditure on preventive medicine and on the fight against some major endemic diseases is now being financed to a smaller extent. Deprived of the finances in the face of a growing population, the quality of the public service is deteriorating. And since the poorer states depend more than the others on a larger share of funds from the centre, they are automatically the ones that have suffered more from the adjustment.

IS IT POSSIBLE TO REMAIN ECONOMICALLY NON-ALIGNED?

Since independence, and particularly since the Third Five-Year Plan (1961-6), large 'projects' set up in the public sector made it possible to produce synthetic drugs and not galenic preparations alone as during the colonial period. But 'India has not succeeded in doing without transnationals' (Chapelet 1998). 'It was not possible to achieve self-sufficiency, there was no alternative to the technology brought in by foreign subsidiaries' (Chapelet 1998). When, for instance, the production of insulin was started, it was dependent on Russian or American technical assistance. Thus half the stake in the large Indian pharmaceutical firms is foreign. Even when the laws (Foreign Exchange Regulation Act) attempt to restrict the role of these companies, it is they, in their capacity as possessors of the technology, who decide on the production trends. Only the small industries remain purely Indian. In spite of recommendations aimed at promoting national self-sufficiency, the public sector manufacturers of drugs (Indian Drugs and Pharmaceuticals Limited) have never been able to cover more than one-third of the needs in drugs (Baru 1998) and even less in medical equipment. The burden borne by Indian imports needs however to be put into perspective. Medical and pharmaceutical products accounted for less than 1 per cent of imports in 1997-8 (*Hindu Survey of Indian Industry 1999*).

The multinationals have progressively strengthened their position. The reduction in duties on import of technology in 1997-8 has even helped them set up establishments in the country. The penetration in the Indian market remains, however, unpredictable, and success erratic. There is the example of the joint venture with the American company Bausch and Lomb (Ray Ban) which, after having invested capital at the start of liberalization in 1990 in the market for visual prosthesis, lost a great deal of money for several years as it had miscalculated the local purchasing power. They were selling their contact lenses at a price four to five times higher than their competitors and imitations began to emerge of their glasses. In order to become profitable, the company then decided to organize training sessions for 1,800 ophthalmologists at the L.V. Prasad Eye Institute in Hyderabad. The result has been that this company has now captured more than half the Indian market. This has served to attract many other aggressive competitors (Lacoste, Benetton, Novartis and Johnson and Johnson). Industrial strategies can also prove to be effective when they rely on funds from the World Bank. In the market for medical imaging equipment, Wipro GE looks after the maintenance of 4,000 pieces of equipment in the hospitals of Karnataka, thanks to funds granted by the Bank which make up effectively for the unstable public outlays. Supplying to public hospitals involves, however, some risks since the latter can obtain duty free supplies from the world market. It is only a recent national order that reversed this possibility.

The price control on 74 of the most commonly sold medicines by the Drug Price Control Order (revised in 1995), obliges national companies to keep small margins of profit on these price-controlled products. While these companies complain of the taxes imposed by the state, their position in the world market does not result in bad business. Low prices enable them to export, particularly to the African and Russian markets (ibid.). In fact, globalization means also the possibility for a country like Brazil to buy the synthetic molecules it uses in its state laboratories for the production of drugs from India where drugs for the treatment for AIDS are, on an average, five times cheaper than elsewhere (Dutilleux 2000). The Brazilian government suggested to the African countries that they do likewise.

It is a known fact that the prices of medicines do not reflect the price of production but also include the cost of research. They depend also highly on their places of production. Cipla, a company in Mumbai, after having kept a margin of the extent of 200 to 300 per cent, was selling AZT at less than $ 1.5 in 1999. At the same time, in the United States, it was valued at nearabout $ 6 (Laing 1999). It is therefore quite understandable that a trial of strength is pitting the United States and Europe against the poorer countries and NGOs on the matter of 'compulsory licences' (WHO 1999)[6] for the production of drugs. India would like to protect the access to drugs by people in developing countries by urging industrialists to put an end to single prices worldwide and to take recourse to the practice of higher prices in richer countries, and lower prices elsewhere.

Medicines are not like any other product. Large numbers of people suffer and die today in the world for lack of a genuine globalization. However some initial measures show that certain laboratories in the countries of the South, and in India particularly, are beginning to react to the large price differential. For instance, Ranbaxy, an Indian manufacturer of generic drugs, has bought out the generic activity of Bayer in Germany to thus find an opening into the German market (Bouscharain 2000).

For India, the arrival of foreign enterprises has proved to be ambivalent. On the one hand, they bring with them international standards of quality, but on the other hand their ways can interfere with national political decisions. The Supreme Court has banned the sale of an antispasmodic (Baralgan) in India. Manufactured by Hoechst, it was not being marketed in Germany on account of its possible secondary effects (Sen Gupta 1999). A position of subordination can also sometimes constitute a serious disadvantage when a multinational decides to withdraw a drug from the Indian market while the local industrialists are not able, or do not want, to supply an equivalent. This is the case at present for Adexolin, a vitamin A and D supplement, which Glaxo laboratories wants to withdraw on account of its low profitability, whereas it constitutes the basis of a widespread public health programme (vitamin supplement for children) (Gopalakrishnan 1999). Again, the government decision to disseminate in its public health system free treatment against tuberculosis ran into difficulties of supply in its domestic market in 1996. These were finally surmounted through purchases in the world market. Indeed, quite often, local industrialists, rather than produce, import base components in bulk and only finish the formulation in India. On account of government deregulation, industrialists are tempted to produce only those medicines which bring in the highest profits (Chapelet 1999). Orchid Chemicals and Pharmaceuticals of

Chennai and Cipla of Mumbai, rather than undertake an effort towards improving public health in the country, prefer to turn towards making copies of Viagra by slightly modifying the manufacturing process, which is enough to afford them protection in the eyes of Indian laws. Their sales would be directed towards the countries which do not protect the final end product.

By signing the GATT agreements and particularly TRIP (Trade Related Intellectual Property Agreement), India is obliged to recognize invention patents and not manufacturing ones alone, from the year 2004. The Indian Patent Act was a device introduced in 1970 in order to dissuade multinationals from bringing in new drugs. Conversely Indian companies were incited to copy these drugs. The new international provisions mean that all companies must launch their own research programmes or pay royalties, which would appear to be absolutely impossible for the thousands of small enterprises whose survival thus seems endangered. The prospect of having to compete involves the restructuring of the Indian pharmaceutical industry. Strategic alliances, already under way for the past few years, have enabled the creation of some industrial giants (Glaxo-Wellcome). What is going to be the fate of the Indian firms?

On the whole, it seems that the danger of India's dependence on transnationals will increase and that generic drugs will be the only slot left for small and medium enterprises to fill. But like all basic medicines, they are less profitable. This explains the 'shortages' in India of anti-tubercular drugs or iodized salts for fighting goitre or again of chloroquine for treating malaria. Finally, the local production seems ill-adapted to meet the majority of the needs of the people. For instance, while India's production of anti-malarial drugs has stagnated at around 35 tonnes a year, imports of these drugs have jumped from 52.8 to 166.3 tonnes between 1978 and 1982.

Many ups and downs have thus forced the Indian government, over a period of time, to 'align itself' in spite of its professed claims (Boquérat 1997). This however is because a part of the local population also benefits from this globalization.

ENDOGENOUS MUTATIONS OF THE HEALTHCARE SYSTEMS AND REGIONAL DIFFERENTIATION

The picture of an India committed, like Great Britain, to the liberalization or even Americanization, of its healthcare system is an attractive one which to a certain extent, corresponds to reality. It should however, not blind us to some aspects. True, opulent hospitals have been opened; but how many people do they affect? How many people go there? It is very difficult to put a figure to the number of people who go to this type of establishment as they offer a multiplicity of services, which are moreover governed by quotas of free service which they try to get around. According to Baru (1998: 121), they do not work to full capacity as the wealthiest still prefer to go abroad. While some well-off families are indeed beginning to make use of these large hospitals with all kinds of specializations, the middle class often remains content with smaller sized establishments, while clerks and workers take recourse to even smaller centres.

As we have said, the government permits imports and often allows, with the municipalities, private hospitals to come up on the condition that they include an initiative of a charitable nature. The authorities may, for instance, give total exemption from import duties or facilitate construction by selling urban land at cheap rates, or again turn a blind eye to corporate rates of taxation. In this way, the authorities act in a pragmatic fashion by bearing in mind that these establishments are, in a way, conducting a public service. In exchange, it is anticipated that a percentage of the activity will be reserved for supplying free service. A quarter of the beds in Delhi are thus reserved in principle for the poorest patients. As verifications are not commonly conducted, deviations have been noted everywhere and for long. 'Under the semblance of an infrastructure of care of the charitable type, the KG hospital has become a hospital complex for persons of high socio-economic status and the other hospitals are following suit' (Eliot 1993). Mobile camps and sporadic free treatment offered by these centres in the neighbouring countryside, often remain the only traces of non-profit activities.

The bonds between the public hospital and the private sector are ambivalent. The professionals of the former provide the latter with clients by urging the patients to go for consultation to private clinics where the doctors of the public sector also work, in principle after their prescribed hours of duty. When in 1983 in Andhra Pradesh a ban was issued on practice in both sectors by the Telugu Desam Party, 300 doctors left to go abroad without resigning from their posts, thus paralysing the system by preventing recruitment to the public sector (Baru 1998: 140). This state, often unsuccessfull in being firm with its doctors, just as is the case with Bihar or Uttar Pradesh, also sees them fleeing in large numbers to 'nursing homes' and hence draws no benefit from the investment made in medical training institutions. It is therefore not surprising that Hyderabad has since 1985 rapidly become the starting point of a network of private healthcare establishments set up generally with local capital, expanding to branch out towards the rest of the large cities of India (Rihouey 1997). In a federal system, local decisions, such as the firmness of some states with their doctors, enters the picture to differentiate regions and acts as a spur to this branch of the economy.

In the same way, local forces contribute towards structuring more or less rapidly a supply of modern and private healthcare. Thus in Coimbatore (Tamil Nadu), industrial groups set up in the 1950s some hospital complexes which were in existence before liberalization. Large groups or trusts manufacturing textile machinery or irrigation pumps (KG Group of Companies, Lakshmi Machine Work, etc.), have gone into the field of healthcare to improve an availability totally out of step with the demand. Some personal tragedies, the outcome precisely of a lack of high quality medical services, were often at the origin of these charitable investments. One of the founders of the textile industry in this city, Kuppuswamy Naidu, after having lost his sister and his child, invested in 1948 in an institution for mother and child care, helped in the venture by the government of the then Madras state. This latter assistance was subsequently reimbursed. When the son of the same benefactor was stricken with cancer in 1958, a radiation therapy unit was set up. Other donations enabled, in 1974, the opening of a cardiology and a cardio-thoracic surgery service, the only one then in the whole of south India. Following these legendary pioneers, a series of other more profit-oriented establishments came up. Financed by shares in 1990, a public company constructed, for example, the Kovai Hospital, a 200-bed establishment which possesses laser equipment among other facilities. Several less grandiose, hospitals bring together a conglomerate of doctors, sometimes all from the same family (Balaji Nursing Home). These small units themselves account for 74 per cent of the infrastructure providing hospital treatment in Coimbatore. Everywhere in India they constitute a powerful pressure group which has always succeeded in defeating all plans for regulation and taxation in this field.

Coimbatore, the city with the second largest number of millionaires in the state of Tamil Nadu after Chennai, and the tenth largest city of India, is hence home to an absolutely astonishing healthcare availability. These hospitals, often the best equipped in south India and even sometimes in the whole of India (KG Hospital has 'the largest intensive care unit in the country') (*Frontline* 1998), can boast of some of the firsts in Indian medical history. They conduct an impressive number of sophisticated surgical operations. They are practically the first in India to have obtained international standards of certification (ISO 9002). However, this striving for quality does not extend up to the structuring of transportation in cases of emergency (Marechal 1999).

As elsewhere in the world, profit constitutes an active driving force explaining these recent mutations. Still, there is no consistency in the cost of surgical operations in all the Indian metropolises. The fees depend roughly on the ranking of the city and this goes in favour of Coimbatore, enabling it to boast of less expensive charges. Thus an eye operation, billed at Rs. 12,500 in an establishment in this city, costs Rs. 18,000 in Chennai and Rs. 32,000 in Mumbai (*Frontline* 1998). The cost of kidney transplants varies according to the place, ranging between Rs. 75,000 and Rs. 400,000. Leaving aside what legendary accounts would have us believe, the financing of the 65 medical trusts by industrial groups on a charitable basis does indeed lead to a real reduction in fees, even if there is not a truly high proportion of free medicare. The captains of industry of Coimbatore who belong to the dominant castes, maintain an attitude of public service and they are undoubtedly loyal to the region. The logic of commerce is not totally devoid of territorial concerns.

From more than one point of view, the extreme segmentation of Indian society makes it unique and the privatization taking place can in no case be equated with Americanization. Tensions between Muslims and Hindus, and their different ways of looking at the world, make patients turn to doctors of their own religion. This situation, not peculiar to India, stands out here with an intensity that is revealing. It is borne out for instance in the fact that when new hospitals come up in Muslim areas, all the employees are found to be followers of this religion. Even more revealing is the fact that the different Hindu socio-religious groups, even having the same standard of life, each have specific attitudes in the matter of health. Indeed, whenever the need arises, they prefer to go to a doctor of their own caste. The names of the founders of the large healthcare establishments are a pointer to their identity. It can be said that the hospitals are 'caste-branded' (Vaguet et al. 1995). These benefactors, often prominent personalities, also attract people to their hospitals on account of their personal fame, their worldly wisdom, or some might prefer to say their image-building ability which brings them a substantial social prestige. Treatment in such an establishment is like putting oneself under the protection of powerful persons, and taking advantage of a social network that may turn out to be useful when misfortune strikes. It is then possible to obtain loans and reductions in fees for operations, or then to get admitted to hospital while availing of its free services (where care is bestowed by doctors at the start of their career), while attempting to later obtain, once admitted, the services of better specialists. In a word, knowing the right people makes all the difference between anonymity and empathy and one can take advantage of the small improvements, that make life less difficult.

CONCLUSION

The question of globalization, for being widely topical and very often debated, becomes very quickly meaningless if we do not take care to join to it a sub-theme and a space to test arguments on different scales. Globalization in India, from the healthcare angle, has arrived with the privatization of allopathic treatment, but it does not seem for all that to have erased every specific cultural traits and even less to have eliminated from the scene the practitioners of the various non-Western systems, themselves often competing with each other. The same phenomenon can be observed in the wealthier countries, starting with the practices bound to the cult of the body, the New Age practices and alternative therapies, often inspired by or originating from the other end of the world. Who is influencing who? Viewed this way, the process of globalization is contingent and variable according to the territory concerned. From one standpoint India is a centre for the dissemination of and even innovation in the matter of healthcare. Numerous persons in the world are practising yoga and attending meditation sessions. This remedy, albeit a very special one, remains underestimated. Why should it not be taken note of?

Pessimists will find arguments on reading these pages to conclude that globalization helps in strengthening inequalities of access to care in a country like India. One can equally find reasons for hope. The initial period had not given such good results in the field of health as to make one look back on them with nostalgia. It would seem that Indians have acquired in the course of the development of the private sector some additional choices. People want the private sector to develop in order to allow for a rapid dissemination of biomedical techniques. Even those living in the mushrooming slum areas go for the treatment of minor ailments mostly to the private sector. They shun the dispensaries that continue to be financed by government–these will have some day to be either better equipped or else closed down in order to strengthen the services rendered by the large public hospitals that are totally submerged by the most destitute[7] (Yesudian 1999).

The Western model is, willy-nilly, proving a success. This biomedical model allows for a multiplicity of declensions, and one can easily observe its spatial variability according to the different societies in which it is deployed.

The fluctuating options of the political parties in power can direct the economy towards greater or lesser protectionism and national preference. India's healthcare systems, however original they may be, have been the outcome of continuous international contacts. It would be a matter for surprise if globalization were to destroy totally all diversity without the concerned people desiring it or reacting against it.

NOTES

1. According to the National Family Health Survey of 1992-3.
2. 'The infant mortality rate remained at 96 per thousand in 1991 (6 per thousand in France in 1994)' (Véron 1997: 138).
3. 1,750,000 seropositive cases in 1995 as against 700,000 in Thailand (E. Eliot, 1999). In early 2002 their number had risen to 4 million. This figure is most likely to be an underestimate.
4. See the terminological debate on traditional medicine in Janes, 1999. For this author, 'Traditional' means 'without change' which is not the case. 'Indigenous' implies 'ethnic' whereas the major systems have influences each other. To conclude and for lack of anything better, the author prefers the term 'non-Western medicine'. But still, one must consider that Western homeopathy is spreading rapidly among Siddha practitioners .
5. That is to say Uttar Pradesh, Bihar, West Bengal, Orissa and Madhya Pradesh.
6. The involvement of a compulsory or authoritarian licence comes in when the judicial or administrative authority is authorized by law to grant a licence, without the authorization of the holder of the patent, for a diversity of reasons in the general interest.
7. The disastrous quality of the healthcare in the small units attracts no one, while the large hospitals avail of the services of real doctors, even if they are prone to absenteeism.

REFERENCES

Bazin, S., 'Analyse du système public de santé dans un milieu urbain: Coimbatore (Inde du Sud)', Masters Dissertation, Department of Geography, Rouen, 1996.

Baru, R., *Private health care in India. Social characteristics and trends*, Delhi: Sage Publications, 1998.

Bhat, R., 'Characteristics of Private Medical Practice in India: a Provider Perspective', *Health Policy and Planning*, vol. 14, no.1, 1999.

Boquérat, G., *Les avatars du non-alignement: L'Inde et les politiques d'aide américaine et soviétique de l'indépendance à la conférence de Tachkent (1947-1966)*, Sorbonne Publications, 1997.

Carrière, P., 'Santé et nutrition dans un village indien', Medical Doctorate Dissertation, Rouen, 1983.

Chapelet, P., 'Le médicament en Inde entre le local et le global', Masters Dissertation, Department of Geography, Rouen, 1998.

Chapman, G.P., *The Changing Geography of Asia*, London & New York: Routledge, 1992.

Dutilleux C., 'Le Brésil, pirate humanitaire', *Libération,* 12/05/2000.

The Economist Intelligence Unit, 'Profile–business opportunities and constraints in India's healthcare sector', *Healthcare Industry*, 2nd quarter 1999, London.

Eliot, E., 'Les classes moyennes et l'offre de soins à Coimbatore (Tamil Nadu, India)', Masters Dissertation, Department of Geography, Rouen, 1993

——, 'Les lieux du sida en Inde', Master Dissertation, Department of Geography, Rouen, 1999.

Filiozat, J., *La doctrine classique de la médecine indienne,* 1st edn. 1949, rpt. 1975, Maisonneuve.

Frontline, 'A leading centre for medical care', 9 Oct. 1998.

Guilmoto C.Z. and Vaguet, A. (eds.), *Essays on Population and Space in India*, French Institute of Pondicherry, 2000.

Gupta, H.S. and Bagel, A., 'Infant mortality in the Indian slums: case studies of Calcutta Metropolis and Raipur City', *International Journal of Population Geography*, vol. 5, 1999.

Hibon, B. (ed.), *La privatisation des Etats*, Karthala, 1999.

Hoyez, A.C., 'Les recours de santé non médicalisés: l'exemple de la méditation, Coimbatore', Masters Dissertation, Department of Geography, Rouen, 1999.

Janes, Craig R., 'The health transition, global modernity and the crisis of traditional medicine: the Tibetan case', *Social Science and Medicine,* 48, 1999, p. 1803.

Jules, G., 'L'offre privée des systèmes médicaux: Ayurveda et Siddha. à Coimbatore, Inde du Sud', Masters Dissertation, Department of Geography, Rouen, 2000.

Kanna, K.P. et al., *Health status in rural Kerala,* Trivandrum: Kerala Sasthra Sahithya Parishad, 1991.

Maréchal, V., 'La privatisation du système de santé indien. Médecins et recours d'urgence, Coimbatore (Tamil Nadu)', Masters Dissertation, Department of Geography Rouen, 1999.

Patkar, C.N. et al., 'Resurgence of malaria and drug resistance in *Plasmodium falciparum* and *P. vivax* in Bombay', *Journal Association of Physicians in India*, 43, 1995.

Rihouey, F., 'L'émergence de nouveaux réseaux de soins en Inde. Hyderabad, un centre d'innovation', *Espace, Populations, Sociétés,* 2/3, 1997, pp. 265-78.

Saradamma, R.D., Higginbotham, N. and Nichter, M., 'Social factors influencing the acquisition of antibiotics without prescription in Kerala State, South India', *Social Science and Medicine*, vol. 50, 2000.

Thakare, J.P., 'Japanese encephalitis in Sangli district in Maharashtra', *Indian Journal of Medical Research*, May 1999.

Tulasidhar, G.P., 'Expenditure compression and health sector outlays', *Economic and Political Weekly,* 6 November 1993.

Vaguet, A., Rihouet, and F., Eliot, E., 'La géographie de la santé dans les villes indiennes, matériau pour une géographie culturelle', *Espace, Populations, Sociétés,* 1995/1, pp. 81-90.

Véron J., 'La transition démographique en Inde', *Espace, Populations, Sociétés,* Lille, 2/3, 1997.

Visaria, L. and Visaria, P., 'India's population in transition', *Population Bulletin*, vol. 50, no. 3, Washngton, 1995.

W.H.O., *Mondialisation et accès aux médicaments. Perspectives sur l'accord ADPIC de l'OMC.* Economics of Health and Drugs Series, no. 7, 1999.

Yesudian, C.A.K., 'Pattern of Utilisation of Health Services. Policy Implications', *Economic and Political Weekly*, vol. 34, no. 5, 1999, pp. 300-4.

Zimmermann, F., *Le discours des remèdes au pays des épices. Médecine et société*, Payot, 1989.

E. resources:

Bouscharain, P., 'Histoires de labos', *Forum E-Med*, 9/05/2000.

Dr Sen Gupta, 'Internet discussion forum on essential drugs', *E-Drug*, 1999.

Dr Gopalakrishnan, 'Internet discussion forum on essential drugs', *E-Drug*, 1999.

Laing, R., 'A visit to India: drug prices, research and global access', forum *E-Drug*, 8/02/1999.

The Limited Globalization of the Electricity Sector

Joël Ruet

There are at least two reasons for undertaking a study of the political economy of India's power sector. Given that it is placed under the joint responsibility of the centre and the states, its evolution reflects the relations between the two levels of the Indian federal system. Besides, the recent implementation of guidelines which have found favour with a large number of foreign countries could camouflage a subtle relationship with globalization which, in the case of India, is determined largely by the power equations within the country. Indeed, the reform path chosen integrates two elements: the argument that reforms have become necessary on account of the inefficiency of public sector organizations whose modes of functioning are inherited from the Indian bureaucratic system; and that , there are political and economic forces who demand reforms as an essential element of their political strategy. In particular, contrary to the classical view, the opening up of the electricity sector to the foreign private sector could in reality be equated with a relative strengthening of the centre *vis-à-vis* the states. It could also turn out to be to the advantage of some very local components, such as consumers' associations.

CHOICES FOR WHOM?

The electricity sector involves, like other network infrastructures, questions of economic development, the financial redistribution between different sectors and between different social needs, and, *in fine,* politics.

- Electrical energy is an important input for industries and for an agriculture dependent on irrigation. Thus in India the existence of an emerging middle class gives manufacturing industry an important margin of growth; also, the agricultural sector conserves a strategic character.
- The effects of electrification and of the growth of production are variable from one sector to another, while the financing of electrical plants reduces the possibility of financing other types of investment.
- The costs of electrification and of operating the electrical networks vary widely, depending on whether they are in remote mountainous areas or in large cities.[1] At present the tariff structures are not differentiated geographically within each state.
- Moreover, the electrical network constitutes an entity whose costs are difficult to attribute with certainty to the different categories of users, when the nature of their connection and of their consumption vary. Moreover the cross-subsidies to different types of consumers are large: farmers pay on an average 14 per cent of the cost, industrialists pay 166 per cent of the average cost (Planning Commission 1997).

Yet the crux of the matter is that over and above these techno-economic characteristics, the redistributive implications of choice necessarily brings politics into the picture. Indeed, if we assume that the productive efficiencies of the respective players are known, economic analysis can predict only the effects that a given re-distributive choice will have on production. Over and above that, economics is not capable of arbitrating between political objectives (social equity, town and country planning, national independence in terms of agriculture or of development of an industry, etc.) and production objectives (in terms of GDP). The entire role of politics, then, lies in its capacity to decide between domains of a different nature, which in this instance cannot be reduced to the single financial criterion that economic analysis is able to handle (Giraud 1998). The economic factor therefore simply cannot be the sole criterion for the allocation of resources to one sector rather than to another. Hence the necessity, when replying to the questions dealt with in this paper, of approaching the initial etymological significance of the term 'economics'—the *administration* of the world, by exploring the field of political economics.

We will make use of economic analysis *stricto sensu* to assess, whenever possible, the redistributive and productive consequences of the decisions by distinguishing it from the political context of decision making. In a historical perspective, we will adopt an approach of the political economics type, by observing the evolution of the sharing of the centre-state responsibilities in the development and management of the sector.

THE HISTORICAL INFLUENCE OF THE STATES IN THE IMPLEMENTATION OF POLICIES ON ELECTRICITY: LIMITS OF PLANNING

The development of the electricity sector, according to the terms of the Indian Constitution, falls in the concurrent list of the centre and the states. The 1948 Act concerning the organization of this sector sets out its practical modalities. It entrusts to the Centre, via the Planning Commission, the Central Electricity Authority (CEA) and the Ministry of Power, the formulation of policy. Implementation is left to the electricity departments, administrations under each state which in the 1960s became the State Electricity Boards (SEBs). From 1998 onwards, this organization is been gradually complemented with a Central Electricity Regulatory Commission (CERC), and State Electricity Regulatory Commissions (SERC). By July 2002, nineteen states had set up their SERCs. The main institutions, the SEBs, are in charge of generation, transmission and distribution of electricity and they come under their respective state governments. The Planning Commission is entrusted with fixing the volumes of investment and with ensuring financial coordination through budgetary transfers and bank allocations. Particularly during the initial plans, it placed the electricity sector at the service of rural electrification and the development of heavy industry (Chakravarty 1987). The centre thus approved through electricity large redistributive transfers from the cities towards the countryside, and from the private sector towards industry in the public sector. This was done in the very special political context of the near hegemony of the Congress party which, for twenty years following independence, sought to ensure the cohesion of the polity by dealing out a subtle share of responsibilities and reciprocal concessions between the centre and the states (Khilnani 1997). As this initiative took place within the Congress party, the question of the relative shares of the centre and the states is undoubtedly a question of political analysis for this period. But institutional analysis makes it possible to bring out the real influence of the states, which came to light after the end of the Congress rule.

The states have a large say in the implementation of the investment programmes in this sector, since they control 64 per cent of the generation and the near totality of the distribution.[2] This enables them to bend, in practice, the policies decided upon by the centre. Moreover, institutional control by the centre is quite ineffective: the Planning Commission keeps no *ex-post* check on the expenses of the SEBs, nor does the CEA or the Ministry. The Ministry plays the role essentially of administrative coordination (requests for authorizations for implementing projects, monitoring of the coordination between different entities, collecting data, etc.). The CEA for its part defines the technical norms and standards, and its technico-economic endorsement is required for large investments (the trend having been to relax the level of investment from which the *imprimatur* of the CEA is necessary). This control by the CEA is based solely on the adherence to technical criteria and on maintaining costs of projects within 'reasonable' limits. The economic efficiency of the project (an analysis of the opportunity costs or studies of the impact of the project on the costs connected with the networks) is not questioned. There is therefore no control *stricto sensu* over the economic effectiveness of the implementation of the electrical policy. The Ministry at the centre naturally plays the role of helmsman, but its steering is not based on actual controls. For instance a system of allocation of subsidies from the centre towards the states exists which is only partially indexed on incentives to collect bills and to restrict the rates of energy loss. In this context the reports are produced 'for government purpose only' (Gridco 1998), which show such results as will enable them to obtain subsidies. These reports have no relation to reality. Thus, in the case of Orissa, the rates of energy loss have since long been shown at half their real value, and this is a generalized phenomenon.[3]

Implementation, and notably the policy on tariffs, is mainly within the province of the states. One may even consider that it is no longer strictly speaking a matter of implementation as of re-orientation. The states follow their own logic which does not necessarily fall in line with the pursuit of long-term efficiency. Indeed, experts as well as various official reports (World Bank 1996, 1997; Gridco 1998) concur to assert that there is political interference from the state governments in the management of day-to-day matters. From the point of view of investment, particularly, the under-sizing of the transmission and distribution networks compared to generation capacity, which the Planning Commission deplores each year, is easily explained by the creation of local jobs and by financial misappropriations through bribes. Similarly, the priorities of rural electrification follow a very precise place and time calendar, fixed in consonance with the electoral schedule and dictated nearly from one day to the next by the guardians of the concerned strongholds. In the field of employment also, Rajiv Gandhi used to call the SEBs 'state employment boards'. The management of careers depends thereafter largely on politically oriented decisions on transfers taken at the state level.

Over and above this shift of the centre of gravity to the states, there is a need to note also a difference in its nature from that planned by the centre. While through the Planning Commission the centre fixes the policy objectives, the implementation involves an execution based on economic efficiency. In other words, the Planning Commission communicates objectives and leaves it to the bodies entrusted with achieving these to do so by the most cost-effective means. The state governments go about it in a different way. Indeed, they often do not remain content with laying down general policy objectives but, through their near daily interference in the management of the SEBs, give direct instructions concerning execution. One can assess the impact of this in the matter of rural electrification. The Planning Commission fixes the amounts to be invested, in keeping with the rates of electrification to be achieved over a period of five years. Officially, the SEB is therefore free to develop its network in the manner which is the most effective to achieve this objective. Conversely, the priorities based on the imperatives of the electoral schedule, or other fluctuating objectives, or an anxiety to launch eye-catching projects, lead to hurried technical choices being made, in unsuitable locations for the investments and causing their dispersal. In other words, these interventions, the investment remaining constant, lead to choices different from those provided in the Planning Commission models, as well as to an inferior structuring of the networks and of their long-term effectiveness. This has been acknowledged in various official reports (cf. for instance Quraishi 1998) or during interviews with this author. Thus a director of an SEB admitted that he was regularly summoned by his minister a few weeks before the elections to find projects with 'visibility', to be launched urgently, although initially planned to be deployed over a period of several years. Similarly, as regards human resources, officials, aware of the political clout that some of their employees or consumers enjoy, often capitulate and disregard the role entrusted to them of ensuring certain criteria of management. The overall effects are clear. In 1997-8, for instance, the subsidies doled out by the Government of Andhra Pradesh to its SEB, hailed by experts as being one of the least inefficient, to balance its accounts, represented 1.6 per cent of the GDP of the state and constituted 46 per cent of its public deficit (World Bank 1999).

To sum up, more than making redistributive transfers different from those fixed by the centre, what characterizes the Indian power system is the fact that the states substitute the policy directives communicated by the centre (expected to be freely, hence efficiently, implemented) with their own executive instructions. In this way, consequences relating to efficiency get juxtaposed to those relating to redistribution. Indeed, from the point of view of the employee of an SEB, it is more rational to try to follow as best he can instructions which keep changing[4] than to strive for efficiency which at the worst will bring him problems, and for which at best he will in the end not be favoured (Ruet 2002a). In this context, not only is efficiency a moot point to the extent to which it is not required of the employees, but even any step meant to increase it has an unpredictable effect, in the sense that the result will depend *in fine* only on instructions resulting from choices made out of political considerations external to economic efficiency.[5]

All in all, as long as the minimal conditions of separating choices from political considerations and of implementing projects in consonance with economic criteria are not achieved, economic analysis is no longer in a position to predict the effect of the policies assigned to the SEBs. It can simply note that on account of the loss of efficiency, even the initially sought after redistributive effects are no longer achieved. For instance, following the technical deterioration of the networks (in terms of quality and continuity of service), the farmers pay more for repairing their pumps than for their electricity bills. Similarly, industrialists face growing costs following the halts to their production process, or on coping strategies.[6]

As for the political economy, it is the states that are the real masters of a pursuit which, it is true, has become demeaning. To borrow Khilnani's categories (1997), the vision of a central planning striving to make policy choices on a scientific basis, hence publicly contestable through a democratic system focused on the citizen, has been substituted by political management, liable to change from day-to-day, with its emphasis on civil society, that is to say the perception of a democracy as composed of interest groups, where obviously more powerful groups have more voice and effective power than weaker groups.

DISENGAGEMENT OF THE PUBLIC SECTOR AND RELATIVE ADVANTAGE TO THE CENTRE: AN INDIAN DYNAMICS OR THE EFFECT OF GLOBALIZATION?

In the face of the factual pre-eminence of the states, an attempt by the centre to regain the upper hand began in the 1980s. To meet the growing energy needs of the country, the centre set up directly under its supervision some companies in the public sector for production and transmission of electricity. In the framework of the 1948 Act, it bases its legitimacy on the inter-state nature of the plans formulated for a project of a large capacity power station meant to serve several states. In this field covering the inter-state redistribution through allocation of shares of the generation, the centre is perfectly within its legitimate framework of intervention. The main companies are the National Thermal Power Corporation (NTPC), and the National Hydro Power Corporation (NHPC). The NTPC, set up in 1984, also developed and managed high tension lines for evacuation from its power stations to the networks of the states. In 1992, this latter activity was transferred to Powergrid, a newly set up central undertaking, for developing interconnections between the states and building a single national network out of the five present Indian regions.

This comeback of the centre on the scene of activity has been successful since it controls 32 per cent of the generation (as against 64 per cent of the SEBs and 4 per cent for the private sector). In practice, this restores the influence of the Ministry of Power which is entrusted with overseeing relations between these entities and the SEBs when projects are developed and when disputes need to be settled. From the mid-1990s particularly, some financial mechanisms have been set up for settling arrears of payment by the SEBs to the NTPC and the NHPC. The accounts of the main clients of the SEBs are escrowed and this makes it possible to settle accounts with the two corporations in the event of a default in payment by the SEB. Through this mechanism, the centre is regaining control over a part of the financial flows and thus increasing its negotiating power in the deployment of the policies laid down for the electrical sector. This mechanism culminated in 1997 in the taking over by the NTPC of the Thalcher thermal plant, which was under the Orissa SEB, by way of settlement of unpaid dues. In the same line of ideas, the centre has secured for itself the authority to take over by way of settlement of arrears up to 15 per cent of the central budget outlays initially allocated by the Planning Commission. This amount is directly reassigned to the corporations under the centre.

From the institutional standpoint also, the centre has taken the initiative to create the Power Finance Corporation (PFC), a public body in charge of financing projects for the SEBs outside the classic public investment financing systems. From 1989 itself, the PFC has begun to fix some conditionalities on loans, based more on a system of declaration of intent (Operational and Financial Action Plans). Since 1997, the PFC has been setting up a system of conditionalities aimed at bringing in institutional reforms, along with a system of control over their implementation.

To what extent can the recent developments in this sector be explained by the influence of internal forces and to what extent are they due to the external pressure exercised by lending organizations? It is true that following the 1991-2 foreign exchange liquidity crisis affecting the whole of India, the centre undertook a certain number of reforms. The World Bank also decided to place conditions on its loans to the states for the power sector, requiring the introduction of structural reforms in the SEBs (conversion of their legal status into corporations, separation of various activities, and partial privatization). But the earlier institutional analysis underlines the fact that during the 1980s a debate had begun over the need to reduce the authority of the states in the power sector. Similarly, while the centre does authorize the setting up of such patterns of structural reform, it does not impose them on the states. To make the matter clearer, let us analyse the reforms undertaken and the arguments on which they are based.

In 1991-2, the Government of India decided to open up the generation of power to private investment, including foreign investment. The financial crisis had precipitated the decision, but, in fact, this opening up was presented as arising out of the necessity to develop large generation capacities and the inadequacy of public funds. The centre having acquired a greater control over generation than it had over the transmission and distribution networks, it was simpler and quicker at the time to open up generation alone. Moreover, this enabled it to avoid entering into a debate over the matter of a public service on a network enjoying the status of a monopoly. In reality, the argument is not acceptable from the sole techno-economic point of view. First, there exists a large number of investments that the state can make, with a very short time of return, sometimes even as short as one or two years—as in the case of Haryana and Uttar Pradesh (World Bank 1997 and 1999). These investments, whether of an individual amount or of very varied magnitudes, have this fact in common that they relate to maintenance and renovation, including also the networks, in the order of relative priority assigned to the development of new projects for production. The main effect of this type of investment is an economy of energy, reduction of losses, and generation of more energy from a given installed capacity. All this at a smaller cost than involved in the development of new power stations, including those producing under more efficient conditions. In this sense the World Bank agrees with the diagnosis of the Planning Commission (1997), and these results are common to the whole of India (Ruet 2001). The real limit to the setting up of this kind of programme lies in the mode of management characterized above, where it is the political objectives that are overriding and not those of efficiency.[7] The second criticism against the opening up of investment to generation alone is that this does not really attract investors.. Even if the absence of an effort at efficiency in the SEBs *ex-post* makes the hypothesis of a need for new capacities valid, some financially moribund SEBs are not creditworthy enough for investors. Consequently, it has been necessary to give financial guarantees. These have been in the form of financial 'counter-guarantees' by the centre in the event of default of payment by the states, and regulations guaranteeing a 16 per cent rate of profit to independent producers, as against the earlier regulation of 3 per cent. Despite that, out of the 20 GW envisaged from the private sector by the Planning Commission for the Eighth Plan (1992-7), only 2.7 GW has been realized. Figures are not yet available for the Ninth Plan, but, by January 2001, only 5.4 GW had been fully commissioned (IEA 2002). In spite of media publicity, this opening up has met with failure as few investors have responded to it. Among those who have, some have even confided to us that they felt that the magnitude of the investment to which they had committed themselves was too large.

In this first phase (1991-6), the opening up of the electricity sector was considered as triggered by an external crisis and by pressures exerted by the lending bodies. It should however be noted that action would in any case have been necessary. Indeed, right from the mid-1990s, many SEBs listed accumulated debts of an amount equal to their assets, which had moreover been over-valued.[8] Hence it was no longer so much a matter of subsidies on the sidelines as of a latent bankruptcy of the SEBs. Over and above that, while the World Bank was not inclined to direct loans for reforms in public sector and had encouraged the emergence of a private sector, the solution has resulted largely out of an Indian context. Indeed the choice of the first reforms arose out of an analysis still marked by the practices of development and of implementation in force since Independence. This was so first, to the extent to which a quantitative vision of the power sector had been maintained, in terms of levels of investment and of capacities for development, at the expense of a vision consisting in more systematically questioning the modes of management of the SEBs by seeking to make a choice between investment and less costly maintenance with a given result. Second, the centre acted within its purview, which is generation, without attempting to enter into a political struggle with the states on the subject of reforms in the SEBs.

The second phase of the reforms, initiated in 1995, can bring out unexpected results in the relations between the centre and the states. In 1996, at a conference of chief ministers and representatives of the Government of India, it was advocated that states could open up transmission and distribution to private investors. It was also agreed in principle that a Central Electricity Regulatory Commission (CERC), and a State Electricity Regulatory Commission (SERC) would be created, independent of the governments. This agreement did not fix the modalities for the setting up of these commissions, nor yet their attributions. It is notable that while the conference was encouraged by the World Bank and while it marked symbolically the turning point in the 'globalization' of the sector, the Government of India organized it at a time when it was experiencing no particularly pressing financial problem, and was not bound by any loan conditionality. This programme has then been pursued, at a more or less slow pace during electoral phases, by successive governments. As for the states, a former Joint Secretary for Power, acknowledged during a conversation that the chief ministers did not really feel greatly bound by this declaration, which opened up a possibility of an inflow of private capital but without specifying the constraints it would bring on the Commissions. A law has finally established the creation of these Commissions in 1998. In fact, from 1996 to 1998, the centre has tried to impose a restrictive framework for the states. In particular, it has considered making it compulsory to set up SERCs, enjoying the status of courts, which would fix in part the tariffs on the basis of the performances of the SEBs, or of those of the companies having obtained a license. It has also considered a minimal tariff for farmers, fixed at 50 paise per kWh.[9]

This disengagement of the states and opening up to private capital has several advantages for the Centre. It is, in the last resort, the financial guarantor of the states, and the burden, in terms of work as of public investments, of deficit sectors is considered too heavy today as compared to the small operational control that it exercises over them. This absence of control proceeds from two factors. First, the tariff and redistributive policies appear ill-adapted to the objectives of the centre, the subsidies going more to the rich farmers than to the poor peasants, whereas the social cost of the sector is large since a considerable share of the budget transfers is used up by the power sector at the expense of direct social programmes. Secondly, the use of the sector for electoral ends does not bring it any direct advantage and even works against it. That is why it has extended to all the generators, and therefore to itself, the possibility of formulating tariffs on the principle of a profitability of 16 per cent of the assets and imposing cuts on the SEBs which are bad debtors. The effect has been to place the NTPC, acknowledged as technically efficient, in a favourable situation. This has also resulted in accentuating the financial pressure on the SEBs and therefore the pressure exerted by the centre on the states, thus forcing them to undertake reforms.

The states for their part have tried to oppose the centre on the Regulatory Commissions, and the Electricity Regulatory Commissions Act was adopted in 1998 without fixing a minimal tariff (but while maintaining most of the other characteristics, which by itself constitutes a forward thrust by the centre). The Commissions are presently being set up in most of the ctates. In some, major institutional reforms are under way. Orissa in 1995, Haryana in 1998, and Andhra Pradesh in 1999, have adopted their own reform laws, validated by the centre. The three states have opened up the path of reforms to the extent of offering a majority shareholding to private investors interested in the activities of generation and distribution. In these three cases, extensive powers have been given to the Regulatory Commissions for the validation of the investments made by companies and the fixing of tariffs. The only Commission having had a sufficiently long term in office, that of Orissa, has shown a certain strictness on the matter of increase in tariffs granted to the companies which have succeeded the SEB, asking for significant improvements in management.

Ultimately, only Orissa (in 1999) and Delhi (in 2002) have undergone privatization of the distribution of electricity. Both experiments have shown that improvements take longer than anticipated. There again, one may wonder about the influence the lending organizations enjoy and about the motivations specific to the governments of the states in undertaking this type of reforms. In interviews conducted with the Power Secretaries of some reforming states, some political advantages intrinsic to the undertaking of reforms were brought out. They arise out of the fact that the financial burden incurred over the years had become too heavy for the states to bear, with the governments becoming hostages to the extravagant promises made to garner votes. The justification for setting up a Regulatory Commission fixing tariffs in an independent manner was to be found in the fact that it freed the politicians of their responsibilities. In the short term the decision to enter into the path of reforms seems to result from having to settle between an untenable financing by the old methods and electoral risks, even risks of maintenance of law and order. Indeed, in the short term, the main danger is that peasant revolts could multiply, for instance in agricultural states such as Haryana or Andhra. These can be sparked off by tariff increases or by campaigns for recovering billing amounts, hence in a context of reforms, but also if the SEB is not able to supply electricity—which is likely to happen in the end in the absence of reforms, with the NTPC threatening for instance to stop the supply.[10] The state governments have to be tactful in the way they make the people aware of the necessity for reforms. The political responsibility for the creation of the Commissions, and hence for increases in tariffs, seems to be minimized by the local decision makers. In the middle term, indeed, they count on an 'amnesia effect', and present the creation of the Commissions as an idea emanating from the centre. It is therefore in the interest of the states to endow the Commissions with the powers to fix tariffs, which the 1998 Act does not force them to do.

Over and above the creation of a Regulatory Commission, the states also have an incentive to undertake privatization. Indeed, the expected tariff hike also has its downside for the government. There is the risk that the Commissions will be more particular about efficiency, especially over the detection of non-technical losses (thefts, under-billing and other lax practices relating to bill collections), creating a delicate situation in the face of the electorate as well as internal difficulties in implementation by the SEBs (massive strikes occurred in Uttar Pradesh in January 2000). Ultimately, it is up to the regulated company to make a request for a tariff hike, which therefore involves the political responsibility of the government in the case of a public company. For all these reasons, going one step further, that is privatization that enables politicians to disengage from this situation.

The influence of a little blend of ideology should probably also not be denied. While 'minimal' managerial reform appears necessary, it is not established that privatization is the only path open to the states. It is a possibility offered by the centre, but it is in particular not a conditionality of the PFC and hence of the Government of India, which seeks primarily the financial improvement of the SEBs, even if under the public sector system. Kerala, for instance, is not inclined to privatize, and other states have not yet openly expressed their inclinations. Beyond that, privatization presents problems of commitment by investors. Indeed, as is evidenced, foreign direct investments in the generation sector have been few in number. As for distribution, in Orissa and Delhi, where privatization of distribution companies occurred to the extent of 51 per cent in 1999 and 2002 respectively, the private parties concerned have ultimately been Indian ones. No foreign electrical company had initially made an offer, and the American company which took over central Orissa had come in a second round of negotiations with the State of Orissa later in the year 1999, and has ultimately resigned during 2001.[11]

Over and above the influence of ideology, the analysis of the motivations of the centre as of those of some reforming states has shown that the changes under way have largely been the outcome of a conjunction of factors pertaining to the Indian political scene itself. As for the real globalization of the power sector, in the sense of the opening up to foreign private capital, it is for the time being restricted and could remain so for a while. In the states which have attempted privatization, the loans from development agencies do go, it is true, partly to foreign suppliers and manufacturers of equipment, but the major supply comes from the Indian market. The main outcome of the opening up of the Indian power sector could then very well be the relative recuperation of an advantage by the centre over the states, more than any significant opening up to the private sector. This opening up could similarly remain for quite long restricted to the Indian private sector alone,[12] and hence constitute the pursuit of an Indian dynamics, at any rate that of certain Indian interests, even if under the guise of globalization.

A HETERODOX ANALYSIS OF THE ISSUE OF PRIVATE *VERSUS* PUBLIC: A POSSIBLE SPACE FOR LOCAL DYNAMICS

From the presentation of the mode of working of the SEBs, it has been seen that decision making does not depend on criteria based fundamentally on costs, but rather on a choice between various social, electoral, technical and eventually financial objectives relating to outlays, these choices being made *in fine* in favour of whatever procures political gains. Pushing the analysis of their internal working further, it is seen that they have a strong internal rationality, based on the affinity between instructions that are enforceable, criteria not related to costs, a system of unorganized and unreliable information, and a budgetary system fitting into the public sector mould (with non-transferable allocations of budgets). These various elements strengthen each other reciprocally, for the politician, giving instructions that are enforceable, finds it beneficial to avail of a system where information is deficient. Indeed the costs entailed by his interventions are then not apparent. In this context, the employees of the SEB take advantage to increase the margin of their theoretically non-existent discretionary powers, strengthening thereby the need for the political decision makers to give direct instructions. The state then needs budgetary tools imbued with the rigidity of a public budget in order to restrict this margin of manoeuvre by the SEBs. Moreover, the employees lack the means to develop a rationality based on the search for efficiency, and only executive instructions and a control based on the respect for procedures can ensure that the targeted objectives will be suitably pursued. The system is of mutual defiance. It is this system which needs to be changed and replaced by a mode of decision making based on costs, even if it is in the framework of political instructions routed through regulation.

Considering this, the matter of making a choice between recourse to the private or a reform within the public system does not necessarily become a burning issue, and dynamics that are more local in nature can quite rapidly be put to use advantageously.

Let us analyse first of all the effects of a successful reform, by defining it as being capable (i) of cutting down in the short run the large levels of technical and non-technical losses inherited from the mode of administered management, and (ii) of improving efficiency in the long run, in terms of costs spread over the total activity. Such a reform would make it possible to solve the problems that have distanced the sector from the general distribution policies that had been assigned to it. It is compatible with both economic efficiency and the setting up of the targeted social subsidies.

This type of reform leads in the short run to putting at a disadvantage the clients who were drawing profit from the earlier system and in favouring industrialists and above all the poor, on the supposition that the economies achieved would be partly allocated to them (which, keeping in mind the system of debiting from budgetary transfers, is plausible). In the long run, the gains in efficiency should make it possible for all to be winners. It is this manner of reasoning which underlies and justifies the reforms that aim at bringing the private sector, be it the way the World Bank supports it in India, or as proposed by other economists (see Ruet 2002).

Short term	• undeclared consumers or those tampering with their meters	—
	• farmers, domestic consumers	—
	• industrialists	+
	• taxpayers and beneficiaries of social programmes	++
Long term	• all legal consumers	+
	• taxpayers and beneficiaries of social programmes	+

INSET 1: Redistributive effects of a successful reform

The elements crucial to the success of a reform and therefore to its redistributive consequences arise hence out of hypotheses made on the efficiency achieved. Reformers are generally sceptical about the ability of the public sector to achieve, or at least to achieve rapidly, this short-term efficiency, the risk being that the *a priori* beneficiary categories are smaller than predicted; hence the credo of privatization. But conversely, too rapid a privatization will necessarily take place in very reduced conditions of visibility for the investor. This can then lead to a reduction in the value of the assets and the benefits drawn out of them; economically this is not necessarily disturbing but it can become a serious handicap for the political feasibility of such a reform. In addition, a bid in conditions of inadequate information does not guarantee that the best investor, the one who would turn out to be the most efficient, is chosen, the absence of information not being, *a priori,* identically distributed. This has consequences in the end on efficiency and can also lead to negative consequences on distribution in the long run, this time for all clients.

In this framework, it is probably not cardinal to decide in the short term on the issue of private versus public. It is more important to come out of the administered system and to increase the available information to then choose to go in for privatization on this basis. To this end, some local dynamics could be put to use. Indeed, one of the major problems of the SEBs is the management of the consumers on the level of transmission, and the major problem of the consumers is the quality and continuity of the supply. The possibility might be considered of entrusting the management of consumer services to village associations in rural or sectional areas, or again to real estate developers in the urban areas. Some examples are being explored in the rural areas in Maharashtra, and some upstream feasibility studies are being financed at present for a more urban framework.[13] This kind of initiative could be based on strategies of social marketing and be guided by the fairly numerous experiments conducted by some NGOs in hydro-electric programmes. Besides, the development of these services by real estate companies offers to the latter the advantage of a total control over the project. From the point of view of the SEB, payment for consumption is guaranteed. If the power is sold at a higher level of tension than that of transmission, which can happen, even the sale at a lower tariff can then be advantageous to the SEB. The latter by this means frees itself of the responsibility of the maintenance of a part of its distribution network; and an average income per kWh sold could be absolutely comparable to the earlier one since it gets paid for all of its sold energy, while it leaves to others the burden of collecting the bills. Finally, the reduction of losses achieved by franchisees can leave the SEB with more power for the zones remaining under its responsibility, thus precluding costly purchases from independent producers.

In tandem with the prospects of 'globalization', the reforms in the Indian power sector, perceived more and more by its actors as being necessary, could on condition that the governments become aware of their advantages, open up opportunities for the development of dynamics of a very local nature.

CONCLUSION

The analysis of the evolution of the power sector, a sector that is of an extensively distributive nature, makes it possible to throw light on one facet of the 'globalization' of India. The dominant fact of this globalization is not the economic or political emancipation of the states with relation to a supposed subjugation to the centre. Similarly, the quantitative significance of this globalization is limited, at any rate if the latter is defined as the opening up to foreign capital.

Indeed, within the public sphere, it is more a matter of a vertical reconstitution of the centre-state power equations in which it is New Delhi which has gained the upper hand. The centre encourages the states to disengage from sectors which are economically too costly and bring them little politically, to bring to the fore its own pawns, that is to say its administrations, corporations and other structures of financing. In this framework horizontal inequalities arise inevitably between states for attracting private capital. These can to a certain extent be seen by New Delhi as an opportunity to regain some means of effective control, and not simply those planned on paper, over the management of outlays, by recovering from the states an ascendancy which it had lost for a moment.

At all events, it would be wrong to think that the reforms considered or undertaken have been forced solely from outside. They have been fertilized by a debate which existed already in India and they correspond to advantages clearly defined for the different political levels concerned.

It is not certain at present that the power sector has sparked off enthusiasm among foreign investors. The examples of production and of transmission go to prove this. The opening up to the private sector is witnessed therefore undoubtedly among Indian groups, giving preference there again to Indian dynamics.

Finally, keeping in mind the nature of the reforms to be undertaken in the management of the sector, there is the promising possibility of an integration of local dynamics, based on consumer or developer associations.

If 'globalization' is suggested as being the element that is the driving force of reforms in the power sector in the discourses that refer to it, sing its praises, incriminate it, or stigmatize it, it seems that the reality encompasses above all Indian dynamics. This relates to a reassignment from the states towards the centre, of the balance of power in the matter of allocation between sectors, social categories, geographic zones, etc. If we accept the analysis by Khilnani (1997) of Indian policy, the driving forces of the timid advances towards 'globalization' in the power sector can be interpreted as the continuation of a system based on a vertical struggle to take hold of the horizontal redistributive issues on public expenditure, which are sources of political legitimacy. The novel element, for the time being a very tenuous one, could be the arrival on the scene of local players in the form of rural or sectional consumers' associations.

NOTES

1. The costs are inadequately known and depend on the statistical division made between the different densities of habitation. On the basis of the example of France, a factor of two to three between cities and countrysides is plausible.
2. Source: Planning Commission, 1997. Some private companies do exist, particularly for distribution in Bombay or Calcutta, and for production in Ahmedabad, but they constitute a minor part of the electrical sector in India. Very recent developments have taken place, in privatising the distribution in Orissa in 1999 and in Delhi in 2002.
3. The officials in the Ministry communicate only official figures, on the basis of which they work. They declare that they do not know the real figures although they admit that they are aware of the unofficial estimates that are doing the rounds.
4. An employee must cover himself as best he can by being able to show that he has adhered to a fixed procedure.
5. For a more detailed analysis of the decision making and the internal rationality of the SEBs, see Ruet, 2002.
6. Thus the World Bank has assessed at $ 2.5 billion dollars, on the basis of reforms combining tariff increases and improvement of the quality of the supply, the profit converted to current value, over a period of ten years, to consumers of Andhra Pradesh alone (World Bank 1999).
7. Not only is the choice between two alternative solutions not based on a criterion of economic efficiency or of financial profitability, but even the logic of a procedural rationality among the employees can in a number of situations prevent these alternative solutions from even being considered.
8. These debts are essentially due to the governments of the states, but in addition the SEBs owed in 1997 $ 2.9 billion to the companies managed by the centre.
9. For an average cost of supply at Rs. 2.07 per kWh in 1997, that is a subsidy 'restricted' to 75 per cent instead of the present 86 per cent.. Electricity is almost free for farmers, including large farmers, in some states, or even free as in Punjab.
10. Such a risk is very real in Haryana where, for reasons of litigation connected with the collecting of bills, riots took place in 1997 leading to the burning down of railway stations, or in Andhra Pradesh where the burning of public buses is the usual mode of protest, again noticeable during the Winter 2000-1.
11. Apparently out of fears relating to the inadequacy between the supposed expectations of the Regulatory Commission and the possibilities of medium term improvement of efficiency of the companies offered for sale. For more details, see Ruet 2002.
12. All the more so as during conversations several investors who till now have

followed the trends in this sector, declare today that that they no longer consider India as 'strategic' to their diversification efforts.

13. Particularly by the Tata Energy Research Institute.

REFERENCES

Chakravarty, Sukhamoy, *Development Planning. The Indian Experience*, Delhi: Oxford University Press, 1987.

Giraud, Pierre-Noël, *Economie le grand satan*, coll. Textuels, Paris: Gallimard, 1998.

——, "Economie et propriété dans less socialismes", seminar at Cerisy, 1999, unpublished working document, Paris: CERNA, 2000.

Gridco, *Reform in Gridco, Revenue Improvement Action Programme*, Bhubaneshwar, 1998.

IEA, *Electricity in India*, Paris: International Energy Agency, 2002.

Khilnani, Sunil, *The Idea of India*, London: Penguin, 1997.

Planning Commission, *Annual Report on the Working of SEBs for the year 1996-97*, Government of India, 1997.

——, *Annual Report on the Working of SEBs for the year 1997-98*, Government of India, 1998.

——, *Report on the Financial Performance of SEBs from 1991-92 to 1994-95*, New Delhi, March 1998.

——, *Annual Report on the Working of SEBs for the year 1998-99*, Government of India, 1999.

Quraishi, S.Y., 'Power sector regulation and restructuring: Haryana's experience', paper presented at the International forum on Power Sector and Restructuring, New Delhi, 1998.

Ruet, J., 'Investment profitability in bridging the power gap in India', *Indian Journal of Economics*, vol. 49, no.2, October-December 2001.

——, 'Investment Needs and Possible Incomes in Indian Power Sector to Bridge the Energy Gap', *Indian Economic Journal*, October-December 2001(a).

——, 'The State Electricity Boards: Private vs. Public "Enterprisation"', *Indian Journal of Public Administration*, vol. XLVII, no. 1, pp. 29-49, IIPA, New Delhi, 2002.

——, *Against the Current: Organizational Restructuring of State Electricity Boards*, Manohar Publishers, New Delhi, 2002(a).

World Bank, *Staff Appraisal Reprot, Orissa Power Sector Restructuring Project*, Report no. 14298-IN, 1996.

——, *Project Appraisal Document, Haryana Power Sector Restructuring Project*, Report 17234-IN, 1997.

——, *Power Sector Reform and the Privatization of Distribution in India*, main author H. Salgo, Internal Working Document, March 1998.

——, *Staff Appraisal Document, Andhra Pradesh Power Sector Restructuring Project*, 1999.

Endogenous Development and Globalization: An Industrial District in Tamil Nadu

Loraine Kennedy

In the last couple of decades, processes popularly grouped under the term 'globalization', have led to increased competition in international and domestic markets. For firms in India, this challenge may appear even greater since they have until recently benefited from a certain amount of protectionism. One of the key elements of economic liberalization, which has accompanied globalization in India as elsewhere, is the opening of borders to international trade. This destabilizes the domestic structure of economies and necessitates a redefinition of the public and private sectors and of relations between large and small enterprises. In this context, it is noteworthy that there has been a general resurgence of interest in decentralized forms of production and in small and medium enterprises, which occupy a central place in the economic fabric of numerous countries. Hence,

*This research was conducted in the framework of a joint programme of the Social Sciences Department of the French Institute of Pondicherry and REGARDS (CNRS-IRD), Bordeaux.

one of the paradoxes of globalization is that it tends to focus attention on territories and on local resources for economic development.

A concept that has attracted a great deal of interest in recent times is that of the 'industrial district', defined as the spatial concentration of small and medium enterprises, specialized in a particular sector of activity. Indeed, in a number of countries where this configuration is found, it constitutes a competitive form of production, able to withstand the rigours of international competition.[1] The success of the industrial district is attributed to its flexibility, its technical and organizational ability to respond rapidly to changes in demand, and to its strategy of constant innovation. This 'flexible specialization'[2] strategy is one form of the 'new competition', a paradigm that is seen to be replacing mass production.[3]

It is significant that these research areas, once pertaining to Europe and North America, have now begun to attract attention in developing countries where numerous examples of industrial districts are found. Now these districts, also called 'industrial clusters',[4] do not necessarily bring together all the characteristics of the industrial district, such as a high level of inter-firm cooperation or an important division of labour between the enterprises. Nevertheless, some of them have proved to be dynamic, capable of innovating and competing in export markets.

The aim of this study is to ascertain the importance of this form of industrial organization in the Indian context[5] and to explore in particular its ability to respond to the challenges of globalization and of the 'new competition' that it imposes. After a review of the literature on these issues, I will analyse the path taken by an industrial district so as to throw light on the factors on which its dynamism and competitiveness depend. This will be on the basis of a specific case in south India in the tanning sector. This sector's interaction with the world economy through trade and technological exchanges and also non-trade related issues, is also touched upon. Using a recent example, I will show the collective response of this district when confronted with pollution controls, a question of a global nature whose influence is felt locally in a growing number of developing countries. Finally, we look at the main challenges of globalization for these enterprises and for the region in which they are deeply rooted.

An important pivot on which this research revolves is the role the state plays in the development of industrial districts and more generally in the improvement of the competitiveness of small and medium industries with relation to imports, on the one hand, and export markets on the other hand. A new form of public support resulting from the experience of the industrial districts throughout the world consists in helping the enterprises to set up joint structures for making decisions and taking action. These structures aim at facilitating communication and cooperation between enterprises working in a given sector in the same locality, hence among enterprises competing with each other. They also work towards coordinating the representation of the districts in their relations with the higher authorities and towards putting 'real services'[6] at their disposal.

THE CONCEPTUAL FRAMEWORK

The industrial district model has attracted attention because of its high degree of success. When the Fordist crisis was in full force, exerting increasing strain on the dominant mass production model, it was noted that some regions withstood it and even flourished. Flexibility in production, the possibility of producing in small series, as well as constant technical innovation on the part of a qualified labour force are some of the characteristics that could explain this performance. The growing importance, from the 1970s, of quality and variety in production, driven by demand, required new forms of management (Piore and Sabel 1984). Two variants of an emerging model of *flexible specialization* have been identified, one on the basis of large firms, the other on small ones. The Italian case is the most representative of the latter, in the central and north-eastern regions called the 'Third Italy'.[7] Other zones have been identified in Germany, France[8] and the United States. This model, which has become an ideal type, includes elements that go beyond the economic organization of production to encompass equally important social and territorial dimensions. Since the basic components are rather well known I will only briefly review them here.

The Keys to Collective Efficiency

The good performance of the industrial district relies on a certain number of economic principles. First of all, the spatial concentration of enterprises specialized in a single sector leads to *positive externalities*, also called agglomeration effects. Thus, for instance, investments undertaken by an enterprise on technology, new forms of management, or training tend to benefit sooner or later the other enterprises of the district. These gains may be external to the individual enterprise but they remain within the district and collectively benefit the enterprises that constitute it. Similarly, it is on the scale of the district, not the firm, that economies of scale arise. Production costs are reduced due to the easier access of an enterprise to the services and specialized trades that set up shop in the proximity of the district, bringing gains to the cluster. New arrivals can find an experienced workforce in the local labour market. Finally, an 'industrial atmosphere', to borrow Marshall's expression (1919), promotes innovations and learning effects as well as the rapid dissemination of new techniques and know-how.

Such 'passive' external economies, resulting from the proximity of the enterprises to each other, can be considerably increased if they are accompanied by more active cooperation on the part of the enterprises. It is the combination of passive and active economies which brings about the concept of collective efficiency (Schmitz 1995). Active cooperation is required, for instance, when enterprises have recourse to sub-contracting for certain operations, if not for the entire production process. Similarly, in some districts, the enterprises are vertically integrated, in the manner of a large firm, and together they produce goods by specializing in one or several stages of the production process, hence resulting in economies of scale. Outside the productive sphere too, firms can undertake various forms of collective action, through consortiums or producers' associations, for example. The latter, by taking on the responsibility of representing the interests of the local producers in their relations with decision-makers, or by circulating trade-related information, contribute towards improving the competitiveness of the district. However, it should be remembered that cooperation between the enterprises of a district coexists with competition. To the extent to which many firms produce the same goods or services, a high degree of horizontal competition generally prevails within the district.

Recent studies have underscored the crucial importance of trust between economic actors, regardless of the form in which the cooperation between enterprises in the industrial district takes place. A sentiment of trust among entrepreneurs is based in many cases on a common culture and a shared identity (ethnic, religious or political), that is strengthened by the sense of belonging to the same locality or region and to the same profession. Sharing a socio-cultural milieu and political ideology has been identified, in the case of Italy, as a key input in the industrial district model (Trigilia 1986). It is felt that trust between economic actors, while difficult to evaluate, contributes towards reducing transaction costs within the district by reducing risks. Indeed, the probabilities of defection (cheating) are much smaller when all the economic players belong to the same locality and the same community (Nadvi 1999).

Beyond trust in interpersonal relationships, social institutions contribute to circumscribing individual behaviour by fixing and strengthening norms, in such a way as to contain the risks of defection, which tend to increase in a context of severe competition. While trust between players cannot be decreed, and takes varied forms in time and space, it grows with experience when the result of the transactions proves satisfactory for all parties concerned. Consequently, in some districts 'ascribed' trust is progressively being replaced by 'earned' trust (Humphrey and Schmitz 1998). In vertical relations between buyers and suppliers, it is often the latter that prevails, particularly when the 'players' live in different countries.

The social cohesion of a district is closely linked to its roots within a territory, particularly when they are historically grounded. Industrialization processes naturally contribute to organizing space, but space (*territoire* in French) also contributes towards defining local production forms. More than a stock of resources, *territoire* has to be seen as a 'matrix of social organization and interactions' (Veltz 1996: 10). Thus, it generates different types of social relationships in accordance with the dominant social and economic institutions.

The emphasis till now has been on the local level, but districts are involved in relationships with other levels, sometimes in an intensive manner. Their capacity to manage these relationships appears to be crucial. It is by means of vertical relations with clients or trader middlemen that enterprises receive information about market conditions, new inputs, equipment, and techniques (Nadvi 1997). In a world economy characterized by rapid exchanges and dissemination of techniques as well as by a constantly fluctuating demand, access to information is obviously of primary importance.

Industrial Districts in Developing Countries

Numerous examples of industrial districts, that conform more or less to the ideal type, have been noted in developing countries.[9] In fact, the success of this model is explained in part by its correspondence with observed reality. According to Courlet and Pecqueur, 'The theoretical revival that has been conducted on the basis of work on the industrial districts . . . makes it possible to give a theoretical consistency to numerous experiments in industrialization located [in developing countries]' (1996: 92-3). Indeed, small-scale industry constitutes a predominant component in the productive landscape of many countries, where it is, moreover, often concentrated geographically and sectorally.

However, empirical studies have highlighted some elements specific to districts in developing countries. First of all they tend to be less homogeneous, harbouring enterprises very different from one another in terms of size, financial outlays, technologies and end markets (Nadvi and Schmitz 1994: 12). These internal hierarchies have an influence on the relationships between the enterprises within a district. The distinction between flexibility and exploitation of labour is also difficult to discern. Indeed, examples of burgeoning flexible specialization and 'sweatshops' coexist (Pederson, Sverrisson and Van Dijk 1994: 5). Various factors help explain the tendency to adopt strategy based on low salaries: a surplus of labour, a shortage of qualified workers and the weakness of the trade union movement. Finally, it seems that local authorities play a less significant role in many developing countries, as a result of their relative political and financial weakness.

Some theoretical studies point out the advantages of decentralized forms of organization, such as the industrial district, for emerging economies. Smaller initial costs for setting up an enterprise, as it may be involved in only one stage of the production process, for instance, signifies an easier access to entrepreneurial initiatives. Moreover, the pattern of the industrial district is a form particularly adapted to manufacturing, a sector in which developing countries enjoy comparative advantages. This does not mean that the industrial district is a transposable model. What it can provide is an analytical framework that is useful for understanding the internal working of enterprise *clusters*, wherever they may be found, and for explaining their performance.

Turning now to India, the industrial district corresponds to a fairly common configuration in numerous regions. Indeed, some localities have an historical specialization in the manufacture of specific goods (textile, shoes, metalwork) often linked to a traditional craft. Local forms vary enormously in technical, organizational and commercial terms,[10] a fact which makes it difficult to evaluate the true significance of this pattern in the industrial development of India (Cadène 1998). However, the debate is open and it appears that the present political climate of economic liberalization is promoting the development of the districts, particularly those that focus on external markets, like the example examined here.

For the last fifty years, the Indian government has sought to promote and protect modern and traditional small-scale industries with a view to safeguarding employment (as the techniques are more labour intensive that in large enterprises), promoting entrepreneurship and encouraging rural industrialization. In addition to various types of assistance (subsidized loans, tax benefits, import concessions), policy aims to protect small-scale industries from large national firms and foreign production. As critics have pointed out, by giving undue importance to size as compared to other criteria like efficiency, this policy has neglected technical improvements, leading in the end to heavy social and economic costs.[11] In the present context of liberalization, the small-scale sector, which forms the basis of most districts, is exposed to an increasingly competitive market, a situation for which protectionism did little to prepare them. At present, one sees significant changes in policies, at both state and central levels, which take account of the upcoming removal of quotas and other protective measures, in the framework of the WTO agreements.[12]

LEATHER DISTRICTS IN THE PALAR VALLEY

In the middle Palar Valley, in northern Tamil Nadu, several small towns are specialized in leather production (Map 1). Over an 80-km stretch, one can find more than 600 tanneries, most of which are concentrated in and around five small towns (Table 1). Although the majority of these are small enterprises, the towns of the Palar Valley are among the primary leather centres of the country, generating around 45 per cent of total production. In its spatial and productive organization, this industry encompasses many of the characteristics of the industrial district.[13]

Tanning in this region is quite an old specialization, dating back at least a century, which explains the strong territorial mooring that this activity enjoys. This is an example of endogenous economic development, as it is mainly based on local entrepreneurial and financial

TABLE 1: THE TANNERY CENTRES OF THE PALAR VALLEY

Town I	Population (1991) II	Number of Tanneries (1998) III
Ranipet	45,583	224
Melvisharam	26,613	25
Ambur	75,911	95
Vaniyambadi	92,307	136
Pernambattu	36,195	77

SOURCE: Column II: Government of India (1991). Column III: field investigations.

MAP 1

TAMIL NADU state in India

VELLORE district in Tamil Nadu

VELLORE district Leather industry in the PALAR valley

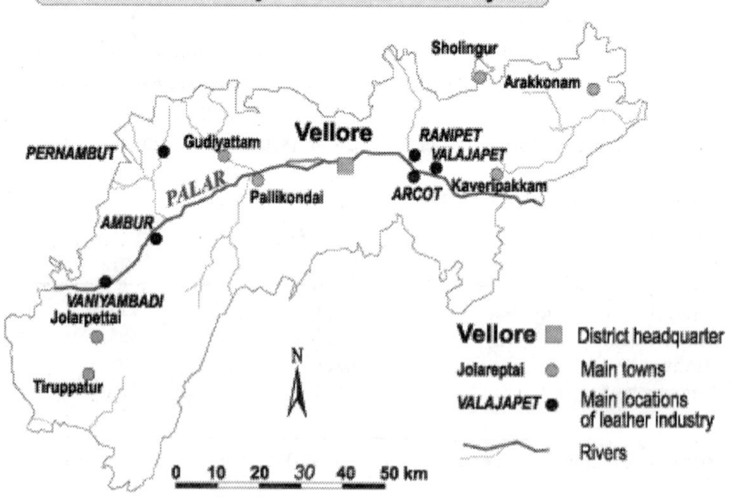

initiatives. This industry is associated with the local Muslim community (Labbai), whose ancestors were the first to organize the manufacture of leather along modern industrial lines (Dupuis 1960: 215-34). It was until then a decentralized, village-level activity, catering to the needs of the local economy. Looked down upon in the Hindu value system due to its impurity, only the lowest castes processed leather. This undoubtedly explains the historical absence of Hindu investment in this activity and the Muslim predominance that is visible even today.

The entrepreneurs who established the first tanneries in the Palar Valley were responding to the growing demand that the colonial presence promoted. For one thing, the colonial administration increasingly needed boots and saddles and for another, numerous British businessmen were trading on an international scale. During a first phase the Indian producers were required to pass through British agents to export their leather. South India in particular developed its industry at the end of the nineteenth century and established a reputation in the London market for the good quality of its semi-finished cow and buffalo leather. This was exceptional at a time when the other regions of India were mainly exporting unprocessed raw hide (Usha 1984: 38 ff.). First World War stimulated the demand for leather and initiated an upward trend that continues to this day, although with great fluctuations.

Numerous factors explain the location of tanneries in the Palar Valley, which quickly became, along with Chennai (formerly Madras), one of the major production centres in south India. The valley was attractive on account of the abundance of water (and probably its quality), and the proximity of the Mysore plateau, from where tannins were supplied, has also been cited as an important factor (Dupuis 1960: 217-18; Sharma 1946: 156). The fact that the towns of the valley were situated near Chennai, and connected to it by railway, certainly played a crucial role. In addition to its port, which opened out to world markets, this large colonial city itself represented an important market for leather.

The strong presence in the industry of Muslims is probably a factor of dynamism.[14] Field investigations confirm that local Muslims are motivated by a strong ethnic identity and constitute a close-knit community.[15] Local Muslim tanners thus do indeed belong to the same 'socio-cultural milieu' and are moreover united by various ties (professional, kinship, friendship). Moreover, most of the entrepreneurs of the leather industry, whatever their community affiliation, come from the region and hence share a territorial identity. They have opportunities to gather together in their professional associations, as well as at other civic meeting places, such as the Rotary and the Lions clubs. Finally, keeping in mind the century old presence of tanning in this region, the local population shares a kind of leather culture. All these elements point to an affinity with the ideal industrial district described earlier.

It is necessary nonetheless to highlight the problems that arise from borrowing the notion of 'socio-cultural milieu' in the case being studied, and in the Indian context generally. While the research on Italian districts underscored the importance of an egalitarian ethic in local work relations, such an ethic is not present in our study. Generally, social relations in Indian society are hierarchical and the workplace is no exception. In the Palar Valley, the owners and managers of the leather industry are mainly Muslim, while the workers are mainly Hindu (or Christian converts) hailing from the lowest social strata of society, people whose traditional occupation was tanning. This occupational specialization is explained by the Brahmanical tradition, and the caste system that forms its base, that relegated to the lower castes the most impure tasks in accordance with an established ritual hierarchy. Even if working conditions in the factory and the evolution of mentalities have contributed towards some social change, the fact remains that tannery work is looked down upon in India, as is manual labour generally.[16] Hence, the idea of a social management of the market, based on a common local subculture (Trigilia 1986); needs to be relativized in this case, and in other industrial districts in India to the extent that traditional social hierarchies are strong and egalitarian ideology less prevalent.[17] In the Palar Valley there is no single sub-culture common to the entire local population, capable of circumscribing individualist behaviour, but partial regulatory systems can be observed, based on criteria of community or class, as we shall see further.

Internal Structure of the Districts

The local leather industry has undergone spectacular change in the last twenty-five years. From a traditional industry specializing in the production of semi-finished leather, it has made the transition to finished leather, particularly from the 1970s. In the last fifteen years, a certain number of tanneries have 'vertically integrated', and have moved up the value chain. They now manufacture leather goods (footwear, shoe uppers, gloves, garments, etc.). Although some industrialists have invested only in the final manufacturing stage, the most successful firms are present in the entire chain, having a solid base in the tannery and supplying leather to their own manufacturing units.

But change is not apparent everywhere in the valley. Most of the tanneries remain relatively small[18] and many are still family-owned. Most of the districts of the valley have a pyramidal configuration. At the base are numerous small firms, followed by some larger units and finally by a small number of very large firms. The latter are often vertically integrated, and directly export their produce, in collaboration with foreign partners.

Many small enterprises specialize either in the initial processing of the skins, which gives semi-finished leather, or in the finishing process which yields finished leather. While some work independently, purchasing the raw material and selling their production in the market, most undertake sub-contracting, at least occasionally. Others work exclusively on a sub-contracting basis. They produce for other tanneries which lack capacity or which require their specialized skills,[19] or for agents or intermediaries. It is common for several enterprises to get together to form a more or less stable production network and here one can observe the importance of family and community bonds in the choices made for collaboration and partnership.

These different practices ensure a certain flexibility of production, typical of industrial districts. This being so, the interactions between the enterprises of the valley do not appear as significant as in many districts, in frequency or intensity. This is explained partly by the nature of the tanning processes, especially when producing semi-finished leather, which it is not easily broken down into separate steps. Like for the tile factories described by Das (1996), these 'primary' tanneries all employ similar technologies and produce a nearly generic product (when starting with raw material of an equivalent quality). There is consequently intense price competition. Specialization exists above all at the finishing stage, which necessitates numerous machines. Here, some micro-enterprises (job units) invest in a single machine, realize only a single stage of finishing, and are paid on a piece-rate basis.

The last twenty years have seen a growing diversification among and within the districts of the valley, as a consequence of an important modernization campaign promoted by the state. This policy has contributed towards increasing interaction between firms, particularly in the form of sub-contracting (for reasons of capacity as well as specialization), and has encouraged the development or reactivation of collective institutions. Each town of the valley has its professional tanners association, which disseminates information to the producers and represents them in their relations with the trade unions[20] and the decision-making bodies at the regional and national levels. Several towns host cooperative societies, which offer services to local producers, akin to the 'real services' mentioned in the theoretical literature. They have been set up with the help of the state to assist the enterprises in making the transition towards greater value added production. This has been the thrust of public policy for the leather industry since the 1970s, which has had a tremendous impact on local industry.

In 1973, acting on the recommendations of a committee of specialists, the Indian government decided to progressively reduce the export of skins and hides and semi-finished leather. This policy was formulated in the context of a complex world situation. It drew its inspiration from the industrial policies of several Latin American countries, aimed at increasing value addition within their borders by banning export of raw material. This decision had a very destabilizing effect on the industry in south India, which had specialized in semi-finished leather. Finishing necessitated new techniques and machines and, more intimidating, new markets abroad. This crisis was handled differently by different enterprises of a single district and by the five districts of the valley, each adapting in a distinct way.

We can now see that this strong policy constraint has opened up new opportunities in the valley, for industrialists and for workers. To begin with only a few tanners rose to the challenge, while the majority indulged in a wait-and-see attitude, having been forced to give their semi-finished leather over to units capable of carrying out the finishing process, or to traders or other intermediaries, who proliferated. With the passage of time, inspired by the success of some of the more dynamic enterprises, other producers in the valley and new entrepreneurs have followed their example,[21] hoping for social mobility. However, for many of the small producers at the bottom of the chain, the best security against the vagaries of the market consisted in tying up with one or several large enterprises, even if it meant accepting smaller margins.

In response to the demands of the industry, the government has developed support measures, particularly in fiscal matters, in order to stimulate and encourage private initiatives.[22] From the 1980s onwards, the local industry has been making the transition to the last stage of a vertical integration with the opening of the first manufacturing factories. Today it is estimated that footwear factories alone employ 16,000 women in the valley. A large number of firms in the valley are now producing high value added leather meant for international markets and are, in annual national competitions, among the winners in all categories.[23] It is significant moreover that the industrialists in the valley occupy the highest positions in various national associations such as the powerful Council for Leather Exports, with its headquarters in Chennai.

The local industry is thus well placed in its relations with political decision-makers, whose continued interest in the leather industry is explained by the large contribution made by the sector to the country's exports. One may wonder, however, about the response of the government to the less efficient or non-exporting industrial districts. It is well known that local governments avail of insufficient financial means to evolve economic initiatives. They even find it difficult to fulfil their statutory functions, and fieldwork suggests that they often lack legitimacy in the eyes of the entrepreneurs.[24] It is probable that we will see private-public collaborations increasing, calling on international capital to solve the problems of infrastructure, as has been done recently in the industrial district of Tiruppur, a large textile centre of Tamil Nadu.

From the standpoint of the national industry, the policy of modernization has achieved its objectives as the structure of exports has undergone a vast change during the last twenty years (Table 2).

GLOBAL CONSTRAINTS AND LOCAL RESPONSES

Globalization does not concern only goods and services but also the ideas, and their underlying norms and values. In this context, it is significant that the producers in developing countries are being increasingly subjected to pressures from industrialized countries, for instance with respect to the environment and work conditions. These pressures coincide largely with changing norms in the importing countries, whose consumers are determined to use their collective purchasing power to modify practices that they consider morally unacceptable. It is probable that in future these questions will be progressively governed by agreements between countries, for example, within the framework of the World Trade Organization (WTO), but for the time being these preferences are conveyed generally by market forces. It is the clients, the firms placing the

TABLE 2: INDIAN EXPORTS OF LEATHER AND LEATHER PRODUCTS, 1976-96

(share of each category in the total exports)

Year	Semi-finished leather	Finished leather	Shoes	Shoe uppers	Garments	Other leather goods
1976-7	47	36	9	2	1	4
1977-8	40	40	7	6	1	7
1978-9	29	51	6	5	2	7
1979-80	20	60	5	7	1	7
1980-1	13	57	8	11	1	10
1981-2	12	52	7	18	2	10
1982-3	14	50	5	20	2	10
1983-4	12	45	5	26	2	10
1984-5	8	53	5	23	2	10
1985-6	7	44	5	29	3	12
1986-7	6	43	9	26	7	10
1987-8	6	39	10	26	8	10
1988-9	3	40	8	26	10	12
1989-90	1	34	8	26	16	14
1990-1	—	31	11	22	22	13
1991-2	—	23	14	22	24	17
1992-3	—	22	14	16	28	19
1993-4	—	21	16	20	26	18
1994-5	—	25	18	14	24	19
1995-6	—	22	19	15	24	21

NOTE: The figures may not total up to 100 as they have been rounded off.
SOURCE: Calculated on the basis of data supplied by the DGCIS, Calcutta Market Research Unit, CLE, Chennai.

orders, which play the role of global mediators by means of the orders they place and the conditions attached to them. They may in some cases help the producer enterprises to conform to the norms laid down,[25] or they may simply inform them of the new constraints that they must adhere to, or risk losing their contract. It is obvious then that the capacity of firms in developing countries to adapt to the new norms depends on the quality of their networks and the kind of relationships they maintain with their partners.

Western norms are also conveyed through international organizations such as the WTO and the ISO (International Standards Organization). This latter defines in specific fields and per sector a series of criteria that give the right to a label. This system of labelling, which has been deployed in each country through ISO approved intermediaries, enables the enterprises fulfilling the required conditions to obtain a label which can constitute a business advantage.

Indeed, choosing suppliers who hold an ISO label is a means for purchasers to ensure the quality of their products.[26]

Apart from pressures, it is undeniable that awareness about the environment has spread to all regions of the planet, although with variable intensity. Economic development that is sensitive to environmental issues has taken on a growing importance in numerous countries as well as in the field of international cooperation, illustrated at the Rio Conference of 1992 and subsequent meetings. In the following example, I analyse the response of small producers in the leather industry to recent pollution controls.[27] Although the initiative came in this case from a local association determined to denounce the lax attitude of the authorities in the application of rules, it concerns a 'global' matter *par excellence*, which has become the subject, in other contexts, of extra-national pressures.

The Pollution Crisis

In May 1995, the Supreme Court of India ordered the closure of those tanneries in the Palar Valley which were not equipped to treat their effluents. Almost 200 factories came under this category. The Court decided not only to impose strict controls, but ordered the Government of Tamil Nadu to make an assessment of the 'loss of ecology' in the valley, to determine the victims of pollution[28] and estimate the compensation to be given to them by the tanneries. The scope of the judgement and its severity indicate a will, on the part of the courts at least, to go forward in the field of pollution control.

The vast majority of the tanneries have opted for a collective solution. They have set up CETPs (Common Effluent Treatment Plants) for treating the waste water. As it happens, the spatial organization of the leather industry in the valley, the enterprises being clustered together, sometimes even contiguous, has lent itself quite naturally to centralized treatment facilities. (Most of the enterprises had neither the space nor the capital required to construct individual installations.)

The concept of the CETP, quite common in Europe, had been suggested to the tanners by government authorities well before the crisis provoked by the decision of the Supreme Court, but in the absence of enforcement, few enterprises had built installations. In 1995, in an atmosphere of crisis, an assistance package was announced, extending up to half of the total cost (25 per cent each from the central and state governments) for the construction of CETPs in all the clusters of the valley. The tanners are required to finance the rest, but they can in some cases avail concessional interest rates for loans from public sector banks. This crucial state support shows both concern for this export-oriented industry and the influence of the leather lobby.[29] The social cost that would result from a massive closure of the tanneries also promoted a quick political response.

The pollution control authorities in Tamil Nadu conduct regular checks, but the responsibility for the proper functioning of the CETP is to be shouldered by the tanners. The heads of the member enterprises elect from among themselves a managing director and a board for this purpose. It is a heavy burden to carry as any malfunctioning can lead to the closure of all member tanneries. At the same time, the CETP is the cause of great tension at the local level between individual and collective interests, as each producer is expected to produce only within certain limits so as not to jeopardize the functioning of the central treatment unit. Now the difficulty in supervising the tanneries makes 'free-rider' behaviour a definite possibility.

Consequently, the efficiency of the CETP, and therefore the survival of the local industry, depends on the cooperation between members. Field investigations show that personal bonds, often of kinship, and affiliation to the same community, as well as a common local identity have promoted cooperation and facilitated the setting up of a systematic management of the CETP, including a system of surprise checks and penalties. Social control also serves as an effective measure of dissuasion for, in the event of non-cooperation, the leaders generally put pressure on the individual and his close relatives. Naturally the personality of the manager is important. He must be able to command the respect of his peers and exercise enough authority over them to be able to ensure their adherence to strict rules.

Collective response to the environmental crisis in the form of the CETP has enabled the survival of the leather industry in the valley. In 1998, seven CETPs connected approximately 400 tanneries to each other and several CETPs were under construction. It is not only the small enterprises that benefit from this, but in fact the entire district. It may be recalled that in an industrial district the enterprises are interdependent. Its strength depends on the flexibility that results from the cohabitation of a large number of firms within a single sector or within a branch of activity, these firms dividing the work among themselves in accordance with the capacities and specialization of each.

However, the response to the challenge was not uniform in the different districts of the valley, and some fared better than others. It is perhaps not surprising that those that managed the crisis best are generally more dynamic and enjoy higher value added production. This was so at least for the leading enterprises. In those cases where failure was most patent, the enterprises were less modernized (as regards mechanization, management, and diversification of production), and most of them continue to manufacture a kind of semi-finished leather for the manufacture of inexpensive sandals (*chappals*) for the domestic market. In addition to the level of value added which characterizes their production, the analysis of the trend followed by the different districts has underlined the importance held by a past experience of collective action.

Indeed, the modernization undertaken in response to the political measures of the 1970s had obliged the local producers to get organized differently, individually as also collectively, for fear of losing everything. This experience, by prompting cooperation, helped the districts to respond to the second crisis, all the more so as their forced reorganization has led, in each case, to social reorganization. We have witnessed since then the emergence of modern and dynamic enterprises and remarkable leadership that is still present. The way things are going it would seem as if these districts had acquired a 'cooperative capital' that they have been able to invest in the management of the pollution crisis. It raises the question of whether this experience will in turn make it possible to accumulate capital which could serve to face other kinds of challenges, among these being globalization and the 'new competition'. A recent study, based on the experience of four districts, suggests a response in the affirmative. It shows first, that in times of crisis, local cooperation increases in the districts, particularly on the vertical level (with suppliers or sub-contractors) and second, that it increases most in those enterprises which are the most efficient (Schmitz 1999b: 11). Indeed, in three of the four cases examined, there exists a statistical correlation between the efficiency of an enterprise and the extent to which it cooperates at the local level.

Although it is too soon to judge if the Palar districts will be able to benefit from the growing local cooperation brought about by the pollution crisis, some observations suggest that the response will be variable. In one case where the social cohesion is particularly remarkable, the district has almost emerged stronger. It is seeking to put to advantage its experience of collective action and to showcase its efforts towards an 'ecological' production of leather. In another case, although it concerns a district whose enterprises yield very high economic returns, the producers, particularly the larger ones, are not able to get along together within the CETP, and are threatening to withdraw and to each conduct individually the treatment of its effluents. Such a decision would have grave consequences.

CONCLUSION

In the 'new competition' which is becoming a generalized phenomenon, competitiveness does not depend solely on prices but concerns also quality and speed. Consequently, Indian industrial enterprises can no longer count on relatively low salaries to establish their competitiveness, all the more so as other countries are succeeding better than India on this level. Whether with relation to imports, which have become more and more liberalized, or to export markets, economic performance depends increasingly on the capacity of firms to integrate the norms defined at the global level, with regard to quality, but also to the environment and perhaps in the near future to working conditions. These are some of the implications of globalization, and ones that pose perhaps the greatest challenge to Indian industry.

Among new industrial models characterized by flexible organization of production and responsiveness to changes in demand, the industrial district has emerged as one of the more promising configurations. There are in India numerous clusters of small and medium industries with attributes of this model. Strong social institutions (kinship, caste or community) can constitute an advantage by reducing costs of transactions and facilitating collaborations, but they may also represent a handicap on account of the rigidity and the hierarchy that they impose.

It is necessary, however, to underscore the limits of this model in India. On a technical level, the production of certain clusters is not sufficiently complex or diversified to promote a vertical break-up. Research has shown that cooperation is more likely to occur between enterprises whose production is complementary than among enterprises that manufacture identical products. Second, the social distance separating managers and workers, a legacy of social history, constitutes an obstacle to the setting up of an environment favourable to the learning process, a necessary condition for constant innovation. It contributes to the unfortunate trend of taking advantage of surplus labour to give low salaries, even if the example of the 'high-tech' sector in Bangalore does suggest that this can be overcome or reduced in certain cases (Holmström 1994). Finally, internal heterogeneity of many districts in terms of size, technologies and final markets, is reflected in hierarchical relationships between enterprises that do not share the same perspectives for growth.

Be that as it may, India appears to have a certain potential for developing industrial districts. The state can play a positive role in this field, not to create but to support and facilitate. As the example of the Palar Valley shows, public policies can lead to intense modifications in the structure and organization of the districts. During the recent pollution crisis, the government supplied crucial assistance. By encouraging the setting up of joint decision-making and implementation structures, it provided producers with the means to come together and develop an internal dynamic. In addition to the effectiveness of such support measures, this type of intervention has the advantage of not necessitating large financial resources. However, long-term policies, such as research for better quality and design and training, will be equally necessary to improve the global performance of the industry and to remedy the inadequacies which hamper it in its race towards global markets.

NOTES

1. The Italian case is the most famous, and it was in that context that the concept of the industrial district, originally formulated by A. Marshall (1919, 1920), was revived. See particularly Brusco (1982) and Pyke, Becattini and Sengenberger (1990).
2. The expression is from Piore and Sabel (1984).
3. According to Best (1990), the new competition is characterized by a flexible organization of production and by a synergy between conception and realization. At the centre of the new competition is the entrepreneurial firm, which strives at every moment to improve its methods, products and processes (Best 1990: 2).
4. Nadvi and Schmitz (1994: 4).
5. See in particular Cadène and Holmström (eds.), 1998.
6. This concept refers to the various services supplied to enterprises by local governments or by professional associations with a view to helping them in a concrete manner in their productive and commercial activities (quality control, technical expertise, legal or tax advice, information on regulations).

7. As opposed to the 'first' Italy of the north where large industry is dominant, and the 'second' Italy of the south, the *Mezzogiorno*, which has remained largely agricultural and less developed economically.
8. For studies on France see Ganne (1990), Benko and Lipietz (1992), Courlet and Soulage (1996).
9. See, for example, Nadvi and Schmitz (1994, 1999) and Abdelmalki and Courlet (1996).
10. See, for example, Cawthorne (1995), Dupont (1995), Jeyaranjan (1997), Kennedy (1999), Knorringa (1996) and the various cases presented in Cadène and Holmström (eds.) (1998).
11. For a review of the critical literature, see Kennedy (2001).
12. Explicit references to industrial districts can be found in policy documents. The New Delhi office of UNIDO has conducted studies on districts with an aim to generate policy recommendations.
13. For purposes of clarity and keeping in mind their differences, each concentration is considered as a district, even if the idea of a single district on the scale of the valley can be entertained.
14. The study towns have a high proportion of Muslims, sometimes a majority, as compared to the average for the state of Tamil Nadu (5.5 per cent of the total population and 10 per cent of the urban population in 1991).
15. On the ethnicity of Tamil Muslims, see Mines (1984).
16. Based on my field investigations, it seems that in general the men from lower and middle (non-SC) castes refuse to work in the tanneries. However, women belonging to these same castes may find irregular employment in tanneries as helpers, usually through a jobber.
17. See in particular Knorringa (1996) on the shoe manufacturing industry in Agra.
18. Based on my field investigations, 68 per cent of the total tanneries in the five towns have the capacity to process less than 1,000 kg. of hides per day. In some towns, like Vaniyambadi, the percentage is considerably higher, just below 90 per cent (121 out of 136 tanneries).
19. Capacity sub-contracting and specialization sub-contracting, according to the distinctions made by Lazerson (1990).
20. In principle, there is 'collective bargaining' every three years in each district, but my field surveys indicate that they are rarely followed in reality.
21. See Ramaswami (1982).
22. The state supports research institutes specializing in leather, such as the Central Leather Research Institute, whose main branch is located in Chennai, and which directly benefits the enterprises of the valley.
23. Organized every year by the Council for Leather Exports, the results are published in the magazine *Leder Informant*, based in Chennai.
24. See Kennedy 1992. These field investigations were conducted in Tiruchengodu, a small dynamic industrial town in Tamil Nadu, in the framework of a programme at the French Institute of Pondicherry (dir. M.-L. Reiniche).

25. Regarding child labour in particular, some major brands and distribution companies have devoted their energies to ensuring that their partners do not employ children. Motivated by their desire to protect their image, they conduct surprise inspections and in some cases have contributed towards setting up schools or orphanages where the young workers are 'rehabilitated'.
26. The series relevant for this study pertain to quality (9000) and the environment (14000).
27. For more detail, see Kennedy (1999).
28. Among the victims mentioned are tannery workers exposed for years at a stretch to toxic chemical substances, and peasants whose land became infertile as a result of the pollution of the water used to irrigate it. Although no official figures are available, an article in *Frontline* mentions 20,000 ha having been affected (8 October 1999).
29. It was the clout of the industrial interests along with the lack of will of the public authorities that explain the lax application of the measures for environmental protection during the earlier decades.

REFERENCES

Abdelmalki, L. and Courlet, C. (eds.), *Les nouvelles logiques du développement*, Paris: L'Harmattan, 1996.

Baud, I.S.A. and De Bruijne, G.A., *Gender, Samll-Scale Industry and Development Policy*, London: IT Publications, 1993.

Bénéï, V. and Kennedy, L. (eds.), 'Industrial Decentralization and Urban Development. A Workshop on a MOST/UNESCO Project', *Pondy Papers in Social Sciences*, no. 23, French Institute of Pondicherry, 1997.

Benko, G. and Lipietz, A. (eds.), *Les régions qui gagnent*, Paris: PUF, 1992.

Best, M., *The New Competition: Institutions of Industrial Restructuring*, Cambridge: Polity Press, 1990.

Brusco, S., 'The Emilian Model: Productive Decentralisation and Social Integration', *Cambridge Journal of Economics*, vol. 6, no. 2 (1982): 167-84.

——, 'The Idea of the Industrial District: Its Genesis', in Pyke, F., Becattini, G. and Sengenberger, W. (eds.), *Industrial Districts and Inter-Firm Cooperation in Italy*, Geneva: International Institute for Labour Studies, ILO, 1990.

Cadène, Ph., 'Conclusion', in Cadène, Ph. and Holmström, M. (eds.), *Decentralized Production in India. Industrial Districts, Flexible Specialization and Employment*, New Delhi: French Institute of Pondicherry and Sage, 1998, pp. 393-403.

Cadène, Ph. and Holmström, M. (eds.), *Decentralized Production in India. Industrial Districts, Flexible Specialization and Employment*, New Delhi: French Institute of Pondicherry and Sage, 1998.

Cawthorne, P., 'Of Networks and Markets: The Rise and Rise of a South Indian Town, The Example of Tiruppur's Cotton Knitwear Industry', *World Development*, vol. 23, no. 1 (1995): 43-56.

Central Leather Research Institute, *Report on Capacity Utilisation and Scope for Modernization in Indian Tanning Industry* (Prepared for the Industrial Bank of India and the State Bank of India), Chennai, 1990.

——, *Directory of Tanneries in India*, Chennai, 1992.

Courlet, C. and Pecqueur, B., 'Districts industriels, systèmes productifs localisés et développement ', in Abdelmalki, L. and Courlet, C. (eds.), *Les nouvelles logiques du développement*, Paris: L'Harmattan, 1996.

Courlet, C. and Soulage, B. (eds.), *Industrie, territoires et politiques publiques*, Paris: L'Harmattan, 1994.

Das, K., 'Collective Dynamism and Firm Strategy: The Flooring Tile Cluster in Gujarat, India', *Working Paper Series*, no. 76, Ahmedabad: Gujarat Institute of Development Research, 1996.

Dupont, V., *Decentralized Industrialization and Urban Dynamics. The Case of Jetpur in West India*, New Delhi: Sage, 1995.

Dupuis, J., *Madras et le nord du Coromandel*, Paris: Adrien-Maisonneuve, 1960.

Ganne, B., *Industrialization diffuse et systèmes industriels localisés. Essai de bibliographie critique du cas français*, Série bibliographique 14, Geneva: Institut International d'Etudes Sociales, ILO, 1990.

Government of India, *Census of India, Series 23, Religion (Table C-9)*, 1991.

Holmström, M., 'Bangalore as an Industrial District: Flexible Specialization in a Labour-surplus Economy?', *Pondy Papers in Social Sciences* 14, French Institute of Pondicherry, 1994.

——, 'Introduction: Industrial Districts and Flexible Specialization, the Outlook for Smaller Firms in India', in Cadène, Ph. and Holmström, M. (eds), *Decentralized Production in India.*, New Delhi: French Institute of Pondicherry and Sage, 1998, pp. 7-41.

Humphrey, J., 'Introduction', *World Development*, vol. 23, no. 1 (1995): 1-7.

Humphrey, J. and Schmitz, H., 'Trust and Inter-Firm Relations in Developing and Transition Economies', *Journal of Development Studies*, vol. 34, no. 4 (1998): 32-61.

Jeyaranjan, J., 'Beyond Tiruppur: Issues for Exploration' in Bénéï, V. and Kennedy, L. (eds), Industrial Decentralization and Urban Development. *Pondy Papers in Social Sciences* no. 23, French Institute of Pondicherry, 1997, pp. 139-43.

Kennedy, L., 'The Functioning of Local Government: A Study of the Administrative and Political Networks between Tiruchengodu Municipality and the State Government of Tamilnadu', presented at the European Conference on Modern South Asian Studies, Berlin, September 1992.

——, 'Cooperating for Survival. Tannery Pollution and Joint Action in the Palar Valley (India)', *World Development*, vol. 27, no. 9 (1999): 1673-91.

——, 'Protégée ou condamnée ? Les politiques publiques à l'égard de la petite industrie en Inde', *Revue Tiers Monde*, Paris, vol. 42, no. 165 (2001): 105 28.

Knorringa, P., *Economics of Collaboration. Indian Shoemakers between Market and Hierarchy*, New Delhi: Sage, 1996.

Lazerson, M., 'Sub-contracting as an Alternative Organizational Form to Vertically-Integrated Production', *Discussion Paper*, no. 20, Geneva: International Institute for Labour Studies, ILO, 1990.

Marshall, A., *Industry and Trade*, 3rd edn. (1927), London: Macmillan, 1919.

——, *Principles of Economics*, 8th edn., London: Macmillan, 1920.

Mines, M., 'Islamization and Muslim Ethnicity in South India', in Imtiaz, A. (ed.), *Ritual and Religion among Muslims in India*, New Delhi: Manohar, 1984, pp. 65-89.

Nadvi, K., *Small Firm Industrial Districts in Pakistan*. Doctoral Thesis, Institute of Development Studies, University of Sussex, Brighton, 1996.

——, 'The Cutting Edge: Collective Efficiency and International Competitiveness in Pakistan', *Discussion Paper* 360, Institute of Development Studies, Brighton, 1997.

——, 'Shifting Ties: Social Networks in the Surgical Instrument Cluster of Sialkot, Pakistan', *Development and Change*, vol. 30, no. 1 (1999): 143-77.

Nadvi, K. and Schmitz, H., 'Industrial Clusters in Less Developed Countries: Review of Experiences and Research Agenda', *Discussion Paper* 360, Institute of Development Studies, Brighton, 1994.

—— (eds.), Special issue on Industrial Clusters in Developing Countries, *World Development*, vol. 27, no. 9 (1999).

Pedersen, P.O., Sverrisson, A. and Van Dijk, M.P. (eds.), *Flexible Specialization. The dynamics of small-scale industries in the South*, London: IT Publications, 1994.

Piore, M. and Sabel, C., *The Second Industrial Divide*, New York: Basic Books, 1984.

Pyke, F., Becattini, G. and Sengenberger, W. (eds.), *Industrial Districts and Inter-Firm Cooperation in Italy*, Geneva: International Institute for Labour Studies, ILO, 1990.

Pyke, F. and Sengenberger, W. (eds.), *Industrial Districts and Local Economic Regeneration*, Geneva: International Institute for Labour Studies, ILO, 1992.

Rabellotti, R., 'Is there an "Industrial District" Model? Footwear Districts in Italy and Mexico Compared', *World Development*, vol. 23, no. 1 (1995): 29-41.

——, *External Economies and Co-operation in Industrial Districts: A Comparison of Italy and Mexico*, London: Macmillan, 1997.

Ramasami, K.S., *Entrepreneurship and Modernization of Industry. A Study of the Tanners of North Arcot*, Doctoral Thesis, University of Madras, 1982.

Schmitz, H., 'Collective Efficiency: Growth Path for Small Scale Industry', *Journal of Development Studies*, vol. 31, no. 4 (1995): 529-66.

——, 'Collective Efficiency and Increasing Returns', *IDS Working Paper* 50, Institute of Development Studies, Brighton, 1997.

——, 'Does Local Co-operation Matter? Evidence from Industrial Clusters in South Asia and Latin America', *IDS Working Paper*, Institute of Development Studies, Brighton, 1999.

Sharma, T. R., *Location of Industries in India*, Bombay: Hind Kitab, 1946.

Trigilia, C., 'Small-firm Development and Political Subcultures in Italy', *European Sociological Review*, vol. 2, no. 3 (1986): 161-75.

Usha, P., *Leather Industry of Tamil Nadu. A Study of Structural Change During 1960-1980, with Special Reference to the 1973 Export Trade Control Policy.* Doctoral Thesis, University of Madras, 1984.

Veltz, P., *Mondialisation, villes et territoires. L'économie d'archipel*, Paris: PUF, 1996.

The Saga of the Diesel Engines of Kolhapur (Maharashtra)

Pierre Lachaier

THE SOCIO-ECONOMIC NETWORKS

Genesis of the Industrial Development of Kolhapur

In 1985, at Sangli in south Maharashtra, a small Digambara Jain industrialist dealing in mechanical equipment spoke to me with nostalgia about the neighbouring kingdom of Kolhapur (Lachaier 1989: 136-47). President of the local association of small industrialists of the Industrial Cooperative Zone of Sangli and member of the Kolhapur Engineering Association, he told me about the high regard in the region for Shahu Maharaj, sovereign of the erstwhile kingdom of Kolhapur (1894-1922) whose policy of socio-economic development

* I thank the industrialists, as well those in charge of the institutions and associations of industrialists of Kolhapur, who very kindly granted me some of their valuable time to talk to me about their enterprises. I am particularly grateful to S.G. Bhanushali, the author of the works to which this study is indebted, for the interview he granted me and the contacts which he had the kindness to facilitate. I remain, naturally, entirely responsible for this present study and the points of view that are developed in it.

(the 'Kolhapuri renaissance') had led to the emergence of numerous entrepreneurs who set about manufacturing diesel engines. And others too who talked to me about the story of the diesel engine manufacturers of Kolhapur, have often described it as an extraordinary adventure, something heroic and exemplary, to which the region owed its present industrial development.

Kolhapur, with its 500,000 inhabitants, the centre of an agricultural market and capital of an important Maratha kingdom till 1949, has become an important seat of the engineering industry with an important impact on the neighbouring market towns and districts, one of these being Sangli, where several Kolhapuri enterprises have been set up. Located around 40 km east of Kolhapur, the town of Sangli (200,000 inhabitants) was till recently the stronghold of Vasant Patil, a great politician and leader of the cooperative movement, who promoted the establishment here of the largest sugar mills in Maharashtra (Sirsikar 1995; Lachaier 1989). And 15 km from Kolhapur, the smaller town of Itachalkaranji with 80,000 inhabitants, has become one of the largest textile centres of Maharashtra. In addition to engineering equipment, as also the agro-industry of sugar, and textiles, Kolhapur and its district are known also for other craft activities, among these being the making of *chappals*, leather sandals made in the local style, that have been exported to countries as far away as Italy.

What are the socio-economic factors which made this emergence possible? How were the main players, who are said to have originated from circles of craftsmen and the peasantry, able to acquire the indispensable technical know-how? What has been the structure of this industry? And what was the dynamics which was able to lead a small industry of local dimensions to reach out today to international markets?

From the Gazetteers and investigations conducted by Sovani (1948, 1951, 1952), it would appear that a diesel engine industry evolved first of all in response to the growing demand for *gul* or molasses made by traditional methods in the cottage industry sector (*Gazetteer Kolh.* 1960: 355). Indeed, the cultivation of sugar cane, whose vegetative cycle exceeds ten months and which requires fertile, well manured and irrigated soil, has been long practised in the southern part of Maharashtra. On account of the topography of the land, it is well irrigation which is the most practical to use, so that people hastened, towards the end of the nineteenth century, to install motorized pumps on the wells so as to increase the acreage under cultivation. But the well-off farmers were almost the only ones who were able to mobilize the capital required, by borrowing more and more from money-lenders of the north Indian merchant castes and communities, who took on the responsibility of marketing the crop and the *gul*.

We will, therefore, first examine what roles these traders and moneylenders may have played at the initial stages of the engine industry, that encouraged its future development. Then we will examine how this small local industrial sector has reached a stage where it forms part of an international network of enterprises. We have depended mainly on the results of field surveys conducted in September 1997, and on one of the most important work done at the Shivaji University of Kolhapur on the engineering industry, *Entrepreneurship Development, An Interdisciplinary Approach*, published in 1987 by S.G. Bhanushali. The situations typical of industrialists dealing in diesel engines and the different phases of their career are illustrated by the cases of R, M, H, S and Ram Menon.

From the Cottage-Industry Manufacture of Gul to Industrial Sugar Mills

Commonly located in the corner of a field, the nineteenth-century equipment for the manufacture of *gul* consisted of at least one animal hauled mill (*ghana*) and a cooking vat with a capacity of 400-500 ls. Some 16 bullocks, 17 workers and several members of the village community, the *balutedar*, were required to make it work.[1] The manufacture of *gul* was of great social and economic importance (*Gazetteer Kolh.* 1960: 355), and it took on a ritual nature. Mills and sugar vats were seen almost everywhere (*Gazetteer Sat.*1885: 167) and in the region of Kolhapur, it was generally rich farmers or Gujarati traders who owned the equipment and who eventually hired it out (*Gazetteer Kolh.*1886: 158).

In the mid-nineteenth century the kingdom of Kolhapur was already known for its production of *gul* which reached around 3,000 t/year.[2] In 1881-2, sugar cane was cultivated on an area extending over 4,000 ha. Around 1945-6, 12,150 ha of cane went into the manufacture of *gul* and 800 into that of industrial sugar. The *gul* manufacturing plants were then using around 1,332 animal hauled crushers, 10,000 simple *moths*,[3] as also 740 motor driven pumps and 475 motorized crushers. In 1951-2, 18,900 ha were under sugar cane cultivation in the district of Kolhapur, and in 1953-4, 23 plants for manufacturing *gul* were registered under the Factory Act. A first industrial sugar mill, the Kolhapur Sugar Mills, was launched in 1932 (*Gazetteer Kolh.*

1960: 353). From 1942 to 1948, it produced 25,000 to 50,000 tonnes of cane per year, and in 1947, its plantations used 70 motor driven pumps for irrigation. But it was only after 1956 that other large industrial sugar mills came into being in the form of cooperatives.

Sugar Cane Farmers and the Gul Trade: The Case of R

In the nineteenth century, in the southern part of Maharashtra, money lending and usury were among the rare possibilities that those capable of putting by some savings could invest in. These were, in the rural areas, the landowners, large farmers and village chiefs, generally Marathas or Digambar Jains. In the urban areas this applied to some among those practising the liberal professions and some government officers (the latter in general Brahmins), and here and there, some moneylenders and traders who were often Gujarati and Marwari immigrants (*Gazetteer Kolh.* 1886: 42, 86). A similar situation prevailed in the less prosperous regions of Satara and Belgaum (*Gazetteer Sat.* 1885: 1811; *Gazetteer Belg.* 1884: 291). It was above all these large farmers and landowners who went on to develop the production of *gul*, and the immigrant moneylenders and traders were the ones who marketed it.

In 1895, the new trading area of Shahupuri was laid out near the recently built Kolhapur railway station. Shahu decided to locate there the wholesale market of groundnut and *gul*, and in 1899 he attracted traders towards it by granting them tax concessions and plots of land. The *gul* market of Shahupuri soon became the largest in the Deccan. The exports of *gul* (and of a little sugar) valued at Rs. 600,000 in 1894-5 soared to 3 million rupees in 1921 (Lathe 1924: 115 quoted by Sovani 1951: 134).

In 1938, following (Table 1) the recommendations of a Trade Inquiry Committee, several procedures of control as well as a system of licenses were imposed on the traders of Shahupuri. The data collected in 1945-6 by Sovani (1951: 135-41) show the division of work of the brokers and the role that the Gujaratis played among these.

The brokers (*dalal* or *kacha adatiya*), numbering 122 at the time of the investigation, used to give short term advances to the *gul* producers. But these advances were generally financed to the extent of 8-12 per cent by the commission agents (*kharetidar* or *pacca adatiya*), mostly Gujaratis, who worked for clients outside the town of Kolhapur.[4] Having got into debt with the commission agents, the brokers were sometimes obliged to sell them the *gul* below the market price. A cooperative society, the Kolhapur Cultivator's Purchase and

TABLE 1: BROKERS AND COMMISSION AGENTS IN THE SHAHUPURI MARKET IN 1945-6

Categories of agents (1946-7)	License (Rs/year)	No. of registered agents	Sovani's observations in 1945-6
No. 1 brokers	100	2 × 3 categories	Are 122 in all:
No. 2 brokers	50	according	52 Marathas, 42 Jains,
No. 3 brokers	25	to turnover:	27 Lingayats,
			1 Muslim
No. 1 Commission Agent	100		Are more than 200,
No. 2 Commission Agent	50	340 in all	majority being Gujaratis
No. 3 Commission Agent	25		
Weighmen	10	91	92
Transporters	4	22	NA
Porters	2	300	NA
Truck drivers	20	6	ND
Retailers	2	559	ND

Sale Society, registered in 1939, did indeed try to circumvent the moneylenders of Shahupuri. But, unable to recover the advances given to its members, it found itself on the brink of bankruptcy and was taken over in 1941 by the State Cooperative Department. After independence, the Registrar General for Money-Lenders assessed the advances for the production of *gul* of the commission agents affiliated to the Shahupuri Merchants' Association at 10 million rupees a year (Gazetteer Kolh. 1960: 395, 422) while those of the cooperatives only rose to 2.4–6 million rupees during the years 1949-50 and 1950-1 respectively. Some commission agents themselves had access to the resources available with organized banks, both private and co-operative ones (*Gazetteer Kolh.* 1960: 404).

Gul was exported mainly to Gujarat. Between 1934 and 1944, up to 70 per cent of the *gul* coming to Kolhapur was regularly exported to Kutch, Kathiawar, Baroda and Palampur (Sovani 1951: 143-6), and the rest, generally of not such a good quality, was sold in the Bombay Presidency and in the region of the present Karnataka. After independence, the exports of *gul* declined while remaining high all the same. According to the *Gazetteer of Kolhapur* (1960: 475), the exports to the Gujarat mainland and Kathiawar even jumped from 42.5 per cent to 50.1 per cent from 1952 to 1956.[5]

Thus, several merchants from the north owned cottage industry style installations for the manufacture of sugar, and their advances on the harvests contributed towards developing the cultivation of the cane. Later, the Gujarati commission agents dominated the *gul* market of Shahupuri, at least till the time when the large sugar mills and cooperative banks took over during the 1960s. It is likely that some big Gujarati merchants even tried to control the industrial production of sugar,[6] but few, like R below, ventured into the manufacture of diesel engines.

Originally from Jamnagar (Kathiawar),[7] the Rs traded in agricultural products or inputs like *gul* and fertilizers in the Kolhapur region. Formerly, says R, Kolhapur used to produce up to 4 million cakes of *gul*, a good part of which was exported to Gujarat, particularly Jamnagar and Kutch. However, the first industrial sugar mill of the district, started in the 1930s followed by the advent of large sugar cooperatives during the years 1960-5, led to a sharp fall in the production of *gul*. Moreover, under the aegis of leaders and politicians of the cooperative sugar lobby, the most famous of these being Vasant Patil,[8] Sangli became the main trading market of south Maharashtra, to the detriment of Kolhapur. It was in 1960, therefore, at the time when the cottage industry production of *gul* declined giving place to the industrial production of sugar, that the Rs set up in partnership an enterprise for manufacturing diesel engines, while continuing to carry on their trade in agricultural products and inputs.

Social Origins of the Engine Manufacturers

For his survey, Bhanushali took a sample of 125 units out of the 993 registered between 1947 and 1981 in the District Industrial Centre (DIC) of Kolhapur.[9] We summarize his results in Table 2 in which are listed the activities undertaken by those working in the engines industry as manufacturers of engines, manufacturers of spare parts for engines, 'job workers',[10] foundry workers and machine repair engineers. Those which do not directly concern this industry have been classified as miscellaneous.[11]

TABLE 2: SOCIAL COMPOSITION OF THE DIESEL ENGINES SECTOR

(*Sampling Bhanushali, 1987:120*)

Castes	Engines	Spare parts	Job work	Foundry workers	Repair engineers	Misc.	Total
Brahmins	2	5	6	3	1	5	22
Marathas	6	18	14	7	7	18	70
Other Hindus	0	0	4	1	1	3	9
Jains	4	4	1	4	0	5	18
Muslims	0	0	1	0	1	0	2
Christians	0	1	0	0	1	0	2
Others	0	0	1	0	0	1	2
Total	12	28	27	15	11	32	125

We note that:

- most of the industrial units carried on activities directly related to the engines industry;
- the members of the immigrant Gujarati and Marwari trader castes, with rare exceptions (the case of R) did not venture into industrial enterprises;
- Marathas, Brahmins and Jains were predominant in number;
- the proportion of manufacturers of engines was small, from which we can deduce that there were numerous and concentrated networks of interdependence;[12]
- the engine manufacturers were mainly Brahmins, Marathas or Jains;
- the majority of the manufacturers of engines, spare parts of engines, 'job workers' and foundry workers, were Marathas;
- although relatively few among them were manufacturers of engines, the Marathas were overall predominant in number;
- the backward castes and other 'other Hindus' were found above all in the 'job work' category;
- the artisan castes, eventually placed in the category of 'other Hindus', played practically no role. However, a number of Marathas, Brahmins or Jains had undertaken cottage industry jobs, as workers or managers of a workshop, although that is not their traditional calling.

Their proportion in the population being large, the Marathas are the most numerous among the farmers and dominant landowners of the Kolhapur region. They are in the majority in all the associations and cooperatives set up by industrialists dealing in mechanical engineering goods. The Digambara Jains are generally well-off farmers in the region (and not the Svetambara Jain immigrant merchant castes from Gujarat or Rajasthan). As Kolhapur has been (and to a smaller extent, continues to be today) an important centre of the anti-Brahmin movement formerly supported by Shahu Maharaj, the Brahmins have kept a low profile here. However, after reservations were instituted in government service during the 1970s, they have tended to send their children to technical education institutes and to set up industrial enterprises, as they began to find it difficult to enter into the jobs of their preference. The Muslims who are found today in small numbers in the engine manufacturing industry, are said to have taken to it right from its start. They often traded in semi-finished articles of iron before independence (*Gazetteer Kolh.* 1886: 208).

Those who experienced the Kolhapuri renaissance under Shahu Maharaj and their direct descendants, have been deeply influenced by it and it is from among them that several leaders of the cooperative movement have emerged, as well as the pioneers of the mechanical engineering industry. 'Persons born during this period of transformation when they came to the age of choosing an occupation, favoured largely independent ventures. . . . It establishes a firm relationship between the renaissance, the emergence of the middle class and the development of entrepreneurial talent with a gap of about a quarter century.'[13] But the impact of the Kolhapuri renaissance is not enough to explain the development of the diesel engine sector in the decade following independence (the *Kolhapur Gazetteer* published in 1960 hardly mentions it). For at this time, several other engineering industries were also developing in the rural zones elsewhere in India, as for instance in the Kheda district in Gujarat, and particularly in Punjab where the same kind of diesel engines as those of Kolhapur were beginning to be manufactured (Rutten 1995: 46, 48, 80; Gulati 1997).

There is a tendency to underline the diverse social origins of the industrialists. This was certainly true of the pioneers.[14] But subsequently, those who were, directly or otherwise, involved in the manufacture of engines came mostly from these same castes as the more well-off farmers, dominant landowners, village chiefs and indigenous moneylenders who were the first to be able to venture into the development of sugar cane cultivation in the nineteenth century.[15] It should be noted again that for the period under consideration, the untouchable castes practically did not participate in the industrial development of Kolhapur (Dahiwale 1989).

Born in 1933, M was the eldest of three brothers who have recently separated from each other. In 1952, after having worked for large engineering companies, like Coopers and then Kirloskar at Kirloskarwadi, his father borrowed Rs. 4,500.00 from a firm at 12 per cent interest to start a small mechanical engineering workshop in Kolhapur. The owner of the firm that gave him the loan was a Brahmin. But inter-caste relations were not a barrier, underlines M. His father became a client of this firm and bought tools and materials from it. The workshop was set up in a hut rented at Rs. 25.00 a month. It was equipped with a single horizontal lathe bought second hand, and the tools were sharpened on the neighbour's grindstone. M was then 19 years old. He had just completed his Secondary School Certificate and went to help his father in the workshop.

M began to work on the lathe in 1953. They undertook repairs to internal combustion engines, sugar cane crushers and centrifugal pumps. The business worked well, and by 1954, both loan and interest had been paid back. Around 1956, they had been able to put by Rs. 4,500.00 which was however not enough for the purchase of a second lathe, which cost Rs. 9,000.00, because at the time banks did not finance the small-scale industry. Fortunately, the National Small-Scale Industry Corporation granted 85 per cent of the required amount at 69 per cent interest, reimbursable over a period of 6 years. The loan application was accepted within a month and the lathe delivered a month later. M remained ever grateful to the government for this and he then helped other entrepreneurs desiring to enter into the business, to avail of similar loans.[16] In 1967 a machine to grind crankshafts was bought for Rs. 105,000.00. But all the customers were those living in the nearby areas and they were experiencing the effects of the crisis which was then affecting the diesel engines market. Today, M's firm employs a little more than ten people one of these being the workshop head.[17] The main building consists of two or three offices and a workshop. Fairly spacious, this latter harbours a large-sized computer controlled machine, some old lathes and a machine specially designed by the enterprise itself. M worked with his younger brother till 1996. Then they separated, and the younger one took away the milling machines from the workshop. As for the other younger brother, he has an enterprise in Belgaum and seems to have never worked with M.

FROM THE LOCAL TO THE GLOBAL

When the industrial take-off started, the artisans and small industrialists had no know-how or technical knowledge. Where and how did they acquire these? In the view of Bhanushali (1987: 29), these came from three main types of activities and workshops. These were the repair workshops for imported engines (among which were those used by the large Kolhapur Sugar Mill which started in 1934), the automobile repair workshops (the road network was developing rapidly), and the traditional metalworking skills. The data from industrial investigations available in the *Gazetteers* of *Kolhapur* of 1886 and 1960, as well as the results of those prepared by Sovani (1951) substantiate this view. But one can still wonder at how these various know-hows were coordinated in such a way as to lead to the manufacture of a diesel engine. In what follows, I will try to reconstruct the pattern of the starting off and development of an engineering industry by non-specialists while concentrating on the formation and the dynamics of networks of enterprises.[18]

The Phase of Acquisition of Various Techniques

It was under Shahu, during the Kolhapuri renaissance and a little after it, that the first institutes were set up for professional teaching (Edward Agricultural Institute in 1912; Rajaram Industrial School in 1920, Jaysingra Technical School in 1921) as also the first agricultural exhibitions (in Pune in 1926 and in Kolhapur in 1927, then in 1929), the first imported engines and the development of automobile transport (*Gazetteer Kolh.* 1960: 207). According to Graham, in 1854 there were in Kolhapur 40 generalist blacksmiths (who were neither cutlers nor gunsmiths, see Sovani 1951: 74). The first automobile repair workshop was opened in 1912. In 1926, Bal Krishna found no more than 26 smithies employing 17 persons in all and 9 workshop-stalls specialized in repairs of engines and employing 13 workers (Sovani 1951: 77). An industrial concentration and specialization was taking place. A circle of small engineering artisan employers and workers got constituted progressively from the starting point of stalls and workshops where traditional articles of common use, and others imported from Europe, were repaired. They were thus familiarizing themselves with various modern techniques while barely possessing the means to deploy them, except perhaps in the biggest workshops.

The Phase of Manufacture of Components: The Case of M

In 1947, Sovani listed in Kolhapur 25 metalworks employing 65 workers who forged, made casts and shaped, as required, still without machines. But there were also 16 general engineering workshops and 23 workshops specialized in the repair of internal combustion engines (1951: 74). The general workshops employed 94 persons in all and repaired various machines, bicycles, automobiles and diesel engines, of which they replaced and adjusted some spare parts with the help of lathes, drills and small tools, for customers coming from the entire Kolhapur region. The 23 engine repairing workshops employed 145 persons and each repaired on an average 100 engines a year. They manufactured spare parts on order with the help of equipment which continued to be simple. Their customers were mostly local but came sometimes from even 80 km away. It should be recalled however that in 1945-6, the cultivation of sugar cane and the manufacture of *gul* was mechanized to a small extent and that water for irrigation was drawn mostly with *moths*.

M illustrated with the help of drawings, the kind of difficulties that the manufacturers of spare parts had to surmount when crankshafts were required to be replaced.

> First of all, he said, we shaped the crankshaft directly in a large block of metal of simple shape. The rough-hewing operation was a long one; there was a large amount of metal scrap and moreover, these crankshafts very often broke. We understood then that it was preferable to get a piece close to that of the final crankshaft, forged by a *lohar* [traditional artisan blacksmith]. These forged crankshafts were then more solid.

Indeed, in a spare part of forged metal the crystals have a tendency to align in the direction in which they have been stretched, and what is called a 'fibrous' structure forms which confers properties of resistance to distortion which a part of the same shape that has been cast, cannot possess. In other words, in addition to the quality of the metal itself, the choice of the manufacturing process is decisive here. And without any technological knowledge nor a study of the material sciences, this choice was not an obvious one. The people had therefore 'tinkered' around looking for a solution, to begin with by experimenting with what seemed the most immediate processes. One could certainly illustrate other cases of laborious learning concerning pistons, piston rings, etc. These are matters of major difficulties which are experienced even today with recent technologies and which are avoided by manufacturing under foreign license.

The Phase of Gathering Together, Learning and Know-how

Once they had learnt how to manufacture the main components of the engines, the pioneers in engineering tried to manufacture a complete one. Towards 1934, the government of the kingdom invited S.Y. Kulkarni to manufacture an 11 horse power diesel engine on the occasion of the visit of the viceroy of India. It was the first manufactured in Kolhapur (Bhanushali 1984: 65-7). Several other pioneers also tried to manufacture an entire engine with the help of foreign designs, or by copying the engines or products imported by Kirloskars, Coopers and particularly Ruston.

> S.A. Patil tried to manufacture an engine on the basis of drawings prepared in England. His idea was to manufacture an entire oil engine under one shed. But the experiment could not succeed (towards 1951-52). Vishnupant Utkur copied Ruston prototype and became successful. Y.P. Powar tried to copy a Czechoslovakian model but failed and so turned to the manufacture of the Ruston type engine prototype and became successful. (Bhanushali 1984: 67-8)

Once the prototypes had been adjusted, an attempt was made to manufacture several engines in a single workshop, which implied that all the components would be gathered together there, tested, adjusted and assembled. One could then proceed according to two opposing principles: either manufacture all the components oneself, or get them supplied by other enterprises. Keeping in mind the small size of the enterprises which were almost all family ventures, and the small capital they availed of, and in view of the dispersal of the know-how over a multiplicity of workshops, some of which were already capable of supplying some good quality components, it was the second solution which was inevitable and was widely preferred.

Thus, when this same Y.P. Powar and two partners founded the enterprise PAKCO, this and another enterprise Autowork, were the first to promote sub-contracting in Kolhapur. They granted interest free loans to those who wanted to start a workshop, said M who, with his father, availed of this benefit. The borrowers, naturally, had to manufacture components, or conduct operations as demanded by their creditors.

As it turned out, it seemed a little as if the engines had been empirically rediscovered, or 'reengineered'. But while some pioneers and promoters distinguished themselves particularly in this adventure, its success was due finally to the formation of a collective agency which incorporated in the engines made by some producers the dispersed, as also originally disparate empirical skills of the multitude of its members, manufacturers of components and providers of miscellaneous services.

The Phase of Promotion of Sub-contracting Networks: The Case of R

The DIC registered the first manufacturer of diesel engines between 1951 and 1960, then another in 1961, and 3 other manufacturers in 1962 (Bhanushali 1987: 38-40). When R started his engine enterprise in the early 1960s, there were in all 18 engine manufacturers.[19] All were then producing the same type of Ruston Hornby engine whose patents had come into the public domain. All the components were then available with the enterprises and in the spare parts market from where even Ruston ordered its supplies.

But this market was, or has become, more highly organized than R makes it out to be. The 125 entrepreneurs in Bhanushali's sample were helped by, and they in turn helped, other entrepreneurs, relatives, friends and employees, to set up their own enterprise. Each of the 34 entrepreneurs promoted another entrepreneur, 36 others promoted two each and 11 three each (Bhanushali, 1987: 214). Out of the 125 entrepreneurs, 81 therefore promoted 139, out of which 124 met with success! The assistance from the promoters was of various kinds, but a common feature was that the promoter-entrepreneurs gave job work especially to the budding man, so that he was relieved of the worries of marketing his produce. In other words, numerous entrepreneurs were sub-contractors and job-workers who had at best only a limited commercial access to the spare parts market.

Formation of an Industrial District

The diesel engines sector has had the following characteristics typical of an industrial district (Nadvi and Schmitz 1998):

- The engineering equipment industrialists were mostly from Kolhapur and the region, and they belonged in the majority to some castes which shared a long tradition of neighbourhood and common social relationships. With few means at their disposal, they had collectively succeeded in manufacturing the diesel engines which have brought them fame.
- Their enterprises were almost all structured round the family or were partnerships which themselves brought together members of a single family, if not the same caste. Many among them had relationships of interdependence with others, either because the heads of the enterprises were related to each other or because they were each others clients through sub-contracting.
- The first industrial zone, Shivaji Udyam Nagar, was promoted by the Kolhapur municipality in 1941-2. The workshops which were earlier dispersed throughout the town, came together there and tended to form a centre for technical exchanges and links of complementarity. Several of the pioneering enterprises of the Kolhapuri industry have maintained there till today a workshop, and even their headquarters, despite the establishment of two new spacious industrial zones outside Kolhapur.
- There was a strong and age old tendency to form groups working in cooperation. Moreover, the sugar cooperative movement developed alongside the engine industry. The industrialist entrepreneurs formed several associations in Udyam Nagar where they are still active. These are the Kolhapur Engineering

Association (founded in 1947), the Kolhapur Udyam Cooperative Society Ltd. (1957), the Kolhapur Productivity Council (1958) and the Kolhapur Chamber of Commerce and Industry (1983).

By and large, Kolhapur's small industry has often availed of the incentives offered by government authorities. After independence, when, under the impetus of the First Five-Year Plan, the demand for motorized pumps increased along with the acreage under cultivation, two measures contributed particularly towards the boom in the engine industry. These were firstly, the ban imposed by the central government on the import of diesel engines in 1950-1 (Bhanushali 1987: 30), and secondly the grant of easy *taccavi* loans to farmers for the purchase of engines of the Kolhapuri type, less expensive than others. These measures marked the start of the golden age of the Kolhapuri diesel engine which was to continue till the early 1960s.

Is it because this small industrial centre, concentrated then at Udyam Nagar was a highly friendly one that it is still recalled with such great emphasis? Social relations, it is said, are no longer what they were, and workers today demand more salaries rather than attempt to learn respectfully from their bosses how to set up enterprises on their own! It is doubtful whether the atmosphere of this old industrial area has been able to perpetuate itself in the vast new industrial zones.

CRISES AND DIVERSIFICATION: THE ARRIVAL OF THE LARGE EXTERNAL PRINCIPALS

Several crises were experienced by the engineering industry (1962-3, 1971-2, 1977-8, 1981-2, according to Bhanushali 1987: 171). The engine sector was particularly affected by the first, when several states stopped standing surety for the *taccavi* loans on account of the difficulty they experienced in recovering them. The *taccavi* loans had greatly promoted the sales of the Kolhapuri engines which were inexpensive and sturdy, but copied and adapted from models which were already technically outdated at the time when several entrepreneurs began to manufacture them. The diesel engines of Kirloskar and of Coopers, of another type and more effective, supplanted those of Kolhapur (Bhanushali 1987: 31-3).

According to R, during the 1965-70 period, when vertical engines of the Peter type began to be manufactured, which turned faster (1,500 t/mn instead of 350-500 t/mn), and which were more compact and

TABLE 3: NUMBER OF MANUFACTURERS OF ENGINES IN OPERATION, ACCORDING TO R

Years	Number of manufacturers	Types of production; engines/year
1960	18-19	Ruston Hornby type
1980	10	Peter type
1990	3-4	
1997	3 (R., X. and Y.)	R: 18-20,000 engines/year X: 2,000 Y: 2,000

lighter, many of the 18 or 19 manufacturers of engines present on the scene during the 1960s, could not follow suit. The diesel engines industry underwent several other crises which forced most of the manufacturers to discontinue their activities or to switch over to something else in one way or another.

The most typical among the paths chosen by the enterprises in Kolhapur for surmounting the crisis were those of techno-commercial development, giving up of earlier activities and conversion to others, widening of the clientele, sub-contracting for large principals, and also 'stagnation'.

Technical and Commercial Development: The Case of R

Like other manufacturers, R produced a range of horizontal engines of the Ruston type of 5 to 19 HP which he marketed under his brand name till 1966. From 1968, however, he was among those who managed to manufacture vertical engines of the Peter type. The production of the horizontal engines was transferred to another establishment started in Ahmedabad (Gujarat) and R took on the status of a private limited company. But R was to experience another recession in 1969. His losses soon mounted to the level of his capital, and from 1970 to 1980, the Kolhapur enterprise was in great financial difficulty. The credit that his sub-contractors gave him and exceptional overdrafts from his bank enabled him to pursue his production and concentrate on the development of new markets. An agreement was signed with a subsidiary of Tatas which resold R's engines under its brand name. In 1982, an improvement in sales enabled him finally to pay off the debts of the enterprise, and in 1987-8, another marketing agreement concluded with a Bombay firm enabled him to optimize the utilization of his production capacity. In 1989, a range of four new portable engines which R had designed, developed and had patented, was launched. And in 1992, R entered into a marketing agreement for these portable engines with Kirloskar Oil Engine Ltd. (a Pune manufacturer of diesel engines). Orders began flowing in from all over India and in 1993, a new factory was built in one of the new industrial zones close to Kolhapur. The production capacity reached 40,000 to 50,000 engines a year. Today R employs 250 persons and has dealings with 70-80 sub-contractors, some of whom supply exclusively to him.

At the height of the difficulties of 1970s, R continued to receive credit although he was practically in a state of insolvency. It is likely that the situation was a fairly dramatic one at the time since people seemed to prefer to give him further loans rather than lose everything. But there is also the fact that at that time, R already had some technical and commercial plans under way, and in all likelihood it was this which enabled his creditors to pin their hopes on a revival of the enterprise. R was the only major survivor among the engine manufacturers because of his technological investments, even though he had to get his products marketed by other large engine manufacturers, some of whom sold his engines under their own brand name.

Relinquishment and Conversion: The Case of H

Several enterprises which relinquished the production of engines, began to manufacture agricultural machine tools and equipment and spare parts for sugar cooperatives whose numbers had increased.

The senior H started in 1947 a small engineering goods workshop and in 1965 he started with a partner the manufacture of horizontal diesel engines which he sold under his own brand name. It was perhaps out of anxiety to keep a check on the quality of its products that the new enterprise tried to manufacture them to the largest extent possible on its own. Unfortunately, in 1972, the diesel engines market collapsed and the enterprise had to sell its written off machines as scrap. The enterprise survived by doing job work for other local firms, but not for the automobile industry. Today, the small group of H's enterprises works essentially for the twelve sugar cooperatives operating in the Kolhapur district. He employs 11 to 13 persons and has a turnover of 1-1.2 million rupees.

Diversification and Search for New Clients: The case of M

Other enterprises which had not till then ventured outside the region of Kolhapur, tried to procure orders from Maharashtra and elsewhere in India.

For M and his father, business progressed well enough to enable them, as we have seen, to purchase in 1967 a machine for grinding crankshafts costing Rs. 105,000. But as the customers were all from the neighbourhood, they also were experiencing the cyclic depressions which were affecting the local diesel engines market. To protect himself against this, M tried, right from 1968, through correspondence, to find customers in other regions. He succeeded in finding one in Hyderabad and another in Bombay. He went to meet the latter, from whom he received some orders. This effort at diversification of sources of orders continued during the 1970s. M found three in Bombay, one for punched pieces, another for components of injection moulding machines for plastic material, and another for components of cinematographic projectors. Despite the enormous diversity of the work to be executed, the financial situation remained sound. But the enterprise was unable to grow.

Sub-contracting for the Large Principals and Stratification of the Networks: The Case of M

A number of enterprises accepted orders for components which some large principals producers of engines or of motorized vehicles had moreover already begun to place in Kolhapur right from 1960 (Bhanushali 1984: 72). The sub-contracting networks got further stratified, while the principal-sub-contractor relationships evolved in terms of new strategies of management and organization. These drew their inspiration from Japan, having been introduced in practice in India around 1984 with the launching of the Maruti-Suzuki factory in Gurgaon.[20]

In the 1980s, M found other sources more compatible with the technical capability of his enterprise and which he has kept to this day. These are Mahindra and Mahindra (Jeeps and tractors), TELCO of Jamshedpur (trucks), Maruti Udyog of Gurgaon (cars), then Bharat Earth Movers (earthmoving equipment) and Tata Cummins who place orders for large quantities of spare parts conforming to the QS 9000 norm. These principals keep a close watch over their sub-contractors. They grant them technical assistance, give them drawings of machining frames, but do not advance them any money. Mahindra came to conduct an investigation, TELCO assigns marks to its 'Vendors', Maruti came to inspect the workshop, Tata Cummins sent instructors to train M's staff.

M subcontracts some rough hewing and preliminary cutting work to about ten other workshops which are located mostly in the old industrial area of Udyam Nagar. Some workshops work exclusively for him, others receive orders from one or two others also. Their level of education is variable. Some speak English, several among them have even studied at the Kolhapur Engineering Institute. M chooses them for their competence and their sense of organization, but it has happened that one of his large principals has also insisted on approving them himself. M tends to help and checks his sub-contractors also a little like he himself is helped and checked by those who place orders with him. He gives them drawings and gauges, systematically notes their qualitative and quantitative performances. These practices have become very common in Kolhapur, specifies M.

As the automobile industry is going through a period of recession (September 1997), M has less work. To continue to keep a part of his employees and his machines running, he has kept on the rough hewing work at the expense of his sub-contractors who, in technical terms, serve as 'shock absorbers'. M acknowledges that his sub-contractors are in a subordinate position. But, as he comments, their position is just similar to his, on a lower level.

The Small Sub-Contractors and 'Job-Workers': The Case of S

The enterprise belonging to M stands at an intermediary level in the sub-contracting networks. It experiences the pressures of its large principals, so as to adapt to the technically demanding and complex norms which they themselves try to maintain. It contributes in turn towards passing these on to its own sub-contractors as can be illustrated in the case of S.

S was born in 1934. In 1964, after having worked in two engineering workshops, he took a loan to buy a lathe and founded his own workshop in the area of Udyam Nagar. He then received some components to shape, and did job work for some enterprises. S, who speaks English quite well, says that he has studied engineering, and his sons are doing business studies in a college in Kolhapur. The enterprise possesses 'two-three' lathes and 'four-five' milling machines. In normal times, according to S, it employs 30 to 40 people and has a turnover of around 1.5 million rupees. S shapes uncut connecting rods for smithies for some 'OEMs'.[21] They come reportedly from Punjab (tractor rods), from Uttar Pradesh (Maruti Udyog), and from Gujarat. S tells us mournfully that the activity of his enterprise has made more or less no progress since it started.

ACCESS TO THE GLOBAL MARKET FOR COMPONENTS

Some entrepreneurs were quick to understand that the development of the engines industry, and particularly the vehicle engines industry, could lead to the creation of a wide market for high technology components. But since liberalization in 1991, and in 1993 for the automobile industry in particular, the large pan-Indian market for automobile components has also become a challenge for the larger international constructors and suppliers of equipment. What role do these players, the Indian government and our industrialists of Kolhapur desire to play in it, and above all can they face up to it?

The large international automobile industry is in the process of systematically reorganizing its division of work on the global scale. This reorganization has, directly or otherwise, consequences for some tens of thousands of production units, from the biggest to the smallest ones. It involves mainly:

- the concentration of the large international constructors who tend to circumscribe their field of action to activities considered to be of strategic importance (research, development, international marketing, global organization of work, standardization);
- the reduction of the number of manufacturers-suppliers of sub-assemblies and of systems and an increase in their specialization at a high technological level of conception and realization;
- the reorganization of the relationships between major constructors, their main suppliers and their sub-contractors through a just-in-time organization as regards logistics, supply networks and production;
- the worldwide geographic distribution of the different categories of suppliers and sub-contractors according to techno-economic criteria of efficiency, and other political factors;
- the organization of the networks of suppliers and of sub-contractors in many tiers, and the setting up of appropriate measures of control at each level.[22]

After the success of the Maruti enterprise launched in 1983-4, and particularly after the liberalization of 1991, the larger Indian engineering enterprises tried increasingly to fall in line with this model, generally by concluding minority partnership agreements with large worldwide constructors (Ford and Mahindra, Fiat and Premier Automobiles Limited, Mercedes and Tata, Toyota and Kirloskar, Hindustan Motors and Mitsubishi or General Motors) and with large manufacturers of systems which are often connected to them (Delphi Automotive System and General Motors, Visteon Automotive Co. and Ford, Magneti-Marelli and Fiat) and which also came and established themselves in India, or else developed some already existing establishments, despite an economic situation that was deemed to be uncertain.[23]

The Indian government has imposed on constructors of vehicles the condition of utilizing a minimum quota of components manufactured in India and of exporting a part of their production. But as the Indian enterprises have great difficulty in conforming to the specifications of foreign constructors, the latter tend to encourage their own suppliers to come and join them in India. This is so, among others, for the constructor Hyundai Motor India from Korea, around fifteen of whose Korean suppliers have opened establishments in India by entering into partnership agreements with Indian firms.[24] In this way, the quality of the components and of the vehicles produced in India is getting closer to international norms and these can be more easily exported. The large constructors are interested in the Indian market and moreover they desire to make India one of their bases for the export of components.

The worldwide strategies of division of work involve an increasingly strict coordination of the processes of manufacture and a worldwide uniformity of quality of the products (Cabanes 1996). The norms of the International Standard Organization (the ISO 9000 series), to which relatively few Indian small and medium enterprises can conform, have now been excelled by those called 'QS 9000' which the three large American manufacturers of Detroit are practically in the process of imposing on a large part of the world market. Only some Indian manufacturers of components, among these being Menon Piston Ltd. of Kolhapur, are capable of producing in accordance with these norms.[25]

M shares his office with his son who has joined him after two years of technical training. He has been busy for six months with analysing the QS 9000 norm which Tata has asked them to implement. This norm, which concerns all the operations, all the control and all the control devices, involves a thorough statistical processing of the results and the periodical standardization of the measuring instruments, the templates and gauges, in accordance with international procedures of reference. It necessitates from its users a good level of technical and theoretical qualifications which, as M acknowledges, have gone out of the reach of non-technicians, including himself.

Norms of this kind can moreover be supplemented by others which go to the extent of specifying certain modalities of the relationships which the tier one suppliers can have with those of tier two[26] (as we have seen M's principals took an interest in his relations with his own sub-contractors). The degree of conformity to these quality norms is synthetically assessed by the proportion of rejected parts per million (ppm). Thus, Nissan claims that in Japan the rate of rejection is 15 ppm and it requires of its suppliers a maximum rate of rejection of 200 ppm, a rate which has become an international benchmark.[27] But the Indian manufacturers of components, with the exception of some,[28] have much higher rejection rates, going up to 30,000 ppm.[29] This is a big handicap which will force the majority among them to settle for lower levels of sub-contracting networks which the large Indian manufacturers and their foreign partners are also setting up in order to carve a place for themselves in international markets.[30]

Tata Industries, which aims at becoming the main supplier for the large manufacturers of international vehicles, has promoted the setting up of TACO (Tata Auto Components Systems).[31] TACO has signed more than 15 collaboration agreements with leading approved international manufacturers of components, and is considering the establishment, in several stages, of a hundred units in large cities such as Pune, Bangalore, Chennai and Delhi. These units would be distributed over two tiers. Those of tier one would have technically highly competent foreign partners, and those of tier two would be manufacturers of basic products having Indian partners. Proceeding in accordance with a similar strategy, Hindustan Motors has classified its suppliers into four categories in a hierarchy in accordance with their technical level and the relations that they have forged with foreign firms.[32]

Industrialists of Kolhapur: The Case of Ram Menon

South Maharashtra has become an industrial zone for the sub-contracting units of the large makers of Indian engines and vehicles, and in particular for those of Pune,[33] which itself, with Chennai, Delhi and Mumbai, has become one of the large centres of Indian automobile engineering.

The Maharashtra Industrial Development Corporation (MIDC) has promoted two new industrial zones near Kolhapur. In Gokul-Shirgaon, 491 buildings have been allotted, and a large number of the 627 buildings in Shiroli have already been occupied.[34] Moreover, Kolhapur contains several old industrial zones like Vikram Nagar, and the old area of Udyam Nagar which still accounts for a good 100 small and large industrial units. In 1997, the Kolhapur Engineering Association, which has its headquarters there, listed 490 members, of which 133 were foundries installed in Kolhapur and its new industrial zones as also at Sangli, and in the neighbouring smaller towns of these two administrative centres. In the district of Kolhapur alone, in addition to 14 sugar mills and 10 export-oriented cotton spinning mills, there are reportedly 7,000 small SSI enterprises, and 100 units which supply their products on varied contractual bases to TELCO (trucks), Mahindra and Mahindra (tractors and Jeeps), Maruti Udyog (cars), Ashok Leyland (trucks and buses), Bajaj (scooters and *rickshaws*), and Kirloskar (diesel engines, compressors, cars).[35] The engineering industry of Kolhapur has also diversified, particularly with the setting up of the Manugraph Industries Ltd., a large enterprise which manufactures printing equipment and which has its own specialized sub-contractors. But most of the enterprises work for the makers of engines and motorized vehicles.

The living symbol of the development of Kolhapuri mechanical engineering equipment is most certainly the large industrialist and self-made man, Ram Menon.[36] His *curriculum vitae* specifies that Ram is the president of the Menon Group (a group made up of the totality of the family enterprises), the managing director of Menon Piston Ltd. and the president of three other Menon companies. He is also the president, director, trustee, magistrate, promoter, etc., of local and regional associations or organizations which have relevance to the activities of his enterprises.[37] Appointed special executive magistrate, he is, besides, the president of the Kolhapur Institute of Technology, elevated to this position by the industrialists of Kolhapur in 1984. He is a member of the Council of the Private Education Society and a member of the local Rotary Club.

Born in 1929 in a family of wealthy farmers, Ram joined his elder brother, Chandra, who had set up a small workshop in Kolhapur, described as a 'job work unit'. Then, in 1965, Ram launched his own car reconditioning workshop and from 1971 he started manufacturing pistons for diesel engines. With the help, considered today as substantial, of Kirloskar Cummins Ltd.,[38] Menon Piston succeeded in supplying its products to large manufacturers of diesel engines and to the automobile industry, among these being the three large companies of Kirloskar diesel engines, the large car manufacturers (Maruti Udyog, Mahindra and Mahindra, TELCO) and manufacturers of tractors (Escorts, Eicher, Gujarat Tractors). In 1997, the Menon Group was made up of 13 companies and firms of varied importance; it employed 2,300 persons and it had a turnover of 1 billion 500 million rupees.

Some of Menon's clients who have played a capital role in the development of the group have been able to, or can even still, absorb by themselves a large share of the production capacity of the Menon factories, and in order to free themselves from their hold, the Menon family cannot but set their sights on widening their clientele to extend it to the pan-Indian and the international market. To achieve this objective, they have entered into cooperation agreements with foreign firms of repute (with Nippon Piston Ring Co. in 1976, Sakura Kogyo Co. Ltd. in 1982, Izumi Industries Ltd. in 1996), and have got their reliability certified by quality control organizations of international repute (ISO 9000 and 9002, QS 9000 certificates, etc.), or by their largest clients 'Best Vendor Performance' by Maruti Udyog in 1994, 'Ship to Use Status' by Kirloskar Cummins in 1995; 'Self-Certified Vendor' by Kirloskar Pneumatics in 1996), or again by some professional associations (National Quality Award, instituted by the Auto Component Manufacturers Association).[39]

It did not take Ram long to understand that the supply of highly technical components for engines and automobiles had a greater future in India than the other avenues of diversification that the local mechanical engineering sector offered. He has amply participated in the saga of the diesel engines of Kolhapur, and his large family, the Menon Group testifies to the fact that this saga has indeed taken place. Originally from Kerala, Ram has become a true son of the soil and its most prestigious representative.[40]

THE SAGA AND ITS HIGHLIGHTS

To conclude, after having summarized the saga of the diesel engines, we shall attempt to bring out its highlights in terms of relationships between networks and territories.

The inhabitants of Kolhapur owe to Shahu Maharaj the initiation of the social and economic development of the region. Under the Kolhapuri renaissance, some pioneer entrepreneurs from various castes tried to construct diesel engines the demand for which grew to the extent that the Gujarati merchants of Shahupuri could develop markets for the export of the *gul* produced locally.

It was the entrepreneurs of the subsequent generation, their origins mostly in the dominant local Maratha, Jain and Brahmin farming castes, who set up the diesel engine industry in Kolhapur. Their numerous workshops formed an assemblage of a highly collective nature in Udyam Nagar, an industrial district, within which the relationships were well-knit, cooperative and even warm. With the advent of the large sugar cooperatives, this was the golden age of Kolhapur's diesel engines.

But these Kolhapuri engines were only adaptations of engines which were already technically obsolete even as compared to others being manufactured in Maharashtra during the same period. Not concerned with modernization of their products, nor with finding outlets for them in larger markets, the industrialists in this area soon saw themselves forced to become sub-contractors for other engine manufacturers. With the passage of years, the region became little by little one of the large sub-contracting zones for the Maharashtrian and later the pan-Indian industry for engines and motorized vehicles.

After the liberalization of 1991, and particularly since 1995-7, the large foreign manufacturers, who aim at making India a base for the production and export of automobile components, have begun to impose their norms and their ways in the organization of the networks of supply. But even a large Kolhapuri industrial group such as that of Ram Menon remains small as compared to the big manufacturers of Indian systems.

At present it would seem that the Indian automobile engineering enterprises will occupy only a subordinate position in the worldwide division of work organized by multinational firms. This is so for reasons similar to those which prevented the Kolhapuri engines industry from developing, these being the small size of the enterprises, the lack of capital and above all, in our view, technical inadequacy.

To the extent that it is possible to make a judgement keeping in mind the limits of this study, the saga unfolded in three phases corresponding to three different configurations of spatial relationships. During the first and third phases, two systems of economic organization in networks, one predominantly agricultural and the other industrial, found themselves being set up in supra-state spaces while during the second phase, the industrial district was formed within the protected economic space of the national Indian territory.

In the first phase (of Shahu at the turn of independence), the development of the engine manufacturers' district was due to the conjunction in Kolhapur of material and human factors related to spaces of different scales and natures:

- on the local scale (the kingdom of Kolhapur): the soil, favourable for the cultivation of sugar cane grown mostly by Maratha and Jain farmers, was irrigated to advantage by drawing water out of wells
- on the regional scale (British India): merchants from Gujarat were attracted to Kolhapur
- on the intercontinental scale (Europe and British India): techniques imported from the West were progressively adapted by the Kolhapuri farmers.

But this remains too sketchy to enable the portrayal of the relationships in space as actually experienced by the main players, members of castes separated from each other by differences in socio-religious customs, languages and callings. Indeed, the spaces of the identity references of these players are those through which their caste networks cross, which have been woven out of different logics of action for conducting their activity. These networks do not coincide with each other, nor with the territories of the political entities in which their members carry on their activities. It needs to be specified that the kingdoms of Marathas and Brahmins, with many enclaves, were not mutually exclusive. The Digambara Jains, found in large numbers in Karnataka, represent generally their own religious space, which distinguished them from the Hindus, by itineraries of pilgrimages they undertook right up to north India. And the Gujarati networks extended from East Africa to Malaysia while crossing through north India, where they were often subordinated to the British.

Quite often, one of these networks was predominant in one of the agglomerations of the present Maharashtra. Thus, Pune is reputed to be a city of Brahmins (it was the seat of the powerful Peshwa Brahmins who attracted their caste associates there) and even till the 1990s, the city of Kolhapur was considered as the Maratha capital, a rival to Pune (Shahu had been a leader of the anti-Brahmin movement), whilst in Bombay, in business circles, the majority of businessmen are still Gujaratis.

Governed by their respective centres of gravity, these networks are nonetheless travelled by 'their members from 'the top downwards' and from 'the bottom upwards' in accordance with a logic dependent on their social status. Rich Gujaratis who have emigrated to Africa remained members of the community of their ancestral village where they used to return to participate in festivals, while even today, some

Marathas of noble lineage, active in the sugar industry in Sangli, go in search of spouses of an equivalent lineage, to Tanjore (in Tamil Nadu, former seat of a small Maratha dynasty).

This first type of economic organization in which producers who are members of specific peasant or artisan castes depend on supra-state merchant networks to market their production, has been common.

In a second phase (from independence to the 1960s), the former Indian empire was restructured. New states were created by separating the Muslim majority provinces (the two Pakistans), abolishing the kingdoms (more than 500), annexing the last colonial trading posts (Goa and Pondicherry), creating regional states on linguistic bases (the State of Bombay created in 1956 was subdivided in 1960 into Maharashtra and Gujarat), and redefining administrative sub-divisions (the district of Sangli was carved out of that of Satara). On the whole, by creating, in the likeness of the Western nations, states as politico-administrative entities organized in a hierarchy that tend to be culturally homogeneous, a logic of territorial sovereignty was more or less successfully imposed on the various spatial networks.

The industrialists who manufactured engines benefited from the measures accompanying the policy of substitution of imports and of the development of agriculture followed by independent India. On the one hand, the import of diesel engines was banned in the country, and on the other hand, agricultural loans were granted at the districts level by the states to promote in turn the purchase of low cost but sturdy engines.

But a decisive crisis occurred as soon as several regional states stopped granting loans. Farmers then preferred to purchase more efficient engines, among which were those being manufactured in Pune by the Brahmin industrialist Kirloskar. The Kolhapur industrialists had soon to remain content to work for this firm through sub-contracting. The engine industry which had developed for the purpose of supplies meant for the local clientele, got integrated little by little in the wider sector of the Maharashtrian and then the national engineering industry.

During this same period, the Gujarati trader networks got restructured over the national territory while their expatriate branches tended to migrate towards America and Europe (for instance the refugees from Uganda in 1972) rather than return to India.

During the third phase (from the 1991 liberalization to the present), protectionist barriers have been partially removed. Foreign companies are investing in India, and the former manufacturers of Kolhapuri engines are once again finding themselves in a subordinate position in the hierarchy of the sub-contracting networks. Among the industrialists, the relationships of intra- and inter-caste interdependence have practically disappeared, giving place to techno-economic relationships between enterprises that could be considered as almost neo-feudal.

The trader networks of emigrant Indians (the 'Non-Resident Indians' of Canada, Great Britain and Africa) are evolving to cover a wider field of action than that of the former British Empire and they are making investments in industry. Their caste associations are tending to federate on the Indian and global levels (opening up of Internet sites).

From the first to the third phase of the saga, the transition has been effected from an economic organization in supra-state networks to a different economic organization in which networks of firms and enterprises tend to delocalize and transcend administrative and political limits. *A posteriori*, the coming into being of the industrial district of diesel engines may appear as a transitory stage in the movement towards the globalization of capitalist economies. And this movement can very often profit from the local developments which nurture it, as it has done in the case of the small diesel engines district, a fine adventure launched by the enthusiastic sons of peasants who have rightly attempted to perpetuate its memory, even though aware of its final outcome.

NOTES

1. The *balutedar* is the equivalent in Maharashtra of the *jajmani* system in north India. It needs to be underlined that there are two categories of specialists, some called by names of technical functions, and others by the name of the reckoned/alledged profession of their caste, or by the name of their caste itself. The place for crushing becomes the 'evening resort of all the village' and the patron farmers give cane, whether in the form of juice or sugar, in generous quantities, extending up to 20 to 25 per cent of the production, which attracts a horde of beggars (*Gaz. Kolh.* 1886: 178-9; *Gaz. Sat.* 1885:167).
2. Graham, *Statistical Report,* 1854, p. 221, quoted by Sovani, ibid., 1951, p. 123.
3. Large leather pouches hauled by several pairs of bullocks to draw out the water.
4. It is to be noted that a division of work of this kind, between brokers coming from the local farming casts (Maratha, Jain, Lingayat, etc.) and commission agents immigrants from the north (Gujarati, Marwari, etc.) is found again in

1985-6 in the spice exchange market of Sangli, where the main commodity of transaction is turmeric. The former were expert in evaluating the state of the produce bought from the farmers, the others sold them to the firms in Pune, Bombay and in north India (Lachaier 1989: 82).

5. The data in figures available for the overall period 1934-56 comes from different sources and is heterogeneous. See also the data of the Merchants' Association of Shahupuri for the years 1944-5 and 1945-6, which indicates smaller quantities. Registered in 1927, by 1946-7 it had 353 members, which included and most of the merchants of Shahupuri (Sovani 1951: 290).
6. The *Gazetteer of Kolhapur* (1960: 353) mentions the starting of a first industrial sugar mill, the Kolhapur Sugar Mills, in 1932. But it says nothing about the Godavari Sugar Mill which is said to have been started around 1936 in the district of Kolhapur. It was shifted to Karnataka in the 1960s on account of the unfavourable political environment: 'Private agricultural farms were nationalized and the cooperative movement accelerated the process of final closure' (according to a publicity brochure of the Somaiya Group received in 1996 and an interview with Sh. K. Somaiya). Moreover, according to Mulraj Ruparel, two Kutchi 'sugar barons' are famous: Gordhandas Jadavji Ruparel who launched the Kolhapur Sugar Mills and Karamshi Jethabhai Somaiya (father of Sh. K. Somaiya). See Mulraj Ruparel, 'Bijun Kutch Mumbai', *Kutch Tari Asmita*, special issue of *Kutchmitra*, Vishesh Prakashan, Bhuj, 1995, pp. 243-58.
7. There was no indigenous merchant caste in Maharashtra. A first wave of merchants invited by the Peshwa Bajirao I arrived from Gujarat in the eighteenth century. A second batch arrived from the Muslim kingdom of Jamnagar (Saurashtra) after 1918 (Lachaier 1989: 82 ff.).
8. Right from 1940, Vasant Dada Patil tried to control the networks of informal credit by setting up credit-cooperatives (P. Lachaier 1989: 74 ff).
9. Bhanushali's results are proportionately similar to those of the list of the DIC.
10. The category includes very small workshops and small sub-contractors doing piecework, or on order, and which rank generally at the lowest level of the tiered sub-contracting networks.
11. This category includes manufacturers of metallic furniture, agricultural tools, sugar machinery, machine tools, etc.
12. 'Most of the units were engaged in ancillary production and job work' (Bhanushali 1987: 45).
13. Bhanushali 1984: 61.
14. Bhanushali's version is not unambiguous: 'All first generation (1948-58) entrepreneurs in Kolhapur were in this way self-made persons. They all were invariably artisans. . . . Of significance, they were local people coming from the lower strata of the society. Economically, they were from the middle class.' How is one to understand the contradiction here between 'lower strata' and 'middle class'? Several obituaries in the journal of the Kolhapur Engineering Association, *Kolhapur Udyog Varta*, are those of small

industrialists belonging to the artisan castes (see the special Dipavali issues of 1993, 1995 and 1996).

15. However, we find no Lingayat, although several did later start some foundries, in Sangli for instance.
16. At that time and till recently, Kolhapur was a bastion of the complex Maratha-Cooperatives-Congress and had easy access to public funds. But 'when the Shiv Sena-BJP alliance came to power in 1995, one of its first targets was the very politically powerful sugar region of West Maharashtra' (*India Today*, 15 September 1997).
17. This was a period of recession, and the workshop was practically empty when I visited it in September 1997.
18. Bhanushali, who examines the engineering industry in general, and who tries to capture the development of the industrialists as efficient entrepreneurs, has suggested a carving out into entrepreneurial periods. After a period of pre-conditioning of the beginnings, the Kolhapuri renaissance, there have been: (1) the era of the internal combustion engines 1948-58, and the first generation of artisan entrepreneurs, (2) a second phase of entrepreneurial development, the crisis of the diesel engines and the arrival of the large principals, and (3) the era of diversification during the 1970s. I distance myself here from this pattern whose validity I do not deny, in order to concentrate on the matter of formation and evolution of the networks of enterprises.
19. They probably did not get themselves registered as such with the DIC, as it became compulsory only after 1971.
20. Narayana (1989) suggests a pattern for the sub-contracting networks in which the very small workshops do not appear. See also P. Lachaier, 1989 and 1999.
21. In the jargon of the profession, Original Equipment Manufacturers, that is to say enterprises approved by the big constructors to supply them with the initial starting-off equipment or parts, or to supply the market with what are called 'original' or 'approved' spare parts. As it happens, small sub-contractors prefer not to mention the intermediaries who come between the prestigious big firms placing orders, the OEMs and themselves. S did not want to allow us to visit a workshop deserted by a part of his workers who had been retrenched.
22. According to K. Lederer, president of the German manufacturers of ITT systems, the structure of the global market will tend to comprise 25 to 28 large constructors who together would supply more than 40 million clients via 50,000 distributors; their suppliers would be distributed over four levels of hierarchy into 2,500 manufacturers of systems, 30,000 manufacturers of components and 250,000 other suppliers of levels 3 and 4 (Lederer 1995).
23. According to *Business India* (19 April–2 May 1999, 'An Imminent Shakeout', pp. 113-16), the firm Delphi-General Motors has the following characteristics: turnover of 28 billion dollars, 200,000 employees, 169 factories in 36 countries, and in India an overall investment above 3.5 billion rupees in Bangalore, Noida and Gurgaon. The firm Visteon-Ford, for its part, has invested 6.5

billion rupees in Pune and Maraili Nagar (Chennai). According to *The Economic Times* ('Global Battle on Indian Turf', 23-9 April 1999), Visteon-Ford Motor Company had a turnover of 18 million dollars in 1998, and was the second largest supplier of systems after Delphi, and had operations in 21 countries with 81 factories and 81,000 employees. According to its President P.C. Mulhauser, 'we will be tier I suppliers and they (Indian small and medium ancillary units) will in turn be tier II suppliers. . . . Worldwide, vehicle manufacturers are shifting their risks relating to investment, design, engineering and assets to suppliers. That's where global players like Visteon come in.'

24. 'Korean auto-part makers track Hyundai with tie-ups', *Economic Times,* 6.12.97.
25. 'The Auto Components Bazaar', *Indian Auto,* October 1997, pp. 33-6.
26. *Automobile Management,* December 1995, 'Ready for New Challenges', p. 3. This is the case with the MS 9000 norms of Ford which supplement the QS 9000.
27. *Automobile Management*, December 1995, p. 42.
28. Sundaram Fasteners has been recognized as the best supplier of the year from among the 30,000 suppliers worldwide of General Motors ('GM Award again for Sundaram Fasteners', *Motor India,* October 1998, p. 24).
29. *Auto Review,* October 1997, ibid., p. 33.
30. 'The [Indian manufacturers] may not remain tier one much longer . . . most of them will become tier two or even tier three suppliers . . . Even the strongest . . . cannot match the money power of the international giants . . ., (*Business India*, 19 April–2 May 1999, pp. 113-16, 'An Imminent Shakeout').
31. 'The Auto Component Bazaar', ibid., October 1997, p. 37; and 'Tata Autocomp well ahead with JVs plan', *The Hindu,* 12 December 1998.
32. 'The Auto Component Bazaar', *Indian Auto*, October 1997, ibid., pp. 36-7.
33. 'Pune: India's Auto Capital', *Business World*, 17-21 October 1998, pp. 99-103.
34. According to the registration lists of the MIDC, Kolhapur, received in September 1997.
35. 'Give better deal to Kolhapur, Sangli', *The Hindu*, 9 July 1996.
36. According to the documents received in the course of an interview with Ram Menon. See *Menon Pistons Ltd., A Profile,* 1997, and *Biodata of Mr. Ram Menon,* as also according to Seshan 1996.
37. Such as the Chamber of Commerce, the Industrial Zone Association, the Association of Manufacturers of Diesel Engines, the Kolhapur Engineering Association, the Confederation of the South Zone Engineering Industry, the Confederation of Indian Industry, the Productivity Council, the People's Cooperative Bank of Kolhapur, the Maharashtrian Engineering Cooperative Society.
38. The American firm Cummins manufactures diesel engines in Poona. Before joining up with Tata, it had a partnership with Kirloskar.
39. This pan-Indian association has some 400 of the largest suppliers or sub-contractors of the automobile engineering industry.

40. It may be recalled that R is from Gujarat. He and Ram, among the most remarkable of the entrepreneurs of the Kolhapuri engines industry, are not natives of Kolhapur.

REFERENCES

Bhanushali, S.G., *Entrepreneurial Development in Engineering Industry in Kolhapur,* Kolhapur: Dept. of Economics, Shivaji University, 1984.

——, *Entrepreneurship Development (An Interdisciplinary Approach),* Bombay: Himalaya Publ. House, 1987.

Cabanes, R., 'Notes sur l'entreprise et la qualité au Brésil', in Cabanes, R. and Lautier, B., eds., *Profils d'entreprises au Sud. Les politiques de gestion face aux cultures et aux statuts,* Paris: Karthala, 1996, pp. 253-64.

Dahiwale, S.M., *Emerging Entrepreneurship Among Scheduled Castes of Contemporary India, A Study of Kolhapur City,* New Delhi: Concept, 1989.

Gazetteer of the Bombay Presidency, *Belgaum,* ed. J.M. Campbell, vol. XXI, Bombay, 1884; *Kolhapur*, vol. XXIV, 1886; *Satara,* J.M. Campbell, vol. XIX, 1885.

Gulati, Mukesh, *Restructuring and Modernisation of Small Medium Enterprise Clusters in India,* Report, UNIDO, 20 November 1997.

Humphrey, J., Kaplinsky, R. and Saraph, P.V., *Corporate Restructuring, Crompton Greaves and The Challenge of Globalisation,* New Delhi: Sage, 1998.

Karnataka State Gazetteer, *Belgaum District*, ed. S. Kamath, Bangalore, 1987.

Lachaier, P., *Firmes et entreprises en Inde, La firme lignagère dans ses réseaux*, Paris: Karthala-IFP-EFEO, 1999.

——, 'Réseaux marchands et industriels au Maharashtra. Castes. sous-traitance et clientélisme', Ph.D., EHESS, Paris, 1989.

Lathe, A.B., *Memoirs of His Highness Shri Shahu Chhatrapati Maharaj of Kolhapur*, 1924.

Lederer, Klaus, 'The Global Automotive Village, Only 25 Global Players?', *Automobile Management International*, Germany: Landsberg, December 1995, pp. 32-3.

Maharashtra State Gazetteer, *Kolhapur District*, revd. edn. of vol. XXIV of the original of the Bombay Presidency, Bombay, 1960, *Sangli District*, Bombay, 1969.

Nadvi, K. and Schmitz, H., 'Industrial clusters in less developed countries: review of experiences and research agenda', in Cadène, Ph. and Holstrom, M., eds., *Decentralized Production in India,* Delhi: Sage Publications and French Institute of Pondicherry, 1998, pp. 60-138.

Narayana, D., *The Motor Vehicle Industry in India,* Centre for Development Studies, Occasional Paper Series, Delhi: Oxford & IBH, 1989.

Rutten, Mario, *Farms and Factories, Social Profile of Large Farmers and Rural Industrialists in West India,* Bombay: Oxford University Press, 1995.

Seshan, S., 'Quality Drive, The Menon group', *Business India*, 12-15 August 1996, pp. 81-2.

Sirsikar, V.M., *Politics of Modern Maharashtra,* Bombay: Orient Longman, 1995.

Sovani, N.V., *The Social Survey of Kolhapur City,* Gokhale Institute of Politics and Economics, vol. I: 'Population and Fertility', 1948, p. 83; vol. II: 'Industry, Trade and Labour', 1951, p. 346; vol. III: 'Family Living and Social Life', 1952, p. 330.

'The Price of Progress': A Large Planned Project with Different Players

Gérard Heuzé

BIRTH DURING THE EMERGENCY

The beginning and the evolution of the mining and industrial conurbation of Singrauli (Madhya Pradesh) is a remarkable illustration of the way the associations between the global and the local have melded, within the framework of 'the largest democracy in the world', into the various types of interactions between the upper and the lower strata of society, as well as into the disparate city-countryside relationships. Set up in 1960, this region is flourishing today. The framework of its development was designed during the period of the Emergency (1975-7) when the central administration strengthened its prerogatives and power on the local level found itself considerably diminished. Networks of wheeler-dealers, whether within political circles or otherwise, stood in for the official hierarchical orders.[1] In the matters of industrial policy and development, this period was characterized by the cohabitation of three trends which, during a crisis, often intensified pre-existing features.

The first was the predominance of rhetoric and populist dictums, summarized in the 'Twenty-Point Programme' of Indira Gandhi. The second was the upsurge of technocracy, the reasoning having come from the top and the technical considerations being expected to take precedence over a parliamentary democracy which had been thrown to the winds, over the lower echelons of a particularly disregarded people's representation, and even more over the wishes of those coming to terms with development plans. In Nehru's time, a small body of engineers and administrators inspired by these principles had begun to assert itself. It increased its prerogatives under cover of the state of Emergency. The last trend was the active collaboration of the government with large private firms. The Maruti project[2] notably was launched, and *in tandem* with the ban on strikes, imprisonment of assertive trade union leaders and the freezing of salaries, the rulers gave other important concessions to employers, among these being the take-over of numerous sick textile mills and the grant of subsidies to enterprises shifting their production premises towards the rural areas. In the name of law and order and efficient functioning of the infrastructure, the large entrepreneurs supported the emergency, which explains partially the magnitude of the wave of strikes which accompanied in several regions the advent to power of the Janata Party.[3]

The period of the Emergency thus saw both the intensification of the trend towards populism to the detriment of market principles (particularly as regards the land-owning regulations) and the germ of what were later to be called the 'reforms' or the 'opening up'. The desire to export, which is considered to be of recent origin, also existed. It was, for instance, during the Emergency that a national programme was launched for promotion of the export of knotted carpets, a niche which has today become a major source of revenue. This activity is centred around the regions of Mirzapur and Varanasi (Benares), just a little to the north of the Singrauli zone, and some of those working at home in the framework of this programme live in Singrauli itself.[4]

BIRTH OF AN INDUSTRIAL REGION

Singrauli became the pole of attraction for development projects in 1960 when Nehru inaugurated a kilometre long barrage on the Rihand River, around 200 km to the south of Varanasi. Situated in Uttar Pradesh, this structure led to the submersion of 330 sq km of territory and the displacement of 80,000 peasants. The 30 km long dam straddles the border between Uttar Pradesh and Madhya Pradesh, at this time respectively the most populated and the largest of the provinces of India. During public meetings, the peasants had received the assurance that the benefits that irrigation brought them would be sufficient compensation for their misfortune. It is difficult to judge today to what extent the officials of the central government, those of the local governments and the employees of the National Hydro Power Corporation (NHPC) were aware that it was a fool's bargain Inferior lands were distributed at the expense of forests, and the compensations given were miserably inadequate. There was no further mention of irrigation thereafter. No village was electrified. On the other hand, the Birla group installed an aluminium factory at Renukot, very close to the barrage so as to use the major part of the electricity produced (300 MW). As the barrage experienced falls in production, the private firm got a thermal power station of 600 MW, constructed utilizing the water of the reservoir for its cooling process. The coal came from the nearby plateau where the prospectors of the National Coal Development Corporation (the first public firm in this sector[5] set up in 1956) had brought to light the existence of large reserves of bad quality coal. In 1975, the players on the ground were therefore only the central government, two of its firms and one large private enterprise. The local population could well have been non-existent. This being the attitude, the state of confusion in which these new entrants found themselves and their lack of preparedness, along with a certain technological fervour for 'development for development's sake' was added on to the distance already separating the anglicized strata of society from the rural folk. There was also the arrogance of government officials, inherited from colonial times. The provincial governments did have prerogatives at their disposal and they had interests to defend, but their influence was inadequate.

In 1976, faced with a serious shortage of electricity, the government set up the National Thermal Power Corporation (NTPC). Created to overcome the shortcomings of the provincial governments and of the existing power stations, it was constructed in the name of productivity with a very probable eye on centralization. It aimed at improving two ratios considered unfavourable for the country's economy. These were the number of megawatts per employee, which were intended to be doubled, and the rate of utilization of the production capacities. This latter was particularly low, being around 45 per cent in the public sector.[6] The NTPC was assigned the objective of exceeding 75 per cent. The collieries had been nationalized in two phases, in 1971 and 1973, particularly because the private sector proved incapable of putting in the enormous investments required in this sector (Kumar 1982).

The Birlas expanded their aluminium factory. A factory for producing soda and another for carbon black came to supplement the industrialization of Renukot. Right from 1977, the NTPC started the construction of a 2000 MW thermal power station named Shaktinagar ('the city of energy'). Several other installations were planned. There was talk of an integrated development plan with the end objective of producing 25,000 MW of electricity based on 70 million tonnes of coal. It was then that the situation of the inhabitants of the region became dramatic.

The NTPC took over large portions of land to instal its power stations, its areas for the spreading of ash and the estates for housing its staff.[7] An outline plan was launched in 1977 by the NTPC and the National Planning Commission. A special development zone was set up spanning the two states and integrated within a regional development plan based on industry. No investment was provided for agriculture, an activity in which 90 per cent of the population was involved before the establishment of the power stations. The planners had deliberately ignored pre-existing institutions such as the *panchayats* (village councils) and the *zilla parishads* (district councils).[8] The administration entrusted with development remained, however, embryonic. The plans aimed at perfecting it under the guidance of the Planning Commission evolved incessantly, the successive versions tending to contradict each other.[9] The project managers had to adjust to these variations. They paid no attention at first to the problem of displaced persons, which was attended to by ill-qualified and unmotivated people. Right from 1977, the first rehousing zone ('rehabilitation colony') was set up on sterile land. This measure was accompanied by the allocation of unskilled work to the heads of the landowner families. The managers of the projects and the administrators felt they were being extremely generous.[10] Certain of their right, and moreover, of the legitimacy of their intervention, they repeatedly displaced entire families and groups of populations. In 1988, a group of families assessed at about one-twentieth of the population had been obliged to destroy and then reconstruct their houses five to six times. A large mass, estimated at 30,000 persons (one-third of the population) had done it three times.

The new authorities of the Rihand Valley could not, for several reasons, understand the gravity of what was happening. The managers, in accordance with the ways of the public sector (devised for the purpose of preventing corruption) could not remain in one place for more than two years. This was so also for those in charge of law and order and high officials. No project in charge could have, had he wished, gone to the roots of what was going to become a conflict. The region did indeed have three members in the regional legislative assemblies of Madhya Pradesh and Uttar Pradesh. They had not been done away with as the village councils had been (it is true that the zone voted for the Congress party, which dominated the political scene in both provinces). But these seats were reserved for 'tribals',[11] which fact led mostly to weak and easily manipulable persons being co-opted. No political mediation could therefore make up for the indifference or the inadequacies in management shown by the administration. There was also the existence in the latter, of a pioneering spirit justifying its indifference towards social matters by putting forward the plea of having put to good use a territory that was wild and barren before industrialization (brochure published by the Birlas in 1988).

The peasants had never been happy at the measures taken for 'their' benefit. These people, who were attached to their own ways of living, readily considered that they had been despoiled by a foreign power. Their positions became more and more violent.[12] They had been tricked and were being tricked again since each displacement was accompanied by promises of a coming stability. The development of the mines, ensured by Northern Coal Limited (NCL),[13] and the setting up of rail and road infrastructure, aggravated the situation. The creation in 1978 and 1981 of the Special Area Development Authorities (SADA), expressed itself, notably in Madhya Pradesh, by a quickening in the pace of certain projects and the downslide of some others. There was one in each province. They were territorial entities provided with all administrative and political powers, whenever other overriding powers did not enter into the picture. The NTPC never accepted their tutelage. For the people, inclusion in a SADA meant the abolition, on a larger scale, of local representative institutions, for the benefit of the discretionary power of the engineers of the public works department and of administrators appointed by the provincial governments. While the same ways prevailed in the factory towns of the NTPC and the mining colonies, the managers of the NTPC were more efficient and less corruptible.[14] This worsening trend greatly widened the gap between the displaced persons and those in charge of the projects.

The record for the years 1977-83 was noteworthy on the plane of mobilization of men and capital. Almost thirty thousand people had emigrated from the rural areas of Uttar Pradesh, Madhya Pradesh and Bihar. At the place where the villagers had earlier been rehabilitated two giant thermal power stations arose. The social landscape was controlled with an iron hand by institutions which lacked neither funds nor incentives. A pioneering spirit, as if this valley had been an 'unpeopled land',[15] still drove the more motivated among the officials, who were qualified men[16] coming mostly from large cities and availing, on account of their distant stationing, of substantial allowances. Their disregard for the peasants was added on to their fear of the latter's primitive way of life, to create a mindset justifying the superiority complex of the migrants. No great contradiction showed up between the major players on the scene.

A new category of not very visible persons and who were not represented, made its appearance with the massive recourse to precarious migrant labour. Its constituents were much more discreet than the people who had been evicted, although they had been relegated to the margins. Contrary to the latter, they were indispensable to the implementation of the projects. Workers belonging to this category were lodged in the interstices, ravines, marshy zones or on the hills.[17] Trade unionism was either in its embryonic stage or non-existent. The over-exploitation of the forest which, for different reasons, public enterprises, wood sellers and the local population indulged in, led to no debate despite the promulgation in 1982 of a new forest policy meant to save the Indian forests as also to secure returns from them.

THE APPEARANCE OF NEW PLAYERS AND THE GREAT INCREASE IN THE LEVELS OF INTERVENTION

It took five years for awareness to dawn that there was need for a reappraisal of this paradise of state productivity[18] and, to a smaller extent, of private business (sale of wood, sub-contracting, illegal transportation). In 1988, the NTPC and the Uttar Pradesh State Electricity Board (UPSEB) began the construction of four power stations (Shaktinagar, Rihand, Vindhyachal, Anpara), the first being the only one to supply electricity. The setting up of a grid for the distribution of high tension current had increased the problems of displaced persons, driven away also from those areas where they had found refuge, on account of the commissioning of nine of the eleven open-cast mines.[19] Even before a single kilogram of coal had been extracted, this latter being located at a depth of a 100 m, vast expanses of land were required for depositing the rubble, as the mine face extended over an area of 30 km. The construction sites proved to be much more expensive than anticipated. On the national scene, Rajiv Gandhi's government had spent a great deal on arms and on subsidies for fertilizers, electricity, etc., as vote-catching devices. The salaries of government employees had been doubled. Even though the NTPC called on a growing mass of casual employees, among them a large number of qualified persons, all the costs were soaring, particularly those on the purchase of technology. In order to become competitive and to ensure an optimal production, the thermal stations had called on Anglo-American (Shaktinagar), Russian (Vindhyachal), British (Rihand) and Japanese (Anpara) advisers. This was profitable only at the time that invitations for bids were made. Subsequently, with the continuous devaluation of the rupee, this recourse to the services of foreigners became very costly.

The NTPC, for whom the Government of India had stood surety, as also the coal mines, had to take loans. An application was made to the World Bank in 1987 for a loan of a billion dollars. The latter accepted, in view of the 'exemplary' manner in which the construction was being executed. The Corporation had the reputation of completing its constructions within the schedule and of exceeding the initial estimates less regularly than was the case with regional institutions. The pressure on the forests then became the centre of an extensive debate. The Bank found itself subjected to pressure by American ecologists, warned by Gandhian 'philanthropists', particularly Prem Bhai, a local personality associated with a network of NGOs, and R, a New Delhi personality known among circles critical of the development process. A question was even even in the House of Representatives of the United States of America. The Bank then insisted that the borrowers that take note of the environmental problems (discharge of ash, acid rain, toxic waste, deforestation). It also mentioned in internal documents the 'sufferings of the people'. In 1988, EDF International won the contract for conducting an investigation concerning the environment, and secondarily the socio-economic problems created. Numerous players intervened. The reasonings brought forward and the interests defended became more and more complicated. It was no longer a matter of only working for the progress of the nation.

In 1985, the displaced persons (*udvasit*) succeeded in surmounting their extreme divisions, of villages and castes, and joined together to form a committee of defence, soon coupled with an Organization of

Workers displaced by Development Projects, the *Pariyojna Udvasit Shramik Sangathana.* Up to 50,000 persons demonstrated against the policy of the large companies, to obtain jobs, or to protest against the government. Since 1960, an entire generation had experienced forced displacements, calamitous rehabilitation and unkept promises. Small groups of educated volunteers, generally from the upper castes, came and asserted themselves. As these persons had received an education in Hindi, the national language and also the official language of the two concerned provinces, they were handicapped in their discussions with the federal administrators, the planners and those in charge in the public sector companies. Most of these latter knew Hindi but feigned to know only English, in order to assert their personal status or to defend the interests of their enterprise. A group of lawyers and of migrant journalists or sons of migrants therefore served as a link for some local politicians and representatives of Indian NGOs. The atmosphere in which each played his role was one of mistrust. With a hundred thousand people having arrived in the region (a hundred and fifty thousand in 1991, three hundred thousand were expected in 2000), the development of power and industrial growth had become a major stake. Political circles woke up to this awareness with some delay. Between 1985 and 1991, several attempts were made to create a regionalist movement. However, there was unanimity over one thing, and that was opposition to the party in power. In 1991, for the first time in its history, the region voted in men of the Bharatiya Janata Party (BJP).

It was at this time that the EDF International team produced its report on the situation in Singrauli. It was a long text, drawn up for the NTPC but over which the World Bank had repeatedly tried to exert pressure.[20] Its 'socio-economic' portion underlined the gravity of the situation, particularly with regard to displaced persons and migrant casual workers, the absence of coordination between the institutional players and the internal spirit of colonization[21] which still prevailed in the region. It is not certain that the NTPC paid any heed to these observations. On the other hand, it received all the instalments of its loan. It was even able to ask for another one.

NEW LEVELS AND NEW RELATIONSHIPS?

The venture thus no longer remained a 'saga of progress'[22] orchestrated by the public sector and seconded by some dynamic private firms. In 1988-90, the aluminium factory in Renukot was modernized and its capacity was doubled. New players emerged, as well as new alliances between these players, corresponding to new stakes and fields of intervention. Among the former figured the local defence organizations, various groups claiming to represent the 'poor' and the 'tribals', national and local political parties, committed journalists, trade union workers and the displaced persons union, the internal organizations for conciliation within the enterprises, the Indian sub-contractors recruiting casual labour, the SADAs, the Uttar Pradesh electricity department, the two provincial administrations (outside of SADA), the (national) forest department, the Indian Railways, the multinational power firms and, if required, the governments of their countries of origin, Indian NGOs such as Prem Bhai's Ashram,[23] some North American NGOs and some international financiers dominated by the United States of America.

All this was accompanied by a multiplication of the ways of reasoning underlying the actions of the players. At no time had the scene come down to being a struggle of the forces of progress against an untamed nature, which portrayal had been so popular with the public enterprises as with private firms, nor to the struggle of the 'enlightened elements of the nation against feudal, reactionary and caste-ridden forces', the second pertinent position adopted when it was the 'social' elements that came to the fore. The members of the local administration and numerous officials of the large enterprises were at least as attached to caste identity and to the new ideas that arose therefrom as were the peasants of the region, but it was their own caste and their family networks which interested them. In the public sector and in this specific region, the logic of profit combined with that of caste has always been important. Sub-contracting agreements were mostly entered into with members of the families of the officials or of administrators or persons belonging to the same circles. In the private sector, profit was the primary motivation of these establishments mobilizing an enormous amount of capital, while the caste networks partially shaped the relations between entrepreneurs and officials. The small bureaucracies in place ferociously defended their prerogatives, as they would territories, by subscribing to the procedures of organizational status. The logic of 'assistance', which combined forced eviction with an unequal redistribution of minor benefits presented as generous gifts, was at the centre of the relationship between the (very) large and the (very) small players, the large firms and the displaced people. It was the most glaring demonstration of an inequality that widely disregarded democratic relations. Physical violence was not absent either. It was the outcome generally of the dispossession of the indigenous folk and was rarely countered. It was resorted to by the police, the militia of the factories and of the Central Industrial Security Force,[24] by labour recruiting agents and sometimes the evicted indulging in illegal acts (pilfering of wood) or, more rarely, openly refusing the promises and injunctions of the public sector firms.

In 1991, it had become difficult to find a way out of this situation with the result that the planning of projects was whittled down while new bodies came to the fore and numerous conflicts broke out. The organizations for the defence of the inhabitants of the region, the trade union (Pariyojana Udvasit Shramik Sangathana) and the peoples' committee (Lokit Samiti) were gaining recruits in two main sectors, the rehabilitation colonies, sorely lacking in facilities and more and more congested, and the peasantry in the Waidhan (or Baidhan) plain, a fairly prosperous agricultural zone threatened with total extinction by the construction of buildings to house the administration and other infrastructure. The core of the local movement was composed of sons of peasants recruited from the factories or the mines, who knew and depended on the adversary. The endangered peasantry was divided between the desire to refuse industrial expansion from the standpoint of idealizing rural life, and the desire to obtain permanent jobs in exchange for their land. A small number of people in the camps held such jobs and their regret over the land they had given up became gradually an argument for presenting demands. The majority who did not have these jobs spent the larger part of their time begging for them or demanding them. These jobs were given only to (large or medium) landowners.[25] This was in compensation for the loss of the property they had declared. The peasants who cultivated land without owning it, in which category about half of the initial population fell, and the poorest (30 per cent) found themselves without any compensation. The landowners possessing documents to this effect, proved to be particularly easy to buy off since they were entitled to jobs. It was nevertheless they who became the most committed among the elements who opposed the large planning and production bodies. They were the torch-bearers of local pride and culture.

The organizations representing the people of the area were born out of the remains of the former local democratic institutions. As earlier underscored, the first thing the SADAs had done was to dissolve the village *panchayats* and make the transition to an administrative management of the kind that already existed in the factory township of Renukot or in the official housing complexes constructed by the Renusagar power station. The private sector acted like the public sector and would not hear of elected municipalities. The positions adopted by Rajiv Gandhi, followed by the BJP, in favour of local democracy had no effect on the region. In 1989, 1991 and 1995, the region covered by the SADAs extended finally over an area of 1600 sq km, corresponding to 180 villages.

The annihilation of the local democratic institutions and of their means of intervention gave rise to mixed feelings. The members of the lower castes and the agricultural workers, and these categories often coincided, felt that they were in fact better off without the village *panchayats*. This opinion was due to the fact that the payment made for casual work was twice as much as for agricultural labour. These groups had moreover no nostalgic memories of the *panchayats* from which they had excluded. The members of the upper castes and the well-off peasants on the other hand, regretted the loss of a representation which although it did not yield any tangible result, did add to their prestige and a sense of identity. Those involved in the representation of the 'locals' by way of the trade unions or of the movements like the defence committees, criticised the public enterprises and the state, but they could conceive of no other situation either. The return to the system of local representation would have deprived them of the substance of their arguments and, in a number of cases, of their employment. They had crossed over from the way of thinking of notables accustomed to consensus to the logic of demand which made them, in the wider sense, clients of the state or of more important politicians, or turned them into more or less aggressive people availing of state assistance.

They maintained moreover diverse types of relationships with the non-governmental organizations devoted to the environment and to the cause of the social condition of the locals, hesitating between solidarity, being kept under domination, and reciprocal manipulation. The Delhi organizations and those of the United States held a comparable position, but the former mistrusted the latter. An ambiguousness of a different kind presided over their relations with the World Bank. This latter, through its special envoys made up of sociologists and anthropologists, on several occasions made use of the situation of the evicted persons to try to influence the decisions of the Indian government, the Planning Commission, or the NTPC. Its representatives offered more money in exchange for the right of inspection. It is not possible to say if the institution served its own interests as an organization, the interests of a nation-state (the United States[26]) or a group of influential states, or again its international reputation as a lender or as an advisor in matters of development. It is not unlikely that it was a combination of all these various preoccupations. As regards displaced persons and their descendants, it was noted that on several occasions, the representatives of organizations (in 1990 particularly), as well as individual peasants, attempted to access the World Bank by short-circuiting the NTPC (which managed the rehabilitation colonies), the Indian government (which was at the origin of the planning and had stood surety for the enactments that were implemented to the detriment of the evicted persons) and the provincial states. The representatives of the Bank appeared to be flattered at these attitudes but they refused any direct negotiations.[27]

The district councils (*zilla parishads*), whose financial means had tripled with the establishment of the factories and mines, proved to be totally inefficient. They were ill-prepared for these transformations and the higher powers agreed to relegate them to the background. The dominant players as also the intermediaries (NTPC, NCL, Indian sub-contractors) easily bought over the politicians at the local level. All they had to do was to invite them to the VIP guest-house of the NTPC at Shaktinagar where excellent meals were followed by drinking sessions.[28] Attempts to use conventional political channels had earlier been made to counterbalance the activities of the SADAs which depended on the state governments. This had resulted in more intensive efforts by the rural 'development blocks', institutions managed by the provinces and the *zillas* into which the central government and enterprises such as the NTPC could inject funds so as to influence their functioning but without much result, because there was nothing to start from and neither the state nor the large firms were keen to achieve anything. The disastrous state of the infrastructure and of irrigation in the proximity served the interests of the large enterprises, both public and private, by encouraging a large number of peasants to enter the casual labour market. Getting the local employees to compete with the migrants who had come from afar seemed a rather good proposition. The centres of the new townships were covered with posters glorifying the quantities of megawatts, the progress achieved and the NTPC, while the permanent employees put up a hidden resistance.[29] Casual labour and the introduction of new techniques compensated for this resistance, for the demonstrations of the peasants, and for political pressures. In 1995, the best hospitals and schools of the region were those of the NTPC, collieries and private institutions functioning in Renukot. There was also a central government school at Shaktinagar. SADAs could not compete.[30] In the centre of the zone managed by the SADA of Madhya Pradesh, the town of Waidhan which some planning projects had anticipated would have a million inhabitants by the year 2015, had barely 30,000 in 1996. Its infrastructure remained inferior to that of Renukot, which dated back to 1965.

CONFLICT AND ORGANIZATION OF THE PLAYERS INTO A HIERARCHY

One of the most apparent among the characteristics of the situation at the start of the 1990s, in relative contrast with the one that prevailed at the end of the Emergency, was the enormous increase in conflict. There were conflicts not only between the local population, the large public enterprises and the other agents responsible for evictions (railways, SADAs, etc.) but tension had multiplied even among the large enterprises. Two crucial confrontations took place for very different reasons. There was first of all an image-building quarrel between the leaders of the collieries (NCL) and those of the NTPC. The former no longer used casual labour; they organized their rehabilitation colonies better and evicted fewer persons, mainly for technical reasons related to the situation of the mining zone over a forested plateau.[31] In addition, they only took the land on lease for 99 years, whereas the NTPC purchased it compulsorily for ever, the NCL tried to promote the argument that its functioning was more compatible with social norms. Those in charge of the NTPC reacted with extreme bitterness,[32] but the conflict remained a symbolic one. The other conflict which was a very concrete one, opposed, then brought together the NTPC and the collieries (its ups and downs were relayed by the press). The NTPC produced power which it distributed all over India. It did not sell to individuals but to the State Electricity Boards. These latter, which also have their own power stations, then enjoy a monopoly over its resale. The SEBs had always proved to be incapable of getting their rural clients (80 per cent of the population of Uttar Pradesh and about 70 per cent of that of Madhya Pradesh) to pay their bills. As they were not able to get a large part of their urban clients to pay their dues either, they found themselves, as consumption increased, unable to pay for the current supplied by the

NTPC. For its part the latter refused to pay for the coal it used. There followed a succession of episodes bringing such great tension between the two enterprises that the transit of coal to the power stations was stopped several times.[33] After efforts at conciliation through meetings under the aegis of the SADA and the Planning Commission, the NTPC and the collieries joined together to put pressure on the SEBs. In the case of the Anpara Power Station of Uttar Pradesh, the worst of the defaulters, the situation was simpler since it was a matter of a conflict between the collieries and the provincial Board. The power station was forced to stop production for several months. This conflict led to others. The large public enterprises put on the mat the politicians in the provinces for carrying out populist measures at the expense of the nation.[34] The centre, for its part, accused the state governments of bad management and of squandering away their resources.

At other levels, conflict increased manifold. In 1995, the entire special development zone was still cut in two by the Uttar Pradesh–Madhya Pradesh border. The workers of Shaktinagar, who worked at the power station (situated in Uttar Pradesh) could find themselves blocked by the road octroi barriers between their residences and their place of work. This was systematically done with trucks carrying goods, whereas passenger vehicles used to make a long detour so as to not pay the octroi tax, one of the rare resources of the *zillas*. The NTPC and the collieries suffered less from this practice than people in general or small enterprises. Their transits not being affected in the name of 'national interest', they did not intervene directly. The SADAs had been created to unify and coordinate development efforts in the zone, but as there were two of these involved and they experienced sometimes contradictory pressures coming from Bhopal and Lucknow, they embodied often an additional divisive element. The Madhya Pradesh SADA was moreover infinitely richer and better organized than the one of Uttar Pradesh. The latter, in keeping with the general destitution of the province, hung on to its prerogative of collecting octroi dues, which forced its 'other unequal partner' to do the same.

When the question arose of the profitability of the public sector and of liberalization of exchanges in the framework of the 'opening up' to the international market, another conflict emerged. It was discovered that numerous sub-contracting contracts had been over-valued, some billed work simply not having been done.[35] There followed a campaign of 'clarification and clean-up' which, in 1993-4, pitched the public enterprises against their sub-contractors, beginning with the smallest and (politically) least protected ones among the latter. It was not the politicians but the administrators in the collieries and the NTPC who had made corrupt deals with the private sector. The press and public opinion, as well as the administrators of the large firms, however once again accused the politicians, because of the (national) conflict setting the congress party, in power at the centre, against the Bharatiya Janata Party (BJP) in the majority in Uttar Pradesh and with a very large following in Madhya Pradesh. This accusation also illustrated an old internal cleavage within the state apparatus in India, between, on the one hand the 'technocrats', the men of the state of Emergency, and on the other hand the elected representatives suspected by the former of being at the root of inefficiency, weakness and corruption.

All the conflicts between Indian partners were ambiguous. They pitted against each other parties who, considering the logic of the projects and their overall position, should have had very close relationships, or else they set against each other enemies who could not have been able to survive without their adversary or the framework which provided the mechanism for the settlement of their confrontation, considering that the state and its international financiers had done everything to make the situation irreversible. It was inconceivable that the NTPC, the displaced persons, the new immigrants, the provincial governments, the SADAs or the SEBs should disappear from the scene. Only the private sector could have considered the possibility of shifting its worn-out installations, at least before their modernization in 1989.[36]

The interventions by foreign agents evoked mixed reactions. On the one hand, being foreigners they were seen to be non-partisan and objective and were therefore widely appreciated. On the other, the same agents, because of their foreign origin, were assumed to be indulging in unfriendly acts and hence demonized. The World Bank did not need the NTPC for its survival. The converse was less true. American ecologists did not depend for anything on the Government of India. The small local players placed them right at the top of the hierarchy, with the most odious role being played by the lowest ranked labour sub-contractors who were close to the casual workers and highly involved in local politics.[37] The big players such as the Government of India or the major political parties (BJP and Congress) could negotiate at close quarters with these external powers and they largely succeeded in getting round them. Yet it was from among them that the most serious accusations were made against the intervention of the distant players. They were accused mostly of exploiting underdeveloped countries, of under mining the independence of the country and of collusion (this concerned the United States of America) with rival Pakistan. The most frequently heard argument was that the fate of the local people was only a pretext used by these very distant interlocutors who were hardly involved in the matter, to gain ascendancy and derive political mileage and material gains.

It appears that the intervention of distant agents enabled the local players, in ever increasing numbers, to indulge in limited, but conspicuous, activities of subversion of the hierarchical order, established at the beginning of the industrialization of the region. It had become more complex as the political context in India evolved and with the appearance of new players in the field, without much change in the criteria. In 1991, the casual workers and the tribal people who lived by exploiting the forests were at the lowest rung of the hierarchy.[38] Then came the ordinary peasants, the displaced persons, then the factory workers (represented by their trade unions). Among the administrations present, effectively capable of intervening in the situation (to pollute, displace, or not displace), the NTPC and the collieries were on top followed by the SADA of Madhya Pradesh, then the railways, the provincial states (other administrations), the large (public) sub-contracting enterprises, the Uttar Pradesh and Madhya Pradesh SEBs, and finally the small sub-contracting enterprises and the local defence committees. There was a hierarchical order even within the police. The Central Industrial Security Force was superior to the police forces of Uttar Pradesh and Madhya Pradesh, the special forest guard being between the two.

The intrusion of the World Bank, American NGOs and New Delhi NGOs made it possible for representatives of groups such as the tribes to receive sustained attention in the newspapers, and for the committees for the defence of displaced persons, to negotiate as equals with representatives of the large enterprises. This did not last long. It seems that the interference of the NGOs and foreign benefactors, to whom a lot of publicity was given by the media, pleased nobody, least of all the World Bank. The latter had been able to make use of media attention with remarkable skill, to influence the public sector firms and the Government of India. It was however not in its interest to see this kind of practice becoming systematized, its concepts of development not being contrary to those of the collieries or of the NTPC. The power of the representatives of the 'locals' was, moreover, rapidly reduced as migrants gradually arrived and environmental protection measures were taken.[39] What is more, their leaders (among these being the secretary of the *Lokit Samiti*), could easily be bought over or won over.

By the end of the 1990s, the Singrauli scandal no longer interested anyone. The events concerning the Narmada[40] have overtaken it and they have been concluded to the disadvantage of the displaced persons.

THE CONSEQUENCES OF GLOBALIZATION

While the change of direction of the Indian state towards the world market was officially proclaimed in 1991, it had been heralded in 1985 by the 'New textile policy' of Rajiv Gandhi's government. We have seen that the Emergency itself was the harbinger of a nebulous trend in this direction. We will support, in the light of the presentation of the situation of Singrauli, three main propositions as regards the evolution of power equations and levels of intervention. The first is that private sector–public sector opposition cannot serve as a lead. The second is that liberalization or globalization has not occurred in a sudden or univocal manner. These phenomena have always been there combined with other contradictory or parallel processes. The rhetoric which cites these as grounds has often served to mask other, generally older conflicts. Finally, the phenomenon of globalization had had neither positive effects, nor negative ones, on the situation of the local players. It has introduced an additional dimension without changing old power equations. It has accompanied the emergence of additional players but has not given rise to it. The rather limited dimension of the Indian opening up may be at the source of this trend. It is however also possible that the structural characteristics of Indian society, subjected for long to the external world but organized in a complex manner, has played the role of a buffer.

PUBLIC SECTOR AND PRIVATE SECTOR

The opposition between the private and public sectors is not very pertinent to the understanding of the evolution of the Singrauli region and its relationships with the different decision-making levels. Some nuances, true, can be brought out. The private sector, not desiring involvement in the rehabilitation of evicted persons, avoided displacing people.[41] Only the public sector made it statutory for a certain limited percentage of displaced persons to be recruited among its workforce (less than 10 per cent of the families even in 1992) and the grant of plots in the rehabilitation colonies. As for the organized opposition, whether from the 'locals' or from anyone else, the public sector dealt with it in a definitely less high handed manner than the private sector. It did not ask for help from *goondas* but called the police which adhered to certain norms. The private sector, the Birlas notably, marginalized the trade unions which had not pledged their loyalty to it,[42] while the public sector practised a form of joint management with all the national organizations and ended up by making contact even with the defence committees. The small private entrepreneurs brooked no opposition to their power or methods. The relations of the private firms and the public firms with the central and provincial governments were not similar but were not conflicting either. The centre exerted pressures through members of parliament so as to guarantee monopolies and privileges. The provincial states enjoyed the right of listing priorities and granted contracts, which made it possible to eventually buy off the elected representatives.

The two categories of industrial players were however always in agreement over the attitude to be adopted with regard to the local people ('natives' in the colonial sense of the word would be quite fitting).[43] A mixture of scorn and disregard was combined, in both sectors, with respect for legal procedures which have always worked to the detriment of the locals, and with a certain dose of (private) charity or (public) assistance. The expressions of local democracy, whether the *panchayats* or the *zilla parishads*, were either abolished or disdained equally by the public as well as the private enterprises. The public and private enterprises had moreover close links. This was not in the form of contracts alone as the private firms used coal belonging notably to the state.[44] Under the aegis of the SADA, the managing council of the region kept away the locals and all autonomous political representation, but it brought together the large enterprises, the administration and the private enterprises. On the sociological plane, as the field investigation has shown, the officials of the two sectors tended to constitute an overall united if not homogeneous whole. They sent their children to the same reputed schools and went to the same Lions and Rotary clubs. The authorities of both sectors shared, moreover, a common ignorance, whether out of self-interest or naiveness, of casual work. Finally, they shared the same idealizing of city life combined with a profound disdain for the peasantry. These prejudices and reactions are part of the common legacy of numerous contemporary elite societies. They were however intensified by the fact that a number of officials of the NTPC and collieries (a large majority in the case of the SADAs and of the SEBs) came from the well-off upper caste *rural* strata of society.[45] The external players such as the World Bank, noting an old and deep-seated intermingling of interests, never favoured the private over the public or the other way round. They only insisted on greater transparency and a greater competitiveness in the invitations for international bids. This attitude boomeranged, as it seems that the World Bank was not very happy about the choice of a French (nationalized) firm for conducting the environmental impact assessment!

A PROGRESSIVE GLOBALIZATION

In this region there has never been any massive or sudden swing towards globalization. A certain degree of opening up has been there since a very long time. Right from its conception, the NTPC had entered into collaboration agreements with foreign firms. The same trend was to be seen in the collieries, set up as far back as 1973, at the time of the Leftist populist trend in the Congress party. It is true that a notable part of the collaboration agreements and technology imports were in partnership with the Soviet Union in the framework of partially non-commercial relationships (barter agreements, etc.). By increasing manifold the sources of collaboration and of financing, India aimed at being independent in the power sector. A certain degree of insularity also goes back to the beginning and this has been maintained to this day. At the time they were set up, neither the NTPC nor the collieries had any foreigners or permanent representatives of foreign interests within their managerial bodies. This was so also the case with the Birla firm. Nothing has changed since then. The opening up of the power and the mining sectors (no concrete shape has yet been given to the latter) has not led to the arrival of new industrial players in the region. With the help of their purchases of patents and spare parts, the thermal power stations of Singrauli are nevertheless important sources of profit for large foreign firms. The latter have also drawn great benefit from their major role in the conception of the projects.

What one would call the 'consequences of the opening up' was therefore visible ten years before they became official. The same trend was found in Coal India too. Its accelerated mechanization, taking recourse to North American, Russian, Polish and French equipment, dated back to the early 1980s. This enabled it to do without casual labour. In 1985, it was the house of Birla who took the least recourse to modern foreign techniques. It sold, like the NTPC and the NCL, its entire production within India. The rhetoric of globalization and opening up was pertinent in Singrauli only on specific levels which did not influence the in-depth situation. The collapse of the Soviet Union destroyed a reference point and a model appreciated by a part of the officials of the public sector and even of the private sector. The new Russia lost all capacity to innovate and even to follow up the Vindhyachal project which was completed thanks to the staff of the NTPC.[46] The putting into play of the principle of free competition, which leaves some room for profitability, could have promoted the interests of displaced persons. But nothing of the sort occurred. In 1995, the collieries inaugurated their new administrative buildings which had necessitated the clearance of 4 sq km of fertile irrigable land in the Waidhan plain. The logic of inter-institutional competition for status seemed more important, in a number of circumstances, than the logic of the market.

New trends were often a matter of lip service. References in praise of globalization and market forces increased manifold. They came up notably during debates between the NTPC, NCL and the SEBs. No enterprise was more consistent than the other in these matters. Such concepts were even used as arguments against the monetary demands of the trade unions. As the salaries had risen greatly during the 1990s, there was a greater recourse to casual labour. It was also by invoking the imperatives of global competition that the Government of India and the management of the NTPC (NCL having long accepted practices of this kind without making them official) refused to give legal sanction to the inheritance by children of the jobs held by their parents. The establishment of Singrauli is characterized by the fact that it brought nothing to the peasants of the region. On the other hand, the perspectives and needs of the small, well-off and anglicized sections of society were gratified. It was in this framework, and not in that of the social, political or environmental setting of Singrauli, that the upsurge of the rhetoric on globalization needs to be viewed. Those who would have shunned all talk of this in 1977 spoke of nothing but this ten years later. It was during the Emergency that money being transferred abroad and the peddling of influence within the public sector and the administration took on increasing proportions. It was these phenomena, affecting entire classes of people, that prepared the elite and the dominant classes for new perspectives. To this extent Singrauli was a laboratory, one among others, of globalization, after having been a major arena for the interpenetration of the public and the private sectors.

THE SOCIAL IMPACT OF THE OPENING UP

I have underlined the ambiguous nature of the globalization that took place in the industrial conurbation of Singrauli. As regards the appearance of new players in the regional field, including foreign governments and supranational institutions, these facts are only partially the outcome of the globalization of activity during the 1980s. Right from the 1960s, the Ford Foundation was to a large extent financing the Green Revolution. Ten years later, the World Bank devised the 'Food for Work' programmes before participating at all levels in the establishment of the Integrated Rural Development Programmes (IRDP). American ecologists had already begun to show interest in India from the early 1980s, particularly in the matter of the dams in the Himalayas and in deforestation. At the other end of the scale, on matters of status and power the local players (including the organizations for the defence of displaced persons or the pressure groups of vegetable traders[47]) took on prominence from the middle of 1985 when globalization began. These subjects gained popularity due to the growing conflicts between dominant sectors. These confrontations, which used to take place earlier in the name of national interest or of Socialism, changed their discourse and began to invoke economic liberalism, but most of those who found themselves engaged in these debates were hardly bothered over this new[48] universal model.

The belief may have prevailed that the direct intervention of the World Bank in the formulation of these projects had promoted the emergence of the basic players. This in turn enabled a strengthening of the already dominant position of the institution. The projects were revised and whittled down in 1988, then again in 1992, but it does seem that it was considerations of cost, with their technical imperatives, which got the better of the interests of displaced persons. As regards these latter, the perceptions of those in charge in the Bank were not different from those of the Indian promoters of the projects. What had happened was deplorable, but it was the 'price of progress' (*vikas ki kimat*[49]). The primary preoccupation of the Bank was, it seems, to not compromise its public image amongst American parliamentarians or the Government of India. That was why it laid emphasis on the environmental protection aspect. All the major players, situated at the upper fringes of the 'organized sector' (World Bank, Government of India, NTPC and NCL particularly) knew very well that the large works at Singrauli were required for the well-off residents of the

Indian cities so that they could, among other things, avail of air-conditioning. No one, not even the ecologists who were fascinated by the talk of the 'good wild tribal' who had to be protected,[50] found fault with the fact that the peasants of the villages surrounding the five giant power stations themselves had no electricity. This might have polluted their culture more certainly than the acid rains[51] did.

DEMOCRACY AND THE INCREASING COMPLEXITY OF THE SCENE

The Singrauli arena has numerous new players and has witnessed the intervention of forces and institutions situated at a great distance. It would be tempting to wonder, by way of conclusion, whether this has had a positive effect on democracy. Keeping as a criterion of comparison the national experience in the matter of popular representation and participation, the present situation in Singrauli appears ambiguous. As compared to the countryside in Uttar Pradesh, for instance, the region is still very wanting in local democracy.[52] The only compensation is a trade union power, but this too has greatly declined since the expansion of casual work in the NTPC. The dynamics of caste shape the social and electoral trends in the region, including the 'progressive' upsurges such as the assertiveness of the lower caste parties.[53] The Singrauli region appears also to be underdeveloped and heavily dependent on the state. This zone is, on the other hand, much less affected than its hinterland by the activities of armed groups or the manipulations of vote-seeking politicians.

If we compare it with what it was twenty years ago, the area has witnessed enormous change, especially in the matter of procedures of negotiation and of representation. It does not seem however as if there has been much in-depth change in the major structural characteristics, such as the order of hierarchy of the players, the tendency to ignore those interests and persons that cause annoyance, or the absolute dominance of the well-off urban sections. They have only softened their positions as the field of relationships has become more complex. It is thanks to the members of the local legislative assembly, to the movements for defence of the evicted families, and to the trade unions that the people's claims to hereditary employment and to the exchange of land against jobs have finally been accepted. These weak forces are precisely the chosen targets of the local supporters of liberalization and of opening up. The growing influence of the logic of finance, considered as being above such players and above democracy, has widely compensated for the expansion in the number of players and the introduction of new norms, including legal ones.[54] It is noteworthy that no one among the evicted persons or the salaried ones, has contemplated the idea of privatization of the NTPC or of the collieries. Everything leads them to the conclusion that this would only cause a deterioration in their conditions, as was seen in the Dabhol-Enron power station affair in Maharashtra.

NOTES

1. Cf. S.A. Kochanek (1974) and M.J. Zins (1992).
2. Maruti, whose use became widespread during the 1980s, was a small family car consuming little fuel and steel, which was then lacking in the country. Sanjay Gandhi was one of its initiators. The project, which aimed at responding to the needs of the well-off urban classes, availed of public funds, but was set up as an autonomous body in partnership with Suzuki.
3. Founded in 1977, the Janata Party was a united response of the opposition to the Congress party, comprising elements ranging from the Hindu rightist Jan Sangh to the Socialists. It was dissolved in 1980 but a party by this name remained for a long time on the political scene.
4. See G. Heuzé 2000.
5. See Heuzé 1989 for the conditions of life and work in the mining basins of eastern India.
6. Till 1991, private power stations operated to meet the needs of factories and mines. It was the job of the public sector to supply the general public and small industries with power.
7. The power generating firms, which had to adhere to the rules laid down by the Bureau of Public Enterprises (set up in 1965) had to provide lodging to their employees if they worked more than 8 km away from home. The word 'colonies' also used in this context in Hindi, was the term indicating the zones where displaced families were relocated. Each had the right to a piece of land 20 ft wide and 30 ft long (6 × 10 m). The word 'colony' served also to indicate the housing complexes of miners, dispersed over a 40 km stretch along the coalface.
8. This was confirmed by the official in charge of town planning for the NTPC estate of Vindhyachal during an interview in 1990. The village councils had been abolished over the entire area managed by the NTPC (around 28 sq km) because they could not but 'impair law and order'. This testimony was not quoted in the investigation report by Duclos et al. (1991) on the request of its author. This text of 244 pages, to which are appended 140 pages of documents (*Socio Economics, Basic Documents*) brings together the analysis of the results of an investigation through 1,400 questionnaires covering the entire zone of development, several qualitative targeted investigations, and a background and analysis of the situation. The investigation was conducted by

Indians and French from 1989 to 1990. The nationalized firm did not consider it necessary to mention the names of those in charge of the investigation and the text, written mainly by G. Heuzé. This 'final report' (it was the term used by those who had commissioned it) tries to cover the entire population present in the zone while taking note particularly of the factors of income, migrations and caste origins. The impact of industrialization, the methods of displacement, compensation and relocation were then spelt out. The report came to the conclusion that the rehabilitation had failed due to social causes and the attitude of the industries. Highly critical of the NTPC (which had commissioned it), the report was however accepted by this firm. One of the most serious issues raised by the text was the abolition of the small existing democratic institutions, following the takeover of the village lands. The increase of tension between migrants and locals was also dealt with.

9. See Duclos et al. 1991.
10. If the remarks made in 1989 by the managers of the Rihand and Shaktinagar power stations are to be taken seriously.
11. Since the early 1950s (the first general elections were held in 1952), 7 per cent of the seats in Parliament and a variable percentage of seats in the local assemblies are reserved for the *adivasis* (aborigines) as a whole. Similarly, 15 per cent of the seats are reserved for the 'untouchables'. These clauses, which remain in force, are part of a group of measures aimed at promoting the advancement of underprivileged social groups. It applies also to the educational system and to employment in the public sector.
12. On the arguments of the displaced persons, see G. Heuzé 1993.
13. Coal India Limited (CIL) was represented in the field by seven companies corresponding to different geographic zones.
14. The 'factory townships' of the NTPC embody a kind of utopia marked by an implacable spatial reproduction of the factory hierarchy and a near total cutting off from the outside world. One of the biggest preoccupations of those in charge was to get high boundary walls constructed, to isolate these towns extending over several square kilometres (Heuzé 1990).
15. One can recall in this context the slogan of the pioneers of Israel, 'an unpeopled land for a people without land'; the 'colonies' for displaced people bear quite a good resemblance to the Palestinian camps. The comparison, made by the members of the defence committee themselves, ends there.
16. At the time of the investigation, there was no woman working among the managerial staff of the NTPC, the NCL or the SADAs. The matter of recruiting women was being debated in the framework of a policy of reservations.
17. See the appendices to the final report which analyse the spatial configuration and the mode of installation of the precarious housing zones for the migrants.
18. The cult of productivity took several concrete forms. Propaganda in the form of posters and speeches, laying great stress on the needs of 'the nation' for generating more and saving electricity, was launched within the enterprises

and in the townships belonging to the enterprises. Systems for grant of bonuses were introduced which proposed a form of joint management with a view to imbuing a sense of responsibility in the trade unions. The most effective measure which was not a matter for argument, seems to have been the introduction of qualified casual workers, a practice banned till then by the trade unions, and the shortage of this kind of labour.

19. See the chapter of the final report analysing the processes that were the cause of grave traumas locally.
20. Notably during a trip made to Washington by the author and D. Duclos in 1989, as well as during informal meetings in Paris with an emissary of the World Bank.
21. The term 'colonial' is overly simplified and does not appear anywhere in the explicit positions of the powers present in the zone. The spirit that prevailed in Singrauli is, however, not rare in the development processes of those countries that have undergone a long domination, nor those where inequality persists between cities and countryside including other processes of domination. This spirit was expressed in a totality of composite elements which were noted during talks between 1988 and 1990. There was notably the omnipresence of paternalist and hierarchy-oriented metaphors placing the newcomers at the apex, a scorn for the countryside, for rural ways of life and values, the conviction that the elected representatives of the people had no legitimacy and could be shamelessly manipulated, the feeling that one had to do good to the people, even if it was against their will and their 'short term' interests, the free hand given to voracious exploiters such as labour contractors and wood contractors and, the overall conviction that 'this fine land' was lying neglected, vacant or inhabited by primitive tribals from whom nothing but 'stagnation' or 'backwardness' could be expected. It was just waiting to be 'developed' and 'civilized'.
22. A term repeatedly mentioned in numerous documents of the NTPC.
23. This institution founded in the 1960s was situated on the south bank of the lake, the least inhabited and the most forested. Those in charge had specialized in giving legal assistance to displaced persons, in local development and in bringing morality into public life. They had an authoritarian and paternalistic style but they clashed for a long time with those in charge of the Rihand project of the NTPC.
24. The CISF is a special police entrusted with protecting the enterprises of the Government of India and its properties, including their townships. Its intervention in social conflicts has on several occasions led to firing.
25. In 1990, according to the survey conducted in the framework of the investigation, less than 10 per cent of the displaced families had a permanent job. Out of these, 3 per cent had two or three jobs.
26. This state had a relative majority of the capital of the Bank and the right of veto over the decisions of the institution, a privilege which it continues to enjoy.

27. In 1989, at the start of the setting up of the investigation, the representatives of the Lokit Samiti gathered outside the Shaktinagar guest-house and shouted slogans to draw the attention of the World Bank representatives who were staying there. But they were led away by the police.
28. The management of the NTPC availed of three types of guest-houses which offered very varied types of facilities and services. They used the different facilities available with a sharp sense of management of tensions. Thus, those in charge of EDF International (paid for by the NTPC) were lodged in the ordinary guest-house, while the representatives of the World Bank and parliamentarians were sent to the deluxe establishment.
29. The Essential Services (Maintenance) Act of 1981 puts a ban on strikes in the power sector.
30. Access to the hospitals managed by the collieries or the NTPC, free for the permanent employees, was subject to the payment of a deposit equal to two weeks' salary for all the other inhabitants of the region.
31. Since 1980 and following the launching of opencast mines in the east-central coal fields Indian collieries have witnessed numerous conflicts with displaced villagers. (Eastern Collieries and the BCCL of Dhanbad employed 400,000 persons in 1983.) Those in charge have become experienced negotiators.
32. Notably by sharing their complaints with me when I had gone there as an investigator (1989-90). This point has not been dealt with in the final report. Despite some very detailed analyses, the sharpness of the statistical system used and the development of the flaws in the attitude of the large firms, this text had to remain within certain bounds, imposed by those who had commissioned it.
33. The two sectors of power and mines are classified as 'essential' according to the Indian nomenclature, which means that strikes in them are practically banned (1981 Act), and it is the watchword of those in charge to do all within their purview to ensure that production is never stopped. This indicates the gravity of these inter-administration confrontations which took place between 1992 and 1997.
34. 'NTPC: no dearth of power', *The Pioneer,* 9 March 1990.
35. Interview with P.K. Sinha, in charge of the Northern Coal Ltd., in March 1990.
36. The Birla aluminium factory has been reconstructed, changing in the process its production procedures and its organization of work (using more casual workers).
37. These sub-contractors (*thekedars*) collected the migrant casual labourers from their area and brought them to the work place, usually in their trucks. Caste polarizations were flagrant. In 1988, the NTPC paid Rs. 35 a day to the unskilled casual workers whom it employed directly. The *thekedar,* acting on behalf of the enterprise, which was the common practice, kept back Rs. 20 out of this sum. See Heuzé 1991.
38. The category of 'tribal' is to be treated with caution in India where the legacy

of colonial anthropology is a particularly onerous one and is aggravated by high caste depictions. At Singrauli, the 'tribal' was omnipresent in the discourse on assistance and in political interventions but very difficult to meet in reality.

39. These were of the kind that are called 'cosmetic changes', which in fact often aggravated the situation. What seemed important was to be able to show to the press and to critics a catalogue of measures that could be enumerated in terms of figures, the number of trees planted, for instance.
40. The development of the Narmada valley is an undertaking of pharaonic proportions also financed partially by the World Bank. The three thousand engineering works, including around fifty large barrages and an immense reservoir near the Gujarat border, are meant to irrigate Gujarat, but the 500,000 persons whose eviction is anticipated have opposed, in a very dispersed manner, the starting of the work all through the 1990s. The *Narmada Bachao Andolan*, led by Medha Patkar waged a legal fight and a non-violent agitation on the spot, and was finally defeated.
41. These measures had become compulsory since 1894. The compensation procedures were intensified during the 1990s following the incidents that had taken place at Singrauli and in other major construction work sites. Fifty thousand people have reportedly been displaced since 1960, but less than one-fifth of these have been 'rehabilitated'.
42. At Renukot where the Birla factory is situated, a section of the INTUC (the trade union of the Congress party) supported by the management was well entrenched there while the representatives of the CITU and the AITUC (Communists) hid their affiliations after the 1974 strike which had led to numerous dismissals.
43. The official government terminology speaks of 'poor *adivasis*', while the displaced persons used the term *udvasit* ('evicted') or *sthaniya log* ('locals').
44. The public monopoly was broken only by some private captive mines working for some steel mills or thermal power stations, without access to the market.
45. While the NTPC and the collieries did their recruitment from all over India, their employees requested generally that they be stationed close to where their family resided. During the investigation, it was found that the majority of the middle level officials of all the enterprises, with the possible exception of the Birla aluminium factory, came from Madya Pradesh, Uttar Pradesh and Bihar, the three states closest to the zone. Higher officials and casual workers shared the common factor of coming from further away.
46. The Vindhyachal project, which makes use of 3,000 ha to produce 3,000 MW, appears to be the most wasteful in terms of space and the most polluting.
47. They put pressure on the administrators of the SADAs and the Members of Parliament to ensure that no agricultural investment was made in the region (interviews with those in charge in the SADA of Madhya Pradesh, winter 1989-90).

48. The element of novelty is valid only for Independent India (from 1818 till 1947 the Indian subcontinent had a 'liberal', even hyper-liberal, economic system), and it is as ambiguous as it is limited.
49. This was the title—as a rejoinder to the NTPC's slogan 'The Saga of Progress'-- of a booklet published in Waidhan in 1986 by the committee for the defence of displaced persons. It gave a background of the despoiling along with judicial arguments (the author was a lawyer) and made a call for mobilization. The translated version of this text was presented to those in charge in the NTPC who had never taken note of it.
50. This position which attaches value to a so-called state of nature forms part of the Anglo-Saxon liberalism but it can match the Gandhian idealizing of the village. It was in its name that the eradication of local democracy was often justified. How could these people govern in any way when they were 'all naked in the forest' (interview with the person in charge of the city factory of Vindhyachal, in 1990)?
51. Acid rain put in an appearance after the inauguration of Shaktinagar. Its effect was aggravated by the nature of the soil. The electrostatic filters seemed to be inadequate. Moreover, the Singrauli coal, which contains 30 to 40 per cent of non-combustible elements, produces an enormous quantity of waste matter.
52. The Ambedkarist movement does not exist in Singrauli, although it has a very large following in Uttar Pradesh. This despite the presence of a high concentration of Chamars.
53. The Bahujan Samaj Party, the party of the (oppressed) majority, which claims to follow the ideals of Ambedkar and of Buddhism, has become the second or third largest political force in Uttar Pradesh. In Madhya Pradesh, it is powerful enough to tilt the electoral balance between the Congress and the BJP.
54. The rehabilitation norms notably have been greatly improved.

REFERENCES

Aneja, D., *Potential Environmental Problems Due to Coal Fired Power Plants around Singrauli*, Delhi: Tata Energy Research Institute, 1983.

Anonymous, 'The State and Development in India', *Economic and Political Weekly*, vol. XXIV, no. 33 (1989): 1877-84.

Bhadouria, B.P.S. and Dubey, V.B., *Panchayati Raj and Rural Development*, Delhi: Commonwealth Publishers, 1989.

Bharti, I., 'Power Generation at Cost of People', *Economic and Political Weekly*, vol. XXV, no. 44 (1990): 2360.

Boillot, J.J., 'Régulation et développement. Le modèle indien depuis 1947', Ph.D. Dissertation, University of Paris X, 1989.

Centre for Science and Environment, *Green File, a selection of clippings on the environment*, Delhi: CSE, 1988.

Crozier, M., *Le phénomène bureaucratique*, Paris: Editions du Seuil, 1965.

D.N., 1988, 'Coal India Modernisation Programme', *Economic and Political Weekly*, vol. XXIII, no. 8 (1988): 347-8.

Dubey, K.N. (ed), *Planning and Development in India*, New Delhi: Ashish Publications, 1990.

Duclos, D., Heuzé, G., Mankodi, K. and Meynaud, H., *Environmental Study of Singrauli Area, Main Report*, vol. 2, Ch. 3: 'Socio-Economics', New Delhi: National Thermal Power Corporation, 1991.

Editor, *The Land Acquisition Act, 1894*, Lucknow: Eastern Book Company, 1988.

Environmental Service Group, *Environmental Status of Mining in Madhya Pradesh*, New Delhi: World Wildlife Fund India, 1983.

Heuzé, G., *Ouvriers d'un autre monde*, Paris: Maison des Sciences de l'Homme, 1989.

——, 'Les nouvelles villes industrielles en Inde', *Acta Geographica*, III, 83 (1990): 2-18.

——, 'Les paysans et l'emploi industriel dans l'Inde contemporaine', *Annales*, 46, I, 1991.

——, 'Les grands projets d'aménagement et les déplacements de populations en Inde: 88' dits 'd'acteurs oubliés', *Revue Tiers-Monde*, vol. XXXIV, no. 133, 1993.

——, 'Le travail à domicile en Inde contemporaine. Peu d'exotisme et beaucoup d'enseignements', *Syndicalisme et société*, vol. III, no. 1, 2000.

Hindustan Times Correspondent, 'Police Picket to Detect Illegal Connections', *Hindustan Times*, 16 January 1989.

Jauhari, S.C., *Development at Singrauli*, Singrauli: Town and Country Planning Organization, 1983.

Kochanek, S.A., *Business and Politics in India*, Princeton: Princeton University Press, 1974.

Kulkarni, S., 'Towards a Social Forest Policy', *Economic and Political Weekly*, vol. XVIII, no. 6 (1983): 191-2.

Kumar, R., 'Nationalisation by Default: the Case of Coal in India', *Economic and Political Weekly* (25 April and 1 May 1981): 757-68 and 824-30.

——, *The Indian Coal industry after Nationalisation*, Oxford: Oxford University Press, 1982.

Laidi, Z., *Enquête sur la Banque mondiale*, Paris: Fayard, 1989.

Lokit Samiti, *Vikas Ki Kimat*, Baidhan, 1985.

Madhya Pradesh State Electricity Board, *About Us in Figures*, Jabalpur : Statistical Cell of MPSEB, 1988.

Mehetre, M.G., *Energy Crisis in India*, Allahabad: Chugh, 1990.

Mitra, A., *The Hoodlum Years*, Bombay: Orient Longman, 1979.

Mukherji, S., *Mechanism of Underdevelopment, Labour Migration and Planning Strategies in India*, Calcutta: Prajna, 1981.

National Thermal Power Corporation, *Integrated Power Development at Singrauli in Uttar Pradesh and Madhya Pradesh*, New Delhi: NTPC Technical Services Division, 1981.

——, *Rihand Super Thermal Power Project, Interim Environmental Impact Assessment*, New Delhi: National Thermal Power Corporation, Government of India, 1988.

National Working Group on Displacement, *National Policy on Developmental Resettlement*, New Delhi: Lokayan, 1988.

Pant, A.D. and Gupta, S.K., *Bureaucracy, Development and Change*, New Delhi: Segment Publishers, 1990.

Prasad, P.H., 'Neglected Aspects of India's Development Planning', *Economic and Political Weekly*, vol. XXIV, no. 28 (1989): 1591-5.

Rathore, J.S., Mathur, K.C. and Shukla, U.M., *Environmental Situation at Singrauli Coal Mines and Super Thermal Power Complex and Proposed Environmental Impact Studies (an approach paper)*, Rewa: Rural Division of Environmental Planning and Coordination Organisation, Government of Madhya Pradesh, APS University, 1982-3.

Rathore, J.S. et al., *Human Settlement Pattern: a Case Study of Shifting Population of Nine Villages at Singrauli*, Rewa: Rural Division of Environmental Planning and Coordination Organisation, Department of Housing and Environment, 1982-3.

Rodrigues, D., 'Rallying against Planned Disaster', *Economic and Political Weekly*, vol. XXIV, no. 39 (1989): 2183.

Roy, D., 'Environment and Politics', *Economic and Political Weekly*, vol. XXI, no. 46 (1986): 1980.

Sanwal, M., 1989, 'Panchayati Raj: the Next Steps', *Economic and Political Weekly*, vol. XXIV, no. 42 (1989): 2365-9.

Sapru, R.K., *Environment Planning and Management in India*, New Delhi: Ashish Publishing House, 1990.

Sarangi, S. and Billorey, R., 'The Nightmare Begins. Oustees of Indira Sagar Project', *Economic and Political Weekly*, vol. XXIII, no. 17 (1988), 829.

Sengupta, M., *Energy and Power in India*, New Delhi: S. Chand Publications, 1985.

Sengupta N., *Topdown and Bottom Approach: Some Cases of Regional Planning in India*, Bangkok, International Labour Office, paper presented at the seminar on 'Rural Development and Regional Planning in the 80s', 1981.

——, *Fourth World Dynamics: Jharkhand*, Delhi: Author Guild Publications, 1982.

Sharma, B.D., *Rehabilitation of Tribals Displaced by Irrigation Projects: An ecologically viable and socially compatible approach*, New Delhi: Government of India, 1986.

Sharma, N.K., 'Large Dams: a Necessary Development Choice', *Bhagirath*, vol. 33 (1986).

Sharma, R., *Scope of Study and Environmental Impact of the Development in Singrauli*, Bhopal: Environmental Planning and Coordination Organization, 1983.

Sharma, R.B., *Singrauli Area Development: A Report*, Bhopal: Town and Country Planning Organization, Government of Madhya Pradesh, 1983.

Singh, S., *Impact of Electrification on Agricultural and Industrial Development of Rihand Grid Area*, Varanasi: Bhoogol Parishad, 1976.

Social Action, 'Number on Displacement and Rehabilitation', *Social Action*, vol. 38, no. 3, 1988.

Sudarsen, V. and Kalem, M.A. (eds.), *The Uprooted People: Displacement, Resettlement, Development*, New Delhi: Gian Publications, 1989.

Thorner, D. and Thorner, A., *Land and Labour in India*, Bombay: Asia Publishing House, 1962.

Town and Country Planning Organization, *Development Plan for Singrauli Area*, New Delhi: Goverment of India, Ministry of Urban Development, 1987.

Varma S.C., *Dub main anevalon ke sath manaviya byobhar jarur hai*, New Delhi: Gandhi Peace Foundation, 1985.

Weiner, M., *Sons of the Soil: Migration and Ethnic Conflict in India*, New Delhi: Oxford University Press, 1978.

World Bank, *India: Economic Issues in the Power Sector*, Washington: World Bank, 1979.

Zins, M.J., *Histoire politique de l'Inde indépendante*, Paris: Presses Universitaires de France, 1992.

Globalization and Self-sufficiency: A Tentative Revolution in Oilseeds

Bruno Dorin

This paper deals with the oils and oilseeds industry in India, and with a governmental mission set up during the 1980s in order to achieve self-reliance in edible oils.

Self-reliance is not a new objective in India: it is the leitmotif of the non-alignment movement and, above all, of the economic policy conducted by the country since its independence in 1947. The concept remains, nonetheless, ambiguous. In the large majority of cases, it is used and understood in the sense of self-sufficiency to indicate that the country is in a position to meet the needs of its population on its own. In other words, it does not depend on imports or foreign support. Within this framework, no matter what the methods, what matters is to be self-sufficient, to be independent of the outside world, to be able to function in isolation if necessary. This concept of autonomy clearly reflects a process of locking into oneself ('locked-autonomy'), in which 'the social being, totally obscure to itself, withdraws into itself, making inconceivable every path, every response that has not already been instituted' (Dupuy et al. 1983: 21–2).

Actually, autonomy can also be quite the opposite: a matter of ever-increasing relationships and dependencies with the outside world. Indeed, every opening process allows a process of mutual specification between an inner and an outer world (the outside specifies the inside which specifies the outside, and so on), process which leads each world to become more and more dependent on the other. Then, very ironically, one's increasing dependency and fragility widen one's scope of expression and activity in the outside world, and therefore one's strength, self-fulfilment and self-reliance within it. This idea of 'open-autonomy', which might also be called 'self-organization' or 'auto-organization', owes much to cybernetics (with von Neuman and von Foerester in the lead), as also to philosophers such as Cornelius Castoriadis, Edgar Morin, and biologists such as Francisco J. Varela. The works of the latter are for example hinged on the concepts of *autopoiesis* and of 'structural coupling', where the mutual specification of the components of a system is not only in the heart of the production (*poiein*) of self (*autos*), but also the surest way to evolve without disintegration in an environment where each one's structural plasticities lead each to select the other's path.

This intuition of what is 'open-autonomy' surely helps us see differently the specific human endowment and power in the world, the inner challenge of globalization in which we are just entering, and the lead (not always fortunate since not always 'plastic') taken by the United States of America in a world which seems to call us for an emancipation rooted in an ever-increasing interaction and solidarity towards nature and our neighbours. This text is rooted in this peculiar and unfinished theory of autonomy, and will come back to it after having tried to show how this idea of autonomy can express itself and help us to appreciate how fortunate or unfortunate are certain situations.

The first part of this chapter starts with the internationalization of the American soya bean complex to explain how the later managed to reconfigure the world of oils and oilseeds, including in India. Indeed, thanks to an outstanding capacity of continual organization, a network and its agents (from peasants to multinationals including governmental institutions) were able, after a protection granted to the fledgling industry, to adapt themselves to the various circumstances of time and place, achieving fruition well beyond the narrow limits of their borders. Meanwhile, in India, the protection granted to the oils and oilseeds industry, as well as the adoption of a planned and centralized economy, led on the contrary to an ossified system that finally went against the interests of both producers and consumers, as well as the balance of payments (huge imports of edible oils). It was then that Sam Pitroda arrived on the scene, with the ambition to change, through five missions including one on oilseeds, 'the work ethos of the government and the bureaucracy'. The goals and means of this mission for self-reliance are developed in a second part, while a tentative assessment of this local policy for global autonomy is done in a third and final section.

NEW DEALS FOR OIL SEEDS

Internationalization of the American Soya Bean Complex

Until First World War, with Senegal (groundnut), China and Manchuria (soya bean), India indisputably dominated the international market for oilseeds: up to 60 per cent of the domestic production of rapeseed and 50 per cent of the production of groundnut were exported from the subcontinent. However, a few decades later, a totally different configuration prevailed, following the internationalization of a 'soya bean complex'.

Soya bean put in an appearance in American statistics in 1924 only, but right from 1928, agricultural producers and processing firms were already organized and associated through the American Soya bean Association (ASA). Two years later, this lobby obtained from the government to restrict the imports of oilseeds so that domestic prices and production be boosted. This protectionist policy was strengthened in 1947 when the American producers of margarine undertook to incorporate in their product only soya bean produced within the country. Meanwhile, the soya bean–maize model had already come to the fore in the United States, in crop rotation and livestock feed. The oilcake, obtained after extraction of the oil, became indeed an excellent new use of soya bean: its high protein content perfectly completes the carbohydrate inputs of an animal diet based on cereals, as for example grains or silage of maize. And it was on the basis of these assets that the American soya bean complex began to gain popularity on an international scale from 1945.

The Marshall Plan provided the first opportunity to export large volumes of soya bean beyond the Atlantic, especially to the Netherlands and the Federal Republic of Germany, as well as to set up and control factories for seed preparation and expelling. An agreement in 1961 helped to achieve a solid entrenchment in Europe. For its Common Agricultural Policy, the European Community did indeed choose the custom protection of oils, and the elimination of trade barriers for oilseeds and oilcakes in view of encouraging their use in the production of meat, as also of legitimizing levies in the sector of cereals and milk products. The model 'animal feed = cereals + (imported American) soya bean' could then penetrate Europe in a big way. The Europeans, realizing more specifically after the 1974 embargo the importance of the deal, then decided, despite calls to order from the GATT, to subsidize their domestic production of oilseeds. While these have become a major subject of dispute between the European Union and the United States, the former continues nevertheless to import massive quantities of soya beans and oilcakes from the American continent (USA and Brazil).

A judicious utilization of the well-known Public Law 480 (PL 480) also enabled the United States to dispatch soya bean oil to the developing countries. Indeed, during the 1980s, the world demand for oils was partly sustained by countries (India, Pakistan and Latin-America) which in fact faced important difficulties in financing their imports: 'it was the food aid policies of America and Canada, often along with policies of short-term loans, which made it possible to ensure a certain stability of demand by banking on a future solvency, and to maintain the prices of oils at a relatively high level at least till 1985' (Bertrand et al. 1988: 270). Food aid was thus a means of popularizing soya bean oil, not only in developing countries but also in a solvent continent such as Europe since it is through the channel of the PL480 that large capacities for seed trituration have been set up in Spain which, in 1976, just after the death of its dictator Franco and a few years before its entry into the Common Market, had a potential in this field three times higher than that of France.

The outcome of this remarkable strategy is that despite the development of the production of sunflower (USSR, EU, Argentina), of rapeseed (China, EU, Canada) or, even more, of palm oil (Malaysia), soya bean became not only the must traded oilseed but also the primary source of oil on the planet. During the mid-1980s, it represented around 20 per cent of the volume of production out of 17 oils and fats of plant and animal origin (or 14 million tonnes out of 70 million oil-equivalent tonnes in 1985–6), the other sources not exceeding 11 per cent. In this reconfiguration of the production and of the world trade, India hardly figured, for it was concentrating on its wheat and rice Green Revolution.

India's Conversion into Massive Import of Edible Oils

Until the mid-1960s, India, despite competition from soya bean, remained a net exporter of oils and oilseeds thanks notably to the organizational efforts of businessmen to meet the post-War demands through the world. But after that, the tables were totally turned: the domestic prices of oils rose incessantly, and sharply during the droughts of 1971, 1972 and 1973. American food aid (between 30,000 and 100,000 tonnes every year till the mid-1970s) was insufficient to bring about a stabilization in prices. The production of oilseeds, which had been set aside by the Green Revolution, increased by a little more than 1 per cent per year on an average, falling far behind the rate of growth of the population. Soaring prices of oil, virulently castigated by consumer associations such as Mrinal Gore's in Bombay or by political movements such as Navnirman in Gujarat, forced the centre to modify in 1976–7 its protectionist stance, and to import 400,000 tonnes of edible oil. In the years that followed, the supply from abroad exceeded a million tonnes, making India the foremost importer of vegetable oils in the world. The country purchased a record amount of 1.9 million tonnes between April 1987 and March 1988, to which volume should be added 100,000 tonnes of foreign donation during that year of severe drought.

Until 1989, vegetable oils constituted the second Indian largest imports after petrol. From 1981–2 to 1988–9, these imports were valued on an average at 7.2 billion rupees per year (around 4 per cent of the total import bill): this expenditure was all the more burdensome as it made serious inroads into the foreign currency reserves which were already showing signs of depletion. Moreover, and this could not last long, India was deriving full benefit from the competition raging at that time between countries battling in the international market to either sell their surpluses (rapeseed oil from Europe and Canada, soya bean oil from Brazil, etc.) or to boost an export spearhead such as the Malaysian palm oil (a product to which India gave preference on account of the geographic proximity as also as a way to assert a bilateral political cooperation). Thus, between 1981–2 and 1989–90, the average annual price of the oils bought abroad ranged between Rs. 3.6 and Rs. 8.1 per kg, far below the domestic prices of groundnut or rapeseed/mustard oil.

But this worrying situation was only the visible aspect of the iceberg. Indeed, within the country itself, powerful forces were also working towards widening or maintaining this import burden so embarrassing for a nation officially self-sufficient on the food front. The imports of edible oils, as well as their distribution, did in fact give to the different parties involved—or involving themselves in the operations—the opportunity to make large profits, whether officially or unofficially.

On the top of the list was the central government, since it used to charge 45 per cent customs duty on imported oils between 1982 and 1988 (1.4 million tonnes per year at Rs. 6.56 c.i.f. per kg on an annual average): a yearly average income of 4.1 billion rupees to which has to be added 2.8 billion rupees coming from the sale of a part of these imported oils to the public or semi-public industries dealing in vanaspati (a blend of hydrogenated oils that remain solid at room temperature). Thus, the total rose to 6.9 billion rupees per year on an average from 1982 to 1988. In other words, each kilogram of imported oil brought back more than 4.9 rupees into the coffers of the central government during that period of heavy imports.

True, from these incomes a certain amount should be subtracted as expenses inherent in the operation, notably a 2 per cent commission *ad valorem* charged by the STC (State Trading Corporation of India), a public enterprise which in 1978 was given the monopoly for the import of oils. In 1988, this one single activity (import of vegetable oils) accounted for more than 60 per cent of the STC turnover. Similarly, vanaspati manufacturers gained from these imports: 500,000 tonnes of vegetable oils were sold to them by the Ministry of Food and Civil Supplies at a price that was at least Rs. 6 per kg less than the price of the oils most widely purchased in the domestic market. These imported oils, legally blended with those produced on Indian territory (only vanaspati manufacturers were at this time allowed to blend edible oils), led to vanaspati becoming a particularly attractively priced product, specially as compared to butter which has the same appearance.

Finally, Indian states get some imported oil for the Public Distribution System (PDS) which releases to the poor essential commodities at cheap prices. In that process, from 1982 to 1988, almost 1.8 billion rupees a year got back to the states,[1] more than enough to cover their everyday expenses. It was therefore in their interest to avail of a maximum allocation of imported oil since every kilogram intended for the PDS returned about 2 rupees. In fact, according to a study conducted in Bombay, Bangalore and other large consumer centres, 80 per cent of the groundnut and coconut oils sold in the free market proved to be blended with imported palm oil. From this, it can reasonably be deduced that, on an average in India, half of the volume of the vegetable oil meant for the PDS actually found its way into the domestic market where the ruling prices were at least Rs. 6 per kg higher than the sale price 'recommended' for the deprived households of the population. In other words, corrupt officials and dishonest oil merchants pocketed about 2.7 billion rupees a year between 1982 and 1988 (Dorin 1994: 115–18).

All in all, between the value of the imports at the borders (1.4 million tonnes a year at Rs. 6.56 per kg on an average) and their minimum value in the domestic market in India (Rs. 18.50 per kg on an average), there is an annual difference of 17.1 billion rupees, of which 51 per cent went to central and state governments, 17 per cent to vanaspati manufacturers, 16 per cent to corrupt dealers, and only 16 per cent to the PDS. It was therefore not the Indian consumer who benefited the most from the massive wave of imports of edible oils until 1988.

As for the domestic producer of oilseeds, it became very difficult for him to survive. The high domestic price of the finished product (oils) did not imply that farmers were obtaining a high price for their product (oilseed): oil-millers and traders were sufficiently well connected and organized (Dorin 1994: 97–9) to purchase oilseeds at the lowest price during the harvesting times, and to sell vegetable oils at a high price a few months later. Moreover, it regularly happened that imported oils were released on the domestic market just at the time of the harvest, leading to an even further fall in farm prices. And that is not the whole story: to these market-related risks must be added the monsoon-related risks which can dash a farmer's hope of income, since oilseeds were mostly relegated—after the Green Revolution—to non-irrigated rainfed seasons or regions not suitable for the high-yielding varieties of cereals (Dorin 1999).

A MISSION FOR SELF-RELIANCE

Pitroda's Will to Change

After Rajiv Gandhi took office in January 1985, the entire administrative machinery of Delhi found itself in the grip of feverish activity. 'Panchsheel' had been Nehru's slogan, 'Garibi Hatao' was the watchword of his daughter Indira Gandhi, while 'India in the twenty-first century' was the formula that the new and young prime minister seemed to favour. Like a manager enamoured of new technologies, Indira's son asserted a will to work faster, with less red tape, greater efficiency, honesty and modernity. Inter-ministerial committees met thereafter at a rapid pace and devoted their attention to the most diverse matters. Five of them were named Technology Missions. This was in fact a very discreet designation, in the sense that the mass media—and even some ministers—happened to know the existence of these missions only after the arrival of Sam Pitroda in late 1987. The latter then openly spelt out the grand designs for which he wanted henceforth to specifically mould them: to change the work ethos of the government and the bureaucracy for radically changing a system that had remained colonial and feudal even forty years after independence (*Financial Express*, 13 April 1989; *City Scan*, June 1989).

Within a few years, Sam Pitroda had become an influential advisor of Rajiv Gandhi. The two men had known each other since the early 1980s, when Pitroda had presented to Mrs Gandhi and to her son a plan for restructuring—as recommended by the Sarin Committee—the Indian telecommunications network. The initiative was a happy one, for after numerous deliberations, the Union cabinet finally approved it in February 1984. In a few months, and despite a limited budget of 350 million rupees, the C-DOT system came into being, devised for India by Pitroda's engineering in order to be functional in the difficult and varied conditions of temperature and hygrometry prevailing in the subcontinent. For Pitroda, it was only another opportunity to confirm a know-how and a talent in the matter, since he was granted numerous patents all over the world for similar achievements, and made that way his fortune in the United States where this son of a very modest family of Orissa had lived for twenty-two years, just after the end of his studies in Baroda.

As was inevitable, Pitroda was suspected of taking advantage of his recent proximity to Rajiv Gandhi to pursue some personal ambitions. For example, the 'rejuvenation plan' he proposed in January 1986 (at Rajiv Gandhi's request) to the Congress party led some to assert that Indians could do without sermons from this go-getter who had no scruples in the past to amass a fortune hand in hand with Americans. However, on the whole, the press remained prudent, more inclined to show in him an interest tinged with kindly irony (if not respectful admiration) rather than open and caustic hostility. It is true that one of the favourite words of this man was 'communication', to which, according to him, modern India should give more attention. As a matter of fact, after he was appointed in October 1987 to head the National Technology Missions (NTM) and after he had spelt out the ambitious plans that he wanted them to fulfil, journalists kept an eye on this 'adventurer and peddler of utopian ideas' (*Probe India*, March 1988) and on this 'gloss of high-tech jargon' (*Business India*, 21 March–3 April 1988) coming from an 'Ivory Tower' (*Economic and Political Weekly*, 7 October 1989): although they remained distant, they almost dared to believe this man, who asserted that in twelve years India could achieve what it had not been able to do in forty.

How then should one view the pessimism of some intellectuals? Harsh Sethi denounced 'a paternalist corporate model of management' which, while giving primacy to action, paid hardly any attention to the institutional structures that had been progressively set up by the society (*Economic and Political Weekly*, 14 May 1988). As for Rajni Kothari and Shiv Visvanathan, they saw in Sam Pitroda the 'meteor' of those technological programmes which revel in the high-flown language of science and progress, but which—though launched with the best of intentions—end up in the 'destruction of our civil rights' (*Seminar*, February 1989). No doubt the 'meteor' in question would have put forward the point, as in 1988, that 'we require people who want to make a career out of solving problems and not those who want to spend time identifying and analysing them. We have enough of them' (*National Herald*, 17 May 1988). After six pages of reflection on the matter, Rajni Kothari on his part concluded thus: 'Let the Technology Missions too be conceived in the framework of movements from below instead of so much fiction perpetrated from above. I'd better stop here. Advising others is so easy to do. It is not what I normally enjoy doing. Except with exceptionally motivated people. Like Pitroda' (*Seminar*, February 1989: 17).

Casting and Recasting the 'Technology Missions'

In November 1985, the development programmes of the Seventh Plan were drawn up and released to the public. A special chapter planned for the setting up of Technology Missions. Their main objective was to bring together researchers and users of technologies at the first stage of the innovation cycle so as to convert laboratory knowledge into concrete applications in sectors where the need was considered pressing. Were the earlier successes in the fields of agriculture, space, defence and atomic energy not due mainly to a similar strategy?

Thirteen sectors of action were then proposed, mainly targeted towards research and development in rural areas. Five of these were retained with a budget allocation in the Plan of 70 billion rupees: oilseeds, drinking water in non-urban zones, immunization of children and pregnant women, adult literacy, and telecommunications in rural area. These five Technology Missions, which were expected to fulfil ambitious objectives considering the time limit granted to them, were progressively set up during the course of the year 1986. A sixth was added in August 1988, on dairy development.

In October 1987, when Sam Pitroda became the national head of the Technology Missions, there was no question of modifying the concrete and ambitious objectives which had been fixed for these on the horizons of 1990, 1995 and 2000, or of revising their budget. (Either of these could have been feasible as there was general agreement on the fact that the Technology Missions had remained virtually dormant until then.) In fact, for Pitroda, even if the Missions did indeed have an obligation to achieve tangible results, their real challenge and scope was of a totally different nature: becoming self-reliant, thanks to four keys which had received too little importance till then: 'management', 'community participation', 'information and communications', and 'centre–state coordination'. These four keys to self-reliance were hammered out and explained in the course of numerous seminars and press conferences. They were also printed in red in a glossy brochure with the pompous title 'The Will to Change' (NTM 1989).

Management should be paid greater attention in order to 'mobilize resources from various places' (*National Herald*, 8 February 1988). On this point, Pitroda specified that his role at the head of the Technology Missions was restricted to a 'catalyst'. His first months in office were for that matter devoted to making an (apolitical) survey in the different states, in which talks with those at the top of the hierarchy (chief minister, chief secretary, etc.) were supplemented by visits to the field. Pitroda then insisted on the necessity for clarifying the responsibilities and the commitments of all the providers of a service. And since an articulation of concise objectives could help in the matter, the new NTM's management did its utmost to print within three months booklets detailing the various objectives to be reached by each Mission.

As far as community participation is concerned, it meant primarily that 'we must make every Indian aware of these missions and their importance' (*National Herald*, 8 February 1988). 'The Missions can only strike sparks. It is the people who must nurture the flame. This is why community participation is a vital part of Mission design. The people are empowered to make their own decisions and act' (NTM 1989: 4). On numerous occasions, Pitroda insisted on the necessary collaboration with cooperatives or with non-governmental organizations (grouped together under the designation of 'voluntary agencies'). Twenty-five among these came from all over India to interact, during a meeting organized in Delhi in February 1988, with persons in charge of various administrative departments (Rural Development, Health and Family Welfare, Education, Agriculture, etc.). In May 1988, the government also announced a special training programme for 50,000 retired officials whose experience could be of help in the execution of the national objectives, since 'even if 1,000 of these people could be mobilized every year, we could go a long way in achieving success in our programmes' (*National Herald*, 17 May 1988).

As regards information and communication, Pitroda noted sadly that 'most of the information at our disposal is not relevant, sometimes obsolete, and at times even fabricated' (*National Herald*, 8 February 1988). He then promised that in August 1988, the 430 districts of the country would be connected through computers thanks to the NICNET network that the Technology Missions were already using. The information gathered had in fact to be systematically standardized, stored and made easy to consult. It was also important that the information and awareness campaigns make use of all communication channels: radio, television, press, newsletters, national and regional seminars, posters, audio recordings, and so on. In July 1988, the prime minister's advisor also set up the Council for Social Audit (CSA) which, under the chairmanship of a former chief justice of the Supreme Court, brought together five eminent citizens recognized for the services they had rendered to the nation. This Council needed no legal standing since, in the same spirit as that of the Missions, the idea was to not create new bureaucracies. Its role was 'to increase people's participation in the Missions, conduct qualitative assessments, perform concurrent evaluations, suggest improvements for delivery and heighten people's awareness' (*The Hindu*, 7 July 1988). Every citizen could moreover write directly to the CSA at its very simple address: PB-55, New Delhi 110001.

Finally there had to be better centre-state coordination in order to restrict large losses of energy and to promote the convergence of governmental action with that of associations, non-governmental organizations, private and international agencies. Consequently, rather than centralized decision-making in New Delhi, 'Mission implementation takes place very largely at state level' (NTM 1989: 4). In this respect, it was assumed that the latter would finance three of these Missions (drinking water, literacy and oilseeds) in equal shares with the Union. First and foremost, there had to be a close cooperation between the Mission's director at the Union level, the Mission's director or coordinator at the state level, and the Mission's Committee of Advisers at the state or district level. This very informal organization chart, often portrayed by the triad 'States-Centre-Voluntary Agencies', illustrates the 'Pitrodian' concept of development. The challenge is to skilfully short-circuit the inertia of the far too compartmentalized Indian administration, to offer a sufficiently flexible framework to welcome voluntary involvement and promote adjustment to local circumstances, and to make the different agents more dependent on each other so as to be more self-reliant. As it was highlighted in the brochure of the NTM, no other policy makes sense than self-reliance in the long term, and nothing else makes development change truly sustainable than self-help at the local level (NTM 1989: 4).

It was in the same tone and with the same conviction that the close collaborators of Sam Pitroda sought to inspire a new dynamics: 'we need local solutions in which the people are involved' (Gerson Da Cunha, Communications Consultant for the NTM), 'we are showing people a problem-solving approach' (Jairam Ramesh, Officer in the Planning Commission on special duty with the NTM), 'the Missions are trying to create a climate of contagious enthusiasm' (Avik Ghosh, consultant for the Technology Mission on Literacy), 'the Mission is trying to reconcile the interests of everyone' (P.V. Shenoi, Director of the Mission on Oilseeds), and so on (*City Scan*, June 1989). In short, fine phrases were voiced, but some relativism also: 'the Missions are basically old wine in an old bottle with new lemons' (Jairam Ramesh). These new lemons appeared at any rate to be highly appreciated since soon was mooted the idea of setting up new Missions, on cotton, pulses, floods control, tea, wastelands development,[2] etc. Manifestly, for oilseeds, the dynamics engendered had not remained fruitless. In 1987–8, India had paid its largest ever bill for vegetable oil imports despite a long series of programmes in favour of oilseeds development, but three years later, the escalation of the trade deficit was really checked, and was even forgotten since the volume of imported oil in 1987–8 had since then been divided by ten.

The Technology Mission on Oilseeds

The revised Technology Mission on Oilseeds (TMO) saw the light of day in 1988 when its objectives and strategies were explicitly stated and published. This operation provided an occasion for Dr P.V. Shenoi, IAS, its new director, to make two statements.

The first was that of the failure of the programmes adopted till then towards oilseeds, because they had led to:

- an incessantly growing and alarming bill for imports of vegetable oils;

- a particularly low annual growth rate of the production of oilseeds since the early 1970s;
- a high concentration of the domestic production on groundnut and rapeseed/mustard, on poor and rainfed land, with a profit margin grabbed by middlemen and speculators;
- a large growth in demand, particularly since the liberalization of imports and the access to very attractive prices in the international market;
- a very inequitable satisfaction of the nutritional needs, to the grave detriment of low income groups.

The second statement was that of the success of the strategy adopted for cereals, cotton, jute, sugar and milk, which transformation from import-reliance to self-reliance was brought about by a four-pronged strategy introduced in the mid-1960s:

- agricultural research institutions were re-organized to speedily develop high-yield crops;
- research and development paid a special attention to storage and processing technologies;
- a host of institutions were built to provide farmers with seeds, fertilizers, pesticides, irrigation, credit, etc.;
- others institutions, like the Food Corporation of India (FCI), helped to stabilize and increase farm prices so that farmers can make profit and invest in turn in new technologies.

Consequently, with this wealth of experience behind the country, and also its well-established infrastructure for supplying modern agricultural inputs and services, the TMO flaunt three rather ambitious objectives:

- to reduce by half the import bill before 1990, that is to say to 300 million US dollars (5 billion rupees instead of 10);
- to harvested 18 million tonnes of oilseeds in 1989–90 (the last season of the Seventh Plan), the equivalent estimated for the production of 5 million tonnes of edible oil;
- to produce 8 to 9 million tonnes of edible oil by the year 2000 (or 26 million tonnes of oilseeds) in order to secure a daily per capita supply of vegetable oil of 25 gm.

The objectives having been set out, the TMO then proposed that it be a kind of consortium that, extending beyond the frontiers dividing public and private agencies as well as administrative departments, would mobilize and coordinate the existing potential so as to 'develop a holistic and harmonized programme to achieve the common objective of self-reliance' (TMO 1989: 6). To make coordination easier, the national committee of the Mission (whose members were some senior government officials and some representatives of the different agencies or departments mobilized) was subdivided into four mini-missions. The same sub-division existed on the level of the eighteen states in which the Mission had chosen to target its action. Each of these four mini-missions took over one of the four thrusts of success enunciated above, and brochures were printed to describe—sometimes with great precision—their objectives, the paths or means to be adopted, and the division of responsibilities and financing between various central and state organizations (see Appendix 1).

PERFORMANCE OF A LOCAL POLICY OF GLOBAL AUTONOMY

The Illusions of Self-Sufficiency

The first two objectives fixed for 1990 have evidently been achieved. First of all, the production of the nine oilseed crops (groundnut, rapeseed/mustard, soya bean, sesame, sunflower, castor, safflower, linseed and niger) rose to 16.9 million tonnes (18 million tonnes had been produced the year before due to an excellent monsoon). Along with the other oil-producing materials (rice bran, cottonseed, copra, sal, neem, mahua, mango, etc.) whose potential was far to be fully exploited, the domestic production of vegetable oil reached 5.5 million tonnes in 1989–90, of which 5 million were edible oil (Dorin 1994: 88–96).

The import bill for vegetable oil, for its part, was not simply halved but reduced to practically one-fifth in two years, from 9.7 billion rupees in 1987–8 (a year which endured the severest drought of the century) to no more than 2.1 billion rupees in 1989–90 (293,000 tonnes of vegetable oil). Even if India, on the verge of financial bankruptcy, could hardly have imported more, the union government had reason to be satisfied. Not only was this bill by far the most modest of the whole decade, it was accompanied by a large increase in exports of oilcakes (particularly soya bean) and, to a smaller extent, oilseeds (particularly sesame). Finally, in 1989–90, for the first time since many years, there was a positive trade balance, with a surplus of

5.6 billion rupees. This increase in value corresponds, naturally, to an increase in the volume exported, and testifies also to a clear-cut offensive outside the Rupee Payment Area (between India and the USSR), an initiative that was all the more fortunate as there was an enormous dearth of dollars in India (Dorin 1994: 111–16).

After the Green Revolution (cereals) and the White Revolution (milk), there was much talk then of a Yellow Revolution. The speed of its execution even conferred on it the merit of better performance than the others, all the more so since its budget was relatively modest (although higher than those for the earlier programmes in favour of oilseeds). It is true that with a budget of 3 to 4 billion rupees extending over the five years of the Seventh Plan, the TMO could claim, on this count, to have put public funds to highly profitable use.

Beyond 1986 and 1987 speeches of good intentions, what exactly has been done to reach so impressive results? In 1986, when appeared for the first time the acronym TMO, the recipe for success was quite simple: to carry out a transfer of technology of the same type as that which had been undertaken, twenty years earlier, for cereals. As a matter of fact, four ingredients were mixed to boost the production of oilseeds at the end of the 1980s: high yielding seeds (selected by the research institutions and then spread to farmers through minikits or other means), water (distribution of sprinklers, assistance in digging of wells, electricity subsidy), fertilizers, and pesticides (various incentives for their use, including the Indian high rate of subsidy for fertilizers). When Sam Pitroda revived the Technology Missions in October 1987, the Mini-Mission III was entrusted to disseminate this package in oilseeds-producing areas, the responsibility for the research aspects being given to the Mini-Mission I. Out of the four mini-missions, these two kept enjoying financial priority since at least three-fourths of the five-year budget of the TMO was given to them. The Mini-Mission III alone availed of 2.5 to 3 billion rupees.

The implementation of this old recipe had of course some effects. *A posteriori*, it is noted that from 1986–7 to 1989–90, the volume of production of the nine oilseeds crops increased by more than 15 per cent per year, which was more than double the average annual rate of growth noted between 1980–1 and 1984–5. 7 per cent can be attributed to an increase in area, and 8 per cent to an increase in yields. This latter rate can partly be explained by the good monsoons at the end of the decade. However, this should not detract from the real transfer of technology that took place and which was in fact carefully followed up by the Agricultural Finance Corporation

(Bombay) appointed in 1988 by the TMO to conduct detailed and season-wise 'impact studies' in the field.

Encouraging and/or subsidizing the use of modern inputs led also to an increase in the area under oilseeds by more than 4 million ha from 1986–7 to 1989–90, to cross to 23 million ha at the end of the decade. Only a small part of this high increase can be attributed to an intensification of rotations and of mixed crops. The main part is due to either an extension of mono-cropping, or encroachment on other crops. Neither is sustainable. As well known to agricultural producers (Dorin 1994: 254–7), mono-cropping impoverishes the fertility of the soil and increases risks of parasites. Farmers also noticed that the progress of irrigation and of the near permanent cultivation of land work to the detriment of shrubs and of cattle whose excreta is yet an essential source of organic matter for the soil. As far as encroachment by oilseeds on other crops is concerned, it led to debates and controversies among economists (Gulati et al. 1996; Bansil 1997; Dorin 1999) whether it was profitable or not. Whatever be the conclusions, we may wonder if we could in fact expect other results from the Green Revolution's recipe. When the latter was under way, crops like oilseeds and pulses were relegated to risk-prone zones and seasons, to areas where—and to periods when—water supply is small or uncertain. Twenty years later, the machinery is programmed a little more in favour of oilseeds, which in turn expanded. It is a mechanical adjustment, and this Delhi-controlled machine does not provide its components with the flexibility which is now obviously needed to overcome the limits inherent in the Green Revolution model of agricultural production.

Learning and Experimenting with Autonomy

Mini-Missions I and III were not the only responsible for the sharp increase in the cultivated area in oilseeds. The Mini-Mission IV (price support, storage, processing and marketing) also played a very important part in it. But this mission was to reflect more faithfully what Pitroda wanted primarily to see: a public policy calling for the active support and involvement of numerous members of the civil society, rather than few specialized departments and savoirfaire of the unwieldy Indian administration.

Indeed, from the centre to the districts, from the local to the national levels, the new TMO intended to build bridges and cooperations between public and private agents, as also between the numerous departments of the state administrations. The new discourse was explicit enough to see the TMO no longer motivated by some objective and recipe of self-sufficiency, but rather by a more spirited ambition: that of autonomy, which can also be spelt out as 'auto-nomy', so that there is no doubt about its meaning here: work and result by which agents (individuals as well as institutions) become transformed into agents capable of changing their situation instead of behaving in such a way as to reproduce it. Being autonomous no longer meant being independent, but being capable of negotiating one's dependence within a natural and human environment that one cannot structure alone any more, an environment of growing uncertainty and complexity in which every knowledge and means are limited, and in which 'joint innovation' (*innovation solidaire* in French) is the surest guarantee for greater 'better-being'.[3] To be the 'catalyst' of this autonomy, in which agents are firstly governed by themselves and not as mere cogs in a wheel, means not only to make them confront their responsibilities, but also to informed them of the issues and of their common dependence, as well as to enable them to express their perception of the situation and of its evolution. As all this seemed to be the prime ambition of Pitroda and the new technology missions, the latter had no option but to transform the missions into a pole of information and mediation in which technology logically steps aside and recedes into the background, behind management, community participation, information and communication, and centre-states coordination. As asserted at the time P.V. Shenoi, the main thing was more about a change in attitude and thinking rather than a matter of technology.

Few years later, in the early 1990s, the Mini-Missions I and III, victims perhaps of their big budget and of the obligatory nature of their scheme, hardly seemed to have extricated themselves from a fragmented mode of management in which each public department (the private sector was not really consulted) still tended to shelter behind the narrow limits of its official fields of competence. And that was really a major source of dysfunction (as also of waste of money), as it could be noted, for instance, in Andhra Pradesh, as regards seeds, fertilizers, credit, and training (Dorin 1994: 254–66). The spirit of the mission appears nevertheless to have energized people into action, since these important problems of communication and negotiation seem thereafter to have been brought to the fore, as they should have been a long time earlier. As for the Mini-Mission II on post-harvest technologies, it hardly had the opportunity to make an in-depth study: private entrepreneurs, the main concerned parties, were not invited to the round table parleys. As a matter of fact, the state Centres for Scientific and Industrial Research worked rather in isolation, on rice-bran stabilization, which is undoubtedly an important field, among many others that should also have being investigated (storage, drying, shelling, processing of by-products, valorization of oilcakes). Mini-Mission IV, on the contrary, created upheaval in the Indian oils and oilseeds economy, thanks to the NDDB which was the kingpin of this movement, from research to marketing of vegetable oils.

The National Dairy Development Board—based in Anand—is not exactly a public sector undertaking, but rather a powerful cooperative antenna which federates millions of producers who have revolutionized the Indian dairy sector through a skilful management of foreign gifts of milk powder. On the strength of its success and autonomy, the NDDB decided, right from 1977, to get involved in the oils and oilseeds sector, a sector with which it was in competition (butter/vegetable oil) and with which it was also dependent (oilcakes for cattle feed). Its strategy was similar to the one it had deployed ten years earlier: to recycle the gifts in kind—which in this case were American, Canadian and European vegetable oils—for the development of cooperative societies of oilseeds growers which would vertically integrate the sector. From 'Operation [White] Flood', the NDDB set in motion 'Operation Golden Flow'. Its presence on the political scene remained relatively discreet to the mid-1980s, busy as it was taking possession of donations, a favour which the central government finally granted to it. But subsequently, its voice rose in pitch, until it vociferously denounced in 1987–8:

- the release of imported oils—purchased at one-third of the domestic market price—into the Indian territory right in the harvest season, leading to a catastrophic crash in farm harvest prices;
- a pro-imports lobby which drew large profits from these purchases abroad as well as from the malfunctioning of the PDS (see above);
- a large-scale tax evasion arising out of prohibitive rates of duties and taxes imposed on the processing activities.

In short, an upright organization like the NDDB felt not placed in a fair environment of competition enabling it to assert itself and ensure a decent income to the hundreds thousands of oilseeds growers that it now brought together. Whether as a consequence of this altercation or not, in April 1989 the NDDB was officially given the responsibility of leading the Market Intervention Operation (MIO), a programme worked out a year earlier by the TMO (Dorin 1994: 123–5). This delegation of power to Anand caused some unrest among administrative circles in New Delhi, as well as among business circles in Bombay. The objective of the MIO was indeed an ambitious one. It aimed at reorganizing the market to ensure that the farmer received a remunerative price without penalizing the consumer at the same time. For that, the NDDB firstly intended to channel a part of the imported volumes to market them during periods and at places that it considered opportune. Secondly, it planed to make purchases of seeds and oils in the regions where, and during the seasons when, the production was abundant. The NDDB also considered setting up throughout the Indian territory a network for storage, transport and packaging, so as to reduce the gaps in supply and demand between regions and seasons, gaps that speculators were taking full advantage of. Finally, it planned to popularize the sale of packaged oil, on the one hand to create a parallel market likely to mitigate the impact of the operations of speculation on bulk sales, on the other hand to discourage adulteration. The implementation of this programme was accompanied by a wealth of developments and of controversies. Two of its major effects need to be noted.

In the early 1990s, the Indian market for oils and oilseeds had become a field offering real opportunities: different strategies could now compete with each other. New agents did indeed enter the scene, on top of the list being the NDDB which the TMO have helped to emancipate. The NDDB, for its part, had gone on to prove that the oils and oilseeds market could be a strategic field for expansion as long as the management of men and techniques was strict and uptodate. It was then that, in turn, some para-public organizations such as the National Cooperative Development Corporation, or some agro-food giants such as Indian Tobacco Company, Lipton India, or Britannia, came on the scene, and made their presence felt. Some of them opted for the newly-opened market for packaged oils. Others evolved policies of vertical integration, treading, by so doing, into areas which had till then been closed to them, whether by the public authorities (seeds, distribution of agricultural inputs, research and development, crop production technologies, risk management, farm incomes, etc.), or by some private processors and traders (storage, transport, post-harvest technologies, marketing of oils and oilcakes, etc.). In this 'meso-system' (see Appendix 2) made up of very heterogeneous agents, some organize themselves, and others get disorganized or are forced to reorganize. The net slowing down of the import of oils in 1989, for instance, forced an organization such as the Hindustan Vegetable Oil Corporation to consider a form of cooperation with the NDDB that would have been inconceivable a few years earlier. As for the vanaspati industry, it was now clear that it had to resume the research and development activity that had been too quickly abandoned, during the 1980s, for the benefit of a lobbying activity in favour of cheap imported oils.

At the beginning of the 1990s, the oil and oilseeds sector had become a field full of opportunities because it was so for the farmers also: cultivated areas in oilseeds increased, along with their prices. Since 1989, year from which the MIO truly began its operations, the prices did indeed constantly rise, at a rate which largely exceeded that of the general wholesale price index. In the momentum, the seasonal fluctuations stabilized: the NDDB was since long denouncing—and with reason—the perverse nature of these fluctuations in an agricultural activity which was already hampered by other irregularities, those of the erratic water supply. But while the farmer was profiting more or less from such an evolution which enabled him to cover, with greater certainty, his costs of production, this was not so for the consumer, who had in fact to support most of this price increase. And it aggravated an already worrisome situation: in 1993–4, 67 per cent of the Indian population (80 per cent rural and 28 per cent urban) could afford such small quantities of vegetable oils that the lipids of their diet provided less than 15 per cent of the total dietary energy supply, that is to say less than the minimum of the Indian and international nutritional recommendations. Moreover, 15 per cent of the Indian population (19 per cent rural and 5 per cent urban) had such a low supply of lipids (less than 18.6 gm per day per capita) that it could not meet even the very basic requirement of essential fatty acids (Dorin 1999).

Since the TMO started functioning, the Indian Union has therefore greatly increased its production of vegetable oil, and has simultaneously solved its balance of trade problems. But before ensuring to each inhabitant a daily supply of 25 gm in the year 2000, the Mission must redouble its efforts, or accept imports once again: this is in fact what India has chosen to do since the mid-1990s, after having dismantled the TMO and its MIO which were politically too disruptive. In 1999, these imports exceeded 4 million tones, while huge stocks of cereals rotted in the Indian public godowns.

CONCLUSION

The economy shapes matter, energy, information and human resources in order to create some human 'better-being', physically (through food and arrangement of the external environment) and socially (with relation to the group and its values). In this activity, organization is of capital importance. To stress this point underlined years back by René Passet (1979), we can make use of Philippe Lorino's islets/continents image:

> This shaping activity is done in large historical phases, with thresholds effects: below a certain level of structuring, organization (neguentropy[4]) is the exception and entropy (disorder) is the rule. Economics can then deal with organization as being an exception, delegating it to theories of management. There are islets of organization in an ocean of entropic competition: the islets hardly bring any upheavals in the large oceanic movements. In modern societies, this approximation is no longer acceptable. As René Passet notes in his book *L'économique et le vivant*, the 'mayonnaise of organization' is in the process of getting gelled and the organizational phenomena become economically decisive: 'Economy is a negentropic structuring activity which has the effect of incorporating some structural information into matter. . . . The new advances to be expected get displaced from accumulation towards organization. . . . By crossing certain critical levels of development, a system experiences functional modifications which deeply alter its mechanisms'. The islets are connected to each other and form continents. One can no longer study oceanic movements without taking them into account. (Lorino 1989: 168)

While organization became of capital importance in the economy, it is necessary nonetheless to bring out the difference between an 'artefact' (simply organized) machine, and a living 'self-organizing' (or 'auto-organizing') machine (this difference has been suggested by von Neumann):

> The 'artefact' machine is made up of extremely reliable components (the engine of an automobile for instance, is made up of parts which have been checked and manufactured in the most durable and the most resistant manner possible in accordance with the work they have to perform). However, the machine, as a whole, is much less reliable than each of its components considered in isolation. Indeed, if even one of its components is impaired, the entire whole gets jammed, breaks down, and can only be repaired through external intervention (mechanic).

> On the other hand, with the living (self- or auto-organized) machine, things work very differently. Its components are not very reliable: they are molecules which deteriorate very fast, and all the organs are evidently made up of these molecules; in this respect, we see that in an organism, the molecules, like the cells, die and are renewed, to such an extent that an organism remains identical to itself even though all its components have been renewed. Hence, as opposed to the artificial machine, the overall reliability of the whole is large and the reliability of the components is small. This not only shows the difference in nature and logic between the auto-organized systems and the others, it also shows that there is a consubstantial link between disorganization and complex organization, since the phenomenon of disorganization (entropy) continues its course in the living even more rapidly than in the artificial machine; but, in an inseparable manner, there is the phenomenon of reorganization (neguentropy). Here lies the basic link between entropy and neguentropy, which is in no way a manichean opposition between two contrary entities [. . . .] Entropy, in a way, contributes to the organization that it tends to ruin and [. . .] the auto-organized order can not become more complex without disorder. [And] while the auto-organizing system gets detached from the environment and differentiated from it, by virtue of its autonomy and individuality, it binds itself more and more to it through the increase in opening and exchange which accompany every advance of complexity: it is auto-eco-organizing [. . . .] The environment is hence within it and [. . .] it plays a co-organizing role. The auto-eco-organizing system can therefore not suffice unto itself, it can only be totally logical by introducing into itself the foreign environment. (Morin 1990: 43, 46)

This process towards auto-eco-organizing systems can be called 'auto-eco-nomy', or even 'auto-(eco)nomy' (Dorin 1994: 214–20). And it seems that it is towards the latter that the Indian mission on oilseeds have tried to work, at least for a while. As says R. Devarajan, 'every country has its own culture based on social, economic, and political milieu in which it operates. From that culture springs forth the national ethos, which provides its population with the principles and guideline of life, which in other words, is the mission for that nation'. But 'converting a [nation] to a new mission is akin to converting a community to a new religion. It has all the pains and characteristics of proselytism' (*The Hindu*, 5 January 2000) in a world which still seems to feel more secure and independent–in India as elsewhere–when it sticks to its own 'business as usual'.

APPENDIX 1: THE MINI-MISSIONS ON OILS AND OILSEEDS

Mini-Mission I	CROP PRODUCTION TECHNOLOGY
Objectives	To increase the yields of the crops by 20 to 50 per cent To reduce the duration of occupation of the land by 5 to 25 days To evolve varieties of seeds resistant to parasites To increase the oil yield of seeds by 6 to 25 per cent To exploit tissue cultures of coconut and palms To produce seeds for multiplication on a large scale To develop appropriate cultivation materials and techniques
Coordination	Department of Agricultural Research and Education
Main partners	Indian Council of Agricultural Research (ICAR); Department of Biotechnology; The 26 State Agricultural Universities; International Crops Research Institute for the Semi-Arid Tropics (Hyderabad); Directorate of Oilseeds Research (Hyderabad); All-India Coordinated Research Projects; National Research Centre for Soybean (Indore); Central Plantation Crops Research Institute (Kasaragod); Central Research Institute for Dryland Agriculture (Hyderabad); All-India Coordinated Agronomic Project (Modipuram); Central Soil Salinity Research Institute (Karnal); All-India Coordinated Research Project on Micronutrients (Ludhiana); Coordinated Soil Test Crop Response Project (Hyderabad); Central Institute of Agricultural Engineering (Bhopal); All-India Coordinated Research Projects on Implements and Machinery and Post-harvest Technology (Bhopal)
Mini-Mission II	POST-HARVEST TECHNOLOGY
Objectives	To develop integrated modern processing chains To develop technologies for processing of non-traditional oilseeds (cotton, rice bran, extraction through solvents, etc.) To develop technologies leading to an increase in the oil yield of the raw material To improve the quality of the oils and of the oilcakes produced in the traditional units
Coordination	Department of Scientific and Industrial Research
Main partners	Council of Scientific and Industrial Research (CSIR); Department of Civil Supplies; 7 Regional Research Laboratory (Trivandrum, Hyderabad, etc.); Central Mechanical Research Institute (Ludhiana); Central Food and Technology Research Institute (Mysore); private manufacturers

Mini-Mission III	INPUT AND SERVICE SUPPORT TO THE FARMERS
Objectives	To strengthen the transfer of technologies to farmers through the National Oilseeds Development Project (NODP) and the Oilseeds Production Thrust Project (OPTP) To rationalize the production and distribution of seeds To rationalize the supply and distribution of seeds, pesticides and materials (particularly for irrigation and seedbeds) To organize, under the authority of NABARD, the distribution of specific funds by cooperatives (PACS), rural regional banks and commercial banks
Coordination	Department of Agriculture and Cooperation
Main partners	State Agricultural Departments; National Dairy Development Board (NDDB); National Bank for Agriculture and Rural Development. (NABARD); National Oilseeds and Vegetable Oils Development Board (NOVODB); International Crops Research Institute for the Semi-Arid Tropics (Hyderabad)
Remarks	NODP: Devised in 1984–5 and reformulated in 1987–8, this project was now targeted towards 180 districts in 17 large oilseeds-producing states. Its budget allocation in the Seventh Plan was 1.7 billion rupees, 1 billion being taken care of by the union government, the rest by the concerned states. The programme consisted in conducting demonstrations, in improving the quality of the services offered by the district to the farmers, and in distributing or subsidizing new seeds, fertilizers, rhizobium, chemical products against pests and diseases, and equipment. The union also financed the production of first-generation seeds for distribution to the states free of charge. OPTP: Noting that around 85 per cent of oilseeds production revolved around groundnut, rapeseed/mustard, soya bean and sunflower, this project, devised in 1987–8, targeted its action towards these four crops alone. But it covered 246 districts in 17 states, among which were 151 (out of 180) districts of the NODP. Totally financed by the union government, the budget allocation for the last three years of the Plan was of the order of 1 billion rupees. It was meant to encourage the use of good quality seeds, of different types of sulphides (such as gypsum) and of agricultural equipment, to improve the effectiveness of the protection against parasites and the marketing of the products. On the principle of 'seeing is believing', an important component of the project consisted in carrying out field

	demonstrations on plots of land belonging to the farmers. The transfer of technology that these two projects aimed at was also effected through the already proven systems of Village Extension Workers (VEWs) and Training and Visit (T&V). Brochures, bulletins, posters, radio broadcasts, etc., also formed part of the programme.
Mini-Mission IV	PRICE SUPPORT, STORAGE, PROCESSING AND MARKETING
Objectives	To guarantee a fair price to the agricultural producer (minimum incentive price displayed before the sowing season, fight against speculation and price fluctuations, . . .) To extend and modernize the capacity for storage of seeds and oils To set up and develop modern processing chains in the co-operative sector To modernize the existing processing infrastructure of the private sector To modernize the existing marketing system (correct weights, quality controls, authorization for certain mixtures of oils, . . .) To introduce packaging systems To ensure a fair price for the consumer
Coordination	Department of Agriculture and Cooperation
Main partners	National Cooperative Development Corporation (NCDC); National Dairy Development Board (NDDB); National Agricultural Cooperative Marketing Federation (NAFED); Department of Civil Supplies; Khadi and Village Industries Commission (KVIC); National Oilseeds and Vegetable Oils Development Board (NOVODB)
Remarks	While the NAFED was in charge of the minimum prices programme, it was the NDDB which had to intervene in the market to check the high seasonal fluctuation of prices (through purchases, storage, sales, and so on). The Civil Supplies Department, for its part, was responsible for the distribution of oils at reduced prices to the poorest sections of the population (through the Public Distribution System). This mini-mission also had to turn its attention to non-traditional oilseeds, such as rice bran or cotton. But for seeds originating in the forests, only the Tribal Cooperative Federations (TRIFEDS) were permitted to prospect with a view to developing the exploitation of these resources.

APPENDIX 2: THE MESO-SYSTEM

In the *Traité d'Economie industrielle* (Treaty of Industrial Economics), Jacques De Bandt devotes to the 'meso-system' a few pages where we can read the following (Arena et al. 1988: 242–9):

1. The meso-system is 'an organised and finalised set of relationships, which is endowed with an autonomous dynamics, but which is nonetheless open to—and in interaction with—other subsystems. In contrast to the image of the static "mechanics of flux" that every table of inter-industrial exchanges conveys, here it is a question, while integrating also the relations of exchange of goods between suppliers and clients, of seeing how an autonomous and thereby specific dynamics gets constructed. This [dynamics] is based, on the one hand, on the modalities of organisation of all the relations which develop between agents, and, on the other hand, on the confrontations and interactions between the projects of the agents between themselves and with the constraints linked to circumstances of time and place'.

2. 'The agents or units which make up the system are heterogeneous as regards the nature of the activity, the stage of manufacture, the organizational characteristics, the statutes, ... We have to lay stress particularly on the functional heterogeneity: while the activity of certain agents relates to production, others conduct activities which concern distribution or again finance, training, research, . . ., being understood that outside of activities of this type which are conducted in a horizontal manner, that is to say in a way which is undifferentiated in all commodity-chains, these activities can be conducted in a [more] specific manner and it is because of this that they truly constitute a component of the meso-system'.

3. 'These agents or units, which have obviously a certain autonomy and a logic of functioning that is proper to them, can, if required, get integrated into two, even several meso-systems.' But these 'agents and units share, to a certain extent, what could be called a common destiny. They are indeed inter-dependent on a certain number of common data—concerning materials, techniques, markets, . . . —and common macro-economic constraints arising out of the modalities of working, of regulation and of performance specific to the overall productive system in which they are placed. These agents and units are linked together by a whole assembly of relationships. These trade and non-trade relationships enter within the fold of a specific organisational, including institutional, framework.'

4. 'Thus presented, the meso-system is therefore an organised assembly of relationships. But it is also a strategic space. The meso-system is defined with reference to the strategic action of agents who, *vis-à-vis* the common data and constraints which have been mentioned above, continuously possess or create for themselves some degrees of liberty. It is the strategic action of the agents which defines the field of variables and targets and thereby the concerned space. More than a place of any relationships whatsoever, the meso-system thus defined with reference to the strategic action of the agents, becomes the place par excellence of

conflicting/co-operative relationships, always within a given organizational framework. It is understood that the confrontations of the strategic actions of the agents, each one seeking to exploit for himself the degrees of existing liberty, are likely to modify the organisation as well as the contours and the structures of the meso-system. It is the specific modalities of organization of the relations of interdependencies between the agents, and more particularly the confrontations of the strategic actions of these agents, under constraints, which condition and determine the dynamics proper to the commodity-chain. This in turn rebounds on the dynamics of the overall productive system.'

5. The productive meso-system revolves around 'the production of a certain type—or of several associated types—of products, goods, or services. In other words, the meso-system fulfils a certain function in terms of use value. It can obviously be goods for different purposes, that is to say, depending on the case, consumer goods, capital goods or intermediary goods. This means that the meso-system cannot be defined, in a statistical or abstract manner, without reference to this function.'

6. The 'meso-system is, in a certain way at least, a fuzzy space, that is to say its contours are partly indeterminate. This is so partly because by definition it is not possible to know the strategic spaces of the agents, as long as their strategic actions are not made concrete through decisions and actions that are observable on the one hand and, on the other hand, because the degrees of freedom are all the greater when we explore alternatives more distant from the existing structures and configurations. In other words, the fields and variables which are the object of strategic actions likely to have the greatest impact due to the magnitude of the structural transformations that can result from them, are those which are found at the borders of the fields of activity and of relationships pertaining to the earlier practices.'

NOTES

1. At least, that is what we come to if we apply the difference between the STC's issue price (around Rs. 10.5 per kg) and the sale price recommended for the PDS (around Rs. 12.5 per kg) to an average annual allocation to the PDS of 900,000 tonnes.
2. See successively *India Week*, 7 July 1989 (cotton); *The Economic Times*, 22 July 1989 (pulses); *Patriot*, 4 August 1989 (flood control); *The Economic Times*, 14 November 1989 (tea); *The Economic Times*, 5 December 1989 (wasteand development).
3. The use of the word 'well-being' in economics leads us to think of an ideal and universal state of well-being, whereas 'better-being' tries to indicate that this state has to be constantly built and rebuilt in an ever-changing environment. In other words, it is not a static point, but a relative and moving ones which call us for permanent adaptation and innovation.
4. According to the *Encyclopaedia Universalis* (2000, version 5 on CD-ROM),

this word was invented by the French mathematician and physician Léon Brillouin (*Science and Information Theory*, 1956) to replace expressions such as 'negative entropy' used more or less at the same time—but independently—by Norbert Wiener and Erwin Schrödinger (*What is life?*, 1945).

REFERENCES

Arena, Richard, Benzoni, Laurent, De Bandt, Jacques and Romani, Paul-Marie (eds.), *Traité d'Economie Industrielle*, Paris: Economica, 1988.

Bansil, P.C., 'Oilseeds Scenario: Some Issues', *Economic and Political Weekly*, vol. XXXII, no. 52 (December 1997): A191–200.

Bernard, Jean-Pierre A., 'Autonomie', in Ory, Pascal (ed.), *Nouvelle histoire des idées politiques*, Paris: Hachette, 1987: 661–8.

Bertrand, Jean-Pierre (ed.), *Le monde des oléo-protéagineux. Politique des Etats et stratégie des acteurs*, Paris: Economica, 1988.

Boltanski, Luc and Thévenot, Laurent, *De la justification. Les économies de la grandeur*, Paris: Gallimard, 1991.

Dorin, Bruno, 'Food Policy and Nutritional Security. Unequal Access to Lipids in India', *Economic and Political Weekly*, vol. XXXIV, no. 26 (26 June – 2 July 1999): 1709–17.

——, *L'économie oléifère de l'Union Indienne. Evaluation d'une stratégie d'autonomie*, Ph.D. Dissertation (Economics), Université de Montpellier I, Montpellier, 1994.

Dupuy, Jean-Pierre, 'Vers une science de l'autonomie', in *Ordres et Désordres*, Paris: Seuil, 1982: 109–24.

Dupuy, Jean-Pierre and Dumouchel, Paul (eds.), *L'auto-organisation. De la physique au politique*, Colloque de Cerisy, Paris: Le Seuil, 1983.

Gulati, Ashok, Sharma, Anil and Kohli, Deepali S., 'Self-Sufficiency and Allocative Efficiency: Case of Edible Oils', *Economic and Political Weekly*, vol. XXXI, no. 13 (30 March 1996): A15–24.

Lorino, Philippe, *L'économiste et le manager*, Paris: La Découverte, 1989.

Morin, Edgar, *Introduction à la pensée complexe*, Paris: ESF Editeur, 1990.

NTM, *The Will to Change*, New Delhi: National Technology Missions, 1989.

Passet, René, *L'économique et le vivant*, Paris: Petit Bibliothèque Payot, 1979.

TMO, *Technology Mission on Oilseed. Towards Self-Reliance: Progress Report 1986/89*, New Delhi: Ministry of Agriculture, 1989.

Varela, Francisco J., *Autonomie et connaissance. Essai sur le vivant*, Paris: Seuil, 1989.

——, J., *Principles of Biological Autonomy*, New York: Elsevier North Holland, 1979.

World Bank, *The Indian Oilseed Complex. Capturing Market Opportunities*, South Asia Rural Development Series, World Bank, New Delhi: Allied Publishers, 1999.

Explaining the Production of Milk in Gujarat and Haryana: A Matter of Scale

Véronique Alary, Anne-Claire Degail, Rachel Rivière

In 1998, with a production of nearly 74 million tonnes, India became the world's largest producer of milk, surpassing the United States. From depending on international aid to prevent famines in the past, this country has made the transition to self-sufficiency. This achievement is the result of decades of effort on the level of production (improved cattle feed and better livestock practices), procurement, and distribution, made during four Operations Flood, and by projects launched by the gigantic Indian milk cooperative, the National Dairy Development Board. These operations have made it possible, among other things, to ensure the supply of milk to urban dwellers at a reasonable price by procuring stock from a widely dispersed area (Indian farms have on an average 2 animals, their production generally being 3-4 ls/day). In a period of twenty years, the average daily availability of milk per person has jumped from 112 gm/day/ person (1973-4) to almost 204 gm (1997-8).[1]

However, with a population growth of 1.8 per cent per year and its desire to become self-reliant in basic products such as milk, India has to further boost its production. Efforts are on in the field of selection of breeds thanks to the spread of artificial insemination (free or at nominal rates) and to the fixing of a minimum price for milk in some states. The problem today is of the acute shortage of green fodder for the animals, all the more so as Indian farms extend on an average to about 1 to 2 ha of land (Seetharaman et al. 1998). To encourage the production of milk, some cooperatives offer an animal feed of dry fodder enriched with proteins (a development of the silage technique).

But how do the producers react? What are the main constraints on the level of farms? What are the main factors leading to the decision to intensify the production of milk and to sell it? To study some trends concerning production and sale and to bring out the cleavages between individual decisions and decisions on the national scale, we investigated 95 producers in Haryana and Gujarat. These states have witnessed different modes of development and organization in the milk sector, notably on account of the distinctly disparate nature of their cooperative movements. The recourse to a typology will help in formulating some hypotheses on the main constraints of the livestock systems in terms of the structures of the farms as also of the regional elements.

HYPOTHESES AND CHOICES OF INVESTIGATION

After the famines of the early part of the 1960s, all the political, social and economic decisions of the country were directed towards self-sufficiency in food. The successive agricultural policies adopted by the Indian government mainly concerned the cultivation of two cereals, wheat and rice (the Green Revolution), and oilseeds (the Yellow Revolution) as also the output of milk (the White Revolution). These initiatives were designed to meet the food needs of the population on a massive scale: to achieve self-sufficiency, followed by food security. Cereals and oilseeds were to be the sources of energy, and milk, proteins.

The development of animal husbandry is generally linked with the agro-climatic conditions in relation to the species of animals, their diet and their milk output. Considering the extent of the areas covered by livestock activity, it is hardly possible to conduct an exhaustive approach covering all the regional situations. For choosing from among the different regions, the latest classification, made by the Agro-Climatic Regional Planning (ARPU 1998; Basu and Guha 1996), gives a synthesized view of the Indian territory while taking into account the natural characteristics of the surroundings (soil, climate, relief) as also the main productive agricultural and livestock systems. On the basis of this classification, which divides the country into 15 agro-climatic regions and 73 sub-regions, two areas were chosen for their agro-climatic characteristics and the institutional modes of development of their milk production.

The zone of the trans-Gangetic plain (zone VI), which covers Haryana, Punjab, Delhi and some districts of Rajasthan, is one of the largest agro-climatic regions with a cultivated area of 14.8 million ha (Chaudry and Singh 1990). It encompasses a sub-humid zone in the north, a semi-arid zone in the east, characteristic of the 'wheat/rice' production systems resulting from the rapid development of irrigation and finally an arid zone to the west with diversified production systems (small millet, soya bean, rapeseed, cotton). We see the emergence, by way of these agro-climatic and crop pattern differences, of different strategies of production and marketing in the matter of milk. Haryana constitutes a mosaic of the different systems prevalent in the zone. Gujarat, where the National Dairy Development Board was born, has witnessed a vast development in milk production. It accounts today for nearly 4.1 per cent of the total bovine population of India and is responsible for almost 7 per cent of the total production of milk (Vaishna 1990). As less than 20 per cent of the cultivated area in Gujarat is irrigated, the production of milk is not simply an activity bringing in a supplementary income but has become for the farmers a veritable economic alternative.

These two states have witnessed a disparity in the evolution of their cooperative systems: Haryana had 2,296 cooperative societies in 1996, as against 11,430 in Gujarat. Some institutional and geopolitical factors can explain this difference. The NDDB deliberately established its headquarters at Anand, the place where the first village cooperative was born, which was far away from the political and bureaucratic interference of Delhi. Moreover, the milk production activity is seen as a source of revenue in poor and neglected zones and has therefore been privileged as an activity.

CHOICE OF THE DISTRICTS

Haryana is subdivided into three large zones. There is an arid zone (less than 320 mm/year of rainfall), a semi-arid one (around 560 mm/year) and a sub-humid one (with more than 890 mm/year) (Map 1). The two large semi-arid and arid zones are characteristic of the main production systems in north India, the 'wheat/rice' system for the subsistence crops and the sorghum/alfalfa for the fodder crops which cover a large part of the alluvial zones of north India. Then there are some more diversified systems encompassing the traditional subsistence crops (small millet, sorghum) and the cash crops (cotton, rapeseed, mustard) characteristic of the more arid zones of the rest of India.

The arid zone is represented by two districts: the district of Hisar, a zone largely irrigated by the canal and dominated by wheat and cotton, and the district of Bhiwani, whose wheat, rapeseed and millet crops are greatly affected by the problem of salinity. The semi-arid zone, for its part, is represented by the district of Karnal where the capital intensive 'wheat/rice' rotation systems, requiring inputs and irrigation, are dominant. Livestock farming on pasture land is very insignificant in Haryana which has a rural density of more than 328 inhabitants/sq. km (Table 3).

Gujarat (Map 1) is divided into 7 sub-regions in accordance with the agro-climatic conditions, the means of irrigation in place and the level of development of livestock activity. In north Saurashtra (a semi-arid dry zone with 537 mm of rain per year), the district of Rajkot is characterized by production systems highly oriented towards the cultivation of cash crops (groundnut, cotton, mustard) and what are called 'coarse cereals' (*bajra*, millet). The dominant species in the livestock is the local Kankrej, more resistant to the prevalent agro-climatic conditions and notably those of the dry season. In middle Gujarat (more humid semi-arid zone with 940 mm of rain per year), the former Kheda district (today divided into Kheda and Kaira districts) is characterized by its large number of animals per farm and by the presence of breeds which have been crossed with Holsteins. Morever, the development of irrigation has made it possible to grow commercial crops such as tobacco which is competing today with the milk production activity. The different levels of intensification of milk production in Gujarat are explained by the great differences in the population densities (397 inhabitants/sq. km in Kheda as against 164 in Rajkot), in the crop-growing possibilities related partly to the hydroelectric facilities, and in the disparities in the efforts of the cooperative sector in accordance with the potential of each district.

Two main criteria have been used for making the choice of the villages to be investigated in each district: the availability of irrigation, and the degree of remoteness. The irrigation systems in place make it possible to explain the choice of the crops grown and hence the place given to the livestock activity. For the second criterion, it is assumed

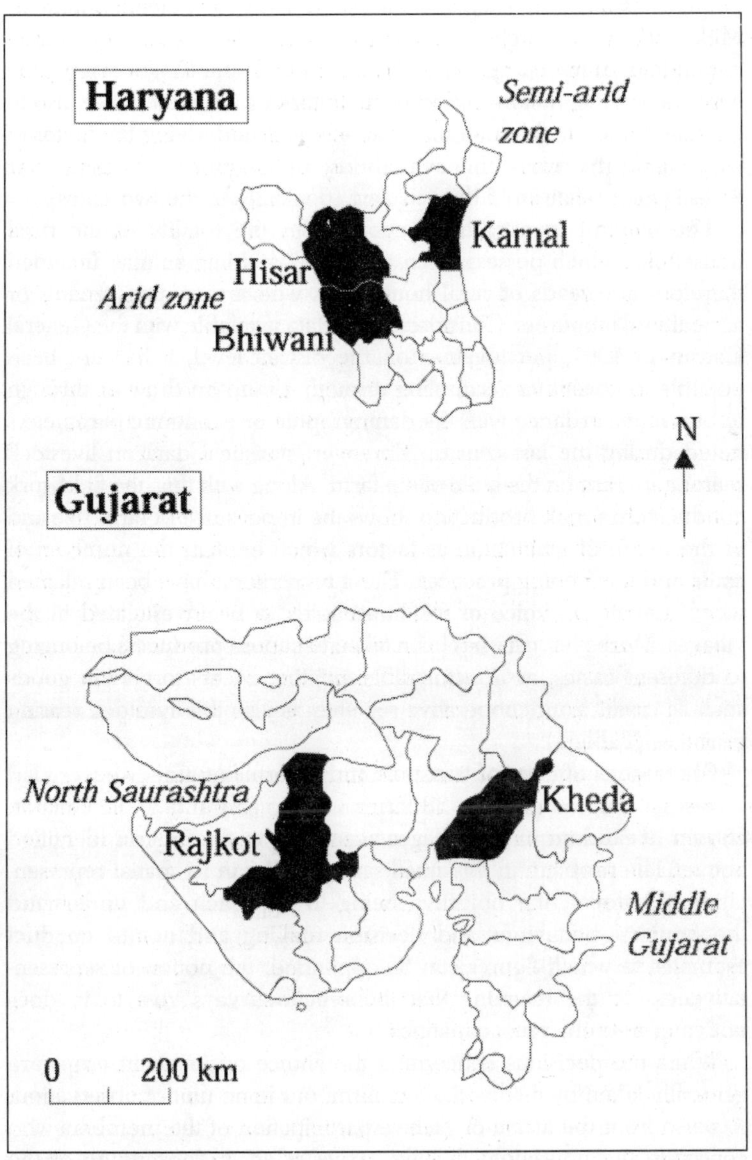

MAP 1: LOCATION OF THE DISTRICTS

that the strategies aiming at increasing the production of marketable crops and at innovations (market garden produce, fruit orchards, poultry farming, etc.) depend greatly on access to potential markets. Milk, which is a highly perishable commodity, is almost entirely dependent on infrastructure for its transport. In the Rajkot district, the types of rearing systems, whether sedentary or nomadic, have also to be taken note of, although this is an element underlying the factor of water and therefore the availability in irrigation. In total, our investigation relates to 5 districts and 16 villages in the two states.

The field of investigation encompasses the totality of the rural households which possess at least one milk yielding animal. Included therefore are heads of rural households who are owners, tenants or agricultural labourers. Considering the data available with the General Census of 1991, put together on the district level, it has not been possible to constitute a sampling through a random draw or through quotas in accordance with the demographic or economic parameters noted during the last census. Moreover, statistical data on livestock rearing are rare on the scale of the farm. Along with this, the fieldwork conducted on milk production shows the importance of farm size and of the mode of cultivation as factors which explain the numbers of cattle and the feeding practices. These two criteria have been retained when making a choice of the households to be investigated in the villages. Moreover, care has been taken to choose producers belonging to different castes, as a factor differentiating access to certain goods such as credit from cooperative societies as also the livestock rearing practices (Table 1).

For reasons of costs of transport and in terms of time, we were led to restrict our sampling to 38 farms in Haryana and 57 in Gujarat, chosen at random in the villages according to the criteria identified above. The problem in this small sampling lies in its spatial representation. However, the objective being to approach and understand the farmers' behaviour and decision making and not to conduct estimates to which figures can be appended, the notion of representativeness in the meaning that theoretical surveys give to it, does not enter into our preoccupations.

While the decisions concerning the choice of the main crops are generally taken by the head of the farm, our main unit of observation, it is also from the active or passive participation of the members who constitute the household that we arrive at an understanding of the coordinated actions conducted on the farm. The unit of observation was therefore the household, a study of the wives, children, elderly

TABLE 1: DISTRIBUTION OF THE SAMPLE PER DISTRICT

District	Sample	Castes (i)	Mode of farm (ii)	Size of farm in acres (iii)
HARYANA				
Karnal	13 farms (35%)	Low: 54 % High: 46 %	Inheritor: 69 % Purchaser: 8 % Sharecropper: 15 % Tenant: 8 % Landless: 0 %	0 to 1.9 a: 8 % 2 to 3.9 a: 23 % 4 to 7.9 a: 23 % 8 to 11.9 a: 23 % >12 a: 23 %
Hisar Bhiwani	25 farms (65%)	Low: 4 % Middle: 84 % High : 12 %	Inheritor: 84 % Purchaser: 0 % Sharecropper: 8 % Tenant: 0 % Landless: 8 %	0 to 1.9 a: 8 % 2 to 3.9 a: 24 % 4 to 7.9 a: 20 % 8 to 11.9 a: 24 % >12 a: 24 %
GUJARAT				
Kheda	29 farms (50.8%)	Low: 24 % Middle: 4 % High: 72 %	Inheritor: 86 % Purchaser: 3.5 % Sharecropper: 3.5 % Tenant: 0 % Landless: 7 %	0 to 1.9 a: 27.6 % 2 to 3.9 a: 10.4 % 4 to 7.9 a: 27.6 % 8 to 11.9 a:10.4 % >12 a: 24 %
Rajkot	28 farms (49.2%)	Low: 18 % Middle: 32 % High: 18 % Muslims: 32 %	Inheritor: 60 % Purchaser: 11 % Sharecropper: 11 % Tenant: 0 % Gift: 11 % Landless: 7 %	0 to 1.9 a: 7 % 2 to 3.9 a: 21 % 4 to 7.9 a: 36 % 8 to 11.9 a: 11 % >12 a: 25 %

NOTES: (i) 'low castes': scheduled castes or tribals; 'middle castes': artisans and farming castes; 'high castes': castes of higher rank in the Indian system and comparable communities (Brahmins, Sikhs, etc.).

(ii) The inheritors consist of the overall households having inherited a part of the land while another part may have been bought or simply taken on rent; the tenants are heads of households owning no land of their own either bought or inherited.

(iii) 1 acre = 0.408 ha.

persons making it possible to achieve an in-depth grasp of the family structure and the internal working of the family group, particularly the distribution of tasks between cultivation and cattle rearing.

Information was collected on different levels (plot, species, age group of the animals), to be then recombined. While there is no direct relation between these different elements, they constitute nevertheless units that are relevant for analysis in order to obtain precise information on the modalities of access to the land or on the management of each type of activity conducted on the farm, as also on the way of reasoning behind the sale or the consumption within the household, which is going to have local and regional repercussions. The different types of statistical units which are included in the observation then define 'the hierarchical structure of the information' (Lebart, Morineau and Piron, 1995).

Such breaking up of the information and of cross-checking it with other elements of the investigation is indispensable for all quantitative data, be it household expenses, recourse to credit, the type of feed given to the cattle or the extent of the cultivated areas. Consequently, several types of individuals within the household were interviewed. Hence persons residing on the farm for more than six months, whether related or not to the head of the household, were included in the households (or 'Peasant Production Units'). This group generally acknowledges the authority of a single person as head of the household. Thus those interviewed were preferably those who made decisions on the agricultural choices. However, by choosing the household unit as a unit of sampling, it becomes possible to encompass these different components in a hierarchical order, as it corresponds to a relatively stable unit in rural surroundings.

Methods of Analysis of the Population

The difficulty in the construction of a typology is to choose a unit of analysis which is relevant to the search for the decision-making processes. Indeed, in the field of livestock rearing, the factors differentiating the productive units can be as varied as the opening up to the market or the entrenchment of the cooperative movement, access to the means of production (notably type of irrigation, mechanical traction), access to land or to pasture land, the forms of mobilization of work (family labour, seasonal labour), the influence of connected activities and incomes in the farming economy, or even the personality of the members making up the household. All these elements give an account of the multiplicity of the modes of management of an agricultural economy, as also the way in which individual decisions are linked to decisions on the scale of the household, the village and the region.

In view of the complexity and sometimes the singularity of the way the livestock rearing systems function in terms of the agro-climatic conditions, the size of the farms, the means of access to water and the efficiency of the cooperative, it is difficult for us to obtain a synthesized view of the types of farms without taking recourse to multidimensional methods of analysis to classify our population and hence be able to reason out any number whatsoever of variables. The multivaried Analysis of Multiple Correspondences (AMC) brings out notably some types of individuals having similar profiles from the standpoint of the criteria chosen to describe them.[2] These criteria are established through the choice of the main variables called 'active variables'. The types of individuals are described with the help of additional 'illustrative' variables.

However, the typology leads necessarily to a structuralist approach. It is consequently assumed that the farmers belonging to a given class will adopt a similar behaviour. Yet the reality and its vagaries are such that things very often happen otherwise. The socio-economic situation of the farmers changes fairly rapidly from one year to the next. In fact, this typology attempts nothing other than painting an orderly picture of the mode of farming.

The investigations conducted reveal the importance of access to the factors of production (land, water and mechanical traction) for understanding the way the farms function. In irrigated areas, the farms enjoy a relative security in the matter of green fodder. With mechanical traction, some producers give up the use of devices drawn by bullocks which often played the role of reproducers. This has promoted the spread of artificial insemination. Consequently, we have chosen to consider as main variables those which make it possible to measure the apportionment of land (cultivated areas, modes of access to the land) and the means of production (irrigation, tractor, etc.). For the activity of livestock farming, the main variables are the capital in heads of cattle owned and the portion of land devoted to the growing of fodder.

As a supplement to the information concerning the structures of production, data concerning cultivation and husbandry practices, modes of management, and the way in which the producers confront the environmental and institutional constraints have been utilized so as to give a more complete description of the factors of differentiation in the sample studied.

THE STRATEGIES OF THE PRODUCERS IN MATTERS OF ANIMAL HUSBANDRY

Figure 1, retracing the first 10 appropriate values, shows the importance of the first three axes as factors for explaining the shade of points, each axis being a linear combination of the modalities of the main variables.

No.	Eigen value	Perc.	Cumulate perc.	
1	.2392	7.88	7.88	**************************************
2	.2200	7.25	15.13	**********************************
3	.1588	5.23	20.36	**************************
4	.1256	4.14	24.50	*********************
5	.1188	3.91	28.41	********************
6	.1058	3.48	31.89	*****************
7	.0981	3.23	35.12	***************
8	.0918	3.02	38.15	*************
9	.0898	2.96	41.11	*************
10	.0871	2.87	43.97	************

FIGURE 1: HISTOGRAM RETRACING THE FIRST 10 APPROPRIATE VALUES

On the first axis of the analysis of multiple congruities, we note a strong link between farm size (total cultivated area), private minor irrigation (wells and tube-wells) and the number of cattle. One distinction is seen already between the producers in terms of possession of sunk capital (land, means of irrigation) and in living capital (number of animals). The proportion of the cultivated area reserved for growing fodder for the livestock as also the share of milk produced and consumed within the household are also strongly correlated to the capital in land and irrigation.

Factor 1 therefore brings into opposition two types of farms. There are the small farms of less than 1 ha making small investments in agricultural equipment and in capital (little irrigation, less than two local buffaloes or cows), and there are the medium and large farms of more than 5 ha, called 'intensive' farms. These account for at least 3 animals per farm and generally they are animals which have been crossed with exotic breeds.

The second axis brings out the divergent nature of the farms in terms of the type of crop, and more precisely of the dominant cash crop grown in the zones irrigated by the canal. It brings out the disparate nature of especially those farms oriented to rice cultivation in the Kheda district and cotton in Hisar. These two types of zone are divergent also on the axis of livestock rearing systems (more precisely of the breeds and of the outlets for the milk). In Kheda, the farmers have adopted high yielding breeds (crossed with Holsteins) and they sell their surplus milk to the cooperative, whereas in Hisar district, the farmers have turned towards the production of buffalo milk for domestic consumption. This has resulted in a differentiation in the use made of the males. In Kheda the males are reserved for reproduction whereas in the Hisar district they are used for traction. Thus, the second axis distinguishes the farms in terms of cash crops and dominant animal husbandry systems in zones that are identical from the standpoint of means of irrigation.

The third axis differentiates the farmers of the dry semi-arid zones from those of the arid zones (Rajkot and Bhiwani) in terms of agro-pastoral conditions as also socio-economic parameters (demographic density). In Rajkot, the farms generally extend over more than 5 ha (as against 1 ha in the Bhiwani district). The former draw their main income from groundnut whereas the latter have turned towards the cultivation of cereals (wheat, *bajra*) for consumption within the household. In Rajkot the farmers keep the male oxen for animal traction whereas in Bhiwani they keep one male for reproduction and a single pair of bullocks for working in the fields, taking recourse preferably to a rented tractor for ploughing work. In Rajkot, the farmers possess a livestock of local cows (Kankrej) which may go up to 9 heads as against an average of 1 head for the Bhiwani farmers. Thus the third axis differentiates two zones well demarcated by the regional administrative framework.

The overall analysis of the factorial plan reveals profiles specific to the animal husbandry economy of the zones investigated, in accordance with the extent of land, the means of irrigation and the use of mechanical traction. In a simplified way, one can talk of:

- mechanized large and medium-sized farms of more than 5 ha which account for more than 3 cows or buffaloes, whose production is meant essentially for covering the needs of the family in milk, while the surplus is converted into *ghee*, the cooking medium for the family's food (Karnal);
- medium-sized farms which invest in genetically selected animals and which sell most of the milk produced to the cooperative society (Kheda);
- small farms of less than 2 ha which keep one or two buffaloes to look after the milk needs of the family (Hisar/Bhiwani);
- medium-sized farms of 4 ha in arid zones which have more than two local cows with a high propensity towards sale of the milk (Rajkot district).

The projection of the additional variables (characteristics of the head of the household, the marketing strategy for the sale of the milk, etc.) makes it possible to enrich the analysis and to diagnose the respective effects of some among them and conversely the absence of other effects.

For instance, a great deal of concordance has been noted between the initial possessions of the producers (means of irrigation, cultivated areas, tractor, number of animals) and the social characteristics of the head of the household, notably his community affiliation. With regard to axis 1, the two types of differentiated farms, whose mode of working depends essentially on private means of irrigation, do indeed correspond to these two major types. There are the small and medium farms held by a majority of heads of households belonging to the 'low' castes, and there are on the other hand the large farms held mostly by heads of households belonging to the 'high' castes. The first axis can therefore also be defined as the axis of social differentiation. It is noted also that the Patels, an upper caste in Gujarat, sell mostly to the cooperatives (managed partly by Patels). A differentiation then exists in the strategies of sale according to the communities.

The practice of a secondary activity (handicraft, salaried work, trade, etc.) has no effect on the degree of intensification of agriculture or on the modes of farming. It has instead a relationship with the mode of management of the expenses within the family and the priorities of the household. It is common to use non-farm income to send the children to study in private institutes or to raise status in the village society by giving larger religious gifts, to the detriment of productive investment.

The smallest farms or the landless farmers buy their green fodder on the market while the large landowners take recourse to permanent labourers to cut it on their own land. So in the small farms, the feed ration comprises a large part of dry fodder, mainly cereal straws. Characteristics of the farms (size, irrigation) therefore explain partly the different strategies for feeding cattle.

At this stage of the analysis, the first three factors give an idea of the main structures of the population investigated in terms of private means of irrigation, size of the farm, and dominant animal breeds (improved or local breeds, buffaloes). Structures which are less solid appear on the axes of higher rank (axes 3 to 5). Thus, an Ascending Hierarchical Classification can make it possible to discover the existence of new types of producers not revealed on the main factorial plane. It leads to some homogeneous regroupings of producers on the basis of the most significant factors. This gives the great advantage

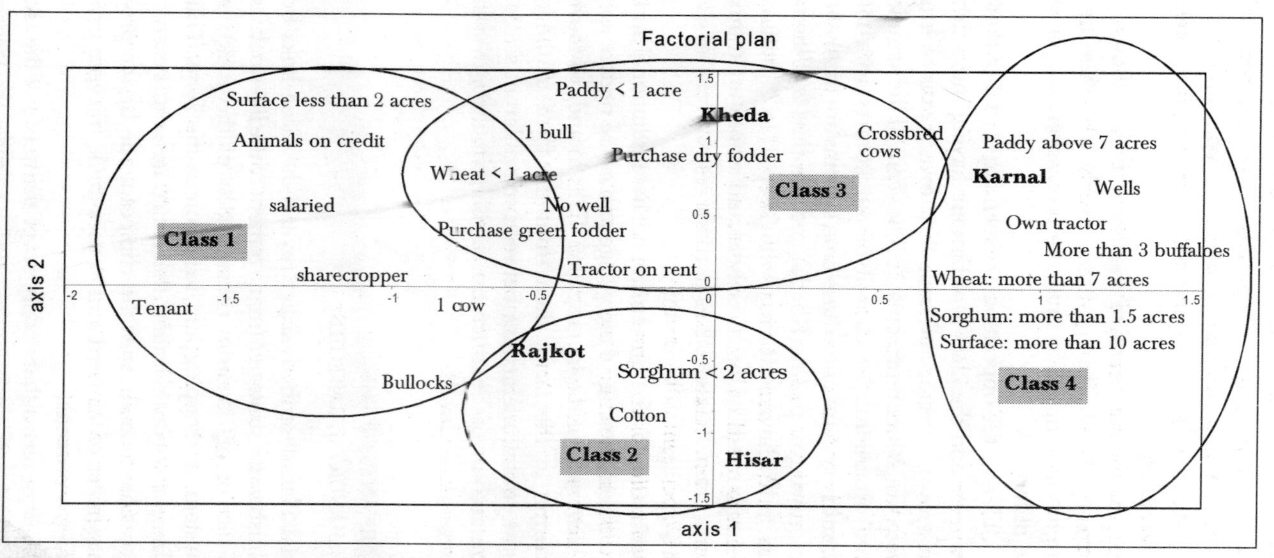

FIGURE 2: FACTORIAL PLAN OF THE FIRST TWO AXES

of obtaining stable groups. Like the Analysis of Multiple Correspondences, this classification is conducted on the basis of active variables which make it possible to define the typical profiles. These are then illustrated (Figure 2) by information arising out of the additional variables.

A perusal of the histogram of the level indices shows a basic partition into 4 classes. This partition clearly identifies the farms according to the presence of a canal, the possession of a private well and the size of farm.

On axis 1, there is the opposition between the class 1 of landless or marginal farmers, and the class 4 of farmers having more than 5 ha who generally own a tractor and have their own means of irrigation. Each of these two classes represents 31.5 per cent of the sample. Axis 2 brings into opposition the class 3 of the farmers with intensive animal husbandry systems and whose crop systems are highly oriented towards the growing of paddy (Kheda) and the class 2 of the farmers of the Hisar and Bhiwani districts who keep 1 to 2 buffaloes for meeting the milk needs of the household and whose main income is derived from cotton. These classes account respectively for 12.3 per cent and 24.7 per cent of the sample.

This classification of the farms brings out the institutional and socio-cultural factors, on the scale of the village and of the region, identified during the setting up of the investigation. This to and fro movement from the region to the farm, then from the farm to the region, underlines the strong interactions between the different scales. Each of these takes account of the structures, the behaviours or the strategies at the lower or higher levels.

THE DETERMINANTS OF THE ANIMAL HUSBANDRY STRATEGIES

The Factorial Plan described earlier reveals the close links between the animal husbandry strategies (management of the livestock farming, strategy of sale or of domestic consumption of the milk) and the dominant system of cropping and irrigation in the zone. Thus, it is only by taking into consideration the entire farming system that it becomes possible to understand the choices made by the producers on the management of the herd and its uses (milk, traction) in a given institutional environment.

Generally, large farms that widely cover the needs of the family in cereals and which sell a substantial surplus to meet the farming and family expenses, allocate more than 1 ha for fodder crops. But in the district of Rajkot where the largest amount of space is available, some farms have had, since 1990, to reduce their livestock on account of the failure of the monsoon and the small level of facilities available for irrigating the land. So the available area is not by itself a determining factor. It is a combination of land area and means of irrigation that explains the intensification of milk production. Indeed, the majority of the farmers who have invested in milk production are found in the Kheda and the Karnal districts. These same farmers generally have 2 or 3 wells with submersible pumps which enable them to secure good crop yields.

At the other end, the small farms that devote less than 0.5 ha to fodder crops register large fluctuations of their yields. They generally do not have more than 2 cows throughout the year. At the extreme end, there are the salaried landless farm workers who do not have the means to make the slightest investment in capital in the form of live animals.

However, the majority of the large landowners of the district of Karnal consume, in the form of raw milk or of processed products (particularly in the form of curd and *ghee*), almost the totality of their milk production while the small landowners conserve 0.5 to 1 l for the daily milk needs of the family and sell the surplus. In the dry arid zones of Rajkot, the majority of the farmers who experience problems of water scarcity, also sell their surplus milk. Consequently, the existence and the stability of water supply influence the milk selling strategies of the producers. This can be explained by the expected income from the crops. The farmers of the arid or semi-arid scantily irrigated zones compensate for the modest inflow of money from the crops they grow by selling their milk. Moreover, in the Kheda district where the cooperative system is firmly entrenched, the farmers who have been able to diversify their crops thanks to the canal, and have changed over to cultivating cash crops such as tobacco, have turned away from milk production. Thus, the irrigation capacity acts indirectly on the strategies of marketing versus household consumption.

To the irrigation and surface availability factors is added the influence of the type of cropping system. In the two zones of our sample covered by the canal, we observe some disparate strategies of sale between the farms. In Kheda, the farms oriented towards the cultivation of paddy, derive a substantial income from their improved livestock by the sale of milk, while the farmers of the Hisar district who grow cotton for sale consume within the household almost the totality of their production of buffalo milk. Thus, the type of crop grown, being a subsistence or a cash crop, although contingent on agro-climatic conditions, does influence the strategies for intensification of milk production for selling purposes.

Percentage of Land Devoted to Fodder in the Strategies of Sale

In the districts of the arid zone of Haryana (Hisar and Bhiwani), the farmers generally devote around 10 per cent of their available agricultural land to fodder crops for herds of less than two cows or buffaloes, whatever be the size of their farm. While the majority of the farmers feed their animals well, few sell their milk products. The major part of the monetary income comes from commercial crops, particularly those of cotton in the rainy season. The sale of milk is resorted to by farmers having more than three dairy cows or buffaloes and who devote up to 20 per cent of their land surface to growing fodder. The latter sell fresh milk occasionally to traders or convert it into *ghee* for sale in the neighbourhood. The income from milk generally does not exceed 20 per cent of their turnover. The majority of the milk (between 20 to 80 per cent of the amount that has been milked) is consumed within the household. These milk production strategies for household consumption are deeply rooted in the food habits of the villagers. Milk is not only the main source of protein, but it is central to the social and village life of the farmers.

In Karnal district, the system of management of the herd and of utilization of the products after milking is identical for small farmers owning less than 1 ha. One-tenth is grown with green fodder (i.e. less than 0.1 ha). The livestock consists on an average of 1 to 3 buffaloes. The milk produced is entirely for household consumption and the land is used mainly for growing cash and subsistence crops. In this case, it is the smaller cost of milk production that motivates the farmer. The income on the capital he possesses in the form of a living animal enables him to satisfy the need for milk for the family tea. In case of extreme need, these producers take plots of land on rent to meet the fodder requirements of their animals.

The 'large' owners of more than 4 ha use almost 10 per cent of their cultivated area for growing fodder crops in order to feed a herd of 3 to 5 buffaloes. Some invest in cows which have been cross-bred with Holsteins so as to get better milk yields. These farmers generally possess substantial irrigation facilities which explain the high crop yields on the plots. The sale of milk accounts for a small part of their turnover as compared to the income from subsistence crops (wheat, rice). Moreover, the major share of milk is consumed within the household (60 per cent). Thus, these farmers have got accustomed to eating *ghee* on their *chapatis* to fortify their three daily meals.

In Haryana, small farmers owning less than 2 ha and landless villagers who work for others, adopt strategies for selling their milk. Milk constitutes the main source of income of the household accounting for up to 70 per cent of their turnover. The children, and more precisely the girls, are in charge of the daily care of the animals while the able-bodied adults work outside as salaried farm labourers. The main place of sale is the village. Few of them sell to the cooperative on account of the higher prices prevalent in the private market, the distance at which some of them are located from the places of collection of the cooperative, and the small involvement of the cooperative in village development, whether it be for the supply of concentrated food for the cattle or by way of social investments (dispensary, schools).

In Gujarat, the majority of the farms are involved in the sale of milk. This activity is very important for farmers owning less than 2 ha of land and around 5 animals, particularly cows obtained out of cross-breeding with Holstein races. The income from milk goes up to 50 to 70 per cent of the turnover of the farm. These latter devote between 30 to 50 per cent of their land for growing fodder crops. Only the large landowners having been able to diversify their cropping system by adopting highly remunerative crops such as tobacco, progressively give up the sale of milk.

In the district of Rajkot where less than a fourth of the cultivated surfaces are irrigated, the producers make substantial use of the supplementary products distributed by the cooperative for maintaining a good feed ration for the animals. In conditions of extreme drought, they sell some animals. The sale of milk constitutes between 40 to 70 per cent of their turnover. The entrenchment of the cooperative in this climatically and infrastructurally underprivileged region has enabled stable revenues to be generated in the rural environment, which was not possible from crops with their excessively unpredictable yields.

Thus, in contrast to the farms of the Karnal district, the majority of those in Gujarat have taken to milk production for sale. For the medium-sized farms (between 2 to 4 ha), which devote 12 per cent of their land to fodder crops, milk constitutes the main income (between 50 to 70 per cent of the turnover of the farm). For the small farms devoting 60 per cent of their land to fodder crops, the sale of milk constitutes the main income of the farm (up to 95 per cent of the turnover). These farms use a very small part of the milk for household consumption (between 3 to 9 per cent of the production). On the other hand, in farms of more than 5 ha which have been able to grow highly profitable cash crops (tobacco), the livestock activity is quite often limited to simply covering the household needs. Thus, the trend followed by these farms is similar to that of the large landowners of Karnal.

Consequently, the production of milk is indeed considered a secondary activity by producers as soon as the agricultural income becomes substantial. Although the small producers mention it as being a subsidiary activity, it represents between 50 to 70 per cent of the annual income and pays for their day-to-day purchases of spices and vegetables which form the base of the daily meals along with the cereals they produce. Milk therefore constitutes a regular source of income in contrast to the sudden fluctuations in prices and yields in the cropping systems. Moreover, the percentage of land given over to fodder cultivation seems to constitute a good indicator of the marketing or the household consumption strategies of the producers. The strategies of sale are confirmed when the farmer devotes more than 10 per cent of his available land to fodder crops and this is so whatever be the size of his farm. In addition, the dynamism of the cooperative movement in Gujarat has certainly promoted the intensification of milk production on the farm level through the input of concentrates and the improvement of fodder yields. But as long as the state continues to grant support prices for commercial and subsistence crops, milk production for purposes of sale will remain limited to the most impoverished. It is moreover with a view towards improving their lot that the strategies and modes of intervention of the cooperative are based. In the process of liberalization that threatens the support prices for crops, and in the event that the prices of milk will remain highly regulated by the cooperative, great changes would take place in the coming years.

Let us not, however, convince ourselves of a strong rationality on the local level that would relegate to the background the human and even cultural characteristics distinct to the development of the Indian milk cooperative system. These are the very characteristics which lend it a peculiar aura with Indian consumers as also beyond the borders of the country. The whole development of the Indian milk production system is not based on a simple, rational and even economics-oriented way of thinking within a nevertheless highly insecure agricultural environment. The analysis of the strategies of the selling of milk by the producers tend to blot out the local specificities, while an institutional analysis on the national scale underscores India's originality and its singularity in the conduct of this activity (Alary 1999). Moreover, the strategies of production and even more of marketing, described in the framework of the Indian farming systems, can hardly be generalized or applied to other countries on account of the specific place that milk occupies in the modes of consumption as also the place that the cow, as a 'sacred animal', occupies in agricultural farms. The allocation of a portion of very scarce land, for feeding one or two cows, or the taking on rent by 'landless' peasants of a plot of land for growing fodder crops, cannot be explained through the unique factors of economic rationality.

CONCLUSION

The factorial plan and the analysis of the farming systems show the extent to which water lies at the core of the cropping systems and consequently the animal husbandry system. The means of irrigation partly dictate the possible crops and the average yields, which in turn determine the financial capacities of the farmers for investing in animal husbandry as also the physical capacities for meeting the feed requirements of the herd. Thereafter, cropping possibilities and area available explain the productive and commercial strategies. When the cultivated area exceeds 8 ha, farmers give up the production of milk for commercial purposes in favour of the cultivation of prestigious crops such as wheat and paddy. As regards the highly profitable cash crops, the farmers change over to these when they own around 5 ha.

The analysis of the increase and intensification of milk production hence necessitates the integrated study of the agricultural area and the means of irrigation, factors that condition the size of the herd and the proportion of land allocated to fodder cultivation. The overall political decisions (agricultural policy and animal husbandry policies) may determine the level of production of milk as also its marketing and therefore the food security in the cities (Desai 1997). Our field-work also brings out the lacuna between the intensification of milk production and the sale of the milk. This is closely related to the food habits and preferences prevalent in India. Thus, the close bonds between the structure of the farm and the mode of raising the livestock, and between individual and local decisions on the one hand, and policy decisions on the national level, on the other hand, have to be examined in-depth if we are to fully understand the conflicts and trade-offs of liberalization in a high priority sector such as that of milk.

NOTES

1. Ministry of Agriculture, Dept. of Animal Husbandry and Dairying, New Delhi, 1997.
2. The principle of this method of data analysis is described by Lebart et al., 1995.

REFERENCES

Alary, V., 'Le système coopératif laitier en Inde face à la libéralisaton', *Economie rurale*, 252 (July-August 1999): 35-41.

ARPU, *Agro-Climatic Regional Planning: Recent Developments*, ARPU Working Paper 10, August 1998, Ahmedabad: 50-9.

Basu, D.N. and Guha, G.S., *Agro-Climatic Regional Planning in India, Vol.I: Concepts and Applications,* Ahmedabad: Concept Publishing Company, 1996.

Chaudry, A.L. and Singh, I.J., *Planning for Agricultural Development in Trans-Gangetic Plains Region (Zone VI) with Emphasis on Haryana State*, Agro-Climatic Planning Unit for Trans-Gangetic Plains Region Zone VI, Hisar: Haryana Agricultural University, 1990.

Desai, Bhupat M., *Agricultural Development Paradigm for the Ninth Plan under Next Economic Environment*, Ahmedabad: Oxford and IBH, 1997.

Lebart, L., Morineau, A. and Piron, M., *Statistique Exploratoire Multidimensionelle*, Paris: Dunod, 1995.

Seetharaman, S.P., Singh, Gurdev and Pichholiya, K.R., *Understanding Fodder Marketing—A Study in Gujarat*, no. 178, Ahmedabad: Indian Institute of Management, 1998.

Vaishna, T.N. *Livestock Development in Zone 13 and 14—Special Reference to Arid Zone*, ARPU Technical Paper 3, Ahmedabad, 1990.

APPENDICES

TABLE 2: GENERAL AGRICULTURAL DATA PER DISTRICT

States and districts	Production systems (1)	Area ha (1)	Net irrigated area 1991 (%) (1)	Rural 1991 density (inhab./ km²)	Number of producers investigated
HARYANA					
Semi-arid zone					
1. Karnal	Wheat/Paddy	372,000	98.60	355	13
Sub-total		4172,500		515	13
Arid zone					
1. Hisar	Wheat/Cotton-Millet	631,500	80.20	236	15
2. Bhiwani	Wheat/ Mustard-Small millet	509,900	39.80	180	10
Sub-total		6,160,600		187	25
Total Haryana		11,680,100		328	38
GUJARAT					
Semi-arid zone					
1. Kheda	Tobacco/Millet	719,000	49.10	397	28
Arid zone					
1. Rajkot	Cotton Groundnut-Millet	1,120,000	26.10	164	29
Total Gujarat		1,839,000		210	57

SOURCES: (1) Agro-climatic zonal planning unit for trans-gangetic plains region zone VI.
(2) *Indian Agricultural Statistics*, vols. I and II, Ministry of Agriculture.

TABLE 3: GENERAL DATA ON LIVESTOCK PER DISTRICT

States and districts	Composition of livestock (%) (1)	Yield in milk (L/animal/ day) (1)	Type of fodder	Area under fodder (% culti-vated area) (1)	Pasture land (% culti-vated area) (1)
HARYANA					
Semi-arid zone					
1. Karnal	Buffalo: 65 Local cow: 29 Hybrid cow: 6	Buffalo: 4.8 Local cow: 3.2 Hybrid cow: 5.8	Sorghum Bersim	9	3
Sub-total	651,000				
Arid zone					
1. Hisar 2. Bhiwani	*Buffalo: 58 *Local cow: 40 *Hybrid cow: 2	*Buffalo: 6.3 *Local cow: 4.25 *Hybrid cow: 6.6	1- Sorghum, Bersim, Millet 2- Sorghum, Bersim, Oats	*17	*0
Sub-total	*771 000				
Total Haryana	6,025,000		11,680,100	12	0.8
GUJARAT					
Semi-arid zone					
1. Kheda	Buffalo: 70 Local cow: 25 Hybrid cow: 5	Buffalo: 5.1 Local cow: 3.1 Hybrid cow: 6.9	Maize, Sorghum, Millet	3	5.3
Sub-total	920,000				
Arid zone					
2. Rajkot	Buffalo: 29 Local cow: 70 Hybrid cow: 1	Buffalo: 6.4 Local cow: 4.5 Hybrid cow: 8.1	Maize, Sorghum, Millet	15	4
Sub-total	571,000				
Total Gujarat	10,742,000		1,839,000	10	2.6

NOTE: *Data available for Hisar only.

SOURCE: (1) R. Saxena, *Comparative Advantage and Competitiveness of the Indian Milk Sector*, Institute of Rural Management, 1998.

Conclusion
From the Top or From the Bottom? Rural Development and Food Security

Frédéric Landy

> *Télerama:* How did you choose [the French peasant whose biography you have written]?
>
> *Alain Corbin:* I did not look for a representative individual. Representativeness is a meaningless idea, considering the social, geographic, anthropological diversity of the peasants in the 19th century. So, why not choose him at random? I chose first of all an area with which I had every likelihood of feeling a certain empathy: Orne, the region of my birthplace where I spent all my holidays with my grandparents. And then I went to the archives of Alencon [the headquarter of Orne district]. I took out one of the volumes of the inventory. I closed my eyes. My finger fell on the village of Origny-le-Butin. In the tables of the registry office for the end of the 18th century, I found, by chance, two names which pleased me. They were Jean Courapied and Louis-Francois Pinagot. The first had died young; I therefore preferred the second who had lived till the age of seventy-eight!
>
> *Télérama* no. 2512, 4 March 1998.

In early 1996, I returned to India to update my 1993 data on the liberalization of the prices of chemical fertilizers. I had followed from France the trend in this sector during the entire course of the earlier year only through the press and through some reports published by New Delhi. I had read that since 1992, no fundamental change had taken place. The price fixed by the government for urea, which accounts for more than half the consumption of fertilizers, had been maintained; but the controls on the prices of all other fertilizers had been removed, even though they still enjoyed some subsidies from the centre. Wanting to be acquainted with the reality of the prices in their regional variations, I went to Karnataka and began my investigations in the Agriculture Department at Bangalore. There I asked if by chance they had any idea about the price range of a particular fertilizer in the state. 'But, of course!' I was told, and a list was held out to me in which there was an MRP in rupees against each fertilizer. They explained to me that MRP meant 'maximum retail price'. The so-called decontrolled prices were reined in by a ceiling which finally served as a control price!

This example has been cited to mention an evidence. Seen from New Delhi (or worse, from Paris), it is not possible to have, on the national scale, an accurate perception of the reality as it exists in the different Indian states, and even less in the villages. What was being presented by the central government and the national press as liberalization, and therefore in tune with the dominant position on the global level and with the desire of the IMF, hid in reality the adoption of a certain price control on the local level. New Delhi was managing in this way to satisfy both the financiers in Washington as well as the farmers of the '600,000 villages' of India. Playing around with scales is shrewd politics.

While restricting itself to rural, agricultural and food-related matters, the first part of this text will attempt to show that the 'complexity' of what is called our 'post-modern' era cannot be used as an excuse for keeping certain concepts vague, and notably the meaning of the words 'global' and 'local'. These ambiguities are maintained because with their help certain interests and ideologies can hide behind a position acceptable to the protagonists. The paper then turns to a reappraisal of the 'national' dimension with the example of the steps taken by different states, and that of the concept of food security. I will then talk of the primacy granted today to the micro-scale, by many researchers and development agencies. Finally, I show that a shift of scale is like changing causality and that one should, as far as possible, adopt a multi-level approach in order not to restrict arguments, diagnoses, or actions.

COMPLEXITY DOES NOT MEAN VAGUENESS

This is the post-modern era. Deconstruction playing its part, an entire trend in social sciences is proclaiming the need for the macro-scale to give place to the micro-scale, as also for preference to the inductive over the deductive (Peemans 1995). The decline of ideologies no longer allows us to believe in modernization or development, whether it be of Marxist or of liberal inspiration (Rist 1996; Gupta 1998). 'Complexity', therefore, has found its place and this in three fields.

First, in the reality of things, since the world seems more and more complicated and seeing that the antagonistic globalization/identity movements working *in tandem* have clouded the outlines of the post-war maps; second, in the perception of this reality by those who try to grasp it, be they economists, philosophers, or sociologists; finally in the taking into account of this complexity by politicians, planners and practitioners of development when they deploy their actions. There is, true, a wide distance between the 'complex thought' theorized by Edgar Morin[1], based on an epistemology of physics or biology, and the more prosaic perception of the multiple interactions of the world in which our societies pulsate. The 'complex' of the philosopher cannot be reduced to the 'complicated' of the developer. But each time the same humility arises when awareness of the reality dawns,[2] and the same desire, bordering on challenge, for a thought or an action that is truly 'multidimensional'. Table 1 drawn by Maxwell (1996) speaks for itself on this score. It may be felt however that it does not go far enough since it considers that the concept of 'development' is still part of the post-modern arsenal while this concept is itself challenged, and some scholars go to the extent of talking today of 'post-development' (Nanda 1999).

Because of the importance it grants to the micro-scale, post-modernism gives preference to the local level approach, all the more so—there is no contradiction in this—as it is acutely aware of the

TABLE 1: MODERN AND POST-MODERN TRENDS IN THE THINKING ON DEVELOPMENT ACCORDING TO SIMON MAXWELL (1996)

	Modern	Post-modern
Underlying reality	Simple, uniform	Complex, diverse
Objectives	Growth	Development
	Preoccupation with macro	Preoccupation with micro
Research approach	Measure	Listen
	Survey	Participatory rural appraisal
	Reductionist	Holistic
	Deduction	Induction
	Abstract models	Complex reality
Planning approach	Plan	Enable
	Model	Interact
	Top-down	Bottom-up
Implementation	Blue-print	Process
	Standardization	Flexibility, innovation

processes of globalization and of cross-fertilizations. However, as we have seen in the introduction to this volume, it hardly succeeds in dissipating the ambiguity over words such as 'globalization' or 'local'. Is this conceptual vagueness or are there ulterior motives of an ideological nature?

During the 1990s, the Farmers Union of the State of Karnataka (KRSS) destroyed the installations of the multinationals Cargill and Kentucky Fried Chicken in Bangalore in the name of the fight against the invasion of large foreign capital. The rioters asserted that they were defending the heritage of the farmers of the 'South' and the necessity for a sustainable development on a planetary scale. The KRSS thereafter became part of the Global Peoples' Action in which these representatives of medium or large farmers, sugar-cane planters or rice growers, rubbed shoulders, strangely enough, with the Brazilian Movement of the Landless or the Mexican Zapatist Front. One can doubt the sincerity of this conversion to a utopian zeal of 'Farmers of all countries, unite!' on the part of a union which in actual fact in no way represents Indian agricultural labourers and which continues to expect subsidies and the continuance of a certain protectionism from New Delhi, being thus closely tied to a national framework and a nationalist ideology.

One position can conceal another, and even more the reality. In 1999, 400 union members of the KRSS and BKU (its equivalent in north India, with a presence particularly in Uttar Pradesh among the dominant Jat community) came to take part in demonstrations in Europe, thanks to tickets 'paid for by their villages'. Speaking before European environmental movements, the French leftist Peasant Confederation or their equivalents, they denounced the liberalism of globalization, the WTO, transgenic seeds, and the dominance of chemical fertilizers, in the name of the defence of the *jajmani* system, the self-sufficient Gandhian village, environmental protection, and the preservation of the fertility of the land. The 'local' was endangered by the 'global'. In the background, one more position was being taken. The pro-urban policy of the Indian government was being accused of maintaining agricultural prices at a low level to satisfy consumers, even at the cost of importing agricultural products. The 'local' was thus also endangered by the 'national'. There was in all this something like a gradient of growing perversity, from the local to the global. At the lower level there was the good village, then the ineffective provincial state, given a rough deal by the requirements of New Delhi; then the anti-farmer centre; finally the WTO, dominated by the international powers desirous of ruling over the markets. This position made it possible to relegate to obscurity the reality of the village and mask the equations of power and exploitation within the local agrarian structures by claiming to speak in the name of the agricultural proletariat, even women.[3] This 'strategy of scales' made it possible to bring out the virtue of the local at the expense of the higher levels.

Two types of local organization are considered today as being in a position to bring about real development. These are the NGOs and the official local institutions which have been empowered through decentralization. But what kind of 'local' do they represent? As Neil Webster (1998) has noted, talk of 'civil society', 'social capital', and 'empowerment' does not exempt one from defining these concepts and knowing precisely what they mean on the ground. Can an 'international' NGO, despite all efforts to arouse the peasants into taking initiatives, or again a village council dominated by notables, claim to represent the local? For whom do organizations such as the Narmada Bachao Andolan speak, concerning the deplorable ecological and human consequences of the dams being constructed and put into operation? In a book that is highly politically incorrect, A. Baviskar (1995), who is in fact a sympathizer of the movement, shows that the aborigines, the main victims of these dams, do not have as ecological a vision of nature as is asserted: poverty forces them to destroy their environment, their religious values and their rituals do not suffice to ensure proper management, and, far from finding it to their advantage to be left in a so-called state of nature, they need the state and its presence, but by way of well conceived development plans.

Who is speaking, for whom, in whose name (Rootes ed. 1999)? This is so also for the voluntary organizations which are trying to organise a better management of urban wastes in India. There are among these two distinct types. There are the 'green' organizations which are concerned above all with the environment and are made up of residents belonging to the upper social classes, and there are the 'red' organizations, seeking rather to improve the lot of the households living on the collection of waste material (Schenk et al., 1998). Like the other levels, the local is therefore a level where disputes and exploitation prevail. It is in them that lie, more or less hidden, many of the roots of poverty. The local is not the ideal.

Hence, corresponding to a specific situation in space and time, the local does not withstand an excessive intellectual reconstruction, a theorization which would set aside its peculiarities. The limits of generalizations on the basis of the local, and of the inductive process, are obvious. Let us be wary therefore of what Webster calls the 'globalization of the local', the blotting out of local characteristics in the name of a reductionist position, of an ideology (not to say a religion) of the local. For it would be like the return of an authoritarian concept of development in a roundabout way. In this connection, the local Indian institutions of the Panchayat Raj, elected by adult franchise and officially revived since 1992, prove to be very problematic:

> on the one hand panchayats are seen to possess greater social capital than local administrations, to be rooted in 'traditional' systems of community management and local governance, but at the same time they are viewed as the 'modern' institutions of local democracy whose role and capacity are being enhanced by the national government to enhance the development process at the local level. The ambiguity in these perceptions appears not to be a problem, at least not for donors, (Webster 1998: 12)

Also, the less said the better of NGOs led by a large city industrialist or a degree holder from Berkeley who wants 'to do something' for his native village which he had left thirty years earlier.

The other ambiguity over the local arises out of the fact that the places classified under this spatial term are of highly variable scale (a village or an urban neighbourhood, a city, even a region). Local can therefore serve as a discreet euphemism for the individual or the enterprise as well as the village or neighbourhood community. The unit of production of a multinational settled there for three years will be, spatially, part of the local but its place in the indigenous society will still have to be evaluate. Giving more power to firms does not necessarily mean more power to the local population, but the confusion is maintained in order to enable some forms of economic liberalization to become acceptable to public opinion. Is it a mere chance that the launching of the *panchayats* (1992) was contemporaneous with the structural adjustment programme (1991)? Giving power to the local is an advance towards liberalization considering that the state is dispossessing itself of some initiatives, but at the same time it satisfies certain aspirations of the people. It is probably no longer possible to assert that the local (soil and sentiment) is Rightist, while the universal (rationality and equality) is Leftist (Bouthillon 1998).

Two nuances however need to be made. In the first place, the liberal policy remains above all a macro-policy based on the respect for equilibrium of budget and balance of payments on the national scale, and takes account of local scale only in this perspective. It is in order to accelerate national economic growth that local development is encouraged, rather than the reverse. 'Methodological individualism attributed to neo-liberal theories is in reality only an ideological individualism' (Chauveau 1997: 207). And to what extent the invoking of local identities, in the name of resistance to capitalism, or of the post-modern denunciation of ideologies and universalities, can lead to the most inflexible nationalism, even to fascism, is well known (Brass 1995).

Moreover, initiatives combining the spirit of enterprise with decentralization are rare. The state of West Bengal, it is true, does desire to develop joint ventures with the *panchayats* so as to set up more rural small enterprises *à la* China. But one comes up soon enough against the ambiguity noted already. Is the unit that goes to make up the local a space (in this case a village, represented by an elected assembly such as the *panchayat*), or is it the individual? This is an important question as the spirit of enterprise is more easily of an individual rather than that of a collective order. Effective self-help groups, made up of persons who get together to avail of a collective loan not unlike the model of the Grameen Bank are still rare, despite government encouragement, and the NGOs appear sometimes to be the only ones who believe in the (more or less) spontaneous achievements of the local bodies. A solar pump installed in Jharkhand to bring irrigation during the dry season to almost all the farmers who volunteered, even the landless ones, finally brought direct benefits to only a few land owning farmers (Landy 1994). The experience with 'biovillages' by the Swaminathan Foundation in Pondicherry, so reputed in India, succeeds above all on the farm scale (cultivation of mushrooms, goat farming), even if on the scale of the village strictly speaking there do exist some operations such as fish farming in community ponds or joint floriculture (Druesne 1999). The local of the liberals, focused on the individual, is far different from the local of the NGOs, often focused on the community.

In the urban environment, neighbourhood committees can certainly take over charge of the management of some kinds of infrastructure and compensate for the deficiencies of the municipality (garbage collection). But can one, for all that, do without city-level integrated management for networks like transport and water (Zerah

1999)? The same questions have to be put on the state level in the matter of heavy infrastructure whose burden neither the private sector nor local initiatives can shoulder. As regards investments in agriculture, one cannot therefore remain satisfied with the present increase in private investment which would be coming in 'to compensate', as some assert, for the lowering of public investment and which would correspond to this much desired 'development from below', for private capital is not interested in large irrigation works, nor in rural electrification, nor in the setting up of marketing structures which disregard short-term profit. Private and public investment are concerned with different priorities and cannot therefore be considered substitutes, whatever the staunchest supporters of a withdrawal of the state might say.

REAPPRAISAL OF THE 'NATIONAL'

This reappraisal is in no way synonymous with putting the 'local' level in the forefront in India, even less than elsewhere, on account of the power of the states of the Union which cannot but benefit from any relative retreat of New Delhi. In fact, the relationships between the global, national and local levels are rendered highly complex by the federal pattern, as is revealed by India's fragile food policy.

Punjab's Food Geo-Economy

Punjab is undoubtedly one of the most forceful (and early) examples of the difficulties of the integration of a state within the Union. To its cultural Sikh peculiarities is added a high level of agricultural development, visible since the nineteenth century thanks to the irrigation works on the Himalayan rivers, but further strengthened by the Green Revolution from the second half of the 1960s. This level of development has been depicted in Map 1 in which on the one hand are shown the central procurement of grains aimed at supporting domestic prices and constituting stocks to ensure food security, and on the other hand, the reallocations of these grains to the states through the Public Distribution System (PDS) which offers wheat, rice (as also sugar, oil or kerosene) at subsidized prices to a part of the population (Landy 1999).

Depending on the years, this system involved between 10 to 20 per cent of the national production and consumption of wheat and rice. This shows its importance. And yet, as the map reveals, it is based almost exclusively on the Punjab and its neighbourhood. Conse-

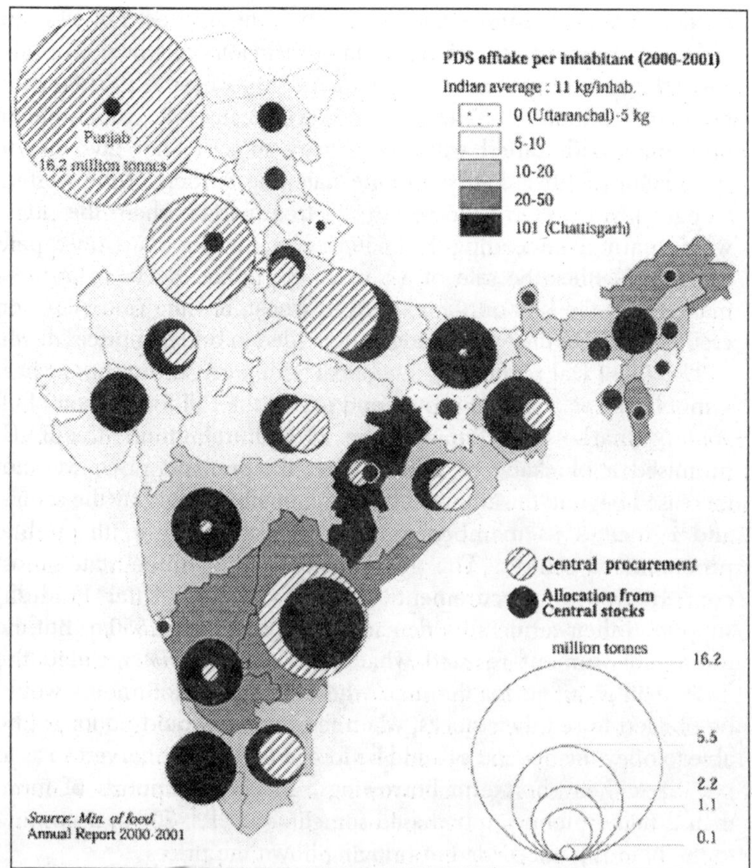

MAP 1: CENTRAL FOODGRAIN PROCUREMENT, ALLOTMENT AND OFFTAKE (2000-01)

quently, conflicts in that zone constitute a danger to the food needs of India's one billion inhabitants. The wheat crisis which occurred in 1997 is revealing on this score.

The national wheat stocks had dwindled in April 1997 to 2.7 million tonnes, a million tonnes less than the norm, and three times less than in April 1996, when the godowns had been overflowing. The factors that had converged to create the crisis were a high demand from the PDS (the prices had not been increased between 1994 to 1997), the expansion of the 'Revamped PDS' (which offered more subsidized products) to most of the underprivileged regions, the resale in the domestic market of more than 6 million tonnes of stocks of wheat in 1995-6, the export of 2 million tonnes, a mediocre wheat crop, the smuggling out of probably a large quantity of wheat to Pakistan, and the small amount of sales to the state because the procurement operations had started with great delay so as to not give rise to speculation. Rather than sell to the state, the farmers of the western Ganges plain preferred to sell in the free market where the prices were soaring, exceeding Rs. 650/q whereas the state only paid Rs. 415. Neither the sale of a part of the public stocks in the free market, nor the ban on the exports of wheat, nor the restrictions on credit granted to the wheat traders succeeded in bringing prices down.

The Akali Dal (Amritsar), a regional Sikh party, burnt some wheat symbolically as a sign of protest and joined the call for boycott of all *mandis* (markets) in Punjab. The agricultural union, the BKU, promised a blockade of Delhi if the procurement price was not increased beyond the additional Rs. 60/q finally granted by the centre, and it incited its members to stop tractors going to the public procurement centres. The governments of the three states most concerned with procurement (Punjab, Haryana, Uttar Pradesh) supported their farmers by demanding a price of Rs. 550/q. But the union government resisted what the *Economic Times* called the 'blackmail', waiting for the time when the speculator-traders would be obliged to sell their stocks, when the farmers would no longer be able to obey the boycott call and be forced to sell their harvest so as to pay back their short-term borrowings, and when imports of more than 2 million tonnes (purchased sometimes at Rs. 700/q, according to the unions!) succeeded in bringing down the prices.

This crisis reveals the complexity of a situation involving numerous players with sometimes contradictory objectives. The central government, in the first place, had wanted to give preference to the export of cereals the earlier year, without keeping in mind the fact that it was then making national self-sufficiency entirely dependent on the coming procurement activity. It is a difficult venture to want one's cake as well as the money from the cake, to open up to exports while remaining as impervious as possible to imports. As for the governments of the three wheat supplying states, in which the Hindu opposition BJP was present, they saw in it the opportunity to criticize the central government both for its stinginess towards the farmers producing surpluses (prices too low!) and its inability to fight the inflation that was plaguing city dwellers and agricultural workers (prices too high!). The agricultural unions, for their part, supported the large farmers, even at the expense of antagonizing consumers and petty farmers who wanted to sell immediately. Locally, the rural circles were indeed divided, and the clamours of the powerful stifled the wails of the 40 per cent of agricultural workers of Punjab and Haryana who depended on their salaries for survival, as they bought grain and did not sell it.

Finally, there was the population of the rest of India to contend with, whose interests and constraints were highly variable. The farmers of Punjab, their union leaders explained, were tired of having to sell their produce at procurement prices that had been fixed too low so that the deficit states could feed themselves easily. Was it so astonishing that a state such as Kerala depended on the PDS for half its consumption of rice, when its farmers had since long converted a number of their paddy fields into more profitable plantations of rubber trees, bananas or coconuts? In Kerala the area under rice cultivation had decreased by 43 per cent between 1975 and 1995. That state was secretly happy as its agricultural exports were growing and the inflows of grain from the PDS came at a cheap price. Yet, there is no doubt that this trend increased rural under-employment (rice is far more labour intensive than the crops that replaced it) and made the task of national redistribution of grain even more difficult.

Central State, Provincial State: The Chemical Fertilizers Scenario

Under the Constitution, the states avail of a great deal of power in the matter of agriculture, health, education and certain industries. The states enjoy a not negligible power of decision making considering that they can fix at least marginally a good part of the prices of agricultural goods and inputs. Moreover, it is at their level that the food policy of the union government functions since a part of the procurement is done through them, and particularly since the larger part of the grain sales at subsidized prices by the PDS is done through them. It is to the states that New Delhi distributes a share of the stocks of federal grains. It is up to the states to fix (to the extent of their budget resources!) the prices and to decide on which social groups will avail of the PDS.[4]

New Delhi has however kept to itself most of its power in the name of 'national interest', a clause mentioned without further clarification in the Constitution. The centre has also drawn benefit from the lack of financial resources of the provincial states which raise few taxes. The tax on agricultural income which is reserved for them, is of a near non-existent amount. The three types of financial transfers made from the centre towards the states are themselves fairly small.[5] In fact, the Eighth Five-Year Plan has been implemented by the states with only 39 per cent of financing by the centre and 2 per cent of the funds of the states themselves. The rest consisted of loans which further aggravated the generally catastrophic financial situation of the states (Kurian 1999).

Despite this financial bottleneck, or on account of it, the states do not hesitate to come into conflict, as we have seen, with the central government. They are undoubtedly helped by the ruling position which advocates that decentralization is a guarantee for effectiveness and justice. Thus in 1998, the Planning Commission suggested that the Central Ministry of Rural Areas and Employment should concede to the states control over the development plans financed by the centre, worth more than 97 billion rupees in 1998-9. The ministry replied that the flawed utilization of these funds by the states was too well known to permit that such a step be taken and that in addition, the day-to-day management of these programmes had already been given over to the states and even to the *panchayats* (*Business Line,* 5 October 1998).

Delicate power struggles between the centre and the states, ambiguous constitutional texts and irresolute policies sometimes give rise to a veritable bungling. The chemical fertilizer sector has been a typical example of this through the 1990s. The culmination of a veritable action-packed drama, urea continues to carry an extremely low price tag fixed in New Delhi. To satisfy the IMF and the World Bank, as also the Finance Ministry, the prices of other fertilizers have been theoretically 'decontrolled', mostly in 1992, after great hesitation and back-tracking (Landy 1997a). But since 1992, we have seen, the responsibility for fixing the ceiling prices of the 'decontrolled' fertilizers had been given over to the governments of the different states. The farmers were not really paying these prices, since they availed of a subsidy, fixed for each fertilizer by the centre, which was directly paid to the producing industry. Thus, if the ceiling price was Rs. 5,000 and the subsidy was of the order of Rs. 200, the farmer only paid Rs. 4,800 and the government paid the rest.

Such a system actually suited no one. The industry complained of the prices being fixed sometimes below their production costs, and of arrears in the reimbursement of the subsidies (till 1994, it was the states which had to pay the sums due to the firms; subsequently, in order to try to simplify the procedures, it was the central government . . . but always on receiving the bills which had to be submitted by the firms to the states. The states were in charge of transferring them to the Government of India). As for the farmers, they complained of the tardiness of the states in fixing the prices, which sometimes forced them to sow their seeds without using the fertilizer as it had not reached the market. And in Madhya Pradesh and Haryana private traders did not have the right to offer subsidized prices! Finally, the states which had fixed the lowest prices found themselves sometimes boycotted by the industrialists who preferred to sell elsewhere, and this led to serious shortages.[6] In March 1997, the central government therefore decided that it would itself henceforth fix the maximum prices and that these would prevail in the whole of India. The industrialists could immediately receive 80 per cent of the subsidies which they claimed, while it was up to the states to then send the sale certificates to New Delhi so that the remaining 20 per cent could be paid.

But rules change quickly in India. In August 1998, the centre changed its views and put an end to the ceiling on fertilizer prices, the industrialists having full freedom to thereafter themselves fix the 'maximum retail price'. In September of the same year came another about-turn. The ceiling on prices reappeared, fixed by the centre, and by the states in the case of simple superphosphate! Centre, states, industrialists, farmers, consumers of agricultural products, international funding agencies, all these numerous players, by dint of too much scattering of decision making and of confusing populism with democracy, seem to be enacting a stage show in the theatre of the absurd.

Global or Local Advantage? India's Food Security

More generally, it is the entire agricultural and food policy which has been put on the mat. In fact, India is in the process of making the transition from the concept of cereal self-sufficiency to that of food security. Already in the forefront when the Grow More Food campaign was launched in 1943, the need for self-sufficiency became more evident at the time of independence in 1947, as a factor of economic and political autonomy, in short, of sovereignty. In the matter of agriculture however, self-sufficiency was put in the background between 1956 and 1965, when an agreement with the United States facilitated imports of wheat. With the Second Plan giving preference to industrialization, investments in agriculture were no longer a priority. But with the Green Revolution during the 1965-6 crisis, the idea of self-sufficiency came again to the fore (even if it involved importing seeds and fertilizers during the early years). In the matter of cereals, success came rapidly. It can be said that from 1977 onwards, India has been almost self-sufficient in wheat and rice, even exporting these articles during some years. This being so, it is practically no longer dependent on others and is reasonably self-reliant on the global level. Till 1991, with its borders almost impervious, agricultural development and the food issue were addressed in India above all within the national framework.

From 1991 however, a slow, chaotic, but real liberalization, brought to light the imperfections of the system. The often clumsy management of the stocks and of the procurement, some incongruous decisions to export or to import, all these elements which till then had appeared like a necessary evil in the name of self-reliance, seemed thereafter, in the light of liberalism, like grave flaws which required to be eliminated. The wheat crisis of 1997 showed how, in a barely opened national framework in which wheat imports remained subject to authorization, price increases in the domestic market could become dramatic. More and more voices rose demanding that wheat be placed on the Open General Licence (OGL) list, which would render international transactions easier and hence curtail speculation in the domestic market. Conversely, the public stocks of 65 million tonnes of grain that the Food Corporation of India had to cope with in 2002 prove that abundance also is difficult to manage.

From then on, it was the concept of food security which was addressed, this being more flexible from a certain point of view than that of self-sufficiency in that it enabled the more intense utilization of the world markets and of comparative advantages. It became a matter of financing imports through exports, instead of trying to produce everything oneself. What did the means matter (national self-sufficiency or imports), it was the end that counted, and this was to achieve a satisfactory nutritional standard for households and individuals. In the agricultural field, costly protectionism to oilseeds could therefore be discontinued, even if it meant that more of this commodity had to be imported, and some international competitiveness in the matter of rice, or even wheat had to be put to good use. And then, rather than promoting only wheat and rice, why not take advantage of the agro-climatic diversity of the country to diversify the agricultural production (flowers, fruit)? While many observers (and some among those in government) considered that too excessive an opening up would be dangerous, almost no one wanted to return to the *statu quo ante*.

Opening up to the 'global'? Certainly. But the notion of food security has another implication. It forces the attention away from the national trade balance towards the nutritional situation of *individuals.* Self-sufficiency for the country does not mean that all Indians be sufficiently well fed, quantitatively (in calories) and even less qualitatively (in proteins, lipids, vitamins, iron). What are highlighted in this case are the inequalities between regions, between social classes or between sexes and generations within a single family (Dreze et al. 1995). While self-sufficiency is determined on the national level, food security takes into account the two extreme levels. Its implementation makes use of the potentialities in the global markets, but it can only be evaluated on the local level (Figure 1).

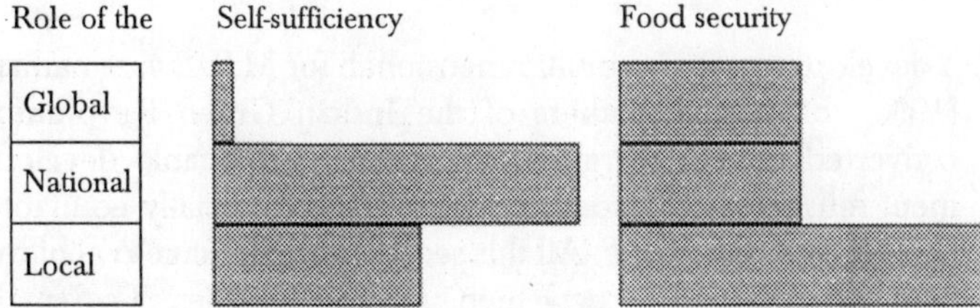

FIGURE 1: FOOD POLICY AND SCALES

The facts, true, are not in accordance with the positions advocated. The Food Corporation of India, entrusted with the purchase of grains for the state, does indeed try to develop the local storage and itself undergoes pressures for a more decentralized management. But serious reforms in this direction are yet to be implemented, as if New Delhi feared that by attempting to change some elements of the food system in India, it would bring about the collapse for good of this heavily criticised system as a whole.

The Revalorization of the Micro-Scale

That the complexity of the world requires the 'complex thinking' dear to Morin is certain. That the world is more complex today than it was yesterday, as some think, is debatable. Today there is an awareness that there is not just one single paradigm for an understanding of the world, and that there is no simple solution to underdevelopment. By looking for the actor behind the structure, by giving preference to the 'micro' as compared to the 'macro', we arrive necessarily at a fragmented view of reality. Is it not because we analyse the present better that we give it a complexity which existed nevertheless in the past, but which has remained buried under the sediments of time?

Perhaps hybridism and cross-fertilization of cultures and people had a less global and a more national or a regional framework in earlier times. Has this prevented nevertheless the spread of ideas or of cultivated species throughout the world? A meticulous historical perspective would perhaps show that 'post-colonialism' (Gupta 1998) has not invented mixing, conflicts and interplay of scales, either in discourses or in facts, since they were already existing in the past. There did indeed exist a pre-modern complexity, albeit to a lesser extent.

Such modesty, seen in the acknowledgement that everything is highly complicated, is accompanied nevertheless by an increased ambition, the ambition to transform everything. There are two major axes:

(*a*) a development that is multidimensional: for M.S. Swaminathan (1996), one of the fathers of the Indian Green Revolution converted to the 'evergreen revolution,' sustainable development must be both economically profitable, socially equitable and ecologically viable. All this seems more difficult to achieve than the adoption of new high yielding varieties. The small success of the 'integrated rural development' programmes in South Asia, launched in the 1980s, shows moreover the extent to which programmes, conceived generally as the outcome of deep and apt reflections on development, can encounter difficulties which in theory it had been believed would be possible to surmount.

(*b*) an action on the most local scale possible. There again, the difficulty is increased. Instead of a Five-Year Plan drawn up by New Delhi, it would be a matter of diagnoses and actions formulated for hundreds of thousands of villages and urban quarters. True, there is no question of descending to the level of the agricultural farm as in France with the 'territorial farming contracts' launched in 1999. (There are less than 700,000 farms in France as against more than 100 million in India.) It is a tough job however for India, made necessary by the awareness of the importance of the local scale in the development process (Friedmann 1981; Peemans 1995). Since 1998, the agro-climatic regional planning of the ICAR has divided India into 15 agro-climatic regions and 73 sub-regions according to relatively precise ecological and agricultural economics criteria. 'Micro-planning' has an already ancient history in Community

Development, then in Panchayati Raj launched in the 1950s. Yet, either because it was simply a matter of political rhetoric, or because of the complexity of the social situation on the ground, such initiatives were doomed to failure, and decentralization remained largely a dead letter. Will the relaunching of the *panchayats* through the constitutional amendment of 1992 make local democracy more dynamic (Chaturvedi ed. 1997)? The 'paradigm shift' (a pronouncement that is repeated *ad nauseam* today in India) towards the local is just a more and more hackneyed mantra.

Concern for the micro-scale is however in line with the general trend in the social sciences. In economics, the theories of endogenous growth bring to the forefront the role of infrastructure, education and health, to explain tardy development. At least as great a stress is laid on the potential of the local level as on the national environment or on the economic policies. Chapters 4 and 5 here are good examples of the importance of the local context woven around entrepreneurs. The family networks, the integration within a 'territory' in the fullest sense of the word, a very real socio-cultural identity, the existence of social capital, are factors at least as important as the role of the state or relations with the national or international centres of gravity. The scale encompassed is more the village and its environs than the region, and *a fortiori* the provincial or the federal state.

For geography or ethnology, the monographs of village, town or individual meet with a scientific and sometimes popular success (Viramma and Racine 1997). For history, it is for instance the return of biography (say, the 'life stories' project of the Centre of South Asian Studies of London University). 'Micro-history' distances itself from the *Annales* French school to celebrate contingency, disparity, freedom (on the fringe) of the actors, and the priority of a certain inductive approach which does not however prevent generalizations (Revel ed. 1996). In the epigraph here, Corbin mentions among the reasons for the choice of the individual being studied factors such as 'my holidays with my grand-parents', 'empathy', 'closing my eyes', and names 'which pleased'. Subjectivity and chance are claimed for this work which is said to be in the field of 'historical anthropology' (Corbin 1998). (It should be noted however that this is an interview reported by a popular weekly journal; I did not note any such openness in his book.)

It is an epistemological irony that the French 'old' geography inherited from Vidal de la Blanche, ridiculed for being excessively detailed and preventing synthesis, and for its regional monographs which rule out generalization, could, in a certain way, prove to be at the cutting edge of science, once it has been properly redrafted. And a modelling geography, which proclaims the existence of 'laws of space' by attempting, notably under the leadership of Roger Brunet, to shake out the dust of a truly French tradition, is now finding itself out of tune with the trends of this discipline in other countries. The revenge of history? Just as today, the European rural areas having missed out on the industrial revolution appear finally to be privileged to become the scene of new activities, similarly the tardiness experienced by a certain French geography in the presence of the Anglo-Saxon progress could well turn out now to be an advantage.

A CHANGE OF SCALE INVOLVES A CHANGE OF CAUSALITY

No micro-analyses, in whichever scientific discipline, are content with using blindly the categories, concepts and processes of the macro. The local is in no event a microcosm, a miniature model (nor an 'illustration', even less a 'proof') of what occurs at the higher levels, even if assuredly the macro-processes may have a visible impact on the micro-scale. In this, the Mauss notion of 'total social fact'[7] which is sometimes used as an all-purpose concept in the social sciences, is particularly dangerous, since it can lead to the belief that a single field study can reconstruct the complexity of a whole society (Revel ed. 1996: 95). The 'principle of the hologram' explained by Morin, according to which in every individual is reflected his society, is not devoid of danger either. True, it is possible that by dint of going down towards the local level and then towards the individual, we reach down to human nature. After all, the whole of the genetic heritage is present in each individual cell: 'the whole is in the part which is in the whole' (Morin 1990: 101). And village studies make it possible, on the basis of a small sample, to generalize on human rationality (Adams, Neale 1997; Landy 1997b). But it is not possible to discover everything through the micro-scale. In this sense, there is no question of seeking out any 'representativeness' whatever of the local level. This latter does not correspond to the sample of the surveys, based on the principle that one need just drink a spoon, not the entire bowl, to know the taste of the soup. It is therefore impossible to have a global view through the intermediary of the local. On the other hand, that this local exists is sufficient to give legitimacy to its analysis, just as, it has been felt, when the skeleton of a dinosaur of an unknown species is discovered, no one waits to find a second one before setting out to study it. To know how it works locally is by itself a worthy task, without wanting to widen the study vertically (towards higher levels) or horizontally (towards other local systems).

The corollary is that it is pointless to hold out a criterion of replicability in the choices of financing of development projects, since each project cannot but be unique.[8] Most sponsors still require that the projects to be financed should be capable of being near-identically reproduced in other settings, as if the same recipes could be used elsewhere, even in the neighbouring village. However, no model can exist considering the peculiarities of each local situation which, if they are not taken note of, will lead straightaway to failure. The expression 'pilot project' needs therefore to be banned, and not only because it involves turning social systems and human beings into guinea pigs.

A change of scale does not mean looking at things in a smaller or a bigger way, but rather in a different way. It is like reading maps. A map on the 1/100,000 scale shows the broad outlines of the space organization (axes of the relief, communication networks, economic polarities), and it would be futile to look for such information on 1/25,000 map. But conversely, the 1/25,000 map could be valuable for reading the different functions of space of a restricted size, specifying the types of urban areas or the forms of rural landscapes, which the 1/100,000 map is unable to do.

Brunet (1990:127) is probably wrong in making a difference between these cartographic 'scales' and the 'levels' of analysis. In his opinion, the variations of scale do not necessarily lead to the appearance of different structures or phenomena ('Changing scales only means changing the ratio of the depiction'), while when we change the level of analysis 'it is not only the extent which increases and the distances which become greater, it is the phenomena which change their nature or content'. These words underestimate the power of cartographic depiction. For changing the scale changes the realities. Every coastline as a fractal object, has a length which varies with the scale of perception. Antonioni in his film *Blow Up* shows how several successive enlargements of a photograph are required before the murder that is concealed within the snapshot can be revealed (Revel ed. 1996:36). I will add that by enlarging too much, one soon sees no more than the dots of the four-colour print and that the photograph becomes indecipherable. We have to know what to look for to choose the proper scale and conversely we must have awareness of the scale of study to know the limits of its results.

SCALE AND CAUSATION

A change of scale changes the realities as also the relations of causality. For geographers particularly, space is not only a framework within which the processes being studied take place. It exists in its own right, as a possible factor in a chain of causality, through the simple fact that it holds distances and proximities within itself. Thus, the fertility decrease in India can be perceived as a response of couples to the emancipation of women and to the evolution of sexuality, which turns it into a phenomenon that is intimate (and difficult to analyse). It goes without saying that no one will stop at this level of analysis alone and that immediately thereafter, the macro-scale structural processes of female literacy or urbanization will be brought out, even if only to show its limits. Nevertheless, by mentioning the socio-regional environment solely as a referent, we risk underestimating the 'independent role of spatial mechanisms', and notably the processes of dissemination related to 'social or cultural contiguities' (Guilmoto 2000: 51) or simply to proximity (what statisticians call spatial auto-correlation). We will run the risk of overestimating the endogenous factors of evolution, while they actually only channel, accelerate or curb dissemination. If Indian space has truly 'changed from a mosaic to a crown-shaped structure' (ibid.: 52), the exclusive micro-analysis loses all legitimacy.

Equally revealing is the example of the Public Distribution System (PDS) which accounts for between 10 to 20 per cent of the Indian consumption of subsidized grains and 40 per cent of sugar. The amounts lost and those leaked out are enormous, because it is a very unwieldy system which functions on the scale of the whole of India, because it includes a clientele which is well-off, and because corruption and dishonesty enable the disappearance of articles subsequently resold in the free market at higher prices. The different levels of analysis of these losses throw light in a variable manner without it being possible to choose one over another. On the national scale, the tonnages having actually passed through the PDS are compared to the quantities actually purchased by consumers according to the National Sample Survey (Ahluwalia 1993; Radhakrishna et al. 1996). On the scale of the *taluk/tehsil*, there is a need to underline the losses in the form of trucks which leave the godowns of the city to take supplies to the rural Fair Price Shops and never reach there (Mooij 1999). On the scale of the village are underlined the misdeeds of those shop managers who want to compensate for an inadequately fixed margin in view of the costs of transport, by declaring sales higher than the reality or by adding sand to the grain (Nawani 1995). On the scale of the household finally, light can be thrown on the middle-class client who purchases subsidized grain of bad quality to feed his maid (just like in the USSR one could sometimes feed the cattle with subsidized bread), or the poor woman who purchases it only in order to resell it in the free market after having removed its impurities.

The observer has therefore to choose the appropriate questioning for the appropriate scale. In an Indian village, social relations and conflicts can only be understood by taking into account the power equations between the different groups and castes on the regional level as much as on the local level (Lerche 1994). Similarly, it is hardly on the scale of the village that the impact of changes in economic policy can be assessed. In 1993, desiring to study the reactions of farmers to the increase in the price of chemical fertilizers, I went to a semi-arid village in Karnataka, devoid of irrigation, where four years earlier, I had spent six months. But it proved to be impossible to assess the impact of the liberalization of prices on the consumption of fertilizers. For lack of irrigation in the village, in the event of inadequate rainfall, half the normal amount of fertilizer is used. The same strategy is adopted if the farmer falls ill or some other misfortune strikes the household. The role of rainfall and the economic fragility of the farms are therefore more important than that of the prices for determining the use of fertilizers (Landy 1997a). To get a reply to my questions I would have had to compare the curve of the rainfall, that of the prices and that of the consumption of fertilizers over a period of several years. All these would be statistical series very difficult to obtain. Finally, I was not able to assess the importance of this one factor (the price of fertilizers) in the absolute. But I was able to situate it in a hierarchical order in comparison with other factors, which was not devoid of some importance. Still, this was not the objective I had in mind.

Let us proceed now to the district of Kurukshetra, in Haryana (Grandcolas 1996). In the village of Mathana, half the farmers questioned had reduced their area under wheat, replacing it particularly by rapeseed-mustard (*toria*). Why? Because of the procurement price of wheat decided by the federal government (national scale)? Or the inadequacy of the allowances added to these prices by the Government of Haryana (scale of the state)? Or the free market prices of wheat and rapeseed (regional scale)? Or could it be a progressive impoverishment of the soil felt by many farmers (scale of the plot) or indeed the lowering of the groundwater level?[9] Alternatively, did this trend correspond to an overall crisis encompassing all these factors? A village study cannot settle the issue.

The macro-scale is not devoid either of risks or of errors in reasoning (Bardhan ed. 1989).[10] This is why numerous observers are worried today over the decline in the areas on which food grains (cereals and pulses) are cultivated. Between 1987-8 and 1995-6, they have declined in India by 3.7 million ha (–3%). Gulati et al. (1996) denounced the policy of encouragement to oilseeds launched in 1986, which sacrificed India's comparative advantages in the matter of cereals on the altar of self-reliance in edible oils. But is it not misleading to simply draw a parallel between cereals and oilseeds, by suggesting a causality which has in no way been proved? That the surfaces on which oilseeds are being cultivated have at the same time grown by 6.2 million ha (almost double the decline in the areas growing cereals) makes it difficult to assume a pure and simple replacement. Above all, so many factors may be playing a role (the abundance of rainfall, or variation in the prices of the inputs and productions) that it is incorrect to attribute these changes to one factor.[11]

On all levels, humility is therefore advisable. On the micro- as on the macro-scale, it is difficult to describe a full-fledged system with all the interrelations between its elements. It is necessary more often than not to remain content with analysing a simple socio-economic 'landscape', while mentioning its components but without always being able to connect them to each other in a viable manner. As for the bridges between the scales, they are limited. A factor that is locally dominant may have a very restricted importance on the scale of the state or the Indian Union, and vice versa.

FOR A MULTILEVEL APPROACH

Since it is difficult to transpose correlations from one level to another, it is necessary to adopt an approach on several levels. If this is not possible for lack of means, it should be taken note of and the reasoning and diagnosis should be limited, since one cannot grasp the entire process studied, that is to say 'the superimposition of numerous factors, each one intervening on a specific scale, from the village or the urban quarter to the universe or the planet' (Le Bras 1997: 6). A 'heaping up of influences' (p. 199) is undoubtedly what shows through multilevel analyses. Well conducted, they make it possible to avoid 'the ecological error when we seek to detect individual behaviour from aggregated measures', as much as 'the atomist error' when we forget the context of individual behaviour (Courgeau and Baccaine 1997: 832). We can see an application of this in the study by Dupont (1997) on mobility in Delhi. She illustrates 'the impact of the history and the characteristics of the city and the neighbourhood on the biographies of individuals' by considering 'the conduct of individuals in the context in which they function. In this framework, the advantage of combining an anthropological type of observation with statistical demographic surveys enhances the efficiency of the system of investigation' (ibid.: 23).

Agronomists, and geographers more particularly, have a now old habit of working in accordance with an embedded structure on three levels. The most favoured is the village level, so well depicted in the *études de terroir* ('village studies') of the 1960s-70s by French-speaking geographers. But the necessity of working beyond this scale is well known, in order to address the 'agrarian' or 'rural systems', the regional data on the environment, the politico-economic or socio-cultural framework. Conversely there is the scale of households, of farming systems, even of individuals, so as to enable a closer study of the strategies of the actors. In the best of cases, these changes of dimension are effected without there being any hiatus in the levels of observation, 'a little like climbing up the steps of a staircase without ever ceasing to hold the handrail which joins the floors' (Cambrezy et al. 1984: 151).[12]

The same article betrays however a certain theoretical vagueness on these changes of scale when it explains that the village monographs on the Senegal Valley 'aim at furnishing a sum of results supplementing each other and *together* representing . . . contributions to an analysis of regional dimension' (ibid.: 147). It is obviously a matter of much more than a simple collage of the pieces of a puzzle. When Jan Breman (1989), after an initial work on agrarian structures on the village scale in Gujarat, undertook a second one on the regional scale on institutional and commercial dynamics, he soon noted that this level of analysis was incongruous considering the issue he was examining. There was a different regional space to match each social class, and the little town at the centre of the so-called 'region' in no way played the role of a relay between the upper level and the village level. It was a third research programme, this one on seasonal migrations, although it had been designed, to start with, on a thematic and not a regional basis, which proved paradoxically to result in a very clear definition of a space (corresponding to the network of the dominant caste). Which goes to show that regions are much less given entities than *a posteriori* constructions.

SUMMARY AND CONCLUSION

That this is the era of 'complex thought' does not therefore legitimize a fuzzy logic. We have seen that a loose usage of terms such as global or local has often made it possible to conceal the double standards of an agricultural union, or to promote the triumph of liberalism in the name of popular initiative. The fact remains that in a multiplicity of ways the intermediary level of the national is called into question. The food policy of India, eroded by the frailty of the Union, is a good example of this. It could be felt that the micro-scale has to be promoted at present to compensate for the excesses of the past. This would however be an error from the methodological point of view, considering that each scale bears a specific causality, with explanatory factors which are not necessarily found at other levels of approach.

Let us close by recalling that just as a culture does not correspond to a compartmentalized space (Appadurai 1996), similarly the local is not a closed entity to be set against a transcending global one, or against the state or the market. The different spaces are interconnected and it is this which enables change and recomposition at each of the levels, thanks to these non-discreet links which ensure that in every local, there is a global. In the discourses of the peasants of western Uttar Pradesh noted by Akhil Gupta (1998), are thus intermingled references to scientific agronomy and quotations from ancient theories based on the heat of bodies. This 'cultural hybridity' (p. 20) leads to the cohabitation between what it is even less appropriate than usual to call 'tradition' and 'modernity', or 'the West and the rest'. The Swaminathan Foundation, which makes no bones over its Gandhian inspiration, promotes hybrid varieties of rice produced by Mahyco, a large Indian enterprise in which the American multinational Monsanto holds 26 per cent of the capital. These 'alternative modernities' (Appadurai) correspond to reinventions by different places, with their distinct history and geography, of a globalizing modernity introduced since colonization. I can journey through the entire planet seeking the global; I will find nothing but the local, and that too in Wall Street itself.

NOTES

1. For Morin (1990), the world is characterized by 'complexity', that is 'uncertainty inside highly organized systems' (p. 49). The classical thought of yesterday was based on three pillars: order (incompatible with disorder), 'separability' (a Cartesian principle according to which it is necessary to break up a phenomenon into its component parts for studying it), and the inductive-deductive-non-contradictory logic. Now these three pillars have collapsed due to recent developments of sciences, from thermodynamics to the theory of chaos and ecological science. A new thinking, 'full of holes', is necessary, taking into account subjectivity and causal feedbacks: the complex thought.
2. 'Complexity is a problem word and not a solution word', writes Morin (1990: 10).
3. 'Without desiring it, the critics of modern science and of modernization influenced by post-modernism are in the process of building the foundations of a non-populist movement which seeks to subordinate modernization to the anti-modern and patriarchal values of the traditional elites', asserts Nanda (1999: 7) about the Indian farmer unions.
4. In 1997, the Targeted Public Distribution System was launched which sought to focus the subsidized prices more towards the really needy populations. Indirectly, it sought to bring homogeneity in the regional situations by extending to the whole of India a 'targeting' which had already been effected by some states. However, the programme has proved to be a failure from this standpoint since some states have managed to maintain their scope for manoeuvre in the fixing of the sale prices and for defining (often in a financially lax manner but which pays off at election time) the number of 'poor' households.
5. The financial resources granted by the centre to the states are in three forms. They receive a share of the federal income tax, fixed every five years for each state, some grants and some loans provided for by the Five-Year Plan, and some non-Plan grants and loans (Delhi Science Forum 1998: 25).
6. Moreover, the states were torn between the temptation to fix the sales tax at a high level and the risk that no industrialist would thereafter want to give them these supplies (like in Karnataka in 1998 when a 3 per cent tax had led to a shortage of potassium fertilizers). The problem has become less acute since the year 2000, thanks to the specification for the whole of India of a minimum sales tax. Henceforth, no state can impose less than 4 per cent tax on chemical fertilizers.
7. For Marcel Mauss (1873-1950), a total social fact is a fact that when studied opens a gateway to the understanding of the whole society.
8. Philippe Jacques, personal communication, March 2000.
9. The acquifer under the Kurukshetra district is utilized to the extent of 178 per cent of its capacity and its level has gone down by 8 m in twenty years, which

leads to additional costs due to the need for further lowering of the submersible pump and further digging by the drills.

10. Particularly the chapters by J. Harriss ('Knowing About Rural Economic Change: Problems Arising from a Comparison of the Results of "Macro" and "Micro" Research in Tamil Nadu', pp. 137-73) and by A. Appadurai ('Small-Scale Techniques and Large-Scale Objectives', pp. 250-82).
11. A similar problem of interpretation appears in the analysis of the agricultural trade balance. When, during some years, India exports cereals, this is not necessarily a sign of prosperity. These exports may correspond to a crisis in the purchasing power (inflation of the consumer price index), the price rises in the PDS (as in 1995 and 2000), a congestion in the domestic means of transport (rail), excessive purchases by the state resulting in overflowing godowns. These are as many negative factors which can express themselves by an indicator which most observers will however consider as positive. It needs to be specified that, conversely, if China imports cereals, it is less on account of the crisis in its agriculture than on account of its economic growth (upsurge in the consumption of meat, urbanization).
12. This to and fro movement between observation and generalization, which enables analysis and synthesis, cannot be broken up between the different social sciences. It seems to me dangerous in particular that geography could be restricted to the study of large agro-ecological zones or at best of small regions (Jouve and Clouet 1984), while anthropology for instance would restrict itself to the lower levels of villages and households. Interdisciplinarity has no need for scales, and each science is entitled to its say at every level.

REFERENCES

Adams, J. and Neale, W.C., 'Institutions, Transactions and Rationality: Evidence from Indian Village Studies', *South Asia*, XX, 2 (1997): 139-56.

Ahluwalia, D. 'Public Distribution of Food in India. Covering, Targeting and Leakages', *Food Policy*, 18, 1 (1993): 33-55.

Appadurai, A., *Modernity at Larg: Cultural Dimensions of Globalization*, Minneapolis: University of Minnesota Press, 1996.

Bardhan, P. (ed.), *Conversations Between Economists and Anthropologists: Methodological Issues in Measuring Economic Change in Rural India*, Delhi: Oxford University Press, 1989.

Bouthillon, F., 'Après l'épistémologie de gauche', *Commentaire*, 83 (1998): 641-51.

Brass, T., 'Post-Script: Populism, Peasants and Intellectuals, or What's Left of the Future?', in Brass, T. (ed.), *New Farmers' Movements in India*, Ilford: Frank Cass, 1995.

Breman, J., 'Extension of Scale in Fieldwork: From Village to Region in Southern Gujarat', in Bardhan, P. (ed.), op. cit., 1989, pp. 127-36.

Brunet, R., 'Le déchiffrement du Monde', in *Mondes nouveaux, Géographie Universelle*, Paris: Hachette-Reclus, 1990.

Cambrezy, L., Couty, Ph., Lericollais, A., Marchal, J.Y. and Raynaut, C., 'La région, territoire de recherche', in ORSTOM, *Le développement rural en question*, Paris, 1984, pp. 123-80.

Chaturvedi, P., *Food Security and Panchayat Raj*, New Delhi: Concept, 1997.

Chauveau, J.P., 'Des "stratégies des agriculteurs africains" au "raisonnement stratégique". Histoire, usages et remise en question d'un concept pluri-disciplinaire', in Blanc-Pamard, Ch. and Boutrais, J. (eds.), *Thème et variations. Nouvelles recherches rurales au Sud*, Paris: ORSTOM Editions, 1997, pp. 179-218.

Corbin, A., *Le monde retrouvé de Louis-François Pinagot*, Paris: Flammarion, 1998.

Courgeau, D. and Baccaïni, B., 'Analyse multi-niveaux en sciences sociales', *Population*, 4 (1997): 831-64.

Delhi Science Forum, *The Indian Economy 1997-98: An Alternative Survey*, Delhi, 1998.

Dreze, J., Sen, A. and Hussain, A., *The Political Economy of Hunger*, Delhi: Oxford University Press, 1995.

Druesne, N., *Révolution doublement verte. Les biovillages à Pondichéry*, CIRAD, Paris: Programme Economie, Politiques et Marchés, Document de travail no. 29, 1999.

Dupont, V., *City History—Life Histories: Changing Equations. Migration Surveys and Biographical Data Collection in Delhi*, Contributions CSH 97/7, Delhi, 1997.

Grandcolas, D., *Les producteurs de blé en Inde: exemple du village de Mathânâ*, M.Phil. Dissertation, University of Paris X-Nanterre, 1996.

Guilmoto, C.Z., 'The Geography of Fertility in India (1981-1991)', in G.Z. Guilmoto, G.Z. and Vaguet, A. (eds.), *Essays on Population and Space in India*, Pondicherry: French Institute of Pondicherry, 2000, pp. 37-56.

Gulati, A., 'Self-Sufficiency and Allocative Efficiency: Case of Edible Oils', *Economic and Political Weekly* (30 March 1996): A.15-A-24.

Gupta, A., *Postcolonial Developments: Agriculture in the Making of Modern India*, Durham: Duke University Press, 1998.

Jouve, Ph. and Clouet, Y., 'La fonction diagnostic appliquée à l'étude des systèmes agraires', *Cahiers de la Recherche-Développement*, no. 3-4 (1984), pp. 41-8.

Kurian, N.J., 'State Government Finances: A Survey of Recent Trends', *Economic and Political Weekly* (8 May 1999): 115-25.

Landy, F., 'Entre villes et campagnes, la politique alimentaire de l'Inde', in Chaléard, J.L. and Dubresson, A. (eds.), *Villes et campagnes dans les pays du Sud*, Paris: Karthala, 1999, pp. 21-45.

——, *Fertilizers, Structural Adjustment and Food Policy*, Pondy Papers in Social Sciences, no. 25, French Institute of Pondicherry, 1997a.

——, 'Ends, Logics, Strategies. Rationalities and Objectives of Tropical Peasant Holdings: A South Indian Example', *Man and Development*, XIX, 3, September (1997b): 70-89.

——, *Paysans de l'Inde du Sud. Le choix et la contrainte*, Paris: Karthala and French Institute of Pondicherry, 1994.

Le Bras, H., *La planète au village*, La Tour d'Aigues, Datar-Editions de l'Aube, 1997.

Lerche, J., 'Is Bonded Labour a Bound Category? Reconceptualising Agrarian Conflict in India', *Journal of Peasant Studies*, 22, 3 (1994): 484-515.

Maxwell, S., 'Food Security: A Post-Modern Perspective', *Food Security*, 21, 2 (1996): 155-70.

Mooij, J.E., *Food Policy and the Indian State. The Public Distribution System in South India*, Delhi: Oxford University Press, 1999.

Morin, E., *Introduction à la pensée complexe*, Paris: ESF Editions, 1990.

Nanda, M., 'Who Needs Post-Development? Discourses of Difference, Green Revolution and Agrarian Populism in India', *Journal of Developing Societies*, vol. XV. 1 (April 1999): 5-31.

Nawani, N.P., *Towards Food for All: Ideas for a New PDS*, Delhi: Ministry of Information and Broadcasting, Govt. of India, 1995.

Peemans, J.P., 'Modernisation, globalization et territoires: l'évolution des regards sur l'articulation des espaces urbains et ruraux dans les processus de développement', *Revue Tiers Monde*, XXXVI, 141 (1995): 17-39.

Radhakrishna, R. et al., *India's Public Distribution System: A National and International Perspective*, Poverty and Social Policy Dept, World Bank, 1996.

Revel, J. (ed.), *Jeux d'échelles. La micro-analyse à l'expérience*, Paris: Gallimard-Le Seuil, 1996.

Rist, G., *Le développement: histoire d'une croyance occidentale*, Paris: Presses de la Fondation Nationale des Sciences Politiques, 1996.

Rootes, C. (ed.), 1999, *Environmental Movements: Local, National, Global*, London: Frank, 1999.

Schenk, H., Beaud, I. and Rameshwari, B., 'Perspectives on Waste in Urban India. On Green and Red "Waste-Oriented" Voluntary Organizations', in Kalland, A. and Persoon, G. (eds.), *Environmental Movements in Asia*, Richmond: Curzon, 1998, pp. 271-85.

Swaminathan, M.S., *Sustainable Agriculture*, Delhi: Konark Publ., 1996.

Viramma, Racine, J. and Racine, J.L., *Viramma: Life of a Dalit*, London: Verso, 1997, New Delhi: Social Science Press, rpt. 2003.

Webster, N., 'In the Name of the Poor: Constructing the Local in Indian Rural Development', 15th Conference of South Asian Studies, Prague, 8-12 Sept. 1998.

Zerah, M.H., *Water: Unreliable Supply in Delhi*, Delhi: Manohar, 1999.

Contributors

Véronique Alary, Agro-economist, CIRAD, Montpellier.

Gilles Boquérat, Historian and Political Scientist, Centre for South Asian Studies (CEIAS), Paris.

Basudeb Chaudhuri, Associate Professor of Economics, University of Caen and Centre for South Asian Studies (CEIAS), Paris.

Anne-Claire Degail, Agro-economist, INAPG, Paris.

Bruno Dorin, Agro-economist, CIRAD, Montpellier.

Gérard Heuzé, Sociologist, CNRS and Centre for South Asian Studies (CEIAS), Paris.

Loraine Kennedy, Socio-economist, ADES-CNRS and Centre for South Asian Studies (CEIAS), Paris.

Pierre Lachaier, Associate Professor of Anthropology, Ecole Française d'Extrême Orient and Centre for South Asian Studies (CEIAS), Paris.

Frédéric Landy, Associate Professor of Geography, University of Paris X-Nanterre, Laboratoire Geotropiques and Centre for South Asian Studies (CEIAS), Paris.

Rachel Rivière, Zootechnician, INAPG, Paris.

Joël Ruet, Economist, Centre de Sciences Humaines, New Delhi.

Alain Vaguet, Associate Professor, Geography, University of Rouen.